Courts and Criminal Justice in America

Second Edition

Larry J. Siegel

University of Massachusetts, Lowell

Frank Schmalleger

Distinguished Professor Emeritus,
University of North Carolina at Pembroke

John L. Worrall

University of Texas at Dallas

PEARSON

Boston   Columbus   Indianapolis   New York   San Francisco   Upper Saddle River
Amsterdam   Cape Town   Dubai   London   Madrid   Milan   Munich   Paris   Montreal   Toronto
Delhi   Mexico City   São Paulo   Sydney   Hong Kong   Seoul   Singapore   Taipei   Tokyo

Editorial Director: Vernon R. Anthony
Executive Editor: Gary Bauer
Development Editor: Elisa Rogers, 4development
Program Manager: Megan Moffo
Editorial Assistant: Kevin Cecil
Director of Marketing: David Gesell
Marketing Manager: Mary Salzman
Senior Marketing Coordinator: Alicia Wozniak
Marketing Assistant: Les Roberts
Team Lead for Project Management: JoEllen Gohr
Senior Project Manager: Steve Robb
Procurement Specialist: Deidra M. Skahill

Creative Director: Andrea Nix
Art Director: Diane Y. Ernsberger
Cover Designer: CFISHDESIGN, Candace Rowley
Cover Image: Angela Waye/Shutterstock.com
Media Project Manager: Leslie Brado
Media Project Coordinator: April Cleland
Full-Service Project Management:
    Jean Smith/S4Carlisle Publishing Services
Composition: S4Carlisle Publishing Services
Printer/Binder: RR Donnelley
Cover Printer: RR Donnelley
Text Font: 10.5/13.5 Goudy Oldstyle Std

Credits and acknowledgments for content borrowed from other sources and reproduced, with permission, in this textbook appear on the appropriate page within the text.

Microsoft® and Windows® are registered trademarks of the Microsoft Corporation in the U.S.A. and other countries. Screen shots and icons reprinted with permission from the Microsoft Corporation. This book is not sponsored or endorsed by or affiliated with the Microsoft Corporation.

Many of the designations by manufacturers and sellers to distinguish their products are claimed as trademarks. Where those designations appear in this book, and the publisher was aware of a trademark claim, the designations have been printed in initial caps or all caps.

Library of Congress Cataloging-in-Publication Data
Siegel, Larry J., author.
    Courts and criminal justice in America/Larry J. Siegel, University of Massachusetts, Lowell;
Frank Schmalleger, Distinguished Professor Emeritus, University of North Carolina at Pembroke;
John L. Worrall, University of Texas at Dallas.—2nd ed.
        pages cm
    Includes index.
    ISBN-13: 978-0-13-345999-9
    ISBN-10: 0-13-345999-3
    1. Criminal courts—United States. 2. Criminal justice, Administration of—United States.
I. Schmalleger, Frank, author. II. Worrall, John L., author. III. Title.
    KF9223.S525 2015
345.73'01—dc23
                                                                    2013030291

ISBN-10:   0-13-345999-3
ISBN-13: 978-0-13-345999-9

THE CRIMINAL COURTS SYSTEM

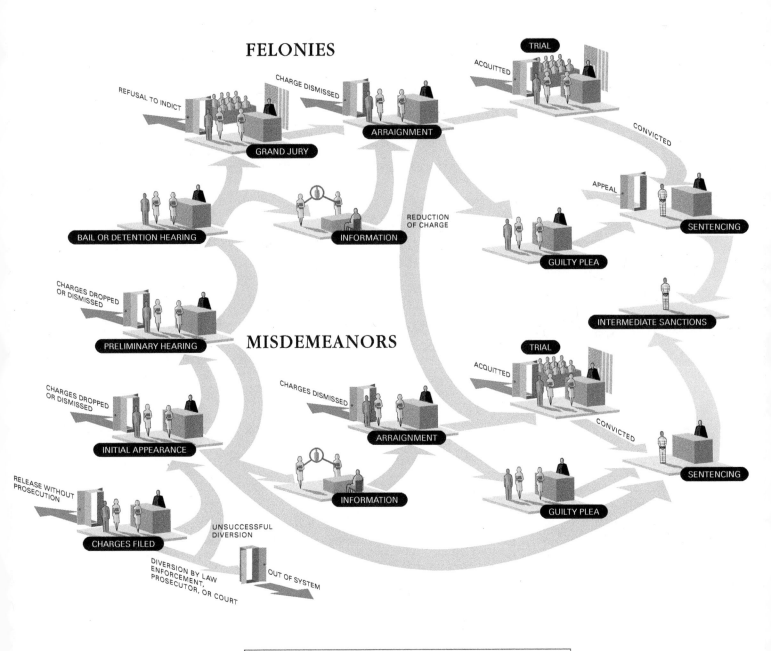

FELONIES

REFUSAL TO INDICT

CHARGE DISMISSED

GRAND JURY

ARRAIGNMENT

TRIAL

ACQUITTED

CONVICTED

BAIL OR DETENTION HEARING

INFORMATION

REDUCTION OF CHARGE

APPEAL

SENTENCING

CHARGES DROPPED OR DISMISSED

PRELIMINARY HEARING

MISDEMEANORS

GUILTY PLEA

INTERMEDIATE SANCTIONS

CHARGES DROPPED OR DISMISSED

INITIAL APPEARANCE

CHARGES DISMISSED

ARRAIGNMENT

INFORMATION

TRIAL

ACQUITTED

CONVICTED

SENTENCING

RELEASE WITHOUT PROSECUTION

CHARGES FILED

UNSUCCESSFUL DIVERSION

DIVERSION BY LAW ENFORCEMENT, PROSECUTOR, OR COURT

OUT OF SYSTEM

GUILTY PLEA

DEFENDANT   DISTRICT ATTORNEY   LAWYER   JUDGE

CONVICT   OUT OF SYSTEM

Brief Contents

Contents

NEW TO THE SECOND EDITION

The second edition has been extensively revised. We have made a number of changes throughout the text:

- Chapter-opening stories that highlight the chapter's theme have been added at the beginning of each chapter.

- Learning objectives replace focusing questions at the start of each chapter to allow for better student access to key ideas.

- The latest statistics and research findings have been integrated throughout.

- "Courts in the News" features have been rewritten and updated to highlight the latest developments in the study of courts.

- "Lasting Impact" features and "What Will You Do?" exercises have been revised and refreshed throughout.

THE GENESIS OF THIS BOOK

In 2003, a woman was raped by an armed assailant who broke into her Salisbury, Maryland, home. Though she was not able to describe her attacker, the police did obtain a sample of the perpetrator's DNA. Six years later, in 2009, Alonzo King was arrested in Wicomico County, Maryland, and charged with first- and second-degree assault for menacing a group of people with a shotgun. As part of a routine booking procedure for this serious offense, a DNA sample was taken by applying a cotton swab or filter paper—known as a buccal swab—to the inside of King's mouth. The DNA was found to match the DNA taken six years earlier from the Salisbury rape victim. King was then tried and convicted for the rape. The key evidence used in gaining the rape conviction was the DNA taken at the time he was booked in 2009; this evidence is what linked him to the earlier rape. When the DNA sample was taken, the procedure conformed to the Maryland DNA Collection Act (1994). The act originally required all convicted sex offenders to submit DNA samples but has since undergone major expansion: In 1999, it was amended to include convicted offenders of violent crimes; in 2002, it began to include all felony convictions and some misdemeanor crimes; and as of January 1, 2009, the DNA law was expanded to include individuals arrested of crimes of violence and burglaries so that DNA samples could be matched with prior crimes, increasing the likelihood of offender identification.

After his conviction, King appealed, arguing that being required to give a DNA sample without a warrant being issued violated his Fourth Amendment right to be free from illegal searches and seizures. The Maryland Court of Appeals agreed, setting aside his conviction and finding unconstitutional the portions of the act authorizing DNA collection from felony arrestees.

On appeal, the U.S. Supreme Court reversed the Maryland court in 2013. They ruled in the case of *Maryland* v. *King* that when police officers make an arrest supported by probable cause and bring the suspect to the station to be detained in custody, taking and analyzing a cheek swab of the arrestee's DNA is like fingerprinting and photographing, a legitimate police booking procedure that is reasonable under the Fourth Amendment. They reasoned that DNA testing may significantly improve both the criminal justice system and police investigative practices by making it possible to determine whether a biological tissue matches a suspect with near certainty. They found it reasonable that Maryland's act authorizes law enforcement authorities to collect DNA samples from persons charged with violent crimes, including first-degree assault. They also noted that a sample may not be added to a database before an individual is arraigned, and it must be destroyed if he or she is not convicted. Nor did the Court find that collecting a DNA overly intrusive: Taking a swab is quick and painless, requires no surgical intrusion beneath the skin, and poses no threat to the arrestee's health or safety.

To some, the *King* case represents a breakthrough that will allow law enforcement agencies to use a relatively new technology to solve crimes and put dangerous criminals behind bars. To others, it creates a slippery slope with both legal and moral ramifications: It paves the way for the construction of a national database containing personal information on every citizen. Cases such as *King*, they warn, give the federal government unlimited power to monitor private citizens and keep track of their activities.

Regardless of which position you take, the *King* case illustrates the power of the courts to define the boundaries between legitimate and illegal behavior. If the Supreme Court had ruled for King, the prosecution would have been forbidden to use his DNA at trial, and he would never have been convicted; in essence, a rapist would have been set free. But because the Court ruled that taking King's DNA was a legitimate exercise of government power, not only does his conviction stand but the ruling also gives a green light to police officers to take DNA swabs of arrestees in all subsequent cases. *King* creates a precedent that will shape law enforcement activities and trial outcomes for years to come.

We have written *Courts and Criminal Justice in America* because of cases such as King that illustrate the tremendous power the court system has to regulate citizens' lives, to shape what is acceptable and what is forbidden, and to ensure that criminal justice policy balances both rights and liberties. It is therefore important for all students to understand the structure of the courts, how they operate, and how they use their power to control behavior ranging from rape to religious freedom and from the taking of a life to the celebration of Christmas.

APPROACH

We take a balanced, modern, and comprehensive approach in this book. It is balanced in the sense that we present all sides of the most controversial issues facing courts today. We firmly believe that there are two sides to every story and that while there may be a convincing argument against a particular set of practices, it is also important to consider the opposing view. For example, the case of racial disparities is taken up in Chapter 15. Many researchers have found evidence of racial discrimination in criminal justice, but to accept such claims on their face leaves much unsaid. What is meant by discrimination? Depending on how it is defined, different conclusions can be reached. We do not take sides in this book; we simply present what is known about various issues confronting the courts and let the readers draw their own conclusions.

Our approach is modern in the sense that we cover a wide range of cutting-edge topics and novel practices. For example, we dedicate an entire chapter to so-called specialized courts, such as homeless courts. We situate them within the historical development of the court system and discuss strategies to solidify their place in the American judicial landscape well into the future. As another example, we also look at the problem of wrongful convictions and DNA-based exonerations, both of which have captured plenty of headlines in recent years. From the beginning of the book to the end, you will find a wide range of topics that stir controversy and enliven discussion as they relate to the courts.

Finally, ours is arguably the most comprehensive introduction to America's courts you will find. *Courts and Criminal Justice in America* covers not only the basics about courts and the personnel who bring them to life but also the context in which they operate and the complexities of human interaction found at every level. This book is also comprehensive in that it does not presuppose any knowledge about the courts or how they operate. We begin with a basic definition of courts and discuss why it is important to have government courts. Then we delve more deeply into the constant struggle for control over the courts that takes place, the many types of courts and the cases that they adjudicate, and the myriad persons and interests that compete for the courts' attention on a daily basis. Rest assured that no stone has been left unturned.

Goals

Our goal is for each reader of *Courts and Criminal Justice in America* to understand the following:

- The importance that courts have in modern society
- Pressures that courts face and the context in which they operate
- Various types of courts that range from the all-powerful U.S. Supreme Court to limited jurisdiction courts
- Professionals who are involved at all stages of the court process (including judges, prosecutors, and defense attorneys)
- The role of victims who participate in the court process
- The role of criminal defendants who are tried in the courts
- Rights that are enjoyed by accused persons (such as the rights to counsel and a jury trial)
- The court process that goes from arrest all the way through to conviction (whether by trial or plea bargaining), sentencing, and appeal
- Reasons that not every case or person is treated the same
- The role of technology that is used in the courts today
- Alternatives to trials that are available
- Difficult issues that courts are likely to face as time goes by

Topical Coverage

Courts and Criminal Justice in America is divided into five parts. Part 1 (Chapters 1 and 2) discusses the legal foundations of America's court system and the many different efforts to control the courts from the outside. Part 2 (Chapters 3–6) presents the main types of courts, beginning with federal and state courts and then moving to juvenile and specialized courts. Part 3 (Chapters 7–10) introduces the people involved in the court process. We begin with the members of the courtroom work group: judges, prosecutors, and defense attorneys. Then we discuss the roles and rights of defendants and victims. Part 4 (Chapters 11–14) takes a close look at the court process, starting with the arrest, the initial appearance, the bail decision, the charges, and the process of discovery; we also look at plea bargaining, guilty pleas, the jury, the trial, the sentencing process, the types of appeals, and even *habeas corpus*. Finally, Part 5 (Chapters 15 and 16) examines current issues and the future of U.S. courts. Topics covered include differential treatment, wrongful convictions, technology, alternatives to courts, and both emerging problems and pressing issues that courts will continue to face.

PEDAGOGICAL FEATURES

Courts and Criminal Justice in America includes a number of special learning features that are designed to enhance student comprehension of key concepts and issues in the study of American courts. "Courts in the News" features contain contemporary feature stories of interest to anyone studying the courts, along with thought-provoking questions that build on each story. One box, for example, discusses federal courts that offer digital audio recordings of their proceedings online; another reviews the 2008 U.S. Supreme Court case of *District of Columbia* v. *Heller*, in which the right to individual gun ownership was upheld; a third covers the issues involved in paying for America's courts; and another examines alternative courts and their possible future.

A second important learning feature is the "Lasting Impact" features found throughout the text that highlight the continued significance of important court cases such as *Mapp* v. *Ohio*, *Gideon* v. *Wainright*, *Terry* v. *Ohio*, *Gregg* v. *Georgia*, *In re Gault*, *Payne* v. *Tennessee*, and *Daubert* v. *Merrell Dow Pharmaceuticals*.

The "What Will You Do?" features provide scenario-based activities that bring focus to issues such as Web-based conferencing in virtual courtrooms, the notion of precedent as it applies to police decision making, and the issue of victim advocacy.

A fourth feature, "Learning Objectives," is located at the beginning of each chapter. These questions are linked to bulleted summary items that refresh students' memory about the chapter's key points. "Review Questions" at the end of each chapter relate back to the "Learning Objectives" posed at the chapter's start.

Other learning features include "Web Extras" and "Library Extras." "Web Extras" lead readers to websites, blogs, and in-depth postings of importance to the study of courts. Following are some of the organizations that the "Web Extras" provide links to:

Administrative Office of the U.S. Courts
American Bar Association's Center for Professional Responsibility
American Judges Association
American Judicature Society
Center for Constitutional Rights
Center for Court Innovation
Center on Wrongful Convictions
Electronic Discovery Blog
Harlem Parole Reentry Court
Innocence Project
National Association of Criminal Defense Lawyers
National Association of Drug Court Professionals
National Center for State Courts
National Council of Juvenile and Family Court Judges
National Youth Court Center
Sentencing Project
U.S. Supreme Court

Some "Web Extras" also feature video segments of relevance to the study of courts, including a few from Brightcove .com, *Frontline*, and responsible postings to YouTube.

"Library Extras" provide links to important court-related documents on the Internet. They focus on topics as diverse as the fundamental nature of the adversarial system, judicial ethics, the judicial process, essential elements of courtroom safety, court cultures, community courts, the exclusionary rule, the issue of plea bargaining, the law of arrest, the process of juror selection, and selected writings of Oliver Wendell Holmes.

SUPPLEMENTS

To access supplementary materials online, instructors need to request an instructor access code. Go to **www .pearsonhighered.com/irc**, where you can register for an instructor access code. Within 48 hours of registering, you will receive a confirming e-mail, including an instructor access code. Once you have received your code, go to the site and log on for full instructions on downloading the materials you wish to use. Online supplements include the following:

- Instructor's Manual with Test Bank (0-13-357668-X)
- MyTest test bank (0-13-346000-2)
- PowerPoint Presentation (0-13-357742-2)

ACKNOWLEDGMENTS

The authors sincerely thank the following reviewers for this edition: Larry D. Creason, Campbellsville University; Thomas A. Dreffein, Triton College; Wendy P. Guastaferro, Georgia State University; Jacqueline M. Mullany, Triton College; Emmanuel Onyeozili, University of Maryland Eastern Shore; Steven Philbrick, Northwest Vista College; Julie Raines, Marist College; Lisa Ratliff-Villarreal, San Antonio College; Douglas D. Shuler, Paris Junior College; and Jason B. Waller, Tyler Junior College.

The authors also thank the following reviewers for the previous edition: Beth Bjerregaard, University of North Carolina at Charlotte; Alton Braddock, University of Louisiana, Monroe; Don Bradel, Bemidji State University; Paul H. Clarke Jr., Northcentral Technical College; Amy Craddock, Fayetteville State University; Chris De Lay, University of Louisiana, Lafayette; Joe D. Dillsaver, Northeastern State University; Robert D. Hanser, University of Louisiana, Monroe; David M. Jones, University of Wisconsin, Oshkosh; Sharon Jumper, Northwestern State University; Michael J. McCrystle, California State University, Sacramento; Elvage G. Murphy, Edinboro University of Pennsylvania; Karen Nielson, Ivy Tech Community College; James J. Ross, The College at Brockport, State University of New York; John Tahiliani, Worcester State College; Cort Tanner, Western Texas College; David Tate, Purdue University; Sarah E. Uselding, Amarillo College; and Elvira M. White, Fayetteville State University.

We also wish to thank the staff at Pearson who have made this book the quality product that it is. Many thanks to Vern Anthony, Gary Bauer, Megan Moffo, Kevin Cecil, JoEllen Gohr, Steve Robb, Diane Ernsberger, David Gesell, and many other staffers (some of whom remain anonymous) who have brought this book to fruition. Special thanks to Elisa Rogers at 4development and Jean Smith at S4Carlisle Publishing, for their development and production assistance. Thank you, each and every one!

Larry J. Siegel was born in the Bronx and graduated from Christopher Columbus High School in 1964. After attending City College of New York in the 1960s, he pursued his interest in social forces and human behavior when he became a member of the first class of the newly created graduate program in criminal justice at the State  University of New York at Albany. After earning his MA and PhD, Dr. Siegel began his teaching career at Northeastern University. He subsequently held teaching positions at the University of Nebraska, Omaha, and Saint Anselm College in New Hampshire. He currently is a professor in the School of Criminology and Justice Studies at the University of Massachusetts, Lowell. Professor Siegel has published books on juvenile law, delinquency, criminology, and criminal procedure. The father of four and grandfather of three, Larry and his wife, Terry, reside in Bedford, New Hampshire, with their two cockapoos, Watson and Cody.

Frank Schmalleger is Distinguished Professor Emeritus at the University of North Carolina at Pembroke. He holds degrees from the University of Notre Dame and The Ohio State University, having earned both a master's (1970) and a doctorate (1974) in sociology (with a special emphasis in criminology) from The Ohio State 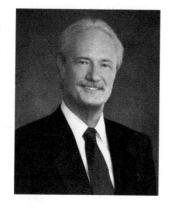 University. From 1976 to 1994, Dr. Schmalleger taught criminology and criminal justice courses at the University of North Carolina at Pembroke; for the last 16 of those years, he chaired the university's Department of Sociology, Social Work, and Criminal Justice. The university named him Distinguished Professor in 1991.

Dr. Schmalleger has taught in the online graduate program of the New School for Social Research, helping to build the world's first electronic classrooms in support of distance learning through computer telecommunications. As an adjunct professor with Webster University in St. Louis, Missouri, he helped develop the university's graduate program in security administration and loss prevention and taught courses in that curriculum for more than a decade. An avid Web user and website builder, Professor Schmalleger is also the creator of a number of award-winning websites.

Dr. Schmalleger is the author of numerous articles and more than 30 books, including the widely used *Criminal Justice Today* (Pearson, 2015), *Criminal Justice: A Brief Introduction* (Pearson, 2014), *Criminology Today* (Pearson, 2015), and *Criminal Law Today* (Pearson, 2014).

Professor Schmalleger is the founding editor of the journal *Criminal Justice Studies*. He has also served as editor for the Pearson series *Criminal Justice in the Twenty-First Century* and as imprint adviser for Greenwood Publishing Group's criminal justice reference series.

Dr. Schmalleger's philosophy of both teaching and writing can be summed up in these words: "In order to communicate knowledge, we must first catch, then hold, a person's interest—be it student, colleague, or policy maker. Our writing, our speaking, and our teaching must be relevant to the problems facing people today, and they must in some way help solve those problems." Follow the author's tweets @schmalleger.

John L. Worrall is Professor of Criminology and Program Head at the University of Texas at Dallas. A Seattle native, he received a BA (with a double major in psychology as well as law and justice) from Central Washington University in 1994. Both his MA (criminal justice) and his PhD (political science) were received from Washington  State University, where he graduated in 1999. From 1999 to 2006, Professor Worrall was a member of the criminal justice faculty at California State University, San Bernardino. He moved to Texas in the fall of 2006.

Dr. Worrall has published articles and book chapters on a wide variety of topics ranging from legal issues in policing to community prosecution. He is also the author of several textbooks, including *Crime Control in America: What Works?* (3rd ed., Pearson, 2015) and *Criminal Procedure: From First Contact to Appeal* (5th ed., Pearson, 2015). He is coeditor of *The Changing Role of the American Prosecutor* (State University of New York Press, 2009) and editor of the journal *Police Quarterly*.

Paul Whitfield (c) Rough Guides

EQUAL JUSTICE UNDER LAW

Legal Foundatio

Hemera/Thinkstock

A young person dressed informally on courthouse steps. Many judges enforce dress codes for those having business before the court. Should they?

INTRODUCTION

The courts conduct serious business, so people should dress accordingly, at least according to some judges.[1] For example, after a woman in Bakersfield, California, showed up to her court date dressed in flip-flops and shorts, the judge ordered her sent home for disrupting courtroom decorum. Another judge held a woman who appeared before him in contempt of court for wearing an offensive T-shirt, and many courts do not allow jeans to be worn into the courtroom. Delaware courts don't permit women to wear skirts that are shorter than four inches above the knee when standing. I know it "sounds like Catholic school," says Timothy Fautsko, an adviser to the National Center for State Courts on security issues; but, he says, the dress codes serves a purpose: "it maintains order in the courtroom."[2]

The court represents the collective conscience of society, serving as an instrument for expressing the revulsion people feel for those who commit particularly heinous crimes. Because they are given the task of punishing wrongdoers, courts serve as an agency of social control, determining which behaviors may be acceptable and which deserve severe sanction. This role is not without ambiguity: What is fair? What is just? How can we determine who should be punished, for how long, and for what?

COURTS AND THEIR IMPORTANCE

The courts are a critical component of American criminal justice because they determine what happens to people charged with violating the law. Courts are important beyond criminal justice, too. Disputes that arise between private parties, businesses, government officials, and the like are brought to court in order to ensure that they are heard in a neutral forum.

What Is a Court?

Despite the fact that courts predate other components of the justice system by thousands of years (police are a nineteenth-century creation, and corrections began in the eighteenth), coming up with a concise yet all-encompassing description of their structure and function is difficult. Even so, the U.S. Justice Department has defined a **court** as "an agency or unit of the judicial branch of government, authorized or established by statute or constitution, and consisting of one or more judicial officers, which has the authority to decide upon cases, controversies in law, and disputed matters of fact brought before it."[3]

This definition emphasizes three distinct elements:

1. To be considered a court, it must have proper legal authority, as spelled out in constitutions or statutes.
2. Courts are generally found in the judicial as opposed to legislative and executive branches of government (there are some exceptions, as we will see in Chapter 3).
3. Courts are empowered to make decisions that are binding. The notion of "[deciding] upon cases, controversies in law, and disputed matters of fact" is known as **adjudication**, or "the process by which a court arrives at a decision regarding a case."[4]

Learning Objective 1

Explain the purpose and functions of courts and the dual court system.

Library Extra
1–1 How Courts Govern America

court
"[A]n agency or unit of the judicial branch of government, authorized or established by statute or constitution, and consisting of one or more judicial officers, which has the authority to decide upon cases, controversies in law, and disputed matters of fact brought before it."[i]

adjudication
"[T]he process by which a court arrives at a decision regarding a case."[ii]

It is important to distinguish between civil and criminal courts, the latter being the primary focus of this book. Civil courts generally resolve disputes between private parties. Criminal courts deal with suspected law violators and thus serve as a mechanism by which society establishes and maintains social norms.

Courts in American Government

It makes sense to have courts be both authorized and limited by the statute. To do otherwise would put control over the courts in the hands of nongovernmental authorities. But why do we have government courts as opposed to private courts? This question is rarely asked, but its answer is important.

In prehistory, prior to the emergence of formal governments and during the time of tribal civilizations such as those of the Goths, Celts, and Franks, disputes were often resolved informally and privately. A person who felt that his or her privacy interests were compromised may have taken steps to confront the alleged violator and resolve the dispute with violence. Similarly, to the extent there was any need to preserve order, this was often accomplished informally.

This all changed during the rise of the Greek city-states and the Roman Empire. The shift moved law enforcement from what was essentially a private affair to a public one. As law enforcement and criminal justice moved in the public direction, formalized courts and other criminal justice institutions came into being.

We have now moved to a point in history where serious conflict is resolved with formal processes, whether that be court proceedings or a suitable alternative. Not everyone buys into the idea completely, but one of the hallmarks of modern society is a more civilized set of procedures for resolving matters of human conflict. The reason we have government courts, therefore, is to deal with conflict in a civilized manner.

Also, there have been changing conceptions throughout history about whom disputes and conflict ultimately affect. Thinking about crime specifically, there is a general consensus today that victims are not just individuals but the state as well. More than 80 years ago, in the case of *Mallery* v. *Lane*,[5] the presiding judge stated,

> The offenses are against the state. The victim of the offense is not a party to the prosecution, nor does he occupy any relation to it other than that of a witness, an interested witness mayhaps, but none the less, only a witness. . . . It is not necessary for the injured party to make complaint nor is he required to give bond to prosecute. He is in no sense a relator. He cannot in any way control the prosecution and whether reluctant or not, he can be compelled like any other witness to appear and testify.[6]

Dual Court System Ours is a **dual court system** that separates federal and state courts. The dual court system is advantageous and desirable because it parallels federalism, a system of government where power is constitutionally divided between a central governing body (i.e., the federal government) and various constituent units (i.e., the states). Federalism requires that laws are made by the central governing authority and by the constituent units. In the United States, the federal government makes law, but federalism also gives the states power to make their own laws.

A quick glance at the U.S. Constitution reveals a system of **dual federalism**, where the only powers of the federal government are those explicitly listed, with the rest being left to the states. In reality, though, ours is more of a system of **cooperative federalism**, meaning that some of the lines between federal and state power are blurred. Article I, Section 8, of the U.S. Constitution gives the federal government the power to regulate interstate commerce, but this authority has been interpreted broadly such that the federal government can control much of what happens at the state level.

Library Extra
1-2 U.S. Courts: Federal and State Jurisdiction

dual court system
A judicial system comprising federal- and state-level judicial systems.

dual federalism
A system of government wherein the only powers of the federal government are those explicitly listed, with the rest being left to the states.

cooperative federalism
A system of government wherein some of the lines between federal and state power are blurred.

While a dual court system is desirable from a federalism standpoint, it also promotes complication and confusion. It would be neat and tidy if the federal criminal law were separate and distinct from state criminal law, but in reality both overlap. For example, certain criminal acts, such as those involving firearms, are violations of *both* federal and state criminal law. This leads to confusion over where it would be best to try offenders or whether they should be tried twice in the two different systems.

The dual court system is only part of the story. At each level, there is a distinct court hierarchy. States often have limited jurisdiction courts (such as traffic courts), trial courts, appellate courts, and supreme courts. At the federal level, there are trial courts, appellate courts, and the U.S. Supreme Court. Each trial court adjudicates different offenses. Appellate courts consider different matters depending on where they lie in the court hierarchy. Appeals from state courts can sometimes be heard in the federal courts. Higher-level courts can control the actions and decisions of lower courts but not the other way around. Despite the apparent complexity, each court has its place.

Functions of the Court System With a definition of the courts in place and an understanding of the need for government courts, we can now think in more detail about the main functions of the courts. Four stand out: upholding the law, protecting individuals, resolving disputes, and reinforcing social norms.

1. *Upholding the law.* Not only are courts authorized by law, but they are called on to *uphold the law.* What is the law, and what is the legal basis for the courts? Throughout history, the concept of "law" has been fluid and changing. Early legal codes, the common law, modern statutes, constitutions, and the like have all built a legal foundation for the justice system (we will look at these in more detail shortly).

   Today, the criminal courts are tasked primarily with upholding criminal codes. Found at the federal and state levels, these codes identify actions that are not acceptable in contemporary society because they cause social harm. The police arrest people for violating them, prosecutors then decide which arrestees should be charged, but courts ultimately decide whether those charged with violations of the criminal law should be held to answer for their actions.

2. *Protecting individuals.* One of the hallmarks of our system of government is a concern with people's freedom and liberties. No less than the preamble to the U.S. Constitution makes this clear:

   We the People of the United States, in Order to form a more perfect Union, establish Justice, insure domestic Tranquility, provide for the common defence, promote the general Welfare, and *secure the Blessings of Liberty to ourselves and our Posterity,* do ordain and establish this Constitution for the United States of America.

   If individual liberties are to be preserved, then the government has to be kept in check. This is accomplished through constitutions, which spell out the rights that people enjoy and set limits on government authority. When it comes to the courts, people are also protected via other means. In the criminal justice context, the adversarial system ensures that *both sides* to a criminal case can tell their story. Also, important presumptions exist in our system of justice that ensure protection for everyone who comes before the courts.

3. *Resolving disputes.* Courts are agencies of dispute resolution. Disputes come in all varieties, but most fall into either civil or criminal categories. By way of preview, criminal disputes are those between the government and an individual accused of violating the law. The actions in question are usually those legislatures have declared harmful to society on the whole. Civil disputes, in contrast, tend to involve private interests, such as duties owed one another.

COURTS IN THE NEWS

Recording the Court Process

Federal courts are now participating in projects to make digital audio and video recordings of courtroom proceedings and make them available to the public online. In the first project, the U.S. District Court in Nebraska and the U.S. Bankruptcy Court for the Eastern District of North Carolina integrated their recording and case management/electronic case files systems to make some audio files available the same way written files have long been available on the Internet. Three other courts—the U.S. District Court for the Eastern District of Pennsylvania, the U.S. Bankruptcy Court in Maine, and the U.S. Bankruptcy Court for the Northern District of Alabama—plan to join the pilot project soon.

The audio files are accessible through the Public Access to Court Electronic Records (PACER) system. More than 700,000 subscribers already use PACER to access docket and case information from federal appellate, district, and bankruptcy courts.

In the second project, 14 federal trial courts are taking part in the federal judiciary's digital video pilot, which started July 18, 2011, and will evaluate the effect of cameras in courtrooms. All 14 courts volunteered to participate in the three-year experiment. No proceedings may be recorded without the approval of the presiding judge, and parties must consent to the recording of each proceeding in a case. The recordings will be made publicly available at http://www.uscourts.gov and may also be on local participating court websites at the court's discretion. The participating courts were selected by the Committee on Court Administration and Case Management (CACM) of the Judicial Conference of the United States in consultation with the Federal Judicial Center, the Judiciary's research arm.

Only the federal district courts participating in the pilot study are permitted to record and provide videos of court

Kevin Dietsch/UPI Photo/Landov

Federal courts are now making audio and visual recordings of trials. Does that violate a crime victim's right to privacy, considering they are often asked embarrassing questions at trial? Does the general public's right to know outweigh a crime victim's right to maintain personal privacy?

proceedings to the public. Districts volunteering for the pilot must follow guidelines adopted by CACM. The pilot is limited to civil proceedings in which the parties have consented to recording. Photographing in the courtroom, as well as broadcasting of judicial proceedings, is prohibited in criminal cases by Rule 53 of the Federal Rules of Criminal Procedure. A presiding judge can choose to stop a recording if it is necessary, for example, to protect the rights of the parties and witnesses, preserve the dignity of the court, or choose not to post the video for public view. Coverage jury selection is prohibited, as is coverage of jurors or alternate jurors.

These projects show that courts are not static institutions and that change and constant efforts at improvement characterize American courts at most levels. Technology, in particular, now plays a central role in the day-to-day business of many courts. ■

DISCUSSION QUESTIONS

1. Who is likely to use the digital audio recordings now offered online by some federal courts?

2. What use might those recordings have?

3. What other technological innovations might we soon expect to see from the federal courts?

Source: Administrative Office of the United States Courts, "Pilot Project Begins: Two Courts Offer Digital Audio Recordings Online," August 6, 2007, available at http://www.uscourts.gov/Press_Releases/digitalaudio080607.html (accessed May 2013); Administrative Office of the United States Courts, Cameras in the Courtroom, http://www.uscourts.gov/Multimedia/cameras.aspx (accessed May 30, 2013).

4. *Reinforcing social norms.* Courts help reinforce social norms. Social norms consist of informal and often unspoken rules concerning standards of behavior. They are often tacit and unnoticed:

[They are] norms that most of us are barely conscious of taking our guidance from, since they are not often supported in a surrounding discourse of general commendation and critique and are not reflected in levels of common or mutual awareness. They may include the norms that govern turn taking in conversation, the use of eyes in relation to others, the distance at which one stands in speaking to another, and a host of such unnoticed but not merely mechanical regularities.[7]

Other "unnoticed" regularities include beliefs about what is and is not acceptable. Legislatures may define criminal acts in statutes, and prosecutors may charge criminal suspects, but the court's role in deciding whether someone is punished highlights its role in reinforcing social norms. The court mentioned at the beginning of this chapter could have treated Michael Vick's actions with a measure of leniency, but it did not, which sent a clear message about what types of behavior society is willing to tolerate.

Learning Objective 2
Outline the history and development of law and the courts.

LEGAL BASIS FOR THE COURTS

Formalized government and criminal justice roughly paralleled societal growth. But before we can more fully appreciate these developments and their effects on American criminal justice, it is important to move backward in time to some of the other nations we just mentioned, for many of their approaches to dispute resolution were adopted in America.

The foundations for modern American criminal justice are several. One was religious. Judeo-Christian values had a key role in the evolution of American government and, of course, criminal justice, beginning with the Declaration of Independence:

> We hold these truths to be self-evident, that all men are created equal, that they are endowed by their Creator with certain unalienable rights, that among these are life, liberty and the pursuit of happiness.

There is often talk of church and state separation, but this does not mean that God was separated from government. The Declaration of Independence recognizes the "Creator" as a source of rights. Biblical morality made an indelible imprint on this nation's founding rules and laws, particularly its Constitution. John Adams once stated this:

> We have no government armed with power capable of contending with human passions unbridled by morality and religion. Avarice, ambition, revenge, or gallantry would break the strongest cords of our Constitution as a whale goes through a net. Our Constitution was made for a moral and religious people. It is wholly inadequate to the government of any other.[8]

Our system of justice was also shaped by ancient legal codes, going back as far as 1760 B.C. There is also a strong common law tradition in this country, that owes much to our British heritage. The common law emphasizes the importance of judicial decisions, not the codified criminal law such as can be found in state penal codes. Still other legal bases for modern criminal justice include modern criminal codes, administrative regulations, and even constitutions.

Early Legal Codes

Code of Hammurabi
The earliest-known example of a formal written legal code.

Perhaps the earliest known example of a formal written legal code was the **Code of Hammurabi**. Also known as Hammurabi's Code and assembled by the sixth Babylonian king, Hammurabi, in 1760 B.C., the code expressed a strong "eye for an eye" philosophy. To illustrate, here is the seventh of the code's "code of laws":

> If any one buy from the son or the slave of another man, without witnesses or a contract, silver or gold, a male or female slave, an ox or a sheep, an ass or anything, or if he take it in charge, he is considered a thief and shall be put to death.[9]

Twelve Tables
The first secular (i.e., not regarded as religious) written legal code, dating from 450 B.C.[iii]

Roman law provides another example of formally codified legal principles. The so-called **Twelve Tables** (450 B.C.) was the first secular (i.e., not regarded as religious) written legal code.[10] The code was named as such because the laws were literally written onto 12 ivory tablets. The tablets were then posted so that all Romans could read them. The Twelve Tables, like Hammurabi's Code, contained a strong element of retributive justice. One of the laws, "*Si membrum rupsit, ni cum eo pacit, talio esto*" translates as follows: "If one has maimed another and does not buy his peace, let there be retaliation in kind."[11]

Despite their shortcomings and harsh character, these early legal codes are important because they signaled the emergence of formalized "law." And while it is difficult to define the term with precision, *law* generally refers to formal rules, principles, and guidelines enforced by *political authority*. This political authority is what began to take dispute resolution out of the hands of citizens and put it under control of governments. Legal codes have changed and evolved considerably over the years, but the use of political or governmental authority to enforce such codes has remained pretty constant.

Common Law and Precedent

After the Norman conquest (A.D. 1066), King William and his Norman dukes and barons moved quickly to consolidate their hold over newly won territories. One method was to take control of the preexisting legal/court system. Once they did this, the judges in their courts not only issued decisions but also wrote them down. These decisions were subsequently circulated to other judges. The result was a measure of uniformity from one court to the next. This was literally the law "in common" throughout England, and it came to be known as the **common law**.

The common law can be better understood when it is contrasted with **special law**, which refers to the laws of specific villages and localities that were in effect in medieval England and that were often enforced by canonical (i.e., religious) courts. Under the reign of Henry II (1154–1189), national law was introduced but not through legislative authority as is customary today. Rather, Henry II implemented a system whereby judges from his own central court went out into the countryside to preside over disputes. They resolved these disputes based on what they perceived as custom. The judges effectively created law, as there was no democratic law-forming process in place at the time.

As more and more judges began to record their decisions, the principles of *stare decisis* and precedent were developed. **Precedent** refers, generally, to some prior action that guides current action. In the common law context, this meant that judges' decisions were guided by earlier decisions. Precedent thus ensured continuity and predictability. If decisions changed radically from one judge to the next, from place to place, or both, the "common" law would be anything but common. It was also easier for judges to fall back on earlier decisions; otherwise, they would have to continually reinvent the wheel. *Stare decisis*, which is Latin for "to stand by things decided," is thus the formal practice of adhering to precedent.

While the common law is usually viewed as a legal concept, it also had social implications: The medieval judge was entrusted with the collective wisdom, values, and morals established by the community and was trusted to apply them to solve disputes between citizens. Even when appointed by the king, the medieval judge represented the community and applied the community's (not the king's) law, thereby maintaining its age-old customs and values.

Early colonists brought this English common law tradition to America. Today, all courts are essentially *bound* to follow earlier courts' decisions as well as decisions issued by higher courts. If a state supreme court issues a decision, all lower courts in that state will be bound to follow it; likewise, if the U.S. Supreme Court issues a decision, all courts must adhere to it. Technically, precedent is binding only on those courts within the jurisdiction (a concept we will discuss later) of the court issuing the decision, but as a courtesy some courts adhere to other courts' decisions across jurisdictional boundaries. Again, the practice promotes consistency.

common law
The law originating from usage and custom rather than from written statutes; also, a term that referred to the law "in common" throughout England following the Norman Conquest in medieval times.

special law
Any law of specific villages and localities that was in effect in medieval England and that was often enforced by canonical (i.e., religious) courts.

precedent
A legal principle that ensures that previous judicial decisions are authoritatively considered and incorporated into future cases.

stare decisis
A term that literally means "to stand by things decided." In the law, it is the formal practice of adhering to precedent.

There is nothing etched in stone about precedent. Times change. Often, early decisions become outdated as technologies change. It used to be, for example, that the U.S. Supreme Court defined the word *search* as basically consisting of physical trespass. These days, there is much the government can do to infringe on people's privacy without actual physical trespass; for example, wiretaps can be used at a distance, without any measure of physical trespass. The Supreme Court recognized this and effectively redefined a search, requiring a departure from earlier decisions.[12]

At the other extreme, there is no need to be concerned with courts issuing new decisions that depart from prior ones on an *ad hoc*, willy-nilly basis. Take the issue of abortion. When there is an open seat on the Supreme Court, questions of a nominee's stance on abortion routinely come up, as if the Court would promptly overturn *Roe* v. *Wade* (the Supreme Court case that legalized abortion) if the nominee were confirmed. But the Supreme Court is not going to suddenly overturn that landmark decision without a very good reason. Even if the Court were composed of a solid conservative majority, there is no reason to expect a dramatic departure from precedent. In fact, prior decisions are *rarely* overruled. The Supreme Court has recently chipped away at the legality of abortion by upholding a law banning partial birth abortions, but it has not overruled *Roe* v. *Wade*.[13]

Library Extra
1–3 Oliver Wendell Holmes: The Common Law

Why Common Law? Common law emerged at a time when legal codes were in their infancy. Judges issued decisions when there were not necessarily formal statutes to criminalize certain forms of conduct. Laws need explanations, clarifications, and modifications from time to time, and were it not for common law, this would not be possible. Oliver Wendell Holmes raised a similar point in this eloquent observation:

> The life of the law has not been logic; it has been experience. The felt necessities of the time, the prevalent moral and political theories, intuitions of public policy, avowed or unconscious, even the prejudices which judges share with their fellow men, have had a good deal more to do than the syllogism in determining the rules by which men should be governed. The law embodies the story of a nation's development through many centuries, and it cannot be dealt with as if it contained only the axioms and corollaries of a book of mathematics.[14]

Other Sources of Law

Besides early legal codes and the common law, other important sources of law include modern legal codes, administrative regulations, and constitutions. These have helped shape America's courts (not to mention the criminal justice system in general) in many ways as well.

Modern Legal Codes Modern legal codes differ from early legal codes because they exist at different levels of government and come in several different forms. The United States Code contains federal laws, and violations of its provisions can lead to federal prosecution. States have their respective codes. Other units of government, such as counties and cities, often have their own ordinances. These legal codes exist in several varieties. States such as California list criminal offenses in more than one code. There, most crimes are spelled out in the Penal Code, but the Health and Safety Code criminalizes drug-law violations. The state has 29 separate legal codes![15]

Legal codes do not just prohibit conduct considered criminal. They also provide important rights. For example, both the states and the federal government have minimum-wage laws that provide the minimum hourly wage an employee can earn. Without such laws, there would be no right to a specific wage.[16]

Administrative Regulations **Administrative regulations** are rules promulgated by government agencies that have been given their authority by the executive branch or legislative branch. Several federal cabinet-level agencies (e.g., Department of Education, Department of Labor) serve as visible examples. There are also independent agencies, such as the Environmental Protection Agency, the Internal Revenue Service (IRS), and the Securities and Exchange Commission, that have been created by Congress and that have adopted rules and regulations to fulfill their mandates. Similar entities can be found at the state and local levels. Together, the rules these agencies adopt and enforce are considered administrative regulations. They carry equal weight and importance relative to legal codes, but violations tend to be regarded as civil rather than criminal matters.

Why do we have administrative regulations and not just laws? When government agencies are created, often they are given a fairly broad mandate. To expect the executive or Congress to completely map out—in advance—these agencies' duties and their limits would be unrealistic. By giving administrative agencies the authority to set their own regulations, this eases the burden on the executive or legislative branch. It also permits the agencies to adapt and change as new laws are passed and new problems present themselves. Consider the IRS. It defines what constitutes a legitimate tax deduction because it would be impractical and overly time-consuming to have outsiders setting such rules.

Administrative regulations can be found in specific statutes, not unlike the legal codes we have already discussed. At the federal level, the **Code of Federal Regulations** spells out the rules and regulations adopted by federal agencies and departments. The regulations are organized into some 50 different titles, covering everything from aliens and nationality to conservation of power and water resources. While violations of administrative regulations may not be considered criminal in the traditional sense, it is important to appreciate that this body of rules closely parallels that of federal and state criminal codes, making it clear that ours is a system of laws.

Constitutions Constitutions are perhaps the most significant source of law. Unlike penal codes, constitutions generally do not prohibit actions on the part of private citizens, and unlike administrative regulations, they tend to steer clear of specifics when it comes to the creation of specialized government agencies. Rather, constitutions generally place limits on government authority. They define, in broad terms, government structure and organization; they also spell out various rights that people enjoy, how government officials will be selected, and what roles various government branches will take on.

The **Bill of Rights**, consisting of the first ten amendments, also announces important limitations on government authority with respect to the investigation of crime. The Fourth Amendment, for example, spells out warrant requirements, and the Fifth Amendment protects people, in part, from being forced to incriminate themselves. The Eighth Amendment prohibits cruel and unusual punishment and so on. Entire books and college courses are devoted to the study of constitutional law for criminal justice (i.e., criminal procedure).

While the federal Constitution receives the most attention due to its status as the supreme law of the United States, it is important to note that each state has its own constitution. These often mirror the federal Constitution, but they often go into much more detail. Some states use an initiative process, where every November voters can decide the fate of proposed constitutional amendments. Other states have used their constitutions to more clearly spell out what they consider prohibited actions, whereas a close read of the federal Constitution suggests that the founding fathers intended something different. In any case, constitutions work together with legal codes, administrative regulations, and the common law to provide an interesting basis for criminal justice as we know it.

State constitutions can be more restrictive than the U.S. Constitution, but no state can relax protections spelled out in the U.S. Constitution. For example, the U.S. Constitution's

administrative regulations
Rules promulgated by government agencies that have been given their authority by the executive branch or legislative branch.

Code of Federal Regulations
The group of rules and regulations adopted by U.S. federal agencies and departments.

Bill of Rights
The first ten amendments to the U.S. Constitution, which place important limitations on government authority with respect to the investigation of crime.

Fourth Amendment spells out search warrant requirements, but the Fourth Amendment is vague in terms of whether a warrant is required in all circumstances. In theory, a state could require warrants for *all* searches, but as a practical matter, most states have followed the U.S. Constitution's lead (and the Supreme Court's interpretation of it).

Role of the Courts

Courts are important to the study of criminal justice for two key reasons: adjudication and oversight. Both of these functions are critically important for the protection of public safety and the smooth operation of the system itself.

Adjudication One of the primary focuses of the courts is dispute resolution and the adjudication of complaints. In the context of criminal justice, this means most often that courts decide who is going to answer for an alleged criminal act. Without this adjudication role, police would be making arrests and prosecutors filing charges in vain. Courts perform the vital function of determining who is and is not guilty.

More than deciding matters of guilt, certain courts (namely, the appellate courts) ensure that lower courts applied the law correctly. This important set of checks ensures that judges who make mistakes and apply the law incorrectly are held accountable for their mistakes. In the extreme, a trial court judge who makes a serious legal error could see the individual charged with the crime walk free due to an appellate court decision.

Oversight Courts also provide an important oversight function in American criminal justice. Our nation's appellate courts decide matters of law (such as by interpreting ambiguous constitutional provisions) that affect how police officers do their jobs on the street. The Supreme Court's famous decision in *Tennessee* v. *Garner*[17] placed limits on the use of deadly force, something of great import to all police officers patrolling America's streets.

While courts oversee the operations of criminal justice officials, this oversight is not direct like it is in a supervisor–subordinate relationship. Rather, the courts get involved only once a particular matter comes to the attention of an appellate court and only then if the decision is publicized and made available for practitioners and other interested authorities to read and implement.

Not all decisions are published, particularly in the lower courts, so this limits the oversight function. It is generally the most serious instances of police misconduct that come to the courts' attention, but even so, thousands of decisions have been issued—and published—over the years that have altered the way criminal justice officials do their work. Police academy training now contains fairly extensive legal education, again highlighting the importance of courts in criminal justice.

Learning Objective 3
Summarize the guiding legal principles underlying the U.S. court system.

GUIDING LEGAL PRINCIPLES

Ensuring that *everyone* can come before a court, regardless of which side of a dispute they represent, is one of the hallmarks of the American justice system. A number of key guiding legal principles exist to make sure that people are adequately protected as they participate in the court process. Presumptions, like the presumption of innocence, and safeguards, like those spelled out in the U.S. Constitution, are of critical importance in a system of criminal justice. Presumptions and safeguards protect the accused, as does our adversarial system. Contrasting our adversarial system with its opposite, an *inquisitorial* system, makes it clear that protection for the accused is paramount in our system of criminal justice.

Presumptions

A **presumption** is a fact assumed to be true under the law. In the world of criminal evidence, there are many types of presumptions. Conclusive presumptions require that all parties agree with something assumed to be true. An example of this would be that a child born to a married couple who live together is the couple's child. It is likely that both parties to a case would agree to this presumption. In contrast to this kind of a conclusive presumption, a *rebuttable* presumption is one that could reasonably be disagreed with. Here is an example of a rebuttable presumption: "Because a letter was mailed, it was received by its intended recipient." This is rebuttable because the letter could actually be lost due to a mistake made by the post office.

Every person charged with a crime is assumed, in advance, to be innocent, which is known as the **presumption of innocence**. The presumption of innocence is both a presumption of law (because it is required from the outset) and a rebuttable presumption (because the prosecutor will present evidence to show that the defendant, the person being charged with the crime, is guilty). The presumption of innocence is a bedrock legal principle. One classic court decision put it this way:

> [The presumption of innocence] is not a mere belief at the beginning of the trial that the accused is probably innocent. It is not a will-o'-the-wisp, which appears and disappears as the trial progresses. It is a legal presumption which the jurors must consider along with the evidence and the inferences arising from the evidence, when they come finally to pass upon the case. In this sense, the presumption of innocence does accompany the accused through every stage of the trial.[18]

Presumptions are essential to the smooth operation of criminal justice. They serve, basically, as substitutes for evidence. Without them, every minute issue that could possibly be disputed would come up during trials. For example, it is presumed that a child born to a married couple who live together is the couple's child. Without presumptions such as these, the process would be slowed down considerably because every minor event, no matter how likely, would have to be proven in court. (Box 1–1 shows popular presumptions that arise in criminal justice.)

presumption
A fact assumed to be true under the law.

presumption of innocence
The bedrock U.S. legal principle that assumes that every person charged with a crime is innocent until proven otherwise.

BOX 1–1 Common Presumptions

- *Presumption of sanity.* All defendants are presumed sane; the burden falls on the defense to prove otherwise.
- *Presumption of death.* It is presumed that a person who has disappeared and is continually absent from his or her customary location (usually after seven years) is dead.
- *Presumption against suicide.* It is assumed that when a person dies, the cause is not suicide.
- *Presumption of a guilty mind following possession of the fruits of crime.* The jury can usually infer guilt if a person is caught "red-handed" with the fruits of crime.
- *Presumption of knowledge of the law.* Ignorance is not a defense to criminal liability.
- *Presumption of the regularity of official acts.* It is assumed, for example, that a proper chain of custody exists, unless the defense can show otherwise.
- *Presumption that young children cannot commit crimes.* Some states presume that children under a certain threshold age (e.g., age seven) cannot form criminal intent and thus cannot commit crime.
- *Presumption that people intend the results of their voluntary actions.* If a person voluntarily shoots another, the jury can presume the shooter intended to do so. ■

Constitutional Rights

The presumption of innocence acts as something of a safeguard to protect the accused from instant incrimination. Constitutional rights are safeguards in the same way: They help ensure that people accused of criminal activity are not rushed to judgment and treated unfairly. Indeed, constitutional rights protect *everyone* in this country, not just suspected and accused criminals. Even noncitizens (except, perhaps, terror suspects, which is an area of ongoing dispute) enjoy the same protections as U.S. citizens. A close examination of the Constitution confirms this point; there is no mention of criminals versus law-abiding persons or citizens versus noncitizens.

As we pointed out earlier, constitutional rights can be found at both the federal and state levels. The U.S. Constitution spells out the rights we all enjoy, and these rights are not boundary-specific; they apply throughout the United States. States also have their own constitutions. The rights spelled out in a state constitution apply only to people within that state. Importantly, states can adopt more restrictive protections than spelled out in the U.S. Constitution, but they cannot adopt looser standards.

For criminal justice purposes and particularly for a study of courts, the constitutional rights of interest to us are those that can be found in the U.S. Constitution's Bill of Rights and in the Fourteenth Amendment (for two others not found in these places, see Box 1–2). The Bill of Rights (as we pointed out earlier) consists of the first ten amendments to the U.S. Constitution (see Box 1–3), and we will begin by discussing it. Then we will turn our attention to the Fourteenth Amendment's **due process clause**. The Fourteenth Amendment is important because the U.S. Supreme Court has used its due process clause to make various protections listed in the Bill of Rights (which is binding only on the federal government) binding on the states. This is known as **incorporation**.

Bill of Rights The Bill of Rights contains a total of ten constitutional amendments, four of which are most relevant in the criminal justice context. They are the Fourth, Fifth, Sixth, and Eighth Amendments. An exception is the Second Amendment, which deals with the right to keep and bear arms, but it has little in the way of implications for court and criminal justice procedures.

1. *The Fourth Amendment.* The Fourth Amendment is perhaps the most well known of all the amendments. It states,

   The right of the people to be secure in their persons, houses, papers, and effects, against unreasonable searches and seizures, shall not be violated, and no Warrants shall issue, but upon probable cause, supported by Oath or affirmation and particularly describing the place to be searched, and the persons or things to be seized.

---

due process clause
The portion of the Fourteenth Amendment that has been used by the U.S. Supreme Court to make certain protections specified in the Bill of Rights applicable to the states.

incorporation
The legal doctrine based on the due process clause of the Fourteenth Amendment that makes various protections listed in the Bill of Rights, which is binding only on the federal government, binding on the states, as well.

BOX 1–2   Other Constitutional Rights of Relevance in Criminal Procedure

ARTICLE III, SECTION 2

. . . The trial of all crimes, except in cases of impeachment, shall be by jury; and such trial shall be held in the state where the said crimes shall have been committed; but when not committed within any state, the trial shall be at such place or places as the Congress may by law have directed.

Note: The right to jury trial has been significantly restricted by the Supreme Court. We look at this more closely in Chapter 13.

ARTICLE I, SECTION 9

The privilege of the writ of habeas corpus shall not be suspended, unless when in cases of rebellion or invasion the public safety may require it. ▪

Note: Habeas corpus provides a means for prisoners to challenge the constitutionality of their confinement. We look at it more closely in Chapter 14.

BOX 1–3   Bill of Rights

AMENDMENT I

Congress shall make no law respecting an establishment of religion, or prohibiting the free exercise thereof; or abridging the freedom of speech, or of the press; or the right of the people peaceably to assemble, and to petition the Government for a redress of grievances.

AMENDMENT II

A well regulated Militia, being necessary to the security of a free state, the right of the people to keep and bear Arms, shall not be infringed.

AMENDMENT III

No Soldier shall, in time of peace be quartered in any house, without the consent of the Owner, nor in time of war, but in a manner to be prescribed by law.

AMENDMENT IV

The right of the people to be secure in their persons, houses, papers, and effects, against unreasonable searches and seizures, shall not be violated, and no Warrants shall issue, but upon probable cause, supported by Oath or affirmation, and particularly describing the place to be searched, and the persons or things to be seized.

AMENDMENT V

No person shall be held to answer for a capital, or otherwise infamous crime, unless on a presentment or indictment of a Grand Jury, except in cases arising in the land or naval forces, or in the Militia, when in actual service in time of War or public danger; nor shall any person be subject for the same offense to be twice put in jeopardy of life or limb; nor shall be compelled in any criminal case to be a witness against himself, nor be deprived of life, liberty, or property, without due process of law; nor shall private property be taken for public use, without just compensation.

AMENDMENT VI

In all criminal prosecutions, the accused shall enjoy the right to a speedy and public trial, by an impartial jury of the State and district wherein the crime shall have been committed, which district shall have been previously ascertained by law, and to be informed of the nature and cause of the accusation; to be confronted with the witnesses against him; to have compulsory process for obtaining witnesses in his favor, and to have the Assistance of Counsel for his defence (sic).

AMENDMENT VII

In Suits at common law, where the value in controversy shall exceed twenty dollars, the right of trial by jury shall be preserved, and no fact tried by a jury, shall be otherwise reexamined in any Court of the United States, than according to the rules of the common law.

AMENDMENT VIII

Excessive bail shall not be required, nor excessive fines imposed, nor cruel and unusual punishments inflicted.

AMENDMENT IX

The enumeration in the Constitution, of certain rights, shall not be construed to deny or disparage others retained by the people.

AMENDMENT X

The powers not delegated to the United States by the Constitution, nor prohibited by it to the States, are reserved to the states respectively, or to the people. ■

Several rights can be distinguished by reading the text of the Fourth Amendment. It refers to the rights of people to be free from unreasonable searches and seizures, and it provides that there are specific requirements guiding the warrant process. Warrants must be issued by a magistrate or judge, supported by probable cause, and sufficiently specific as to what is to be searched and/or seized. The courts have grappled with this amendment's seemingly innocuous language for generations. What is a person? What is a search? What is probable cause? What are the warrant requirements? We will answer some of these questions later on in the book, particularly in the section on court process.

2. *The Fifth Amendment.* The second constitutional amendment of interest to us is the Fifth Amendment. It states,

> No person shall be held to answer for a capital, or otherwise infamous crime, unless on a presentment or indictment of a Grand Jury, except in cases arising in the land or naval forces, or in the Militia, when in actual service in time of War or public danger; nor shall any person be subject for the same offense to be twice put in jeopardy of life or limb; nor shall be compelled in any criminal case to be a witness against himself, nor be deprived of life, liberty, or property, without due process of law; nor shall private property be taken for public use, without just compensation.

This amendment is quite clear, on its face, about which rights people enjoy: Grand juries appear necessary, no one can be forced to incriminate him- or herself, people cannot be put in "double jeopardy," and people cannot be deprived of certain rights without due process. But like the Fourth Amendment, the terms in this amendment are not abundantly clear. What does it mean to be a "witness against himself"? What exactly is "double jeopardy"? Are grand juries really required in all capital and infamous crimes? Despite these ambiguities (which, again, we will seek to clarify later in the book), it is clear that the Fifth Amendment also provides an important safeguarding function.

3. *The Sixth Amendment.* The Sixth Amendment is also of great importance. It specifies the following:

> In all criminal prosecutions, the accused shall enjoy the right to a speedy and public trial, by an impartial jury of the State and district wherein the crime shall have been committed, which district shall have been previously ascertained by law, and to be informed of the nature and cause of the accusation; to be confronted with the witnesses against him; to have compulsory process for obtaining witnesses in his favor, and to have the Assistance of Counsel for his defence.

Of relevance to the study of courts is the Sixth Amendment's language concerning speedy and public trials, impartial juries, confrontation, compulsory process, and especially the right to counsel. Reading between the lines, the Sixth Amendment also suggests that in addition to being public, trials should be open (not closed) proceedings. This ensures openness, which is consistent with democratic governance.

4. *The Eighth Amendment.* The Eighth Amendment is relevant to a fairly limited extent. It is limited in the sense that the other amendments we just introduced have received much more attention by the courts. In any case, the Eighth Amendment states,

> Excessive bail shall not be required, nor excessive fines imposed, nor cruel and unusual punishments inflicted.

Keeping bail to a reasonable level ensures that nondangerous individuals charged with criminal activity do not languish in jail cells needlessly until their trial dates. Likewise, the protection against cruel and unusual punishment ensures that torture, beatings, horrific forms of execution, and the like are not used.

Due Process The Fourteenth Amendment, particularly its language concerning "due process," has profound importance in criminal justice. It is a fairly long amendment, with

BOX 1–4   Unincorporated Rights

- The whole of the Second Amendment
- The whole of the Third Amendment
- The whole of the Seventh Amendment
- The Fifth Amendment's right to grand jury indictment
- The Eighth Amendment's prohibition against excessive bail

only a small portion relevant to the handling and treatment of criminal suspects. It states, in relevant part,

> All persons born or naturalized in the United States, and subject to the jurisdiction thereof, are citizens of the United States and of the State wherein they reside. No State shall make or enforce any law which shall abridge the privileges or immunities of citizens of the United States, *nor shall any State deprive any person of life, liberty, or property, without due process of law*; nor deny to any person within its jurisdiction the equal protection of the laws. [italics added]

First, note that the due process clause (the italicized part) of the Fourteenth Amendment mirrors the Fifth Amendment's due process clause. Remember, though, that the Fifth Amendment, because it is part of the Bill of Rights, is binding only on the federal government. The Fourteenth Amendment's due process clause has been used by the Supreme Court to make certain protections specified in the Bill of Rights applicable to the states. But note that not all rights spelled out in the first ten amendments have been incorporated. The Fifth Amendment's grand jury provision has not been incorporated, which is why some states rely on grand jury indictments and others do not (see Box 1–4 for a full listing of unincorporated rights).

There are two types of due process the courts recognize: (1) substantive due process and (2) procedural due process. **Substantive due process** is concerned with protecting people's life, liberty, and property interests; that is, it protects "substantive rights," like the rights to possess and do certain things. **Procedural due process**, in contrast, is concerned with ensuring *fairness*.[19] One court distinguished between both types of due process in this way:

> [S]ubstantive due process prohibits the government's abuse of power or its use for the purpose of oppression, and procedural due process prohibits arbitrary and unfair deprivations of protected life, liberty, or property interests without procedural safeguards.[20]

There is no constitutional right to privacy, but substantive due process (in conjunction with other constitutional amendments, such as the Fourth) has been used to effectively "create" a constitutional right to privacy.

Adversarial System

Ours is an **adversarial justice system**, particularly when describing the courts. It is adversarial because it pits two parties against each other in pursuit of the truth. Our adversarial system is not what it is, though, because attorneys love to hate each other. Rather, **adversarialism** owes to the many protections our Constitution and laws afford people.

When criminal defendants assert their rights, this sometimes amounts to one side saying that the other is wrong, which ultimately leads to an impasse that must be resolved by a judge. If the defendant's attorney seeks suppression of key evidence that may have been obtained improperly, the prosecutor will probably disagree; after all, such evidence could

substantive due process
The constitutional provision that is concerned with protecting people's life, liberty, and property interests.

procedural due process
The constitutional provision that is concerned with ensuring fairness.[iv]

adversarial justice system
The functional construct of the American court system that features two competing sets of interests (the defendant's and the government's) working against each other in pursuit of the truth, from which stems the many protections our Constitution and laws afford people.

adversarialism
The element incorporated into the American judicial system by the founding fathers to promote argument, debate, and openness as a defense against oppressive government.

form the basis of his or her case. The judge must rule to settle the matter. This is the essence of adversarialism—two competing sets of interests (the defendant's and the government's) working against each other.

Why else is ours an adversarial system? Another, more fundamental explanation lies in the founding fathers' concerns with oppressive governments. Adversarialism promotes argument, debate, and openness. With no defense attorneys and only prosecutors having any say in a defendant's case, there would be untold numbers of rights violations, rushes to judgment, and so on.

Prosecutors and Defense Attorneys: Mortal Enemies?

The answer to the question this heading poses is a resounding "No." Yet by watching courtroom dramas and movies, it would be easy to think otherwise. Hollywood loves to make it look like prosecutors and defense attorneys cannot stand each other, and they are constantly springing surprise witnesses on one another, arguing with each other to the point of fighting, and so on.

While it is true that some prosecutors and defense attorneys are not the best of friends, most know each other and work together on a routine basis. Some prosecutors were once defense attorneys and vice versa. These days, collaboration is popular, too, as prosecutors and defense attorneys are coming to realize that the traditional hard-line adversarial approach to meting out justice is not always helpful for the accused. We will come back to this notion of the opposing parties working together when we look at the courtroom work group in Chapter 2.

Opposite of Adversarialism: Inquisitorial Justice

Adversarial justice can be better understood when compared to its opposite, namely, inquisitorial justice, which is characteristic of an **inquisitorial system**. There are several features of inquisitorial systems that differ from adversarial systems. First, inquisitorial systems do not provide the same protections to the accused (e.g., right to counsel). Second, inquisitorial systems place decision making in the hands of one or a very few individuals. Third, juries are often the exception in inquisitorial systems. Finally, the attorneys in inquisitorial systems are much more passive than in adversarial systems, and judges take on a more prominent role in the pursuit of truth.

Inquisitorial justice is often likened to justice from the past, such as in medieval England, and particularly at the hands of the early Christian church. For the most part, this perception is accurate, but some borderline inquisitorial systems are very much alive and well in this day and age, even in modern industrialized nations. For example, in France, the "juge d'instruction" (i.e., investigating magistrate) engages in fact-finding and performs investigations in cases of serious and complex crimes. American judges, in contrast, focus on legal matters, and in trials by jury, they never engage in fact-finding.

Until as recently as 1996, China had a full-blown inquisitorial system. Since the Chinese adopted significant reforms to their legal system, that has changed. As one researcher observed,

> [U]nder China's inquisitorial system, judges were required to engage in evidence-gathering and criminal investigations. Judges in the post-reform period, however, should be more likely to serve as impartial adjudicators who hear evidence and arguments from both sides and render a decision based solely on this information.[21]

TYPES OF DISPUTES

Another court function we identified earlier is resolving disputes. We rely on courts, not ourselves, to resolve many varieties of disputes. There are exceptions to this rule with recent advents in the area of alternative dispute resolution (see Chapter 16), but when disputes

---

inquisitorial system
A judicial system that is the philosophical opposite of the adversarial system.

Library Extra
1–4 The Adversarial System

Learning Objective 4
Explain the nature of disputes.

escalate to a certain level or when a true impasse is reached, the courts will more often than not get involved.

Chances are this book has been assigned for a courts class as part of a criminal justice or criminology program. In that spirit, most of our energies will be channeled toward courts of the criminal variety, but we would be remiss not to discuss civil procedures. Here is one reason why: We already mentioned the Supreme Court's landmark decision in *Tennessee* v. *Garner*,[22] where standards governing deadly force as they pertain to fleeing felons were adopted. In that case, Garner, age 15, was shot in the back by an officer who was chasing him from the scene of a residential burglary. He was killed, but his surviving family members sued, arguing that the boy's constitutional rights were violated. Specifically, they argued that the boy was seized in violation of the Fourth Amendment (i.e., that the seizure was unreasonable). The case arrived at the Supreme Court via civil process; it was not a criminal case. *Garner*, along with many other important cases, has affected law enforcement, which is why it is important to give some attention to civil procedure.

Civil Law and Procedure

The world of civil law and procedure is distinct from criminal law and procedure (see Figure 1–1 for an overview of the civil process). This was made apparent in the famous 1995 O.J. Simpson murder case. Simpson was acquitted in criminal court, but he was found liable in a subsequent wrongful death lawsuit. The first proceeding was criminal; the second was civil. Both actions were separate and independent from one another. Simpson could have been sued and never charged criminally. This could have happened if the prosecution felt, in advance, that it did not have enough evidence to convict (the standard of proof in civil proceedings is generally lower). Alternatively, he could have been charged criminally and never sued. The point is that each action, civil and criminal, had no bearing on the other.

Nature and Substance of Civil Law
Contemporary criminal law is concerned with actions that are regarded as harmful to society on the whole. That is why criminal cases are often initiated by the government, such as in *State* v. *Jones*, *Commonwealth* v. *Jones*, or *People* v. *Jones*. In contrast, civil law is concerned mainly with disputes between private parties and with the duties private parties owe one another. Private parties can include individual people as well as organizations. The government occasionally gets involved as a party to a civil case as well, often in actions related to administrative law (see earlier discussion).

When an individual is held criminally liable, he or she is often punished. Appropriate sanctions range from fines to death, depending on the seriousness of the crime. In the civil context, courts seek to determine the parties' legal rights and then settle on appropriate remedies. Generally, there are two main types of remedies. One is **monetary damages**; that is, the party considered in the wrong can be ordered to pay money to the other party. In the other type of remedy, the court may order one party to perform certain acts or refrain from certain actions (the latter is known as **injunctive relief**).

It is tempting to view criminal cases as occurring more frequently than civil cases, particularly in light of the press coverage that crimes tend to receive. In reality, though, the opposite is true: Civil cases far outnumber those of the criminal variety. This is not too surprising because, as one famous legal scholar put it, "Every broken agreement, every sale that leaves a dissatisfied customer, every uncollected debt, every dispute with a government agency, every libel and slander, every accidental injury, every marital breakup, and every death may give rise to a civil proceeding."[23]

monetary damages
A court-ordered payment of money by one party in a civil suit to the other party.

injunctive relief
A court order directing one party in a civil suit to perform or refrain from performing certain acts.

Citizen Complaint

The first step in filing a lawsuit normally involves a citizen complaint. In a citizen complaint, the aggrieved party can do one of two things. The complaint can be lodged for the sake of calling attention to inappropriate police conduct *or* the complaint can demand some form of remedial action (e.g., injunctive relief or monetary damages). This latter form of a citizen complaint is considered a demand.

Demand

If whoever files a citizen complaint (the complainant) with the police requests some action on the part of the police, then the complainant will make a more or less informal "demand" of the police, who will then send a "response." This may lead to informal discussions. The complainant could retain the services of an attorney, but the procedures remain largely informal at this early juncture.

Citizen Complaint Board

In some jurisdictions (e.g., Spokane, WA) complainants can further file a complaint with the local citizen complaint board if the police agency in question fails to take satisfactory action. Citizen complaint boards vary considerably in their usage, authority, and terminology, so they are only mentioned here in passing as one alternative dispute resolution mechanism. Other avenues of dispute resolution besides complaint boards may well be in place.

Claim with City/County Clerk

Before they can proceed with a lawsuit, citizens in some states and counties are first required to file a claim with the city, or county, or give the police agency a chance to respond to a formal complaint or a request for damages. This *claim* should be distinguished from a *citizen complaint* discussed above. Claims of this nature differ because they are explicit prerequisites that must be filed before a lawsuit can move forward; they are mandated by law. Their purpose is primarily to inform officials of what is about to transpire. Often a lawsuit cannot be filed until the parties in question are given the opportunity to respond to a claim.

Pre-Litigation Settlement Discussions

There often is an informal "pre-litigation settlement discussion" where both the police and/or their representatives and the complainant and/or their representative work together to achieve a settlement. If no agreement is reached, chances are the complaint/demand will evolve into a full blown lawsuit.

Lawyer's Letter

If the complainant and the police can't work things out among themselves informally, the complainant usually has an attorney send a "lawyer's letter" to the police agency, officer(s) in question, and/or the municipality or county. While there may not be any legal significance to a lawyer's letter, it usually gets a serious response.

Full Blown Lawsuit

A citizen complaint/demand evolves into a full blown lawsuit when all of the foregoing informal proceedings do not meet with the complainants' satisfaction. In order for a citizen complaint/demand to move to the stage of a lawsuit, two actions must occur. First, a "complaint" must be filed with the Clerk of the Court where the lawsuit will be heard. This complaint differs from a citizen complaint; it is a legal requirement. Second, the court or an attorney then issues a "summons" that is "served" on the defendant(s). Sometimes the summons is personally delivered, other times it is sent by registered or certified mail. The parties involved are now known as defendants (the police, their agencies, municipalities, or whoever is named in the lawsuit) and the plaintiffs (the aggrieved party or parties filing the lawsuit). Answer: Once the defendant police officer(s), agency, and/or municipality is "served" with legal process, they must provide their formal "answer" within a prescribed time frame. For obvious reasons defendants in police civil liability cases rarely fail to acknowledge the summons.

Discovery

A lawsuit may involve "pre-trial discovery" in which one or both parties attempt to get evidence as to what happened, perhaps by taking the testimony of witnesses, or examining documents or physical evidence.

Motions

In a lawsuit either side may make "motions" to try to narrow the issues, or compel the other side to do something, or even to have the court decide the matter without the need for a trial. Two common motions in police civil liability cases are raised by the defendants. The first most common motion is the motion to dismiss. Here, defendants attempt to have the case thrown out on the grounds that no question of law or legitimate legal issue is raised. These are rarely granted. A second common motion is a motion for summary judgment. Here, defendants ask the court to find in favor of the police without the need for trial. The majority of these motions succeed, leaving only a few lawsuits which progress to the trial stage.

Trial, Judgment, Post-Trial Motions and Appeals

If a lawsuit progresses all the way to trial, it will either be decided by a judge alone, or with a jury to decide the facts and the judge to decide the law. After the trial the court will "enter judgment" in which the plaintiff, for example, might be entitled to a fixed amount of money. Post-trial motions might be raised in which the losing party tries to convince the original judge that something else is appropriate, perhaps more money, or added relief, or none at all. After that, there may be an appeal by the losing party to a higher court.

Judge's Pre-Trial Conference

Before a trial the court will typically order a "pre-trial conference" to narrow issues down still further, and perhaps to get the parties to agree to a settlement, again attempting to avoid a lengthy trial proceeding.

Collecting the Judgment

The victorious party may have received a judgment stating what he or she is entitled to recover. It is then his or her job to collect the "judgment." Collecting judgments can be a difficult and time consuming process, and is typically put on hold until all relevant appeals are exhausted.

FIGURE 1–1

Stages of a Civil Lawsuit

Source: Adapted from V. E. Kappeler, *Critical Issues in Police Civil Liability*, 2nd ed. (Prospect Heights, IL: Waveland, 1997).

Categories of Civil Law There are five important categories of civil law that are frequently resolved via civil litigation:

1. *Tort law.* **Torts** are civil wrongs recognized by law to be grounds for a lawsuit. Understood differently, **tort law** deals with conduct that leads to injuries not considered acceptable by societal standards. Nearly all personal injury claims stem from civil law. Medical malpractice lawsuits also fall in the tort category, as do many lawsuits against criminal justice officials.

Using tort law to resolve disputes is increasingly popular due to large jury awards and shifting standards of proof. On the subject of shifting standards of proof, much has changed in the world of product liability. It used to be that for a manufacturer of a product to be successfully sued, it was necessary to show the manufacturer acted with negligence. The negligence standard is increasingly being replaced by a strict liability standard.[24] **Strict liability** means that a party will be held liable regardless of culpability.

2. *Contract law.* When people enter into voluntary agreements by signing contracts, such as to purchase a home, this creates important legal obligations between both parties that are covered under **contract law.** When contracts are violated, lawsuits are often filed. Other options besides full-blown lawsuits are often available (we will look at some in this book's last chapter) and indeed required some of the time, but our concern here is with lawsuits.

Some contracts are very simple. Signing a credit card statement after buying a product or eating out in a restaurant is the same as signing a contract, agreeing to pay a specific amount. Other contracts can be described as nothing short of horrendous. Returning to the housing example, most home buyers will never see a more tedious contract in their lives; every contract provision provides a basis for liability. The authors of this book also signed a contract, and both we and our publisher were required to fulfill certain obligations.

3. *Property law.* While some consider it a subcategory of contract law, property law is distinct from contract law for a simple reason: Contracts are enforceable only insofar as the parties to the agreement are concerned, but property rights are enforceable against various unnamed parties, such as people who do not have legal right to use certain premises. **Property law** is thus significantly concerned with the acceptable uses of property, such as those uses spelled out in zoning laws: Some property is zoned commercial, some is zoned industrial, and some is zoned residential. Property law also governs property ownership, not just ownership of real property such as land but also personal property such as cash, conveyances, automobiles, and valuable items. Leases, such as apartment leases, fall under property law as well (and, of course, they are contractual).

4. *Law of succession.* The **law of succession** is concerned with how property is passed from one generation to the next. The law of succession can thus be understood as the law of wills. A **will** is a legal document wherein a person spells out the rights of others over his or her property following the person's death. If a person leaves behind no will (and dies intestate), the state will dispose of that person's property pursuant to applicable statutes. Most often, state laws require that intestate property go to the deceased person's heirs or closest relatives.

5. *Family law.* The area of **family law** is concerned with matters of marriage, divorce, child custody, and children's rights. For example, marital disputes have served as grounds for countless divorces, and once a couple who have children divorce, the courts often resolve disputes over which party gets custody of the children. Family law also spells out requirements as far as who can enter into marriage, what sort of testing (e.g., blood testing) is necessary, what license and

tort
A civil wrong recognized by law to be grounds for a lawsuit; also, conduct that leads to injuries not considered acceptable by societal standards.

tort law
The category of civil law that involves lawsuits to resolve civil wrongs.

strict liability
A standard of guilt that holds a party liable regardless of culpability.[v]

contract law
The category of civil law that involves lawsuits to resolve unfilled legal obligations between parties.

property law
The category of civil law that is significantly concerned with the acceptable uses of property, such as those uses spelled out in zoning laws.

law of succession
The category of civil law that is concerned with how property is passed from one generation to the next.

will
A legal document wherein a person spells out the rights of others with regard to his or her property following his or her death.

family law
The category of civil law that is concerned with matters of marriage, divorce, child custody, and children's rights.

Library Extra
1–5 The Civil Law

fee requirements exist, what waiting periods are necessary, and so on. Since our focus here is on courts and criminal justice, we will effectively abandon all but tort law from here on.

Criminal Law

Criminal law differs markedly from civil law. Acknowledging as much, this section answers several questions: What is a crime? What are the categories of crime? What are the elements of crime? What defenses are available to the accused? How does the criminal law affect the courts?

What Is a Crime? The usual image of crime conjured up in our minds is some physically harmful or sinful act. The definition of **crime** is quite different: A crime is any action that violates a statute duly enacted by the proper public authority. Legislatures typically define what is criminal. More formally, a crime is "an act committed or omitted in violation of a law forbidding or commanding it for which the possible penalties for an adult on conviction include incarceration, for which a corporation can be penalized by fine or forfeit, or for which a juvenile can be adjudged delinquent or transferred to criminal court for prosecution."[25]

Crime is also an offense against society, as opposed to against an individual. Clearly, crimes have victims and therefore affect individual people, but defining crime as an act against society puts it under the purview of the criminal justice system and possibly sends a clearer message that a certain action is unacceptable by *everyone*, not just an individual.

There is also no requirement in our definition of crime that it be physically harmful or even sinful. In Washington State, for example, it is illegal to walk about in public if one has a common cold.[26] This is hardly sinful, and the odds of "hurting" someone from such actions are certainly minor. After all, a common cold is just that: common!

Importantly, the criminal law does not necessarily define all the actions that are most harmful to individuals or society. On the one hand, as new problems begin to present themselves, legislatures must scramble to keep up. Consider terrorism. No one likes to wait around for a terrorist act to prosecute the perpetrators (if they survive) for murder. It is more acceptable to *prevent* such acts and possibly deter would-be terrorists via prosecution. But how do we prosecute someone who has yet to offend?

On the other hand, some have alleged that laws are crafted in a deliberate fashion to foster control of certain individuals, maintain class divisions, and protect the wealthy. Jeffrey Reiman's popular book *The Rich Get Richer and the Poor Get Prison*[27] provides several specific examples, such as how the actions of so-called white-collar criminals are not treated as harshly as those of ordinary criminals.

What Are the Categories of Crime? Crimes can be placed in at least three categories based on the punishments that can (but may not, if courts decide otherwise, as they often do) accompany them. **Felonies** are serious offenses generally punishable by more than one year of incarceration. These are the most serious offenses, and examples include murder, forcible rape, and armed robbery, among others. **Misdemeanors** are less serious and are generally punished with less than a year of incarceration. In fact, the vast majority of convicted misdemeanants never spend time incarcerated. Public drunkenness, social gambling (in states where it is not legally permissible), and vagrancy are common examples. Finally, **infractions** are less serious than misdemeanors and usually consist of violations of state statutes or local ordinances punishable by a fine or other penalty but not by incarceration.[28]

crime
Any conduct in violation of the criminal laws of the federal government, a state, or a local jurisdiction for which there is no legally acceptable justification or excuse.

felony
A serious criminal offense generally punishable by more than one year of incarceration.

misdemeanor
A less serious criminal offense generally punishable by less than one year of incarceration.

infraction
An offense that is less serious than a misdemeanor, that usually consists of a violation of a state statute or local ordinance, and that is punishable by a fine or other penalty but not by incarceration.[vi]

BOX 1–5 Examples of Strict Liability Offenses

- Drunk driving
- Statutory rape
- Most traffic violations
- Illegal dumping
- Most code violations
- Failure to pay child support
- Selling of alcohol to minors ■

What Are the Elements of a Crime? One of the core elements of a crime, the first that must be in place before the government can target any individual for a criminal conviction, is known as *corpus delicti*, Latin for "the body of crime." This could mean the literal "body" of a murdered individual, but more generally it refers to the objective proof (i.e., the reality) of a crime. Simply put, a crime must be committed in order to hold someone liable for it.

Before a person can be convicted of a crime, the prosecution must show first and foremost that the person (as either a principal offender, an accessory to the crime, or an accomplice) committed a criminal act. This is known as *actus reus*, which is Latin for "the criminal act." But a criminal act is not enough—in most cases—for a prosecutor to obtain a guilty verdict.

The prosecutor must also show a degree of intent on the offender's part, which is known as *mens rea*. There are various types of intent, including general intent, specific intent, and negligence. General intent refers to a conscious decision on the offender's part to commit a crime, and general intent statutes do not specify what intent is necessary. Specific intent offenses, by contrast, specify the type of intent necessary for a prosecutor to secure a guilty verdict. Negligence is a failure to use reasonable care or caution. The following "Courts in the News" feature highlights the influence of mens rea in a famous criminal trial.

Earlier we mentioned the doctrine of strict liability. It pops up again here insofar as there are certain criminal offenses for which people can be found guilty regardless of their intent. Examples of some such offenses appear in Box 1–5.

What Defenses Are Available to the Accused? It is important to have a grasp of defenses that are available to people accused of a crime. We just saw that criminal liability attaches when a person commits a criminal act with intent. But what if a person acts *without* intent? What if a person raises an argument at trial such as "I was under the influence of hallucinogens at the time of the crime and so was not responsible for my actions." Or, alternatively, what if a person intends to commit what would be considered a criminal act but has an excuse for doing so? Such is the essence of criminal defenses. There are three main types of defenses:

1. *Alibi.* An **alibi** is available when the defendant (i.e., the person charged with the crime) argues that he or she was somewhere else at the time of the crime, making it impossible for him or her to commit it. There is no single alibi defense; rather, there is a litany of potential arguments that a defendant can make if he or she wishes to present a convincing case that he or she was somewhere else at the time of the crime. For this reason, we will not give alibis any more attention in this book; they come in an infinite variety of forms, so it is not possible to review them in exhaustive detail.

2. *Justification defense.* With **justification defenses**, defendants accept responsibility for the act they are charged with but argue that the act was right under

corpus delicti
A term that literally means "the body of crime." While this could mean the literal body of a murdered individual, it more generally refers to the objective proof (i.e., the reality) of a crime.

actus reus
A term that literally means "the criminal act." The prosecutor has to show that an accused person (as a principal offender, an accessory to the crime, or an accomplice) committed a criminal act.

mens rea
A term that literally means "a guilty mind." The prosecutor has to show that there was a degree of intent on the offender's part.

alibi
A type of defense against a criminal charge wherein the defendant argues that he or she was somewhere else at the time of the crime, making it impossible for him or her to have committed it.

justification defense
A type of defense against a criminal charge in which the defendant admits committing the act in question but claims that it was necessary in order to avoid some greater evil.

COURTS IN THE NEWS

The Jodi Arias Murder Trial

REUTERS/Tom Tingle/The Arizona Republic/Pool

Jodi Arias shown testifying at her trial tried and failed to convince the jury that she lacked a "guilty mind" when she killed her boyfriend Travis Alexander and was in fact a battered woman acting in self defense.

Some cases make headlines around the world, and one such involved the 2008 murder of Travis Alexander in Mesa, Arizona. Soon after the murder, Jodi Arias, Alexander's ex-girlfriend, was charged with the bloody crime: Alexander had been stabbed multiple times, his throat was slit, and he suffered a gun wound to the head. In this case, the question was not who did the deed but why it was done. Did Arias have *mens rea* or the intent to kill Travis Alexander?

Alexander and Arias had met at a conference in Las Vegas in 2006 and began a stormy long-distance romance. In 2007, they broke up but continued to see each other for sex. Eventually, Arias moved to Arizona, and the two continued their relationship. In May 2008, a .25-caliber gun was reported stolen from the home of Arias's grandparents, where Arias had been staying. Then on June 4, 2008, Arias went to Travis's home, where they engaged in sex and then took provocative photographs of each other. While there, Arias killed Alexander and then left for a trip to Utah, where she was seeing another man. When friends found Alexander's body in the shower the next day and called police, they found Arias's hair and bloody palm print at the scene, along with time-stamped photos in a camera discovered inside Alexander's washing machine. At first, Arias denied any involvement in the crime but then changed her story, claiming that two masked intruders had attacked her and killed Alexander. Despite her protestations of innocence, prosecutors charged her with first-degree murder and filed a notice of intent to seek the death penalty. They contended that Arias had planned the attack and killed Alexander in a jealous rage. A year later, Arias changed her story about the killing, claiming self-defense. At her trial, she testified for 18 days, telling jurors that Alexander was physically and emotionally abusive. She said that he turned violent the day of his death, forcing her to fight for her life. She said that she lied about it earlier because she had planned to commit suicide. Her defense brought forth expert witnesses who claimed that she suffered from post-traumatic stress disorder and amnesia, explaining her memory lapses and changing story. Other experts testified that she suffered from battered woman's syndrome.

In May 2013 during their closing arguments, prosecutors described Arias as a manipulative liar who meticulously planned the savage attack. The jury bought his argument and found Arias guilty.

The Arias case aptly illustrates the concept of *mens rea*. If the jury believed that Jodi Arias was a battered woman who killed an abusive boyfriend in self-defense, she would have been found not guilty. However, after weighing the evidence, the jury believed that she went to Travis Alexander's house in a jealous rage, intending to kill him, and so found her guilty of murder in the first degree. Later the same jury deadlocked at the penalty phase of the trial, failing to agree whether Jodi Arias deserved the death penalty for her crime. ▪

DISCUSSION QUESTIONS

1. *Mens rea* is a mental attitude with which an individual acts, and therefore it cannot ordinarily be directly proved but must be inferred from surrounding facts and circumstances. Does this make the law too subjective and create the possibility of error?

2. A beginning driver intentionally switches lanes, knowing that he is on a busy highway, but negligently fails to check his blind spot and causes a fatal collision. Should his negligent behavior be considered *mens rea* sufficient to support a murder conviction?

Sources: Fox News, "Timeline of Key Events in the Jodi Arias Murder Case," May 8, 2013, http://www.foxnews.com/us/2013/05/08/timeline-key-events-in-jodi-arias-murder-case/#ixzz2T08FjpDU (accessed May 30, 2013); Brian Skoloff and Jacques Billeaud, "Jodi Arias Trial: An Over-the-Top Media-Spectacle," *Huffington Post*, May 22, 2013, http://www.huffingtonpost.com/2013/05/23/jodi-arias-trial-media-coverage_n_3324549.html?utm_hp_ref=media (accessed May 30, 2013); Brian Skoloff and Josh Hoffner, "Jury in Jodi Arias Trial Resumes Deliberations ABC News," May 22, 2013, http://abcnews.go.com/US/wireStory/deliberations-resume-arias-trial-penalty-phase-19234768 (accessed May 30, 2013).

the circumstances. Self-defense is an example of a justification defense (we will look at it—and others—in more detail shortly). There are two broad categories of justification defenses: those justified by necessity and those justified by consent. An example of justification by necessity is self-defense; consent is a common defense in rape cases when the defendant argues that the victim consented.

3. *Excuse defense*. With **excuse defenses**, defendants admit that what they did was wrong but claim that they were not responsible for the crime because of some condition that precluded them from forming criminal intent. Examples of excuse defenses include insanity, diminished capacity, age, duress, intoxication, and entrapment. The common thread running throughout excuse defenses is an argument on the defendant's part that he or she lacked the capacity to make an informed decision and therefore did not meet the legal requirement of *mens rea* at the time of the crime. Note that defenses such as these provide methods of avoiding (rather than dodging) criminal liability; dodging could include fleeing the country to avoid prosecution.

excuse defense
A type of defense against a criminal charge in which the defendant claims that some personal condition or circumstance at the time of the act was such that he or she should not be held accountable under the criminal law.

Most criminal defenses are considered "affirmative." Affirmative defenses are those formally raised by the defendant at trial; that is, he or she presents evidence to support an alibi, justification, or excuse. This means that the burden of proof falls on the defendant instead of the government to prove that the defense is legitimate. Additionally, some defenses are known as "perfect defenses." Perfect defenses result in acquittal; that is, the defendant goes free. But not all defenses, even if they are successful, result in the defendant going free. Some defenses are called "imperfect," which means that if the defense is successful, the defendant will be confined to some sort of facility (e.g., a mental institution) other than a prison or that the defendant's conviction will be for a less serious crime (e.g., negligent manslaughter instead of murder).

Library Extra
1–6 Criminal Defenses

How Does the Criminal Law Affect the Courts?

The criminal law is the criminal court's bread and butter. First, the criminal law makes work for the courts due to a need to sort through the complexities and contradictions in statutes. There are gradations of offenses (e.g., first-degree murder and second-degree murder), and frequently there are multiple statutes that effectively criminalize the same conduct. Judges and prosecutors must then decide what laws should be applied, how they should be applied, and what to do when inconsistencies are apparent.

Second, due to the fact that most criminal codes contain gradations of offenses, this affords opportunities for prosecutors to charge defendants with the top offense, which frequently leads to negotiations between the prosecutor and the defense attorney to reduce the charges. On the one hand, this plea bargaining (to which we will return later) saves courts time because it is a means of avoiding trial; on the other hand, judges must "sign off" on plea agreements, so plea agreements make work for them, too. Without complex legal codes containing multiple offenses and gradations of each, this activity probably would not occur.

The typical criminal court not only adjudicates the offense but also settles on a proper sentence. Most criminal statutes specify a range of possible penalties, or at least an upper limit. Due to strong public pressures for legislatures to adopt "get-tough" anticrime legislation, this makes plenty of work for courts, as it is their responsibility for ensuring that such sentences are carried out in the spirit intended by legislative authorities. Judges have been put in a difficult position due to legislative changes, and efforts to curtail their discretion to hand down sentences have complicated matters.

Finally, the criminal law affects the courts in the postsentencing phase. If an individual is convicted of first-degree murder and appeals the conviction, due perhaps to a judge's decision to improperly admit questionable evidence, this further taxes the courts. Allegations that judges improperly applied the law are common in appeals. There are also appeals that challenge the criminal law itself, and many laws have been overturned because they violate key constitutional provisions. To illustrate, a federal judge just recently overturned an Oklahoma law that made it a criminal offense to disseminate violent video games to juveniles.[29] In support of her decision, she argued that the right to disseminate video games is a form of free speech protected under the First Amendment.

CHAPTER › SUMMARY

1. EXPLAIN THE PURPOSE AND FUNCTIONS OF COURTS AND THE DUAL COURT SYSTEM

- A court is an agency or unit of the judicial branch of government, authorized or established by statute or constitution and consisting of one or more judicial officers, that has the authority to decide cases, controversies in law, and disputed matters of fact brought before it.
- The reason we have government courts is to settle disputes in a civilized manner.
- The United States has a dual court system, consisting of state and federal courts. The dual court system owes much to federalism.
- The three main functions of courts are (1) upholding the law, (2) protecting individuals, and (3) resolving disputes.

2. OUTLINE THE HISTORY AND DEVELOPMENT OF LAW AND THE COURTS

- The legal basis for the American court system lies in early legal codes, the common law, modern criminal codes, administrative regulations, and constitutions (federal and local).
- Early legal codes include the Code of Hammurabi and the Twelve Tables.
- The common law is judge-made law, and it prizes the practice of *stare decisis*, or adhering to precedent (past decisions).
- Administrative regulations are rules promulgated by government agencies that have been given their authority by the executive branch or legislative branch.
- Constitutions are found at the federal and state levels. State constitutions can be more restrictive than the U.S. Constitutions, but they cannot relax protections spelled out in the U.S. Constitution.
- Modern legal codes are found at the federal and state levels. State legal codes of interest to us are most often penal codes.
- Courts influence other criminal justice agencies and officials through adjudication and oversight.

3. SUMMARIZE THE GUIDING LEGAL PRINCIPLES UNDERLYING THE U.S. COURT SYSTEM

- People who come before the courts are protected via presumptions, constitutional rights, and the adversarial system.
- Presumptions are substitutes for evidence. The most well-known presumption in criminal justice is the presumption of innocence.
- Constitutional rights of relevance in the courts context stem mainly from the Fourth, Fifth, Sixth, Eighth, and Fourteenth Amendments to the U.S. Constitution.
- Ours is an adversarial justice system, which is particularly reflected in the courts. Our system is adversarial because it pits two parties, the prosecution and the defense, against each other in the pursuit of justice. The opposite of an adversarial system is an inquisitorial system of justice.

4. EXPLAIN THE NATURE OF DISPUTES

- Courts adjudicate both civil disputes and criminal cases. In general, criminal cases involve charges against an individual brought by a government official (i.e., a prosecutor). Civil cases involve disputes between private parties or sometimes between a government entity and a private party.

- Categories of civil law include torts, contracts, property law, the law of succession, and family law.

- A crime is any action that violates a statute duly enacted by the proper public authority.

- Crimes can be categorized by the penalties that attach or by the type of conduct involved. Felonies, misdemeanors, and infractions differ in terms of the penalties that can attach to each.

- The doctrine of *corpus delicti* requires that a crime must be committed in order to hold someone liable for it.

- Elements of a crime include *actus reus* (the criminal act) and *mens rea* (the intent).

- Criminal defenses come in three varieties: (1) alibis, (2) justifications, and (3) excuses.

KEY TERMS

actus reus, 21
adjudication, 2
administrative
    regulations, 9
adversarialism, 15
adversarial justice
    system, 15
alibi, 21
Bill of Rights, 9
Code of Federal
    Regulations, 9
Code of Hammurabi, 6
common law, 7
contract law, 19
cooperative federalism, 3
corpus delicti, 21

court, 2
crime, 20
dual court system, 3
dual federalism, 3
due process clause, 12
excuse defense, 23
family law, 19
felony, 20
incorporation, 12
infraction, 20
injunctive relief, 17
inquisitorial system, 16
justification defense, 21
law of succession, 19
mens rea, 21
misdemeanor, 20

monetary damages, 17
precedent, 7
presumption, 11
presumption of
    innocence, 11
procedural due process, 15
property law, 19
special law, 7
stare decisis, 7
strict liability, 19
substantive due process, 15
tort, 19
tort law, 19
Twelve Tables, 6
will, 19

REVIEW QUESTIONS

1. What is the function of courts in American society, and why do we have a dual court system?

2. What is the legal basis for today's courts?

3. How did courts develop in Western societies?

4. What is the difference between our adversarial system of justice and the inquisitorial systems of justice that have sometimes been used in the past?

5. By what means do courts protect everyone, from law-abiding citizens to hardened criminals?

6. What are the various types of defenses to a criminal charge that a defendant might offer in court?

✔ WHAT WILL YOU DO?

You are the police chief of a small California city. Your liaison officer, who works with the local police fusion center, informed you a few hours ago that intelligence developed by the Department of Homeland Security indicates that terrorists might be targeting your city over the next week to ten days. The nature of the threat isn't clear, but intelligence specialists say that it involves a plot to be carried out by three or four Middle Eastern men who have apparently been living nearby for at least a year. The analysts also say that the target seems to be one of the public transportation services in your city.

You realize that the information you've been provided is far from specific. Public transportation could involve buses, commuter trains, ferries, taxis, and even commercial aircraft. Your city does have a small airport served mostly by commuter airlines that transport around 2,500 people per day. There is a ferry service that runs every four hours during daylight hours, linking your town to an offshore resort island.

You wish you knew just how real the threat is. More than that, it would be very helpful to know what kind of attack is planned. Is it a bombing? If so, could it involve radiological materials? Would it be a suicide bomber? A car or truck bomb? Might the analysts have gotten wind of a planned biological attack? If there is an attack, will the attackers have guns and possibly automatic weapons?

You have already begun thinking of the kinds of measures you will implement in an effort to protect the public. Bag searches on commuter trains and buses are sure to be necessary, as are roadblocks and some vehicle searches on the main highways leading into the city. You will want your officers to be on the lookout for anything and anyone suspicious, and you will have to tell them to pay special attention to men who look as though they might be Middle Easterners. Members of the SWAT team will be deployed in critical areas, and they will have to be heavily armed. Your city has installed security cameras in a number of public locations, and some commercial establishments have agreed to allow police personnel to monitor video feeds coming from their locations. You'll ask your video analysts to be on heightened alert while the threat persists.

You've had the chief's job for five years, and while you've trained for various scenarios involving terrorist threats, this is the first time you've faced the "real thing." You take your job very seriously, and you feel responsible for the safety and security of everyone in your community. While safety and security are foremost in your mind, you also value the personal freedoms that you believe have made our country great. The freedoms to come and go, to move about at will, to speak one's mind, and to generally do as one pleases—all without unwarranted government intervention—represent the American way. It will be necessary, you tell yourself, to temporarily deny members of the public certain freedoms—at least while the terrorist threat remains.

You realize, of course, that your department doesn't operate in a vacuum. Not only are you responsible for the safety and security of community members, but the public holds you responsible for fair and just enforcement of the law. The news media will report on the deployment of police resources and will likely exploit any opportunity to show members of the police department acting aggressively. Additionally, you are well aware of the possibility that any limitations you might place on traditional freedoms could result in lawsuits targeting you and your department.

The questions that you'll need to answer are just how far you can go in implementing security measures and how well you'll be able to defend those measures in court should the need arise. Use your general knowledge of criminal justice and of U.S. Supreme Court cases to decide the kinds of measures that you will be able to lawfully initiate. Ask yourself these questions: If you were to face lawsuits as a result of implementing these measures, would you feel confident of a positive outcome? What is the role of court precedent, specifically previous U.S. Supreme Court decisions, in providing such confidence?

NOTES

i. U.S. Department of Justice, *Dictionary of Criminal Justice Data Terminology*, p. 53.

ii. U.S. Department of Justice, *Dictionary of Criminal Justice Data Terminology*, 2nd ed. (Washington, DC: U.S. Department of Justice, Bureau of Justice Statistics, 1981), p. 12. We use this dictionary throughout this book for definitions where appropriate.

iii. O. J. Thatcher, ed., *The Library of Original Sources*, Vol. III: *The Roman World* (Milwaukee, WI: University Research Extension Co., 1901), pp. 9–11.

iv. *Geddes v. Northwest Missouri State College*, 49 F.3d 426 (8th Cir. 1995).

v. Arguably the most famous case in this area was *Greenman v. Yuba Power Products*, 59 Cal. 2d 57 (1963).

vi. Ibid.

1. J. L. Miller, "Judges Crack Down on Inappropriate Clothes in Court," *USA Today*, August 17, 2010, http://usatoday30.usatoday.com/news/nation/2010-08-16-court-dress-code_N.htm (accessed February 20, 2013).

2. Ibid.

3. U.S. Department of Justice, *Dictionary of Criminal Justice Data Terminology*, 2nd ed. (Washington, DC: U.S. Department of Justice, Bureau of Justice Statistics, 1981), p. 53. We use the same dictionary throughout this book for definitions where appropriate.

4. Ibid., p. 12.

5. *Mallery v. Lane*, 97 Conn. 132 (1921).

6. Ibid., p. 138.

7. G. Brennan and P. Pettit, *The Economy of Esteem: An Essay on Civil and Political Society* (Oxford: Oxford University Press, 2004), p. 282.

8. Charles Francis Adams, ed., *The Works of John Adams, Second President of the United States, 1854*, 9:229 US diplomat and politician (1735–1826), October 11, 1798.

9. Ancient History Sourcebook, *Code of Hammurabi*, c. 1780 B.C., available at http://www.fordham.edu/halsall/ancient/hamcode.asp (accessed January 28, 2013).

10. O. J. Thatcher, ed., *The Library of Original Sources* (Milwaukee, WI: University Research Extension Co., 1901), Vol. III: *The Roman World*, pp. 9–11.

11. Ibid.

12. See, e.g., *Katz v. United States*, 389 U.S. 347 (1967).

13. *Gonzales v. Carhart*, 550 U.S. 124 (2007).

14. From the first of 12 Lowell Lectures delivered by Oliver Wendell Holmes Jr. on November 23, 1880, which were the basis for *The Common Law*.

15. See, e.g., http://www.leginfo.ca.gov/calaw.html (accessed January 28, 2013).

16. See, e.g., http://www.dol.gov/esa/minwage/america.htm (accessed January 28, 2013).

17. *Tennessee v. Garner*, 471 U.S. 1 (1985).

18. *Dodson v. United States*, 23 F.2d 401 (1928).

19. *Geddes v. Northwest Missouri State College*, 49 F.3d 426 (8th Cir. 1995).

20. *Howard v. Grinage*, 82 F.3d 1343 (1996), p. 1350.

21. H. Lu, "Confessions and Criminal Case Disposition in China," *Law and Society Review*, Vol. 37 (2003), p. 555.

22. *Tennessee v. Garner*, 471 U.S. 1 (1985).

23. H. Jacob, *Justice in America* (Boston: Little, Brown, 1978).

24. Arguably the most famous case in this area was *Greenman v. Yuba Power Products*, 59 Cal. 2d 57 (1963).

25. U.S. Department of Justice, *Dictionary of Criminal Justice Data Terminology*, p. 60.

26. RCW 70.54.050. See also http://www.dumblaws.com (accessed January 28, 2013).

27. J. Reiman, *The Rich Get Richer and the Poor Get Prison*, 7th ed. (Boston: Allyn and Bacon, 2007); see especially chapter 2.

28. U.S. Department of Justice, *Dictionary of Criminal Justice Data Terminology*, p. 108.

29. K. Orland, "Oklahoma Violent Game Law Overturned," available at http://www.joystiq.com/2007/09/17/oklahoma-violent-game-law-overturned (accessed January 28, 2013).

© Radius Images/Alamy

ho Controls the Courts?

NING OBJECTIVES

nmarize the ways legislatures exert control over
 courts.

nmarize the ways the executive branch of the
 vernment exerts control over the courts.

3. Describe the hierarchical structure of the courts.

4. Summarize the various other ways in which control is
   exerted over the courts.

INTRODUCTION

In 2011, Judge Roslyn O. Silver, chief of the Arizona federal judicial district, declared a judicial emergency, effectively lengthening the time period allowed for bringing criminal cases to trial to 180 days and calling on Congress to provide additional resources for her beleaguered district.[1] Silver's declaration came after judicial caseloads increased by 65% in her jurisdiction over a three-year period, due largely to expanded efforts by the federal government to enforce immigration laws along Arizona's border with Mexico. As of mid-2013, 31 judicial emergencies had been declared throughout U.S. federal courts, and five of the 13 federal judgeships authorized for Arizona remained empty. At that time, the longest judicial vacancy in the federal court system totaled 2,974 days—and it existed in the U.S. Court of Appeals for the Ninth Circuit.[2]

Our constitutional system of government gives legislatures and the executive distinct powers that serve as "checks" on the courts. Legislatures have been tasked with the role of creating courts, assigning the number of judgeships, setting judicial salaries, and confirming prospective judges. Likewise, executives—whether the president at the federal level or governors at the state level—appoint certain judges to their positions. These checks help ensure that court power does not become excessive; they offer a means of controlling the courts.

At the same time, the very fact that our government consists of three branches also reflects a desire on the framers' part to ensure each branch's independence. For example, the Constitution affords the federal judiciary considerable independence by appointing judges to their posts for life (more on this in Chapter 7). Even so, there has also been a consistent struggle for control of the judiciary beyond the executive and legislative branches.[3] A variety of different interests—inside and outside government—have employed creative strategies to shape decisions, enact laws, and formulate policies that serve *them*. This has resulted in a collision of beliefs, values, and priorities that has taken a substantial toll on the courts, prompting them to react in a variety of ways to maintain and promote their independence.[4]

The Sandra Day O'Connor federal courthouse in Phoenix, Arizona. Why is the federal judiciary short staffed?

Superstock/Glow Images

Learning Objective 1
Summarize the ways legislatures exert control over the courts.

direct control
The ability of legislative bodies to directly control the courts through the power to create them, to set the rules they must follow, and to limit their jurisdiction.[i]

indirect control
The ability of legislative bodies to indirectly control the courts through the power to confirm judicial appointees and to set the budget for the judiciary.

jurisdiction
The power of a court to resolve a dispute.

geographical jurisdiction
The organization of courts in distinct geographic regions.

subject matter jurisdiction
The type of case that individual courts can adjudicate.

hierarchical jurisdiction
The courts' distinct functions and responsibilities at different levels within a single (state or federal) judiciary.

original jurisdiction
"[T]he lawful authority of a court to hear or act upon a case from its beginning and to pass judgment on the law and the facts."[ii]

appellate jurisdiction
"[T]he lawful authority of a court to review a decision made by a lower court; the lawful authority of a court to hear an appeal from a judgment of a lower court."[iii]

Legislative Control

Legislatures exert control over the courts through various means. Article III of the U.S. Constitution gives Congress the power to create courts. With this comes the authority to define courts' jurisdiction. When courts are created, Congress also authorizes a specified number of judgeships, sets judicial salaries, and enacts rules that the courts must follow. Similar arrangements are found at the state level.

We call this type of authority **direct control** because it is constitutionally authorized, but the legislative branch can exert **indirect control** over the courts by confirming judicial appointees and setting the judiciary's budget. Together, the direct and indirect controls that the legislative branch can exert over the courts put it at the top of the proverbial "food chain." We begin with a detailed look at jurisdiction, then we look closer at court creation, rule setting, confirmations, and budgeting.

Jurisdiction

Jurisdiction refers to the power of a court to resolve a dispute. It is defined more formally as "the territory, subject matter, or persons over which lawful authority may be exercised by a court or other justice agency, as determined by statute or constitution."[5] As we already mentioned, the U.S. Constitution's third article spells out the judicial power of the United States. Congress has gone on to create several other federal courts; states have done the same. Part of this court creation process involves setting courts' jurisdictional boundaries. There are several types of jurisdiction, and they are covered in the following sections.

Geographical Jurisdiction **Geographical jurisdiction** refers to the organization of courts in distinct geographic regions. California courts hear only California cases, Maryland courts hear only Maryland cases, and so on. Within each state, courts have their own geographic boundaries, and often they are organized by counties. At the federal level, there are federal districts and appellate districts. Federal districts can take up whole states, or there can be more than one federal district in a single highly populous state. In contrast, the appellate districts overlap several states.

Subject Matter Jurisdiction **Subject matter jurisdiction** is concerned with what types of cases individual courts can adjudicate. Some courts have limited subject matter jurisdiction because they hear only specific types of cases, such as gun cases, drug cases, and domestic-violence cases. Higher-level courts, like state supreme courts or the U.S. Supreme Court, hear mostly appeals, so they actually have jurisdiction over many different types of disputes.

Hierarchical Jurisdiction **Hierarchical jurisdiction** is concerned with the courts' distinct functions and responsibilities at different levels within a single (state or federal) judiciary. Hierarchical jurisdiction can be further subdivided into two types. **Original jurisdiction** is "the lawful authority of a court to hear or act upon a case from its beginning and to pass judgment on the law and the facts."[6] **Appellate jurisdiction** is "the lawful authority of a court to review a decision made by a lower court; the lawful authority of a court to hear an appeal from a judgment of a lower court."[7]

The typical lower-level trial court has original jurisdiction to try specific cases, such as those arising out of violations of distinct penal code provisions. In contrast, higher-level courts, like state appellate courts, the federal appellate courts, and supreme courts (including the U.S. Supreme Court), have very limited original jurisdiction and rarely try offenses or resolve disputes between parties. Their jurisdiction is mostly of the appellate variety, meaning that they hear only appeals arising out of the lower courts. Such appeals most often challenge legal decisions made by lower-court judges.

Federal Jurisdiction Jurisdiction further varies between the federal and state courts. In general, the federal courts have jurisdiction over federal matters, and the state courts have jurisdiction over state matters. Exceptions exist when the U.S. Supreme Court has original jurisdiction over certain cases arising from the states.

Both the Constitution and various federal statutes spell out precisely what kinds of cases the federal courts can hear.[8] There are various types of federal court jurisdiction, but one that is most important in the criminal justice context is the **federal question jurisdiction**, which refers to the authority of federal courts to hear cases touching on the Constitution or other federal laws. Cases falling within these categories are said to raise "federal questions." Recall from Chapter 1 that we briefly referenced the Supreme Court's decision in *Tennessee* v. *Garner*.[9] Surviving family members of a 15-year-old who was shot by a police officer sought relief via a lawsuit, invoking a federal statute and arguing that the boy's right to be free from unreasonable searches and seizures was violated. This case ultimately went to the Supreme Court because it raised a federal question: Is it a violation of federal law (the Fourth Amendment in particular) to shoot an unarmed fleeing felon, and, based on that, can a lawsuit be brought to federal court?

What about criminal cases that involve violations of federal law? On the one hand, criminal cases involving violations of federal law fall under the original jurisdiction (see earlier discussion in this chapter) of the U.S. district courts; on the other hand, violations of federal law are akin to "federal questions," which brings federal question jurisdiction into play. Federal question jurisdiction can come into play at the appellate level as well. Assume, for example, that a district court trial judge admits evidence against a defendant that was obtained in a questionable fashion. If the defendant is convicted, he or she may appeal and allege a constitutional rights violation, in which case the appeal would fall under federal question jurisdiction.

> **federal question jurisdiction**
> One of three main types of federal court jurisdiction that refers to the authority of federal courts to hear cases touching on the U.S. Constitution or other federal laws.

Diversity Jurisdiction **Diversity jurisdiction** refers to the authority of certain federal courts to hear cases where the parties are from different states. The term *diversity* is used specifically in this context to refer to the fact that both parties have different, or "diverse," state citizenship. Giving the federal courts jurisdiction in such cases is sensible because it provides a neutral forum in which to resolve disputes arising out of more than one place. It could be construed as unfair to have a dispute between citizens of two states resolved in one of the states where a party resides.

Diversity jurisdiction cases must involve disputed amounts of more than $75,000. Diversity jurisdiction also extends to disputes between U.S. citizens and foreign citizens and/or companies. If a Texas company sued a Mexican company, this would fall under the federal courts' diversity jurisdiction.[10]

> **diversity jurisdiction**
> One of three main types of federal court jurisdiction. This refers to the authority of federal courts to hear cases where the parties are from different states.

Supplemental Jurisdiction Some federal courts also enjoy what is known as **supplemental jurisdiction** (also called *ancillary or pendent jurisdiction*), or the right to hear a case for which it would not ordinarily have original jurisdiction.[11] Supplemental jurisdiction is also called ancillary jurisdiction or pendent jurisdiction.

> **supplemental jurisdiction**
> One of three main types of federal court jurisdiction that refers to the right of some federal courts to hear a case for which they would not ordinarily have original jurisdiction[iv]; also called *ancillary jurisdiction* or *pendentjurisdiction*.

State Jurisdiction State court jurisdiction is considerably more straightforward when compared to federal court jurisdiction. State courts have either original or appellate jurisdiction and do not have authority to decide matters involving federal questions, diversity issues, or supplemental matters (as in the case of supplemental jurisdiction).

State courts exercise original jurisdiction over various disputes. Most often, these are criminal cases or civil lawsuits. State trial courts have original jurisdiction over criminal cases involving violations of state law, and they also have original jurisdiction over civil lawsuits that do not involve federal questions. In contrast, state appellate courts have appellate jurisdiction.

State courts are similar to federal courts when it comes to geographical or subject matter jurisdiction and are divided along specific geographic boundaries; for example, most state trial courts are found at the county level. Likewise, state courts (like the federal courts) have distinct subject matter jurisdiction. The lowest state courts have limited jurisdiction over specific matters, such as traffic violations.

Types of Direct Controls

Jurisdiction is not the only example of direct control of the judiciary by the legislature. Legislative bodies can further exert direct control over the courts through creating them, setting the rules they must follow, and limiting their jurisdiction.[12]

Creating Courts Article III of the U.S. Constitution gives Congress the authority to create courts as it sees fit. New courts have appeared throughout history, others have been eliminated, and still others have had their names and jurisdictions changed. Legislatures perform the same functions at the state level as well.

Legislatures also maintain authority to decide personnel issues. At the federal level, Congress defines the number of judgeships, thereby determining how many judges will be available to settle disputes in the federal courts. Congress also sets judicial pay. Article III bars Congress from reducing judicial salaries, but the ability to set the initial salaries is still important.

The influence of Congress on judicial salaries was recently made apparent in a report by the **American Bar Association (ABA)**, a group that accredits U.S. law schools, and the Federal Bar Association; the report observed that "the current salaries of Federal judges have reached such levels of inadequacy that they threaten to impair the quality and independence of the Third Branch."[13]

Setting the Rules Legislatures also have rule-making authority. At the federal level, Congress has the authority to set the rules of practice, procedure, and evidence in the federal courts. It has delegated this responsibility to the Judicial Conference of the United States (see Chapter 3 for more detail on the Judicial Conference), but it retains the right to modify or reject proposed rule changes. The **Rules Enabling Act of 1934**[14] spells the arrangements out in more detail. A summary of the federal rule-making process can be seen in Table 2–1.

There are five sets of rules that dictate the procedures to be followed in federal court cases. The Federal Rules of Civil Procedure govern the processing of civil cases,[15] and the Federal Rules of Criminal Procedure do the same for criminal cases.[16] The federal appellate courts follow the Federal Rules of Appellate Procedure, but bankruptcy cases have their own set of rules, found in the Federal Rules of Bankruptcy Procedure. Finally, the Federal Rules of Evidence govern the admissibility of evidence in federal cases (e.g., when hearsay is admissible, what evidence is deemed relevant, what forms of scientific evidence are admissible). All federal courts must follow these standard rules, but many have developed their own "local rules" to help them deal with local issues and problems. But like the relationship between states' constitutions and the federal Constitution, the local rules cannot supersede or contradict the federal rules. Local rules often involve simple twists to ensure that a court's day-to-day operations flow smoothly; for example, a local rule may govern which type of paper a claim must be submitted on. The federal rules' intent is to ensure uniformity and consistency in the federal courts.

American Bar Association (ABA)
A professional organization founded on August 12, 1878, whose mission today is "to be the national representative of the legal profession, serving the public and the profession by promoting justice, professional excellence and respect for the law."[iv]

Rules Enabling Act of 1934
The U.S. federal legislation that gave Congress the authority to set the rules of practice, procedure, and evidence in the federal courts.[vi]

TABLE 2–1 Federal Courts' Rule-Setting Procedures

Summary of Procedures

Action	Date
Step 1	
There is a suggestion for a change in the rules (submitted in writing to the secretary).	At any time.
It is referred by the secretary to the appropriate advisory committee.	Promptly after receipt.
It is considered by the advisory committee.	Normally at the next committee meeting.
If approved, the advisory committee seeks authority from the Standing Committee to circulate to bench and bar for comment.	Normally at the same meeting or the next committee meeting.
Step 2	
There is a public comment period.	For six months.
There are public hearings.	During the public comment period.
Step 3	
The advisory committee considers the amendment afresh in light of public comments and testimony at the hearings.	About one or two months after the close of the public comment period.
The advisory committee approves the amendment in final form and transmits it to the Standing Committee.	About one or two months after the close of the public comment period.
Step 4	
The Standing Committee approves the amendment, with or without revisions, and recommends approval by the Judicial Conference.	Normally at its June meeting.
Step 5	
The Judicial Conference approves the amendment and transmits it to the Supreme Court.	Normally at its September session.
Step 6	
The Supreme Court prescribes the amendment.	By May 1.
Step 7	
Congress has a statutory time period in which to enact the legislation, reject it, modify it, or defer the amendment.	By December 1.
Absent congressional action, the amendment becomes law.	December 1.

Source: http://www.uscourts.gov/RulesAndPolicies/FederalRulemaking/RulemakingProcess/SummaryBenchBar.aspx (accessed January 29, 2013).

Limiting Their Jurisdiction Congressional efforts to tinker with court jurisdiction have become so prevalent in recent years that a term has been assigned to the practice: court-stripping. Also called jurisdiction stripping,[17] **court-stripping** has been defined as "the attempt to take jurisdiction away from courts to review matters."[18] Attempts to limit court jurisdiction have most often come in the form of legislative proposals by members of Congress (or state legislators) as a means of voicing their displeasure with controversial court decisions.

Two examples of court-stripping are the Antiterrorism and Effective Death Penalty Act of 1996 (AEDPA)[19] and the Immigration Reform and Immigrant Responsibility Act of 1996 (IRIRA).[20] AEDPA states, in part, "Notwithstanding any other provision of law, no court shall have jurisdiction to review any final order of removal against any alien who is removable by reason of having committed a criminal offense." Note how the "no court shall have jurisdiction" language strips courts of their authority. Likewise, the IRIRA contains provisions for summary deportation of illegal aliens seeking political asylum, at border checkpoints, with no judicial review, and it was upheld in a Supreme Court ruling.[21]

court-stripping
"[T]he attempt to take jurisdiction away from courts to review matters"[vii]; also called *jurisdiction stripping.*[viii]

Indirect Controls

Legislatures also exert indirect control over the courts through two important indirect channels: confirmations and budgeting. At the federal level, the Senate must confirm judicial appointees by a simple majority, a process that has become intensely political in recent years. Congress also sets the budget for the federal judiciary as well as the salaries of individual judges.

Confirmations The Senate ultimately decides who becomes a federal judge, even though the president nominates potential judges to serve on the federal bench. The Senate has taken a hands-on approach to this important role because since 1789 more than 34 Supreme Court nominees (out of about 150) were not confirmed, suggesting that the Senate can indeed control who gets on the bench when there is sufficient support to do so.[22]

One of the more contentious debates of a judicial nominee involved President Reagan's nomination of Robert Bork to serve as associate justice on the Supreme Court. When Bork was nominated in 1987, Senator Ted Kennedy promptly reacted by stating, "Robert Bork's America is a land in which women would be forced into back-alley abortions, blacks would sit at segregated lunch counters, rogue police could break down citizens' doors in midnight raids, schoolchildren could not be taught about evolution, writers and artists could be censored at the whim of government."[23] Bork's nomination was defeated; now when a nomination is blocked, it is often described as being "borked."

A number of observers have expressed frustration with the politicized nature of the confirmation process these days. According to legal expert Ryan Becker, partisan division has entered the confirmation process with a vengeance.[24] It is not uncommon for judicial nominees to wait months for their confirmations.

Library Extra
2–1 Judicial Budgets

Budgeting Congress sets the budget and thus appropriates money for the judicial branch to operate. While the judiciary's budget is a pittance compared to what it costs to run other government programs (such as the military), it is still possible to exert substantial control of the courts through this "power of the purse." Similar observations can be traced all the way back to 1788, when in the *Federalist No. 79* Hamilton argued that "we can never hope to see realized in practice the complete separation of the judicial from the legislative power, in any system, which leaves the former dependent for pecuniary resources on the occasional grants of the latter."[25]

The federal judiciary is funded by Congress following a back-and-forth process: The Committee on the Budget of the Judicial Conference of the United States presents a budget to Congress, defending its various funding proposals; Congress then responds, usually with a somewhat reduced budget. This is fairly typical of the budgeting process for other federal agencies.

Much the same process plays out at the state level, and it can be political there as well.[26] A recent survey of court administrators and other personnel involved in court budgeting revealed just this.[27]

How would legislatures influence court decisions? Nearly 30 percent of the survey respondents claimed that elected legislators either directly or indirectly threatened the courts with budget reductions as a means of protesting unfavorable decisions, and almost 20 percent of the survey respondents claimed that their legislatures *had* reduced courts' budgets in response to such decisions. As for pressures to raise revenues, the researchers found that courts have been pressured to increase court fees and monetary sanctions, such as fines and forfeitures. They noted that "pressuring courts to raise more money creates the potential for biasing court decisions; for example, judges might be inclined to impose the maximum fine in all cases in order to increase funding."[28]

EXECUTIVE CONTROL

Learning Objective 2

Summarize the ways the executive branch of the government exerts control over the courts.

executive control
A measure of control over the courts exercised through the executive's power to appoint judges to the bench and the daily presence of the prosecutors—each of whom is a member of the executive branch—who work in the courts.

Our system of government ensures that the executive branch has a measure of control over the courts. At the federal level, **executive control** is applied through the appointment process. The executive branch also has a significant presence in the courts: Whether at

COURTS IN THE NEWS

Tan Yong and Li Yan: Domestic Violence and the Chinese Court System

AP Photo/Xinhua, Zhou Wenjie

Chinese courts are controlled by political doctrine and must toe the party line. In the US, courts are designed to be objective and non-political institutions. Do you believe they have met that standard?

Before they married in 2009, Tan Yong admitted to Li Yan that he had beaten his three previous wives. He promised to change, but he did not; soon after the wedding, Mr. Tan began abusing his wife. He stubbed out cigarettes on her face and legs. He would take her hair and hit her head against the wall. He locked her on the balcony for hours in the winter. The abuse went on for more than a year. Finally, Ms. Li could take no more and killed him during an argument in November 2010. After killing her husband, she cut him up and boiled some of the body parts. She currently is in a jail in Sichuan Province, China, awaiting execution for murder. The case underscores the severe sentences often imposed on women who fight back, injuring or killing abusive husbands.

Those who support her cause believe that she lost control because of the battering. However, the court did not take the abuse into account when determining her sentence. Lawyers, deputies to the National People's Congress, and Amnesty International have appealed to Chinese authorities not to execute Ms. Li. But at the time of this writing, she remains on death row.

Women's jails are filled with women who have injured or killed abusive husbands; they account for 60 percent of inmates in one jail in Anshan, Liaoning Province, and 80 percent of women serving heavy sentences in a jail in Fuzhou, Fujian Province. In a study by Xing Hongmei of China Women's University, of 121 female inmates in a Sichuan jail who were serving time for attacking or killing abusive partners, 71 were originally sentenced to life in prison or to death (sometimes commuted, delayed, or overturned on appeal), and 28 more were sentenced to at least 10 years. This means more than 80 percent received the heaviest possible sentences for murder or bodily harm. While Li's sentence was severe, she is not alone. While exact statistics of the death penalty in China are unavailable (as they are considered a state secret), it is estimated that thousands of executions take place on an annual basis—which is more than the rest of the world combined.

The harsh treatment meted out by Chinese courts stands in contrast to China's position as a global superpower. Not too long ago, a member of China's nine-man Politburo Standing Committee clearly stated the government's opposition to independent courts in an address published in a state-run magazine on February 2, 2007. Mr. Luo Gan, citing the need to protect against threats to national security, called on Chinese legal departments at all levels to adhere to the "correct" political stance—which he defined as "where the party stands"—in dispensing justice in Chinese courts.

Luo's address served to warn officials throughout China's legal system that the democratic concept of independent courts will not be tolerated. Instead, courts are expected to toe the line set by the country's Communist Party leadership, thus ensuring the Party's continued control.

Many people—even the Chinese themselves—admit that politics plays a central role in the administration of courts in China. As this news box shows, even high-ranking Chinese officials believe that such control is necessary for the effective administration of justice. Western-style democracies, however, often espouse the ideal of an independent judiciary. ■

DISCUSSION QUESTIONS

1. What are the likely consequences of political control over the courts, as appears to be the case in China?

2. What agencies or groups influence courts under the American style of government?

3. Does politics play a role in the operation of American courts?

4. Should American courts operate more independently? If so, how?

Sources: Didi Kirsten Tatlow, "Chinese Courts Turn a Blind Eye to Abuse, *New York Times*, January 29, 2013, http://www.nytimes.com/2013/01/30/world/asia/chinese-courts-turn-a-blind-eye-to-abuse.html?_r=0&pagewanted=print (accessed May 11, 2013); Joseph Kahn, "Chinese Official Warns against Independence of Courts," *New York Times*, February 3, 2007, http://www.nytimes.com/2007/02/03/world/asia/03china.html?_r=2 (accessed May 30, 2013).

the state or the federal level, prosecutors, who are members of the executive branch, work in the courts on a daily basis. The executive branch also asserts its control—or at least its autonomy—by ignoring or modifying certain court decisions.

Executive Appointment Process for the Judiciary

The president is given authority, via the Constitution, to appoint federal judges, but given how many federal judgeships there are, it is unrealistic for the president to be heavily involved in all the nominations. Particularly for vacancies in the lower courts, the president will routinely consult with senators and other elected officials in an effort to identify qualified candidates. Deference is often given to senators when there is a vacancy in their states. The president also consults with the ABA, an issue we discuss later in this chapter.

Executive Presence in the Courts

The executive branch's influence on the federal courts can also be observed in the activities of the Department of Justice, an executive agency that is responsible for prosecuting individuals who violate federal laws and for representing the government in civil cases Executive employees, particularly the U.S. attorneys and their subordinates, routinely interact with the federal courts and argue cases before them. Second, other executive agencies either work in or work closely with the courts. For example, the U.S. Marshals Service provides security for federal courthouses and judges. Finally, some other federal agencies routinely adjudicate disputes arising from administrative law in the federal courts.

Reshaping the Judiciary?

Shortly after Franklin Roosevelt was elected to the presidency in 1936, he unleashed a proposal called the Judiciary Reorganization Bill of 1937. In it, he called for presidential authority to appoint an additional Supreme Court justice to the U.S. Supreme Court for every sitting justice who was over 70½ years of age, up to a maximum of six new justices. Roosevelt's intentions were to "stack" the Supreme Court such that it would uphold important New Deal measures. His plan eventually failed when it was defeated in the Senate, but it nevertheless signaled that the president *could* restructure the judiciary. After all, the Constitution is silent on the appropriate number of Supreme Court justices.

Learning Objective 3

Describe the hierarchical structure of the courts.

CONTROL FROM ABOVE

There is a distinct hierarchy to the court system at both the federal and the state level. Higher courts have considerable influence over lower courts due to this hierarchical structure; at the same time, lower courts do not necessarily "follow the rules" to the letter and have developed various means to cope with influential decisions from the higher courts.

Courts are subject to direct control from higher-court officials, just as they are subject to direct control from the legislative branch. Higher courts, including the judges in higher courts, exert direct control over the lower courts in two ways: jurisdictional authority and rule setting. Higher courts also seek to influence lower-court judges' decisions, but, as we will see, this is not always possible.

Jurisdictional Authority

Recall that hierarchical jurisdiction referred to the organization of courts within a distinct state (or federal) system. This means that the higher courts have direct control over the lower courts. Related to this was geographical jurisdiction, referring to the organization of courts within distinct geographic areas; for example, a state supreme court has jurisdiction over the other state courts within its boundaries.

Jurisdictional authority thus refers to the authority of higher courts to issue decisions that are binding on the lower courts within their jurisdiction. For example, an appellate court may reverse a lower court's decision (more on this process in Chapter 14). In an ideal world, lower courts would follow higher courts' decisions to the letter, implementing them without any resistance or second-guessing, but in reality, lower courts have developed creative methods of adapting to higher-court decisions, of giving the appearance of following them without necessarily doing so.

Rule Setting

Every court is part of an administrative structure. For example, at the state level, trial courts fall under the state administrative office of the courts. State administrative agencies—which often have councils and committees made up of people appointed by judges within each state—set various rules and guidelines that lower courts must follow. The same process occurs at the federal level. The Administrative Office of the U.S. Courts and its various components basically supervise the lower federal courts. (We look more closely at the makeup of these administrative bodies in the next two chapters.)

Interpretation of Higher-Court Decisions

Lower-court judges, like prosecutors and police officers, have enormous discretion. Indeed, judges may have even *more* discretion than these other officials due to both the historically independent nature of the judiciary and the protections that judges enjoy in their professional capacities. Federal judges are protected by lifetime employment and thus do not fear losing their jobs for issuing unfavorable decisions or running their courts as they see fit. State judges, some of whom are elected, need not fear losing their jobs as long as the electorate is satisfied with their decisions. The result? Judges can take a measure of liberty in interpreting and applying higher-court decisions.

Importance of Interpretation Nearly all high-court decisions are subject to interpretation simply by the way they are written. For example, in the famous school desegregation case of *Brown* v. *Board of Education*,[29] Chief Justice Warren's implementation order (also called an implementation decree, issued following the Court's opinion in the case, spelling out details on how the decision was to be implemented by the lower courts) said the following:

> [T]he cases are remanded to the District Courts to take such proceedings and enter such orders and decrees consistent with this opinion as are necessary and proper to admit the parties to these cases to public schools on a racially nondiscriminatory basis with all deliberate speed.[30]

What is meant by "all deliberate speed"? There was no easy answer to this question, which meant that the lower courts had considerable license to interpret it. The implementation order also referenced a "prompt and reasonable start toward full compliance with the ruling."[31] What did Chief Justice Warren mean by this? Again, there was no easy answer, and the result was room for interpretation by the lower courts.

Consider a criminal justice example. In the landmark *Katz* v. *United States*[32] decision, the Supreme Court defined a search as consisting of government action that infringes on a "reasonable expectation of privacy." What is a reasonable expectation of privacy? Yet again, there is no easy answer. To provide a concrete example, there is some dispute as to whether an exploratory drug dog "sniff" of a public school student constitutes a search. This is an important issue because if such a sniff is a search, then an officer must have probable cause before conducting the search. If dog sniffs do not amount to searches, this gives officers considerable latitude to discover illicit drugs. Currently, the federal circuits are divided over the issue: In *Horton* v. *Goose Creek Independent School District*,[33] a lower court ruled that dog sniffs are indeed searches, but the Seventh Circuit has disagreed.[34] These courts have been unable to agree on what constitutes a "reasonable expectation of privacy."

Methods of Dealing with Higher-Court Decisions Lower courts employ a range of methods for dealing with higher-court decisions simply because of how many of the former there are. Researchers are mixed on the issue of how compliant lower-court judges are with higher-court decisions.[35] A number of studies have found that lower-court judges' decisions closely mirror those of the higher courts and that they follow the same ideological trends.[36] But other researchers have found that lower-court judges frequently resist higher-court decisions with which they disagree.[37] For those judges who resist higher-court decisions, they tend to employ two strategies:

1. *Ignoring the higher court's decision altogether*. This type of defiance is rare. A judge may act in this way by disposing of a case on procedural grounds before the point where the controversial higher-court decision may need to be applied. For example, the judge could decide that the plaintiff in a civil case does not have standing to sue.

2. *Implementing a higher court's decision sparingly*. Most cases are factually distinct from one another. Little twists and turns in the facts can make one case seem sufficiently different that a judge will not apply a controversial higher-court decision and thus "distinguish" the case before him or her, effectively issuing a new decision.

In summary, despite the judiciary's historical independence, it is very much subject to control. This control comes, in part, from the other two branches of government: the legislative and the executive. Higher courts, too, exert control over the lower courts, but this control is not unbridled; the lower courts resist some of the time. The struggle for control does not end within the halls of government. In the remainder of this chapter, we look at control from the people and from the legal profession. We conclude with a look at strategies that individual courts employ from within to cope with pressure from above and from outside (by other government officials, the public, and the professional community).

Learning Objective 4

Summarize the various other ways in which control is exerted over the courts.

Library Extra
2–2 Public Trust and Procedural Justice

OTHER FORMS OF CONTROL OVER THE COURTS

In addition to being controlled by legislatures, the executive, and higher courts, America's courts are also controlled by a range of other forces. This includes, first and foremost, the people through their voting behavior. The legal profession is also important, especially its many and influential professional associations. Finally, courts control themselves internally through different mechanisms. We introduce each of these sources of control in the remaining sections of this chapter.

Voter Behavior

If democracy vests authority in the people and they choose their representatives through elections, then elections can most definitely be used to exert a measure of popular control over the courts. This occurs directly through the election of judges, and it occurs indirectly through the election of executives who select judges to serve on the nation's higher courts.

Election of Judges

A number of judges are elected. However, judicial elections are held only at the state level, most often for judgeships in the lower courts. Some state supreme court justices are elected, but most judicial elections play out in the lower tier of states' court systems (we look at judicial elections more closely in Chapter 7).

Elections serve as a powerful tool for voters to exert their control over the judiciary. When a judge is elected to his or her post, it is presumably because the majority of voters are satisfied that he or she will do a good job on the bench. Judges who fail to satisfy their constituencies can sometimes face removal during the next election.

Why is there such a contrast between the federal judiciary, where judges are appointed for life, and state judiciaries, where elections are commonly held? Do judicial elections not threaten the independence of the judiciary? Do elected judges really behave differently due to the possible threat of losing their positions? We answer some of these questions in Chapter 7 when we give additional attention to the various methods of judicial selection.

Election of Executives

Federal judges are appointed to their positions. This would seem to suggest that the public cannot exert direct control over the judiciary. While this is certainly true, voters can *indirectly* influence the judiciary through executive elections. If voters select a Republican president to serve in the Oval Office, it is likely that he or she will appoint judges to the federal bench who share similar views; in contrast, a Democratic president would nominate judges who share his or her ideas and beliefs.

Indirect control over the courts through executive elections is very definitely *indirect*. Even if voters succeed in putting a new political party in the White House, there is no guarantee that judges sympathetic to their views will be nominated—and even if such judges *are* nominated, there is no way to predict how they will behave on the bench. Throughout history, there have been examples of judges who, through their opinions, "switched sides" after assuming their posts. Earl Warren, appointed by then-President Eisenhower because he was a leading conservative, turned into the most liberal chief justice in the nation's history. Former Supreme Court Justice David Souter was appointed by conservative President George H. W. Bush, but he was usually associated with the liberal wing of the Court.

Public Participation

Control over the courts is also accomplished through public participation. Openness ensures that government power does not get out of hand and that decisions are made in a transparent fashion to ensure conformance with applicable laws, constitutional requirements, and the like. Allowing the public to openly participate in the court process thus helps ensure that judiciaries do not become excessively powerful.

By law and custom, the American court system is an open institution. The Sixth Amendment requires that trials be open to the public, so anyone who wishes to observe a court in action, even Supreme Court oral arguments, can do so. All that is necessary is to pay a visit to the courthouse, check the calendar, and watch the proceeding. Sometimes the popular proceedings can get rather crowded and the prospects for getting in become slim, but this openness is a hallmark of the American judiciary and promotes transparency and openness. It ensures that justice is not meted out in secret behind closed doors.

Web Extra
2–1 Alaska Judicial Council

In this technological era, court openness is also being promoted via televising court programs and streaming trials over the Internet. It is easier now than ever before for someone to watch a trial, even from the convenience of his or her own home.

Interest Group Formation

To some extent, the right to observe a court proceeding is largely symbolic because it is unrealistic to expect that observers can directly influence the proceedings at any given time. For example, if one is fortunate enough to observe Supreme Court oral arguments, he or she is required to sit in silence and simply listen to the proceeding. One thing citizens *can* do to give themselves more of a "voice" is to form interest groups.

interest group
An organized private nongovernmental group whose mission is to influence political decisions and policy.

These groups can have considerable influence throughout government. **Interest groups**, whose mission is to influence political decisions and policy, do everything from contributing money to political campaigns to taking legislators out for lavish meals to sharing information and providing services to their members. For example, the National Rifle Association provides magazine subscriptions to its members (among other services), but it is also a lobbying organization of the first order, working hard to protect the rights of gun owners across the country. Victims' advocacy groups also represent a powerful interest group; they often seek to influence the courts by calling for harsh punishments (we look more closely at victim advocacy in Chapter 10).

test case
A court case that is likely to test the legality or constitutionality of a particular tactic or statute.

Test Cases Interest groups attempt to influence court cases either as litigants in specific cases or through the provision of resources to other litigants. They are especially drawn to so-called **test cases,** which are cases that are likely to test the legality or constitutionality of a particular tactic or statute.

One of the most famous test cases was the familiar *Brown* v. *Board of Education* school desegregation case.[38] While the case was a lawsuit filed by Linda Brown against the Board of Education of Topeka, Kansas, the National Association for the Advancement of Colored People supplied the legal assistance and finances to support Ms. Brown's case.

Another famous test case was *Wisconsin* v. *Yoder,*[39] wherein the Supreme Court held that Wisconsin's compulsory school attendance law violated the free exercise of religion clause in the First Amendment. The lawsuit in that case was filed by Amish plaintiffs (they objected to formal education beyond the eighth grade due to its apparent threat to family values), but it was financially assisted by an interest group called the National Committee for Amish Religious Freedom.

Interest groups are active in criminal justice as well. For example, the debate over gun control continues to be fought between interest groups. On one side is the pro-gun organization, the National Rifle Association. On the other side are groups like the Brady Center to Prevent Gun Violence. Sentencing policy has also seen its share of interest group involvement. Organizations such as Families against Mandatory Minimums oppose tough federal sentencing laws, but pro–law enforcement organizations such as the National District Attorneys Association tend to be supportive. For a listing of these and other well-known criminal justice interest groups, see Box 2–1. At the end of the box is a citation of a book where additional details concerning criminal justice interest groups can be found.

BOX 2–1 Some Major Criminal Justice Interest Groups

American Bar Association
American Civil Liberties Union
American Correctional Association
American Council for Drug Education
American Society for Industrial Security
Brady Center to Prevent Gun Violence
Children's Defense Fund
Drug Policy Alliance
Families against Mandatory Minimums
International Association of Chiefs of Police
Law Enforcement against Prohibition
Mothers against Drunk Driving
National Association of Attorneys General
National Association of Criminal Defense Lawyers
National Center for Rural Law Enforcement
National District Attorneys Association
National Organization for Victim Assistance
National Organization of Black Law Enforcement Executives
National Rifle Association
National Sheriff's Association
Society of Police Futurists International ■

Sources: http://faculty.ncwc.edu/mstevens/415/thnktank.htm (accessed January 29, 2013); M. A. Hallett and D. J. Palumbo, *U.S. Criminal Justice Interest Groups: Institutional Profiles* (Westport, CT: Greenwood Press, 1999).

Amicus Curiae Briefs *Amicus curiae*—a written document that seeks to persuade a court to decide in a particular way—means, literally, "friend of the court." As described in *Black's Law Dictionary,* "A person with strong interest in or views on the subject matter of an action, but not a party to the action, may petition in court for permission to file a brief, ostensibly on behalf of a party but actually to suggest a rationale consistent with its own view."[40] This definition references a "person," but *amicus curiae* briefs are very commonly filed on behalf of various interest groups. In fact, filing *amicus curiae* briefs is the easiest way for interest groups to get involved in cases and thereby influence court decisions and policy.[41]

An **amicus curiae** brief can be filed, but there is no guarantee that a judge will agree with an interest group's stance on a particular issue because in controversial cases it is not uncommon for various briefs to be submitted on behalf of groups representing both sides. But a persuasive brief has the potential to shape a court's decision significantly.

Just how influential are *amicus curiae* briefs? At the U.S. Supreme Court level, *amicus curiae* briefs are filed in almost every case the Court elects to hear.[42] Even before the Court elects to hear a case, *amicus curiae* briefs urging the Court to take a particular case are filed, and the presence of these briefs appears to increase the likelihood of a grant of *certiorari* (i.e., the Court agrees to hear the case).[43] Researchers have also found that *amicus curiae* briefs influence the chances of litigant success.[44]

Why are *amicus curiae* briefs successful? Is it because they provide judges with an impression of how many people stand on one side of an important issue, or is it because they provide "information" to assist judges in their decisions? One study suggests that the "information" explanation is most significant.[45]

amicus curiae
A term that literally means "a friend of the court." It is a legal brief filed by a "person [or group] with strong interest in or views on the subject matter of an action,"[ix] seeking to influence the court "ostensibly on behalf of a party but actually to suggest a rationale consistent with its own views."[x]

The Legal Profession

The legal profession also has considerable involvement in the courts. For example, the ABA accredits law schools around the country, which in turn affects the training of attorneys and thus the courts themselves. Research think tanks, too, issue reports and offer guidelines and recommendations for courts.

It should come as no surprise that the legal profession is influential in the courts. For one thing, the vast majority of judges are themselves attorneys; in addition, the sheer size of the legal profession ensures the courts must be responsive on some level. Figure 2–1 shows the number of lawyers per 10,000 residents in each state and the District of Columbia. The number of lawyers per person in the United States dwarfs the same statistic in many other industrialized nations.

Most professions have their own professional associations, and the legal profession has several. Lawyers in this country are often members of the ABA as well as their own state's bar association. In addition, there are professional associations for different types of lawyers. Many defense attorneys belong to the National Association of Criminal Defense Lawyers, and many prosecutors belong to the National District Attorneys Association. Then there are defense attorney and prosecution professional associations at the state level. Two of the most influential professional associations are the ABA and its equivalent state-level organizations.

Web Extra
2–2 American Bar Association

The ABA The ABA was founded on August 12, 1878. The association's first constitution called for "the advancement of the science of jurisprudence, the promotion of the administration of justice and a uniformity of legislation throughout the country."[46] The mission of the ABA today is "to be the national representative of the legal profession,

FIGURE 2–1

Lawyers per 10,000 People

Source: Based on data from http://www.averyindex.com (accessed January 29, 2013).

serving the public and the profession by promoting justice, professional excellence and respect for the law."[47]

The ABA has approximately 400,000 members, consisting of roughly half the attorneys in the United States. In addition to providing law school accreditation, the ABA provides professional training for attorneys, legal information, initiatives to improve the legal system, and, most important, programs to assist lawyers and judges with their work.

Not only is the ABA a professional association, but it is also an interest group. In this capacity, it often takes firm stances on various legal policy issues; for example, the ABA has repeatedly called for a moratorium on the use of capital punishment in the United States. The ABA has offered policy recommendations on nearly all criminal justice matters, ranging from the war on drugs to domestic violence to juvenile justice to grand jury policy.

To provide a specific example of the influence of the ABA over the courts, consider its ratings of nominees to the federal judiciary. For more than 50 years, the ABA's Standing Committee on the Federal Judiciary has been ranking nominees as either well qualified, qualified, or not qualified. These ratings have been relied on strongly by various presidents in their efforts to identify candidates for the federal bench. According to the ABA,

> The Committee's goal is to support and encourage the selection of the best-qualified persons for the federal judiciary. It restricts its evaluation to issues bearing on professional qualifications and does not consider a nominee's philosophy or ideology. The Committee's peer-review process is structured to achieve impartial evaluations of the integrity, professional competence and judicial temperament of nominees for the federal judiciary.[48]

At a glance, it would seem that the ABA has performed a valuable service, but many researchers have questioned the ABA's objectivity in this endeavor. Most of the research has centered around the ABA's ratings of Clinton and Bush nominees. One study found that "a Bush appointee with good credentials—both private and government practice experience, a top-10 law school education, law review experience, and a federal court clerkship—has a lower probability (32%) of getting the highest ABA rating than a Clinton appointee who has none of these credentials (48%)."[49] Another stated, "There is some evidence that on average Clinton nominees have been treated more favorably than Bush nominees, but the estimates do not always indicate a consistent statistically significant difference."[50]

Together, these studies suggest that the ABA may have shown a liberal bias in its recommendations, something that the ABA of course denies. The issue is important because political bias can adversely affect the selection of federal judges, which could in turn shape court decisions and ultimately public policy.

State Bar Associations For aspiring lawyers, state bar associations are all-important. State bar association tests (the so-called bar exams) must be passed before law school graduates can practice law in their home states. Like the ABA, state bar associations also provide a variety of services to the legal occupation, including training, information, and policy recommendations. State bar associations also supply evaluations of judicial candidates to assist governors in their nominations. Finally, state bar associations sponsor legislation and review bills bearing on the legal profession.

Much of the discussion in this chapter has concerned threats to judicial independence. Legislative and executive efforts to shape and control the judiciary suggest that the judiciary is far from independent. Bar associations, however, frequently engage in efforts to promote the independence and autonomy of their states' judiciaries. To illustrate, one of the core values of the New York State Bar Association is what it calls "independence of the courts, independence of the bar."[51]

Think Tanks

Just as professions have their professional associations, most professions are of interest to various research organizations, or "think tanks" as we call them. In the policing context, organizations like the Police Executive Research Forum and the Police Foundation conduct research and perform training to assist the profession. The courts have followed the same pattern. Two of the most visible and influential in the court context are the National Center for State Courts and the comparatively newer Center for Court Innovation.

The **National Center for State Courts** (NCSC), with offices in Virginia and Colorado, is a think tank that seeks "to improve the administration of justice through leadership and service to state courts, and courts around the world."[52] The NCSC's Research Division supports states' efforts to improve their judiciaries through identifying trends and recent developments as well as researching effective practices. Its many reports and publications, often authored in collaboration with the ABA, offer recommendations and best practices, all in the name of improving and shaping court policy at the state level. As we discuss in Chapter 4, the NCSC has been instrumental in state court performance measurement.

The **Center for Court Innovation** was initially formed as a partnership between the New York State Unified Court System and the Fund for the City of New York. It has since grown into a "non-profit think tank that helps courts and criminal justice agencies aid victims, reduce crime and improve public trust in justice. The Center combines action and reflection to spark problem-solving innovation both locally and nationally."[53] The center has been particularly instrumental in the formation of innovative problem-solving courts.

Judicial Restraint and Activism

Judges are put on a pedestal (quite literally), suggesting a degree of infallibility, but they are human like everyone else. They bring their own emotional baggage, political beliefs, agendas, and biases to the bench. Some judges see their role as a lawmaker rather than just an interpreter of the law, but others steer clear of "making law" to the fullest extent possible by focusing solely on legal matters and deferring to legislative authorities, such as by refusing to declare certain statutes unconstitutional.

Judicial restraint is the philosophy of limiting decisions to the facts of each case, deciding only the issues that need to be resolved in a particular situation. Judicial restraint also entails avoiding unnecessary decisions on constitutional questions that have yet to be posed. In the area of criminal procedure, a judicially restrained judge will look to the Constitution for guidance, and if the Constitution is not entirely clear, he or she will attempt to understand the framers' intent. One way to think of judicial restraint is that it is interpretive, seeking nothing other than interpretation of the Constitution. Yet another way to understand judicial restraint is with regard to precedent; the judicially restrained judge will defer to precedent as much as possible and avoid setting new guidelines and rules.

Judicial restraint is a philosophy found at the end of a larger spectrum of judicial philosophies, and at the other end is **judicial activism**. A judicially active judge is one who sees his or her role as more than interpreting the Constitution or laws; he or she avoids precedent and hands down decisions with sweeping implications for the future. Further, a judicially active judge favors "judge-made" law and looks more to the future than the past.

Sidebar (margin notes)

National Center for State Courts
A nongovernmental research, consulting, publishing, and educational service that seeks "to improve the administration of justice through leadership and service to state courts and courts around the world."[xi]

Center for Court Innovation
"[A nongovernmental] non-profit think tank that helps courts and criminal justice agencies aid victims, reduce crime and improve public trust in justice."[xii]

Web Extra
2–3 National Center for State Courts

Web Extra
2–4 Center for Court Innovation

Web Extra
2–5 ABA Center for Professional Responsibility

judicial restraint
The philosophy of limiting decisions to the facts of each case, deciding only the issue or issues that need to be resolved in a particular situation.

judicial activism
The philosophy of using one's power as a judge to do more than interpret the Constitution or laws by avoiding precedent and handing down decisions with sweeping implications for the future. A judicially active judge favors "judge-made" law and looks more to the future than the past.

To illustrate the activist view, consider the Supreme Court's decision in *Kyllo* v. *United States*,[54] where it decided on the constitutionality of warrantless thermal-imaging (infra-red) searches. The Court held, "Where, as here, the Government uses a device that is not in *general public use*, to explore *details of the home* that would previously have been unknowable without physical intrusion, the surveillance is a 'search' and is presumptively unreasonable without a warrant."[55] Notice how sweeping and general this language is—the Court did not focus on thermal imagers but instead handed down a decision addressing a wider range of technology. This, according to some critics, violates the philosophy of judicial restraint.

Why do we care? Activist judges issue decisions with broad implications for criminal justice. The "not in general public use" standard in the *Kyllo* decision suggests that law enforcement should be cautious with the use of not only thermal imagers but also any other technologies that ordinary citizens cannot readily get their hands on. This, critics of the decision have argued, makes it increasingly difficult for the police to do their job. Maybe if the Supreme Court showed more restraint, then officers could—at least for the time being—use *other* technologies to apprehend lawbreakers. A contrasting view is not that the Supreme Court was being activist but rather that it was being "forward-looking," realiz-ing that multiple technological advances raise constitutional questions—and will continue to as they are developed.

The Courtroom Work Group

In an effort to control their daily activities, courts have developed a number of in-formal and unwritten procedures for the processing of cases. In the criminal context, there are variations from one jurisdiction to the next in terms of how specific cases are handled. These variations impact the people who must work together in the courts on a daily basis. The three main parties to this relationship are the prosecutor, the de-fense attorney, and the judge; together, these three officials constitute the **courtroom work group**.

As we saw in Chapter 1, prosecutors and defense attorneys are not mortal enemies. They work together on a daily basis, and it is in their interest to ensure the efficient move-ment of cases through the criminal process. These attorneys frequently present their cases before the same judges, so they also learn how judges decide. The judges stand to benefit from a measure of uniformity in terms of how cases are handled. Finally, uniformity in the treatment of cases allows courts to adapt to the pressures and desires of outside influences. For example, people in one city may feel that people who drive with revoked licenses should be dealt with harshly, whereas in another jurisdiction people may not feel the same way. The courtroom work group can adapt its activities and decision making in response to such sentiments.

Even if prosecutors, defense attorneys, and judges cannot get along, there is still a measure of predictability in the cases they shepherd through the criminal process. If one were to ask a judge, a prosecutor, or a defense attorney from the same courthouse what would happen to a defendant who has a certain type of criminal history and who allegedly committed a specific offense, then any one of these actors could probably come up with an accurate estimate of what will happen to the defendant. They may agree that the case will be plea-bargained; alternatively, they may all feel that the case will go to trial and that the sentence will be pretty standard. The point is that there is a degree of predictability to the criminal court process—and there has to be. If the outcome of every case were totally unpredictable, if prosecutors, defense attorneys, and judges could not work together in a dignified manner, then the wheels of justice would slow to a crawl.

courtroom work group
The professional courtroom actors, including judges, prosecuting attorneys, defense attorneys, public defenders, and others who earn a living serving the court.

CHAPTER SUMMARY

2

1. SUMMARIZE THE WAYS LEGISLATURES EXERT CONTROL OVER THE COURTS

- Legislative control over the courts is manifest through jurisdiction setting, Article III authority for the legislative branch to create courts, rule setting, confirmations of nominees to judgeships, and budgeting.

- Court-stripping refers to legislative efforts to take jurisdiction away from the courts.

2. SUMMARIZE THE WAYS THE EXECUTIVE BRANCH OF THE GOVERNMENT EXERTS CONTROL OVER THE COURTS

- Executive control over the courts is manifested through appointments to the bench and executive participation in the courts (e.g., federal prosecutors appear before the courts on a regular basis).

- The Constitution is silent on the number of Supreme Court justices. In theory, the president could attempt to add more justices, but congressional approval would be required.

3. DESCRIBE THE HIERARCHICAL STRUCTURE OF THE COURTS

- Courts are subject to control from higher courts in the judicial hierarchy. This control is manifested through higher courts' jurisdictional and rule-setting authority.

- Despite the fact that lower courts are controlled by higher courts through jurisdictional and rule-setting authority, lower courts have developed various strategies to react to higher-court decisions. Higher-court decisions require interpretation and are sometimes ignored or applied sparingly.

4. SUMMARIZE THE VARIOUS OTHER WAYS IN WHICH CONTROL IS EXERTED OVER THE COURTS

- The people control the courts through several means, including the elections of judges and the elections of executive officials (presidents, governors) who nominate judges.

- Interest groups influence the courts through assisting with and/or funding test cases (cases that test controversial laws and policies) and through filing *amicus curiae* ("friend of the court") briefs. *Amicus curiae* briefs attempt to persuade the court to decide in a particular manner.

- The legal profession controls the courts through professional associations and think tanks. Professional associations are most noted for accrediting law schools and authorizing attorneys (by passing a state bar exam) to practice law.

- Think tanks influence the courts through training, research, and policy recommendations.

- Despite the many controls from outside and above, courts have adopted strategies to control themselves from within. Examples include judicial restraint and the concept of the courtroom work group.

- Judicial restraint is the philosophy of limiting decisions to the facts of each case, deciding only the issues that need to be resolved in a particular situation. Judicial activism is its opposite; so-called activist judges are those who issue decisions that are sometimes unpopular with legislators, the executive branch, and other interest groups.

- The courtroom work group consists of the prosecutor, the defense attorney, and the judge. These officials work together on a daily basis, and it is in their interest to work well together to ensure the efficient administration of justice.

KEY TERMS

American Bar
    Association, 32
amicus curiae, 41
appellate jurisdiction, 30
Center for Court
    Innovation, 44
courtroom work group, 45
court-stripping, 33
direct control, 30
diversity jurisdiction, 31

executive control, 34
federal question
    jurisdiction, 31
geographical jurisdiction, 30
hierarchical jurisdiction, 30
indirect control, 30
interest group, 40
judicial activism, 44
judicial restraint, 44
jurisdiction, 30

National Center for State
    Courts, 44
original jurisdiction, 30
Rules Enabling Act of
    1934, 32
subject matter
    jurisdiction, 30
supplemental
    jurisdiction, 31
test case, 40

REVIEW QUESTIONS

1. How do legislatures control the courts? What kinds of controls are available to legislatures?

2. How do government executives exercise control over the courts? What kinds of controls are exercised by government executives?

3. What kinds of controls do the higher courts exercise over lower courts? How does the interpretation of higher-court decisions by the lower courts help to shape such controls?

4. What kinds of controls does the public have over the courts? What is the role of interest groups in exercising such controls?

5. How does the legal profession influence the courts? What are some of the most influential professional associations?

6. What is judicial activism? How does judicial activism influence the courts?

WHAT WILL YOU DO?

You are an attorney and a member of your state's commission on higher education. Your committee is charged with assessing applications from out-of-state educational institutions wishing to offer courses for college-level credit in your state. "College-level credit" is defined by the legislature to include undergraduate offerings, professional school courses, graduate school courses, and law school classes. Courses approved by your committee will be accepted for transfer credit into appropriate programs in state universities.

Recently, a well-known out-of-state educational institution has applied to your commission for authorization to offer for-credit online law school courses to state residents seeking law degrees both in and out of state; the courses for which authorization has been requested are mostly in the area of criminal law. The applying institution notes in its supporting documentation that there is a nationwide need for public defenders, something that is also true in your state. By preparing more attorneys for practice in the area of criminal law, the institutional application argues, the needs of your state will be well served—especially as those needs relate to the creation of a cadre of attorneys capable of serving as public defenders.

The chair of your committee, however, has raised a number of objections to the application. Primary among them is her concern that online education does not provide a medium appropriate to the training of criminal attorneys. This, she says, is because both prosecutors and defense attorneys are required to practice within an adversarial system of justice, and that means a system that requires face-to-face personal confrontation.

The educational institution making application appears to have anticipated this objection and notes in its documentation that courts at many levels are moving toward greater use of the Internet and electronic media. Some hearings, the institution says, are being held over closed-circuit television, and attorneys frequently appear and argue in front of judges (and with one another) through the use of such virtual media. The day will likely come, says the institutional application, when much of any court's business will be handled in virtual fashion. The application goes on to note that online education is a widely accepted format in higher education today and that it often involves instructional personnel who are highly dedicated to the educational process and who provide intense one-on-one instruction, exceeding even the level of personal attention possible in traditional classrooms.

When the time comes to vote for or against the institutional application, how will you vote?

NOTES

i. Mecham, *Understanding the Federal Courts*.

ii. U.S. Department of Justice, *Dictionary of Criminal Justice Data Terminology*, p. 117.

iii. U.S. Department of Justice, *Dictionary of Criminal Justice Data Terminology*, p. 117.

iv. For two leading cases, see *Owen Equipment and Erection Co. v. Kroger*, 437 U.S. 365 (1978) and *United Mine Workers of America v. Gibbs*, 383 U.S. 715 (1966).

v. American Bar Association. Available at http://www.abanet.org/about/history.html (accessed September 22, 2009).

vi. 28 U.S.C., Sections 2071–2077.

vii. D. S. Dobkin, "Court Stripping and Limitations on Judicial Review of Immigration Cases," *Justice System Journal* 28 (2007):104–108.

viii. T. J. Weiman, "Jurisdiction Stripping, Constitutional Supremacy, and the Implications of *Ex Parte Young*," *University of Pennsylvania Law Review* 153(2005): 1677–1708.

ix. *Black's Law Dictionary*, 6th ed. (St. Paul, MN: West, 1990), p. 82.

x. Ibid.

xi. National Center for State Courts. Available at http://ncsconline.org/D_About/index.htm (accessed March 4, 2009).

xii. Center for Court Innovation. Available at http://courtinnovation.org/index.cfm?fuseaction=page.viewPage&pageID=471 (accessed January 4, 2009).

1. John R. Emshwiller and Alexandra Berzon, "Decree in Arizona Eases Trial Limit," Wall Street Journal, January 26, 2011, http://professional.wsj.com/article/SB10001424052748704013604576104510607653374.html?mg=reno64-wsj (accessed February 20, 2013).

2. Administrative Office of the U.S. Courts, "Judicial Emergencies," available at http://www.uscourts.gov/JudgesAndJudgeships/JudicialVacancies/JudicialEmergencies.aspx (accessed May 2, 2013).

3. C. G. Geyh, *When Courts and Congress Collide: The Struggle for Control of America's Judicial System* (Ann Arbor: University of Michigan Press, 2006).

4. See, e.g., D. W. Jackson, "Judicial Independence in Cross-National Perspective," in American Bar Association, Division for Public Education, ed., *Judicial Independence: Essays, Bibliography, and Discussion Guide* (Chicago: American Bar Association, 1999).

5. U.S. Department of Justice, *Dictionary of Criminal Justice Data Terminology*, 2nd ed. (Washington, DC: U.S. Department of Justice, Bureau of Justice Statistics, 1981), pp. 116–117.

6. Ibid., p. 117.

7. Ibid.

8. See, e.g., http://www.fjc.gov/history/home.nsf (accessed January 29, 2013).

9. 471 U.S. 1 (1985).

10. See, e.g., *Grupo Dataflux* v. *Atlas Global Corp.*, 541 U.S. 567 (2004).

11. For two leading cases, see *Owen Equipment and Erection Co.* v. *Kroger*, 437 U.S. 365 (1978); *United Mine Workers of America v. Gibbs*, 383 U.S. 715 (1966).

12. Much of the discussion that follows draws from L. R. Mecham, *Understanding the Federal Courts* (Washington, DC: Administrative Office of the U.S. Courts, Office of Judges Programs, 2003).

13. American Bar Association and Federal Bar Association, *Federal Judicial Pay Erosion: A Report on the Need for Reform*, p. i, available at http://news.findlaw.com/hdocs/docs/aba/abafedjudpy1213.pdf (accessed January 29, 2013).

14. 28 U.S.C. Section 2071–2077.

15. Available at http://www.law.cornell.edu/rules/frcp (accessed January 29, 2013).

16. Ibid.

17. T. J. Weiman, "Jurisdiction Stripping, Constitutional Supremacy, and the Implications of *Ex Parte Young*," *University of Pennsylvania Law Review*, Vol. 153 (2005), p. 1677.

18. D. S. Dobkin, "Court Stripping and Limitations on Judicial Review of Immigration Cases," *Justice System Journal*, Vol. 28 (2007), pp. 104–108.

19. Pub. L. No. 104-132.

20. Pub. L. No. 104-208.

21. *Reno v. American-Arab Anti-Discrimination Committee*, 525 U.S. 471 (1999).

22. H. B. Hogue, *Supreme Court Nominations Not Confirmed, 1789–2004* (Washington, DC: Library of Congress, Congressional Research Service, 2005), available at http://www.fas.org/sgp/crs/misc/RL31171.pdf (accessed January 29, 2013).

23. See http://en.wikipedia.org/wiki/Robert_Bork#Supreme_Court_nomination (accessed January 29, 2013).

24. R. T. Becker, "Comment: The Other Nuclear Option: Adopting a Constitutional Amendment to Furnish a Lasting Solution to the Troubled Judicial Confirmation Process," *Penn State Law Review*, Vol. 111 (2007), pp. 981–1008.

25. The Federalist No. 79, available at http://www.constitution.org/fed/federa79.htm (accessed January 29, 2013).

26. For some classic studies, see C. Baar, *Separate but Subservient: Court Budgeting in the American States* (Lexington, MA: D. C. Heath and Co., 1975); R. W. Tobin, *Funding the State Courts: Issues and Approaches* (Williamsburg, VA: National Center for State Courts, 1996); R. W. Tobin, *Trial Court Budgeting* (Williamsburg, VA: National Center for State Courts, 1996).

27. J. W. Douglas and R. E. Hartley, "The Politics of Court Budgeting in the States: Is Judicial Independence Threatened by the Budgetary Process?," *Public Administration Review*, Vol. 63 (2003), pp. 441–454.

28. Ibid., pp. 450–451; also see J. P. Nase, "The Revenue Role of State Courts: Implications for Administration and Adjudication," *Judicature*, Vol. 76 (1993), pp. 195–200.

29. *Brown v. Board of Education*, 347 U.S. 483 (1954).

30. *Brown v. Board of Education*, 349 U.S. 294 (1955), p. 301.

31. Ibid., p. 300.

32. *Katz v. United States*, 389 U.S. 347 (1967).

33. *Horton v. Goose Creek Independent School District*, 690 F.2d 47 (5th Cir. 1982).

34. *Doe v. Renfrow*, 631 F.2d 91 (7th Cir. 1980).

35. D. R. Songer, J. A. Segal, and C. M. Cameron, "The Hierarchy of Justice: Testing a Principal-Agent Model of Supreme Court-Circuit Court Interactions," *American Journal of Political Science*, Vol. 38 (1994), pp. 673–696.

36. For just a few examples, see L. Baum, "Response of Federal District Judges to Court of Appeals Policies: An Exploration," *Western Political Quarterly*, Vol. 3 (1980), pp. 217–224; S. C. Benesh, *The U.S. Court of Appeals and the Law of Confessions: Perspectives on the Hierarchy of Justice* (New York: LFB Scholarly, 2002); J. Gruhl, "The Supreme Court's Impact on the Law of Libel: Compliance by Lower Federal Courts," *Western Political Quarterly*, Vol. 33 (1980), pp. 502–519; D. Songer and R. S. Sheehan, "Supreme Court Impact on Compliance and Outcomes: *Miranda* and *New York Times* in the United States Courts of Appeals," *Western Political Quarterly*, Vol. 43 (1990), pp. 297–319.

37. See, e.g., J. W. Peltason, *Fifty-Eight Lonely Men: Southern Federal Judges and School Desegregation* (New York: Harcourt Brace, 1961); N. T. Romans, "The Role of State Supreme Courts in Judicial Policy Making," *Western Political Quarterly*, Vol. 27 (1974), pp. 38–59.

38. *Brown v. Board of Education*, 347 U.S. 483 (1954).

39. *Wisconsin v. Yoder*, 406 U.S. 205 (1972).

40. *Black's Law Dictionary*, 6th ed. (St. Paul, MN: West, 1990), p. 82.

41. G. A. Caldeira and J. R. Wright, "Organized Interests and Agenda Setting in the U.S. Supreme Court," *American Political Science Review*, Vol. 82 (1988), pp. 1109–1127.

42. L. Epstein and J. Knight, "Mapping Out the Strategic Terrain: The Informational Role of *Amici Curiae*," in C. Clayton and H. Gillman, eds., *Supreme Court Decision Making: New Institutionalist Approaches* (Chicago: University of Chicago Press, 1999), p. 221.

43. See, e.g., H. W. Perry, Jr., *Deciding to Decide: Agenda Setting in the United States Supreme Court* (Cambridge, MA: Harvard University Press, 1991).

44. See, e.g., J. D. Kearney and T. W. Merrill, "The Influence of Amicus Curiae Briefs on the Supreme Court," *University of Pennsylvania Law Review*, Vol. 148 (2000), pp. 743–855.

45. P. M. Collins, Jr., "Friends of the Court: Examining the Influence of Amicus Curiae Participation in U.S. Supreme Court Litigation," *Law and Society Review*, Vol. 38 (2004), pp. 807–832.

46. American Bar Association, available at http://www.abanet.org/about/history.html (accessed January 29, 2013).

47. Ibid.

48. American Bar Association, available at http://www.americanbar.org/content/dam/aba/migrated/aging/PublicDocuments/hist_aba.authcheckdam.pdf (accessed January 29, 2013).

49. J. Lindgren, "Examining the American Bar Association's Ratings of Nominees to the U.S. Courts of Appeals for Political Bias, 1989–2000," *Journal of Law and Politics*, Vol. 17 (2001), p. 19.

50. J. L. Lott, "The American Bar Association, Judicial Ratings, and Political Bias," *Journal of Law and Politics*, Vol. 17 (2001), pp. 41–61.

51. New York State Bar Association, *2006–2007 Report to the Membership* (New York: New York State Bar Association, 2007).

52. National Center for State Courts, available at http://stage.ncsc.org/about-us.aspx (accessed January 29, 2013).

53. Center for Court Innovation, available at http://www.courtinnovation.org/who-we-are (accessed January 29, 2013).

54. *Kyllo v. United States*, 533 U.S. 27 (2001).

55. Ibid., p. 2046.

© LightScribe/Fotolia

Federal Cour

INTRODUCTION

Inscribed on the wall of the U.S. Supreme Court building in Washington, D.C., are these words: "It is emphatically the province and duty of the judicial department to say what the law is." Those words come from the Court's holding in the famous 1803 case of *Marbury* v. *Madison*,[1] which arose from a failure by the U.S. Secretary of State to deliver the paper documents necessary to complete the appointment of some federal judges following the inauguration of President Thomas Jefferson. Courts don't create statutory law, but they do interpret it. Whenever a law is unclear or in cases where two laws appear to contradict one another, it is up to the courts to determine how the law should be interpreted and applied. In *Marbury*, the interpretation of the law took an interesting twist, which you can read about in the Court's decision at http://www.law.cornell.edu/supct/html/historics/USSC_CR_0005_0137_ZS.html. Documents relating to the original handwritten decision, penned by Chief Justice John Marshall, can be viewed at the U.S. federal government's online archive at http://www.ourdocuments.gov/doc.php?flash=true&doc=19.

U.S. Supreme Court Chief Justice, John Marshall. Marshall wrote the now famous 1803 decision of *Marbury v. Madison*, which established the Court as the final arbiter on issues of law in the United States. What is the historical significance of that decision?

Learning Objective 1

Outline the history and development of federal courts.

BRIEF HISTORY OF THE FEDERAL COURTS

A full appreciation of the modern court structure, functioning, and intricacies cannot be obtained without first considering American court history and identifying the three key turning points in the history of federal courts. These include (1) the U.S. Constitution, (2) the Judiciary Act of 1789, and (3) the Judiciary Act of 1891.[2]

U.S. Constitution and the Courts

The U.S. Constitution spells out the structure and function of the judiciary in Article III, but the Constitution did not create America's courts. Courts were in place and operating before the Constitution was ratified—and they existed in Europe long before colonists arrived here. It was the debate over their role in society that led to considerable discussion during the preconstitutional era.

Preconstitutional Era The Articles of Confederation and Perpetual Union,[3] known more commonly as the Articles of Confederation, was the first governing document in the United States. The final draft was authored in the summer of 1777, adopted by the Second Continental Congress in November of that year, and later ratified on March 1, 1781, when the last of the 13 states signed the document.

The document had a very short history, and it quickly became apparent that it was lacking in several respects. For example, the federal government was not given taxing authority, almost all government power under the Articles of Confederation was vested in a single chamber legislature called Congress, there was no separation of legislative and executive powers (as is the case today), and, more important, no national judiciary was anticipated. In fact, there was almost no reference to courts or to a judiciary in the document.

At the Constitutional Convention in Philadelphia in 1787, delegates gathered in an effort to correct the Articles' deficiencies and adopt a more effective document, which we know of today as the U.S. Constitution. Even at the Convention, however, there was considerable disagreement over the role of a judiciary and what form it was to take.[4]

James Madison drafted a plan for a new national government, known widely as the **Virginia Plan**.[5] It proposed a strong national government with three branches: legislative, executive, and judicial. The executive called for a president and vice president, the legislature was to consist of one house, and the judiciary was to consist of a Supreme Court and lower federal courts.

Opponents of Madison's plan drafted the so-called **New Jersey Plan**,[6] which did not envision the existence of lower federal courts. Its drafters felt that state courts were best positioned to handle disputes that would have otherwise been resolved in the Virginia Plan's lower federal courts. The New Jersey Plan also called for legislative power to be shared between two houses of Congress—the House of Representatives and the Senate. The two-chamber plan was created to ensure that larger states did not have more power than smaller ones. Ultimately, of course, it was the two-chamber plan that was adopted, but the Virginia Plan's proposal for lower federal courts also became law.

Virginia Plan
The plan for a new national government drafted by James Madison.[i]

New Jersey Plan
The plan for a new national government drafted by opponents of Madison's Virginia Plan.[ii]

Postconstitutional Era The compromises that led to the ratification of the U.S. Constitution were several. There are now three distinct branches of government, as proposed in the Virginia Plan, but the legislative branch is structured such that less populous states enjoy the same power (in the Senate) as highly populous ones. Another compromise is found in Article III, which states, in relevant part, "The judicial power of the United States shall be vested in one Supreme Court, and in such inferior courts as the Congress may from time to time ordain and establish."[7] This article effectively created a judiciary that was independent from other branches of government, an innovation that the framers considered important.

Two specific Article III provisions make clear the independence of the judiciary. First, Article III says, in part, "The judges, both of the supreme and inferior courts, shall hold their offices during good behavior." This has been interpreted to mean that judges hold their positions for life, ensuring that they will not be dismissed with changes in Congress or executive turnover. Second, Article III also provides that judges' compensation "shall not be diminished during their continuance in office." This means that neither Congress nor the president can reduce the salary of a federal judge in an effort to exert some measure of control over him or her.

Despite the judiciary's independence, there are limits placed on it. Article III's language concerning the authority of Congress to establish courts as it sees fit limits the reach of the federal judiciary: The only way the federal judiciary can expand is through legislative authority; Congress must agree, and the president must also sign off. Second, Article III recognizes—through what it does *not* say—that the states have the authority to establish their own courts in order to try offenses and resolve disputes that arise within their boundaries. Finally, Article III reinforces the practice of federalism (referenced earlier) when it clearly establishes a federal judiciary, but it is not an "overreaching" judiciary in the sense that there are no limitations on the creation of courts at the state and local levels.

Landmark Legislation

Most changes to the structure of the federal judiciary stem from legislation enacted following the Constitution's ratification. More than a dozen significant laws have been enacted (see Figure 3–1 for an overview), but two of particular note are the Judiciary Act of 1789 and the Judiciary Act of 1891. Each significantly altered the federal court landscape.

Judiciary Act of 1789   Once the Constitution went into effect on June 21, 1788, Congress acted quickly with respect to the judiciary. The first bill introduced in the Senate addressed federal court organization. Many of the same individuals who debated the role of the federal judiciary at the Constitutional Convention were members of the first Congress, and because of this, there was plenty of lively debate over whether additional courts were necessary. Fear was expressed that an overreaching federal judiciary would usurp the power of the state courts. Others, however, felt that there would be too many inconsistencies at the state level and that litigants from different states or counties might be treated unfairly or unjustly. The law that emerged from this first meeting of Congress was the **Federal Judiciary Act of 1789**.[8]

The Judiciary Act of 1789 ushered in a number of reforms. First, it effectively created two sets of lower federal courts beneath the Supreme Court; it also spelled out the jurisdiction of the lower federal courts, placing fairly significant limitations on them. Next, it spelled out the requirements for the way lower court judges would be selected to ensure that judges served in courts within their states of residence, which meant they were at least somewhat accountable to their constituents. There are at least three other important components of the act:

1. The United States was divided into 13 judicial circuits, in each of which was a district court presided over by a district judge. District courts were to meet four times annually.

2. The 13 circuits were divided into three districts (the eastern, the middle, and the southern), the courts for which were called circuit courts. The circuit courts were presided over by two justices of the Supreme Court and one district judge and met twice annually. The Supreme Court justices were forced to travel throughout the circuits.

3. The Supreme Court was to consist of a chief justice and five associate justices.

These arrangements, while perhaps an improvement on the Constitution's requirement that there be one U.S. Supreme Court, were not without their limitations. The Supreme Court justices who were forced to travel between the circuits were particularly upset. This **circuit riding** was such a burden on the justices that in 1793 Congress modified the Judiciary Act of 1789 such that only one Supreme Court justice and one district court judge needed to preside over cases in the circuit courts.[9]

Near the end of John Adams's term as president, Congress eliminated circuit riding and further extended the jurisdiction of the lower federal courts.[10] Thomas Jefferson (the president following Adams) opposed this action, and Congress subsequently repealed it. The Circuit Court Act of 1802 reinstated circuit riding by Supreme Court justices and expanded the number of federal circuits; importantly, though, it also allowed circuit courts to be presided over by one district judge, which proved to be significant because district judges could preside over *both* district courts and circuit courts, giving them more power.

Despite the relief these reforms provided to the generally elderly (and often ill) Supreme Court justices, the federal caseload (particularly that of the Supreme Court) was on the rise, making it especially difficult for the Supreme Court justices to meet their obligations both at home and on the road. In 1869, Congress approved a measure that provided for the appointment of nine new circuit judges, thus providing welcome relief to the road-weary

Federal Judiciary Act of 1789
The federal law that established the organization of the federal courts, which emerged from the first meeting of the first Congress.[iii]

circuit riding
The early practice of requiring two U.S. Supreme Court justices and one district judge to ride between each of the three districts established within the 13 judicial circuits to preside over trials.

Library Extra
3–1 Understanding the Federal Courts

Web Extra
3–1 Federal Courts Locator

FIGURE 3–1

Timeline of Landmark
Federal Judicial Legislation

Source: http://www.fjc.gov/history/
home.nsf.

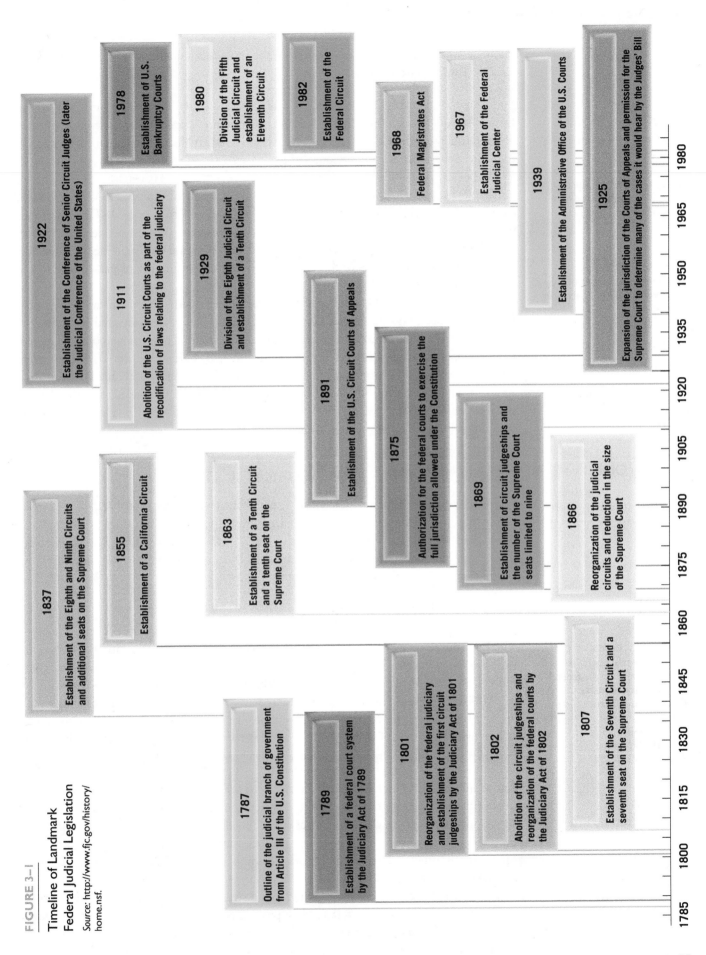

Supreme Court justices, but even this did not provide sufficient relief to caseload issues faced by the Supreme Court.

Judiciary Act of 1891 On March 3, 1891, the Judiciary Act of 1891[11] (also called the Evarts Act, named for the senator who was its primary sponsor) was enacted; the act is also referred to as the **Courts of Appeals Act of 1891**. Its main accomplishment was the creation of the 13 U.S. Circuit Courts of Appeals.[12] (These courts' names were changed in 1948, though, as we will discuss more fully later.)

The act also specified what types of cases the U.S. Circuit Courts of Appeals would hear, namely, appeals from the district courts (the lower federal trial courts). The old circuit courts remained for the time being, and the new courts were to consist of one circuit judge, one U.S. Circuit Court of Appeals judge, one district judge, and one Supreme Court justice. Two judges constituted a **quorum**, which is the minimum number of judges required to decide a particular matter.

In the wake of the Judiciary Act of 1891, the federal court system had two trial courts: the district courts and the circuit courts. Later, in 1911, Congress enacted legislation to abolish the old circuit courts. Finally, the act had the benefit of easing much of the Supreme Court's appellate caseload. Recall that before the U.S. Circuit Courts of Appeals were created, there was no court other than the Supreme Court that was charged with hearing appeals from lower courts, but the act fixed this problem and was heralded as ending "one of the most enduring struggles in American political history."[13] Since 1911, the federal court structure has remained largely unchanged.

STRUCTURE OF THE FEDERAL COURTS

Recall that Article III of the Constitution mentioned a Supreme Court and such inferior courts as Congress sees fit to "ordain and establish." Congress has indeed ordained and established several inferior courts, yet the federal judiciary is relatively uncomplicated. There are three tiers of federal courts: The district courts are the lowest, followed by the courts of appeals and then the U.S. Supreme Court.

U.S. District Courts

The **U.S. district courts** are the federal trial courts, and they are the entry point into the federal judicial system. District courts are where federal civil cases are decided and where individuals charged with violations of applicable federal laws are put on trial. Today, there are 94 district courts. There are considerably fewer appellate courts in the federal system and only one Supreme Court, so inevitably the vast majority of federal cases are resolved at the district court level. Indeed, a very small percentage of actual trials occur due to the practice of plea bargaining (we look more at plea bargaining in Chapter 12).

Early Days Earlier in this chapter, we discussed the Judiciary Act of 1789, the legislation responsible for creating the first federal district courts. Section 2 of the act established 13 district courts: There was one district court for each of the 11 states in the union at the time; the other two were for portions of Massachusetts and Virginia that were to become Maine and Kentucky. This led to the practice of district court boundaries being the same as state boundaries.

The Judiciary Act of 1789 also required that district court judges come from the districts in which they resided. Unlike today, when prospective federal judges are effectively sought out, early district court judges wrote letters to the president, the vice president, and members of Congress seeking their appointment.[14]

Courts of Appeals Act of 1891
The federal law that created the 13 U.S. Circuit Courts of Appeals[iv]; also called *Judiciary Act of 1891*[v] or *Evarts Act.*

quorum
The minimum number of judges required to decide a particular matter.

Learning Objective 2
Describe the structure of the federal court system and the various types of federal courts.

U.S. district court
The federal trial court that is the "entry point" into the federal judicial system within each federal judicial district.

Library Extra
3–2 The Structure of the Federal Courts

As time went on and the union grew, more district courts were added. At one point, President Washington was given the opportunity to offer judgeships to 33 people.[15] One account stated that "all of the judges he appointed were members of the bar, and all but seven had state or local legal experience as judges, prosecutors, or attorneys general."[16] This practice of presidents appointing judges with substantial public service backgrounds and/or accomplishments as attorneys continues to this day.

As even more states came into the union and their populations grew, some states were divided into several federal districts. For example, the populous states of California, New York, and Texas now have four federal districts each. There is no consistency or rational ordering to the lines of federal districts today. Some districts have very few people; others have many. Districts were also created for the District of Columbia and for various territories that came under the control of the United States over the years.

Present-Day Organization Of the 94 federal districts in place today, 89 of them are found in the 50 states, and there is a district in the District of Columbia, in Puerto Rico, in the Virgin Islands, in Guam, and in the Northern Mariana Islands (see Figure 3–2 for the locations of each of the federal districts within and outside the 50 states and the District of Columbia).

While the original districts had single judges, Congress has since made changes. For example, the Federal Judgeship Act of 1990 contained provisions for 74 new positions, bringing the current total to 678 authorized judgeships.[17] Today, there is more than one judge in every district. The largest is the Southern District of New York, which includes both Manhattan and the Bronx, and it has a total of 28 authorized judgeships.[18] The benefit of having more than one judge in each federal district, of course, is that multiple trials can be held at the same time, which cuts down on delays and improves efficiency. The allocation of judgeships across districts also corresponds to workloads.

District Courts as Federal Workhorses The district courts are the workhorses in the federal system. As we have indicated, they are the trial courts where most disputes

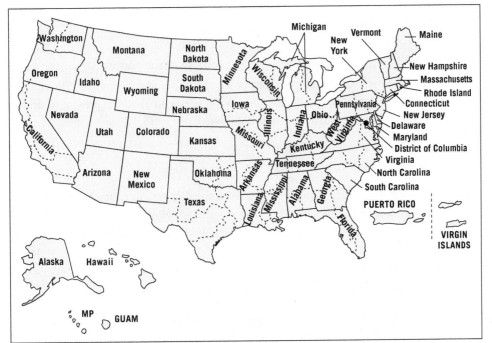

FIGURE 3–2

Federal Judicial Districts

Source: http://www.uscourts.gov/courtlinks.

are resolved. District court judges do much more than preside over trials—they approve plea agreements in those cases that do not go to trial, they supervise settlements in civil cases, and they apply higher-court rulings.

District court judges also hear petitions from prisoners. Known as *habeas corpus* petitions (see Chapter 14 for more details), these are efforts on the part of prisoners to challenge the constitutionality of their confinement, due perhaps to a wrongful search and seizure or an improperly secured confession, and they number in the thousands annually. There is no express constitutional requirement that such petitions first be filed with a district court, but many are, making additional work for district court judges.

consent decree
A judgment by consent of the parties to a lawsuit where the defendant agrees to stop the alleged improper or illegal activity.

Federal district court judges also supervise so-called **consent decrees**, judgments by consent of the parties to a lawsuit where the defendant agrees to stop the alleged improper or illegal activity. These decrees result from what have been branded "institutional reform" litigation,[19] and they cover everything from employment discrimination[20] and school desegregation[21] to prison conditions[22] and reapportionment of electoral districts.[23] One of the better-known consent decrees in criminal justice involves the Los Angeles Police Department, stemming from the department's famous Rampart corruption scandal. The decree, which has been in effect since 2000, set forth in its 93 pages a number of requirements intended "to promote police integrity and prevent conduct that deprives persons of rights, privileges, or immunities secured or protected by the Constitution or laws of the United States."[24]

Fortunately, while district court judges are saddled with many responsibilities, they are spared from deciding bankruptcy cases, which number in excess of a million each year. There are 352 bankruptcy judges who work in 90 distinct U.S. bankruptcy courts, which operate by statute alongside the district courts. Bankruptcy judges are appointed for 14-year terms by the judges of the local U.S. Court of Appeals, and most of the cases they decide involve individuals (rather than corporations) who cannot pay their bills. There are also some other federal trial courts that Congress has created, partly out of a need to limit district court judges' workloads.

U.S. magistrate judge
A federal trial judge who is appointed to serve an eight-year term in a U.S. district court, who decides certain civil cases with the consent of the parties, and who assists in pretrial matters.

Web Extra
3–2 U.S. District Courts

District court judges are also assisted by **U.S. magistrate judges**. These judges are appointed by the district courts to eight-year terms and perform four main functions:

1. Conduct most of the initial proceedings in criminal cases (including search and arrest warrants, detention hearings, probable cause hearings, and appointment of attorneys).
2. Conduct trials of certain criminal misdemeanor cases.
3. Conduct trials of civil cases with the consent of the parties.
4. Conduct a wide variety of other proceedings referred to them by district judges (including deciding motions, reviewing petitions filed by prisoners, and conducting pretrial and settlement conferences).[25]

Appellate Courts

Rarely does one hear about decisions from the federal appellate courts on the evening news; the Supreme Court has the spotlight. Even so, the appellate courts make up an especially important—and powerful—component of the federal judiciary. The Supreme Court issues decisions on less than 100 cases per year. The rest of the cases successfully appealed from the district courts are issued from the appellate courts, so this gives the appellate courts considerable power and influence.

Changing Roles and Names We began this section with reference to federal "appellate courts." This terminology was used deliberately because the formal name for the federal appellate courts has changed over time. Recall from the earlier discussion of court history that the federal appellate courts were called circuit courts. It was the Judiciary Act of 1789 that created these circuit courts, three of them in total. It would not be until 1869, however, that Congress expanded the number of circuit courts; by then, there were nine courts total. These courts heard trials and thus were not technically "appellate" courts. They remained in place until January 1912, when Congress abolished them.

The Courts of Appeals Act of 1891 (also called the Evarts Act), which we touched on earlier, marked a watershed in the evolution of the federal judiciary when it created the U.S. Circuit Courts of Appeal. These worked alongside the circuit courts until 1911 and took on a distinctly appellate function. The creation of these courts also lightened the Supreme Court's caseload. By the 1920s, each of the courts of appeals had no fewer than three judgeships, which also lightened the workload of the judges who worked alone in the beginning.

Initially, there were nine circuit courts of appeal. In 1893, Congress established a court of appeals for the District of Columbia, and the tenth and eleventh courts came into being in 1929. In 1982, Congress combined both the U.S. Court of Customs and Patent Appeals and the U.S. Court of Claims into one court, called the U.S. Court of Appeals for the Federal Circuit. Thus, there are 13 federal circuits at present, and a map of them appears in Figure 3–3.

Congress, in the Judicial Code of 1948, changed the formal name of the district courts of appeal to the U.S. Court of Appeals for the ___ Circuit (e.g., the U.S. Court of Appeals for the Ninth Circuit). Colloquially, they are known as **courts of appeal**, the federal courts of appeal, or even circuit courts (not to be confused with the circuit courts that are no more). The 13 courts have a total of 179 authorized judgeships, but fewer judges than this are actually active as of this writing.[26]

court of appeal
The colloquial name given to the U.S. Court of Appeals (formerly, the U.S. circuit court, renamed by the Judicial Code of 1948) within each respective federal circuit.

Review Function   The federal courts of appeal mostly hear cases that originate beneath them in the district courts. Generally, if a party to a district court's decision is unsatisfied with a judge's decision, he or she may appeal. A defendant who disagrees with a judge's decision to admit questionable evidence may appeal if convicted; the same can apply in the civil context when one of the litigants disagrees with a judge's decision, perhaps to allow

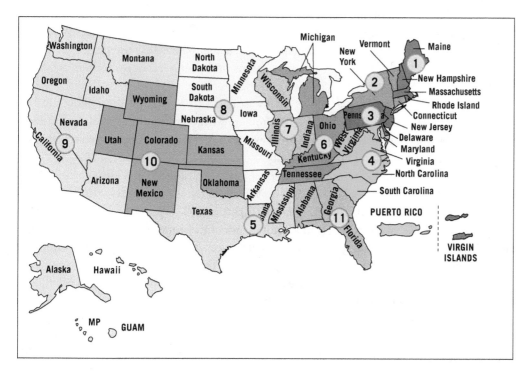

FIGURE 3–3

Federal Circuits

Note: The U.S. Court of Appeals for the District of Columbia is referred to as the Twelfth Circuit; and the U.S. Court of Appeals for the Federal Circuit is called the Thirteenth Circuit.

the testimony of a questionable witness. These sorts of appeals are the "bread and butter" of the courts of appeal. At the same time, though, the federal courts of appeals have no direct control over the types of cases they are asked to review, and their cases can range from completely frivolous to those of significant constitutional importance.

The federal appellate courts do not engage in fact-finding; that is, they are not trial courts charged with rendering verdicts in civil and criminal cases. They fulfill a review function, their primary responsibility being to review alleged errors made by district court judges. The appellate courts review the records of the lower court's proceedings and render decisions as to whether the judges presiding over such proceedings rendered decisions in conformance with applicable laws.

The federal courts of appeal also manage to screen cases for Supreme Court review. Since appeals arising out of the district courts most often end up in the courts of appeals before they arrive at the Supreme Court, the courts of appeals can have considerable say over which issues ever come to the attention of the Supreme Court. A particular appellate court may decline to hear a case, which means it may never arrive at the Supreme Court for consideration.

The appellate court review function sounds a bit tedious, involving plenty of legal minutia, but the courts of appeals often act as policy makers. Consider the controversial case of *Hopwood* v. *Texas*,[27] a case brought after the law school's admission policy was challenged in district court. In it, the Court of Appeals for the Fifth Circuit (Texas) decided that the University of Texas Law School could no longer give preference to African-American or Mexican-American applicants. The U.S. Supreme Court then declined to hear the case (this decision process is discussed below), which means that the Fifth Circuit effectively set policy. Its decision became binding on all the schools within its jurisdiction, including those in Texas as well as those in Louisiana and Mississippi. The following "Courts in the News" feature shows how the Circuit Court uses Supreme Court decisions to guide their decision-making process.

Courts of Appeals at Work The Supreme Court has enormous discretion in deciding which cases it will hear, but this is less true of the federal appellate courts. Even so, the judges in these courts have developed methods to screen cases and thereby lighten their workloads. For example, similar claims are often combined into one to minimize duplication, a process that also promotes a uniform decision. Although the appellate courts may decide to hear a case, this does not mean that oral arguments are actually held because judges often rely on their staff and law clerks for recommendations and then simply issue their decisions in writing.

How are cases assigned? Cases are normally assigned to a panel of three judges rather than all the judges in the circuit. If there is a problem with conflicting decisions by different panels of appellate court judges, all of the judges within the circuit will sit in what is known as an ***en banc*** **proceeding**. This is generally the exception in large circuits, such as the Ninth Circuit, which includes several western states, stretching from Washington through California and into Arizona; a large panel substitutes for a full panel in the Ninth Circuit.

If oral arguments are held, lawyers from both parties will make their arguments before a panel of judges. They are each given a limited amount of time (generally 10 to 15 minutes) in which to present their case in the formal session. Throughout, the judges often ask questions about legal and other matters related to the case, and then they discuss the case privately and render their decision. Judges are required to follow precedent as needed, and two of three judges must agree on a decision before it is issued.

On the one hand, decisions may be announced quickly and be accompanied by a brief order, called a ***per curiam*** **opinion**, that is agreed to by all the judges. On the other hand, if there is an issue that is of considerable importance and/or one that requires lengthy

en banc **proceeding**
A term that literally means "in bench." This proceeding is typically called when there is a problem with conflicting decisions by different panels of appellate court judges and is attended by all of the judges within the circuit.

per curiam **opinion**
An appellate opinion that is agreed to by judges and tends to be short.

COURTS IN THE NEWS

Equal Protection in Sentencing: The Case of Crack Cocaine

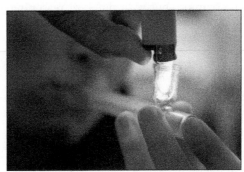
© Alec Macdonald/Alamy

Lighting up a crack pipe. Is it wrong for the government to disproportionately punish crimes that cause the greatest social harm? Why or why not?

On May 17, 2013, the U.S. 6th Circuit Court of Appeals ruled People convicted of crack cocaine offenses have a right to resentencing hearings under the Fair Sentencing Act, a 2010 law that lessened penalties for possession and dealing of crack cocaine. The court ruled that the Fair Sentencing Act applied to people whose cases played out before the law's passage, potentially opening the door for thousands of inmates to ask federal judges to lower their prison time. The Fair Sentencing Act was passed in reaction to complaints that federal sentencing guidelines mandated much higher sentences for possession of crack cocaine than it did for the powdered form. The existing law was considered racially suspect because African-Americans were more likely to be convicted for crack possession than European-Americans who favored the powdered form. The new law lowered the disparity between crack cocaine sentences and powder cocaine sentences from 100 to 1 to about 18 to 1.

The ruling, handed down in the case of two Kentucky men, Cornelius Demorris Blewett and Jarreous Jamone Blewitt, each sentenced to 10 years in prison for possession and distribution of crack cocaine, was based on a U.S. Supreme Court decision in two cases *Dorsey* v. *United States* and *Hill* v. *United States* (2012), in which the justices ruled that people who committed crack cocaine crimes before more lenient penalties took effect and received their prison sentence afterward should benefit from the new rules.

The high court did not specify if the law applied to people whose cases were over before the passage of the law. Judge Gilbert Merritt, writing for the 6th Circuit majority, said the law "can and should" be interpreted to replace "the old, discriminatory mandatory minimums," which weighed heavier on black defendants. Letting discriminatory sentences go forward is unconstitutional. He said, "Like slavery and Jim Crow laws, the intentional maintenance of discriminatory sentences is a denial of equal protection."

The ruling opens the door for thousands of appeals by inmates sentenced under the old laws and who are currently doing more time than they would under the new more lenient rules. About 30,000 federal prisoners, accounting for about 15 percent of all inmates, are now serving crack cocaine sentences; more than 80 percent of those inmates were black.

In 2010, before the Fair Sentencing Act passed, almost 4,000 people, predominantly black, received mandatory minimum sentences for crack cocaine. Among them were 35-year-old Cornelius "Stuff" Blewett and Jarreous Blewitt, both of Bowling Green. The two men pleaded guilty in 2005 to conspiracy to distribute and possession with intent to distribute crack cocaine. Each was sentenced to a decade in prison. Both men sought sentence reductions after the passage of the Fair Sentencing Act, and a federal district judge turned them down. On appeal, the Federal Circuit Court decided to push the legal envelope. In this case, neither prosecutors nor the attorneys for Blewett and Blewitt raised the issue of equal protection under the law. The justices took it up without asking for briefs or argument from either side before basing their ruling on that issue. "We should not allow the government's legalism to undermine the purpose of the Fair Sentencing Act and its more lenient punishment system for crack cocaine," Merritt wrote in his decision. ■

DISCUSSION QUESTIONS

1. Do you agree that punishment should be revised for a crime if there are racial differences among those who commit the crime?

2. Despite this ruling, a person possessing or selling crack is punished more heavily than someone doing the same for powdered cocaine. Should both crimes receive exactly the same punishment? If you disagree, on what do you base your opinion?

Sources: U.S. v. *Cornelius Demorris Blewett and Jarreous Jamone Blewitt,* http://www.ca6.uscourts.gov/opinions.pdf/13a0141p-06.pdf; Associated Press, Court: Law applying crack sentences retroactive Kentucky New Era.com, http://www.kentuckynewera.com/web/news/article_f50480e8-bf8f-11e2-a0ef-001a4bcf887a.html; *Dorsey* v. *United States,* No 11-5683, and *Hill* v. *United States,* No. 11-5721.

opinion
The court's decision in written form with supporting rationale, reference to appropriate precedent, and so on.

concurring opinion
An opinion that supports the opinion but offers different reasoning.

dissenting opinion
An opinion that disagrees with the main opinion.

U.S. Supreme Court
The final arbiter in the U.S. judicial system and the highest court in the United States; also called *the Court.*

discussion and even leads to disagreements among the judges, a lengthier **opinion**, which is basically the court's decision in written form with supporting rationale, reference to appropriate precedent, and so on, is authored by one of the judges. Sometimes opinions are accompanied by concurring opinions and or dissenting opinions. **Concurring opinions** support the opinion, but with different reasoning; **dissenting opinions** disagree with the main opinion.

U.S. Supreme Court

The **U.S. Supreme Court** (also called "the Court"), the final arbiter in the U.S. judicial system, is the highest court in the land and has the proverbial "last word" with respect to interpretation of the Constitution, laws, and treaties. The Court's decisions *can* be altered by constitutional amendment, but such alterations are exceptionally rare. To illustrate, consider the so-called *Miranda* warnings, the Supreme Court's requirement that police officers must advise individuals who are subjected to custodial interrogation of their right to remain silent, have an attorney present, and so on. When the Supreme Court issued its *Miranda* v. *Arizona* decision,[28] some members of Congress were upset. There was a perception that the decision opened up a loophole through which guilty criminals could escape justice. Accordingly, Congress enacted a statute that said, in part, that a confession "shall be admissible in evidence if voluntarily given."[29] The statute remained dormant for a while, but in a recent case the Court ruled,

> We hold that *Miranda*, being a constitutional decision of this Court, may not be in effect overruled by an Act of Congress, and we decline to overrule *Miranda* ourselves. We therefore hold that *Miranda* and its progeny in this Court govern the admissibility of statements made during custodial interrogation in both state and federal courts.[30]

Not only is the Supreme Court the most powerful tribunal in America, it is also unique in the world,[31] mainly because of federalism. Since the founders provided for both federal and state government, it was necessary to have one court that could have the final say on matters arising in each. It would be strange, for instance, to have a state court resolve matters involving federal legislation; likewise, to have a state court issue the final decision on a dispute arising between states would lead to inconsistencies and possibly inequity. The Supreme Court thus resolves such matters—and more. This all-powerful role has led to considerable controversy over the years. Supreme Court historian Charles Warren made this observation:

> Nothing in the Court's history is more striking than the fact that while its significant and necessary place in the Federal form of Government has always been recognized by thoughtful and patriotic men, nevertheless, no branch of the Government and no institution under the Constitution has sustained more continuous attack or reached its present position after more vigorous opposition.[32]

Caseload The Supreme Court has both original and appellate jurisdiction. Its original jurisdiction is narrow and spelled out in Article III, and cases that fall within the Court's original jurisdiction are mostly beyond the scope of criminal justice classes. Of interest to us, then, is the Court's appellate jurisdiction, which accounts for the overwhelming majority of its caseload; that is, most of the Supreme Court's business is concerned with hearing appeals from the lower federal courts and from the state courts.

Most criminal cases originate at the state level. This should be obvious because there are 50 state court structures and only one federal court system. Also, the state laws criminalizing certain types of conduct vastly outnumber federal laws with the same objective. But just because most cases are heard in state court does not mean they are prevented from being heard at the federal level. State-level cases can arrive at the U.S. Supreme Court if they raise a federal question, which is usually a question concerning the U.S. Constitution. First, such cases must proceed through several steps. Before it will be considered by the Supreme Court, a state case must move all the way to its state supreme court, meaning that a case cannot jump from a state-level intermediate appellate court to the U.S. Supreme Court. Figure 3–4 summarizes how cases arrive at the Supreme Court.

The U.S. Supreme Court decides (as do many appellate courts) whether it wants to hear a case. The party seeking a decision by the U.S. Supreme Court must file documents with the Court, asking to be heard. If the Supreme Court agrees the case is worth deciding, it issues what is known as a **writ of *certiorari***, which is an order by the Court requiring the lower court to send the case and a record of its proceedings to the U.S. Supreme Court for review. Four of the nine U.S. Supreme Court justices must agree to hear a case before a writ of *certiorari* will be issued, a process known as the **rule of four**. If four justices do not agree to hear the case, the lower court's decision stands.

It cannot be overstated that only a small handful of cases ever reach the U.S. Supreme Court. It is not uncommon for the Supreme Court to review thousands of petitions for review and then only grant *certiorari* in a fraction of the cases. The Court generally issues written opinions for fewer than 100 cases each term. Most cases that are appealed stop short of the Supreme Court, so it is necessary to find out at what level the final decision was reached.

Important Eras George Washington, the first president of the United States, appointed the first Supreme Court justices. John Jay was selected as chief justice, and the Supreme Court met for the first time on Monday, February 1, 1790, in the Royal Exchange, a building in the Wall Street section of New York City.[33] There were no cases to decide at this early juncture, so the Court began by choosing a clerk, selecting a seal, and admitting several lawyers to argue cases before it in the future. Over the next 10 years, the Court decided only about 50 cases, considerably fewer than it decides each year today.

With John Marshall serving as chief justice from 1801 until his death in 1835, the Supreme Court began a new era.[34] Marshall assumed a more prominent role as chief justice, and he encouraged the justices to settle their disagreements privately so that the Court's opinions would be more uniform when presented to the public because he felt that publicly aired dissents undermined the Court's authority.

Under Marshall, the Court also issued a number of important decisions. One was the famous case of *Marbury* v. *Madison*,[35] where the Court asserted its authority to overrule acts of Congress—and decisions by the executive—that run counter to the Constitution.[36]

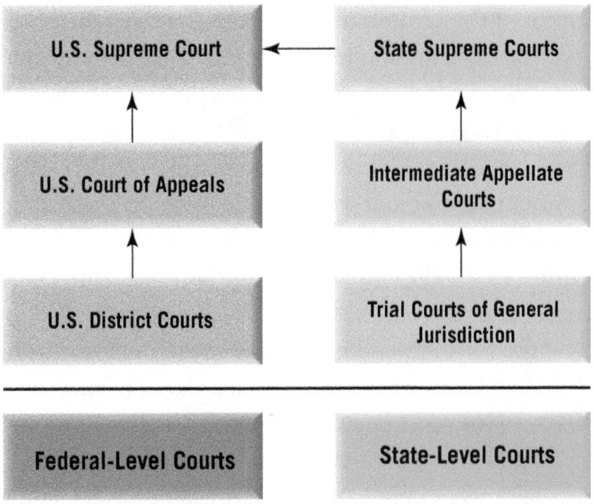

writ of *certiorari*
An order from a higher court that requires a lower court to send a case and a record of its proceedings to the higher court for review.

rule of four
The U.S. Supreme Court rule that requires the agreement of four justices to grant a writ of *certiorari*.

FIGURE 3–4

Means by Which Cases Arrive at the Supreme Court

Source: J. L. Worrall, *Criminal Procedure*, 2nd ed. (Boston, MA: Allyn and Bacon, 2007), p. 21.

To give a sense of the magnitude of this decision, it would not be for another 50 years before the Supreme Court struck down another federal statute.[37]

Under Chief Justice Marshall, the Supreme Court also laid claim to the right of judicial review, the power of the Court to review decisions from other levels or branches of government to ensure their consistency, legality, and conformity with the Constitution. This is important because the Constitution does not explicitly reference the practice of judicial review in Article III; in other words, judicial review is an implied power. The Court exercises considerable restraint in this area:

1. The Court will not pass on the constitutionality of legislation in a friendly, nonadversary, proceeding.
2. The Court will not "anticipate a question of constitutional law in advance of the necessity of deciding it."
3. The Court will not "formulate a rule of constitutional law broader than is required by the precise facts to which it is to be applied."
4. The Court will not pass on a constitutional question, although properly presented by the record, if there is also present some other ground on which the case may be disposed.
5. The Court will not pass on the validity of a statute upon complaint of one who fails to show that he is injured by its operation.
6. The Court will not pass on the constitutionality of a statute at the instance of one who has availed himself of its benefits.
7. "When the validity of an act of the Congress is drawn in question, and even if a serious doubt of constitutionality is raised, it is a cardinal principle that this Court first ascertain whether a construction of the statute is fairly possible by which the question may be avoided."[38]

After Marshall died, the Supreme Court, under the leadership of Chief Justice Roger Taney, continued to decide several cases concerning the relationships between federal and state government. Also, whereas Marshall favored a strong role for the federal government, Taney and his colleagues felt states should enjoy more power.

The exception to this tendency was the Taney Court's role in the debate over slavery. In *Moore* v. *Illinois*,[39] the Court held, in part, that "any state law or regulation which interrupts, impedes, limits, embarrasses, delays or postpones the right of the owner to the immediate possession of the slave, and the immediate command of his service, is void," thus dealing something of a blow to states' sovereignty. Taney's Court also decided *Dred Scott* v. *Sanford*,[40] holding that people of African descent, whether slaves or not, could never be citizens of the United States, a case that was partly responsible for the Civil War.

Following Taney's departure, the Court spent much of its time interpreting post–Civil War amendments to the Constitution (e.g., the Thirteenth, which abolished slavery). Under Chief Justices Salmon Portland Chase (1864–1873), Morrison Remick Waite (1874–1888), and Melville Weston Fuller (1888–1910), the Court also decided several important cases credited with establishing the doctrine of substantive due process[41] (for more on substantive due process, see the discussion in Chapter 1). Under the Edward Douglass White (1910–1921) and William Howard Taft (1921–1930) Courts, the substantive due process doctrine reached its peak; for example, the Court's decision in *Gitlow* v. *New York*[42] made the First Amendment's free speech provisions binding on the states.

Under Chief Justices Charles Evans Hughes (1930–1941), Harlan Fiske Stone (1941–1946), and Frederick Moore Vinson (1946–1953), the Court channeled much of its energies into New Deal cases, such as *West Coast Hotel Co.* v. *Parrish*,[43] where minimum-wage laws were upheld. When Earl Warren became chief justice (1953–1969), the Court decided several cases dealing with issues of equal treatment for minorities and other disadvantaged groups. Many of the Court's decisions through the latter part of this era were rather liberal, one example being the Court's decision in *Brown* v. *Board of Education*[44] which overthrew racial segregation in public schools.

The Court gradually grew more conservative once Warren Burger became chief justice (1969–1986). Although his Court invalidated state death penalty laws in *Furman* v. *Georgia*,[45] it reinstated the death penalty in *Gregg* v. *Georgia*[46] just four years later. He also strongly dissented from the Court's majority holding in *Solem* v. *Helm*[47] that a life sentence for a fraudulent check in the amount of $100 constituted cruel and unusual punishment. This trend continued through William Rehnquist's tenure as Supreme Court justice (1986–2005).[48]

By most accounts, the current Roberts court is maintaining a largely conservative stance, though some cases would seem to depart from this tradition. A prime example is *U.S. Department of Health and Human Services* v. *Florida*, a case in which the Court upheld the so-called individual mandate portion of the Affordable Care Act (i.e., Obamacare).[49]

Supreme Court at Work By law, the Supreme Court starts its annual term on the first Monday in October, and sessions usually continue until June or July. One may encounter a reference to something like the "2006 Term," which refers to the period from October 2006 through the end of the term in 2007, meaning that some 2006 term decisions actually get handed down in 2007.

Supreme Court terms are divided into two periods: sittings and recesses. Sittings are when the justices hear cases and deliver opinions; recesses are generally when they consider business before the Court (such as the many petitions for review the Court receives) and write their opinions. These sittings and recesses alternate at roughly two-week intervals.

Oral arguments are usually scheduled from Monday through Wednesday during the sittings, in sessions running from 10 A.M. until noon and from 1 P.M. until 3 P.M. With few exceptions, each side is given a short 30 minutes to argue. The attorneys must apply and be approved to argue cases before the U.S. Supreme Court.[50] The Court usually hears four cases on any given Monday through Wednesday, so as many as 24 cases can be heard during one sitting. The Court is able to move quickly in this regard because it serves a review function—it does not adjudicate offenses and thus does not rely on juries and witness testimony.

On Wednesday afternoons during a sitting, the Court holds a conference to discuss the cases argued on Monday, and the Court also holds a Friday conference, when cases argued on Tuesday and Wednesday are discussed. The justices also discuss the *certiorari* petitions during these conferences. These meetings are held behind closed doors; interestingly, no formal records of the justices' discussions are kept.

As far as reaching decisions goes, all nine justices participate in the vast majority of Supreme Court decisions. Sometimes one or more justices will not participate, perhaps because one of them is ill, there is a vacancy, or a conflict of interest exists. What if this occurs? A quorum for a decision in the Supreme Court is six justices, so as many as three of the justices need not participate for the Court to reach a decision. After a tentative decision is reached, the Court's opinion is assigned to an individual justice. If the chief justice is in the majority, either he or an assigned justice in the majority will write the opinion, but if the chief justice is in the minority, then usually the most senior justice in the majority will author the opinion or make the assignment. The opinions begin as drafts, which are then shared with other justices in the majority and in the minority. The author of the opinion usually seeks to persuade the other justices to side with his or her opinion, but unanimous decisions are not particularly common. Frequently, concurring opinions and/or dissents accompany the final written opinions (these concurring and/or dissenting opinions are essentially identical to those introduced in the earlier Court of Appeals section).

District of Columbia, et al. v. Dick Anthony Heller (2008)

Dick Anthony Heller, a special police officer within (and a resident of) the District of Columbia, wanted to register and keep a handgun in his home. He could not legally do so because D.C. law banned handgun possession "by making it a crime to carry an unregistered firearm and prohibiting the registration of handguns; provid(ing) separately that no person may carry an unlicensed handgun, but authoriz(ing) the police chief to issue 1-year licenses; and requir(ing) residents to keep lawfully owned firearms unloaded and dissembled or bound by a trigger lock or similar device."[1]

When Heller applied to register his handgun, the District of Columbia denied his application. Heller sued, "seeking, on Second Amendment grounds, to enjoin the city from enforcing the bar on handgun registration, the licensing requirement insofar as it prohibits carrying an unlicensed firearm in the home, and the trigger-lock requirement insofar as it prohibits the use of functional firearms in the home."[2] The District Court's dismissal of the suit was reversed by the D.C. Circuit, which held that "the Second Amendment protects an individual's right to possess firearms and that the city's total ban on handguns, as well as its requirement that firearms in the home be kept nonfunctional even when necessary for self-defense, violated that right."[3]

The U.S. Supreme Court's holding in *District of Columbia, et al. v. Dick Anthony Heller* (2008) was sweeping and unambiguous. The decision clearly declares the Second Amendment protection of "an individual right to possess a firearm unconnected with service in a militia, and to use that arm for traditionally lawful purposes, such as self-defense within the home."[4] It goes on to clarify specific limitations on those Second Amendment protections[5] and concludes with a characterization of the District of Columbia's "total ban on handgun possession in the home (as) amount(ing) to a prohibition on an entire class of 'arms' that Americans overwhelmingly choose for the lawful purpose of self-defense [that] fail(s) constitutional muster."[6]

Analysis of the *Heller* decision reveals the Court's thorough examination of its own precedents on Second Amendment questions. Most notable, however, is the Court's clarification of the nature of the Second Amendment's prefatory clause.

The Second Amendment reads as follows: "A well regulated Militia, being necessary to the security of a free State, the right of the people to keep and bear Arms, shall not be infringed."[7] Gun-control advocates have long interpreted this language to mean that the right of the people to keep and bear arms was justified only by the need to maintain a well-regulated military that is necessary to the security of a free country. Thus, they claimed, the Second Amendment's operative clause limited gun ownership by stating that it "shall not be infringed" only as long as the gun owner is a member of the aforementioned "well regulated militia."

In *Heller*, the Court resoundingly rejected that interpretation, specifically identifying the prefatory clause as an announcement—not a limitation—of the operative clause. In doing so, it is a breathtaking example of the power of the courts to provide citizens with a means to seek redress of governmental laws or actions that they believe adversely affect the citizenry.

Heller laid to rest many arguments that had long been made about gun control in the United States. The victors, it seemed, were gun ownership advocates, who saw their claims to Second Amendment protections vindicated. In *Heller*, however, the U.S. Supreme Court overturned laws that the District of Columbia felt were necessary in order to prevent gun violence or at least to keep it from spiraling out of control. ■

Notes

1. *District of Columbia, et al. v. Dick Anthony Heller* (2008). Available at http://www.law.cornell.edu/supct/html/07-290.ZS.html (accessed July 29, 2009).
2. Ibid.
3. Ibid.
4. Ibid., pp. 2–53.
5. Ibid., pp. 54–56.
6. Ibid., pp. 56–64.
7. Ibid., pp. 2–3.

Source: District of Columbia, et al. v. Dick Anthony Heller (2008), available at http://www.law.cornell.edu/supct/html/07-290.ZS.html (accessed May 2013).

DISCUSSION QUESTIONS

1. Why did it take so long for the U.S. Supreme Court to provide a definitive answer to the question of gun ownership and possession?

2. Should states and cities have the authority to make laws about important issues, such as gun ownership, without interference from the federal government (in this case, the U.S. Supreme Court)? Why or why not?

3. Does the decision in *Heller* mean that anyone can own a gun? What lawful restrictions on gun ownership might still be allowed under *Heller*?

Supreme Court as Policy Maker The Supreme Court, like the U.S. Courts of Appeals, is more than just a body of judges that reviews lower courts' decisions. It is a policy maker in the truest sense of the term—more so, some would argue, than the lower courts—because when the Supreme Court decides on a case, by definition the case is usually pretty important (after all, it is the "cream of the crop" that the Court decides to rule on). Also, since the Supreme Court is the court of last resort, its decision will be not only final but also binding on all other courts throughout the United States.

Supreme Court decisions have covered all manner of governmental and social issues, each with some interesting federal or constitutional question. In the realm of criminal justice, the Court has also been quite influential, with entire books and college courses now being devoted to the Supreme Court's interpretation of the Constitution as it applies to criminal justice. Police cadets are now trained in the nuances of constitutional law for criminal justice, all because of the Supreme Court's influence over criminal justice. We will look at a number of specific cases later in Part 4.

Web Extra
3–3 The U.S. Supreme Court

Other Article III Courts

Federal district courts, courts of appeals, and the U.S. Supreme Court do not make up the whole of the federal judiciary. There are two other noteworthy courts that collectively are known as **Article III courts**, which references the fact that they fall under Article III of the Constitution and thus are considered part of the federal judiciary. They include the U.S. Court of International Trade and a court stemming from the Federal Intelligence Surveillance Act of 1978, namely, the Foreign Intelligence Surveillance Court.

Article III court
A special category of federal courts established by Article III of the U.S. Constitution and considered part of the federal judicial branch. They include the U.S. Court of International Trade and the Foreign Intelligence Surveillance Court authorized by the Federal Intelligence Surveillance Act of 1978 (FISA).

U.S. Court of International Trade
The **U.S. Court of International Trade**, which resolves disputes involving international trade, is an outgrowth of the **Customs Courts Act of 1980**, perhaps the most significant federal legislation affecting international trade disputes. Prior to 1980, trade disputes were resolved in the U.S. Customs Court, but the Customs Courts Act increased the power of this court—and changed its name to the Court of International Trade.

The court is made up of nine judges appointed by the president with the advice and consent of the Senate, but only one judge is necessary to decide a case. The judges are appointed for life, which is what puts the court under Article III of the Constitution; that is, the judges enjoy Article III protection. They can also be appointed temporarily by the chief justice of the U.S. Supreme Court to perform functions in the appellate or district courts.

The court's geographical jurisdiction extends throughout the United States, and it is also authorized to hear some cases in other nations. The court's subject matter jurisdiction is rather limited, but generally it can decide any dispute arising out of laws pertaining to international trade. One of the sponsors of the Customs Courts Act of 1980 described the court's purpose in this way:

> (P)ersons adversely affected or aggrieved by agency actions arising out of import transactions are entitled to the same access to judicial review and judicial remedies as Congress has made available for persons aggrieved by actions of other agencies.[51]

The matters that come before the Court of International Trade are rather tedious, so it is no surprise that a single court has been formulated to resolve them. In one recent case, a U.S. company sought to recover some of the duties it paid on a printing press it imported from Germany.[52] Issues such as these are only loosely connected to the criminal justice system, but it is important to see that there are other federal courts besides those that receive most of the attention.

U.S. Court of International Trade
An Article III court that is an outgrowth of the Customs Courts Act of 1980. The court's geographic jurisdiction extends throughout the United States, and it is also authorized to hear some cases in other nations. Its subject matter jurisdiction is rather limited; generally, it can decide any dispute arising out of laws pertaining to international trade.

Customs Courts Act of 1980
The most significant federal legislation affecting international trade disputes.

Foreign Intelligence Surveillance Court
The U.S. Foreign Intelligence Surveillance Court was created pursuant to the **Federal Intelligence Surveillance Act of 1978 (FISA)**, which spelled out procedures for conducting foreign intelligence surveillance. The act has been amended more than once, most significantly by the 2001 PATRIOT Act (an acronym for Uniting and Strengthening America by Providing Appropriate Tools Required to Intercept and Obstruct Terrorism Act of 2001), legislation enacted in the wake

Federal Intelligence Surveillance Act of 1978 (FISA)
The U.S. legislation that spelled out procedures for conducting foreign intelligence surveillance.

of the September 11, 2001, attacks. The PATRIOT Act's amendments to FISA now assist the government with gathering intelligence against suspect terrorists.

The **U.S. Foreign Intelligence Surveillance Court** (or the FISA court) oversees requests for surveillance warrants against suspected foreign intelligence agents operating inside the United States and has thus been called "America's Secret Court."[53] Its proceedings have been described thusly:

> The FISA court conducts all of its hearings in a secret windowless courtroom, sealed from the public by cipher-locked doors on the top floor of the Department of Justice. It considers surveillance and physical search applications that have been reviewed and forwarded by the Office of Intelligence Policy and Review, which is the Department of Justice's section that deals with foreign intelligence matters.[54]

It is somewhat risky, on the one hand, to call the FISA court an Article III court because it is composed of seven judges "borrowed" from the district courts and chosen by the U.S. Supreme Court's chief justice. Each serves a nonrenewable seven-year term, and the court's membership is staggered such that a new judge is brought on each year. On the other hand, since the judges are already district court judges for life, they once again enjoy Article III protection.

Article I Tribunals

Chapter 1 defined the term "court" by referencing the judicial branch. To be sure, the vast majority of courts are considered part of the government's judicial branch, but there are exceptions, notably **Article I tribunals**, or legislative courts. All the administrative law courts, for example, hail from Article I, and the Board of Patent Appeals and Interferences is another. The U.S. bankruptcy courts, the Merit Systems Protection Board, and many others also fall into this category. We will limit our attention to four of the more visible Article I tribunals: the U.S. Tax Court, the U.S. Court of Appeals for Veterans Claims, the U.S. Court of Federal Claims, and the courts falling within the armed forces.

U.S. Tax Court   The **U.S. Tax Court** consists of 19 presidentially appointed members who are appointed for 15-year terms, not for life, and the court specializes in settling disputes over federal income taxes. Tax disputes can be settled in various courts, but what makes the U.S. Tax Court distinct is that disputes can be heard and settled there before the tax amount in dispute has been paid in full. Other federal courts, like the district courts, require that the disputed amount be first paid in full and that a lawsuit be filed to recover the disputed amount.[55]

U.S. Court of Appeals for Veterans Claims   The **U.S. Court of Appeals for Veterans Claims** reviews decisions from the Board of Veterans' Appeals. The latter makes decisions on appeals arising from decisions made by the secretary of veterans' affairs, who oversees the U.S. Department of Veterans Affairs, a cabinet-level agency. Disputes that first arrive at the Board of Veterans' Appeals and then the U.S. Court of Appeals for Veterans Claims generally involve denial of various veterans' benefits, such as health care or education benefits. The mission of the Court of Appeals for Veterans' Claims is as follows:

> The Court provides veterans an impartial judicial forum for review of administrative decisions by the Board of Veterans' Appeals that are adverse to the veteran-appellant's claim of entitlement to benefits for service-connected disabilities, survivor benefits and other benefits such as education payments and waiver of indebtedness. In further-ance of its mission, the Court also seeks to help ensure that all veterans have equal access to the Court and to promote public trust and confidence in the Court.[56]

The court falls under Article I of the Constitution because it was established as an Arti-cle I court: "[It] is a national court of record, established under Article I of the Constitution

---

U.S. Foreign Intelligence Surveillance Court
An Article III court established by the Federal Intelligence Surveillance Act of 1978 (FISA) that oversees requests for surveillance warrants against suspected foreign intelligence agents operating inside the United States; also called *FISA court.*

Article I tribunals
Federal courts established by Article I of the U.S. Constitution that are not considered part of the federal judicial branch; also called *legislative courts.*

U.S. Tax Court
An Article I court that specializes in settling disputes over federal income taxes.

U.S. Court of Appeals for Veterans Claims
An Article I court that reviews decisions from the Board of Veterans' Appeals, which itself makes decisions on appeals arising from decisions made by the secretary of veterans affairs.

of the United States."[57] The court's judges serve 15-year terms, too, which differs from the lifetime terms for Article III judges. The court is relatively new, as it came into being as a result of the Veterans Programs Enhancement Act of 1998.

U.S. Court of Federal Claims The **U.S. Court of Federal Claims** (formerly the U.S. Claims Court) is another federal tribunal established under Article I of the Constitution whose jurisdiction is described in 28 U.S.C., Section 1491, and it is authorized to issue decisions involving (1) claims for just compensation arising from government taking of private property (eminent domain), (2) refunds of federal taxes, (3) constitutional and statutory rights of military personnel and their dependents, (4) damages for breaches of contract with the U.S. government, (5) claims for back pay from dismissed civil servants, (6) claims involving patent and copyright infringement, and (7) certain claims involving the Indian tribes.

Recently, its jurisdiction has been expanded to include claims concerning injuries attributed to specific vaccines, and it also hears protest lawsuits stemming from failed bids for U.S. government contracts. Finally, certain lawsuits (e.g., other than alleging tort violations) against the federal government involving amounts in excess of $10,000 must be tried before the U.S. Court of Federal Claims. The common theme running through all these types of cases is the requirement that they involve "money claims founded upon the Constitution, federal statutes, executive regulations, or contracts, express or implied-in-fact, with the United States."[58] For a listing of some sample cases, see Box 3–1.

As for the court's composition, 16 judges serve on the court and are appointed for 15-year terms—hence its treatment as an Article I tribunal. It is a busy court; for example, during the 12-month period ending on September 30, 2011, there were almost 7,000 cases on its docket.[59]

Military Justice and Military Tribunals In 1950, Congress adopted the **Uniform Code of Military Justice**,[60] which is basically the military's criminal code, not unlike

U.S. Court of Federal Claims
An Article I court that is authorized to issue decisions involving (1) claims for just compensation arising from government taking of private property (eminent domain), (2) refunds of federal taxes, (3) constitutional and statutory rights of military personnel and their dependents, (4) damages for breaches of contract with the U.S. government, (5) claims for back pay from dismissed civil servants, (6) claims involving patent and copyright infringement, and (7) certain claims involving the Indian tribes. It was formerly the U.S. Claims Court.

Uniform Code of Military Justice
The military's criminal code, akin to state penal codes or the U.S. Code.[vi]

BOX 3–1 Examples of Cases in the U.S. Court of Federal Claims

- A series of approximately 120 contract cases, referred to collectively as *Winstar* cases, involving the collapse of the savings and loan industry in the 1980s and the legislation enacted by Congress in response to the collapse. The Justice Department, at one point, estimated that those cases involved dollar claims of more than $30 billion and over a billion pages of documents.

- A series of 66 contract and takings cases involving claims by electric utility companies that the federal government has breached contracts to remove spent nuclear fuel from their facilities for transfer to the Yucca Mountain repository. While only 11 of these cases have specific dollar claims, those claims still total over $6 billion, suggesting that the remainder of these cases could involve tens of billions of dollars not reflected in docket figures listed above. For example, a 2006 judgment awarded over $40 million in a case without a specific dollar claim.

- A total of 77 cases involving claims by Native American tribes that the government has breached its fiduciary responsibilities. Although these cases generally do not request specific dollar amounts, three cases (involving relatively small tribes) claim more than $550 million in damages.

- Approximately 4,800 vaccine cases involving claims that the measles, mumps, and rubella vaccine or a preservative added to other vaccines (specifically Thimerosal) cause autism. While the initial decisions in these cases are being made by the court's special masters, they will be heard by the judges of this court upon petitions for review. ∎

Source: http://www.uscfc.uscourts.gov/sites/default/files/court_info/Court_History_Brochure.pdf (accessed January 31, 2013).

court-martial
A criminal trial conducted by the military.

U.S. Court of Appeals for the Armed Forces
An Article I appellate court created by the U.S. Congress in 1950 to extend a measure of civilian authority into military law.

summary court-martial
A type of court-martial that handles charges of minor misconduct.

special court-martial
A type of court-martial that is akin to civilian courts of general jurisdiction. This type of court is adversarial and tries more serious offenses than those tried by summary court-martial.

general court-martial
A type of court-martial that is reserved for the most serious violations of the Uniform Code of Military Justice, including cases that may result in a penalty of death.

military tribunal
A group authorized by an executive military order shortly after the September 11, 2001, terrorist attacks on the World Trade Center and the Pentagon to deal with alleged terrorists and individuals the government alleges could threaten national security.

state penal codes or the U.S. Code. This code also provides protections for armed services members brought before **courts-martial**, criminal trials conducted by the military. In 1950, Congress also created the **U.S. Court of Appeals for the Armed Forces**, a court that consists of five civilian judges who are, once again, appointed by the president for 15-year terms. This was done to extend a measure of civilian authority into military law.

There are various types of courts-martial, which is why we selected the general term "military justice."[61] First, **summary courts-martial** handle charges of minor misconduct; usually one individual, a "judge advocate," decides the matter, and punishments are relatively minor. Second, **special courts-martial**, which try more serious offenses and are adversarial, are akin to civilian courts of general jurisdiction. Finally, **general courts-martial** are reserved for the most serious violations of the Uniform Code, and the highest possible penalty is death.

Convictions by special or general courts-martial can be appealed to the appropriate Court of Criminal Appeals (e.g., the Army Court of Criminal Appeals for . . .). Death sentence appeals are mandatory. Appeals can then proceed, subject to various rules, to the U.S. Court of Appeals for the armed forces and then to the U.S. Supreme Court.

On November 13, 2001, shortly after the September 11 attacks on the World Trade Center towers in New York City, President Bush issued a military order titled "Detention, Treatment, and Trial of Certain Non-Citizens in the War against Terrorism." In it, **military tribunals** were authorized as a means of dealing with alleged terrorists and similar individuals who the government feels could threaten national security. Those who came before the tribunals did not see a judge or even necessarily go before a court; instead, their fate was decided by between three and seven commissioned officers of the U.S. military. Also, many of the protections that an ordinary criminal defendant would enjoy were not available in the military tribunal context.

In *Hamdan* v. *Rumsfeld*,[62] the Supreme Court held that these military tribunals' procedures did not comply with U.S. military law. Approximately six months later, the Military Commissions Act of 2006 was enacted and had as its stated purpose to "authorize trial by military commission for violations of the law of war, and for other purposes."[63] Then, in *Boumediene* v. *Bush*,[64] the Supreme Court declared part of the act unconstitutional and ruled that the Guantanamo Bay detainees who were subject to the military tribunals could challenge their confinement in civilian court.

Military tribunals are nothing new. Similar methods were used as early as during the Civil War to deal with suspected confederates. Since then, other tribunals have been used, and the Supreme Court has had several occasions to decide on their constitutionality. For the most part, the Court has sanctioned the use of certain tribunals, but that makes them no less controversial.[65]

Learning Objective 3

Summarize the administration in and caseload trends of federal courts.

FEDERAL JUDICIAL ADMINISTRATION AND CASELOADS

Federal judicial administration is concerned with the day-to-day operation of the federal courts, such as how records are kept and when cases are scheduled. Important to those involved in judicial administration are caseload trends, as these can have dramatic effects on everything from workloads to budget concerns.

Administrative Levels

Federal judicial administration takes place at several levels. The individual courts have the most responsibility, but regional and national bodies have an important role in court administration.

Court Level Each federal court is tasked with its own administrative functions, including everything from hiring staff to overseeing spending and managing court records. Each court uses a hierarchy not unlike that of a business. The chief judge acts as leader and oversees the operations of the court as well as the actions of his or her subordinates. Policy decisions tend to be made by several judges.

Web Extra
3–4 Administrative Office
of the U.S. Courts

Although the chief judge is akin to the chief executive officer of the court, it is the court clerk who handles most of the administrative responsibilities. At the district court level, such individuals generally report directly to the chief judges, follow and implement applicable court policies, and are otherwise tasked with the following:

- Maintaining the records and dockets of the court
- Paying all fees, fines, costs, and other monies collected for the U.S. Treasury
- Administering the court's jury system
- Providing interpreters and court reporters
- Sending official court notices and summons
- Providing courtroom support services[66]

Regional Level: Circuit Judicial Councils Within each federal circuit is a **circuit judicial council**, which consists of both a chief judge who serves in the role of chair and an equal but undefined number of district and circuit court judges. These councils are charged, by law, with the task of making "all necessary and appropriate orders for the effective and expeditious administration of justice within its circuit."[67] The councils further set circuit policy and implement orders from their superior, the Judicial Conference of the United States. Each council also appoints a circuit executive who works with each chief circuit judge. Other responsibilities of the councils include "reviewing local court rules for consistency with national rules of procedure, approving district court plans on topics such as equal employment opportunity and jury selection, and reviewing complaints of judicial misconduct."[68]

circuit judicial council
A council established within each federal circuit that is charged, by law, with the task of making "all necessary and appropriate orders for the effective and expeditious administration of justice within its circuit."[vii]

National Level: Judicial Conference of the United States Congress created the so-called Conference of Senior Circuit Judges in 1922 that was to serve as the main policy-making body of the federal judiciary; in 1948, Congress enacted 28 U.S.C., Section 331, and changed the name to the **Judicial Conference of the United States**. District judges were added to the conference in 1957.

The purpose of the Judicial Conference is to make policy for the federal courts. It also has the following responsibilities:

- Make a comprehensive survey of the conditions of business in the courts of the United States.
- Prepare plans for the assignment of judges to or from courts of appeals or district courts, where necessary.
- Submit suggestions to the various courts in the interest of promoting uniformity of management procedures and the expeditious conduct of court business.
- Exercise authority provided in Chapter 16 of Title 28, U.S. Code, for the review of circuit council conduct and disability orders filed under that chapter.
- Carry on a continuous study of the operation and effect of the general rules of practice and procedure in use within the federal courts, as prescribed by the Supreme Court pursuant to law.[69]

Judicial Conference of the United States
The main policy-making body of the federal judiciary. It was formerly called the Conference of Senior Circuit Judges.

The Judicial Conference also supervises the director of the Administrative Office of the U.S. Courts. The **Administrative Office of the U.S. Courts** carries out the

Administrative Office of the U.S. Courts
The federal agency that carries out the policies of the Judicial Conference and "provides a broad range of legislative, legal, financial, technology, management, administrative, and program support services to the federal courts."[viii]

policies of the Judicial Conference and "provides a broad range of legislative, legal, financial, technology, management, administrative, and program support services to the federal courts."[70] Below are other areas for which the Administrative Office is also responsible:

- Collecting and reporting judicial branch statistics
- Developing budgets
- Conducting studies and assessments of judiciary operations and programs
- Providing technical assistance to the courts
- Developing training programs (taught in the Federal Judicial Center)
- Fostering communications within the judiciary and with other branches of the government and the public[71]

The Judicial Conference is presided over by the chief justice of the U.S. Supreme Court. Other members include the chief judge of each judicial circuit, the chief judge of the Court of International Trade, and a judge from each federal district.

Caseloads

The Administrative Office of the U.S. Courts (as mentioned above) has been tasked with gathering data on caseload trends and other issues affecting the federal judiciary. The last few subsections in this chapter look briefly at caseload trends in the federal district courts, the courts of appeals, and the Supreme Court. The statistics we are about to present should be placed in context: While the federal courts are certainly busy, the vast majority of court cases in this country are handled at the state and local levels. According to the most recent data, state criminal filings outnumber federal filings by a factor of 80 to 1.[72]

**Library Extra
3–3** The Federal Judicial Process

District Courts Table 3–1 contains an overview of trends in cases commenced, terminated, and pending in the federal district courts from 1982 through 2008; the number of authorized judgeships is presented as well. These numbers are used to estimate the number of cases decided each year per judge.

Clearly, the federal district courts—and their judges—have been busy. First, the number of cases before the district courts has doubled from 1982 to 2006, and the cases per judgeship went up considerably during this period as well. Table 3–1 also shows that a large portion of the growth in federal court cases owes to the war on drugs.

Courts of Appeals and the Supreme Court The courts of appeals have been equally busy. Figure 3–5 shows which types of appeals are most often filed. A recent surge in criminal appeals (especially during 2005) has been attributed to a 2004 Supreme Court decision *Blakely* v. *Washington*,[73] in which the Washington State sentencing system was declared unconstitutional. The surge occurred primarily in 2006 because prisoners first had to exhaust state-level remedies before seeking relief in the federal courts.[74] The increase also owed to the Supreme Court's decision in *United States* v. *Booker*,[75] where it held that mandatory application of the U.S. Sentencing Guidelines violates a defendant's right to trial by jury under the Sixth Amendment.[76]

The U.S. Supreme Court is also busy but not on as grand a scale as the appellate and district courts due to the fact that it is only one court. According to the most recent data available as of this writing (from 2010), 86 cases were argued during the Court's term.[77] Eighty-three of those cases were disposed of by full opinions, and three were set up for re-argument. A total of just 90 cases were granted review.

TABLE 3–1 Criminal cases commenced, terminated, and pending, and judgeships authorized in U.S. District Courts 1982–2010

		Cases Commenced[a]				
	Judgeships Authorized	Number	Cases per Judgeship	Drug Cases	Terminated	Pending[b]
1982	515	32,682	63	4,218	31,889	16,659
1983	515	35,872	70	5,094	33,985	18,546
1984	515	36,845	72	5,606	35,494	19,938
1985	575	39,500	69	6,690	37,139	22,299
1986	575	41,490	72	7,893	39,328	24,453
1987	575	43,292	75	8,878	42,287	25,263
1988	575	43,607	76	10,603	41,878	28,776
1989	575	45,792	80	12,342	42,933	32,666
1990	575	46,568	81	11,547	43,296	35,308
1991	649	47,123	73	11,954	43,073	39,562
1992	649	48,366	75	12,833	44,147	34,078
1993	649	46,786	72	12,238	44,800	28,701
1994	649	45,484	70	11,369	45,129	26,328
1995	649	45,788	71	11,520	41,527	28,738
1996	647	47,889	74	12,092	45,499	32,156
1997	647	50,363	78	13,656	46,887	37,237
1998	646	57,691	89	16,281	51,428	40,277
1999	646	59,923	93	17,483	56,511	42,966
2000	655	62,745	96	17,505	58,102	47,677
2001	665	62,708	94	18,383	58,718	49,696
2002	665	67,000	101	19,184	60,991	55,518
2003	680	70,642	104	18,973	65,628	59,218
2004	679	71,022	105	18,414	64,621	65,900
2005	678	69,575	103	18,198	66,561	69,932
2006	678	66,860	99	17,429	67,499	71,916
2007	678	68,413	101	17,046	67,851	73,418
2008	678	70,896	105	15,784	70,629	73,340
2009	678	76,655	113	16,636	75,077	79,068
2010	678	78,428	116	15,785	78,069	79,427
Percent change 2009 to 2010	0%	2.3%	2.7%	−5.1%	4.0%	0.5%

[a]Data for criminal cases commenced include transfers with the exception of drug cases, which exclude transfers.

[b]Beginning in 1993, pending totals exclude cases in which all defendants were fugitives for more than 1 year.

Note: Data for 1982–87 are reported for the 12-month period ending June 30. Beginning in 1988, data are reported for the Federal fiscal year, which is the 12-month period ending September 30. Some data have been revised by the Source and may differ from previous editions of SOURCEBOOK.

Sources: Administrative Office of the United States Courts, *Annual Report of the Director, 1991,* p. 90; *1992,* p. 66; *1997,* p. 20 (Washington, DC: USGPO); and Administrative Office of the United States Courts, *Judicial Business of the United States Courts: 2002 Annual Report of the Director,* p. 23; *2007 Annual Report of the Director,* p. 26; *2010 Annual Report of the Director,* p. 24 (Washington, DC: USGPO). Table adapted by SOURCEBOOK staff.

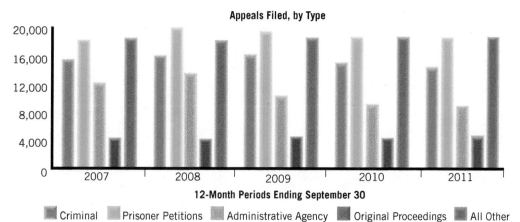

Appeals Filed, by Type

12-Month Periods Ending September 30

■ Criminal   ■ Prisoner Petitions   ■ Administrative Agency   ■ Original Proceedings   ■ All Other

FIGURE 3–5

Source: Administrative Office of the United States Courts, *2011 Annual Report of the Director: Judicial Business of the United States Courts* (Washington, DC: Administrative Office of the U.S. Courts, 2012), p. 13. http://www.uscourts.gov/uscourts/Statistics/JudicialBusiness/2011/JudicialBusiness2011.pdf

CHAPTER SUMMARY

3

1. OUTLINE THE HISTORY AND DEVELOPMENT OF FEDERAL COURTS

- Article III of the U.S. Constitution spells out the structure and function of the federal judiciary.

- Landmark judicial legislation, notably the Judiciary Act of 1789 and the Judiciary Act of 1891, has extended the reach of the federal judiciary and created additional courts.

2. DESCRIBE THE STRUCTURE OF THE FEDERAL COURT SYSTEM AND THE VARIOUS TYPES OF FEDERAL COURTS

- There are three main types of courts in the federal judiciary: district courts, courts of appeals, and the U.S. Supreme Court.

- District courts are the federal trial courts. There are 94 of them in the United States and its territories. District courts are the federal court workhorses insofar as they do much more than hear cases (e.g., they monitor consent decrees).

- The U.S. courts of appeals mostly review decisions from the district courts, and they do their work via three-judge panels.

- The Supreme Court is the highest court in the federal judiciary. It reviews decisions from the lower federal courts and state supreme courts, and it has original jurisdiction in certain cases.

- Of the nine Supreme Court justices, four must agree to hear a case before a writ of *certiorari* is issued.

- The Supreme Court has progressed through several distinct eras, usually as a result of an influential chief justice. The Court, like the courts of appeals, issues sweeping decisions with significant policy implications throughout government, including criminal justice.

- Other Article III courts (owing to Article III of the Constitution) include the U.S. Court of International Trade and the Foreign Intelligence Surveillance Court.

- Article I tribunals, or legislative courts, are created pursuant to Article I of the Constitution. Examples include the U.S. Tax Court, the U.S. Court of Appeals for Veterans Claims, the U.S. Court of Federal Claims, and military courts-martial. Military tribunals fall under this category as well.

3. SUMMARIZE THE ADMINISTRATION IN AND CASELOAD TRENDS OF FEDERAL COURTS

- Federal judicial administration is concerned with the day-to-day operation of the federal courts, such as how records are kept and when cases are scheduled. It is carried out by the federal courts themselves, the circuit judicial councils, and the Judicial Conference of the United States.

- Federal judiciary caseloads have increased considerably over the past several decades, but civil cases still far outnumber criminal cases.

KEY TERMS

Administrative Office of the U.S. Courts, 71

Article I tribunals, 68

Article III court, 67

circuit judicial council, 71

circuit riding, 54

concurring opinion, 62

consent decree, 58

court-martial, 70

court of appeal, 59

Courts of Appeals Act of 1891, 56

Customs Courts Act of 1980, 67

dissenting opinion, 62

en banc proceeding, 60

Federal Intelligence Surveillance Act of 1978, 67

Federal Judiciary Act of 1789, 54

general court-martial, 70

Judicial Conference of the United States, 71

military tribunal, 70

New Jersey Plan, 53

opinion, 62

per curiam opinion, 60

quorum, 56

rule of four, 63

special court-martial, 70

summary court-martial, 70

Uniform Code of Military Justice, 69

U.S. Court of Appeals for the Armed Forces, 70

U.S. Court of Appeals for Veterans Claims, 68

U.S. Court of Federal Claims, 69

U.S. Court of International Trade, 67

U.S. district court, 56

U.S. Foreign Intelligence Surveillance Court, 68

U.S. magistrate judge, 58

U.S. Supreme Court, 62

U.S. Tax Court, 68

Virginia Plan, 53

writ of *certiorari*, 63

REVIEW QUESTIONS

1. How did the federal courts develop historically? Include a discussion of the influence of the U.S. Constitution and important federal legislation in your answer.

2. What is the structure of federal courts in America today?

3. How are the federal courts administered, and what are their characteristic caseloads?

WHAT WILL YOU DO?

You are a court administrator for a federal district court and work with personnel from the Administrative Office of the U.S. Courts in scheduling hearings, hiring support personnel, coordinating with other agencies and offices, purchasing needed supplies, and generally ensuring that the business of the court runs smoothly. Like officials in many other government agencies—including those at the federal, state, and local levels—you have faced increased budgetary constraints.

Although budgets have constricted, the workload of the court has continued to increase. This morning the judge charged with overseeing the district in which you work called you into his chambers and instructed you to develop a new budget instituting a 12 percent cutback in expenditures.

You're now sitting at your keyboard wondering how to implement his instructions. You have pretty much been given carte blanche to do whatever needs to be done to save money, which includes the possibility of altering the hours during which the court is in session, negotiating new pay schedules for transcriptionists, publishing lower pay schedules for expert witnesses, changing the thermostat in the courthouse to save money on heating oil and electricity, cutting back on supplies, moving to more paperless forms of document handling, and deferring orders for new computers and furniture. As you think about these issues, you ask yourself what other budgetary items might be available for cutting and then prioritize your overall list of cost savings. What will that list look like?

NOTES

i. M. Ferrand, ed., *The Records of the Federal Convention of 1787*, rev. ed., 4 vols. (New Haven, CT: Yale University Press, 1937).

ii. M. Ferrand, ed., *The Records of the Federal Convention of 1787*, rev. ed., 4 vols. (New Haven, CT: Yale University Press, 1937).

iii. 1 Stat. 73.

iv. R. Wheeler and C. Harrison, *Creating the Federal Judicial System*, 3rd ed. (Washington, DC: Federal Judicial Center, 2005).

v. 26 Stat. 826.

vi. 10 U.S.C., Sections 801–941.

vii. 28 U.S.C., Section 332 (d)(1).

viii. L. R. Mecham, *Understanding the Federal Courts* (Washington, DC: Administrative Office of the U.S. Courts, Office of Judges Programs, 2003), p. 28.

1. *Marbury v. Madison*, 5. U.S. 137 (1803).

2. R. Wheeler and C. Harrison, *Creating the Federal Judicial System*, 3rd ed. (Washington, DC: Federal Judicial Center, 2005).

3. Available at http://www.usconstitution.net/articles.html (accessed January 31, 2013).

4. B. Bailyn, ed., *The Debate on the Constitution: Federalist and Anti-Federalist Speeches, Articles, and Letters during the Struggle over Ratification* (New York: Library of America, 1993).

5. M. Ferrand, ed., *The Records of the Federal Convention of 1787*, rev. ed., 4 vols. (New Haven, CT: Yale University Press, 1937).

6. Ibid.

7. U.S. Constitution, Article III, Section 1.

8. 1 Stat. 73.

9. The Judiciary Act of 1801 reduced the size of the Supreme Court from six to five justices. 2 Stat. 89. This statute was then repealed. See, e.g., http://www.fjc.gov/history/home.nsf for a thorough overview of pertinent federal judicial legislation (accessed January 31, 2013); also see Wheeler and Harrison, *Creating the Federal Judicial System*.

10. L. Baker, *The Circuit Riding Justices* (Supreme Court Historical Society, 1976), pp. 48–53.

11. 26 Stat. 826.

12. Wheeler and Harrison, *Creating the Federal Judicial System*.

13. R. Richardson and K. Vines, *The Politics of Federal Courts* (Boston: Little, Brown, 1970), p. 26.

14. M. J. Friedman, *Outline of the U.S. Legal System* (Washington, DC: U.S. State Department, 2004), available at http://www.america.gov/media/pdf/books/legalotln.pdf#popup (accessed January 31, 2013).

15. Ibid.

16. Ibid., p. 37.

17. For the latest numbers by district and court type, see http://www.uscourts.gov/Statistics/JudicialFactsAndFigures/JudicialFactsAndFigures2010.aspx (accessed January 31, 2013).

18. Ibid.

19. A. Chayes, "The Role of the Judge in Public Law Litigation," *Harvard Law Review*, Vol. 89 (1976), pp. 1281–1316.

20. See, e.g., *Franks v. Bowman Transp. Co*, 424 U.S. 747 (1976); *Kirkland v. New York State Department of Correctional Services*, 520 F.2d 420 (2nd Cir. 1975).

21. See, e.g., *Brown v. Board of Education*, 347 U.S. 483 (1954).

22. See, e.g., *Hurto v. Finney*, 437 U.S. 678 (1978), pp. 685–688; *Gates v. Collier*, 501 F.2d 1291 (5th Cir. 1974), pp. 1299–1322.

23. See, e.g., *Connor v. Finch*, 431 U.S. 407 (1977).

24. Consent Decree, p. 1, available at http://www.lapdonline.org/assets/pdf/final_consent_decree.pdf (accessed January 31, 2013).

25. Administrative Office of the U.S. Courts, available at http://www.utd.uscourts.gov/judges/qa_magjudge.html (accessed January 31, 2013).

26. http://www.uscourts.gov/uscourts/Statistics/JudicialFactsAndFigures/2010/Table101.pdf (accessed January 31, 2013).

27. *Hopwood v. Texas*, 78 F.3d 932 (5th Cir. 1996).

28. *Miranda v. Arizona*, 384 U.S. 436 (1966).

29. 18 U.S.C., Section 3501.

30. *Dickerson v. United States*, 530 U.S. 428 (2000), p. 431.

31. C. Huges, *The Supreme Court of the United States* (New York: Columbia University Press, 1966).

32. C. Warren, *The Supreme Court in United States History* (Boston: Little, Brown, 1923), p. 4.

33. P. C. Hoffer, W. H. Hoffer, and N. E. H. Hull, *The Supreme Court: An Essential History* (Lawrence: University Press of Kansas, 2007).

34. R. Steamer, "Congress and the Supreme Court during the Marshall Era," *The Review of Politics*, Vol. 27 (1965), pp. 364–385.

35. *Marbury v. Madison*, 5 U.S. 137 (1803).

36. Other important decisions under Marshall included *Fletcher v. Peck*, 10 U.S. 87 (1810); *McCulloch v. Maryland*, 17 U.S. 316 (1819); *Dartmouth College v. Woodward*, 17 U.S. 518 (1819); *Cohens v. Virginia*, 19 U.S. 264 (1821); *Gibbons v. Ogden*, 22 U.S. 1 (1824); *Worcester v. Georgia*, 31 U.S. 515 (1832); and *Barron v. Baltimore*, 32 U.S. 243 (1833).

37. *Dred Scott v. Sanford*, 60 U.S. 393 (1856).

38. *Ashwander v. Tennessee Valley Authority*, 297 U.S. 288 (1936), pp. 346–349.

39. *Moore v. Illinois*, 55 U.S. 13 (1852), p. 17.

40. *Dred Scott v. Sanford*, 60 U.S. 393 (1856).

41. Examples include *Lochner v. New York*, 198 U.S. 45 (1908), and *Adair v. United States*, 208 U.S. 161 (1908).

42. *Gitlow v. New York*, 268 U.S. 652 (1925).

43. *West Coast Hotel Co. v. Parrish*, 300 U.S. 279 (1937).

44. *Brown v. Board of Education*, 347 U.S. 483 (1954).

45. *Furman v. Georgia*, 408 U.S. 238 (1972).

46. *Gregg v. Georgia*, 428 U.S. 153 (1976).

47. *Solem v. Helm*, 463 U.S. 277 (1983).

48. C. E. Smith, "The Rehnquist Court and Criminal Justice: An Empirical Assessment," *Journal of Contemporary Criminal Justice*, Vol. 19 (2003), pp. 161–181.

49. *U.S. Department of Health and Human Services* v. *Florida*, No. 11-398 (2012).

50. Bar admission forms can be found here at http://www .supremecourt.gov/bar/baradmissions.aspx (accessed January 31, 2013).

51. Available at http://www.cit.uscourts.gov/AboutTheCourt .html (accessed January 31, 2013).

52. *Windmoeller and Hoelscher Corporation* v. *United States*, Slip Op. 07-166 (2007).

53. See, e.g., H. Schuster, "Inside America's Secret Court," *CNN.com*, available at http://edition.cnn.com/2006/US/02/ 13/schuster.column/index.html (accessed January 31, 2013).

54. P. S. Poole, *Inside America's Secret Court: The Foreign Intelligence Surveillance Court*, available at http://encryption_ policies.tripod.com/us/poole_98_court.htm (accessed January 31, 2013).

55. Available at http://www.ustaxcourt.gov/about.htm (accessed January 31, 2013).

56. Available at http://www.uscourts.cavc.gov/ (accessed January 31, 2013).

57. Ibid.

58. Available at http://www.uscfc.uscourts.gov/about-court (accessed January 31, 2013).

59. Administrative Office of the United States Courts, *2011 Annual Report of the Director: Judicial Business of the United States Courts* (Washington, DC: Administrative Office of the U.S. Courts, 2012), p. 291.

60. The code is codified in 10 U.S.C., Sections 801–941.

61. For details, see *Manual for Courts Martial, United States*, 2012 edition, available at http://www.au.af.mil/au/awc/ awcgate/law/mcm.pdf (accessed January 31, 2013).

62. *Hamdan* v. *Rumsfeld*, 548 U.S. 557 (2006).

63. Military Commissions Act of 2006, Public Law No. 109-366, p. 1, available at http://frwebgate.access.gpo.gov/cgi-bin/ getdoc.cgi?dbname=109_cong_bills&docid=f:s3930enr.txt .pdf (accessed January 31, 2013).

64. *Boumediene* v. *Bush*, No. 06-1195 (2008).

65. For some additional information on the use of military tribunals throughout history, see R. O. Everett, "The Role of Military Tribunals under the Law of War," *Boston University International Law Journal*, Vol. 24 (2006), pp. 1–14.

66. L. R. Mecham, *Understanding the Federal Courts* (Washington, DC: Administrative Office of the U.S. Courts, Office of Judges Programs, 2003).

67. 28 U.S.C., Section 332 (d)(1).

68. Mecham, *Understanding the Federal Courts*, p. 28.

69. Available at http://www.uscourts.gov/FederalCourts/Judicial Conference.aspx (accessed January 31, 2013).

70. Mecham, *Understanding the Federal Courts*, p. 28.

71. Ibid., pp. 28–29.

72. See http://www.courtstatistics.org/Criminal/20121Criminal.aspx and http://www.uscourts.gov/uscourts/Statistics/Judicial Business/2011/US_District_Courts%E2%80%94Criminal_ all.pdf (both accessed January 31, 2013).

73. *Blakely* v. *Washington*, 542 U.S. 296 (2004).

74. J. C. Duff, *2006 Judicial Business of the United States Courts, Annual Report of the Director* (Washington, DC: Administrative Office of the U.S. Courts, 2006).

75. *United States* v. *Booker*, 543 U.S. 220 (2005).

76. Duff, *2006 Judicial Business of the United States Courts, Annual Report of the Director*.

77. Administrative Office of the United States Courts, *2011 Annual Report of the Director*, p. 58.

© SeanPavonePhoto/Fotolia

4

State Courts

LEARNING OBJECTIVES

1. Outline the history and development of state courts.
2. Summarize the differing structures of state court systems.
3. Describe the workload of state courts.
4. Summarize the administration of state courts.
5. Be familiar with recent developments in state courts.

John Peter Zenger being carried by a celebratory crowd after his courtroom victory in 1734. Zenger's lawyer observed that the outcome of the trial affected everyone in America. What was the trial about?

INTRODUCTION

Like federal courts, discussed in the last chapter, state courts have their own unique history. In the early American colonies, courts existed long before the formation of the United States. In 1691, for example, the New York Assembly, established what was intended to be a permanent judicial system through passage of "An Act Declaring What are the Rights and Privileges of Their Majestyes Subjects Inhabing within Their Province of New York."[1] One of the most famous cases tried in New York prior to independence involved John Peter Zenger, who was hired by the publishers of the *New York Weekly Journal* to print issues of their independent newspaper. In 1734, Zenger (but not the publishers) was charged with the crime of seditious libel, which was defined at common law as "the intentional publication, without lawful excuse or justification, of written blame of any public man or of the law, or any institution established by the law."[2] According to precedent, the Crown's prosecutor did not have to prove that the published statements, charged as libel, were in fact true. Further, the role of the jury in a seditious libel case was limited to merely deciding whether the person charged was responsible for the allegedly libelous statement. If that was the jury's finding, then it was up to the judge to examine the printed text to determine if the statements constituted seditious libel. Zenger was vindicated, however, when his defense attorney convinced the jury that the trial was not about libel, but about liberty—and that their decision would be far reaching. Zenger's attorney successfully argued that "in its consequence [the trial would] affect every free man that lives under a British government on the main of America."[3] Learn more about the Zenger case at **http://tinyurl.com/ajewkbh**.

Learning Objective 1

Outline the history and development of state courts.

HISTORY OF STATE COURTS

Unlike federal courts, state courts were shaped not by fear of an intrusive central government but by the geography of early America. The demands for justice in the largely undeveloped rural areas coupled with the relative difficulty of getting from one place to the next helped mold a variety of distinct judicial systems whose differentiating characteristics remain important today.

Colonial Period

During the colonial period, most political authority rested with governors who were appointed by the king of England.[4] These governors basically exercised legislative, executive, *and* judicial power, so there was no real need for an elaborate court system. The governors appointed justices of the peace to handle minor cases; county courts were the main trial tribunals, and appeals from these lower courts were brought before the governor and his council.

Justice of the peace courts were the workhorses during the colonial period. The justices generally had no formal training and were little more than representatives of the communities from which they came. In this sense, one historian has argued that justice of the peace courts were "an informal, discretionary agency for solving the problems of community affairs" and that the justices' decisions were based largely on "private ties of kinship, friendship, or economic relationship."[5] These arrangements made the justice of the peace courts rather unique:

> The informality and the desire to reinforce community norms [were] so powerful that people were punished for "offenses" that were not specified by statute. Massachusetts, for example, convicted and punished people for defamation and slander, on the indirect grounds that they represented a breach of the peace.[6]

At the county level, the Virginia county courts, which met once per month by the eighteenth century,[7] consisted of anywhere from 10 to 15 justices, but only four were necessary for a quorum. In contrast, the New York courts met less often—semiannually in the rural areas and quarterly in the populous areas. Justice continued to be meted out in an informal fashion, but gradually the process became more official and routine.

Public prosecutors came onto the scene during the seventeenth and eighteenth centuries, and some counties even had district attorneys appointed by the governors. Even so, officials exercised broad discretion in disposing of cases, and defendants enjoyed relatively few rights. Defense attorneys began to gain a presence around the 1730s, prior to the American Revolution, and so began to emerge the more adversarial system we recognize today.[8]

Early State Courts

After the American Revolution (1775–1783), governmental powers were significantly curtailed and taken over by legislative bodies. The former colonists were also nervous about seeing the development of a large-scale judiciary with broad, sweeping powers. State legislatures kept a close eye on the courts: They sometimes removed judges from their posts and abolished certain courts that issued unpopular decisions. As some courts began to declare legislative actions unconstitutional, tensions between legislatures and the courts grew.

The criminal court structure changed little through the nineteenth century. County courts continued to try offenders but were plagued by the same problems of partisan politics and corruption that befell other public and criminal justice agencies. State governors appointed the justices (as is true today), and the county courts in turn appointed other officials such as sheriffs, county attorneys, clerks, and jailers. According to one historian, "This process offered rich opportunities for graft. Corruption was so rampant that the job of sheriff and other positions were literally put up for auction."[9]

Another area of continued controversy concerned selection of judges. During the mid-1800s, all judges were appointed by the governor in Massachusetts, and in Michigan judges were elected to their posts. Other states combined these approaches. These tensions further contributed to the distinct judiciaries we see from state to state today.

Following the Civil War (1861–1865), America entered a period of rapid industrialization and growth, which led to increases in population and, consequently, a surge in caseloads. The courts were on the receiving end of all the new litigation and the growth in criminal activity. States were thus forced to modernize and expand their judiciaries. Some cities created their own courts to handle low-level problems like drunkenness and prostitution; others formed specialized courts to handle specific types of cases, like those involving small claims or family relationships.

Rapid changes in state judiciaries led to various successes and failures. In Chicago, for example, there were 556 separate courts operating in 1931, with most set up to handle minor offenses, but the jurisdictional boundaries were unclear, so cases could effectively be moved around to the right court that would issue a favorable decision.[10]

At the opposite extreme was the court system of Alameda County, California.[11] Between 1870 and 1910, cases were organized in terms of their seriousness, and many were filtered out early on (e.g., due to lack of evidence), much as they are today. Plea bargaining also surged with the advent of probation in California, which thus lightened the courts' trial workload. Alameda County's courts were not without their faults, however. Historians Lawrence Friedman and Robert Percival called it "legalism set amidst great informality." They went on to state,

> [I]n the same court that entertained technical objections to the form of complaints, clucking chickens were introduced as evidence in theft cases. The same judge who presided over an endlessly technical *voir dire* once fined himself $50 for being drunk.[12]

Contemporary State Courts

From the mid-1900s onward, state courts have continued to grow in numbers and specializations. States developed their own court structures to meet specific needs: Some developed new courts to meet the demands of increasing caseloads, others added new courts to cover specific geographic areas, and still others developed more courts to target specific problems. In many areas, this caused considerable confusion, especially since many courts' jurisdictional boundaries overlapped.

This fragmentation in the state court systems prompted many people to speak out against it. Indeed, as far back as 1906, then-dean of the Harvard Law School Roscoe Pound called the American judiciary "archaic" in its multiplicity of courts and a waste of judicial power, and he and others called for unification (or consolidation) of the state courts. Change often begets fear, however, so there were certainly critics of unification, including judges and other courtroom personnel who were sometimes leery of reform. In any case, unification has occurred in a number of states.

court unification
The simplification of state court structures to address such problems as overlapping jurisdiction and to achieve centralized control over state judiciaries.

Web Extra
4–1 New York State Unified Court System

Court Unification **Court unification** is concerned, first and foremost, with simplifying state court structures to address some of the problems just mentioned, such as overlapping jurisdictions, and it is also concerned with centralizing control over state judiciaries. Five principal elements of court unification have been identified:

1. Consolidation of a state's numerous trial courts into a one- or two-tier system
2. Centralized management of the judiciary by an accountable body
3. Grant to the state supreme court of procedural and administrative rule-making authority
4. State funding, with the state assuming complete financial responsibility for the expenses of the judiciary
5. Unitary budgeting[13]

Court reformers have envisioned that a centralized organization (like the federal Judicial Conference discussed in Chapter 3) would make rules, supervise personnel, and streamline budgeting, and they have also envisioned stronger state supreme courts and centralized budgeting authority. In short, unification is concerned with making state court structures look more coherent and bureaucratic, arranged by authority.

It is difficult to fault governments for seeking to improve their efficiency through procedures such as court unification. Besides efficiency, supporters of unification have argued it will provide more flexibility in personnel arrangements and use of facilities, improved cost-effectiveness, and enhanced prestige of the court system.[14]

Once again, there are two sides to every coin. Some critics have argued that we should spend more time focused on case flow rather than trying to reshape entire judiciaries to resemble some ideal hierarchical model,[15] whereas others have found that states' efforts to model their court structures after ideal standards, such as those set by the American Bar Association, have fallen short.[16] Still other critics have argued that unification makes it difficult for certain groups to participate effectively in the judicial process. Interestingly, state judiciaries have very recently started to address this critique through forming so-called community courts.[17] (We will look at this issue more closely in Chapter 5.)

Thus far, the concept of unification may be somewhat vague. It can be more fully appreciated, however, with a look at the differences between two state court systems, one that has been unified and another that has not been fully unified. An example of the former can be seen in California (see Figure 4–1). Notice how in California there is one state supreme court and one type of appellate court as well as general jurisdiction courts (superior courts) in every county.

California first experimented with the idea of unification back in 1992 when then-Senator Bill Lockyer (California treasurer as of this writing) introduced Senate Constitutional

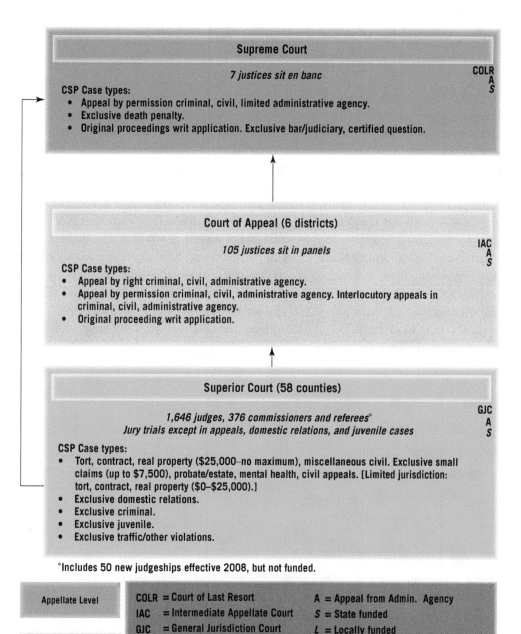

FIGURE 4–1

Example of a Unified Court System (California)

Source: Court Statistics Project, http://www.courtstatistics.org/Other-Pages/State_Court_Structure_Charts/California.aspx (accessed February 1, 2013).

Amendment 3, proposing certain unification reforms.[18] It failed, but Lockyer went on to introduce Senate Constitutional Amendment 4 (SCA 4) during the 1995–1996 legislative session, and the legislature passed a revised version of SCA 4 in June 1996. Since the legislation was to be a constitutional amendment, it had to go before the voters. California voters passed the amendment, as Proposition 220, on June 2, 1998.[19] In general, the constitutional amendment provided for voluntary unification of municipal and superior courts into one type of court: The former municipal courts had jurisdiction over misdemeanors, some felonies, traffic violations, and other matters, and the superior courts generally handled felonies, juvenile cases, and various civil cases involving amounts larger than $25,000, among others. The majority of superior court judges in a county must vote on unification for it to go forward. Proposition 220 also has other provisions:

- It established an appellate division in each unified superior court to hear matters formerly heard within the superior court's appellate jurisdiction.
- It required any newly appointed judge of a unified superior court to have been a member of the state bar for at least the ten years immediately preceding appointment.
- It provided for the countywide election of superior court judges of the unified courts.[20]

Offering something of a contrast to California's judiciary is that of Indiana (see Figure 4–2). There are several noteworthy differences, not the least of which is ten different types of courts, in contrast to California's three. There also appears to be some jurisdictional overlap. While Indiana's court system looks fragmented, it is not alone. Several other states, such as Massachusetts and Texas, have similarly complex structures.[21]

Number of Courts   Strange as it seems, counting the number of courts—particularly state courts—is all but impossible. First, a look at the definition of *court* in *Black's Law Dictionary* reveals no less than 16 different types of courts. Second, as this chapter makes clear, there is no uniformity across states in the names of their courts. Third, some states (like Texas) call their judgeships "courts," whereas other states define their courts as conglomerates of judges (an example of this approach is California). These considerations make it exceedingly difficult to estimate the number of state courts. Even so, the National Center for State Courts (NCSC) has estimated that there are approximately 16,000 state courts throughout America.[22]

Web Extra
4–2 State Courts Directory

Learning Objective 2
Summarize the differing structures of state court systems.

Web Extra
4–3 State Court Structure

STATE COURT STRUCTURE

Whereas the federal judiciary has three levels of courts, many states have four levels:

1. Courts of limited jurisdiction such as traffic courts and misdemeanor courts
2. General jurisdiction courts for felony cases
3. Intermediate appellate courts
4. State supreme courts

Limited Jurisdiction Courts

limited jurisdiction courts
Courts with original jurisdiction over only that subject matter specifically assigned to them by law.

Limited jurisdiction courts constitute roughly 90 percent of all courts.[23] They have been defined as trial courts "having original jurisdiction over only that subject matter specifically assigned to it by law."[24] Most often, the subject matter consists of minor offenses, including everything from traffic infractions and code violations to misdemeanors. The sanctions these courts impose are usually very minor and include fines or, at worst, relatively short jail terms; they also try civil cases involving small amounts of money.

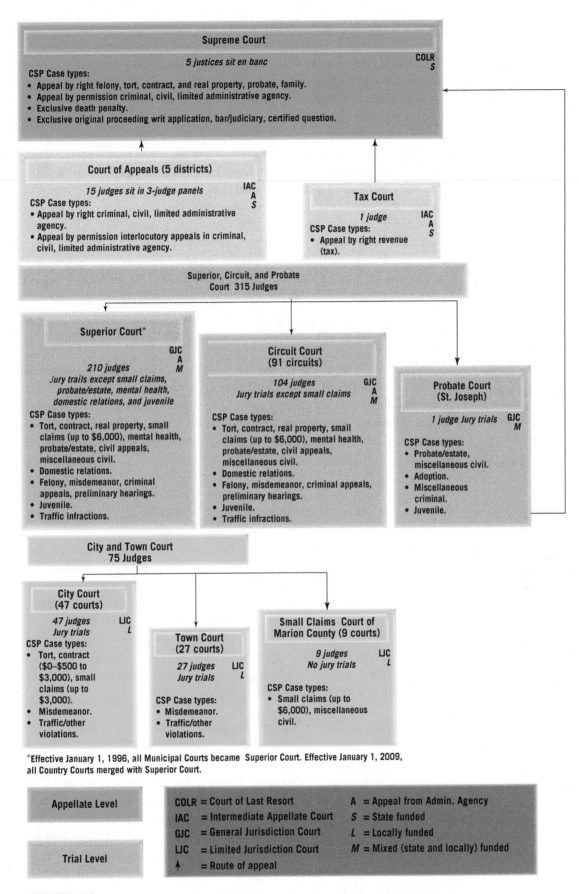

FIGURE 4–2

Example of a Fragmented Judiciary (Indiana)

Source: Court Statistics Project, http://www.courtstatistics.org/Other-Pages/State_Court_Structure_Charts/Indiana.aspx (accessed February 1, 2013).

Records of limited jurisdiction court proceedings are not kept, in contrast to the main trial courts (known as "courts of record"). Without a record of the proceeding, it is difficult to appeal the court's decision. Accordingly, appeals from limited jurisdiction courts usually go before the general jurisdiction courts as a new trial, known as a "trial *de novo*," but this type of trial is relatively uncommon.

Courts of limited jurisdiction differ from general jurisdiction courts in several other ways as well. Judges in these courts sometimes have no formal legal training. Limited jurisdiction courts are frequently plagued by resource shortages, forcing them to meet in temporary facilities like community centers and other government buildings, and their cases are often disposed of in large numbers and at the same time, meaning that full-blown trials are very rare. Finally, some limited jurisdiction courts hold preliminary hearings in felony cases.

justice of the peace (JOP) courts
Low-level courts, found only in Arizona, Delaware, Louisiana, Montana, and Texas,[i] that have original jurisdiction over so-called Class C misdemeanors (e.g., various traffic violations, bail jumping, bad check writing) and minor civil matters and that sometimes issue search and arrest warrants, perform wedding ceremonies, and even serve as coroners in the least populous counties.

Justice of the Peace Courts **Justice of the peace (JOP) courts** are found in five states: Arizona, Delaware, Louisiana, Montana, and Texas.[25] In Texas, the constitution requires that each county in the state establish between one and eight justice of the peace precincts; as a result, there are more than 800 of these courts in the state. Some are simply called "justice courts."

The Texas JOP courts have original jurisdiction over "Class C misdemeanors," which include various traffic violations, bail jumping, writing of bad checks, and others. The JOP courts also have jurisdiction over minor civil matters, such as small claims (an action to recover money that does not exceed $10,000). Finally, justices of the peace sometimes issue search and arrest warrants, perform wedding ceremonies, and even serve as coroners in the less populous counties.

magistrate courts
Low-level courts found only in Alaska, Georgia, Idaho, New Mexico, South Carolina, South Dakota, and West Virginia,[ii] with responsibilities similar to those of justice of the peace courts. While magistrate judges also hold preliminary hearings in felony cases and issue warrants, there are no jury trials in magistrate courts.

Magistrate Courts **Magistrate courts** are similar to JOP courts and can be found in Alaska, Georgia, Idaho, New Mexico, South Carolina, South Dakota, and West Virginia.[26] In Georgia, for example, magistrate courts have jurisdiction over civil claims of $15,000 or less, certain minor criminal offenses, county ordinance violations, check fraud, and other issues, and the magistrate judges also hold preliminary hearings in felony cases and issue warrants; there are no jury trials in the magistrate courts.

Currently, there are 159 magistrate courts in Georgia, each supervised by a chief magistrate.[27] These chief magistrates, who assign cases, set court dates, and otherwise act as the general court administrator, are elected to their posts and serve four-year terms. The requirements to hold the position of chief magistrate are relatively lax compared to those for judges of general jurisdiction courts—Georgia only requires one year of residency in the county and a high school diploma.

municipal court
A type of city-level court, found in most large cities, which typically has jurisdiction over misdemeanors.

Municipal/City/County/Metropolitan Courts Most large cities have their own city-level courts, called **municipal courts**, which usually have jurisdiction over misdemeanors. Before unification, California had municipal courts, but now they have merged with the higher-level general jurisdiction courts. In New Jersey, municipal courts are similar to JOP or magistrate courts. They are limited jurisdiction courts that have jurisdiction over a narrow class of minor offenses. These include moving violations, parking tickets, municipal ordinance offenses (such as code violations), fish and game violations, and minor criminal offenses (e.g., simple assault). Also, their jurisdiction is limited to the city in which they are located. While the municipal courts have limited jurisdiction, they are the courts that people are most likely to come into contact with.[28]

Texas also has county courts. Each of the state's 254 counties has one such court presided over by a county judge. These are known as constitutional county courts. They have original jurisdiction over civil actions involving amounts between $200 and $10,000, misdemeanors with fines greater than $500 or jail sentences, juvenile matters, and some other cases. The state also maintains statutory county courts (also called county courts at law). The jurisdiction of these courts varies by the statutes that created them.

Other Specialized Limited Jurisdiction Courts   The limited jurisdiction courts just introduced have fairly broad jurisdiction over various minor offenses and disputes. Several states have other limited jurisdiction courts whose jurisdiction is truly limited to just a handful of cases. For example, Alabama and some other states have dedicated probate courts, which help dispose of the assets of deceased individuals; Connecticut calls these family courts. Delaware operates so-called alderman courts, which combine features of justice of the peace and municipal courts. Other interesting types of courts include orphans' courts (Maryland), housing courts (Massachusetts), workers' compensation courts (Nebraska), and environmental courts (Vermont).

Justice in the Lower Courts   How is justice administered in these busy lower courts? According to Malcolm Feeley's popular book *The Process Is the Punishment: Handling Cases in a Lower Criminal Court,*[29] justice is meted out swiftly and informally. While observing the court process in New Haven, Connecticut, he found that few defendants (in the 1,600 or so trials he observed) insisted on an attorney; he also found that most trials took mere seconds to conduct and that the "lengthy" ones rarely went over a minute. How is this possible? Almost every defendant pleaded guilty and received a fine or some other community penalty.

Feeley concluded that the process for adjudicating minor offenses was the real penalty in petty cases. Pretrial bail costs, attorney's fees, and lost wages took more of a toll than the fines defendants were required to pay at the end of their trials. In this sense, the process was the punishment!

Feeley's work is important because it shows us that criminal trials are not at all like what Hollywood would have us believe. For one thing, most crimes are minor, and for another, most of them are dealt with swiftly. To do otherwise would take a significant financial toll on an already overworked criminal justice system.

Library Extra
4–1 Bureau of Justice Statistics: State Court Organization

General Jurisdiction Courts

Most states have one set of courts that serves as the major trial courts. Some of these courts also specialize in hearing certain types of cases (e.g., juvenile cases), but the common thread is the element of seriousness associated with each case. These courts also serve an appellate function some of the time. Recall that since limited jurisdiction courts are not courts of record, appeals from those courts occasionally become new trials (trials *de novo*) in the general jurisdiction courts.

General jurisdiction courts often go by names like superior courts, circuit courts, or even district courts, and they are typically organized along political boundaries. In California, for example, the general jurisdiction courts are divided along county lines; in contrast, Louisiana organizes its district courts by parishes, which are similar to counties. General jurisdiction court judges must be highly qualified to serve in their positions, with law degrees and experience often being required (we look at these requirements further in Chapter 7).

general jurisdiction courts Courts with authority to decide all types of cases, civil and criminal, that are not subject to the exclusive jurisdiction of another court. General jurisdiction courts adjudicate serious cases, and some also have appellate jurisdiction.

Criminal Cases   General jurisdiction courts are perhaps best known for conducting high-profile felony cases before full juries. These superior courts are often quite large, are concentrated in populous urban centers, consist of several different courtrooms, and are sometimes staffed by dozens of judges and hundreds of staff. For example, Minnesota's Fourth Judicial District, which includes Minneapolis, is staffed by over 60 judges and 500 court personnel.

Web Extra
4–4 California Courts Online

Civil Cases   General jurisdiction courts also try the more significant civil cases, such as those involving dollar amounts over some specified threshold; for example, Florida's circuit courts have jurisdiction in civil cases involving more than $15,000. General jurisdiction

COURTS IN THE NEWS

New York State Courts Examined

The state of New York operates two court systems. One, the New York Unified Court System, is funded by the state. The second system, known collectively as the Justice Courts System, is a conglomerate of the almost 1,300 town and village courts and 2,154 town and village justice positions, the majority of which are filled by minimally trained nonlawyers. These local courts have jurisdiction over the largest number of cases in the criminal justice system, including misdemeanors, violations and traffic infractions, and the initial stages of felony crimes. In the 21 counties, town and village Courts are the sole overseers of justice in the vast majority of criminal prosecutions. Although many have no legal training, justices in the town and village courts have the power to imprison people for up to one year, evict people from their homes, set bail that can result in lengthy pretrial incarceration for people awaiting their day in court, and impose substantial fines.

There has been mounting public criticism of the justice courts. In testimony before a public, Daniel M. Murdoch, chair of the Fund for Modern Courts Task Force on Town and Village Justice Courts, stated that because the justice courts are funded by the localities they serve, they "operate without the comprehensive oversight of the New York State Judiciary and Office of Court Administration."[1] Corey Stoughton, staff attorney at the New York Civil Liberties Union, testified before the Judiciary Committee of the New York State Assembly that though they wield this great power, town and village courts are not equipped to use it wisely, and the results are predictably alarming. News reports detail stories of judges calling an African-American litigant "that colored man"; telling a victim of domestic abuse that "every woman needs a good pounding every now and then"; and explaining, when confronted by state disciplinary officials, that he "follows [his] own common sense" and "the hell with the law." Stoughton told the committee that there have been stories of a justice who routinely jailed people who were unable to pay fines for minor violations and, when confronted over this practice, explained that no one had told him to do any differently. Another judge ruled on a case based on secret personal interviews of one side's witnesses, explaining when confronted that she had never heard of the rule barring such meetings. And yet another justice allowed the local prosecutor to write her decision denying a motion to suppress evidence that had been seized illegally by the

Mitch Wojnarowicz/The Image Works

During his long career Justice Franklin Wendell, the Town of Mohawk, NY, received many awards and accolades before he died in 2012. Not all town and village judges in New York areas respected as Justice Wendell, a fact that has caused the utility of the entire system to be questioned.

police, claiming that she did not "really have time to puzzle [it] out."

Such complaints about this 300-year-old system are not new. In 1926, then-Governor Alfred E. Smith called the justice courts "a farce."[2] However, the efforts of numerous commissions and conferences, the investigations of numerous state agencies, and the interventions of powerful past governors such as Franklin Delano Roosevelt and Nelson Rockefeller have not been able to curb the power wielded by these courts or reform the manner in which they operate.

Some say that New York's system of town and village courts is a holdover from America's early colonial days and is unsuited to meet the needs of contemporary society. Others argue that the justice courts free higher courts to pursue more serious cases and allow for the informal handling of minor offenses in the community where they occurred. Because justice courts, like justice of the peace courts in other states, can deny individuals their liberty, many ask whether the justices who preside over them should be more formally trained. ■

DISCUSSION QUESTIONS

1. Should New York's town and village court system be retained?

2. Should the educational and training requirements for justices who serve in justice courts be elevated?

Notes

[1]   Fund for Modern Courts, *Task Force on Town and Village Justice Courts,* "Transcript of Public Hearing on the State Justice Courts," November 14, 2006. Available at http://www.moderncourts.org/Advocacy/town/index.html (accessed August 3, 2009).

[2]   William Glaberson, "How a Reviled Court System Has Outlasted Critics," *New York Times,* September 27, 2006. Available at http://www.nytimes.com/2006/09/27/nyregion/27courts.html (accessed August 3, 2009).

Sources: "Proposals to Reform the New York State Justice Courts, Testimony of Corey Stoughton, Staff Attorney at the New York Civil Liberties Union before Judiciary Committee of the New York State Assembly regarding Proposals to Reform the New York State Justice Courts," 2013, available at http://www.nyclu.org/content/proposals-reform-new-york-state-justice-courts (accessed May 2013); Fund

(continued)

for Modern Courts, *Task Force on Town and Village Justice Courts*, "Transcript of Public Hearing on the State Justice Courts," available at http://www.moderncourts.org/Advocacy/town/index.html (accessed May 2013); New York State Office of Court Administrations, "Action Plan for the Justice Courts," available at http://www.courts.state.ny.us/publications/pdfs/ActionPlan-JusticeCourts.pdf (accessed May 2013); William Glaberson, "State's Justice Courts to Face Scrutiny by Assembly Panel," *New York Times*, October 14, 2006, available at http://www.nytimes.com/2006/10/14/nyregion/14courts.html (accessed May 2013); William Glaberson, "In Tiny Courts of N.Y., Abuses of Law and Power," *New York Times*, September 25, 2006. Available at http://www.nytimes.com/2006/09/25/nyregion/25courts.html?_r=1 (accessed May 2013); William Glaberson, "How a Reviled Court System Has Outlasted Critics," *New York Times*, September 27, 2006, available at http://www.nytimes.com/2006/09/27/nyregion/27courts.html (accessed May 2013).

courts also have jurisdiction over several other types of civil matters, ranging from domestic relations and estate matters to landlord–tenant cases and contract disputes.

Web Extra
4–5 Texas Courts Online

Intermediate Appellate Courts

Most state judiciaries also have at least one **intermediate appellate court**, "an appellate court of which the primary function is to review the judgments of trial courts and the decisions of administrative agencies, and whose decisions are in turn usually reviewable by a higher appellate court in the same state" (e.g., the state supreme court).[30] These are akin to the federal appellate courts, and their primary responsibility is to review appeals from the lower courts.

Appellate court organization and titles vary from state to state. For example, Alabama organizes its appellate courts along the lines of specific case types: the court of civil appeals and the court of criminal appeals. Other states, such as California, organize their appellate courts by district, which are often combinations of counties. Some states, usually the less populous ones, simply have one court of appeals.

The state appellate courts usually consist of three or so judges who serve as "panels" and review lower courts' appeals. California has the largest of the intermediate appellate courts, with over 100 authorized judgeships and 88 active judges.[31] The numbers also vary by state in terms of how many judges participate in deciding whether to grant review and how many are necessary to grant review.[32]

intermediate appellate court
"[A]n appellate court of which the primary function is to review the judgments of trial courts and the decisions of administrative agencies, and whose decisions are in turn usually reviewable by a higher appellate court in the same state" (e.g., the state supreme court).[iii]

State Supreme Courts

State supreme courts have the last word over matters arising from the lower courts—any appeal in a criminal case that is not satisfactorily resolved at the intermediate appellate court level may be brought before the state supreme court. But like the U.S. Supreme Court, state supreme courts are often petitioned with more cases than they can possibly review in a single term, so each state has its own rules for selecting cases, with most leaving the decision in the hands of the judiciary. As might be expected, the vast majority of appeals are never selected for review.

While every state has at least one court of last resort, Oklahoma and Texas both have two. In Texas, the court of criminal appeals is the highest court for criminal cases, and the Texas Supreme Court is the court of last resort for civil and juvenile cases; Oklahoma follows a similar model. The rest of the states, however, have a single court of last resort, usually called a supreme court. Exceptions include Maine and Massachusetts, which use supreme judicial courts, and West Virginia, which calls it the supreme court of appeals. To keep things simple, we will refer to state supreme courts.

Some states (specifically, Delaware, Maine, Nevada, New Hampshire, Rhode Island, South Dakota, Vermont, West Virginia, and Wyoming) and the District of Columbia have no intermediate appellate courts, so their supreme courts do not have the discretion to decide which cases they will review. For example, Nevada law requires that every case appealed from its district courts (Nevada's general jurisdiction courts) be considered by its state supreme court. We should also mention that some types of cases, such as death penalty appeals, usually bypass the intermediate appellate courts (if there are any) and go directly to state supreme courts.

state supreme courts
The highest courts in the state court systems. They have the final word on cases arriving to them from the lower courts. Like the U.S. Supreme Court, some state supreme courts have original jurisdiction over certain types of cases.

Policy Making   State supreme courts have profound policy-making authority. One reason for this is that there are 50 state supreme courts and a single U.S. Supreme Court, so while only a few cases make it to the state supreme courts, far more make it there than ever make it to the U.S. Supreme Court. Another reason state supreme courts have strong policy-making authority is that not all types of cases can move from them to the U.S. Supreme Court. Recall that for a state-level case to arrive at the U.S. Supreme Court, the case must involve a critical federal question; since many state cases do not involve federal questions, the "buck stops" at the state supreme court, and their decisions are subsequently binding on state legal policy.

Even when they do involve federal questions, these cases often do not move to the federal courts, the result being that state courts (not just state supreme courts) adjudicate cases involving federal questions. This is but one example of **judicial federalism,** the sharing of judicial power between the states and the federal government,[33] which is an inevitable feature of a court system in which the vast majority of cases are adjudicated at the state level. There is simply not enough time and resources for the federal courts to decide all federal matters, and state courts gain a measure of power. One team of researchers observed that "the constitutional rights of individuals in the United States depend in part on the state in which they happen to be at any given time."[34]

State supreme courts have not always been active in setting policy, as Charles Lopeman has argued:

> For much of [the twentieth] century most state supreme courts have taken a back seat in establishing and changing policy for their states. They regularly agreed with the policy embedded in the laws adopted by their states' legislatures. They affirmed the policy that earlier courts had developed and that had become the doctrine of their states' common law. When an unusual case presented a unique problem that existing policy did not answer or answered unsatisfactorily, the state supreme courts looked to their legislatures to come up with a solution.[35]

More recently, though, state supreme courts have become quite active in setting policy through their decisions.[36] One key criminal justice example is the New York Court of Appeals and its decision to declare the death penalty unconstitutional in that state.[37] New York was thus the first state to declare the death penalty unconstitutional since the U.S. Supreme Court reinstated it in *Gregg v. Georgia.*[38]

State supreme courts' policy influence is apparent across the gamut of social issues, not just those concerned with criminal justice. The courts have influenced policy on everything from how local school districts can obtain funding to whether victims of drunk-driving accidents can sue bar owners.[39] State supreme courts are also important because they serve as intermediaries between the U.S. Supreme Court and local criminal justice agencies: "State supreme courts are of vital significance in [criminal justice] for they interpret Supreme Court decisions and apply them within their own states."[40] Finally, even if state legislatures take steps to curtail their supreme court justices' ability to influence policy, the justices can do a number of other things to still exert their influence:

1. Present judicial views in court opinions that hopefully will be seen and considered by the legislators.
2. Interpret current statutes so restrictively that they become essentially ineffective with the intent of forcing their legislatures to revise the law.
3. Present policy preferences in dicta.
4. Use informal personal contacts between judges and legislators for the exchange of views.
5. Lobby in a systematic and well-organized fashion in order to influence the votes of congressmen on bills important to their courts.[41]

judicial federalism
A term used to refer to the sharing of judicial power between the 50 states and the federal government.

STATE COURT WORKLOADS

Since there are so many state courts, it is not surprising that they bear the brunt of America's caseload. But just what is the nature of this caseload? How many cases come before the lower courts, and how likely are convictions in these courts? Which offenses are more likely to result in convictions in the lower courts? This section answers some of these questions.

Caseload Statistics

The NCSC has tracked caseload trends in the state courts for many years. Figure 4–3 shows the trend for civil cases in state courts that report data to the NCSC, and Figure 4–4 does the same for criminal cases.

Lower Courts The total incoming trial caseload for lower state courts exceeds 100 million in any given year.[42] The majority of the cases involve traffic violations (56 percent); the rest of the breakdown can be seen in Figure 4–5. Criminal cases are the next most common type. Civil cases are the third most common, with almost 20 million civil cases entering the state court system in any given year.

Appellate Courts There are several important considerations that must go into examining state appellate court workloads. First, appellate courts have both appellate and original jurisdiction; for example, many state *habeas corpus* petitions are first reviewed at the appellate level, not in general jurisdiction courts. Second, appellate courts vary in terms of their mandatory and discretionary caseloads. Some cases are reviewed only if the judges elect to do so; others, however, must be reviewed. Mandatory review, as we have seen, is required in certain types of cases and in certain types of courts. Finally, the Supreme Court sometimes

Learning Objective 3

Describe the workload of state courts.

Web Extra
4–6 National Center for State Courts

Library Extra
4–2 National Center for State Courts Annual Report

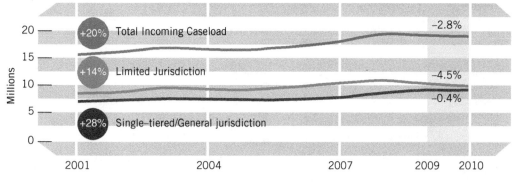

FIGURE 4–3

Total Incoming Civil Caseloads Reported by State Courts, 2001–2010

Source: R. LaFountain, R. Schauffler, S. Strickland, and K. Holt, *Analyzing the Work of State Courts: An Analysis of 2010 State Court Caseloads* (Williamsburg, VA: National Center for State Courts, 2012), p. 8, available at http://www.courtstatistics.org/Other-Pages/~/media/Microsites/Files/CSP/DATA%20PDF/CSP_DEC.ashx (accessed February 1, 2013).

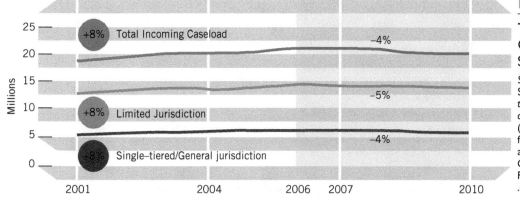

FIGURE 4–4

Total Incoming Criminal Caseloads Reported by State Courts, 2001–2010

Source: R. LaFountain, R. Schauffler, S. Strickland, and K. Holt, *Analyzing the Work of State Courts: An Analysis of 2010 State Court Caseloads* (Williamsburg, VA: National Center for State Courts, 2012), p. 20, available at http://www.courtstatistics.org/Other-Pages/~/media/Microsites/Files/CSP/DATA%20PDF/CSP_DEC.ashx (accessed February 1, 2013).

FIGURE 4–5

Incoming Caseload
Composition in State
Courts

Source: R. LaFountain, R. Schauffler,
S. Strickland, and K. Holt, *Analyzing
the Work of State Courts: An Analysis
of 2010 State Court Caseloads*
(Williamsburg, VA: National Center
for State Courts, 2012), p. 4, available
at http://www.courtstatistics.org/
Other-Pages/~/media/Microsites/
Files/CSP/DATA%20PDF/CSP_DEC
.ashx (accessed February 1, 2013).

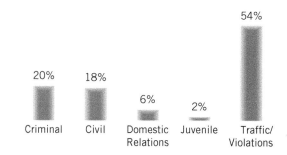

issues opinions that alter trends in appellate caseloads at the state level. Table 4–1 shows the population size and appellate caseload by state for the most recent data available (2010).

In Chapter 3, we briefly referenced the case of *Blakely* v. *Washington*, decided by the Supreme Court in 2004,[43] which held that the right to a jury trial barred judges from increasing criminal sentences based on facts not decided by the jury or admitted by the defendant. This resulted in a modest increase in the number of cases that required resentencing.

TABLE 4–1 Total Incoming Cases in Appellate Courts, 2010

State	Total Incoming Cases	Population Rank	State	Total Incoming Cases	Population Rank
California	34,077	1	Minnesota	3,016	21
Florida	28,952	4	North Carolina	2,968	10
Texas	19,106	2	Maryland	2,885	19
New York	15,898	3	Kansas	2,825	34
Pennsylvania	15,868	6	Massachusetts	2,446	14
Ohio	12,782	7	**Nevada**	2,288	36
Illinois	11,303	5	New Mexico	2,241	37
Louisiana	10,646	25	**District of Columbia**	1,745	51
Michigan	8,137	8	**West Virginia**	1,668	38
New Jersey	7,658	11	Nebraska	1,567	39
Puerto Rico	6,816	29	Idaho	1,545	40
Washington	5,668	13	Utah	1,503	35
Indiana	5,474	15	Arkansas	1,287	33
Virginia	5,206	12	Connecticut	1,188	30
Georgia	5,144	9	**New Hampshire**	1,073	43
Arizona	5,049	16	Hawai'i	842	41
Alabama	4,996	23	**Delaware**	770	46
Missouri	4,863	18	**Maine**	684	42
Oregon[1, 2]	4,520	27	**Montana**	650	45
Colorado	4,408	22	Alaska	629	48
Wisconsin	3,934	20	**Vermont**[1]	479	50
Oklahoma	3,638	28	**Rhode Island**	418	44
Tennessee	3,424	17	North Dakota	406	49
Iowa	3,322	31	**South Dakota**	345	47
Kentucky	3,224	26	**Wyoming**	270	52
South Carolina[1]	3,124	24			

TOTAL INCOMING CASES 272,975

[1]Oregon Court of Appeals, South Carolina Court of Appeals, and Vermont Supreme Court data are for 2009.

[2]Oregon Supreme Court data are for 2008.

Notes: States in bold do not have an IAC.

Mississippi did not provide incoming caseload data.

Incoming caseloads ranged from approximately 270 (Wyoming) to a little more than 34,000 (California) during the 2010 reporting period. In most instances, states with higher populations had larger total caseloads, but an examination of population rankings of the states shows this is not always the case. For example, Louisiana ranks 25th in population, but its appellate courts have the 8th highest incoming caseload.

Source: R. LaFountain, R. Schauffler, S. Strickland, and K. Holt, *Analyzing the Work of State Courts: An Analysis of 2010 State Court Caseloads* (Williamsburg, VA: National Center for State Courts, 2012), p. 40, available at http://www.courtstatistics.org/Other-Pages/~/media/Microsites/Files/CSP/DATA%20PDF/CSP_DEC.ashx (accessed February 1, 2013).

TABLE 4-2 Appellate Caseload Composition in Select Courts, 2010

	Courts of Last Resort				Intermediate Appellate Courts			
	Case Type Total	Total Incoming for Reporting Courts	Percent of Total	Number of Courts Reporting	Case Type Total	Total Incoming for Reporting Courts	Percent of Total	Number of Courts Reporting
Appeal by Right	9,164	38,369	24%	26	88,662	118,947	75%	28
Appeal by Permission	30,336	53,453	57%	34	10,300	66,635	15%	14
Death Penalty	317	30,220	1%	12	13	1,198	1%	1
Original Proceeding/ Other Appellate	9,705	33,407	29%	22	12,265	77,457	16%	16

Source: R. LaFountain, R. Schauffler, S. Strickland, and K. Holt, *Analyzing the Work of State Courts: An Analysis of 2010 State Court Caseloads* (Williamsburg, VA: National Center for State Courts, 2012), p. 45, available at http://www.courtstatistics.org/Other-Pages/~/media/Microsites/Files/CSP/DATA%20PDF/CSP_DEC.ashx (accessed February 1, 2013).

Many defendants were resentenced in their trial courts, but several went directly to state appellate courts, a process termed the **Blakely** bounce:

> The "*Blakely* bounce" appeared as a 3 percent increase in mandatory jurisdiction criminal appellate filings. In some courts, such as Alaska, the "bounce" was more apparent; much of the 56 percent increase of that state's appellate caseload has been attributed to *Blakely*.[44]

As for the workload in intermediate appellate courts versus state courts of last resort, see Table 4–2. State courts of last resort decide many more cases than one may expect; in contrast, at the federal level, there is a significant drop-off in the numbers between Supreme Court decisions and appellate court decisions.

Blakely bounce
The modest increase in the number of cases that required resentencing that arose from the U.S. Supreme Court's holding in *Blakely* v. *Washington* (2004)[iv] that the right to a jury trial barred judges from increasing criminal sentences based on facts not decided by the jury or admitted by the defendant.

Dispositions

The sheer numbers of cases that come before state courts are impressive, but how many defendants who come into these courts are convicted? In a similar vein, which offenses are more likely to result in convictions? Data from the Justice Department's Bureau of Justice Statistics provide some answers.

Convictions and Sentences per Arrest Table 4–3 lists the number of arrests, convictions, and sentences for seven serious offenses. There are three important observations that can be made. First, the most serious offenses have the most convictions per arrest—68 of every 100 murder

TABLE 4-3 Felony Convictions, Sentences, and Rate per 100 Arrests

	Murder, Nonnegligent Manslaughter	Rape	Robbery	Aggravated Assault	Burglary	Motor Vehicle Theft[a]	Drug Trafficking
Adults arrested	21,360	21,840	83,710	377,580	213,030	109,100	282,590
Felony convictions	8,400	12,310	38,850	94,380	93,870	16,910	201,760
Number of felony sentences							
To incarceration	7,730	10,960	33,800	68,900	70,400	14,540	139,210
To prison	7,480	8,490	27,970	40,580	46,000	6,930	78,690
Rate per 100 arrests							
Number of felony convictions	68	56	46	25	44	16	71
Number of felony sentences	63	50	40	18	33	13	49
To prison	60	39	33	11	22	6	28

[a]When vehicle theft could not be distinguished from other theft, the case was coded as other theft. This results in a conservative estimate of motor vehicle theft convictions.

Note: The offenses shown above were selected because they have the greatest comparability across reporting series and are widely defined as felonies by states. Offense designations for convictions and sentences are for the most serious offense.

Source: http://bjs.ojp.usdoj.gov/index.cfm?ty=pbdetail&iid=1533 (accessed February 1, 2013).

and nonnegligent manslaughter defendants are convicted. This is still a fairly modest amount because roughly one-third of such cases never result in convictions, according to the data. Interestingly, drug-trafficking defendants are convicted at a higher rate than murderers.

Second, Table 4–3 makes it clear that there are certain serious offenses where an arrest is highly unlikely to result in a conviction. Motor vehicle theft, not surprisingly, results in the fewest convictions: While over 100,000 people were arrested for this crime, fewer than 20,000 were convicted. The data tell a similar story for the crime of aggravated assault, with only 25 out of 100 arrestees ever being convicted for this crime. Third, remember that these are serious crimes. Less serious crimes are far more common, they result in even fewer arrests, and even fewer arrestees are convicted. We cannot say, however, that this is any fault of the courts.

LASTING IMPACT

Ewing v. California (2003)

California's three-strikes law provides that a defendant convicted of a felony must receive an indeterminate life imprisonment sentence if he or she has previously been convicted of two or more serious or violent felonies. His or her parole eligibility date is calculated by reference to a minimum term, which in this case is 25 years.

Gary Ewing, on parole at the time of his arrest for stealing three golf clubs (each worth $399), was subsequently convicted at trial of felony grand theft. In compliance with the three-strikes law, the prosecutor included a record of Ewing's previous convictions for four serious or violent felonies in the presentencing report to the court.

Refusing to exercise her discretion to reduce the conviction to a misdemeanor or to dismiss the allegations of some or all of his prior relevant convictions, the trial judge sentenced Ewing to 25 years to life. The State Court of Appeal affirmed, rejecting Ewing's claim that his sentence was grossly disproportionate under the Eighth Amendment, reasoning that enhanced sentences under the three-strikes law served the state's legitimate goal of deterring and incapacitating repeat offenders. When the California State Supreme Court denied review, Ewing petitioned the U.S. Supreme Court.[1]

In affirming the appellate finding, the Court cited three specific considerations. First, it addressed Ewing's claim that the sentence was cruel and unusual because it was grossly disproportionate to the crime he committed. Justice O'Connor's opinion rejected that claim on grounds that "[t]he Eighth Amendment has a 'narrow proportionality principle [that] applies to noncapital sentences.'"[2] In a concurring opinion, Justice Kennedy explained that the "Eighth Amendment does not require strict proportionality between crime and sentence [but] forbids only extreme sentences that are 'grossly disproportionate' to the crime."[3]

The Court's articulation of its second consideration recognizes that "state legislatures enacting three strikes laws [make] a deliberate policy choice" to isolate recidivist felons "whose conduct has not been deterred by more conventional punishment approaches."[4] This recognition derives from the Court's tradition of deference to state legislatures as makers and implementers of such important public policy choices.

Finally, the Court's well-crafted explanation of its reasoning on the third consideration supported the trial judge's discretionary decision not to extend leniency by citing the facts that Ewing "has been convicted of numerous offenses, served nine separate prison terms, and committed most of his crimes while on probation or parole" and that his "prior strikes were serious felonies including robbery and residential burglary."[5] The Court went on to state that when "weighing the offense's gravity, both [Ewing's] current felony and his long history of felony recidivism must be placed on the scales," concluding that the "sentence is justified by the State's public-safety interest in incapacitating and deterring recidivist felons and amply supported by his own long, serious criminal record."[6]

Ewing exemplifies the role of the courts in a federal system. Simultaneously, courts provide the forum in which the state imposes legislatively enacted sanctions on miscreants while affording those same miscreants the opportunity—via the appellate process—to obtain relief from sanctions thought to be unreasonable or excessive. ▪

Notes

1. Adapted from *Ewing* v. *California* (2003), available at http://www .law.cornell.edu/supct/html/01-6978.ZS.html (accessed May 30, 2013).
2. *Ewing* v. *California* (2003), available at http://www.law.cornell.edu/ supct/html/01-6978.ZO.html (accessed May 30, 2013), pp. 8–18.
3. Ibid., pp. 8–11.
4. Ibid., pp. 11–15.
5. Ibid., pp. 15–18.
6. Ibid.

DISCUSSION QUESTIONS

1. What is your opinion of Ewing's claim that the sentence was cruel and unusual because it was grossly disproportionate to the crime he committed?

2. Is California's three-strikes law too punitive? Recall that it applies if an individual is convicted of two violent felonies and then commits *any* third felony.

Felony Convictions by Offense Table 4–4 provides some more details on convictions for specific felonies. Today, there are over 1 million convictions for felonies in state courts. The largest category of convictions consisted of drug offenses, followed by property crimes and then violent crimes. Needless to say, the state courts keep very busy.

TABLE 4–4 Felony Convictions in State Courts

Most Serious Conviction Offense	Felony Convictions	
	Number	Percent
All offenses[a]	1,078,920	100
Violent offenses	194,570	18.0
Murder, nonnegligent manslaughter[b]	8,400	0.8
Murder	5,660	0.5
Nonnegligent manslaughter	2,740	0.3
Sexual assault, rape	33,190	3.1
Rape	12,310	1.1
Other sexual assault	20,880	1.9
Robbery	38,850	3.6
Armed	8,990	0.8
Unarmed	8,950	0.8
Unspecified	20,910	1.9
Aggravated assault	94,380	8.7
Other violent offenses[c]	19,750	1.8
Property offenses	310,680	28.8
Burglary	93,870	8.7
Residential	15,100	1.4
Nonresidential	18,230	1.7
Unspecified	60,540	5.6
Larceny	119,340	11.1
Motor vehicle theft	16,910	1.6
Other theft[d]	102,430	9.5
Fraud, forgery, embezzlement	97,470	9.0
Fraud	48,560	4.5
Forgery	48,910	4.5
Drug offenses	362,850	33.6
Possession	161,090	14.9
Trafficking	201,760	18.7
Marijuana	22,180	2.1
Other	60,650	5.6
Unspecified	118,930	11.0
Weapons offenses	33,010	3.1
Other offenses[e]	177,810	16.5

[a] Detail may not add to total because of rounding.

[b] In a small number of cases where it was unclear whether the offense was murder or manslaughter, the case was classified under nonnegligent manslaughter.

[c] Includes offenses such as negligent manslaughter and kidnapping.

[d] When vehicle theft could not be distinguished from other theft, the case was coded as other theft. This results in a conservative estimate of vehicle thefts.

[e] Composed of nonviolent offenses, such as receiving stolen property and vandalism.

Note: These data are from the National Judicial Reporting Program (NJRP), a biennial survey of state felony courts. Data were collected for the U.S. Department of Justice, Bureau of Justice Statistics, by the U.S. Census Bureau. The 2004 NJRP survey was based on a sample of 300 counties selected to be nationally representative. The sample included at least one county from every state except, by chance, Nevada, South Dakota, and Wyoming. Only offenses that state penal codes define as felonies are included. Excluded are federal courts and state or local courts that did not adjudicate adult felony cases. Data specifying the conviction offense were available for the estimated total of 1,078,920 convicted felons. These data are estimates derived from a sample and therefore are subject to sampling variation.

Source: http://bjs.ojp.usdoj.gov/index.cfm?ty=pbdetail&iid=1533 (accessed February 1, 2013).

Learning Objective 4

Summarize the administration of state courts.

STATE COURT ADMINISTRATION

State court administration is fairly similar to that found in the federal courts. Every state has its own administrative body, and individual courts have their own administrators, as well. Since state courts try so many more cases than the federal courts, they have taken more steps than the feds to manage their workloads.

Administrative Office of the Courts

Each state's administrative office of the courts performs several functions, including budget preparation, data collection, education and training, research, personnel management, and facility management, among others. Some states, such as Nebraska, also run their juvenile and adult probation systems through the administrative offices of the courts. It is surprising to some that some probation departments, which have traditionally been aligned with corrections, are actually administered by the judiciary and that the U.S. Probation and Pretrial Services System is currently administered under the U.S. Administrative Office of the Courts.

When considering what probation officers do (in addition to supervising probationers), it is easy to see why some states place probation under control of the judiciary:

- They gather and verify information about persons who come before the courts.
- They prepare reports that the courts rely on to make release and sentencing decisions.
- They supervise persons released to the community by the courts and paroling authorities.
- They direct persons under supervision to services to help them stay on the right side of the law, including substance abuse treatment, mental health treatment, medical care, training, and employment assistance.[45]

California's Administrative Office of the Courts is one of the larger such agencies nationwide, owing to the size of the state's population. Under the leadership of the Administrative Director of the Courts, its departments perform a range of functions commonly found in other states' administrative offices.

Management of the Workload

State courts, through their administrative bodies and with the assistance of national organizations like the NCSC, have taken significant steps to improve their efficiency and responsiveness. Case-flow management systems have become popular, as have efforts to engage in performance measurement.

case-flow management
"[T]he court supervision of the case progress of all cases filed in that court. It includes management of the time and events necessary to move a case from the point of initiation (filing, date of contest, or arrest) through disposition, regardless of the type of disposition."[v]

Case-flow management is "the court supervision of the case progress of all cases filed in that court. It includes management of the time and events necessary to move a case from the point of initiation (filing, date of contest, or arrest) through disposition, regardless of the type of disposition."[46] Case-flow management is thus an administrative process. It has nothing to do with the circumstances of individual cases; rather, its sole concern is with ensuring the smooth and efficient flow of cases through the courts.[47]

How does a court know if it has a case-flow management problem? There will be several symptoms: One is if filings outpace dispositions, which means more cases are coming in than are being resolved, leading to backlogs and delay; another is if the "age" of the pending caseload exceeds ideal standards; that is, if cases have been languishing for too long without resolution, there may be a case-flow management problem.

A specific example of how case-flow management problems can affect everyone involved in the court process concerns **adjournment**, which literally means "to put off" and is a continuance of a scheduled event. Having too many adjournments, often at the request of the attorneys because they are not ready, leads to the scheduling of more cases, which leads to further delay. Control of adjournments is thus critical: "(1) [A]djournments contribute to delay; (2) an adjournment policy influences attorney and litigant perceptions of court commitment to caseflow management; and (3) a lenient adjournment policy undermines a predictable system of event date certainty."[48]

adjournment
The continuance of a scheduled event. The verb "adjourn" means "to put off."

Courts have also become increasingly concerned with their performance. Two main developments were responsible.[49] First, during the mid-1980s, many of America's criminal courts were faced with considerable increases in their drug caseloads,[50] and these increases prompted judges and court managers to think long and hard about the priorities of the courts. As one practitioner noted, "The drug crisis is propelling us to look at this issue of who are we and what are we doing in a very different way than we've historically done."[51] Second, during the 1980s, courts also revisited the problem of delay.[52] This prompted concerns with improving efficiency, but it also prompted thinking about court goals in general.

In 1987, the NCSC received a grant from the Bureau of Justice Assistance to create its **Commission on Trial Court Performance Standards**, which was charged with developing performance standards that could be used by state courts. The commission worked for three years before releasing its measures and standards in 1990. The document was endorsed by numerous organizations, including the Conference of Chief Justices, the Conference of State Court Administrators, the National Association for Court Management, and even the American Judges Association.[53] In short, the standards caused the state judicial community to take note.

Commission on Trial Court Performance Standards
A commission established by the National Center for State Courts in 1987 that was charged with developing performance standards that could be used by the state courts.

What do the standards look like? There are five areas of performance:

1. *Access to justice.* Trial courts should ensure that the structure and machinery of the courts are accessible to those they serve.

2. *Expedition and timeliness.* Trial courts should meet their responsibilities in a timely and expeditious manner.

3. *Equality, fairness, and integrity.* Trial courts should provide due process and equal protection of the law to all who have business before them.

4. *Independence and accountability.* Trial courts should establish their legal and organizational boundaries, monitor and control their operations, and account publicly for their performance.

5. *Public trust and confidence.* Trial courts should work to instill public trust that courts are accessible, fair, and accountable.[54]

Within each area are a total of 22 distinct standards. Together, the areas and standards represent the fundamental purposes and responsibilities of the courts.

Web Extra
4–7 Florida State Courts Online

RECENT DEVELOPMENTS

Learning Objective 5
Be familiar with recent developments in state courts.

Caseload statistics and management strategies only tell so much about the state of the state courts. The reality is that state courts are in something of a difficult spot today: Funding has been cut, staffing levels have been reduced, and the courts' relationships with other branches of government have become increasingly strained in some states. Indeed, "Justice in Jeopardy" was the title chosen by a recent American Bar Association report.[55] The news is not all doom and gloom, however, because courts are reinventing themselves and innovating at unprecedented rates (we look at this further in Chapter 6).[56]

Budget Cuts

State court budgets, just like the budgets in pretty much every public agency across the board, are shrinking. According to the most recent data, a number of serious cuts have been made. These have far-reaching implications for the administration of justice. Examples include the following:

- 42 states have reduced their court budgets
- 39 states have suspended filling clerk vacancies
- 34 states have laid off court staff
- 27 states have increased fines and fees to offset lost revenue
- 23 states have reduced operating hours
- 9 states have seen delays or relied less on jury trials.[57]

Time Constraints

Judges in particular are becoming increasingly busy. It is not that they are deciding more cases per se but rather that the types of cases they are deciding can take more time. Recent advances in the realm of problem-solving courts (see Chapter 6) have required more of judges' time. For example, judges in drug courts see defendants more frequently to track their progress, and these courts also require a measure of participation among various public and private agencies, with the judiciary assuming most of the responsibility of coordinating such efforts.

Library Extra
4–3 Essential Elements of Courtroom Safety

Judges' time has also been affected by federal truth-in-sentencing laws, which mandate that prisoners serve 85 percent of their original sentence and which have abolished parole boards that have traditionally assumed responsibility for deciding when prisoners are released. Now who does it? Judges! The U.S. Justice Department has strongly encouraged so-called reentry courts (see Chapter 6) that effectively require judges to assume some of the roles parole boards once fulfilled.

Public Support and Political Problems

There are plenty of pressures and problems facing the court from the outside. Public opinion has become particularly important. Surveys of citizens' and court users' opinions of their court experience have become popular, and the information resulting from these surveys has been used to usher in various reforms and changes to the way courts traditionally operate. Unfortunately, through all this, various political problems have emerged as courts and legislators continue to vie for power and control over the judiciary.

Public Opinion Historically, the public's involvement in the judiciary was minimal at best. To some extent it still is, but courts are increasingly being forced to respond to public pressures for efficiency, accountability, and fairness. A problem in this regard is that many people are not particularly supportive of the courts, and many view them in an unfavorable light. A recent survey of people's perceptions of the courts led researchers to draw this conclusion: Perceptions that courts are too costly, too slow, unfair in the treatment of racial and ethnic minorities, out of touch with the public, and negatively influenced by political considerations are widely held. Overall, more Americans believe that the courts handle cases in a poor manner than believe courts handle cases in an excellent manner.[58]

Politicizing of State Judiciaries It has been said that the judiciary is "the branch that holds the representative branches to their responsibilities."[59] This role has caused more than a little controversy over the years, and relationships between state judiciaries and their legislatures have become rather contentious, with several explanations being offered for this phenomenon:

- State budget crises
- National interest group pressure in state courts (e.g., by representing one set of interests in environmental lawsuits)
- Lawsuits filed by citizens challenging legislation
- Court decisions with sweeping policy implications[60]

Florida's experience with the case of Terri Schiavo, who was removed from life support in 2005 due to being in a "persistent vegetative state," illustrates how the judiciary can become politicized. In the wake of a Florida court's decision in support of Schiavo's husband's wish to remove his wife's feeding tube over her family's objection, Congress went so far as to pass an act (which President Bush signed), dubbed the **Palm Sunday Compromise**, that transferred jurisdiction over Schiavo's case from the Florida state courts to the federal courts.[61] All of Schiavo's parents' subsequent federal court petitions and appeals (to keep Schiavo alive) failed, however, and she died on March 26, 2005. Although it applied only to Schiavo's parents, the legislation was significant because it not only signaled legislative meddling in judicial affairs but also signaled *federal* meddling in *state* affairs.

Schiavo's case was exceptional, and others like it have not surfaced of late, but when viewed in the context of other legislative efforts to control the courts, some have alleged a pattern is emerging. For example, some states have introduced bills barring their courts from having jurisdiction over school funding challenges.[62] Other states have proposed legislation that takes rule-making authority away from state supreme courts and gives it to legislatures. These recent developments make it clear that court-stripping, which we introduced in Chapter 2, is very much alive and well today.

Palm Sunday Compromise
A significant piece of U.S. legislation that signaled not only legislative meddling in judicial affairs but also federal meddling in state affairs.[vi]

SUMMARY

CHAPTER 4

1. OUTLINE THE HISTORY AND DEVELOPMENT OF STATE COURTS

- During the colonial period, governors appointed by the king of England had executive, legislative, and judicial power. Both justice of the peace and county courts were under control of the governors.
- After the American Revolution, state courts came under control of legislatures, but problems of corruption and favoritism persisted. The judiciary grew along with populations.
- Throughout most of the 1900s, state court structures grew more complicated and fragmented, but unification efforts have since combined various courts to streamline state judiciaries.
- The estimated number of state courts in place today is 16,000.

2. SUMMARIZE THE DIFFERING STRUCTURES OF STATE COURT SYSTEMS

- Most states have four levels of courts: limited jurisdiction courts, general jurisdiction courts, intermediate appellate courts, and state supreme courts (or courts of last resort).
- Limited jurisdiction courts, often called justice of the peace courts, magistrate courts, or municipal courts, typically adjudicate infractions and minor offenses.

- Justice in the lower courts is swift. Malcolm Feeley argued that the "process is the punishment" in these courts.

- General jurisdiction courts adjudicate serious criminal cases as well as civil disputes above defined dollar amounts, and such courts also hear trials *de novo*, which are basically appeals from the lower limited jurisdiction courts.

- Intermediate appellate courts review legal decisions from the lower courts.

- State supreme courts and their equivalents are the state courts of last resort, which hear appeals arising from the intermediate appellate courts. State supreme courts have significant policy-making authority.

3. DESCRIBE THE WORKLOAD OF STATE COURTS

- Civil and criminal caseloads continue to increase modestly year by year in the state courts.

- Most incoming cases in state courts are for traffic violations and ordinance violations, followed by criminal cases, civil cases, and others.

- Appellate court caseloads vary from state to state and tend to be higher in states that provide automatic review of lower courts' decisions. Some Supreme Court cases, such as *Blakely* v. *Washington*, have also affected state appellate court caseloads. The workload of state supreme courts (courts of last resort) roughly parallels that of the state appellate courts, but the former do not author as many written opinions.

- In terms of dispositions, drug offenses have the highest conviction rate per arrest, followed by murder/nonnegligent manslaughter, with considerably fewer arrestees being convicted for other offenses. Recent data reveal more than 1 million convictions for felonies each year.

4. SUMMARIZE THE ADMINISTRATION OF STATE COURTS

- State court administration, including budget preparation, data collection, education and training, research, personnel management, and facility management, is the responsibility of each state's administrative office of the courts. Some states, such as Nebraska, also run their juvenile and adult probation systems through the administrative offices of the courts.

- State courts have adopted case-flow management strategies to manage their workloads and track the progress of cases. They have also adopted performance measurement strategies to improve efficiency and responsiveness.

5. BE FAMILIAR WITH RECENT DEVELOPMENTS IN STATE COURTS

- State courts continue to evolve and change.

- Recent problems include time constraints on judges, violence and threats against judges, weak public support, and increased politicizing of the judiciary (e.g., interbranch tensions).

KEY TERMS

adjournment, 97

Blakely bounce, 93

case-flow management, 96

Commission on Trial
   Court Performance
   Standards, 97

court unification, 82

general jurisdiction
   courts, 87

intermediate appellate
   court, 89

judicial federalism, 90

justice of the peace (JOP)
   court, 86

limited jurisdiction
   courts, 84

magistrate court, 86

municipal court, 86

Palm Sunday
   Compromise, 99

state supreme courts, 89

REVIEW QUESTIONS

1. What are the steps in the historical development of state courts in the United States?

2. How are state courts in this country structured? How does court structure differ among the states?

3. How busy are state courts? How do caseloads vary by level?

4. How are state courts administered?

WHAT WILL YOU DO?

Your state has made use of justice of the peace courts since its founding, but recent criticisms have faulted such lower courts because they are informal and because many of the justices who staff them have little formal training in the law. The controversy over justice of the peace courts was recently enhanced when one of the older justices, a used-car dealer, arranged for a woman he knew to purchase a car and pay for it with periodic prostitution services that she was to provide for him—the justice had even created a bill of sale and purchase contract stipulating the services that the purchaser was to provide.

Of course, all professions have their "bad apples," and many citizens value justice of the peace courts because they allow for the relatively informal handling of minor community disputes. To your mind, the movement toward restorative justice, a somewhat new phenomenon in many locales, essentially represents a rehash of the fundamental principles behind justice of the peace courts, including the opportunity for both offenders and victims to be heard informally and the interests of the community to be represented through local justices. Although many justices are not schooled in the law, they have a good sense of the values that characterize their communities; consequently, some say, they are better able to fairly decide cases involving minor offenses than are the judges in higher courts.

You have decided that the best way to make an informed decision about the future of justice of the peace courts is to create a complete list of their pros and cons and to weigh one side of the list against the other. Consequently, you have begun to work on a list detailing both the positives and the negatives about such courts. What will be on your list?

DISCUSSION QUESTION

Judges are occasionally the victims of violence and threats. How serious is the problem?

NOTES

i. D. B. Rottman and S. M. Strickland, *State Court Organization, 2004* (Arlington, VA: National Center for State Courts, 2006), pp. 16–20.

ii. Rottman and Strickland, *State Court Organization, 2004,* pp. 16–20.

iii. U.S. Department of Justice, *Dictionary of Criminal Justice Data Terminology,* p. 55.

iv. *Blakely* v. *Washington,* 542 U.S. 296 (2004).

v. State Court Administrative Office, *Caseflow Management Guide* (Lansing, MI: State Court Administrative Office, n.d.), p. 1/1.

vi. C. Babington and M. Allen, "Congress Passes Schiavo Measure," *Washington Post,* March 21, 2005, p. A1. Available at http://www.washingtonpost.com/wp-dyn/articles/A51402-2005Mar20.html (accessed March 4, 2009).

---

1. The Historical Society of the Courts of the State of New York, "Colonial New York under British Rule," available at http://www.courts.state.ny.us/history/legal-history-new-york/history-new-york-legal-eras-01.html (accessed May 2, 2013).

2. Ibid.

3. *Crown* v. *John Peter Zenger* (1735).

4. M. J. Friedman, *Outline of the U.S. Legal System* (Washington, DC: U.S. State Department, 2004).

5. L. Steffens, *Autobiography* (New York: Harcourt Brace, 1931), pp. 206–207.

6. S. Walker, *Popular Justice: A History of American Criminal Justice,* 2nd ed. (New York: Oxford University Press, 1998), p. 29; also see L. M. Friedman and R.V. Percival, *The Roots of Justice: Crime and Punishment in Alameda County, California, 1870–1910* (Chapel Hill: University of North Carolina Press, 1981), pp. 87, 99.

7. Walker, *Popular Justice.*

8. S. L. Harring, *Policing a Class Society: The Experience of American Cities, 1865–1915* (New Brunswick, NJ: Rutgers University Press, 1983).

9. Walker, *Popular Justice,* p. 71.

10. H. Glick and K. Vines, *State Court Systems* (Englewood Cliffs, NJ: Prentice Hall, 1973).

11. Friedman and Percival, *The Roots of Justice.*

12. Ibid.

13. S. Carbon, L. Berkson, and J. Rosenbaum, "Court Reform in the Twentieth Century: A Critique of the Court Unification Controversy," *Emory Law Journal,* Vol. 27 (1978), pp. 559–607.

14. Ibid.

15. V. E. Flango, "Court Unification and Quality of State Courts," *Justice System Journal,* Vol. 16 (1994), pp. 33–55.

16. C. Baar, "Trial Court Unification in Practice," *Judicature,* Vol. 76 (1993), pp. 179–184.

17. J. M. Broder, J. F. Porter, and W. M. Smathers, "Hidden Consequences of Court Unification," *Judicature,* Vol. 65 (1981), pp. 10–17; also see J. Lamber and M. Luskin,

"Court Reform: A View from the Bottom," *Judicature,* Vol. 75 (1992), pp. 295–299.

18. Administrative Office of the Courts, *Fact Sheet: Trial Court Unification* (San Francisco: Administrative Office of the Courts, 2005), available at http://www.courts.ca.gov/documents/tcunif.pdf (accessed February 1, 2013).

19. Ibid.

20. Ibid., p. 2.

21. See, e.g., D. B. Rottman and S. M. Strickland, *State Court Organization, 2004* (Williamsburg, VA: National Center for State Courts, 2006), pp. 267–319.

22. R. LaFountain, R. Schauffler, S. Strickland, and K. Holt, *Analyzing the Work of State Courts: An Analysis of 2010 State Court Caseloads* (Williamsburg, VA: National Center for State Courts, 2012)

23. Friedman, *Outline of the U.S. Legal System.*

24. U.S. Department of Justice, *Dictionary of Criminal Justice Data Terminology,* 2nd ed. (Washington, DC: U.S. Department of Justice, Bureau of Justice Statistics, 1981), p. 54.

25. Rottman and Strickland, *State Court Organization, 2004,* pp. 16–20.

26. Ibid.

27. Available at http://www.georgiacourts.org/aoc/selfhelp/courts.html (accessed February 1, 2013).

28. New Jersey Judiciary, *Municipal Court Services,* available at http://www.judiciary.state.nj.us/mcs/index.htm (accessed February 1, 2013).

29. M. Feeley, *The Process Is the Punishment: Handling Cases in a Lower Criminal Court* (New York: Russell Sage, 1979).

30. U.S. Department of Justice, *Dictionary of Criminal Justice Data Terminology,* p. 55.

31. Rottman and Strickland, *State Court Organization, 2004.*

32. Ibid. (especially table 24).

33. J. W. Winkle, "Dimensions of Judicial Federalism," *Annals of the American Academy of Political and Social Science,* Vol. 416 (1974), pp. 67–76.

34. S. L. Beavers and J. S. Walz, "Modeling Judicial Federalism: Predictors of State Court Protections of Defendants' Rights under State Constitutions, 1969–1989," *Publius: The Journal of Federalism,* Vol. 28 (1998), p. 43.

35. From *The Activist Advocate: Policy Making in State Supreme Courts* by C. S. Lopeman. Copyright © 1999 by Charles S. Lopeman. Reproduced with permission of ABC-CLIO, LLC, Santa Barbara, CA.

36. Ibid.

37. *People* v. *LaValle,* 3 N.Y. 3d 88 (2004).

38. *Gregg* v. *Georgia,* 428 U.S. 153 (1978).

39. See, e.g., Lopeman, *The Activist Advocate.*

40. N. T. Romans, "The Role of State Supreme Courts in Judicial Policy Making: *Escobedo, Miranda,* and the Use of Political Impact Analysis," *Western Political Quarterly,* Vol. 27 (1974), p. 38.

41. H. R. Glick, "Policy-Making and State Supreme Courts: The Judiciary as an Interest Group," *Law and Society Review*, Vol. 5 (1970), pp. 272–273.

42. LaFountain, R. Schauffler, S. Strickland, and K. Holt, *Analyzing the Work of State Courts: An Analysis of 2010 State Court Caseloads* (Williamsburg, VA: National Center for State Courts, 2012), p. 3.

43. *Blakely v. Washington*, 542 U.S. 296 (2004).

44. R. LaFountain, R. Schauffler, S. Strickland, W. Raftery, and C. Bromage, *Examining the Work of State Courts, 2006* (Williamsburg, VA: National Center for State Courts, 2007), p. 71.

45. Administrative Office of the U.S. Courts, available at http://www.uscourts.gov/fedprob/system.html (accessed February 1, 2013).

46. State Court Administrative Office, *Caseflow Management Guide* (Lansing, MI: State Court Administrative Office, n.d.), p. 1/1.

47. D. Steelman, J. Goerdt, and J. McMillan, *Caseflow Management: The Heart of Court Management in the New Millennium* (Williamsburg, VA: National Center for State Courts, 2004).

48. Ibid., p. 16/4.

49. "Five Areas of Performance" from P. Casey, "Defining Optimal Court Performance: The Trial Court Performance Standards," *Court Review* Winter (1998), p. 25 (Williamsburg, VA: National Center for State Courts, 1998), reprinted by permission.

50. See, e.g., R. D. Lipscher, "The Judicial Response to the Drug Crisis," *State Court Journal* (Fall 1989), pp. 13–15.

51. "The Drugging of the Courts: How Sick Is the Patient and What Is the Treatment?," *Judicature*, Vol. 73 (1990), p. 315.

52. Special Issue on Court Delay Reduction, *State Court Journal* (Fall 1985).

53. National Center for State Courts, *Trial Court Performance Standards with Commentary* (Williamsburg, VA: National Center for State Courts, 1990). Also go to http://www.ncsconline.org/D_Research/TCPS/index.html (accessed February 1, 2013).

54. Casey, "Defining Optimal Court Performance," pp. 24–33.

55. American Bar Association, *Justice in Jeopardy: Report of the American Bar Association Commission on the 21st Century Judiciary*, available at http://www.americanbar.org/content/dam/aba/migrated/judind/jeopardy/pdf/report.authcheckdam.pdf (accessed February 1, 2013).

56. Much of the discussion that follows draws from D. B. Rottman, *Trends and Issues in the State Courts: Challenges and Achievements* (Williamsburg, VA: National Center for State Courts, 2004).

57. C. Flango, A. McDowell, D. Saunders, N. Sydow, C. Campbell, and N. Kauder, *Future Trends in State Courts, 2012* (Williamsburg, VA: National Center for State Courts, 2012).

58. D. B. Rottman and R. M. Hansen, *How Recent Court Users View the State Courts: Perceptions of Whites, African-Americans, and Latinos* (Williamsburg, VA: National Center for State Courts, n.d.).

59. Commission to Promote Public Confidence in Judicial Elections, *Interim Report to the Chief Judges of the State of New York* (New York: Commission to Promote Public Confidence in Judicial Elections, 2003), p. 1.

60. Rottman, *Trends and Issues in the State Courts*.

61. C. Babington and M. Allen, "Congress Passes Schiavo Measure," *Washington Post*, March 21, 2005, p. A1, available at http://www.washingtonpost.com/wp-dyn/articles/A51402-2005Mar20.html (accessed February 1, 2013).

62. Rottman, *The State Courts in 2005*, p. 237.

Chet Gordon/The Image Works

venile Courts

utline the history and development of juvenile
ourts.

xplain the purpose, organization, and process of
uvenile courts.

3. Explain the different ways that transfers to adult
court take place and the issues surrounding transfers.

4. Summarize recent trends and developments in the
juvenile justice system.

A juvenile breaks into a motor vehicle. Why are juvenile courts separate from adult criminal courts?

Gina Buliga/Shutterstock

INTRODUCTION

Juvenile courts are responsible for dealing with underage minors who commit criminal acts and also status offenses, acts that are forbidden to minors, such as running away, being truant from school, or acting disobediently toward one's parents.

The first juvenile courts were created at the tail end of the nineteenth century by reformers called child savers, who were concerned for the welfare of wayward and criminal youth. The first courts were viewed as social welfare agencies that would serve as a surrogate parent acting in the interests of the child. Today, while some juvenile courts still maintain a social welfare orientation, dispensing personalized, individual justice to needy children, others take a more law enforcement-oriented approach to juvenile crime.

Regardless of philosophy or approach, the American juvenile court system is a very busy institution; it processes approximately 1.5 million delinquency cases each year. In the past 15 years, the number of delinquency cases has climbed steadily and juvenile courts across the nation today handle 30 percent more cases than they did 20 years ago.

This chapter reviews the development of the juvenile court system. In doing so, it covers the most important legal cases that shape its process and highlights some of the most important issues facing juvenile courts in contemporary society.

DEVELOPMENT OF CARE FOR CHILDREN

A **juvenile** is a young person who has not yet attained the age at which he or she is treated as an adult for purposes of the law. More formally, a juvenile is "a person subject to juvenile court proceedings because a statutorily defined event or condition caused by or affecting that person was alleged to have occurred while his or her age was below the statutorily specified age limit of original jurisdiction of a juvenile court."[1] Under federal law, a juvenile is a person who has not yet turned 18 years of age.[2] Most states have followed the federal lead, but several treat 17-, 16-, and even 15-year-olds as adults.[3]

Juveniles come into contact with the courts for a number of reasons. Some are exposed to violence in the home and come before the courts in abuse cases, and some need assistance

juvenile
A young person who has not yet attained the age at which he or she is treated as an adult for purposes of the law. More formally, a juvenile is "a person subject to juvenile court proceedings because a statutorily defined event or condition caused by or affecting that person was alleged to have occurred while his or her age was below the statutorily specified age limit of original jurisdiction of a juvenile court."[i] Under the federal Juvenile Delinquency Act, a juvenile is a person who has not yet turned 18 years of age.[ii] Most states have followed the federal lead, but several states treat 16- and 17-year-olds as adults.[iii]

Web Extra
5–1 Office of Juvenile Justice and Delinquency Prevention

status offense
An act or conduct that is declared by statute to be an offense only if it is committed by or engaged in by a juvenile.

due to their life circumstances, such as when they are raised in conditions of extreme poverty. Some commit a **status offense**, conduct that is declared by statute to be an offense only if committed by or engaged in by a juvenile. Examples of status offenses include underage drinking, curfew violations, incorrigibility, smoking, truancy, and running away from home.

Juveniles enjoy distinct legal protections due to their age, but by the same token, there are certain protections afforded to adult offenders that juveniles do not benefit from. As a result, the juvenile justice system emerged in response to the concern by many that treating children as adults may do more harm than good; however, that view may be changing in response to highly publicized violent crimes committed by juvenile offenders.

Even before the emergence of the formal juvenile justice system and certainly before much attention was even given to juvenile delinquency, there were some important historical developments that signaled state involvement in the lives of wayward youth.[4]

Poor Laws

poor law
Several laws introduced by the English parliament throughout the 1500s (culminating in 1601)[iv] that reflected an increasingly compassionate attitude toward the poor, as people came to realize that there were legitimate reasons why some people found themselves destitute (e.g., weak harvests); also called *Poor Law Act* or *Elizabethan Poor Laws*.

A 1601 **poor law**, also known as the Poor Law Act or the Elizabethan Poor Law (in reference to Queen Elizabeth), was one of several laws introduced by the English parliament throughout the 1500s that reflected an increasingly compassionate attitude toward the poor as people came to realize that there were legitimate reasons why some people found themselves destitute (e.g., weak harvests).[5] Children were sometimes victims of these unfortunate circumstances.

The 1601 poor law helped provide work or apprenticeships for orphaned children and children whose parents could not support them, "setting to work the children of all such whose parents shall not by the said church wardens and overseers, or the greater part of them, be thought able to keep and maintain their children."[6] Many such children came under the control of church wardens and other guardians, with consent of the justices of the peace. While poor laws gave the outward appearance of helping the poor, many children were essentially forced into indentured working conditions until they became adults, which set a precedent for state control over those youth who were deemed unable to take care of themselves.

Poor laws were enacted for more than just the care of children. They also set up tax collection schemes, such that monies collected were used to help people in need; they were, to some extent, precursors to modern welfare systems.[7] Families bore the initial responsibility of caring for their poor relatives, with the government stepping in only when it became clear families could not do so. The strong colonial work ethic was reflected in all poor laws, and those who received assistance were expected to contribute to the community by working.

Chancery Courts

chancery courts
English courts created in the fifteenth century by the lord high chancellor to address cases that could not be decided in other common law courts[v]; also known as *equity courts*.

English **chancery courts** were created in the fifteenth century by the lord high chancellor to address cases that could not be decided in other common law courts.[8] Chancery courts were also called "equity courts," as they applied principles of equity rather than law, meaning that they issued decisions based on fairness rather than on strictly formulated rules of law.

The cases of minor children frequently came before chancery courts. For example, as early as the fifteenth century, chancery courts were exercising jurisdiction over infant heirs who lost their parents, and the courts would sometimes compel the infants' guardians to account for the management of the infants' property.

parens patriae
A medieval doctrine that allowed the Crown to replace natural family relations whenever a child's welfare was at risk.[vi]

One of the original guiding principles of the chancery courts was ***parens patriae***, a medieval doctrine that allowed the Crown to replace natural family relations whenever a child's welfare was at risk.[9] This meant that the chancery courts effectively took over when parents could not control their children's behavior.

The *parens patriae* principle was influential in a number of respects. It provided precedent for state involvement in juvenile affairs by suggesting that government can—and perhaps should—intervene in family affairs when the need arises: "[It] represented one aspect of a broad progressive movement to accommodate urban institutions to an increasingly industrial-immigrant population, and to incorporate recent discoveries in the behavioral, social, and medical sciences into the rearing of children."[10]

Parens patriae still serves as the core principle of the juvenile justice system and continues to guide juvenile courts in their decisions concerning the treatment of many people—not just juvenile—who cannot fend for or take care of themselves. A recent example of *parens patriae* is a judge's decision to grant custody of Brittney Spears's children to her ex-husband, Kevin Federline; Spears's bizarre behavior and drug use were partly responsible for the decision. Another example is Kim Delaney, of *All My Children*, *NYPD Blue*, and *Army Wives* fame, who lost custody of her teenage son because of her alcohol problems when a court felt she was not fit to care for the boy.

Library Extra
5–1 A Century of Juvenile Justice

CREATION OF AMERICAN JUVENILE JUSTICE

The foundations of juvenile justice laid by poor laws and chancery courts were transported to colonial America. Poor laws were enacted throughout the colonies, beginning in 1642 in Plymouth and followed by others in Virginia (1646), Connecticut (1673), and Massachusetts (1693). One historian stated that "early American poor laws served a vital function in the settlements by providing public assistance to the colonists, many of whom had been paupers, vagrants, and indentured servants in England and who, therefore, lacked financial resources."[11] It was not always enough to find work for the poor, especially poor children. People came to realize that more needed to be done in the case of children who found themselves in unfortunate circumstances.

Learning Objective 1
Outline the history and development of juvenile courts.

Child Savers

From about 1850 to 1890, a group of reform-minded individuals sought to improve the living conditions of poor urban children. Known today as **child savers**, these people developed groups and organizations whose function was to care for youth, provide shelter for them, and fulfill their educational and other social needs. Among the most prominent were Lucy Flowers, Jane Addams, Elizabeth Clapp, Lewis Pease, Samuel Gridley Howe, and Charles Loring Brace. Among the many fruits of their labors were the Five Points Mission (1850), the Children's Aid Society (1853), and the New York Juvenile Asylum (1851).[12]

Brace and his Children's Aid Society felt that poor and vagrant children should be gathered up and placed with farm families who could supposedly provide the warmth and compassion of a stable family environment—as well as teach these youth morality and work skills. Contrary to the idealized image that children in need quickly found loving homes as part of this placement process, there is evidence that some of the children basically became laborers rather than real members of their host families.[13] On the other hand, there were some success stories of children who later grew up to have extremely productive lives.

child savers
A group of reform-minded individuals in the United States that sought to improve the living conditions of poor urban children from about 1850 to 1890.

Refuge Movement

In 1825, the Society for the Prevention of Pauperism created the **New York House of Refuge**, the first juvenile reformatory in America.[14] The Society for the Prevention of

New York House of Refuge
The first juvenile reformatory in America.

Pauperism condemned the punitive approach common at that time and by 1824 was incorporated by the state of New York through legislation creating "Managers of the Society for the Reformation of Juvenile Delinquents in the City of New York."[15]

The House of Refuge opened on January 1, 1825, with six boys and three girls, a number that grew to more than 1,600 in about ten years. It is doubtful that the House of Refuge resulted in much "reformation," however. The typical inmate's day consisted of labor.[16]

Despite some critics' claims that the House of Refuge was more of a prison than a reformatory, the concept caught on, and similar institutions emerged. Boston formed the House of Reformation for juvenile offenders a year later.[17] Other state and local governments soon formed their own correctional facilities to house juveniles: Massachusetts opened a reform school for juveniles in 1848,[18] and Rochester, New York, followed suit in 1849.[19]

The children who lived in these facilities worked, learned trades, and received basic education. Conditions were poor and disciplinary measures were harsh, but these institutions, coupled with the child savers movement, were significant milestones in the development of juvenile justice in America.

Juvenile Court

No sooner did juvenile detention facilities emerge than juvenile courts began to appear. The first dedicated juvenile court was founded in Illinois in 1899 when the Illinois Juvenile Court Act of 1899 established a court whose sole purpose was to deal with neglected and delinquent children under the age of 16.[20] By 1925, 46 states, three U.S. territories, and the District of Columbia established their own juvenile courts.[21] See Box 5–1 for an overview of some of the early juvenile court cases.

BOX 5–1 Early Cases in Juvenile Court

After years of development and months of compromise, the Illinois legislature passed on April 14, 1899, a law permitting counties in the state to designate one or more of their circuit court judges to hear all cases involving dependent, neglected, and delinquent children younger than age 16. The legislation stated that these cases were to be heard in a special courtroom that would be designated as "the juvenile court room" and referred to as the "Juvenile Court." Thus, the first juvenile court opened in Cook County on July 3, 1899, was not a new court but a division of the circuit court with original jurisdiction over juvenile cases.

The judge assigned to this new division was Richard Tuthill, a Civil War veteran who had been a circuit court judge for more than 10 years. The first case heard by Judge Tuthill in juvenile court was that of Henry Campbell, an 11-year-old who had been arrested for larceny. The hearing was a public event. While some tried to make the juvenile proceeding secret, the politics of the day would not permit it. The local papers carried stories about what had come to be known as "child saving" by some and "child slavery" by others.[1]

At the hearing, Henry Campbell's parents told Judge Tuthill that their son was a good boy who had been led into trouble by others, an argument consistent with the underlying philosophy of the court—that individuals (especially juveniles) were not solely responsible for the crimes they commit. The parents did not want young Henry sent to an institution, which was one of the few options available to the judge. Although the enacting legislation granted the new juvenile court the right to appoint probation officers to handle juvenile cases, the officers were not to receive publicly funded compensation. Thus, the judge had no probation staff to provide services to Henry. The parents suggested that Henry be sent to live with his grandmother in Rome, New York. After questioning the parents, the judge agreed to send Henry to his grandmother's in the hope that he would "escape the surroundings which have caused the mischief." This first case was handled informally, without a formal adjudication of delinquency on the youth's record.

Judge Tuthill's first formal case is not known for certain, but the case of Thomas Majcheski (handled about two weeks after the Campbell case) might serve as an example. Majcheski, a 14-year-old, was arrested for stealing grain from a freight car in a railroad yard, a common offense at the time. The arresting officer told the judge that the boy's father was dead and his mother (a washerwoman with nine children) could not leave work to come to court. The officer also said that the boy had committed similar offenses previously but had never been arrested. The boy admitted the crime. The judge then asked the nearly 300 people in the courtroom if they had anything to say. No one responded.

Still without a probation staff in place, the judge's options were limited: dismiss the matter, order incarceration at the state reformatory, or transfer the case to adult court. The judge decided the best alternative was incarceration in the state reformatory, where the youth would "have the benefit of schooling."

A young man in the audience then stood up and told the judge that the sentence was inappropriate. Newspaper accounts indicate that the objector made the case that the boy was just trying to obtain food for his family. Judge Tuthill then asked if the objector would be willing to take charge of the boy and help him become a better citizen. The young man accepted. On the way out of the courtroom, a reporter asked the young man of his plans for Thomas. The young man said, "Clean him up, and get him some clothes and then take him to my mother. She'll know what to do with him."

In disposing of the case in this manner, Judge Tuthill ignored many possible concerns (e.g., the rights and desires of Thomas's mother and the qualifications of the young man—or more directly, the young man's mother). Nevertheless, the judge's actions demonstrated that the new court was not a place of punishment. The judge also made it clear that the community had to assume much of the responsibility if it wished to have a successful juvenile justice system. ▪

[1]Beginning in the 1850s, private societies in New York City rounded up street children from the urban ghettos and sent them to farms in the Midwest. Child advocates were concerned that these home-finding agencies did not properly screen or monitor the foster homes, pointing out that the societies were paid by the county to assume responsibility for the children and also by the families who received the children. Applying this concern to the proposed juvenile court, the Illinois legislation stated that juvenile court hearings should be open to the public so the public could monitor the activities of the court to ensure that private organizations would not be able to gain custody of children and then "sell" them for a handsome profit and would not be able to impose their standards of morality or religious beliefs on working-class children.

Source: H. N. Snyder and M. Sickmund, *Juvenile Offenders and Victims: 2006 National Report* (Washington, DC: U.S. Department of Justice, Office of Justice Programs, Office of Juvenile Justice and Delinquency Prevention, 2006), chap. 4, p. 95. Copyright © 2006 National Center for Juvenile Justice. Reprinted by permission.

In their early years, juvenile courts were focused on providing individualized decisions that were in the best interests of the children. Relying on the doctrine of *parens patriae*, decisions were more paternalistic than adversarial. For example, rather than handing down harsh punishments, Judge Ben Lindsey, who served on the Denver Juvenile Court from 1901 to 1927, routinely counseled juveniles, and his approach prompted other juvenile court judges around the country to discard formal rules of procedure and serve as therapeutic change agents. Judge Julian Mack, who presided over Cook County, Illinois, once said that "the child who must be brought into court should, of course, be made to know that he is face to face with the power of the state, but he should at the same time, and more emphatically, be made to feel that he is the object of its care and solicitude."[22]

Legal Protections As a consequence of the *parens patriae* philosophy, there were few legal protections in the early juvenile court. Rather than being protected by the Fifth Amendment, children were frequently encouraged to admit their guilt. Also, the standard of proof in the first juvenile courts was a preponderance of the evidence rather than proof beyond a reasonable doubt, which made it easier to hold juveniles accountable.

These relaxed standards were all in the name of "helping" juvenile offenders, but people eventually realized that juveniles deserved the same protections that adults enjoy. Beginning in the 1960s, the U.S. Supreme Court heard a number of important cases that dealt with juveniles' legal rights.[23] These decisions ushered in a due process revolution in the juvenile court, resulting in the development of legal rights for juveniles that has continued to this day. Here are several of those landmark decisions:

1. *Kent v. United States.*[24] Morris Kent, on probation for a previous offense, was charged with rape and robbery, and he confessed to these and other crimes. His

attorney assumed the prosecutor would waive Kent to the adult justice system, so he filed a motion requesting a hearing on the question of which court (adult or juvenile) would exercise jurisdiction over Kent's case. The juvenile court judge did not rule on the motion and instead concluded that the court was waiving jurisdiction after "a full investigation." The judge provided no details concerning the investigation and did not discuss the grounds for treating Kent as an adult. Kent was subsequently found guilty in adult court and sentenced to between 30 and 90 years in prison. The Supreme Court ruled that this action was invalid and held that Kent was entitled to a hearing, assistance of counsel in such a hearing, access to the records considered by the juvenile court in reaching its decision, and statement of the reasons why he was treated as an adult.

2. *In re Gault.*[25] Gerald Gault (a 15-year-old probationer) and his friend made a crank call to an adult neighbor, asking her, "Are your cherries ripe today?" and "Do you have big bombers?" The neighbor recognized who made the call and had both youths arrested. Gault's parents were never advised of his arrest and detention, nor were they informed that Gault had a right to assistance of counsel. Gault's adjudication as a delinquent was based solely on the arresting officer's statement (not under oath) that Gault admitted to making the obscene phone call; the victim did not appear at the adjudication hearing. Gault was sent to a juvenile reformatory until age 21, meaning that he received a six-year sentence for a prank call.

   An attorney obtained for Gault after the trial filed a *habeas corpus* petition, challenging the constitutionality of the boy's confinement. The petition was eventually reviewed by the Supreme Court, which ruled that juveniles are entitled to certain due process protections, including the rights to be notified of charges, to have the assistance of counsel, to confront adverse witnesses (namely the victim), and to be free from compelled self-incrimination.

3. *In re Winship.*[26] Samuel Winship, age 12, was charged with stealing $112 from a woman's purse. An employee at the store where the money was taken claimed to have witnessed Winship running from the scene before the woman noticed the missing cash, but others said the employee was not in a position to see who took the money. Even so, Winship was adjudicated delinquent and committed to a training school because the legal standard for proof of his guilt was a preponderance of evidence rather than the usual proof beyond a reasonable doubt standard. The Supreme Court ruled that the reasonable doubt standard is necessary in juvenile proceedings.[27]

4. *McKeiver v. Pennsylvania.*[28] Joseph McKeiver, a 16-year-old, was charged with various offenses. He met with his attorney before his adjudicatory hearing; the attorney then requested a jury trial, but his request was denied. The state supreme court cited some of the Supreme Court decisions we have already introduced as evidence that concerns with due process protections for juveniles warranted a jury trial. The Supreme Court disagreed, holding that a jury is not essential in juvenile adjudicatory hearings. It further held that its earlier decisions in *Gault* and *Winship* were concerned with enhancing accuracy of fact-finding in adjudicatory hearings and that a judge is just as capable as a jury of doing this.[29]

5. *Breed v. Jones.*[30] Gary Jones, age 17, was charged with armed robbery and was adjudicated delinquent, but at the dispositional hearing, the judge determined that Jones was unfit to be treated as a juvenile and waived the case to adult court. Jones's attorney filed a writ of *habeas corpus*, arguing that the Fifth Amendment's double jeopardy provision (see Chapter 11 for more details) was violated because Jones was already adjudicated delinquent. The reviewing court denied the petition, arguing that Jones's adjudication as a delinquent was not

a trial and thus that double jeopardy did not apply in his case. On appeal, the Supreme Court disagreed, holding that adjudication as delinquent as a juvenile is the same as a criminal conviction.[31]

6. *Oklahoma Publishing Company* v. *District Court in and for Oklahoma City* and *Smith* v. *Daily Mail Publishing Co.*[32] In the first of these cases, the Oklahoma Publishing Company was prohibited by court order from publishing the name and picture of a juvenile offender involved in a court proceeding. The juvenile's name and picture were legally obtained through a reporter's attendance at the adjudicatory hearing when the juvenile's picture was taken as he left the courthouse after the hearing. The Supreme Court held that the judge's order abridged the freedom of the press and therefore violated the First Amendment to the U.S. Constitution.[33] A similar decision was reached in the *Smith* case.

7. *Eddings* v. *Oklahoma*.[34] When he was 16 years old, Eddings killed a police officer and was sentenced to death. His death sentence was vacated when the Court ruled that a defendant's youthful age must be considered as a mitigating circumstance when deciding to impose the death penalty, but this decision was effectively overruled in *Roper* v. *Simmons* (discussed below).

8. *Schall* v. *Martin*.[35] Gregory Martin, a 14-year-old, was arrested in 1977 for robbery, assault, and possession of a weapon. He and two other boys allegedly hit another boy in the head with a gun and took some of his clothes. Martin was charged and then confined during the period leading up to his adjudicatory hearing. The court detained Martin pursuant to a state statute that authorized preventive detention of juveniles who posed a "serious risk" and who "may before the return date commit an act which if committed by an adult would constitute a crime."[36] Martin's attorney challenged the constitutionality of the statute, but the Supreme Court eventually upheld it.[37]

9. *Thompson* v. *Oklahoma*[38] and *Stanford* v. *Kentucky*.[39] These two cases dealt with the appropriate age at which the death penalty could apply to juveniles. Thompson, a 15-year-old boy, was one of four defendants charged with the brutal killing of Keene, Thompson's brother-in-law (court records showed that Thompson killed Keene for allegedly abusing Thompson's sister). Thompson and his codefendants were convicted of first-degree murder and sentenced to death. The Supreme Court concluded that it would be cruel and unusual punishment, in violation of the Eighth Amendment, to execute a juvenile who committed a capital crime when he was 15 years old.

   The Court reached an opposite conclusion in the *Stanford* case. Stanford, who was 17 at the time he allegedly murdered another individual, was tried as an adult, convicted of first-degree murder, and sentenced to death. The Supreme Court consolidated Stanford's case along with that of another juvenile who was convicted of first-degree murder in adult court and who committed his crime at age 16. The Court concluded that the death sentences in both cases did not violate the Eighth Amendment, meaning that 15-year-olds could not be sentenced to death but that those who committed capital crimes at age 16 or older could be. These rulings held until *Roper* v. *Simmons*.

10. *Roper* v. *Simmons*.[40] When he was a junior in high school, Christopher Simmons, age 17 years, planned and committed murder; almost a year later, after he had turned 18, Simmons was convicted and sentenced to death. There was no doubt Simmons committed the crime—his friends testified that he did, and the evidence showed that he planned and did break into a woman's house, bound and gagged her, and then drove to a nearby park and threw her off a bridge, where she drowned in the

In re Gault

In re Gault (1967) was the landmark U.S. Supreme Court decision that substantially reduced the significance of the *parens patriae* doctrine in the juvenile justice arena and initiated meaningful constitutional controls over juvenile courts. Prior to *Gault*, the American juvenile justice system was a hodgepodge of arcana, widely varying by state, that generally denied juveniles even the most elemental constitutional protections during delinquency proceedings. *Gault* extended to juveniles many of the same due process rights as those accorded adults.

At Gault's preliminary hearing, Judge McGhee, a Gila County Superior Court judge functioning in a secondary role as a juvenile court judge, ordered Gault held while he (McGhee) thought about the case. Gault was held for several more days, then he was released and informed that another hearing would be held the following Monday.

At the second hearing, Judge McGhee found Gault to be a delinquent child and ordered him to be confined at the State Industrial School "for the period of his minority." By definition, that meant that Gault was confined until he reached the age of 21 years. Effectively, then, Judge McGhee had ordered Gault to serve almost six years of confinement for an offense for which the maximum punishment that could have been meted out to a similarly charged adult was two months' confinement and a fine of $5 to $50.

Because Arizona law at the time did not permit appeals of juvenile court actions, Gault's parents petitioned for a writ of *habeas corpus* to obtain his release from detention. The Arizona Supreme Court referred the petition back to Judge McGhee's own Superior Court, where it was promptly dismissed. Gault's parents appealed the dismissal of the writ to the Arizona Supreme Court on grounds that it unconstitutionally denied due process. When the state supreme court affirmed the Superior Court's dismissal, the Gaults submitted a writ of *certiorari* to the U.S. Supreme Court.

On May 15, 1967, the U.S. Supreme Court held that Arizona had violated Gault's Fourteenth Amendment due process rights, citing denial of the right to legal counsel, lack of formal notification of the charges, failure to inform Gault of his right against self-incrimination and to remain silent, denial of opportunity to confront his accusers, and denial of his right to appeal his sentence to a higher court as specific due process failures.

Gault led to revisions of juvenile justice practices throughout the United States, including amendment of laws in all states to ensure protection of juveniles' due process rights. It is interesting to note that many states have also incorporated educational programs for minor children to teach them the importance of the Constitution and the court system in protecting them. In 2007, for example, University of Houston Law School students developed a presentation for use in local area schools. That same year, the *Gault* at 40 Campaign, supported by the National Juvenile Defender Center, focused on ensuring excellence in juvenile defense and devised strategies to improve children's access to competent counsel.

In the years since his case resulted in a landmark U.S. Supreme Court ruling, Gerald Gault has remained an advocate of juvenile justice reform and has periodically participated in panel discussions and other events related to his case. In 1987, for example, he spoke at an American Bar Association ceremony at which his attorney, Amelia Lewis, was honored for her role in the case. He recalled that without a lawyer, he had no idea what was happening to him during the hearings in Judge McGhee's court. He also offered remarks during a webcast conducted by the Georgetown University Law Center on April 14, 2008, titled "40 Years after *In re Gault*: The Role of Juvenile Defense Counsel and Obstacles to Zealous Advocacy in D.C." ■

DISCUSSION QUESTIONS

1. What is the significance for today's juvenile courts of the *Gault* case?

2. How might Gault's life have been different if the U.S. Supreme Court had not ruled in his favor?

3. Might we one day see another case with the significance of *Gault*? If so, what would it be likely to deal with?

water below. Despite the heinous and calculated nature of the crime, the Missouri Supreme Court set aside Simmons's death sentence, and the U.S. Supreme Court agreed. Simmons argued that jurors should be allowed to take aggravating (graphic nature of the crime) and mitigating (Simmons' youth) factors into account in deciding whether death is warranted, but the Supreme Court opted instead to adopt the "bright-line rule": The minimum age for the death penalty is 18.[41]

11. *Graham v. Florida.*[42] Graham was 16 when he engaged in an armed burglary. Pursuant to a plea agreement, Graham was sentenced to probation. The trial court later determined that Graham had violated his probation terms by committing additional crimes. The court revoked his probation and sentenced him

to life in prison for burglary. He challenged his punishment under the Eighth Amendment, and the U.S. Supreme Court agreed that it was cruel and unusual.

12. *Miller v. Alabama*.[43] Evan Miller was convicted of capital murder after he and a friend beat and robbed a neighbor, then set his house on fire. He was 14 when he committed the offense. Under Alabama law at the time, offenses of this sort demanded life in prison without regard to the circumstances, including the age of the offender. In a 5–4 vote, the U.S. Supreme Court decided that "the Eighth Amendment forbids a sentencing scheme that mandates life in prison without the possibility of parole for juvenile offenders."

Web Extra
5–2 Changing Perspectives on Juvenile Justice

These Supreme Court cases (see Figure 5–1 for a summary) defined the legal rights of juveniles, but they are not the only cases that did so. The Supreme Court has decided well in excess of a hundred cases addressing all aspects of juvenile justice, ranging from rights during police confrontations and in the preadjudication phase to conditions of confinement and release decisions.[44]

Federal Legislation   In 1968, Congress passed the **Juvenile Delinquency Prevention and Control Act** (JDPCA).[45] The legislation encouraged states to develop community-level plans to prevent juvenile delinquency, and approved programs received federal funding to support their implementation. The act was later replaced by the **Juvenile Justice and Delinquency Prevention Act** (JJDPA),[46] which was passed in 1974. This legislation created three new entities:

1. Office of Juvenile Justice and Delinquency Prevention (OJJDP)
2. Runaway Youth Program
3. National Institute for Juvenile Justice and Delinquency Prevention

The JJDPA legislation was also responsible for some key reforms that affected juvenile justice in general and juvenile courts in particular:

- *Deinstitutionalization of status offenders*. Subject to certain exceptions, status offenders cannot be held in secure detention or confinement, and such offenders should receive treatment and services.

- *Prohibition of juveniles' detainment in adult jails*. Except for limited periods before and after their court hearings, juveniles cannot be placed in adult lockups; however, children who are tried and convicted in adult court are exempt from this.

- *"Sight and sound" separation*. If a juvenile is placed in an adult lockup, contact with adults is prohibited, a provision designed to protect children from physical and psychological abuse inflicted on them by adult inmates.

- *Disproportionate minority confinement*. States are required to do something about the disproportionate confinement of minorities in juvenile facilities.[47]

See Box 5–2 for more details.

Juvenile Delinquency Prevention and Control Act (JDPCA)
The U.S. federal legislation that encouraged states to develop community-level plans to prevent juvenile delinquency.[vii]

Juvenile Justice and Delinquency Prevention Act (JJDPA)
The U.S. federal legislation that replaced the JDPCA of 1968, created several new entities, and enacted key reforms that affected juvenile justice in general and juvenile courts in particular.[viii]

Juvenile Courts Today: Priorities, Organization, and Process

Today, juvenile court priorities vary from state to state, and the same is true of the juvenile court organization and the juvenile court process. We begin with a look at juvenile court priorities.

Priorities

Variation in the way juvenile courts are set up owes in part to the legislative priorities of the juvenile justice system. Some states attempt to follow a "balanced and restorative justice"

Learning Objective 2
Explain the purpose, organization, and process of juvenile courts.

Web Extra
5–3 National Council of Juvenile and Family Court Judges

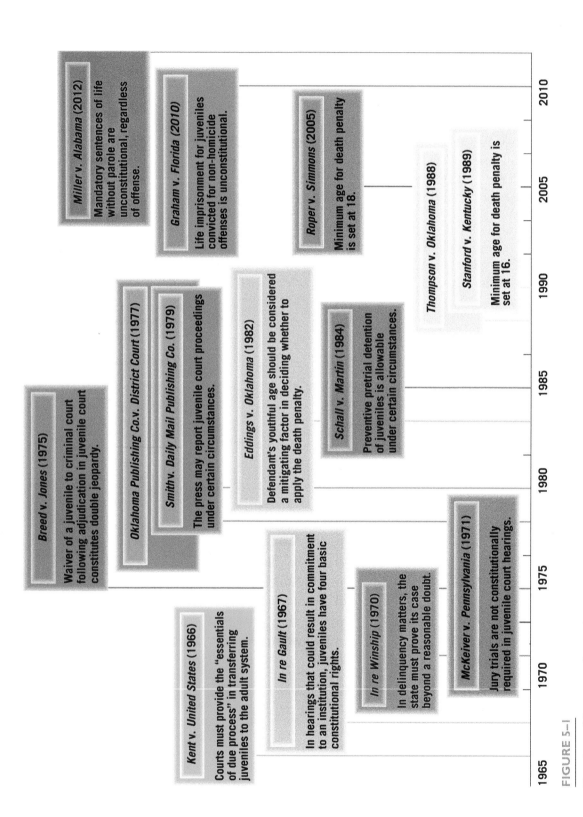

FIGURE 5-1

Timeline of Supreme Court Decisions Dealing with Juveniles

Source: Adapted from H. N. Snyder and M. Sickmund, *Juvenile Offenders and Victims: 2006 National Report* (Washington, DC: U.S. Department of Justice, Office of Justice Programs, Office of Juvenile Justice and Delinquency Prevention, 2006), chap. 4, p. 101. Copyright © 2006 National Center for Juvenile Justice. Reprinted by permission.

LASTING IMPACT

Roper v. Simmons

In early September 1993, Christopher Simmons, then age 17 years, discussed with two of his friends (also minors) the possibility of committing a burglary and murdering someone. On several occasions, Simmons described the manner in which he planned to commit the crime: He would find someone to burglarize, tie the victim up, and ultimately push the victim off a bridge. Simmons assured his friends that their status as juveniles would allow them to "get away with it."

On September 8, 1993, Simmons arranged to meet his friends at around 2 A.M. the following day for the purpose of carrying out the plan. Although the boys met as planned, one bowed out and refused to participate. Simmons and the other boy then went to the home of Shirley Crook to commit a burglary.

After breaking into the home, the boys found Mrs. Crook in bed. Simmons ordered her out of her bed and onto the floor. While the other boy guarded Mrs. Crook in the bedroom, Simmons found a roll of duct tape, returned to the bedroom, and bound her hands behind her back. The boys also taped her eyes and mouth shut before walking her from her home and placing her in the back of her minivan.

Simmons drove the van from Mrs. Crook's home in Jefferson County to Castlewood State Park in St. Louis County, stopping at a railroad trestle that spanned the Meramec River. After Simmons parked the van, the boys began to unload Mrs. Crook from the van. After walking her out on the trestle, Simmons bound her hands and feet together, hog-tie fashion, and covered her face completely with duct tape. He then pushed her off the railroad trestle into the river below; at the time she fell, Mrs. Crook was alive and conscious. The boys then threw Mrs. Crook's purse into the woods and drove the van back to the mobile home park across from the subdivision in which she lived.[1]

Mrs. Crook's body was found later that afternoon by two fishermen. Simmons was arrested the next day (September 10) at his high school. Subsequently tried and convicted, Simmons was sentenced to death. In August 2003, holding that the execution of those who committed crimes while under the age of 18 violates evolving standards of decency and is, therefore, prohibited by the Eighth Amendment of the U.S. Constitution, the Missouri Supreme Court set aside Simmons's death sentence and resentenced him to life in prison without the possibility of probation or parole.

Believing that the Missouri Supreme Court's ruling violated the U.S. Supreme Court's holding in *Stanford* v. *Kentucky* (1989) that executing minors was not unconstitutional, the state of Missouri appealed to the U.S. Supreme Court, arguing that allowing a state court to overturn a U.S. Supreme Court

decision by looking at "evolving standards" would be dangerous because state courts could just as easily decide that executions prohibited by the Supreme Court (such as the execution of the mentally ill in *Atkins* v. *Virginia* [2002]) were now permissible due to a change in the beliefs of the American people.[2]

On March 1, 2005, in a 5–4 decision, the U.S. Supreme Court "ruled that standards of decency have evolved so that executing minors is 'cruel and unusual punishment' prohibited by the Eighth Amendment. The majority cited a consensus against the juvenile death penalty among state legislatures and its own determination that the death penalty is a disproportionate punishment for minors. Finally the Court pointed to 'overwhelming' international opinion against the juvenile death penalty."[3]

Roper captures the essence of the concept of the U.S. Constitution as a living document and exemplifies the procedural checks and balances under which our federal system of government was designed to function. In sequence, the state supreme court of Missouri articulated a finding with which the state government did not concur; the state then exercised its appellate option to obtain federal review of its own state's highest court, and the federal court then articulated its reasoning in announcing its affirmation of the state supreme court's original ruling. *Roper* also displays the vital role of American courts at all levels both in the adaptation of evolving standards of decency to uphold the will of the people and in the preservation of the federalism that is America. ■

Notes

1. *State of Missouri* v. *Christopher Simmons* (Mo banc 1997), available at http://missourideathrow.com/2008/12/state-of-missouri-v-christopher-simmons (accessed May 30, 2013).
2. *Roper* v. *Simmons*, 543 U.S. 551 (2005), available at http://www.supremecourt.gov/opinions/04pdf/03-633.pdf (accessed May 30, 2013).
3. Ibid.

DISCUSSION QUESTIONS

1. In this case, the U.S. Supreme Court ruled that "standards of decency have evolved so that executing minors is 'cruel and unusual punishment' prohibited by the Eighth Amendment." What does the term "evolving standards of decency" mean in the context of this decision?

2. Do you agree with the Court that juveniles should not be subject to capital punishment no matter what their crime?

BOX 5–2   Core Elements of the Juvenile Justice and Delinquency Prevention Act

The Juvenile Justice and Delinquency Prevention Act of 2002 (the Act) establishes four custody-related requirements.

The *deinstitutionalization of status offenders and nonoffenders requirement* (1974) specifies that juveniles not charged with acts that would be crimes for adults "shall not be placed in secure detention facilities or secure correctional facilities." This requirement does not apply to juveniles charged with violating a valid court order or possessing a handgun, or those held under interstate compacts.

The *"sight and sound separation" requirement* (1974) specifies that "juveniles alleged to be or found to be delinquent and [status offenders and nonoffenders] shall not be detained or confined in any institution in which they have contact with adult inmates" in custody because they are awaiting trial on criminal charges or have been convicted of a crime. This requires that juvenile and adult inmates cannot see each other and no conversation between them is possible.

The *"jail and lockup removal" requirement* (1980) states that juveniles shall not be detained or confined in adult jails or lockups. There are, however, several exceptions. There is a 6-hour grace period that allows adult jails and lockups to hold delinquents temporarily while awaiting transfer to a juvenile facility or making court appearances. (This exception applies only if the facility can maintain sight and sound separation.) Under certain conditions, jails and lockups in rural areas may hold delinquents awaiting initial court appearance up to 48 hours. Some jurisdictions have obtained approval for separate juvenile detention centers that are colocated with an adult facility; in addition, staff who work with both juveniles and adult inmates must be trained and certified to work with juveniles.

Regulations implementing the Act exempt a juvenile held in secure adult facilities if the juvenile is being tried as a criminal for a felony or has been convicted as a criminal felon. Regulations also allow adjudicated delinquents to be transferred to adult institutions once they have reached the state's age of full criminal responsibility, where such transfer is expressly authorized by state law.

In the past, the *"disproportionate minority confinement" (DMC) requirement* (1988) focused on the extent to which minority youth were confined in proportions greater than their representation in the population. The 2002 Act broadened the DMC concept to encompass all stages of the juvenile justice process; thus, DMC has come to mean *disproportionate minority contact.*

States must agree to comply with each requirement to receive Formula Grants funds under the Act's provisions. States must submit plans outlining their strategy for meeting these and other statutory requirements. Noncompliance with core requirements results in the loss of at least 20% of the state's annual Formula Grants Program allocation per requirement.

As of 2005, 56 of 57 eligible states and territories were participating in the Formula Grants Program. Annual state monitoring reports show that the vast majority were in compliance with the requirements, either reporting no violations or meeting *de minimis* or other compliance criteria. ■

Source: H. N. Snyder and M. Sickmund, *Juvenile Offenders and Victims: 2006 National Report* (Washington, DC: U.S. Department of Justice, Office of Justice Programs, Office of Juvenile Justice and Delinquency Prevention, 2006), chap. 4, p. 97. Copyright © 2006 National Center for Juvenile Justice. Reprinted by permission.

approach, emphasizing public safety, individual accountability, and offender services.[48] Others follow the Standard Juvenile Court Act, which states,

Web Extra
5–4 National Council on Crime and Delinquency

> [E]ach child coming within the jurisdiction of the court shall receive . . . the care, guidance, and control that will conduce to his welfare and the best interest of the state, and that when he is removed from the control of his parents the court shall secure for him care as nearly as possible equivalent to that which they should have given him.[49]

Still other states follow the *Legislative Guide for Drafting Family and Juvenile Courts*, which lists four purposes of juvenile courts:

1. To provide for the care, protection, and wholesome mental and physical development of children involved with the juvenile court

2. To remove from children committing delinquent acts the consequences of criminal behavior, and to substitute therefore a program of supervision, care, and rehabilitation

3. To remove a child from the home only when necessary for his or her welfare or in the interests of public safety

4. To assure all parties of their constitutional and other legal rights[50]

Some states part ways with this approach and emphasize only juvenile accountability and public protection, whereas others prioritize child welfare over all other concerns. A summary of these five distinct approaches appears in Figure 5–2.

FIGURE 5–2

State Juvenile Code Purpose Clauses

Note: States not listed do not have purpose clauses that fit into these categories.

Source: H. N. Snyder and M. Sickmund, *Juvenile Offenders and Victims: 2006 National Report* (Washington, DC: U.S. Department of Justice, Office of Justice Programs, Office of Juvenile Justice and Delinquency Prevention, 2006), chap. 4, p. 98. Copyright © 2006 National Center for Juvenile Justice. Reprinted by permission.

State	BARJ[1] Features	Juvenile Court Act Language	*Legislative Guide* Language	Accountability Protection Emphasis	Child Welfare Emphasis
Alabama	■				
Alaska	■				
Arkansas		■	■		
California	■	■			
Connecticut				■	
Dist. of Columbia					■
Florida	■	■			
Georgia		■			
Hawaii				■	
Idaho	■				
Illinois	■	■			
Indiana	■				
Iowa		■			
Kansas	■				
Kentucky					■
Louisiana		■			
Maine		■	■		
Maryland	■				
Massachusetts		■			■
Michigan		■			
Minnesota	■	■			
Mississippi		■			
Missouri		■			
Montana	■		■		
Nevada		■			
New Hampshire			■		
New Jersey	■	■	■		
New Mexico			■		
North Carolina				■	
North Dakota			■		
Ohio			■		
Oregon	■				
Pennsylvania	■				
Rhode Island		■			
South Carolina		■			
Tennessee			■		
Texas			■	■	
Utah				■	
Vermont			■		
Washington	■				
West Virginia					■
Wisconsin	■				
Wyoming			■	■	

Organization

A few states have stand-alone juvenile courts, and others adjudicate juvenile cases in family courts. The most common approach is to have juvenile court as part of the state's trial court system. Following is a discussion of three common methods of juvenile court organization.

Stand-Alone Courts Stand-alone juvenile courts are found in relatively few states, including Colorado (in the city of Denver), Georgia, Massachusetts, Nebraska, and Utah.[51] These courts have their own administration, staff, judges, and other personnel. Utah, the state with perhaps the most developed juvenile court system, has 27 juvenile court judges in the state's eight judicial districts.

Some states have a mix of stand-alone juvenile courts and juvenile courts that are part of general jurisdiction courts. In Tennessee, juvenile court jurisdiction is vested with what are called general sessions courts, which are county-level limited jurisdiction courts charged with adjudication of a range of case types. But some counties have created their own stand-alone courts, which are separate from the general sessions courts.

Family Courts Another approach is to adjudicate juvenile cases in dedicated family courts. These family courts have jurisdiction over cases of several types: divorce, child custody, child support, alimony, adoption, and property settlement, to name a few. States with dedicated family courts include Delaware, New York, Rhode Island, South Carolina, Vermont, and West Virginia.[52] Some are independent from general jurisdiction courts; others are separate divisions of general jurisdiction trial courts.

General Jurisdiction Courts The majority of states have opted to process juvenile cases in their general jurisdiction courts.[53] For example, in California, there are three types of juvenile cases adjudicated in superior court: delinquency cases, status offense cases, and dependency cases.[54] In the District of Columbia, juvenile cases are adjudicated in the family court division of the superior court, but note that family court is a *division* rather than a dedicated court. In light of the variability from one state to the next—and continual changes to the jurisdiction of juvenile courts—readers are advised to read up on their own state's legal arrangement.[55]

To further complicate matters, states continue to pass laws and enact new courts that adjudicate juvenile cases. These are stand-alone courts at times, are sometimes tied to family courts, and are often connected to general jurisdiction courts. To muddy the waters even further, some states have juvenile courts dedicated to specific types of juvenile offenses, such as drug abuse and cyberbullying. For more information on specialized courts, see Chapter 6.

Process

The juvenile court process proceeds through four main steps: intake, detention, judicial decision, and judicial disposition. To see how a hypothetical 1,000 cases are disposed of from one of these steps to the next, see Figure 5–3.

Some states have adopted their own procedures that differ from what we present here, so it is best to consider our description of the juvenile court process as a generic one. As the OJJDP has remarked,

> From state to state, case processing of juvenile law violators varies. Even within states, case processing may vary from community to community, reflecting local practice and tradition. Any description of juvenile justice processing in the U.S. must, therefore, be general, outlining a common series of decision points.[56]

COURTS IN THE NEWS

Cyberbullying

While in the past bullies were found in the school yard, they can now use the Internet to harass their victims through e-mails or instant messages. Obscene, insulting, and slanderous messages can be posted to social media sites or sent directly to the victim via cell phones; bullying has now morphed from the physical to the virtual. While it is difficult to get an accurate count of the number of teens who have experienced cyberbullying, a recent study by Justin Patchin and Sameer Hinduja found that more than 20 percent of the youth they surveyed reported being the target of cyberbullying. Adolescent girls are significantly more likely to have experienced cyberbullying in their lifetimes (26 percent versus 16 percent) than boys. Girls are also more likely to report cyberbullying others during their lifetime (21 percent versus 18 percent). The type of cyberbullying tends to differ by gender; girls are more likely to spread rumors, while boys are more likely to post hurtful pictures. There have been a number of cases in which victims of cyberbullying have committed suicide as a result of prolonged abuse, most notoriously Phoebe Prince in Massachusetts and Jessica Laney, a 16-year-old Florida girl who took her own life in 2012 after being tormented on the Internet.

The first prosecution in American history of a cyberbullying case has led to the conviction of a Missouri woman on three of seven charges brought by federal prosecutors. Lori Drew, a 49-year-old mother of three, was convicted of three relatively minor misdemeanor charges relating to unauthorized computer access. She was acquitted of three additional felony charges of deliberately harassing a neighbor girl who ultimately committed suicide. The jury was unable to reach a decision on an additional conspiracy charge.

Prosecutors had contended that Ms. Drew created the fake identity of a 16-year-old boy and used it to establish an online relationship with the 13-year-old girl, Megan Meier, and then led the relationship into abuse by mercilessly teasing and humiliating the girl until she was driven to suicide. Included in Ms. Drew's communications with Ms. Meier was a statement by Ms. Drew, in her role as the fictitious "Josh Evans," that "the world would be a better place" without Ms. Meier in it. Prior to its use in the cyberbullying case, the federal computer crime statute had been used only in computer hacking cases.

The case has put a spotlight on the terms of service that users must agree to in order to use a cybersite's services.

AP Photo/Nick Ut

Lori Drew leaves court during a break in her cyberbullying trial. Her case represents the evolving challenges faced by the courts in the cyber age.

Associate law professor Greg Lastowka of Rutgers School of Law contends that the terms are typically "written to protect the companies you are dealing with." Ms. Drew was ultimately convicted under the 1986 Computer Fraud and Abuse Act of violating the MySpace terms and conditions agreement rather than more serious felony charges, including a conspiracy count.

In a thought-provoking article, one *New York Times* journalist asked this chilling question: "Is lying about one's identity on the Internet now a crime?" At least one other journalist has questioned whether the verdict in this case should be overturned.

It is a reality that laws must evolve to cope with changing technology, but this case raises significant questions. Ms. Drew was convicted of misrepresenting herself online (the conviction was later vacated). What's next? Will an unattractive dweeb be able to sue the beautiful redhead he approached in a bar on Saturday night because she gave him a fake phone number? Imagine the number of such "law violations" that occur in an ordinary bar on an ordinary Saturday night. In the final analysis, it seems that the federal prosecutors fell back on the Computer Fraud and Abuse Act because they could not find a law that fit Ms. Drew's deplorable actions.

Bullying has become a serious problem in society today, and it is a problem on which much media attention is focused. This case is rather unusual, however, in that it does not involve peer-to-peer bullying, as might occur on a school playground between two children. It involves, instead, repeated cyberbullying of a teenager by another girl's mother. The interaction between the parties did not occur face-to-face but occurred online through the medium of the Internet. ■

DISCUSSION QUESTIONS

1. Is cyberspace sufficiently like other aspects of our everyday social world that it should be subject to the criminal laws of wider society?

2. What role should the criminal courts play in the regulation of cyberspace?

(continued)

3. Is new legislation necessary to ensure the safety of today's cyberspace participants? If so, what kinds of new laws are needed?

Sources: Justin Patchin, "How Many Teens Are Actually Involved in Cyberbullying?," April 4, 2012, available at http://cyberbullying.us/blog/how-many-teens-are-actually-involved-in-cyberbullying.html (accessed May 2013); Justin Patchin and Sameer Hinduja, Cyberbullying Research Center, available at http://cyberbullying.us/research.php (accessed May 2013); Guy Adams, "Woman Found Guilty in 'Cyber-Bully' Case," *The Independent*, available at http://www.independent.co.uk/news/world/americas/woman-found-guilty-in-cyberbully-case-1036877.html (accessed May 2013);

William M. Welch, "Mom Indicted in 'Cyber-Bullying' Case," *USA Today*, available at http://www.usatoday.com/news/nation/2008-05-15-myspace-suicide_N.htm (accessed May 2013); Tim Baker, "Lori Drew Cyberbullying Case Raises Profile of 'Terms of Service' Agreements," *Technology*, available at http://www.physorg.com/news147273487.html (accessed May 2013); Brian Stelter, "Guilty Verdict in Cyberbullying Case Provokes Many Questions over Online Identity," *New York Times*, available at http://www.nytimes.com/2008/11/28/us/28internet.html (accessed May 2013); Barbara Sowell, "Should the Lori Drew Cyberbullying Decision Be Overturned?," *Digital Journal*, available at http://www.digitaljournal.com/article/262795 (accessed May 2013).

FIGURE 5–3

Juvenile Court Processing for a Typical 1,000 Delinquency Cases

Note: Cases are categorized by their most severe or restrictive sanction. Detail may not add to totals because of rounding.

Source: Charles Puzzanchera, Benjamin Adams, and Sarah Hockenberry, Juvenile Court Statistics 2010 (Washington, DC: Office of Juvenile Justice and Delinquency Prevention, National Center for Juvenile Justice, 2013), p. 53.

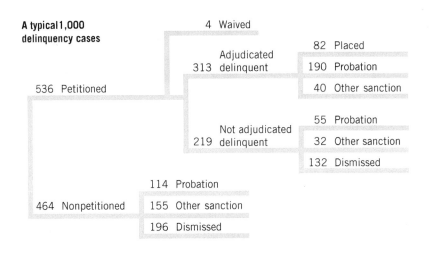

intake

The first step in decision making regarding a juvenile whose behavior or alleged behavior is in violation of the law or could otherwise cause a juvenile court to assume jurisdiction.

petition

"[A] written request made to a court asking for the exercise of its judicial powers or asking for permission to perform some act where the authorization of a court is required."[ix]

Intake At **intake**, a decision is made whether a case should enter the juvenile justice system or be terminated without further action. While some 80 percent of juvenile cases are referred to the juvenile justice system by police officers,[57] a number are also referred by parents, victims, school officials, and probation officers. An example of the latter occurs in California, where probation officers serve as the main gateway to the juvenile justice system. Even if juveniles are arrested by police officers, the officers first approach probation officers, who then decide whether to refer the case to an intake department, usually housed in the prosecutor's office.

Assuming that a case is referred to the intake department, one of two decisions will result. The case will be either petitioned or nonpetitioned. A **petition** is a "written request made to a court asking for the exercise of its judicial powers, or asking for permission to perform some act where the authorization of a court is required."[58] It is the juvenile equivalent of a prosecutor's information or a grand jury's indictment. A case is nonpetitioned if it is handled informally at the intake phase; for example, a prosecutor may feel that the evidence is not sufficient and dismiss the case. There are also other nonpetitioned dispositions:

- *Placement.* Placement involves cases in which youth are placed in a residential facility for delinquents or status offenders or cases in which youth are otherwise removed from their homes and placed elsewhere.

- *Probation.* Cases in which youth are placed on informal/voluntary supervision are called probation.

- *Other types.* Additional options include fines, restitution, community service, and referrals outside the court for services (with minimal or no further court involvement anticipated).[59]

Nearly half of all juvenile cases are handled informally.[60] In contrast, petitioned cases are those that appear on the appropriate court's calendar in response to the filing of a petition. Depending on state law, the prosecutor may file the petition in juvenile or adult court; if the latter option is pursued, a separate judicial hearing may be necessary. The decision whether to waive a juvenile case to adult court is a complex one and varies from state to state, so we devote considerable attention to it later in this chapter.

Detention While the intake process plays out, the juvenile may be held in a secure detention facility. This usually occurs when a juvenile is arrested for a fairly serious offense and is regarded as sufficiently dangerous as to not warrant his or her immediate return to the community. In all states, a hearing must be held within 24 hours of such detentions in order to prevent arbitrary and unwarranted confinement. At the detention hearing, a judge reviews the cases and decides whether continued detention is necessary. Approximately 20 percent of juvenile cases result in detention of the juvenile in the early phases of the process.[61]

Web Extra
5–8 National Center for Juvenile Justice's State Juvenile Justice Profiles

Judicial Decision If a juvenile case is petitioned, the court will either decide to adjudicate the youth or waive the youth's case to adult court. Assuming that the case is not waived to adult court, where the juvenile will essentially be tried as an adult offender, an **adjudicatory hearing**, which is akin to an adult trial but is generally less open and adversarial, is held. All manner of cases result in adjudicatory hearings, as Table 5–1 makes clear.

adjudicatory hearing
The fact-finding process by which the juvenile court determines whether there is sufficient evidence to sustain the allegations in a petition.

TABLE 5–1 Characteristics of Cases Handled by Juvenile Courts

Most Serious Offense	Number of Cases	Younger than 16	Female	White
Total delinquency	**1,368,200**	**52**	**28**	**64**
Total person	**346,800**	**59**	**31**	**57**
Violent Crime Index	71,000	53	19	45
Criminal homicide	1,000	34	13	55
Forcible rape	3,900	57	3	65
Robbery	26,300	48	10	30
Aggravated assault	39,900	56	26	52
Simple assault	237,100	61	36	60
Other violent sex offenses	12,700	69	7	66
Other person offenses	26,000	57	29	67
Total property	**502,400**	**53**	**29**	**66**
Property Crime Index	355,500	52	34	64
Burglary	90,100	52	10	63
Larceny-theft	243,800	52	45	64
Motor vehicle theft	16,100	47	21	57
Arson	5,500	76	14	73
Vandalism	79,400	61	15	77
Trespassing	42,500	53	19	61
Stolen property offenses	14,000	45	15	57
Other property offenses	11,100	45	29	66
Drug law violations	**164,100**	**41**	**18**	**76**
Public order offenses	**354,800**	**49**	**28**	**63**
Obstruction of justice	166,200	41	26	63
Disorderly conduct	101,200	62	35	54
Weapons offenses	29,700	58	12	62
Liquor law violations	16,400	34	32	89
Nonviolent sex offenses	11,200	65	21	74
Other public order offenses	30,000	48	25	74

Percentage of Total Juvenile Court Cases, 2009

Note: Detail may not add to totals because of rounding.
Source: Charles Puzzanchera, Benjamin Adams, and Sarah Hockenberry, *Juvenile Court Statistics 2010* (Washington, DC: Office of Juvenile Justice and Delinquency Prevention, National Center for Juvenile Justice, 2013), p. 9.

At an adjudicatory hearing, the court hears both evidence and testimony. Because there are no juries in the juvenile justice system, the judge decides whether the juvenile should be adjudicated. If the hearing results in a failure to adjudicate, which is akin to an acquittal in an adult case, the petition may be dismissed and the case closed. Alternatively, if the case is not adjudicated, it could be continued in contemplation of dismissal. If this occurs, the juvenile may be ordered to fulfill some obligation prior to dismissal of the charges, which could include paying restitution or attending drug counseling. The case would not be complete until the juvenile completed the obligation.

Cases that result in adjudication (akin to a finding of guilty in adult court) are then sent forward to a disposition hearing. In the interim, probation staff, a social service worker, or other authorized personnel usually prepare a **disposition plan**, a document that includes recommendations concerning the juvenile's education, training, counseling, and support services needs. The state of Vermont describes the use of the disposition report in this way:

> The Plan focuses on the family and/or child, and what they need to do to remedy the problems that brought them to court. All parties, including the court, should receive a copy of the Plan before the hearing. At the hearing, everyone gives their opinion about the report. The judge will either accept or reject the Plan in the Disposition Report and will make a decision about custody of the child at this time.[62]

Note that the disposition report is less of a sentencing recommendation than it is a services recommendation. The intent of the juvenile justice process is to ensure that the needs of delinquent juveniles are met such that they will be dissuaded from breaking the law in the future. This is in contrast to the adult approach, which focuses more on the immediate ends of punishment rather than long-term rehabilitation.

Judicial Disposition The juvenile justice system has at its core a set of **graduated sanctions**, meaning that low-level offenses committed by first-time offenders are generally treated leniently with probation or some other form of community treatment.

If a juvenile is adjudicated delinquent, an appropriate treatment program will be based on his or her "needs and deeds" and may include paying a fine, paying restitution, participating in community service, participating in drug treatment, or serving a term on probation.

Figure 5–4 shows trends in juvenile adjudications over the years by offense type. The adjudications reported in Figure 5–4 were for out-of-home placement, including detention. Note how the lines in the figure peaked in the mid-1990s and either declined or leveled off thereafter.

The following "Courts in the News" feature illustrates the sanctioning process in a well-known juvenile court case.

disposition plan
A document that includes recommendations concerning the juvenile's education, training, counseling, and support services needs.

Library Extra
5–2 Juvenile Justice in California: Facts and Issues

Web Extra
5–9 American Bar Association's Juvenile Justice Committee

graduated sanctions
Sanctions imposed by the juvenile justice system such that first-time offenders who commit relatively minor offenses are treated leniently (with probation or some other form of community treatment). This system may also result in harsher sanctions for those who commit ensuing or repeat offenses or for offenders who commit severe offenses.

Media
Review: Transfer to Adult Court

FIGURE 5–4

Cases Adjudicated Delinquent, Resulting in Out-of-Home Placement

Source: Charles Puzzanchera, Benjamin Adams, and Sarah Hockenberry, *Juvenile Court Statistics 2010* (Washington, DC: Office of Juvenile Justice and Delinquency Prevention, National Center for Juvenile Justice, 2013), p. 46.

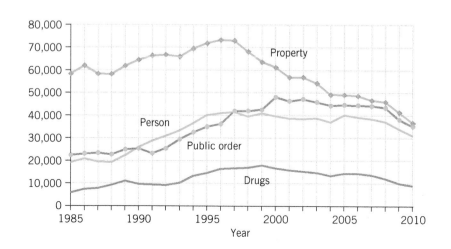

COURTS IN THE NEWS

The Steubenville Rape Case

REUTERS/Keith Srakocic/Pool

Trent Mays, and Ma'lik Richmond, shown here, were found guilty of rape in the notorious Steubenville sexual assault case.

In 2012, two members of a champion football team, Trent Mays, 17, and Ma'lik Richmond, 16, were found to be delinquent because they raped a 16-year-old girl after a night of partying and drinking. Both Mays and Richmond claimed that the sexual acts were consensual. As the facts unfolded, there was no doubt that the girl was "substantially impaired." She did remember drinking at the first big party of the night and then holding Mays's hand as she left with him, Richmond, and others. The next thing she remembers, she told the court, is waking up in the morning naked on a couch in an unfamiliar house. She covered herself with a blanket while she looked for her clothes. She testified that she could not find her underwear, earrings, or cell phone. The defense claimed that the sex was consensual and employed expert witnesses who testified that even when drunk people can engage in consensual acts, such as having sex. On March 17, 2013, Judge Thomas Lipps found Mays and Richmond, who were tried as juveniles, and were found guilty of rape.

Although the young victim had no memory of what happened and therefore could not testify clearly about what happened, prosecutors used this fact to prove that she was incapacitated and incapable of consenting to sex. How did they prove their case? By showing videos posted on the Internet of the young woman being mocked by kids who were at the party and e-mails from people who knew what was going on but did nothing to stop the attack. The prosecution was also aided by the investigations of blogger Alexandra Goddard, who sent captured screen shots and other evidence to the police, including one showing two boys carrying the naked victim. Text messages, pictures, and videos found on the Internet indicated that the girl was barely conscious much of the time the attacks occurred. Texts also showed that Mays had attempted to cover up his actions after police became aware of the attack.

But that was not all: Two teenage girls from Steubenville, Ohio, were arrested after the verdict and charged with sending online threats to the 16-year-old rape victim. One was charged with a misdemeanor count of aggravated menacing for threatening the victim's life; the younger girl was charged with a misdemeanor count of menacing for threatening bodily harm. Prosecutors said that they would convene a grand jury to determine if further charges should be filed against witnesses who failed to report the rape and against adults who might have been aware of the rape but covered it up. Of particular interest is what Steubenville High School football coach Reno Saccoccia and other school officials knew about the crime. By law, they are required to report a suspected crime involving children in their care. Text messages from Mays's phone were offered as evidence and indicated that he had told the coach about the encounters and been assured that the coach would protect him from prosecution. "I got Reno. He took care of it and sh—— ain't gonna happen, even if they did take it to court," Mays said.

The Steubenville case shows that courts are now taking a stand against sexual assaults and are willing to hand out harsh sentences in order to protect victims. ■

DISCUSSION QUESTIONS

1. Should these youths have been tried as adults and been sent to an adult prison? Would that have served justice better?

2. Is covering up this crime equally serious as its commission? Would you recommend a prison sentence for any school official who knew about the crime?

Sources: Tina Susman, "Teens Arrested for Twitter Threats against Steubenville Rape Victim," *Los Angeles Times*, March 19, 2013, http://www.latimes.com/news/nation/nationnow/la-na-nn-steubenville-rape-case-twitter-threats-20130319,0,3670608.story (accessed May 30, 2013); *Plain Dealer* staff, "Steubenville Rape Case: Defense Expert Says Teen Girl Could Have Made Decisions Even after Heavy Drinking," *Cleveland Plain Dealer*, March 16, 2013, http://www.cleveland.com/steubenville-rape-case/index.ssf/2013/03/steubenville_rape_case_defense.html (accessed May 30, 2013); Diana Reese, "Football Wins? Steubenville Coach's Contract Extended despite Allegations in Rape Case," *Washington Post*, April 23, 2013, http://www.washingtonpost.com/blogs/she-the-people/wp/2013/04/23/football-wins-steubenville-coachs-contract-extended-despite-allegations-in-rape-case (accessed May 30, 2013).

Learning Objective 3
Explain the different ways that transfers to adult court take place and the issues surrounding transfers.

Media
Video: Trying Juveniles as Adults

legislative exclusion
A type of juvenile waiver whereby legislative action prohibits trying a juvenile as a juvenile for commission of a specific type of crime[x]; also called *statutory exclusion*.

juvenile waiver
A juvenile judicial action that waives jurisdiction over a juvenile charged with committing a particularly harsh crime to adult court.

discretionary waiver
A type of juvenile waiver that "give[s] juvenile court judges discretion to waive jurisdiction in individual cases involving minors, so as to allow prosecution in adult criminal courts."[xi]

presumptive waiver
A type of juvenile waiver that involves statutory designation of a category of cases in which waiver to criminal court is presumed to be appropriate but that may be rebutted by the defense.[xii]

mandatory waiver
A type of juvenile waiver that requires a case to meet certain age, offense, or other criteria to be waived to adult court. A mandatory waiver differs from legislative exclusion because the case begins in a juvenile court (which is not the case with statutory exclusion).

reverse waiver
A legislative mandate that certain cases initiated in an adult court be sent to a juvenile court for an adjudicatory hearing.[xiii]

TREATMENT OF JUVENILES AS ADULTS

Juvenile courts have always had mechanisms in place for transferring, or waiving, juveniles to adult court. Whether a juvenile can be transferred to adult court varies by state. There are three main mechanisms for treating juveniles as adults: legislative exclusion, waivers, and concurrent jurisdiction. See Figure 5–5 for an overview.

Legislative Exclusion

Legislative exclusion (also called statutory exclusion) refers to the fact that a statute excludes, or bars, a juvenile from being tried as a juvenile. In other words, legislative exclusion requires that certain juveniles be treated as adults; for example, Mississippi excludes all felonies committed by 17-year-olds,[63] whereas Arizona excludes any felony committed by a juvenile as young as 15 years old.[64]

Waivers

The term **juvenile waiver** refers to trying juveniles as adults, or waiving them to adult court. Waivers have been around for some time, and they have been used on occasion when a juvenile commits a particularly harsh crime and there is a desire to charge him or her in the adult justice system. Recent changes have made it easier to try juveniles as adult offenders, a significant departure from the original intent of having a separate juvenile justice system. There are three main types of waivers used with juveniles:

1. *Discretionary waiver.* A **discretionary waiver**, as defined by several states, "gives juvenile court judges discretion to waive jurisdiction in individual cases involving minors, so as to allow prosecution in adult criminal courts. Terminology varies from State to State—some call the process a 'certification,' 'bind-over,' or 'remand' for criminal prosecution, for example, or a 'transfer' or 'decline' rather than a waiver proceeding—but all transfer mechanisms in this category have the effect of authorizing but not requiring juvenile courts to designate appropriate cases for adult prosecution."[65]

2. *Presumptive waiver.* Several state statutes designate a category of cases called **presumptive waiver**, in which waiver to criminal court is presumed to be appropriate. "In such cases, the juvenile rather than the State bears the burden of proof in the waiver hearing; if a juvenile meeting age, offense, or other statutory criteria triggering the presumption fails to make an adequate argument against transfer, the juvenile court must send the case to criminal court."[66]

3. *Mandatory waiver.* Several states use a **mandatory waiver** "in cases that meet certain age, offense, or other criteria. In these States, proceedings against the juvenile are initiated in juvenile court. However, the juvenile court has no role other than to confirm that the statutory requirements for mandatory waiver are met. Once it has done so, the juvenile court must send the case to a court of criminal jurisdiction."[67]

In a twist on these approaches to waiver, some states have **reverse waiver**, which requires that certain cases initiated in adult court be sent to the juvenile court for an adjudicatory hearing.[68] In yet another twist, some state waiver laws have "once an adult, always an adult" provisions, requiring that once a juvenile is waived to adult court, all other offenses he or she commits are to be tried in adult court.[69]

FIGURE 5–5

State Legal Arrangements Governing Treatment of Juveniles as Adults

Most states have multiple ways to impose adult sanctions on offenders of juvenile age

State	Judicial waiver			Prosecutorial discretion	Statutory exclusion	Reverse waiver	Once an adult always an adult	Blended sentencing	
	Discretionary	Presumptive	Mandatory					Juvenile	Criminal
Number of states	45	15	15	15	29	24	34	14	18
Alabama	■				■		■		
Alaska	■	■			■			■	
Arizona	■			■	■	■	■		
Arkansas	■			■		■		■	■
California	■	■		■	■	■	■	■	■
Colorado	■	■		■		■		■	■
Connecticut			■			■		■	
Delaware	■		■		■	■	■		
Dist. Of Columbia	■	■		■					
Florida	■			■	■		■		■
Georgia	■		■	■	■	■			
Hawaii	■						■		
Idaho	■				■				■
Illinois	■	■	■		■		■	■	■
Indiana	■		■		■		■		
Iowa	■				■	■	■		■
Kansas	■	■			■		■	■	
Kentucky	■		■			■			■
Louisiana	■								
Maine	■	■					■		
Maryland	■				■	■			
Massachusetts	■			■	■		■	■	■
Michigan	■			■	■		■	■	■
Minnesota	■	■			■		■		
Mississippi	■				■		■		
Missouri	■						■		■
Montana				■	■	■		■	
Nebraska				■					■
Nevada	■	■			■	■	■		
New Hampshire	■	■					■		
New Jersey	■	■	■						
New Mexico					■			■	■
New York					■	■			
North Carolina	■		■				■		
North Dakota	■	■					■		
Ohio	■		■				■	■	
Oklahoma	■			■	■	■	■		■
Oregon	■				■	■	■		
Pennsylvania	■	■			■	■	■		
Rhode Island	■	■	■				■	■	
South Carolina	■		■		■				
South Dakota	■				■	■	■		
Tennessee	■					■	■		
Texas	■						■	■	
Utah	■	■			■		■		
Vermont	■			■	■	■			■
Virginia	■		■	■	■	■	■		■
Washington	■				■				
West Virginia	■		■						■
Wisconsin	■				■	■	■		■
Wyoming	■			■		■			

Note: Table information is as of the end of the 2009 legislative session.

Source: P. Griffin, S. Addie, B. Adams, and K. Firestine, *Trying Juveniles as Adults: An Analysis of State Transfer Laws and Reporting* (Washington, DC: Office of Juvenile Justice and Delinquency Prevention, 2011).

Concurrent Jurisdiction

concurrent jurisdiction
The legislative authority to try juvenile cases in either juvenile or adult court, with the prosecutor deciding where the case should be tried.

Concurrent jurisdiction means that certain cases can be tried in both juvenile and adult court, and the prosecutor makes a decision as to where the case should be tried. Concurrent jurisdiction sometimes occurs outside of the juvenile justice context as well. For example, if both a federal and a state court could try the same offense, it is said that each has concurrent jurisdiction.

In addition to the jurisdiction issue, the question of a connection between juvenile violence and use of violent video games has been raised in many juvenile court cases. See the "Courts in the News" feature for more details.

Learning Objective 4
Summarize recent trends and developments in the juvenile justice system.

Web Extra
5–10 National Center for Juvenile Justice (NCJJ)

Library Extra
5–3 Models for Change in Juvenile Justice

CHANGING LANDSCAPE OF JUVENILE JUSTICE

Juvenile justice continues to change in ways that make it look more like the adult criminal justice system. Concern over juvenile violence, gang activity, school shootings, and the like has convinced policy makers that the juvenile justice system coddles dangerous young offenders; as a result, there has been a movement to toughen juvenile justice standards and to shift the juvenile court away from its traditional *parens patriae* philosophy as well as an increase in sanctions for juveniles, greater offender accountability, and restrictions in terms of the privacy that juveniles have historically enjoyed.

Increased Sanctions

offense-based sentencing
The practice of sentencing a juvenile based on the severity of his or her crime rather than following the traditional practice of sentencing the juvenile based on his or her need for treatment and rehabilitation.

blended sentence
A form of offense-based sentencing that requires the juvenile to serve both a term of probation and time in an adult correctional facility.[xiv]

extended jurisdiction
The legislative authority for juvenile court judges to commit a juvenile to a correctional facility beyond the age of 18.[xv]

Juvenile sentences have also changed over time and now are more punitive than ever before. For example, many states have allowed juvenile court judges to engage in **offense-based sentencing**, where the sentence reflects the seriousness of the offense. This is in contrast to the traditional practice of sentencing juveniles based not on the offense they committed but on their need for treatment and rehabilitation. Remember, the juvenile justice system was created for the purpose of "correcting" the behavior of wayward youth, not indiscriminately punishing them.

Offense-based sentencing can include the use of **blended sentences**, which require juveniles not only to serve a term of probation but also to spend time in an adult correctional facility.[70] Sentencing guidelines, providing fixed sentences based on offense seriousness and the offender's prior record, are also used some of the time. Further, some states permit **extended jurisdiction**, allowing juvenile court judges to commit a juvenile to a correctional facility beyond the age of 18.[71] With extended jurisdiction, a juvenile could be sentenced to both a juvenile and an adult sentence. The adult sentence may then be "stayed" while the juvenile serves the juvenile sentence, but if he or she violates the terms of the juvenile sentence, the adult sentence will then start. The court's extended jurisdiction would end when the juvenile finishes serving the adult term, perhaps when he or she is well beyond the age of 18 years.

More Accountability

In 2009, the most recent year for which data are available at this writing, about 19 percent of juvenile cases were dismissed at intake.[72] Another 27 percent were handled informally. In more than half of the cases, however, authorities filed a petition and the case was handled formally. These numbers may not in themselves suggest that juveniles are being held more accountable than ever for their actions, but consider adjudication and disposition. In 2009, juveniles were adjudicated delinquent in 59 percent of the petitioned cases, a nearly 45 percent increase from 1985. These numbers signal a movement in the direction of increased accountability for juvenile offenders. Add to this continued use of the juvenile waiver, and it is clear that juvenile crime is being taken seriously.

Also offering evidence of a desire to increase juvenile accountability are changes to state laws affecting how juvenile cases are screened. In 1977, Washington State ceased to rely on probation officers to screen juvenile cases, leaving filing decisions totally in the hands of prosecutors. According to the law, either sufficiently strong cases must be adjudicated in court or the juvenile should be diverted into any number of distinct treatment/rehabilitation programs. Diversion is a slightly less formal approach to handling juvenile crime, but youth still typically sign a contract and agree to abide by program terms; otherwise, they have to go before a judge in a formal hearing. Washington State's decision to elevate the role of prosecutors in juvenile cases signals not only a concern with accountability for young offenders but also a blurring of the lines between the adult and juvenile justice systems.

Less Privacy

Records of juvenile court proceedings have historically been off limits, and offenders' names, records, and personal information were also sealed from prying eyes. But some states have begun to relax their restrictions on access to juvenile records. For example, several states have enacted legislation to give the public and/or media access to the names and addresses of juveniles adjudicated for specific offenses (see Figure 5–6 for an overview). Court records

Library Extra
5–4 Recommendations for Juvenile Justice Reform

FIGURE 5–6

Media Access to Juvenile Identities by State

Source: H. N. Snyder and M. Sickmund, *Juvenile Offenders and Victims: 2006 National Report* (Washington, DC: U.S. Department of Justice, Office of Justice Programs, Office of Juvenile Justice and Delinquency Prevention, 2006), chap. 4, p. 109. Copyright © 2006 National Center for Juvenile Justice. Reprinted by permission.

Media access to identity of juvenile offender in delinquency case

- Access (15 states)
- Access in certain cases (30 states)
- Access with permission (4 states)
- No access (2 states)

■ **Access:** In 14 of the 15 jurisdictions, media can obtain access to the juvenile offender's identity by attending delinquency hearings, which are open to the public. In the District of Columbia, the statute allows the media to attend hearings (although hearings are not public) but prohibits the media from revealing the juvenile's identity.

■ **Access in certain cases:** In 30 states, media can access the juvenile offender's identity for certain cases. Media access is tied to public access to hearings or records, which statutes limit by case characteristics such as the juvenile's age, offense, criminal history, or whether the case is transferred to criminal court.

■ **Access with permission:** In 4 states, media access to delinquency hearings or records (and thus to juvenile offender identities) can only occur if the court gives permission or the media discover the information independently. In these states, statutes require that the court decide the issue on a case-by-case basis.

☐ **No access:** In 2 states, statutes prohibit release of the names of all juvenile offenders.

In 3 states (Maryland, New Jersey, and Wisconsin), under certain circumstances, the media may be prohibited from revealing the juvenile's identity.

FIGURE 5–7

Delinquency Proceedings
and Openness by State

Source: H. N. Snyder and
M. Sickmund, *Juvenile Offenders
and Victims: 2006 National Report*
(Washington, DC: U.S. Depart-
ment of Justice, Office of Justice
Programs, Office of Juvenile Justice
and Delinquency Prevention, 2006),
chap. 4, p. 108. Copyright © 2006
National Center for Juvenile Justice.
Reprinted by permission.

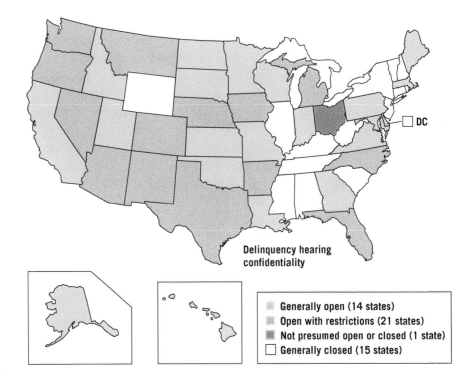

Delinquency hearing
confidentiality

- Generally open (14 states)
- Open with restrictions (21 states)
- Not presumed open or closed (1 state)
- Generally closed (15 states)

are now disclosed more readily, and they can be used in a number of ways, including in central record repositories, data systems, and registries of sex offenders. Finally, some states have increased the period of time before juvenile records can be expunged (i.e., cleared).

States have also moved toward openness in juvenile court proceedings. The legislation that created the first juvenile court in Illinois provided that its proceedings should be open for anyone to see if they so chose, but over time juvenile courts more or less closed their doors to the public.[73] More recently, however, several states have decided that juvenile proceedings should once again be open to the public:

> As juvenile courts became more formalized and concerns about rising juvenile crime increased, the pendulum began to swing back toward more openness. By 1988, statutes in 15 states permitted the public to attend certain delinquency hearings.[74]

Presently, the majority of states provide at least some measure of openness. The norm, however, is for states to also place at least some limitations on openness; for example, a state may allow the public to observe a juvenile proceeding if the juvenile in question was 16 years old at the time of the crime but may not permit such openness for younger offenders. For an overview of these variations by state, see Figure 5–7.

CHAPTER 5 > SUMMARY

I. OUTLINE THE HISTORY AND DEVELOPMENT OF JUVENILE COURTS

- A juvenile is a young person who has not yet attained the age at which he or she is treated as an adult for purposes of the criminal law.
- The 1601 Poor Law helped provide work or apprenticeships for orphaned children and children whose parents could not support them.
- Chancery courts often heard cases involving minor children.

- *Parens patriae*, a guiding principle of the English chancery courts, supported state involvement in the affairs of juveniles.

- The child savers and the refuge movement exerted considerable influence on juvenile justice.

- The Illinois Juvenile Court Act of 1899 established the first juvenile court. Juvenile courts are generally less adversarial than adult courts.

- Legal protections for juveniles tend to be somewhat relaxed (even today) relative to those extended to adults. Federal legislation, including most notably the JJDPA, has also influenced the development of juvenile justice in general and juvenile courts in particular.

- The most important Supreme Court decisions governing the treatment of juveniles include the following: *Kent* v. *United States* (1966), *In re Gault* (1967), *In re Winship* (1970), *McKeiver* v. *Pennsylvania* (1971), *Breed* v. *Jones* (1975), *Oklahoma Publishing Company* v. *District Court in and for Oklahoma City* (1977), *Eddings* v. *Oklahoma* (1982), *Schall* v. *Martin* (1984), *Thompson* v. *Oklahoma* (1988), *Stanford* v. *Kentucky* (1989), and *Roper* v. *Simmons* (2005).

2. EXPLAIN THE PURPOSE, ORGANIZATION, AND PROCESS OF JUVENILE COURTS

- States' juvenile courts vary in their purposes. Some emphasize accountability, others emphasize restorative justice, and still others emphasize other goals.

- There are three types of juvenile courts: stand-alone juvenile courts, juvenile courts that are part of family court, and juvenile courts that are part of general jurisdiction courts.

- Juvenile courts' priorities differ depending on how they are organized.

- The juvenile court process proceeds through four steps: intake, detention, judicial decision, and judicial disposition. Along the way, there are numerous opportunities for informal treatment. A police officer may elect not to arrest, or a prosecutor may elect not to petition the court for an adjudicatory hearing. Even if a juvenile is not adjudicated delinquent, the judge may impose some condition. Most juveniles are placed on probation.

3. EXPLAIN THE DIFFERENT WAYS THAT TRANSFERS TO ADULT COURT TAKE PLACE AND THE ISSUES SURROUNDING TRANSFERS

- Juveniles can be treated as adults through legislative exclusion, waivers, and concurrent jurisdiction.

- Juvenile waivers are discretionary, presumptive, or mandatory.

4. SUMMARIZE RECENT TRENDS AND DEVELOPMENTS IN THE JUVENILE JUSTICE SYSTEM

- Juvenile justice is changing in ways that make it look more like the adult system of criminal justice.

- Recent reforms in juvenile justice include increased sanctioning, more accountability, and less privacy.

KEY TERMS

adjudicatory hearing, 121
blended sentence, 126
chancery courts, 106
child savers, 107
concurrent jurisdiction, 126
discretionary waiver, 124
disposition plan, 122
extended jurisdiction, 126
graduated sanctions, 122
intake, 120

juvenile, 105
Juvenile Delinquency
    Prevention and Control
    Act, 113
Juvenile Justice and
    Delinquency Prevention
    Act, 113
juvenile waiver, 124
legislative exclusion, 124
mandatory waiver, 124

New York House of
    Refuge, 107
offense-based
    sentencing, 126
parens patriae, 106
petition, 120
poor law, 106
presumptive waiver, 124
reverse waiver, 124
status offense, 106

REVIEW QUESTIONS

1. What are the stages in the historical development of the juvenile justice system and of separate treatment for juveniles? What is the philosophy underlying today's juvenile courts?

2. What legal protections are available today to children at both the federal and state levels?

3. What U.S. Supreme Court decisions have been especially influential in the area of juvenile courts? What impact have they had?

4. What are the priorities of today's juvenile courts?

5. How are today's juvenile courts organized?

6. What steps are involved in today's juvenile court process?

7. What are the implications of treating juveniles as adults within the justice system?

8. What do you think juvenile courts will be like in 20 or 30 years? Will they become more like adult courts, or will they retain significant differences?

WHAT WILL YOU DO?

You are a 15-year-old whose best friend, Mallory, was recently taken into custody by juvenile officers from your town's police department. You are concerned for Mallory's future and don't believe that she's done anything wrong. At the time she was apprehended, Mallory had been hanging out with some young people who (she later learned) are gang members. Two of the boys in the group had apparently been carrying concealed handguns, and some others were said to have been in possession of marijuana.

Mallory has always had her sights set high and is not like the other young people with whom she was hanging. She's a good student and a junior varsity cheerleader, and she has plans to go on to college and would like to eventually work in the paralegal area. You're afraid that being in trouble with the law might somehow dash her hopes for the future.

You're not exactly sure why the police took Mallory into custody. You have heard that she was not close to the people who had drugs or were carrying guns, and you know that Mallory does not do drugs. You've also heard some talk that the police may have used an antigang ordinance recently enacted by the city council in order to take Mallory into custody.

Mallory was just released into the custody of her parents; however, she is scheduled to make an appearance in juvenile court in the next day or two.

You have talked to Mallory on the phone and learned that she has no idea what to expect when she goes to court. Moreover, her parents—who are very upset—have been berating her and telling her that she could be found guilty as a "criminal" and sentenced to time in prison.

You realize that there is a lot of confusion at Mallory's household, and you would like to set her mind and that of her parents at rest. As a criminal justice student, you know something about the differences between juvenile and adult courts, but at the same time, you recognize that you are not an attorney and that you cannot give legal advice. Still, you want to do your best to explain the purpose behind juvenile court and to give Mallory and her parents an idea of what is likely to happen when she goes to court.

When you visit Mallory and her parents, what will you tell them about the differences between adult and juvenile court? Should she worry about being sent away? And if not, what do you think will happen to her in court? If you were the juvenile court judge, how would you handle her case?

NOTES

i. U.S. Department of Justice, *Dictionary of Criminal Justice Data Terminology*, p. 118.

ii. 18 U.S.C., Section 5031.

iii. For more details, see the "Shifting Conceptions of Age" section later in this chapter.

iv. For further details, see http://www.elizabethan-era.org.uk/the-poor-law.htm (accessed February 18, 2009).

v. J. Seymour, "*Parens Patriae* and Wardship Powers: Their Nature and Origins," *Oxford Journal of Legal Studies* 14(1994):159–188.

vi. D. Besharov, *Juvenile Justice Advocacy: Practice in a Unique Court* (New York: Practicing Law Institute, 1974); also see J. Albanese, *Dealing with Delinquency: The Future of Juvenile Justice* (Chicago: Nelson-Hall, 1993).

vii. 42 U.S.C., Section 3801; for additional details, see G. Olson-Raymer, "The Role of the Federal Government in Juvenile Delinquency Prevention: Historical and Contemporary Perspectives," *Journal of Criminal Law and Criminology* 74(1983):578–600.

viii. 42 U.S.C., Section 5601.

ix. U.S. Department of Justice, *Dictionary of Criminal Justice Data Terminology*, p. 157.

x. P. Griffin, P. Torbet, and L. Szymanski, *Trying Juveniles as Adults: An Analysis of State Transfer Provisions* (Washington, DC: U.S. Department of Justice, 1998). Available at http://ojjdp.ncjrs.org/pubs/tryingjuvasadult/transfer.html (accessed March 12, 2009).

xi. P. Griffin, P. Torbet, and L. Szymanski, *Trying Juveniles as Adults: An Analysis of State Transfer Provisions* (Washington, DC: U.S. Department of Justice, 1998). Available at http://ojjdp.ncjrs.org/pubs/tryingjuvasadult/transfer.html (accessed February 28, 2009).

xii. P. Griffin, P. Torbet, and L. Szymanski, *Trying Juveniles as Adults: An Analysis of State Transfer Provisions* (Washington, DC: U.S. Department of Justice, 1998). Available at http://ojjdp.ncjrs.org/pubs/tryingjuvasadult/transfer.html (accessed April 1, 2009).

xiii. H. N. Snyder and M. Sickmund, *Juvenile Offenders and Victims: 2006 National Report* (Washington, DC: U.S. Department of Justice, Office of Justice Programs, Office of Juvenile Justice and Delinquency Prevention, 2006), p. 110.

xiv. P. W. Greenwood, "Juvenile Crime and Juvenile Justice," in J. Q. Wilson and J. Petersilia, eds., *Crime: Public Policies for Crime Control* (Oakland, CA: Institute for Contemporary Studies, 2002).

xv. P. W. Greenwood, "Juvenile Crime and Juvenile Justice," in J. Q. Wilson and J. Petersilia, eds., *Crime: Public Policies for Crime Control* (Oakland, CA: Institute for Contemporary Studies, 2002), p. 86.

---

1. U.S. Department of Justice, *Dictionary of Criminal Justice Data Terminology*, 2nd ed. (Washington, DC: U.S. Department of Justice, Bureau of Justice Statistics, 1981), p. 118.

2. 18 U.S.C., Section 5031.

3. For more details, see the "Shifting Conceptions of Age" section later in this chapter.

4. D. S. Tanenhaus, *Juvenile Justice in the Making* (New York: Oxford University Press, 2004); also see L. Stone, *The Family, Sex, and Marriage in England: 1500–1800* (New York: Harper and Row, 1977).

5. For further details, go to http://www.elizabethan-era.org.uk/the-poor-law.htm (accessed February 12, 2013).

6. An Act for the Relief of the Poor, 1601, 43 Eliz., Chap. 2, Section 1 (England).

7. L. M. Gring-Pemble, *Grim Fairy Tales: The Rhetorical Construction of American Welfare Policy* (Westport, CT: Greenwood Press, 2003).

8. J. Seymour, "*Parens Patriae* and Wardship Powers: Their Nature and Origins," *Oxford Journal of Legal Studies*, Vol. 14 (1994), pp. 159–188.

9. D. Besharov, *Juvenile Justice Advocacy: Practice in a Unique Court* (New York: Practicing Law Institute, 1974); also see J. Albanese, *Dealing with Delinquency: The Future of Juvenile Justice* (Chicago: Nelson Hall, 1993).

10. P. W. Greenwood, "Juvenile Crime and Juvenile Justice," in J. Q. Wilson and J. Petersilia, eds., *Crime: Public Policies for Crime Control* (Oakland, CA: Institute for Contemporary Studies, 2002), p. 81.

11. Gring-Pemble, *Grim Fairy Tales*, p. 25.

12. B. Krisberg, *Juvenile Justice* (Thousand Oaks, CA: Sage, 2005), p. 31.

13. A. M. Platt, *The Child Savers: The Invention of Delinquency* (Chicago: University of Chicago Press, 1969).

14. R. S. Pickett, *House of Refuge: Origins of Juvenile Reform in New York State, 1815–1857* (Syracuse, NY: Syracuse University Press, 1969); also see A. M. Knupfer, *Reform and Resistance: Gender, Delinquency, and America's First Juvenile Court* (London: Routledge, 2001).

15. New York State Education Department, *New York House of Refuge: A Brief History*, available at http://www.archives.nysed.gov/a/research/res_topics_ed_reform_history.shtml (accessed February 12, 2013).

16. Ibid.

17. Pickett, *House of Refuge*.

18. Ibid.

19. Ibid.

20. S. J. Fox, "A Contribution to the History of the American Juvenile Court," *Juvenile and Family Court Journal*, Vol. 49 (1998), pp. 7–16.

21. Ibid.

22. J. Mack, "The Juvenile Court," *Harvard Law Review*, Vol. 23 (1909), p. 120.

23. *Kent v. United States*, 383 U.S. 541 (1966).

24. Ibid.

25. *In re Gault*, 387 U.S. 1 (1967).

26. *In re Winship*, 397 U.S. 358 (1970).

27. Ibid., pp. 363–364.

28. *McKeiver v. Pennsylvania*, 403 U.S. 528 (1971).

29. Ibid., p. 543.

30. *Breed v. Jones*, 421 U.S. 519 (1975).

31. Ibid., pp. 528–529.

32. *Oklahoma Publishing Company v. District Court in and for Oklahoma City*, 430 U.S. 308 (1977).

33. See also *Smith v. Daily Mail Publishing Company*, 443 U.S. 97 (1979).

34. *Eddings v. Oklahoma*, 436 U.S. 921 (1978).

35. *Schall v. Martin*, 467 U.S. 253 (1984).

36. Ibid.

37. Ibid., p. 281.

38. *Thompson v. Oklahoma*, 487 U.S. 815 (1988).

39. *Stanford v. Kentucky*, 492 U.S. 361 (1989).

40. *Roper v. Simmons*, 543 U.S. 551 (2005).

41. Ibid., pp. 572–573.

42. *Graham v. Florida*, 560 U.S. ___ (2010).

43. *Miller v. Alabama*, 567 U.S. ___ (2012).

44. For a review all relevant juvenile justice cases, see C. Hemmens, B. Steiner, and D. Mueller, *Significant Cases in Juvenile Justice* (Los Angeles: Roxbury, 2004).

45. 42 U.S.C., Section 3801; for additional details, see G. Olson-Raymer, "The Role of the Federal Government in Juvenile Delinquency Prevention: Historical and Contemporary Perspectives," *Journal of Criminal Law and Criminology*, Vol. 74 (1983), pp. 578–600.

46. 42 U.S.C., Section 5601.

47. Ibid.

48. H. N. Snyder and M. Sickmund, *Juvenile Offenders and Victims: 2006 National Report* (Washington, DC: U.S. Department of Justice, Office of Justice Programs, Office of Juvenile Justice and Delinquency Prevention, 2006), chap. 4.

49. Ibid., p. 98.

50. Ibid., p. 99.

51. D. B. Rottman and S. M. Strickland, *State Court Organization, 2004* (Wilmington VA: National Center for State Courts, 2006), pp. 16–19.

52. Ibid.

53. Ibid.

54. California Administrative Office of the Courts, available at http://www.courtinfo.ca.gov/selfhelp/family/juv/intro.htm#whatis (accessed February 12, 2013).

55. Read Rottman and Strickland, *State Court Organization, 2004*.

56. Snyder and Sickmund, *Juvenile Offenders and Victims*, p. 104.

57. Ibid.

58. U.S. Department of Justice, *Dictionary of Criminal Justice Data Terminology*, p. 157.

59. Office of Juvenile Justice and Delinquency Prevention, available at https://www.ncjrs.gov/html/ojjdp/195420/page2.html (accessed February 12, 2013).

60. Snyder and Sickmund, *Juvenile Offenders and Victims*, chap. 4.

61. Ibid.

62. http://www.vermontjudiciary.org/gtc/Family/Faqs.aspx (accessed February 12, 2013).

63. Available at http://www.ncjj.org/Publications/State_Profiles.aspx (accessed February 12, 2013).

64. Ibid.

65. Available at http://www.ojjdp.gov/pubs/reform/ch2_j.html (accessed February 12, 2013).

66. Available at http://www.ojjdp.gov/pubs/tryingjuvasadult/transfer.html (accessed February 12, 2013).

67. Available at http://www.ojjdp.gov/pubs/tryingjuvasadult/transfer.html (accessed February 12, 2013).

68. Snyder and Sickmund, *Juvenile Offenders and Victims*, chap. 4.

69. Ibid.

70. Greenwood, "Juvenile Crime and Juvenile Justice."

71. Ibid.

72. C. Knoll and M. Sickmund, *Delinquency Cases in Juvenile Court, 2009* (Washington, DC: Office of Juvenile Justice and Delinquency Prevention, 2012), p. 3.

73. Snyder and Sickmund, *Juvenile Offenders and Victims*, chap. 4.

74. Ibid.

© dc_slim/Fotolia

ecialized Courts

RNING OBJECTIVES

ummarize the principles and practices of specialized
ourts.

2. Describe the focus and operations of specialized
   courts.
3. Summarize the issues surrounding specialized courts.

The Allegheny County courthouse in Pittsburgh, Pennsylvania. What are specialized courts and what kinds of offenders do they process?

Jeffrey M. Frank/Shutterstock

INTRODUCTION

A few years ago, Allegheny County, Pennsylvania—home to the city of Pittsburgh—developed the Allegheny County Mental Health Court as an alternative to traditional criminal courts for mentally ill offenders accused of minor crimes. The court uses a soft touch in working with defendants who are brought before it—including handing out certificates of accomplishment, encouraging people to stick with treatment programs, and offering advice on how to dress. Defendants, who are called graduates once they make it through court-ordered treatment and supervision, are diverted from the correctional system, easing crowding in the county's jails. Judge John Zottola, who oversees the court, says, "some people ask, 'Is warm and fuzzy appropriate for the criminal justice system?' But it really works."[1] According to a recent count, there are now about 175 mental health courts nationwide.

ORIGINS AND DISTINGUISHING FEATURES OF SPECIALIZED COURTS

Over the past several years, many nontraditional courts have sprung up across the United States focusing on special problems such as drug addiction, domestic violence, child neglect, and neighborhood quality-of-life issues. Some also serve special populations, like former service men and women and the homeless. These problem-solving courts are called **specialized courts** as well as special jurisdiction courts.[2] Other names used are "specialized courts" or "boutique courts." They include drug courts, domestic-violence courts, community courts, career criminal courts, traffic courts, family treatment courts, mental health courts, gun courts, homeless courts, DUI (driving under the influence) courts, parole reentry courts, and teen courts, among others. Each specialized court targets different problems or populations, but all share a similar mission: to shift the focus from processing cases to achieving meaningful results for defendants by formulating creative individually tailored sentences.

The development of problem-solving courts represents a sea change in the American judiciary, and its magnitude cannot be overstated. As the author of one recent study observed,

Learning Objective 1

Summarize the principles and practices of specialized courts.

specialized court
A type of nontraditional and experimental U.S. court that targets special problems (e.g., drug addiction, domestic violence, child neglect) but shares a similar mission—to shift the focus from processing cases to achieving meaningful results for defendants by formulating creative, individually tailored sentences; also called *problem-solving courts, special jurisdiction courts,*[i] or *boutique courts.*

"The problem-solving court movement is not just significant because of its focus on specialized justice. Such courts are redefining the role of criminal courts altogether."[3]

Specialized courts emerged in response to several factors. Goldstein's concept of problem-oriented policing[4] was influential due to its concern with developing custom-tailored solutions to specific types of crime problems. Wilson and Kelling's broken windows theory, which argued that if minor problems are ignored, serious crime could take hold, was also influential.[5] A number of specialized courts focus on low-level problems with this thinking in mind.

Several other forces helped to set the stage for problem-solving innovations:

1. Breakdowns among the kinds of social and community institutions (including families and churches) that have traditionally addressed problems like addiction, mental illness, quality-of-life crime, and domestic violence

2. Struggles of other government efforts, whether legislative or executive, to address these problems

3. Surge in the nation's incarcerated population and the resulting prison overcrowding

4. Trends emphasizing the accountability of public institutions

5. Advances in the quality and availability of therapeutic interventions, which have given many within the criminal justice system greater confidence in using certain forms of treatment

6. Shifts in public policies and priorities—for example, the way the broken windows theory has alerted people to the importance of low-level crime[6]

Origins and Historical Milestones

Not long after terms like "problem oriented" and "broken windows" became part of the criminal justice vocabulary, Philadelphia implemented the first Protection from Abuse Court, in which one judge was responsible for all civil protection (e.g., restraining) orders stemming from domestic violence.[7] Cook County (Illinois) also established a domestic-violence calendar in one of its criminal courts.

While these two projects represented the first key steps in the specialized court movement, they were overshadowed by the drug court in Dade County (Florida), which opened in 1989 and was the first court to sentence drug offenders to judicially supervised drug treatment. In 1991, Alameda County (California) began the nation's second drug court. Shortly thereafter, Dade County began its own domestic-violence court.

In 1993, the Midtown Community Court opened in the Times Square area of New York City and was among the first to combine punishment and assistance to offenders and victims, focusing largely on minor offenses. According to the Center for Court Innovation, "The nation's first community court, Midtown combines punishment (e.g., community restitution projects) and help (e.g., onsite drug treatment, job training, counseling) to hold low-level defendants accountable for their offenses."[8]

In 1994, Congress passed the Violent Crime Control and Law Enforcement Act, authorizing the attorney general to fund drug courts across the country. By the end of that year, 42 drug courts could be found in the United States. The Violence against Women Act was also passed in 1994, providing funding to states and local communities in the name of combating domestic violence and all its variations. In the same year, the National Association of Drug Court Professionals was founded, further signaling the growth of and interest in specialized courts.

In 1995, the Drug Courts Program Office was established in the U.S. Justice Department, and from 1995 to 2000, it oversaw the creation of more than 275 drug courts. Other problem-solving courts began to emerge at around that time. In 1996, Marion County (Indiana) started its Psychiatric Assertive Identification Referral/Response Program, which amounted to the nation's first mental health court; in the same year, Brooklyn, New York, started the first domestic-violence court that processed felony cases.

By 1997, several states had started drug courts for juveniles. Broward County (Florida) also implemented the first stand-alone mental health court, and the Hartford Community Court also opened in 1997. By 1998, the Drug Courts Program Office reported that nearly 100,000 offenders had entered drug treatment as a result of drug court participation. In 1999, the Office of Justice Programs in the U.S. Department of Justice funded nine reentry courts that assisted parolees in reentering the community. San Diego (California) then implemented the nation's first homeless court, focusing on assistance to the homeless in lieu of adjudication of new criminal offenses. This progression has continued:

> Since 2000, problem-solving courts have continued their growth. Drug courts, do-mestic violence courts, and mental health courts are largely staples on the criminal justice scene. The less prominent courts, such as homeless courts, are also begin-ning to gain a foothold. San Bernardino, California, is currently working on start-ing a homeless court. Teen courts, where teens assume the roles of judge and other courtroom actors, with adult supervision, have gained in popularity. Community courts, such as that found in Brooklyn's Red Hook Community Justice Center, are also becoming more common. What makes this progression so interesting is not just the number of problem-solving courts, but what they are doing to redefine the role of the court.[9]

See the "Courts in the News" feature for more on alternative courts.

Distinguishing Features

The Center for Court Innovation has developed a list of six principles and practices that make problem-solving courts different from traditional courts: focus on outcomes, judicial monitoring, informed decision making, collaboration, nontraditional roles, and systemic change.[10] To these we can add voluntary participation, therapeutic jurisprudence, and com-munity input.

Focus on Outcomes Traditional adjudication is concerned with process and punishment—judges ensure the law is closely followed, and offenders are held accountable for their actions. Left out of the traditional approach to adjudication is a concern with the outcomes that accompany criminal convictions. These outcomes can include the long-term prospects for the offender and the effects of criminal sanctions on family members and relatives. One noted community court judge has observed that "outcomes—not just process and precedents—matter. Protecting the rights of an addicted mother is important. So is protecting her children and getting her off drugs."[11]

Judicial Monitoring In the past, judges may have handed down a sentence and washed their hands of the case, but in problem-solving courts, judges stay involved in the cases from beginning to end. For example, drug-court judges closely supervise offenders who are required to participate in treatment.

Informed Decision Making Problem-solving courts rely on innovative technologies and on-site staff to keep judges more informed about what is happening with offenders. In some community courts, on-site caseworkers evaluate defendants' needs so that judges can hand down appropriate sentences intended to help defendants steer clear from crime.

Web Extra
6–1 City University of New York (CUNY) Dispute Resolution Consortium

Web Extra
6–2 Courtbuilders.org

COURTS IN THE NEWS

Alternative Courts

In 2012, the state of Georgia's criminal justice overhaul bill is expected to raise standards and accountability for a growing wave of drug and mental health courts. "I think we're all really happy about how it is turning out," said Superior Court Judge Kathlene F. Gosselin, who oversees the mental health court at the Hall County Courthouse. Georgia's program offers an emphasis on alternative courts to address substance abuse and mental health issues as well as sentencing reform.

Joshua Hackney, 16, visits with residents at the Fountain Valley Senior Center in Colorado Springs, Colorado. Josh is participating in a restorative justice program and has been ordered to perform community service.

JERILEE BENNETT/Newscom

Georgia is not unique. Alternative courts—also known as problem-solving or problem-oriented courts—have been growing in numbers around the country. They are innovative community measures designed to reduce overcrowding in jails caused by the incarceration of offenders whose repetitive low-level crimes place a heavy burden on already limited resources.

The intent of these courts is to divert habitual petty offenders from incarceration into treatment programs to help them with problems such as alcohol or substance abuse, mental illness, anger management, or other issues that may be contributing to their illegal behavior. Treatment is offered, with judicial pressure as an added inducement. Offenders are also linked up with social service agencies to assist them with other problems that may be compelling their criminal conduct.

The alternative measures simultaneously present the offender with an opportunity to avoid jail while placing the onus on the offender to put forth genuine effort to benefit from the treatment. It's a simple concept: work during treatment to change your behavior, or go to jail.[1]

The impact these repeat offenders have on court and jail resources is far greater than most people realize. Tom Casady is the police chief in Lincoln (Nebraska), where he has to deal with 83 offenders who have each been arrested more than 200 times. "If you can stop that trend in one way or another, there's a huge amount of money that can be conserved," he says.[2]

A typical array of alternative court options is discussed by defense attorney Glen R. Graham on his Oklahoma Criminal Defense blog site. He explains that "the court system in Tulsa County has evolved and adapted to changing times and circumstances"[3] by establishing a drug court, a DUI court, a mental health court, a community sentencing court, and a unique accelerated accountability procedure court to help nonviolent offenders expedite their cases through the

court system. Graham offers a brief explanation of each of these courts on his site. He also hails the application of technological innovations "to provide a multitude of less expensive means of supervising people without expensive prison costs."[4]

Athens-Clarke County (Georgia) Probate Judge Susan Tate captured the essence of the problem when she said, "The [county's] judges finally realized this [repeatedly locking people up] isn't working; we sentence them, we set them loose, and they're right back in here."[5] After an examination of county jail records showed that one inmate had been incarcerated 112 times and that most of its male inmates had been there an average of ten times in the past 15 years, the county established a treatment and accountability court in July 2008.[6]

In theory, alternative courts seem to present a viable method of reducing the almost overwhelming costs associated with repetitive incarceration. It remains to be seen, however, if the effects of the courts will be to actually reduce repeat offenses or merely to divert habitual offenders into repetitive processing through the treatment programs.

Community courts, such as those described here, frequently deal with minor offenders and employ alternative sentencing strategies that place many of those they handle into treatment and counseling programs, allowing them to avoid having to spend time in jail or prison. Proponents of these kinds of courts argue that they save time and money and that they effectively deal with minor repeat offenders. It is not entirely clear, however, whether they shut the revolving door that seems to readmit so many of these kinds of offenders into the system. Critics of these courts argue that diverting offenders who violate the law repeatedly, even for minor offenses, does not impose the kind of justice intended by the law. ∎

DISCUSSION QUESTIONS

1. What kinds of offenses have the repetitive offenders described here generally been convicted of?

2. Why do the courts described here make use primarily of community resources (such as drug-treatment programs and family counseling centers) rather than rely on more

(continued)

traditional sentencing options, such fines, prison, or time in jail?

3. Might the community justice courts described here also prove useful with more serious offenders (including serious recidivists)?

Notes

1 Christian Bourge, "Drug Courts: Viable Alternative to Jail," *UPI Think Tanks*, April 2, 2003. Available at http://www.upi.com/Top_News/2003/04/02/Drug_courts__viable_alternative_to_jail/UPI-82701049327203/ (accessed August 4, 2009).

2 Donna Leinwand, "Alternative Courts Gain Ground for Petty Criminals," *USA Today*, June 9, 2008. Available at http://www.usatoday.com/news/nation/2008-06-09-frequentfliers_N.htm (accessed August 4, 2009).

3 Glen R. Graham, "About Tulsa Drug Court, Tulsa DUI Court, Tulsa Mental Health Court, Tulsa Community Sentencing Court, Tulsa Accelerated Accountability Procedure (AAP) Court," February 9, 2009. Available at http://oklahomacriminaldefense.blogspot.com/2008/09/tulsalternative-courts-tulsa-drug.html (accessed August 4, 2009).

4 Ibid.

5 Leinwand, "Alternative Courts Gain Ground for Petty Criminals."

6 Ibid.

Sources: Aaron Hale, "Criminal Justice Bill Could Boost Alternative Courts," *Gainesville Times*, March 23, 2012, available at http://www.gainesvilletimes.com/archives/65177 (accessed May 30, 2013); Christian Bourge, "Drug Courts: Viable Alternative to Jail," *UPI Think Tanks*, April 2, 2003, available at http://www.upi.com/Top_News/2003/04/02/Drug_courts__viable_alternative_to_jail/UPI-82701049327203 (accessed May 30, 2013); Donna Leinwand, "Alternative Courts Gain Ground for Petty Criminals," *USA Today*, June 9, 2008, available at http://www.usatoday.com/news/nation/2008-06-09-frequentfliers_N.htm (accessed May 30, 2013); Glen R. Graham, "About Tulsa Drug Court, Tulsa DUI Court, Tulsa Mental Health Court, Tulsa Community Sentencing Court, Tulsa Accelerated Accountability Procedure (AAP) Court," February 9, 2009, available at http://oklahomacriminaldefense.blogspot.com/2008/09/tulsas-alternative-courts-tulsa-drug.html (accessed May 30, 2013).

Collaboration Problem-solving courts often work with officials from several public and private agencies, many of whom are often stationed in the courthouse:

> Justice system leaders are uniquely positioned to engage a diverse range of people, government agencies, and community organizations in collaborative efforts to improve public safety. By bringing together justice players (e.g., judges, prosecutors, defense attorneys, probation officers, court managers) and reaching out to potential stakeholders beyond the courthouse (e.g., social service providers, victims groups, schools) justice agencies can improve inter-agency communication, encourage greater trust between citizens and government, and foster new responses—including new diversion and sentencing options, when appropriate—to problems.[12]

Nontraditional Roles There are numerous nontraditional practices that take place in problem-solving courts. Perhaps the best example is the movement away from the time-honored adversarial system, where prosecutors and defense attorneys work against each other, to one where both parties cooperate so that the needs of the offender can be met.

Systemic Change Systemic change refers to the lessons that problem-solving courts have learned and to the changes that they urge other public agencies to make. For example, if a family court lacks access to information, it may encourage the local child welfare agency to improve its record keeping. Systemic change also refers to the combined result of all the forces discussed thus far:

> Instead of adversarial sparring, prosecutors and defenders in some problem-solving courts work together to encourage defendants to succeed in drug treatment. Instead of embracing the tradition of judicial isolation, judges in problem-solving courts become actively involved in their communities, meeting with residents and brokering relationships with local service providers. Perhaps most importantly, instead of being passive observers, citizens are welcomed into the process, participating in advisory boards, organizing community service projects and meeting face to face with offenders to explain the impact of crimes on neighborhoods.[13]

Voluntary Participation It often isn't mentioned that participation in specialized courts is voluntary; that is, defendants are generally given the choice to participate or to take their chances with traditional adjudication. This is both a benefit and a drawback. It is beneficial in the sense that a choice for a nontraditional court may end up helping the defendant in the end, such as by his or her participation in a drug-treatment program. A drawback is that specialized courts draw a particular clientele (in social science research lingo, this is known as a "selection effect"). Defendants select themselves into the courts, meaning that some who may benefit with mandatory participation do not.

therapeutic jurisprudence
A core component of the specialized courts movement that "amounts to seeing law as a helping profession."ii

Therapeutic Jurisprudence At the core of the specialized courts movement is the practice of **therapeutic jurisprudence**, which amounts to seeing law as a helping profession.[14] It arose from the field of mental health law where, traditionally, there was a focus on the legal rights of mental health patients rather than on their treatment needs. It is also concerned with the consequences on social relationships that the law can have; that is, therapeutic jurisprudence views law not as an abstract set of rules that must be obeyed but as a social process that influences people.

Consider domestic violence. The therapeutic jurisprudence approach focuses on issues of victim safety and offender accountability. In the past, if an abuser was arrested, he or she (usually he) may return home after being released from jail and continue a pattern of abuse; further abuse was therefore a side effect, or unanticipated consequence, of traditional justice. Domestic-violence courts seek to minimize such harmful outcomes that can result from an unimaginative traditional response to domestic violence: "[T]he therapeutic jurisprudence approach focuses on offender accountability and victim safety, and it requires those who are making decisions to consider the potential benefits and consequences of their decisions on those involved."[15] See Box 6–1 for more details on therapeutic jurisprudence in the context of domestic violence.

Community Input Another fundamental force behind the specialized courts movement is a concern for community input. Courts have traditionally been cut off from the communities in which they are located. Courthouses tend to be located in urban centers, away from the places most people live, and courts have also been guilty of not keeping community members informed of their decisions. Finally, community members have not had much of a say in what sorts of problems are prioritized or over the sanctions the courts employ. Specialized courts advocates have begun to realize that there can be considerable benefit to improved community involvement:

> Citizens and neighborhood groups have an important role to play in helping the justice system identify, prioritize, and solve local problems. Actively engaging citizens helps improve public trust in justice. Greater trust, in turn, helps people feel safer, fosters law-abiding behavior, and makes members of the public more willing to cooperate in the pursuit of justice (as witnesses, jury members, etc.).[16]

Learning Objective 2

Describe the focus and operations of specialized courts.

VARIETIES OF SPECIALIZED COURTS

Specialized courts are being developed in response to a wide variety of crime problems. Drug courts came first, followed by domestic-violence and community courts. More recently, specialized courts have begun to target everything from gun violence, sex offenses, and homelessness to mental health and reentry. Other specialized courts exist, but here we look at eight—drug courts, domestic-violence courts, community courts, gun courts, sex offense courts, homeless courts, mental health courts, and reentry courts—that have received the greatest amount of attention.

What makes all these specialized courts interesting is that the definition of the American criminal court appears to be changing. Many problem-solving courts are moving away from adjudication to monitoring and service provision, tasks that have historically been handled by probation and parole officers and other treatment providers.

BOX 6–1   Therapeutic Jurisprudence and the Principles of a Successful Domestic-Violence Court

Therapeutic jurisprudence proposes that judges and lawyers be sensitive to the beneficial or harmful consequences that their actions and decisions have on the parties that come before them. In applying the therapeutic jurisprudence approach, the effectiveness of chosen practices depends upon the legal issues involved and the context in which these issues are presented. In essence, therapeutic jurisprudence is what good judges do anyway on a daily basis. The therapeutic jurisprudence approach forces all judges to reflect on and evaluate their effectiveness. As applied to domestic violence, therapeutic jurisprudence suggests that some basic principles can achieve offender accountability and victim safety. These should be applied only where they do not violate other standards of good court performance:

1. When dealing with domestic violence, it is a mistake to try to force what one is doing into the drug court format. Drug courts ordinarily focus on nonviolent offenders whereas domestic violence cases deal with violent crimes against intimates. Although diversion and dismissal of charges may be appropriate after successful completion of a drug treatment program, the slate cannot be wiped clean in domestic violence cases. Rehabilitation of the domestic violence offender is desirable, but offender accountability and victim protection are paramount. Because of the seriousness of violent behavior and the repetitive nature of domestic violence, a legal record needs to be maintained.

2. Judicial demeanor toward defendants and victims can increase compliance with court orders as well as have therapeutic effects. Judges can use their authority to make victims feel welcome in the court, to express empathy for their injuries, and to mobilize resources on their behalf. With offenders, judges can be respectful while insisting that offenders take responsibility for their violence and acknowledge the court's authority over their behavior. Judicial recognition of offender success in treatment, compliance with court orders, and demonstrated alternatives to violence can give the offender a sense of self-efficacy and achievement.

3. One of the most important roles of a domestic violence court is to confront the perpetrator's cognitive distortions. Distorted thinking includes minimizing or denying the violence and blaming the victim. Seize the opportunity provided by the trauma of the arrest to intervene in the perpetrator's life while he is still receptive, and encourage voluntary mental health activities as well as alcohol evaluation and treatment. Be mindful that accepting a "no contest" plea and other compromises or plea bargains can serve to reinforce distorted thinking by allowing the offender to avoid full responsibility for his behavior. It also can be harmful by causing the victim and the offender to believe that the offender can escape responsibility for present and future acts with some degree of impunity. Instead, stress that domestic violence is a chosen behavior and, that contrary to what the perpetrator has believed in the past, it will not get him what he wants.

4. Involve the defendant in contracting with the court and assisting the court in establishing the terms of no contact orders and terms of supervision (e.g., distances, supervised visitation with children, how items of personal property may be obtained). Including input from the offender in fashioning the order can increase compliance. It also lets the individuals know how seriously the court takes the "no contact" and protection orders.

5. We do not like the phrases "fast track" or "rocket docket" but are convinced that these cases need to be acted on immediately with continual court involvement. Otherwise, the court loses judicial effectiveness. Continuances and other dilatory tactics need to be discouraged in every case.

6. Take advantage of the domestic violence dockets to "red flag" children at risk. Appropriate referrals to child advocacy and child welfare agencies should be initiated.

7. Sentencing should be swift but not severe. Some jail time may get the offender's attention that there are consequences for his behavior, but it should be proportionate to his offense. Excessive fines should be avoided as they can rarely be collected and often take needed resources from the family.

8. Routine post-sentencing reviews should be calendared without cause and need to include domestic violence treatment providers, victim advocates, and probation officers to modify

(continued)

restrictions on the offender when there is substantial compliance, as well as to impose graduated sanctions when there is non-compliance.

9. Within the framework of the American justice system, the domestic violence judge who applies therapeutic jurisprudential principles should also be an expert on the special evidentiary issues that arise repeatedly in the context of domestic violence cases. Using his or her familiarity with the law, the judge may also apply these skills to draft custom jury instructions that better frame the issues for jury consideration.

10. Coordinate domestic violence cases with other cases occurring contemporaneously that may involve the perpetrator, victim, or their family. The domestic violence judge should be particularly aware of related dissolution cases, other criminal matters, juvenile court cases, child abuse and neglect cases, and paternity proceedings. In issuing orders, especially those involving "no contact" or protection order provisions, be careful to avoid conflicting or incompatible orders. ■

Source: "Principles of an Effective Domestic Violence Court" by Randal B. Fritzler and Leonore M. J. Simon, *Court Review* (Spring 2000), p. 31 (Williamsburg, VA: National Center for State Courts, 2000). Reprinted by permission.

Drug Courts

drug court
A special state, county, or municipal court that offers first-time substance abuse offenders judicially mandated and court-supervised treatment alternatives to prison.

Drug courts are similar in at least one respect to justice system practices that took place well before the development of problem-solving courts: They emphasize treatment. Treatment is nothing new, and there is a wealth of research available concerning the effects of treatment on recidivism.[17] What makes drug courts different from treatment by itself is that courts and treatment officials work more closely together in the drug-court environment. Historically, a treatment sentence was handed down, but the offender was not monitored by the courts and would return to court only if he or she relapsed and was rearrested. Drug courts are designed to increase the likelihood that drug addicts will stay in treatment and complete it successfully.

Drug courts usually operate in two different ways. First, they can be used to divert offenders out of the criminal process by assigning them to treatment; assuming that offenders complete treatment, they won't carry with them the stigma of a criminal record. Second, postadjudication programs either defer sentencing or suspend it in exchange for successful completion of a treatment program.

Regardless of which avenue is pursued, the drug court will then frequently monitor and supervise offenders. Frequent hearings and regular contacts with judges are common in drug courts. The most common features and elements of drug courts include the following:

- Integration of alcohol and other drug-treatment services with justice system processing
- Nonadversarial approach (prosecution and defense counsel promote public safety while protecting participants' due process rights)
- Early identification and placement in drug-court program
- Access to continuum of alcohol, drug, and other related treatment and rehabilitation services
- Frequent alcohol and other drug testing
- Coordinated strategy to govern responses to participants' compliance
- Ongoing judicial interaction with each drug-court participant
- Monitoring and evaluation to measure achievement of program goals and gauge effectiveness
- Continuing interdisciplinary education to promote effective drug-court planning, implementation, and operations
- Partnerships among drug courts, public agencies, and community-based organizations to generate local support and enhance program effectiveness[18]

Web Extra
6–3 National Association of Drug Court Professionals

Web Extra
6–4 Office of National Drug Control Policy—Drug Courts

Web Extra
6–5 New Jersey's Adult Drug Court Programs

For additional details on what sets drug courts apart from other courts see Figure 6–1.

Drug courts have grown rapidly in number since the first was established in Dade County (Florida) in 1989. Recent estimates indicate the presence of some 800 drug-treatment courts nationwide.[19] Because drug courts have been around for some time, this has given researchers plenty of opportunities to study their effectiveness. Based on the studies that have been conducted, it appears that drug courts have been remarkably effective.[20]

Web Extra
6–6 National Drug Court Institute

Steven Belenko, a noted drug-court researcher, has cautiously concluded that drug courts can favorably affect long-term drug use.[21] Belenko stated, "Drug courts have achieved considerable local support and have provided intensive, long-term treatment services to offenders with long histories of drug use and criminal justice contacts, previous treatment failures, and high rates of health and social problems."[22]

More recently, a team of researchers analyzed the results of 42 separate drug-court evaluations and, after doing so, tentatively concluded that "drug offenders participating in drug court are less likely to reoffend than similar offenders sentenced to traditional correctional options, such as probation."[23] They expressed concern over research designs used to evaluate drug courts. First, they were discouraged by the fact that few researchers used pre–post designs with random assignment to treatment and control conditions. Second, many of the designs "made no attempt to statistically control for differences between drug court and

Web Extra
6–7 National Criminal Justice Reference Service: Spotlight on Drug Courts

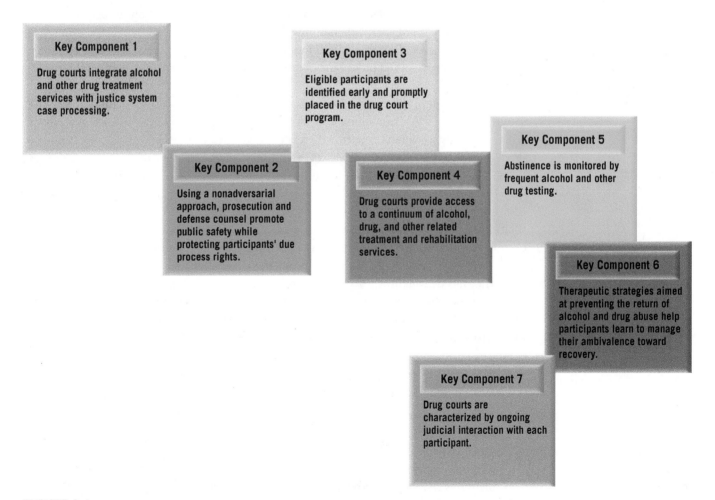

FIGURE 6–1

Key Components of Drug Courts

Source: National Association of Drug Court Professionals, *Defining Drug Courts: The Key Components* (Washington, DC: U.S. Department of Justice, Bureau of Justice Assistance, 1997), pp. iii, 13.

comparison participants, and a common comparison group, drug court drop-outs, has a bias favoring the drug court condition."[24]

In 2011, researchers at the Urban Institute, the Research Triangle Institute, and the Center for Court Innovation completed a five-year study comparing participants in 23 drug courts in seven states to similar defendants whose cases were processed traditionally.[25] The evaluation revealed that drug-court participants were one-third less likely than controls to report drug use in an 18-month follow-up period. It also revealed that success was most likely when participating judges were regarded favorably by drug-court clients: "Having positive perceptions of the judge was also the greatest predictor of reduced drug use and reduced violations of supervision."[26]

Domestic-Violence Courts

To deal with the problem of domestic violence, police departments have been encouraged to adopt mandatory arrest policies, which unfortunately appears to be an unhelpful approach.[27] The failure of mandatory arrest and the uncertain effects of other methods of intervening in domestic-violence situations (some of which we will touch on in Chapter 8) have led to the creation of domestic-violence courts.[28]

domestic-violence court
A special state, county, or municipal court that focuses on tailoring interventions to meeting the needs of victims, closely monitoring the offender, and enlisting community participation.[iii]

Domestic-violence courts focus on tailoring interventions to the needs of victims, closely monitor the offender, and even enlist community participation. Recent estimates suggest that more than 300 courts nationwide are giving specialized attention to domestic-violence cases.[29] Not all of these are stand-alone domestic-violence courts, however; some reserve time for specialized processing of domestic-violence cases within a general jurisdiction court.[30]

One of the more developed domestic-violence courts operates in Lexington County (South Carolina). All nonfelony domestic-violence cases are processed by a specialized criminal domestic-violence court, which is collaborative in the sense that it relies on the services of sheriff's office investigators, a victim advocate, and a full-time prosecutor. A court administrator handles the administrative tasks, and mental health officials work with the court to diagnose offenders and assign them to the proper treatment program; in addition, the court draws on the services of a legal advocate from a local domestic-violence shelter. All parties involved in the court work together to emphasize treatment for offenders and services for victims. Offenders who come before the court often participate in a 26-week group-based cognitive therapy program in exchange for a suspended jail sentence, but if they fail treatment, they serve out their jail term.

New York State operates some 30 different domestic-violence courts.[31] They are located in courts of various levels and in various cities and counties, ranging from the Bronx to Buffalo. New York's domestic-violence courts all share several features in common:

Web Extra
6–8 Specialized Domestic-Violence Court Systems

Library Extra
6–1 New York Domestic-Violence Court Fact Sheet

Dedicated judge. The judge presides over cases from postarraignment through disposition, monitors offenders and their compliance with orders of protection and other court mandates such as program attendance, and promotes consistent and efficient case handling.

Resource coordinator. The resource coordinator prepares offender and victim information for the judge, holds agencies accountable for accurate and prompt reporting, and identifies any problems that challenge court components.

On-site victim advocate. The on-site victim advocate serves as primary contact to victims, creates safety plans and coordinates housing and counseling as well as other social services, and provides victims with information about criminal proceedings and special conditions contained within their orders of protection.

Coordinated community response. A coordinated community response involves increased information sharing, communication and coordination among criminal justice agencies and community-based social services, a consistent and collaborative response to domestic violence, and more opportunities for continued education and training on domestic violence and the courts.[32]

Web Extra
6–9 Center for Court Innovation—Domestic Violence

Evaluations have suggested that domestic-violence courts can be quite successful in gaining more convictions than traditional courts.[33] Whether domestic-violence courts reduce recidivism remains somewhat unclear, however.[34]

In one of the more comprehensive evaluations of domestic-violence courts, Gover and her colleagues concluded that such courts simultaneously increase arrests and reduce recidivism.[35] Specifically, they found that arrests for domestic violence increased following the implementation of a specialized domestic-violence court in Lexington County (South Carolina), stating that "these findings lead to the conclusion that the establishment of a centralized court for processing domestic violence cases increased the responsiveness of law enforcement to this crime."[36] They also found that offenders who were processed through the domestic-violence court were 50 percent less likely to be rearrested. Other evaluations have not been so supportive of domestic-violence courts; for example, researchers who evaluated the Bronx misdemeanor domestic-violence court found fairly high failure and rearrest rates among defendants.[37]

Library Extra
6–2 Community Courts: An Evolving Model

Library Extra
6–3 Center for Court Innovation—Community Court

Community Courts

Drug courts and domestic-violence courts target their own specific problems. **Community courts** are more general in terms of the problems they target and the approaches they take to deal with such problems, and they emphasize partnering and problem solving: "They strive to create new relationships, both within the justice system and with outside stakeholders such as residents, merchants, churches and schools. And they test new and aggressive approaches to public safety rather than merely responding to crime after it has occurred."[38] Elements and practices associated with community courts include the following:

- Community service and other alternative sanctions replace jail and fines.
- Increased court time and resources are devoted to "minor" misdemeanors.
- Extensive inventory of information on defendants is gathered through expanded intake interviews and access to other criminal justice databases.
- Community service work crews or improvement projects are posted as the products of community service.
- Offender compliance with sentence conditions is strictly enforced.
- Community service and treatment programs are immediately started (as opposed to at postrelease).
- Access to a comprehensive package of treatment and social services is gained through a mix of government and nonprofit agencies.
- Dual commitment focuses on changing the lives of individual offenders and improving the quality of life in communities.
- Both treatment and services are components of sanctions.[39]

One of the earliest community courts, the **Midtown Community Court**, opened in New York in October 1993. The court was implemented following a two-year collaborative planning effort between the New York State Unified Court System, the city of New York, and the Fund for the City of New York. The purpose of the court was to provide "accessible justice" for various quality-of-life crimes (e.g., panhandling, loitering, and prostitution)

community court
A neighborhood-focused court that attempts to harness the power of the justice system to address local problems by using creative partnerships and problem solving, creating new relationships within the justice system and with outside stakeholders (e.g., residents, merchants, churches, and schools), and testing new and aggressive approaches to public safety rather than merely responding to crime after it has occurred.[iv]

Web Extra
6–10 Red Hook Community Justice Center

Web Extra
6–11 San Francisco's Community Courts

Midtown Community Court
One of the earliest community courts (October 1993) whose purpose was to provide "accessible justice" for various quality-of-life crimes occurring in and around Times Square.[v]

occurring in and around Times Square. See Figure 6–2 for an overview of how cases flow through the Midtown Community Court.

The Midtown Community Court was developed in response to several concerns.[40] First, traditional courts tended to devote most of their attention to serious crime, not quality-of-life offenses that affect people more directly. Second, community and criminal justice officials were frustrated with the lack of organization in the processing of low-level offenses. Third, community members often felt shut off—and even geographically isolated—from central downtown courts. Fourth, it was felt that community members should have a stake

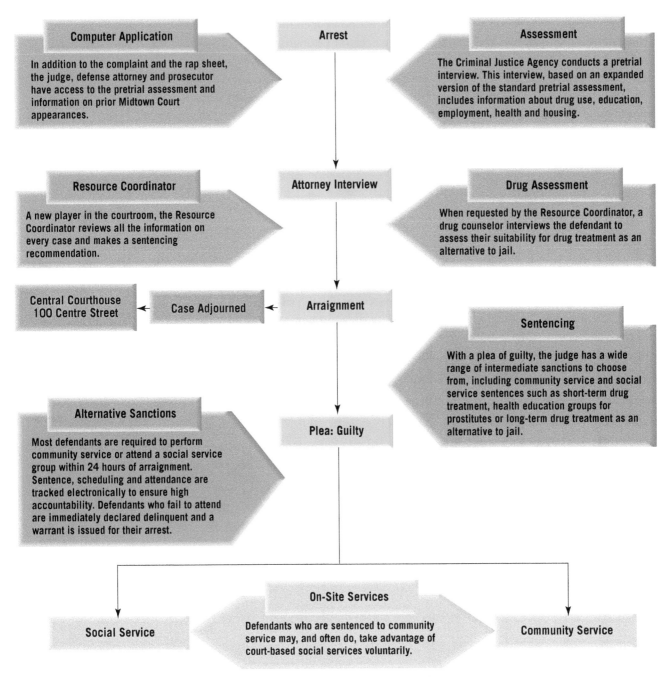

FIGURE 6–2

Midtown Community Court Case-Flow Summary

Source: From *How It Works: A Summary of Case Flow and Interventions at the Midtown Community Court*, by E. Lee and J. Martinez (New York: Center for Court Innovation, 1998), available at http://www.courtinnovation.org. Reprinted by permission.

in the administration of justice because it affected them directly. Finally, there was a desire to have offenders "pay back" the community and assist in restoring it to its original—and hopefully safe—state.

While community courts are popping up all over the country, few of them have been subjected to rigorous research, with many accounts of community court activity being descriptive and anecdotal.[41] According to a recent review of the literature, what few evaluations have been published are far from unanimous in terms of their view on the effectiveness of community courts.[42] They have also had a tendency to focus on outcomes other than crime.[43] One of the few studies that *did* look at postcourt participation criminality and contained a comparison group found virtually no difference between treatments and controls.[44]

Gun Courts

In 1989, Rhode Island passed a tough law that mandated a longer prison term for violent crimes committed with guns, but gun crime continued to be a problem.[45] A 1994 law was then passed that created the nation's first gun court. The court, which was to be located in Providence, represented an effort to take guns even more seriously—particularly to ensure that tough sentences were handed down and that delays were minimized.

Prior to the emergence of the gun court, sentences were imposed in only 67 percent of gun cases, and the average time to disposition was 518 days; the new court required that any case involving a gun be scheduled for trial within 60 days. It appears that since the court's launch, processing time has improved, and considerably more offenders have been sentenced than was the case before a dedicated gun court was formed.[46]

Shortly after the Providence gun court was launched, Philadelphia opened its own gun court,[47] with a focus on educating the defendants about gun safety and providing an infrastructure for quick adjudication and rapid responses to defendants who violated court orders or who were repeat offenders. Like the Providence court, Philadelphia consolidated all gun cases onto a single docket, but the latter court was unique because it also contained pre- and posttrial components.[48] In the pretrial phase, a case manager monitored defendants who were on bail. Posttrial, convicted defendants were required to participate in intensive supervision probation, complete 20 to 50 community service hours, and participate in various education programs covering conflict resolution and anger management. An evaluation revealed that gun-court defendants were rearrested less often than a similar cohort of offenders who did not participate in gun court.[49]

Many of the more recently formed gun courts have focused their energies on gun crimes committed by juveniles: "The juvenile gun court, another type of specialty court, intervenes with youth who have committed gun offenses that have not resulted in serious physical injury. Most juvenile gun courts are short-term programs that augment rather than replace normal juvenile court proceedings."[50] They share several common features:

- Early intervention (in many jurisdictions, before resolution of the court proceedings)
- Short-term (often a single two- to four-hour session) intensive programming
- Intensive educational focus, using knowledgeable, concerned adults from the community to show youth the harm that can come from unlawful gun use, the choices they can make regarding carrying and/or using guns versus nonviolent alternatives for resolving conflicts, and the immediate response by adults in positions of authority that will result when youth are involved with guns
- Inclusion of a wide range of court personnel and law enforcement officials—judges, probation officers, prosecutors, defense counsel, and police—working together with community members[51]

Sex Offense Courts

Web Extra
6–12 Sex Offense Courts
in New York State

One of the most recent specialized courts to emerge is that aimed specifically at sex of-fenses. Having a dedicated sex offense court is advantageous because it requires that judges have specialized knowledge concerning these offenses, that coordination between the court and other stakeholder agencies occurs, and that victim satisfaction is improved.[52] Histori-cally, victims would have to follow the cases from court to court and judge to judge, judges would have to base their decisions on inadequate information about how best to deal with sex offenders, and district attorneys would often plead cases down to misdemeanors when faced with judges who were just not sure what to do with sex offenders. All in all, there has also been a lack of coordination by the various officials involved in the processing of sex offenders.

Library Extra
6–4 Center for Court
Innovation—Sex Offense Court

In January 2006, three counties in New York State became the first to pilot specialized sex offense courts. The mission of these courts is to provide a "comprehensive approach to case resolution, increasing sex offender accountability, enhancing community safety and ensuring victim safety while protecting the rights of all litigants."[53] Core elements of the New York sex offense courts include the following:

- Keeping victims informed
- Scheduling cases promptly
- Having dedicated, trained judges
- Supervising defendants continuously
- Implementing additional judicial monitoring of cases postconviction/postplea
- Building strong relationships with service providers
- Coordinating with probation departments
- Convening regular meetings with criminal justice agencies and service providers
- Providing court personnel and partners with education and training[54]

Homeless Courts

homeless court
A special state, county, or municipal court whose purpose it is to resolve outstanding misdemeanor criminal warrants against homeless people so as to ease court case backlogs, reduce vagrancy, and meet a fundamental need of homeless people by eliminating obstacles to their reintegration into society that deter them from using social services and impede their access to employment.

Homeless courts differ perhaps most of all from traditional courts and other problem-solving courts because instead of being used to process new offenses, they are used to resolve outstanding misdemeanor criminal warrants (see Figure 6–3 for an overview). There are reasons for taking this approach: Several of the homeless are perfectly content remaining homeless and want no part of a justice system intervention, and many of the homeless lack the resources to meet the obligations associated with their criminal convictions (e.g., pay a fine) and do not have the ability to show up at court when they are required to do so. All this can result in a number of warrants that "stack up." Here is how California's Administra-tive Office of the Courts describes the situation:

> Resolution of outstanding warrants not only meets a fundamental need of homeless people but also eases court case-processing backlogs and reduces vagrancy. Homeless people tend to be fearful of attending court, yet their outstanding warrants limit their reintegration into society, deterring them from using social services and impeding their access to employment. They are effectively blocked from obtaining driver's licenses, job applications, and rental agreements.[55]

Despite the obvious need for homeless courts, there is virtually no research on their effectiveness. Only one evaluation has been published, and it was concerned largely with the number of cases resolved following the implementation of a homeless court in San Diego.[56] Whether homeless courts help their clients secure gainful employment, receive appropriate social services, or desist from low-level criminal activity is currently unknown.

Web Extra
6–13 California Homeless
Courts

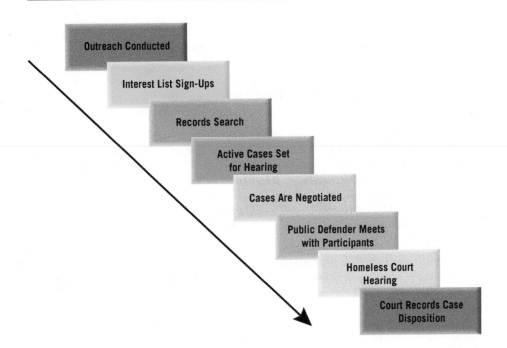

FIGURE 6–3

**Homeless Court Process
Flowchart**

Source: N. Kerry and S. Pennell,
*San Diego Homeless Court Program:
A Process and Impact Evaluation*
(San Diego, CA: San Diego
Association of Governments,
2001). Reprinted by permission
of San Diego Association of
Governments.

Mental Health Courts

Historically, the justice system and mental health agencies have acted independently of one another.[57] **Mental health courts** are intended to bring these entities together in pursuit of a common goal: providing services to mentally ill offenders. This is a significant development because there are many mentally ill offenders processed by the justice system, some of whom "slip through the cracks."[58] In fact, by some estimates there are more than a quarter million mentally ill offenders in America's prisons and jails, and prisons and jails are not generally equipped to deal with mentally ill offenders.[59] These concerns have led criminal justice officials to seek other options.

The four original mental health courts are located in Broward County (Florida), Anchorage (Alaska), King County (Washington), and San Bernardino (California). Participation in the courts is voluntary and is usually reserved for low-level offenders. In the King County Mental Health Court, a court liaison to the treatment community is present at all hearings and is responsible for linking the defendant with appropriate services. Defendants participate in court-ordered treatment programs and can often have their charges dropped on successful completion of treatment; they are also supervised by probation officers with a background in the mental health field who have small caseloads. See Box 6–2 for details on the King County Mental Health Court.

Mental health courts serve a noble purpose, and it is difficult to argue against enhanced collaboration and coordination between the justice system and social services organizations. Whether such courts actually affect the offenders, though, remains unclear. To date, there are few evaluations of mental health courts, particularly their effects on recidivism. An evaluation of the King County Mental Health Court revealed that those who participated in the program spent less time in detention and were booked on fewer new offenses.[60] Another recent evaluation found that mental health court participants had significantly lower recidivism rates than nonparticipants.[61] Otherwise, most researchers' attention has been focused on the effects of mental health courts on the utilization of mental health services. For example, researchers who evaluated the Broward County (Florida) Mental Health Court found that offenders brought before the court were much more likely to receive mental health treatment than offenders in a comparison group.[62]

mental health court
A special state, county, or municipal court that is intended to bring together justice system and mental health agencies to provide services to mentally ill offenders.

Library Extra
6–5 Mental Health Courts

Library Extra
6–6 Mental Health America Net Position Statement: Mental Health Courts

Library Extra
6–7 *U.S. News & World Report*: Mental Health Courts

BOX 6–2 King County District Court's Mental Health Court: How It Works

King County's Mental Health Court offers misdemeanor defendants with mental illnesses a single point of contact with the court system. The defendant will work with their dedicated team including judge, prosecutor, defender, treatment court liaison, and probation officers:

- Defendants may be referred to the Mental Health Court from a variety of different sources. In-custody defendants are often referred by jail psychiatric staff who have screened for mental health issues. Defendants may also be referred for consideration by police, attorneys, family members, or probation officers. A defendant may be referred by another District Court at any point during regular legal proceedings if the judge feels the defendant could be better served by the Mental Health Court. In addition, the Mental Health Court handles all cases in which competency is an issue for the District Courts.

- The Mental Health Court reserves the right not to accept cases into its jurisdiction if a person does not meet eligibility criteria. Likewise, participation in the program is voluntary, as defendants will be asked to waive their rights to a trial on the merits of the case and enter into a diversion or plea agreement with a community-based treatment emphasis. The exception, however, is that cases in which competency issues have been raised are always eligible for transfer to Mental Health Court. If a person is treated and "restored" following a competency proceeding, they then have the right to "opt out" of the Court.

- The Court holds daily (Monday–Friday) first appearance hearings for defendants newly booked into jail. The Court hears status and review hearings on Mondays, Tuesdays, Wednesdays, and Thursdays (in addition to those days' first appearance hearings).

- A court liaison to the treatment community is present at all hearings and is responsible for linking the defendant with appropriate services, developing an initial treatment plan with the treating agency.

- Defendants participate in court-ordered treatment plans, and successful participation may result in dismissed charges, early case closure or reduced sentencing.

- Defendants are placed on probation, and the case is assigned to a Mental Health Court Mental Health Specialist Probation Officer. These officers have mental health backgrounds and carry substantially reduced caseloads in order to be able to provide a more intensive level of supervision and expertise to this traditionally high-needs population. ■

Source: "How It Works," King County (WA) District Court Mental Health Court, available at www .kingcounty.gov/courts/districtcourt/mentalhealthcourt.aspx (accessed February 14, 2013). Reprinted by permission.

No amount of research or evaluation will shake some supporters' faith in mental health courts. An account of one defendant's experience with the Brooklyn Mental Health Court, a court that adjudicates felony cases (most mental health courts target misdemeanors at the present time), follows:

> At age 26, Irwin Smith was living on Long Island in a supported residence for people with mental illness. He had been working for several years, first at a furniture factory and then at a restaurant. He had a lapse in taking his Clozaril, a powerful antipsychotic that requires weekly blood monitoring because of its potentially lethal side effects. (Irwin doesn't recall whether he forgot to take his medication or whether the pharmacy wouldn't renew his weekly prescription because the lab work was missing.) He spotted a car with keys in the ignition and heard a voice telling him to "take the car and have fun." He started driving toward Manhattan but had no money to pay the toll at the Brooklyn-Battery Tunnel—and that's when he was arrested for driving a stolen car. . . . By taking a guilty plea and agreeing to comply with a court-mandated treatment plan for 18 to 24 months, Irwin became a participant in the Brooklyn Mental Health Court, a unique judicial experiment that links offenders with mental illness to community-based treatment. He lives in a supported residence in New York City, attends a day treatment program, has an intensive case manager who helps coordinate services for him, and appears

regularly before Judge Matthew D'Emic, the presiding judge of the Brooklyn Mental Health Court. Irwin has never missed a court appearance, and the reports provided to the court by his housing and treatment providers are consistently positive. He is moving toward employment again, hoping to work at a concession stand in a sports arena. Since coming under the court's supervision, Irwin has been, in all respects, a model citizen.[63]

To learn about another type of specialized court—veterans' courts—see the "Courts in the News" feature.

Reentry Courts

Reentry courts do not adjudicate new offenses; instead, they provide oversight and support services to offenders reentering the community. Take, for example, the **Harlem Parole Reentry Court**, which began its operations in June 2001 and whose purpose was to "test the feasibility and effectiveness of a collaborative, community-based approach to managing offender reentry, with the ultimate goal of reducing recidivism and prison return rates."[64] The court was developed as part of the U.S. Justice Department's Reentry Court Initiative and was developed through the efforts of the New York State Division of Parole, the Center for Court Innovation, and the New York State Divisions of Criminal Justice Services.

Are reentry courts helpful? Do they make a difference in the lives of parolees? Plenty of research suggests that parolees are far from equipped to reenter society as law-abiding citizens. As noted parole researcher Joan Petersilia has written, "Prisoners return home with most of their treatment and vocational training needs unmet, and they will soon learn that they occupy an in-between status; they are back in society but not free."[65] Reentry courts are intended to pick up where parole has traditionally left off; in doing so, they take some of the load off parole officers whose caseloads can border on outrageous. While there is not much research yet available on the successes or failures of reentry courts,[66] some anecdotal accounts suggest that this approach is helpful. The first female graduate of the Harlem Parole Reentry Court said this about her experience:

> It gave me a good start in life, it really did. Because I'm still doing good. They sent me to a class when I first came home, where they teach you how to get jobs, and though I got a job on my own, I was glad for the experience they gave me. Eventually I just started enjoying going over there. I was from Harlem, and when they told me they'd help me with any problems that occurred I was already going through a lot of problems. And I had hard things with them and hard times but I needed that. I had a social worker over there, I had my parole officer. At first I really didn't care about the drug treatment program they sent me to, but I finished it, and I think it's great. I think it's the best thing they ever came up with.[67]

THREATS TO AND KEYS TO SUCCESS FOR SPECIALIZED COURTS

Because of the revolutionary nature of specialized courts, they have faced considerable challenges and threats to their longevity. This section first looks at various criticisms of specialized courts and then wraps up with a discussion of what needs to happen to ensure that these courts last.[68]

Possible Threats

Possible threats to specialized courts are several. Some people think they are simply the latest of several fads that criminal justice has seen over the years, others feel these courts are too far removed from what courts should really do, and still others believe they will fail to

Harlem Parole Reentry Court
A court that was developed as part of the U.S. Justice Department's Reentry Court Initiative to "test the feasibility and effectiveness of a collaborative, community-based approach to managing offender reentry, with the ultimate goal of reducing recidivism and prison return rates."[vi]

Web Extra
6–14 Harlem Parole Reentry Court Toolkit

Web Extra
6–15 Harlem Community Justice Center

Library Extra
6–8 Reentry Courts Toolkit

Library Extra
6–9 Reentry Court in the Superior Court of Delaware

Learning Objective 3
Summarize the issues surrounding specialized courts.

Library Extra
6–10 Prison Reform through Offender Reentry

Library Extra
6–11 Reentry Policy Council: Reentry Courts—An Emerging Trend

COURTS IN THE NEWS

Special Veterans' Courts: Brooklyn's Treatment Program

AP Photo/Don Heupel

Hank Pirowski, right, Veterans Court Project Director, listens to Guy LaPenna about paperwork concerns after appearing in the veterans court session in Buffalo, N.Y. in 2008.

An unfortunate aspect of military service is that the experience adversely affects some of those who serve. The unique stresses of military life, particularly those encountered during combat, too often render former service members unable to cope with the transition back into civilian life—or even with life in general. Not surprisingly, some are left emotionally or psychologically damaged, and their ability to address their difficulties in a healthy, recuperative way is somehow short-circuited; unfortunately, they sometimes make bad decisions in their desperate pursuit of relief from their demons.

Such bad decisions sometimes lead to behavior that involves the breaking of the criminal law. In the past, the troubled veterans would then find themselves in a criminal court that was itself ill-equipped to handle the special problems of these defendant-veterans.

Like other special courts (e.g., drug or domestic-violence courts), the hallmark of the veterans' court is its focus on treatment rather than punishment. Arrangements are made for the veterans to see appropriate mental health or substance abuse professionals, and help is given in their job search. Often, that help comes from one of the cadre of local nonoffending veterans who volunteer to serve as mentors for their troubled comrades.

Brooklyn's Treatment Court program has an independent veterans' treatment program. It's a program designed specifically for vets caught in drug offenses. The court treats addiction as a disease and offers an array of rehab possibilities and social services to keep vets out of jail. Judge Michael Brennan, a former veteran himself, presides over the court. In one recent case, a veteran faced the judge as Margarita Fournier, an e-source coordinator, relayed the offender's progress. "Judge, Mr. Gonzalez [not his real name] has persevered. He has tested clean and attended his outpatient program several times a week," she said. The judge addressed the veteran. "You are a Marine. Once a Marine—always a Marine." Judge Brennan went on to say, "We all know this is not easy." With that, he saluted, and the court gallery broke out in applause because in this court drug offenders are treated with respect.

Judge Brennan believes that veterans are sometimes ashamed of their addiction and too proud to admit it. His court assigns mentors, former veterans themselves, to counsel the offenders and offer encouragement. "I also feel that I'm

a mentor," Brennan says. "I'm a veteran. And I'm sitting up here in a black robe, but I'm going to come down to your level as a brother and sister and work with you." If they persevere, the veterans get gold medallions or coins. On one side is an American eagle and the words "Veterans in Recovery." On the other side, the coin reads, "I came with hope and worked and learned. I have a new life—a life that I've earned." The success rate in Brooklyn's Treatment Court is 78%.

Special veterans' courts have caught on very quickly in other jurisdictions, including California, Illinois, Nevada, and Pennsylvania. While the successes seen in Buffalo have certainly been a factor, the movement gained even more momentum early in 2009 with the introduction of grant funds from the U.S. Department of Health and Human Services. The funds are provided to help communities establish programs that divert people with trauma-related disorders from the criminal justice system. Understandably, many of the troubled veterans who end up in trouble with the law fit the target profile.

Special veterans' courts deemphasize punishment and put the focus on helping returned veterans reenter society. Many of us would agree that veterans are a special group with special problems, but they are not the only special-needs group served by the courts. ∎

DISCUSSION QUESTIONS

1. What is the purpose of special courts such as the type described in this feature?

2. Do you believe that veterans deserve special treatment? If not, why?

3. Can you think of any other types of special courts that might be created? If so, what would they be?

Sources: Chuck Gomez, "Brooklyn Treatment Court: A Second Chance for Drug Offenders," April 22, 2013, available at www.huffingtonpost.com/chuck-gomez/brooklyn-treatment-court_b_3053615.html (accessed May 30, 2013); Libby Lewis, "Court Aims to Help Vets with Legal Troubles," *Morning Edition*, National Public Radio, April 29, 2008, available at www.npr.org/templates/story/story.php?storyId=90016059 (accessed May 30, 2013); Matthew Daneman, "N.Y. Court Gives Veterans Chance to Straighten Out," *USA Today*, June 1, 2008, available at http://usatoday30.usatoday.com/news/nation/2008-06-01-veterans-court_N.htm (accessed May 30, 2013).

thrive without complete judicial buy-in. Specialized courts may also blur historically clear role distinctions, lack a strong enough research base, be soft on crime, work for certain individuals better than others, and even be unconstitutional.

Passing Fad? The criminal justice system, like governments and people in general, is guilty of following fads. Various policies come and go as new presidential administrations come on board, new research studies are published, new sources of funding emerge, and so on. Could specialized courts be but one more example of this? While many of them have emerged out of a genuine concern to fix problems, have all of them been implemented for this reason, or are the developments we are witnessing just politically favorable or tied to the availability of funding for specific types of courts? For example, would we see reentry courts but for the fact that the federal government has decided to fund reentry initiatives?[69] Only time will tell.

Changing of Courts for the Worse So far in this book (with the exception of this chapter), we have conceived of courts in one fairly simple way: They decide cases. When they step outside this traditional function, there is cause for concern. Critics of specialized courts have argued that these courts have no legitimate legal foundation. All the courts we have discussed throughout this book have statutory and constitutional roots, but not all specialized courts do. It has also been argued that specialized courts are not neutral because judges work closely with defendants. Finally, some critics feel that specialized courts are inherently unfair because treatment is essentially threatened (if defendants fail to complete their treatment, off to jail they go):

> [Specialized courts] change the basic nature of the courts. They demonstrate none of the characteristics that would ordinarily add to the rational basis of legitimacy. They are not fair. They are not neutral. In some instances, they are not legislatively enacted. Without a rational basis to exercise authority, the tradition of following the authority of the court, merely because it is a court, will deteriorate. The problem-solving courts are headed for a crisis of legitimacy.[70]

Insufficient Judicial Buy-In A survey of 500 judges nationwide revealed that the vast majority of them favored problem solving,[71] but this does not necessarily mean that the same percentage of judges buy in to the concept of having courts dedicated to specific problems. Change is difficult, and some judges feel that parting ways with their traditional practices and roles could be difficult and possibly risky. Truman Morrison, a judge in the District of Columbia Superior Court, said this:

> I'm concerned about the power that judges have and I'm concerned about giving judges the ability to make decisions that are just borne of their individual worldview. I don't think we should free judges to leave their traditional role and be informed only by their own personal definition of what justice is. . . . That kind of anarchy is what I don't want in courts. I don't think that has to in any way inhibit the creative role of problem-solving courts, but I think it's a risk that we need to pay attention to.[72]

Blurred Role Distinctions Specialized courts are but one part of a significant movement throughout criminal justice that calls for collaboration, information sharing, pooling of resources, and a combination of previously distinct functions. The problem is that this may begin to blur the lines between historically distinct criminal justice functions. For example, juvenile justice reforms (as we discussed in Chapter 5) are making the juvenile system start to resemble the adult system. As another example, the police are starting to partner with probation officers to help them engage in supervision duties, but should this occur? Should police officers collaborate with probation officers? In the case of specialized courts, judges are involving themselves more and more in the supervision of offenders. Is this ideal, or

Library Extra
6–12 U.S. Office of Justice Programs: Reentry Courts— Managing the Transition from Prison to Community

Library Extra
6–13 Harlem Reentry Court Evaluation

have judges stepped outside the realm of what they should be doing? Richard Cappalli, a professor at Temple University Law School, made this observation concerning the role of judges in the specialized courts context:

> When judges move out of the box of the law and into working with individual defendants, transforming them from law-breaking citizens into law-abiding citizens, we have to worry. Because what has always protected the bench has been the law. Whenever a judge is approached by a disgruntled individual saying, "How could you do that?" the judge always says: "That wasn't me speaking—that was the law." If we take the mantle of the law's protections off of the judges and put them into these new roles, we have to worry about judicial neutrality, independence, and impartiality.[73]

Looking at the emergence of specialized courts along with other developments throughout criminal justice has caused a number of researchers some concern. One critic of recent reforms observed,

> There is currently a bewildering array of developments occurring in penal policy and practice, many of which appear mutually incoherent or contradictory. Disciplinary obedience versus enterprising autonomy, incapacitation and warehousing versus correctional reform, punishment and stigmatization versus reintegration, formal criminalization versus informal victim/offender settlements—these inconsistent and sometimes contradictory couples may all be used to describe elements that make up the diversity and incoherence of contemporary penal policy and practice.[74]

Another critic put it this way: "In recent decades penal regimes across the western world have embarked upon a process characterized by relentless expansion and volatile and contradictory patterns of innovation and development."[75]

This incoherence, coupled with the blurring of traditional and comfortable role distinctions, offers an explanation for the emergence of specialized courts. An alternative view is that the apparent contradiction and confusion that exist throughout criminal justice bode poorly for the longevity of specialized courts.

Inadequate Empirical Support
Drug courts have been around for some time and have been extensively researched, but other problem-solving courts have not. Since evaluation tends to lag behind implementation, it will be necessary to wait a while for any sort of definitive answer to the question of whether specialized courts work. The jury is still out, especially outside the drug court context.

Soft on Crime?
Are specialized courts soft on crime? Do treatment, individualized sentences, judicial monitoring, and the like coddle offenders? Some critics answer yes to these questions: "Many judges in problem-solving courts have found themselves derided as 'touchy-feely,' 'soft on crime,' and 'coddling.'"[76]

Once they spend some time in a problem-solving capacity, some judges change their tune and come to regard specialized courts as "smart on crime" rather than soft on crime, as is reflected in this judge's observations:

> I was really skeptical about drug courts at first, thinking that they were one of those liberal touchy-feely programs where you just pat somebody on the back, get them on probation and get them out of the courtroom. But after watching the drug treatment court in Rochester a couple of times, I realized that it was not a social worker type of court. It was the first time that I saw defendants having to take responsibility for their actions. Defendants were immediately accountable. The judge knew whether they were following their program within a couple of days, not months later.[77]

Voluntary Participation
As we pointed out near the beginning of this chapter, some specialized courts won't reach the offenders who are most in need or those who are unwilling

or uninterested in receiving treatment.[78] Others have criticized drug courts because people often assume (sometimes incorrectly) that drug use is a cause of crime. As one researcher has pointed out, even if drug treatment causes an addict to desist in the short term, if the offender still "runs with the same dangerous crowd, perhaps drinking heavily while complaining about twice-weekly drug testing," his or her likelihood of recidivism can go up.[79]

Court Challenges Specialized courts have themselves been challenged in court. In one case, *People* v. *Avery*,[80] the defendant argued that the period between his plea and actual imposition of his sentence (participation in a drug-treatment program) amounted to a period of "interim probation," that he was "sentenced" before actually receiving his sentence. Avery's argument did not succeed, but it signaled a possible desire on some defendants' part to challenge specialized courts' legitimacy.

In another case, *State* v. *Alexander*,[81] the Oklahoma Supreme Court heard arguments concerning the structure of drug courts in that state. The defendant argued that his termination from a drug-treatment program violated the Oklahoma constitution's separation of powers provision because the judge who terminated him from the program was a member of the treatment team. The court denied relief, but a concurring opinion written by one of the justices sided with the defendant, arguing that termination hearings of the sort at issue in this case should be held before a neutral judge.

Keys to Success

While specialized courts face their share of challenges, officials have offered a number of recommendations to ensure that they succeed. Those interested in forming specialized courts should begin by looking for other courts that have been successful and follow their lead. It is also necessary for court personnel to adopt a different mind-set with respect to these courts—the focus should be on underlying problems rather than on single criminal incidents. Additional recommendations to ensure the longevity of specialized courts include pooling resources, attracting support, and training, to name a few. The Center for Court Innovation has offered several strategies that, together, are intended to help promote the continued expansion and development of specialized courts.[82] Following are three of them.

First, perhaps the most significant predictor of future specialized court success is that they need to be viewed differently from traditional courts. Their concern should be with getting to the root of problems rather than simply meting out justice. While specialized courts have emerged as a means of targeting specific problems, it is not always the case that the problems defendants have fit neatly into one type of court; for example, some defendants have mental disorders *and* are addicted to drugs. In such cases, it is advisable for specialized court officials to "cross-pollinate" and do several things:

> [They need to] share information and strategies, to share resources, and to collaborate in creating (or advocating the creation of) new resources. Since, for example, programs for dually diagnosed offenders are often scarce, a team consisting of representatives from both a drug court and a mental health court might be in the best situation to encourage and help shape the creation of services for this difficult population.[83]

Specialized courts are still the exception when their numbers are compared to traditional courts. Moreover, they have had to compete for limited resources to ensure their launch and longevity. Some specialized courts have been launched after grants have been awarded to communities, and others have emerged based on community and corporate contributions.

Web Extra
6–16 Center for Court
Innovation: YouTube Drug
Courts Video

Perhaps the second best way for specialized courts to continue expanding, then, is if they share resources with one another.

Third, like most government initiatives, specialized courts do not go very far without some measure of support from officials in high-level positions. This does not have to mean mayors and other high-level elected officials, however; senior judges with significant political clout can influence the adoption of specialized courts:

Web Extra
6–17 Center for Court
Innovation: YouTube Red Hook
Community Justice Center
Video

> In New York State, the support of the state's two top judges—Chief Judge Judith S. Kaye and Chief Administrative Judge Jonathan Lippman—has been crucial to the development of problem-solving courts. After Kaye called for the establishment of drug courts and domestic violence courts across the state, she appointed Judge Judy Harris Kluger to oversee the development of over 200 problem-solving courts. Kluger's office has fostered the creation of integrated domestic violence, community, mental health, and sex offender management courts.[84]

CHAPTER SUMMARY

6

1. SUMMARIZE THE PRINCIPLES AND PRACTICES OF SPECIALIZED COURTS

- Specialized, or problem-solving, courts emerged in response to several factors, including a concern with low-level crimes and a desire to use the courts to help solve complex problems, ranging from drug abuse to domestic violence.
- Specialized courts have several distinguishing features, including a focus on outcomes, judicial monitoring, informed decision making, collaboration, nontraditional roles, and systemic change.
- Also central to specialized courts are the concepts of therapeutic jurisprudence (the law is a helping profession) and community input.

2. DESCRIBE THE FOCUS AND OPERATIONS OF SPECIALIZED COURTS

- There are many varieties of specialized courts. Some of the more recognized varieties include drug courts, domestic-violence courts, community courts, gun courts, sex offense courts, homeless courts, mental health courts, and reentry courts.
- Of the many types of specialized courts, drug courts have been subjected to the greatest deal of research. Based on several evaluations, they appear quite effective.

3. SUMMARIZE THE ISSUES SURROUNDING SPECIALIZED COURTS

- The threats to specialized courts are varied, and the success of specialized courts hinges on several factors.
- Threats to these courts' longevity include concerns that they (1) represent a passing fad, (2) are changing courts for the worse, (3) suffer from insufficient judicial buy-in, (4) blur traditional role distinctions, (5) lack empirical support, (6) are soft on crime, (7) rely too heavily on voluntary participation, and (8) have themselves been challenged in the courts.
- Experts claim that specialized courts will experience success and become mainstream if (1) information is shared; (2) officials focus on core problems rather than traditional conceptions of courts; (3) officials focus on the core principles of solving problems, being

careful not to get too bogged down in the particulars of specific courts; (4) resources are pooled; (5) judges share information with one another; (6) top-level officials put their weight behind these courts; (7) boundary spanners are identified and used to communicate and share information between various specialized courts and their personnel; and (8) sufficient training occurs.

KEY TERMS

community court, 145
domestic-violence court, 144
drug court, 142
Harlem Parole Reentry
    Court, 151

homeless court, 148
mental health court, 149
Midtown Community
    Court, 145

specialized court, 135
therapeutic
    jurisprudence, 140

REVIEW QUESTIONS

1. What are specialized courts, and how did they originate? How do they differ from other courts?

2. List some kinds of specialized courts that function in the United States today and explain the purpose of each.

3. Have specialized courts been successful? Why or why not?

WHAT WILL YOU DO?

You were discharged from the U.S. Army two months ago and have since been living with your mother in her small apartment. Two days ago, you found yourself involved in a barroom brawl—and ended up being arrested and charged with battery.

Unfortunately, you'd had a lot to drink that night and can't quite remember how the fight started. Witnesses told police that you threw the first punch but that the man you hit was a former Marine who had said some disparaging things about your branch of the service, the infantry. Although the charge of battery is a serious one, neither you nor the man you fought with had been seriously hurt.

You feel that you have served your country honorably, having done two tours of duty in Iraq and seeing some of your friends die. You've heard talk about posttraumatic stress syndrome and believe that you might be suffering from it. You know that you feel constantly on edge, jump at loud sounds, and usually have a few drinks in the evening to help soothe your nerves.

The superior court in your county recently established a special court to handle relatively minor cases of alleged criminal conduct involving former military personnel. You learn that you will be appearing before the judge of that special court.

This special veterans' court functions much like any other trial court and has the power to hear cases and impose sentences, but it also has a reputation for going easy on many of those who come before it. You've heard that some of those who are found guilty are given alternative sentences like community service and don't have to serve time in jail.

You can't afford to hire a lawyer, but you have learned that someone from the public defender's office will be available to help you present your case. You've never been in trouble with the law before and have an honorable discharge from the military. You're hoping that you can convince the judge to go easy on you.

What will you tell the judge? What outcome will you hope for? Even though you may benefit from appearing before this special court, do you believe that your service to the country qualifies you for different treatment than if you were a nonveteran? Should there be special courts for a whole variety of people—immigrants, abused children, and homeless people—or should everyone be treated the same regardless of background or special needs?

NOTES

i. J. Petrila, "An Introduction to Special Jurisdiction Courts," *International Journal of Law and Psychiatry* 26(2003):3–12.

ii. D. P. Stolle, B. J. Winick, and D. B. Wexler, *Practicing Therapeutic Jurisprudence: Law as a Helping Profession* (Durham, NC: Carolina Academic Press, 2000).

iii. K. Little, "Specialized Courts and Domestic Violence," *Issues of Democracy: The Changing Face of U.S. Courts* 8(2003):26–31; J. Weber, "Domestic Violence Courts: Components and Considerations," *Journal of the Center for Families, Children, and the Courts* 2(2000):23–36.

iv. Center for Court Innovation, *Community Courts* (New York: Center for Court Innovation, 2008). Available at http://www.communityjustice.org/index.cfm?fuseaction=page.viewPage&pageID=570&documentTopicID=17 (accessed July 7, 2009).

v. For additional information, see M. Sviridoff, *Dispensing Justice Locally: The Implementation and Effects of the Midtown Community Court* (New York: Center for Court Innovation, 1997).

vi. D. J. Farole, *The Harlem Parole Reentry Court Evaluation: Implementation and Preliminary Impacts* (New York: Center for Court Innovation, 2003).

---

1. Emma Schwartz, "Mental Health Courts," *U.S. News and World Report*, February 7, 2008, available at www.usnews.com/news/national/articles/2008/02/07/mental-health-courts (accessed February 25, 2013).

2. J. Petrila, "An Introduction to Special Jurisdiction Courts," *International Journal of Law and Psychiatry*, Vol. 26 (2003), pp. 3–12.

3. J. L. Worrall, "Prosecutors in Problem-Solving Courts," in J. L. Worrall and M. E. Nugent-Borakove, eds., *The Changing Role of the American Prosecutor* (Albany: State University of New York Press, 2008), pp. 231–243.

4. H. Goldstein, "Improving Policing: A Problem-Oriented Approach," *Crime and Delinquency*, Vol. 25 (1979), pp. 236–258.

5. J. Q. Wilson and G. Kelling, "Broken Windows: The Police and Neighborhood Safety," *Atlantic Monthly* (March 1982), pp. 29–38.

6. G. Berman and J. Feinblatt, *Problem-Solving Courts: A Brief Primer* (New York: Center for Court Innovation, 2001), pp. 5–6, available at www.courtinnovation.org. Reprinted by permission.

7. The discussion in this section draws extensively from Center for Court Innovation, *Problem-Solving Justice* (New York: Center for Court Innovation, n.d.), available at http://courtinnovation.org/index.cfm?fuseaction=page.viewPage&pageID=505&documentTopicID=31 (accessed August 4, 2009).

8. Ibid.

9. Worrall, "Prosecutors in Problem-Solving Courts," p. 233.

10. Berman and Feinblatt, *Problem-Solving Courts*.

11. J. Kaye, "Making the Case for Hands-On Courts," *Newsweek*, Vol. 134 (1999), p. 13.

12. Center for Court Innovation, *Problem-Solving Justice in the United States: Common Principles* (New York: Center for Court Innovation, n.d.), available at www.courtinnovation.org/_uploads/documents/fact_sheets/Problem_Solving_Justice_in_the_US.pdf (accessed August 4, 2009).

13. Center for Court Innovation, *Problem-Solving Courts* (New York: Center for Court Innovation, n.d.), available at www.problem-solvingcourts.org (accessed August 4, 2009).

14. D. P. Stolle, B. J. Winick, and D. B. Wexler, *Practicing Therapeutic Jurisprudence: Law as a Helping Profession* (Durham, NC: Carolina Academic Press, 2000).

15. A. R. Gover, J. M. MacDonald, and G. P. Alpert, "Combating Domestic Violence: Findings from an Evaluation of a Local Domestic Violence Court," *Criminology and Public Policy*, Vol. 3 (2003), pp. 109–132; also see R. B. Fritzler and L. M. J. Simon, "Principles of an Effective Domestic Violence Court," *American Judges Association Court Review*, Vol. 37 (2000), pp. 1–2.

16. Center for Court Innovation, *Problem-Solving Justice in the United States*.

17. See, e.g., J. L. Worrall, *Crime Control in America: What Works?*, 2nd ed. (Boston: Allyn and Bacon, 2008), chap. 11.

18. P. M. Casey and D. B. Rottman, *Problem-Solving Courts: Models and Trends* (Williamsburg, VA: National Center for State Courts, 2003), p. 6.

19. U.S. General Accounting Office, *Drug Courts: Better DOJ Data Collection and Evaluation Efforts Needed to Measure Impact of Drug Court Programs* (Washington, DC: U.S. General Accounting Office, 2002).

20. U.S. General Accounting Office, *Drug Courts: Overview of Growth, Characteristics, and Results* (Washington, DC: U.S. General Accounting Office, 1997).

21. S. Belenko, "Research on Drug Courts: A Critical Review 2001 Update," *National Drug Court Institute Review*, Vol. 4 (2001), pp. 1–60.

22. Ibid., p. 1.

23. D. B. Wilson, M. Ojmarrh, and D. L. MacKenzie, "A Systematic Review of Drug Court Effects on Recidivism," paper presented at the annual meeting of the American Society of Criminology, Chicago, 2002, p. 20.

24. Ibid.

25. S. B. Rossman, J. K. Roman, J. M. Zweig, M. Rempel, and C. H. Lindquist, *The Multi-Site Adult Drug Court Evaluation: Executive Summary* (Washington, DC: Urban Institute, 2011).

26. G. Berman and E. Gold, "Procedural Justice from the Bench: How Judges Can Improve the Effectiveness of Criminal Courts," *Judges' Journal*, Vol. 51 (2012), pp. 20–22.

27. See, e.g., L. W. Sherman and D. A. Smith, "Crime, Punishment, and Stake in Conformity: Legal and Informal Control of Domestic Violence," *American Sociological Review*, Vol. 57 (1992), pp. 680–690; R. A. Berk et al., "The Deterrent Effect of Arrest in Incidents of Domestic Violence: A Bayesian Analysis of Four Field Experiments," *American Sociological Review*, Vol. 57 (1992), pp. 698–708.

28. K. Little, "Specialized Courts and Domestic Violence," *Issues of Democracy: The Changing Face of U.S. Courts*,

Vol. 8 (2003), pp. 26–31; J. Weber, "Domestic Violence Courts: Components and Considerations," *Journal of the Center for Families, Children, and the Courts*, Vol. 2 (2000), pp. 23–36.

29. S. L. Keilitz, *Specialization of Domestic Violence Case Management in the Courts: A National Survey* (Washington, DC: National Center for State Courts, 2000).

30. L. S. Levey, M. W. Steketee, and S. L. Keilitz, *Lessons Learned in Implementing an Integrated Domestic Violence Court: The District of Columbia Experience* (Washington, DC: National Center for State Courts, 2001).

31. Center for Court Innovation, *Domestic Violence Courts: What Are They?* (New York: Center for Court Innovation, 2008), available at http://courtinnovation.org/index.cfm?fuseaction=Page.ViewPage&PageID=600&currentTopTier2=true (accessed August 4, 2009).

32. Ibid.

33. C. C. Hartley and L. Frohmann, *Cook County Target Abuser Call (TAC): An Evaluation of a Specialized Domestic Violence Court, Revised Final Report* (Washington, DC: National Institute of Justice, 2003).

34. N. K. Puffett and C. Gavin, *Predictors of Program Outcome and Recidivism at the Bronx Misdemeanor Domestic Violence Court* (New York: Center for Court Innovation, April 2004).

35. Gover et al., "Combating Domestic Violence," pp. 109–132.

36. Ibid., p. 119.

37. Puffett and Gavin, *Predictors of Program Outcome and Recidivism at the Bronx Misdemeanor Domestic Violence Court*.

38. Center for Court Innovation, *Community Courts* (New York: Center for Court Innovation, 2008), available at www.communityjustice.org/index.cfm?fuseaction=page.viewPage&pageID=570&documentTopicID=17 (accessed August 4, 2009).

39. Adapted from Casey and Rottman, *Problem-Solving Courts*.

40. For additional information, see M. Sviridoff, *Dispensing Justice Locally: The Implementation and Effects of the Midtown Community Court* (New York: Center for Court Innovation, 1997).

41. See, e.g., D. J. Chase, S. Alexander, and B. J. Miller, "Community Courts and Family Law," *Journal of the Center for Families, Children, and the Courts*, Vol. 2 (2000), pp. 37–59; J. S. Goldkamp, D. Weiland, and C. Irons-Guynn, *Developing an Evaluation Plan for Community Courts: Assessing the Hartford Community Court Model* (Rockville, MD: National Institute of Justice, 2001).

42. D. Kralstein, *Community Court Research: A Literature Review* (New York: Center for Court Innovation, 2005).

43. For a thorough review, see K. Henry and D. Kralstein, *Community Courts: The Research Literature* (New York: Center for Court Innovation, 2011).

44. E. Nugent-Borakove, *Seattle Municipal Community Court: Outcome Evaluation Final Report* (Denver: Justice Management Institute, 2009).

45. Office of Juvenile Justice and Delinquency Prevention, *Gun Court—Providence, RI, Profile No. 37.* (Washington, DC: U.S. Department of Justice, Office of Juvenile Justice

and Delinquency Prevention, n.d.), available at http://ojjdp.ncjrs.org/pubs/gun_violence/profile37.html (accessed August 4, 2009).

46. Ibid.

47. First Judicial District of Pennsylvania, *Philadelphia Gun Court Fact Sheet* (Philadelphia: First Judicial District of Pennsylvania, n.d.), available at http://courts.phila.gov/pdf/notices/2005/notice-2005-guncourt-fact-sheet.pdf (accessed August 4, 2009).

48. Ibid.

49. E. Kurtz, R. Malvestuto, F. Snyder, K. Reynolds, J. McHale, and F. Johnson, *Philadelphia's Gun Court: Process and Outcome Evaluation Executive Summary* (Philadelphia: First Judicial District of Pennsylvania, 2007), available at http://fjd.phila.gov/pdf/criminal-reports/Gun-Court-Evaluation-report-executive-summary.pdf (accessed August 4, 2009).

50. D. Sheppard and P. Kelly, *Juvenile Gun Courts: Promoting Accountability and Providing Treatment* (Washington, DC: U.S. Department of Justice, Office of Juvenile Justice and Delinquency Prevention, 2002), p. 2.

51. Ibid.

52. K. Herman, "Sex Offense Courts: The Next Step in Community Management?," *Sexual Assault Report*, Vol. 9 (2006), pp. 65–80.

53. Ibid., p. 66.

54. Ibid.

55. California Administrative Office of the Courts, *Homeless Courts* (Sacramento, CA: Administrative Office of the Courts, 2004), available at www.courtinfo.ca.gov/programs/collab/homeless.htm (accessed August 4, 2009).

56. N. Kerry and S. Pennell, *San Diego Homeless Court Program: A Process and Impact Evaluation* (San Diego, CA: San Diego Association of Governments, 2001).

57. For an introduction, see D. Denckla and G. Berman, *Rethinking the Revolving Door: A Look at Mental Illness in the Courts* (New York: Center for Court Innovation, 2001).

58. A. Watson, D. Luchins, P. Hanrahan, M. J. Heyrman, and A. Lurigio, "Mental Health Court: Promises and Limitations," *Journal of the American Academy of Psychiatry and the Law*, Vol. 28 (2000), pp. 476–482.

59. P. M. Ditton, *Mental Health and Treatment of Inmates and Probationers* (Washington, DC: Bureau of Justice Statistics, 1999).

60. E. Trupin, H. Richards, D. M. Wertheimer, and C. Bruschi, *Mental Health Court Evaluation Report* (Seattle: University of Washington, 2001), available at www.cityofseattle.net/courts/pdf/MHReport.pdf (accessed August 4, 2009). Also see E. Trupin and H. Richards, "Seattle's Mental Health Courts: Early Indicators of Effectiveness," *International Journal of Law and Psychiatry*, Vol. 26 (2003), pp. 33–53.

61. S. Rossman, J. B. Willison, K. Mallik-Kane, K. Kim, S. Debus-Sherrill, and P. M. Downey, *Criminal Justice Interventions for Offenders with Mental Illness: Evaluation of Mental Health Courts in Bronx and Brooklyn, New York* (Washington, DC: Urban Institute, 2012), p. 124.

62. R. A. Boothroyd, N. G. Poythress, A. McGaha, and J. Petrila, "The Broward Mental Health Court: Process, Outcomes, and

Service Utilization," *International Journal of Law and Psychiatry*, Vol. 26 (2003), pp. 55–71.

63. C. Fisler, "Building Trust and Managing Risk: A Look at a Felony Mental Health Court," *Psychology, Public Policy, and Law*, Vol. 11 (2005), p. 587. Reprinted by permission.

64. D. J. Farole, *The Harlem Parole Reentry Court Evaluation: Implementation and Preliminary Impacts* (New York: Center for Court Innovation, 2003), p. vii.

65. J. Petersilia, *When Prisoners Come Home: Parole and Prisoner Reentry* (New York: Oxford University Press, 2003), p. 105; also see B. Western, J. Kling, and D. Weiman, "The Labor Market Consequences of Incarceration," *Crime and Delinquency*, Vol. 47 (2001), pp. 410–428; H. J. Holzer, *What Employers Want: Job Prospects for Less-Educated Workers* (New York: Sage, 1996); M. C. Love and S. Kuzma, *Civil Disabilities of Convicted Felons: A State-by-State Survey, October 1996* (Washington, DC: U.S. Department of Justice, 1997).

66. For a few exceptions, see S. E. Vance, "Federal Reentry Court Programs: A Summary of Recent Evaluations," *Federal Probation*, Vol. 75 (2011), pp. 64–73.

67. Center for Court Innovation, *Reentry* (New York: Center for Court Innovation, n.d.), available at http://courtinnovation.org/index.cfm?fuseaction=page.viewPage&pageID=508&documentTopicID=28 (accessed August 4, 2009).

68. For additional criticisms beyond the scope of those considered here, see T. Casey, "When Good Intentions Are Not Enough: Problem-Solving Courts and the Impending Crisis of Legitimacy," *Southern Methodist University Law Review*, Vol. 57 (2004), pp. 1459–1519.

69. Available at www.reentry.gov (accessed August 4, 2009).

70. Casey, "When Good Intentions Are Not Enough," p. 1504.

71. A. Fox, *A Problem Solving Revolution: Making Change Happen in State Courts* (New York: Center for Court Innovation, 2004).

72. G. Berman, "What Is a Traditional Judge Anyway? Problem Solving in the State Courts," *Judicature*, Vol. 84 (2000), p. 81.

73. Ibid.

74. P. O'Malley, "Volatile and Contradictory Punishment," *Theoretical Criminology*, Vol. 3 (1999), pp. 175–176.

75. S. Hallsworth, "The Case for a Postmodern Penality," *Theoretical Criminology*, Vol. 6 (2002), p. 146.

76. G. Berman and J. Feinblatt, *Judges and Problem-Solving Courts* (New York: Center for Court Innovation, 2002), p. 10.

77. Ibid., p. 11.

78. M. A. R. Kleiman, "Controlling Drug Use and Crime with Testing, Sanctions, and Treatment," in P. Heymann and W. N. Brownsberger, eds., *Drug Addiction and Drug Policy: The Struggle to Control Dependence* (Cambridge, MA: Harvard University Press, 2001).

79. W. N. Brownsberger, "Limits on the Role of Testing and Sanctions," in Heymann and Brownsberger, *Drug Addiction and Drug Policy*.

80. *People* v. *Avery*, 85 N.Y. 2d 303 (1995).

81. *State* v. *Alexander*, 48 P. 3d 110 (Okla. 2000).

82. R. V. Wolf, *Don't Reinvent the Wheel: Lessons from Problem-Solving Courts* (New York: Center for Court Innovation, 2007).

83. Ibid, p. 4.

84. Wolf, *Don't Reinvent the Wheel*, p. 7.

Thinkstock

7

Judges

LEARNING OBJECTIVES

1. Summarize the role and functions of judges.

2. Describe the qualifications and appointment of federal judges.

3. Describe the qualifications and selection of state judges.

4. Summarize judicial ethics and incompetence as well as what constitutes judicial misconduct.

5. Describe judicial decision making and limits on judicial decisions.

INTRODUCTION

In 2013, Michigan domestic violence court Judge Elizabeth Hines became the first recipient of the American Judges Association's *Judge Elizabeth Hines Award*—a prize created in her honor by the national organization.[1] Hines was the natural first winner, as the award honors leadership in the area of domestic dispute resolution. Kevin Burke, immediate past president of the American Judges Association, explained that the award recognizes a judge's "diligence, passion, and concern for every individual standing before her."[2] In applauding Hines, Burke noted that "the award was established in her name because she is a role model for other judges." Hines also runs the Domestic Violence and Street Outreach Court for homeless defendants in Michigan's Washtenaw County. "If I have anything to offer," says Hines, "I hope it's that people feel more comfortable and not afraid when they come to court," she said. "We all see hundreds of people each week, and many of them don't have attorneys. I just want to make sure they understand what's going on and have a fair shot, no matter what the situation is."[3]

Michigan domestic violence court Judge Elizabeth Hines. Hines was recently honored by the American Judges Association. What is the role of a judge?

THE JUDICIAL ROLE AND FUNCTIONS

Learning Objective 1
Summarize the role and functions of judges.

Judicial robes and gavels stand out as perhaps the most visible symbols in America's court system. Just like armed police officers in their distinctive uniforms, judges in black robes who sit behind imposing benches and bang their gavels with authority leave no doubt in people's minds about the significance of their positions. Judges are powerful and significant figures in the justice process—from traffic court to the Supreme Court, judges issue decisions that alter the courses of people's lives and often leave indelible imprints on the justice system itself.

Judges are often described as **triers of law** (or finders of law), meaning that they are generally tasked with resolving any *legal* matter that comes before the court. For example, if one of the attorneys in a civil case goes too far in questioning a particular witness, such as by leading the person in one direction, the judge will make a ruling on the propriety of such action if the opposing party objects. In other words, the judge will determine whether the questioning can proceed. In a criminal case, the defendant's attorney may seek exclusion of evidence that was allegedly obtained improperly, and the judge—being familiar with the Fourth Amendment and relevant state and local rules governing the admissibility of evidence—will decide on the matter. His or her decision will amount to applying the law, either as spelled out in statutes or as interpreted by other courts' decisions.

trier of law
A description often applied to a judge that means he or she is generally tasked with resolving any legal matter that comes before the court; also called *finder of law.*

The opposite of a trier of law is a **trier of fact** (or finder of fact), someone who listens to the evidence and renders a decision as to the facts at question. Assuming that there is a jury trial, jurors are the triers of fact. In a criminal case, they listen to the facts presented by the prosecution and the defense and then render a decision based on which side presented the most convincing case. (Remember that the "facts" presented by the prosecution and the "facts" presented by the defense can differ because what happened before the trial is often disputed.) Since jurors were not present at the time of the crime, they are forced to interpret the facts as presented to them by the prosecution and defense. Jurors' decisions ultimately affect whether the defendant will be held accountable for the crime. At no point does a jury decide on what the law says or how it is to be interpreted. At the most, members of a jury may be presented with different options for verdicts, but these options are presented to them by a judge.

trier of fact
The role of a juror (in a jury trial) or a judge (in a bench trial) that requires one or the other to listen to the facts presented by the prosecution and the defense and then render a decision based on which side made the more convincing case; also called *finder of fact.*

In some cases, judges serve as triers of law *and* fact. This occurs in a bench trial, a trial in which the judge basically replaces the jury. Sometimes defendants waive their constitutional right to a jury trial (more on this in Chapter 13). In other cases, especially those involving low-level offenses like misdemeanors, jury trials are rare, if not barred altogether, which requires that the judges do more than just decide on the legal minutia in the cases. Judges even act as triers of fact to some extent in jury trials, especially in the sentencing phase. They weigh aggravating and mitigating factors and settle on a sanction that is fair relative to the crime in question, something that requires at least some degree of attention to what happened during the case or at least to what the defendant's background was leading up to the case.

Just as there are many types of courts, there are many types of judges. In this chapter, we first look at federal judges, including issues of qualification, appointment, compensation, and careers; we then do the same for state judges. But there is more to judges than just the objective aspects of the job. Judges are human and thus prone to error, and they are also pressured by various parties inside and outside the justice system. This requires some attention to judicial decision making as well as judicial ethics. Finally, while judges exercise considerable authority, their authority is not limitless; there are significant limits to judicial decisions, and we look at these in this chapter's last section. The following "Courts in the News" feature discusses a hot-button case in which a trial judge's impartiality became an important topic.

Learning Objective 2

Describe the qualifications and appointment of federal judges.

Web Extra
7–1 American Judicature Society

Library Extra
7–1 Court Cultures

FEDERAL JUDGES

The main actors in the federal judiciary are the men and women who serve as judges. Federal judges differ from their state and local counterparts not just because there are relatively few of them but because they are appointed by the president. The prospect of being asked by such a powerful individual to serve on the federal bench can serve as an important motivator for someone to seek a career as a judge. Unfortunately for most, the odds of someone being appointed to such an elite position are fairly low.

Backgrounds

Each of the many federal courts we introduced in Chapter 3 has its own judges. The most visible of these judges are the Supreme Court justices, the appellate court judges, and the district court judges. While in principle almost anyone can become a federal judge, history makes it clear that the federal bench has attracted people from a fairly select demographic, usually the middle and upper middle classes.[4]

District Judges   Most federal district court judges were first judges at the state or local level.[5] Some were previously employed in government or high-profile law firms, and a relatively small number began as law professors or attorneys in small law firms, but the norm is to have previously served on the bench, and the average age for district judges is 49 at their time of appointment. The majority graduated from Ivy League schools or private universities.[6] Most district judges are male. Until the presidency of Jimmy Carter (1977–1981), less than 2% were female, but almost half of Bill Clinton's appointees were women or minorities; between 2000 and 2008, George W. Bush also increased diversity on the bench in America's district courts by appointing 54 women and 49 minorities.[7] Despite these advances, the overwhelming majority of district court judges today continue to be white males.[8] In terms of political affiliations, approximately nine out of ten have been of the same political party as the president who appointed them.

COURTS IN THE NEWS

Judicial Impartiality

In 2013 a class-action lawsuit, *Floyd* v. *City of New York*, brought by the Center for Constitutional Rights and other civil rights lawyers, claimed that the New York Police Department (NYPD) had long been stopping and frisking black and Hispanic New Yorkers without evidence they were engaged in criminality, a violation of their civil rights. After listening to two months of testimony on the NYPD's stop-and-frisk practices, Federal Judge Shira A. Scheindlin left little doubt about where she stood on the issue. In federal district court in Manhattan, Judge Scheindlin said, "A lot of people are being frisked or searched on suspicion of having a gun and nobody has a gun, so the point is, the suspicion turns out to be wrong in most of the cases." Observing that only about 12% of police stops resulted in an arrest or summons, Judge Scheindlin focused her remarks on the other 88% of stops in which the police did not find evidence of criminality after a stop. She characterized that as "a high error rate" and remarked to a lawyer representing the city, "You reasonably suspect something, and you're wrong 90% of the time. That is a lot of misjudgment of suspicion," suggesting that officers were wrongly interpreting innocent behavior as suspicious.

During trial, Judge Scheindlin repeatedly asked a city lawyer whether it be appropriate to infer that a police encounter was racially motivated if an officer stopped a black man with no apparent basis. "If the court were to conclude there was no fair basis for the stop, but the stop was made, there has to be a reason," Judge Scheindlin said, suggesting that it might be a fair inference to find that it was a race-based stop.

Other moments revealed Judge Scheindlin to be struggling with an essential difficulty of the case: how to measure the constitutionality of not one single street stop but rather millions of stops conducted over many years. The lawsuit represented all the minority men and women who have been stopped not because their behavior was suspicious but because of the color of their skin. Research shows that about 85% of the people stopped by police are black and Hispanic. The city maintained that this number merely reflects crime patterns, but when a lawyer for the city raised this during the trial, Judge Scheindlin took issue with it, calling it a "worrisome argument." Judge

AP Photo/Richard Drew

Federal Judge Shira A. Scheindlin took plenty of heat for her handling of a civil suit filed against the New York City police department charging discrimination in their stop-and-frisk policy, but she stuck to her guns and issued a decision highly critical of police practices.

Scheindlin wondered if this line of thinking could lead police officers to rely on racial profiling in deciding whom to stop for suspicious behavior. She said that a police officer might lean toward stopping a black person because "it's more likely that he's going to be committing a crime than a white person, so that gives me further reasonable suspicion."

What's interesting about this case was that it became personal. The City went on the offensive against the judge even before the case began. An internal report by Mayor Michael Bloomberg's office painted the judge as biased against law enforcement. The report that was made public showed that she issues an unusually high number of written opinions finding that the NYPD and other law enforcement agencies make illegal searches and seizures and that she ruled against law enforcement in 60% of her written "search-and-seizure" opinions dating to when she started on the bench in 1994. That's the highest rate of any of the 16 current and former Manhattan federal judges. Court records show that she's tossed out evidence such as drugs, ammunition, and wiretaps because she deemed that it was obtained illegally by the NYPD, the U.S. Marshals Service, the Federal Bureau of Investigation, or the Bureau of Alcohol, Tobacco, and Firearms.

In response, the judge called it a "below-the-belt attack" on judicial independence. Of the criticism, she said, "It's very painful. Judges can't really easily defend themselves. . . . To attack the judge personally is completely inappropriate and intimidates judges, or it is intended to intimidate judges, or it has an effect on other judges, and that worries me."

When Judge Scheindlin ruled for the plaintiffs, the City asked an appellate court to intervene. On October 30, 2013, the Second Circuit Court of Appeals blocked Judge Scheindlin's ruling and ordered the decision to be reconsidered by another district court. It also barred the judge from further involvement in the case on the grounds that the judge violated the Code of Conduct for United States Judges, which states, "A judge should avoid impropriety

(continued)

and the appearance of impropriety in all activities" and that "A judge shall disqualify himself or herself in a proceeding in which the judge's impartiality might reasonably be questioned." The appeals court obviously believed that Judge Scheindlin behavior before and during the trial indicated that she could not an objective observer of fact and therefore voided her decision. ∎

DISCUSSION QUESTIONS

1. Let's say that Judge Scheindlin was in fact concerned about racial profiling by police. Should that be enough to force her to recuse herself from the trial?

2. Is it in the public interest to have city officials do research on the judge's past cases? Does that undermine the rule of law?

Sources: Joseph Goldstein, "Judge Criticizes 'High Error Rate' of New York Police Stops," *New York Times*, May 20, 2013, available at www.nytimes.com/2013/05/21/nyregion/judge-skeptical-of-new-york-police-stops-effectiveness.html?_r=0&pagewanted=print (accessed May 30, 2013); Ginger Adams Otis and Greg B. Smith, "Federal Judge to Rule on Stop-and-Frisk Case Bias against Cops: Report," *New York Daily News*, May 15, 2013, available at www.nydailynews.com/new-york/federal-judge-weighing-stop-and-frisk-case-bias-cops-report-article-1.1344293 (accessed May 30, 2013); Larry Neumesiter, "Shira Scheindlin, Judge in Stop-and-Frisk Trial, Calls Criticism 'Below-the-Belt,'" *Huffington Post*, May 19, 2013, available at www.huffingtonpost.com/2013/05/20/shira-scheindlin-judge-in-stop-and-frisk-trial-calls-criticism-below-the-belt_n_3306097.html?utm_hp_ref=new-york (accessed May 30, 2013); Reuters, "Appeals Court Halts New York Stop-and-Frisk Ruling, Removes Judge, October 31, 2013, available at: http://www.reuters.com/article/2013/10/31/us-usa-newyork-stopandfrisk-ruling-idUSBRE99U1A120131031.

Appeals Court Judges Federal appeals court judges are demographically very similar to their district court counterparts. The differences are that they are even more likely to have graduated from Ivy League or private university law schools.[9] They are also more likely to have been actively involved in their respective political parties before arriving on the federal bench. Of the 161 federal appeals court judges who were actively serving in spring of 2013, 110 were male and 51 were female[10]; only 36 were nonwhite.[11]

Supreme Court Justices Since 1789, 108 men and only four women (Ruth Bader Ginsburg, appointed in 1993; Sandra Day O'Connor, appointed in 1981 and retired in 2006; Elena Kagan, appointed in 2010; and Sonia Sotomayor, appointed in 2009) have served on the U.S. Supreme Court.[12] In addition, only three minorities have ever served on the Supreme Court. Thurgood Marshall, who retired in 1991, was the first African-American appointed to the Court, and the second African-American, appointed by President George H. W. Bush, was Clarence Thomas. Sonia Sotomayor, who is of Puerto Rican descent, is the Court's first Hispanic justice. Prior to Thurgood Marshall's appointment, the Court was composed entirely of white males. To this day, there is no Asian or Native American member of the nation's highest court.

The vast majority of Supreme Court justices have come from politically active families, and about one in three has come from a family with a history of judicial service.[13] Unlike the lower federal court judges, only about one in five U.S. Supreme Court justices once served as a judge at the state level or as a judge in any other federal court immediately before their appointment.

Qualifications

Many jobs carry with them a list of formal qualifications a person must possess, but informal qualifications are also important from time to time. The reverse is true for the federal judiciary: There are virtually no formal qualifications, but the informal qualifications are numerous.

Both the Constitution and federal law are silent on the subject of qualifications for Supreme Court justices and federal judges. There are no exams that need to be taken, there are no age requirements and no requirements that a judge be a U.S. citizen (as is required for the position of president), and there is even no requirement that a federal judge have a law degree. To even say that there *are* formal qualifications is a stretch because a position on the federal bench is all about the informal qualifications.

There are a number of informal qualifications that candidates for the federal bench should possess, and these run the gamut from professional competence to the "crapshoot component":[14]

1. *Professional competence.* Just because there is no formal requirement that a federal judge have a law degree and/or previous experience, clearly these competencies can improve a candidate's likelihood of gaining appointment. Tradition has basically created an expectation that, at a minimum, a federal judge have a law degree and some measure of prior law practice, and the expectations go up as the prestige factor increases.

2. *Political qualifications.* Most federal judgeships carry with them significant potential to make law and render decisions that can have sweeping implications for other branches of government. To the extent the appeals courts and particularly the Supreme Court perform a review function (see Chapter 3), it would not be helpful to have a federal judge who is clueless with respect to political issues and pressures.

3. *Political connections.* To a significant extent, positions on the federal bench are given out as "awards" for loyal political service, with those who have been active in politics being more likely to gain appointment than those who have not. Most candidates would not be visible to the president (or other political officials who often send recommendations to the president) except for some level of prior political involvement. As one author put it, "Judging is not a partisan political process, but being fitted for the robe definitely is."[15]

4. *Self-selection.* Many people are content to wait until the right job comes their way. The same is true of most judges, but some judges express their interest in serving on the federal bench. Few will do this actively or openly, but there are many means by which someone could launch a discreet campaign for a position on the federal bench. It all begins, again, with making the right political connections.

5. *"Crapshoot component."* Given that there are relatively few positions on the federal bench, there is an element of chance. At the least, one needs to be a member of the right party at the right time; for example, an openly Democratic judge probably stands no chance of being appointed to the federal bench when a Republican is in the White House. Luck can have almost as much to do with an appointment as qualifications.

Appointment Process

All federal judges are selected in essentially the same fashion. Per Article II, Section 2, of the U.S. Constitution, they are appointed by the president with the advice and consent of the Senate. Although the only judges mentioned in Article II are Supreme Court justices, the same process plays out for selection of other federal judges.

The Constitution suggests only the president and the Senate are involved in federal judicial selection, but there are many other parties also involved:

1. *President.* Technically, the president nominates all judicial candidates; history has shown, however, that the president tends to be more involved in Supreme Court appointments than those to other court positions, which is not unexpected given

senatorial courtesy
A tendency among U.S. presidents to defer to the judgment of senators and local party leaders regarding the qualifications of individuals for appointments to the lower courts.

the sheer magnitude of the federal government and the fact that the president makes numerous appointments beyond the judiciary. Supreme Court appointments are generally seen as more important because of the influence that a justice can have when serving on the highest court in the land. There is also a tendency for presidents to defer to the judgment of senators and local party leaders for appointments to the lower courts; this practice, known as **senatorial courtesy**, means that senators who are members of the president's party and are from the home state of the nominee are asked by the Senate Judiciary Committee (see below) about their thoughts concerning the suitability of one or more candidates.

2. *Justice Department.* The U.S. attorney general and the U.S. deputy attorney general help to screen prospective candidates. One of their key functions in this regard is to seek out candidates and ensure they meet the criteria (e.g., party loyalty) that the president feels are important. This process plays out in consultation with the White House staff and can include senators and other party leaders. The Federal Bureau of Investigation, an arm of the U.S. Justice Department, performs a security and background check to guide appointment decisions for all nominees to federal positions, not just judgeships.

3. *Interest groups.* After a nominee's name is released, various interest groups voice their opinions concerning the desirability (or undesirability) of one candidate relative to another. When Chief Justice Roberts was going through the nomination process, the liberal advocacy group Moveon.org vowed to oppose the nomination of what they called a "right-wing corporate lawyer and ideologue."[16]

4. *American Bar Association.* The Standing Committee on the Federal Judiciary of the American Bar Association (ABA) evaluates professional qualifications of nominees to the federal bench, but it stops short of proposing or recommending specific candidates.[17]

5. *Senate.* Candidates' names are sent to the Senate Judiciary Committee, which conducts its own investigation of the candidates' suitability for the nominated post. If the committee's vote is favorable on a candidate, his or her name is sent to the floor of the Senate, where a full vote takes place. A simple majority vote is necessary; otherwise, a nominee is not confirmed. Senatorial courtesy operates in different ways, depending on the position being voted on:

> For district judges the norm of senatorial courtesy prevails. That is, if the president's nominee is acceptable to the senator(s) of the president's party in the state in which the judge is to sit, the Senate is usually happy to confirm the appointment. For appointments to the appeals courts, senatorial courtesy does not apply, since the vacancy to be filled covers more than just the state of one or possibly two senators. But senators from each state in the circuit in which the vacancy has occurred customarily submit names of possible candidates to the president. An unwritten rule is that each state in the circuit should have at least one judge on that circuit's appellate bench.[18]

We also covered the appointment process and its effects on the court in Chapter 2, and readers are invited to review that chapter to gain further perspective.

Compensation

Federal judges are paid more than their state- and local-level counterparts, which is almost certainly due to the prestige factor that goes along with being a federal judge. According to the Administrative Office of the U.S. Courts, the chief justice of the U.S. Supreme Court earned $223,500 in 2012.[19] Associate justices each earned $213,900,[20] and they can

TABLE 7–1 Federal Judicial Salaries Compared to Congressional Salaries

Year	Senators	Members of the House of Representatives	Circuit Judges	District Judges	Associate Justices	Chief Justice
2012	$174,000	$174,000	$184,500	$174,000	$213,900	$223,500
2011	174,000	174,000	184,500	174,000	213,900	223,500
2010	174,000	174,000	184,500	174,000	213,900	223,500
2009	174,000	174,000	184,500	174,000	213,900	223,500
2008	169,300	169,300	179,500	169,300	208,100	217,400
2007	165,200	165,200	175,100	165,200	203,000	212,100
2006	165,200	165,200	175,100	165,200	203,000	212,100
2005	162,100	162,100	171,800	162,100	199,200	208,100
2004	158,100	158,100	167,600	158,100	194,300	203,000
2003	154,700	154,700	164,000	154,700	190,100	198,600
2002	150,000	150,000	159,100	150,000	184,400	192,600
2001	145,100	145,100	153,900	145,100	178,300	186,300
2000	141,300	141,300	149,900	141,300	173,600	181,400

Source: www.uscourts.gov/Viewer.aspx?doc=/uscourts/JudgesJudgeships/docs/JudicialSalarieschart.pdf (accessed February 14, 2013).

also earn a certain amount each year related to teaching engagements. Federal appellate court judges earned approximately $184,500 during 2012, and district court judges earned approximately $174,000.[21] Federal judges in the non–Article III courts (e.g., bankruptcy courts) earned a little bit less. Table 7–1 shows how federal judicial salaries have compared to those of U.S. senators and representatives over the last several years. Note how salaries have remained constant between 2009 and 2012.

Federal Judicial Compensation in Perspective Many federal employees now earn more than federal judges. For example, thousands of federal employees in certain banking and professional positions can now earn more than district judges.[22] Some federal trial attorneys can earn more than a district court judge, and some law school deans and senior professors easily earn more than some of their students who eventually find careers on the federal bench.[23] Of course, the starting pay at a prestigious big-city law firm may also be higher than that of a federal district court judge, and law partners' pay far outstrips that of the chief justice of the Supreme Court.

Discrepancies such as these have prompted a number of federal judges to leave the bench. When looking at issues of judicial compensation, one federal commission remarked that "the lag in judicial salaries has gone on too long, and the potential for the diminished quality in American jurisprudence is now too large."[24] Chief Justice Roberts has made this observation:

> Inadequate compensation directly threatens the viability of life tenure, and if tenure in office is made uncertain, the strength and independence judges need to uphold the rule of law—even when it is unpopular to do so—will be seriously eroded. . . . If judicial appointment ceases to be the capstone of a distinguished career and instead becomes a stepping stone to a lucrative position in private practice, the Framers' goal of a truly independent judiciary will be placed in serious jeopardy.[25]

Before we take up a collection for members of the Supreme Court, it is important to note that most of them are millionaires. According to the Center for Responsive Politics, here is the average net worth for each of the U.S. Supreme Court justices as of 2011:

- Ruth Bader Ginsburg: $28,090,007
- Stephen G. Breyer: $20,410,031

Web Extra
7–2 National Council of Juvenile and Family Court Judges

- John G. Roberts: $3,680,019
- Antonin Scalia: $2,130,010
- Elena Kagan: $1,835,010
- Samuel A. Alito: $580,004
- Anthony M. Kennedy: $290,002
- Clarence Thomas: $280,001
- Sonia Sotomayor: −$22,500[26]

Judicial Career Stages

If a person has the good fortune of being appointed to the federal judiciary, he or she does not exactly hit the ground running because there is a process of transitioning and easing into the new position. No amount of formal education or previous experience at the state level substitutes for a somewhat lengthy socialization process where new judges learn the ropes from their senior counterparts.

anticipatory socialization
The law school–based process of teaching an aspiring judge important analytic and communication skills and arming him or her with much of the information he or she will need in his or her future job.[i]

freshman socialization
An informal phase of the socialization of a judge, during which he or she learns and adjusts to his or her new role over the short term.

occupational socialization
An informal phase of the socialization of a judge, during which he or she undergoes on-the-job training over the course of his or her career.[ii]

Socialization Besides teaching aspiring judges the nuances of law, law school teaches them important analytic and communication skills. Years of legal practice as a prosecutor or defense attorney (or both) further develop aspiring judges' understanding of how the courts and the law work in reality. This time before a person becomes a judge is known as **anticipatory socialization**,[27] and it arms aspiring judges with much of the information they will need to do their future jobs, but no amount of anticipatory socialization can replace valuable on-the-job experience.

Unlike in many other justice-related careers, there is no formal training period or process for judges. Police officers, on completion of the academy, work with field training officers, and prosecutors, on assuming their posts, work with and learn from senior prosecutors, but judges learn the ins and outs of their jobs much more informally. They begin with a period of **freshman socialization** (learning and adjusting to the new role over the short term) followed by **occupational socialization** (on-the-job training over the course of a judge's career).[28] There is training for new federal judges offered by the Federal Judicial Center,[29] the research and education arm of the federal judicial system, but the vast majority of judges' learning takes place on the job.

Judicial socialization is critical because before an attorney becomes a judge, he or she often specializes in one avenue of law, perhaps defense representation or civil litigation for medical malpractice. Judges, by contrast, are generalists.[30] They may handle primarily civil or criminal cases, but they must become experts in all aspects of law, many of them unrelated to the work they performed before coming to the bench. For example, sentencing is mostly out of the hands of prosecutors and defense attorneys, but criminal court judges need to know a great deal in terms of sentencing options.

Moving from the position of trial court judge to the appellate level requires socialization as well. A new appeals court judge may take longer to write his or her opinion or may defer to senior colleagues. New appellate court judges may stay quieter for a period of time, too, as they absorb their surroundings and learn the job.

Move up to the level of the U.S. Supreme Court, and judicial socialization is much more complex and time-consuming. A new justice may experience a period of indecision given the importance of his or her new role. The task of a Supreme Court justice is not just to correct lower courts' errors—the justices have the authority to make policy, with sweeping implications for the whole justice system, which is a role that some new justices struggle with. Former Justice William Brennan once remarked, "I expect that only a Justice of the Court can know . . . how arduous and long is the process of developing sensitivity to constitutional adjudication that marks the role."[31] Novice justices write fewer opinions, take a more passive stance for a while, and defer to their senior colleagues.[32] Researchers have identified three so-called **freshman effects**[33] that new Supreme Court justices experience:

> First, newly appointed justices are said to be overwhelmed—even bewildered—by the Court's caseload and their own responsibilities for constitutional adjudication on the nation's court of last resort. Second, senior justices allegedly ease the opinion-writing burden on newly appointed justices by assigning freshmen fewer and less complex opinions than are assigned to veteran members of the Court. Finally, freshman justices are believed to avoid alignments with established voting blocs during their early years on the Court, a voting pattern said to be consistent with the uncertainty inherent in the role of freshman justice.[34]

Removal Article III of the U.S. Constitution provides that federal judges will hold their posts "during good Behavior," which has been interpreted to mean for life or until a judge decides to retire or step down for other reasons. A federal judge can be removed from the bench via impeachment in the House of Representatives and conviction by the Senate. **Impeachment** is defined as a "written accusation by the House of Representatives of the United States to the Senate of the United States against the President, Vice President, or an officer of the United States, including federal judges."[35] Following are the steps in the impeachment process:

1. The House Judiciary Committee deliberates over whether to initiate an impeachment inquiry.
2. The Judiciary Committee adopts a resolution seeking authority from the entire House of Representatives to conduct an inquiry. Before voting, the House debates and considers the resolution. Approval requires a majority vote.
3. The Judiciary Committee conducts an impeachment inquiry, possibly through public hearings. At the conclusion of the inquiry, articles of impeachment are prepared. They must be approved by a majority of the Committee.
4. The House of Representatives considers and debates the articles of impeachment. A majority vote of the entire House is required to pass each article. Once an article is approved, the [judge] is, technically speaking, "impeached"—that is, subject to trial in the Senate.
5. The Senate holds trial on the articles of impeachment approved by the House. The Senate sits as a jury while the Chief Justice of the Supreme Court presides over the trial.
6. At the conclusion of the trial, the Senate votes on whether to remove the [judge] from office. A two-thirds vote by the Members present in the Senate is required for removal.[36]

Article III further provides that impeachment is reserved for "treason, bribery, or other high crimes and misdemeanors," meaning that judges are removed only for the most serious of violations. Throughout U.S. history, only 13 federal judges have been faced with **articles of impeachment** (the formal allegation of misconduct, much like an indictment), and only seven have been convicted in the Senate and removed from the bench.[37] Approximately 20 other federal judges have elected to resign their posts on learning that impeachment proceedings may be initiated against them.[38] Here are the details associated with three of the most recent impeachments:

freshman effects
The phenomenon experienced by new U.S. Supreme Court justices wherein they are said to be overwhelmed—even bewildered—by the Court's caseload and their own responsibilities. The senior justice allegedly eases their opinion-writing burden, and the new justices are believed to avoid alignments with established voting blocs during their early years on the Court.[iii]

impeachment
"[A] written accusation by the House of Representatives of the United States to the Senate of the United States against the President, Vice President, or an officer of the United States, including federal judges."[iv]

articles of impeachment
The formal allegation of judicial misconduct, akin to an indictment in a criminal case.

1. *U.S. District Judge Harry Claiborne of Nevada.* Claiborne was charged with failing to report certain income on his tax returns. He shot himself to death in Las Vegas in 2004, apparently due to his battles with cancer and Alzheimer's disease.
2. *U.S. District Court Judge Alcee Hastings of Florida.* Hastings was charged with accepting a $150,000 bribe. Following his removal from the bench, he was elected to Congress and served on the House Committee on Rules.
3. *U.S. District Judge Walter L. Nixon of Mississippi.* Nixon was charged with lying to a federal grand jury. His case went before the Supreme Court, but the Court held that no court can review the impeachment and conviction of a federal officer.[39]

Judicial Councils Reform and Judicial Conduct and Disability Act of 1980
The 1980 U.S. legislation that provided a mechanism for the federal judiciary to respond to allegations that a particular judge is unfit.

Rule of 80
A retirement rule (established in 1984) that allows a federal judge to retire with full pay and benefits if the sum of his or her age and years of service on the bench equals 80, subject to certain restrictions. A sliding scale allows a judge to retire earlier for less pay.[v]

senior status
A category of federal judgeship permitted by the U.S. Congress to federal judges who do not formally retire but who effectively give up their seats and work part time, handling cases based on need. Senior status judges essentially volunteer their services and, together, handle about 15 percent of the federal courts' workload in a given year.[vi]

What about a judge who does not commit "treason, bribery, or other high crimes and misdemeanors" but instead has an obvious conflict of interest in a particular case, or what of a judge whose personal beliefs and perceptions affect his or her behavior more than the law? Can anything be done? When the **Judicial Councils Reform and Judicial Conduct and Disability Act of 1980** took effect, it provided a mechanism for the federal judiciary to respond to allegations that a particular judge is unfit; most judges, however, will excuse themselves in cases where they may face potential criticism for sticking with a particular case. Unfortunately, to remove an Article III judge (one appointed pursuant to Article III's "good behavior" provision), impeachment is the only recourse. We also look at some additional steps for removal of judges from specific trials (as opposed to removal from their positions) in the section titled "Limits on Judicial Decisions" later in this chapter.

Senior Status and Retirement   Allowing federal judges to stay in their positions for life can result in the problem of having some rather elderly judges. Since 1984, federal judges have been allowed to retire with full pay and benefits under the so-called **Rule of 80**[40]: If the sum of the judge's age and years of service on the bench equals 80, he or she qualifies for retirement. This rule is subject to certain restrictions, and there is a sliding scale such that a judge can retire earlier for less pay; for example, the judge who is at least 65 years of age and has 15 years of experience can retire. Congress has also permitted federal judges who do not formally retire to qualify for **senior status**,[41] meaning that these judges effectively give up their seats and work part-time, handling cases based on need. They essentially volunteer their services and, together, handle about 15% of the federal courts' workload in a given year. To retain senior status, judges have to meet certain criteria, which are reprinted in Box 7–1.

BOX 7–1   Requirements for Federal Judges to Retain Senior Status

- Having carried, in the preceding calendar year, a caseload involving courtroom participation which is equal to or greater than the amount of similar work which an average judge in active service would perform in three months [Section 371(e)(1)(a)]
- Having performed, in the preceding calendar year, substantial judicial duties not involving courtroom participation, but including settlement efforts, motion decisions, writing opinions in cases that have not been orally argued, and administrative duties for the court to which the justice or judge is assigned [Section 371(e)(1)(b)]
- Having performed substantial administrative duties, either directly relating to the operation of the courts, *or* for a Federal or State governmental entity [Section 371(e)(1)(d)] ▪

Source: 28 U.S.C., Section 371.

While age typically influences the retirement decision, researchers have found that federal judges sometimes retire for strategic reasons. One study found that judges retire when political conditions favor appointment of a successor who holds similar ideological beliefs and policy views.[42] Another study found that retirement decisions are affected mostly by nonpolitical factors (e.g., age) but that presidential elections exerted some influence over judges' decisions.[43] One author argued that "many jurists view themselves as part of a policy link between the people, the judicial appointment process, and the subsequent decisions of judges and justices."[44]

STATE JUDGES

Learning Objective 3
Describe the qualifications and selection of state judges.

State judges perform many of the same functions as federal judges, but the state judiciary parts ways quite significantly from the federal judiciary in other respects. First, depending on a state's legal arrangements, there may be many more types of judges at the state level. Second, the selection varies from state to state: State-level judicial selection can be intensely political due to the fact that some judges are elected to their positions; procedures for compensation, retention, removal, and retirement also vary to some extent among the states when compared to the federal judiciary.

Types and Qualifications

There are many types of state-level judges. As a general rule, the qualifications for judges who work in limited jurisdiction courts are less stringent than those for judges who work in general jurisdiction courts, appellate courts, or state supreme courts. For example, to become a justice of the peace in Texas, there are six requirements:

1. He or she must be a citizen of the United States.
2. He or she must be at least 18 years of age on the day the term starts or on the date of appointment.
3. He or she must not have been determined mentally incompetent by a final judgment of a court.
4. He or she must not have been convicted of a felony from which he or she has not been pardoned or otherwise released from the resulting penalties.
5. He or she, as a general rule, must have resided continually in Texas for one year and in the precinct for the preceding six months.
6. He or she must not have been declared ineligible for the office.[45]

Similar rules apply for magistrate judges, who adjudicate cases in limited jurisdiction courts throughout the country (see Box 7–2, which lists the qualifications of a city judge in Hamilton, Montana; also see Chapter 4). In contrast, trial and appellate court judges usually must be practicing attorneys. For example, the state of Maryland requires that its judges possess the following qualifications:

- U.S. and Maryland citizenship
- Registration to vote in state elections at the time of appointment
- Residence in the state for at least five years
- Residence, for at least six months preceding appointment, in the geographic area where the vacancy exists
- Age of at least 30 at the time of appointment
- Membership in the Maryland bar[46]

Web Extra
7–3 Federal Magistrate Judges Association

Library Extra
7–2 National Institute of Justice Survey of Judges, Trial Court Administrators, and State Court Administrators

BOX 7-2 Qualifications and Requirements of a City Judge in Hamilton (Montana)

- The individual must be a citizen of the United States and must have been a resident of the county (in this case, Ravalli County) for a minimum of one year.
- The judge must hold office hours from 8:00 A.M. to 5:00 P.M. daily, except on weekends, holidays, and nonjudicial days.
- Each judge must obtain a certificate demonstrating that he or she completed training required by the Montana Supreme Court Commission on Courts of Limited Jurisdiction. This training must be completed *before* the judge takes office. Temporary certificates are issued in some circumstances.
- All city judges must abide by applicable ethical standards and principles.
- Before a city judge can serve, he or she must take a constitutional oath of office.
- The city judge will collect all required payments and disseminate all such payments to the parties entitled to them. ■

Source: Ordinance 102 (part), 1996; prior code, Section 2.12.050, available at www.cityofhamilton.net/codes/Title_2/36/050.html (accessed February 15, 2013).

Selection Process

At a glance, the process of selecting state judges for their posts could seem dry and uninteresting. On closer examination, though, the process is extremely controversial and politicized. Some people feel that courts (especially appellate courts) serve to keep the legislative and executive branches of government in check, so to the extent this occurs, it is important for judges to be removed from the legislative and executive processes. Alternatively, some people feel strongly that judges themselves need to be kept in check, which can occur by making them answerable to the voters. A possible downside of judicial elections, though, is that elections put judges and politics in close company.

Election More than 80% of state appellate court judges and nearly 90% of state trial court judges are elected to their posts.[47] The terms that elected judges serve are generally short, typically lasting between two and four years, which is far from the lifetime appointments that federal judges receive.

While judicial elections can be quite political, they are generally far from presidential or gubernatorial elections in terms of their contentiousness. In addition, many judicial candidates run unopposed.[48] Even so, it is still possible for negative campaigning and publicized disagreements over important issues to creep into the judicial election process, especially in partisan elections (those in which a candidate runs as a member of a known political party). Critics of partisan elections for judges have raised some concerns:

> Elections create concerns about judicial corruption and impartiality. The view is that current elections and campaign financing create an impression of impropriety, bringing into question a judge's ability to impartially interpret and apply laws and administer justice. "There is also a concern that if judges can be influenced by campaign contributions, then they will be unable to resist the difficulties that a judge faces through friendships and associations that come before the court."[49]

Some states rely on nonpartisan elections for judicial selection. These nonpartisan elections help ensure judicial neutrality while keeping judges answerable to the electorate. Judges in these nonpartisan election states are also elected to longer terms, usually from four to 12 years.

While nonpartisan elections may seem ideal, there is a potential downside of this approach: In nonpartisan elections, voters may elect judges based on name recognition and other illegitimate criteria (e.g., race, age) rather than their partisan affiliations. Finally, because nonpartisan judges do not overtly side with one political party over another does not mean that they will avoid negative campaigning. Some have expressed concern that the same dirty politics we see in gubernatorial and presidential elections are creeping into even the most nonpartisan judicial elections.[50]

Merit Selection Merit selection is concerned solely with identifying judges who are qualified and intelligent and who will do the job well. How does merit selection take place? A nonpartisan commission is typically appointed; it then evaluates prospective candidates. The commission selects the best and most qualified candidates and forwards their names to the appointing authority (typically the governor).

One of the more common merit-based selection systems has been dubbed the **Missouri Plan** (after the Missouri Bar Plan adopted in 1940), and it combines appointment and election systems. Three steps take place: First, a commission nominates qualified individuals, thus ensuring that not just anyone becomes a judge; second, the governor or another executive official appoints a nominee to a judicial position; and, third, retention elections follow the initial term.

There are several arguments in favor of merit-based selection:

> Proponents advocate merit selection over election on a number of grounds, including (1) judges should be chosen based upon qualifications (merit) rather than political or social connections; (2) merit selection reduces the negative influence of politics and money pervasive in judicial elections; (3) merit selection retains an electoral feature for removal of judges—a yes/no citizen vote for retention; and (4) merit selection increases representation of women and minority judges.[51]

But there are always two sides to every story, and the merit system has its share of critics. Some feel that it is not shielded from politics, as the appointment commissions can themselves be less than objective[52]; others have pointed out that there has been a decline in support for merit-based systems.[53] This may be due to the fact that merit-based appointment takes some control over who serves as judge away from the voters.

Gubernatorial and Legislative Appointments Many state judges are appointed by state governors. Whether gubernatorial appointment is used depends on the state in question and the type of court. For example, while the governor in California appoints judges to courts of appeal and the supreme court, voters decide who serves as superior court judges.[54] Supporters of gubernatorial appointment feel that this selection mechanism is essential for the promotion of judicial independence. Since appointments usually carry long terms, this can act to protect judges from threat of removal that would result from an election; moreover, appointed judges do not have to worry about voters' approval of their decision making.

Just because a judge is appointed to his or her post does not mean that he or she answers to no one. Governors appoint judges who most likely agree with their positions, and voters select governors who agree with their positions. Thus, even appointed judges can be answerable to the electorate to some extent. Of course, there is always the possibility that an appointed judge will go his or her own way:

> The appointive systems' greatest strength is also its greatest weakness. There is no guarantee that judicial decisions will be decided fairly and impartially even though judges are free from all limits on their decision-making. There is no substantive check

Missouri Plan
One of the more common merit-based selection systems for state judges, based on Missouri Bar Plan adopted in 1940, that combines appointment and election systems.

on judicial decision-making and discretion after the initial appointment. The tradeoff for judicial independence is the risk that judges will pursue personal agendas that are in conflict with their judicial responsibilities.[55]

Appointment Methods and Diversity on the Bench

There has been some interest in the effects of judicial appointment methods on diversity on the bench. Does one system result in more minority judges than another? One study found that appointment and merit systems increase minority representation more than elective systems,[56] but another study concluded that it was the diversity of the nominating commission or authority that made the difference more than the actual appointment mechanism employed.[57] As for women, research reveals that their chances of serving on the bench improve when appointment methods are used[58]; however, their chances are improved only if the court is already male-dominated.[59] For example, governors may use their appointment authority to diversify the bench if there is public pressure to do so.

Compensation

Judges' compensation varies from state to state and court to court. Since the 1970s, the National Center for State Courts has conducted surveys of judicial salaries by state.[60] The center does not survey limited jurisdiction courts for salary information, but it does report on judges' salaries in general jurisdiction trial courts and appellate courts as well as the states' highest courts. The highest-paid chief of a state's top court was paid $218,237 per year in the most recent survey period[61]; in contrast, the lowest-paid general jurisdiction court judge was paid $104,170 per year.[62] Table 7–2 ranks salaries by state for appellate and general jurisdiction court judges. Not surprisingly, California, with its high cost of living, ranks at the top for judicial salaries, and Montana ranks near the bottom.

TABLE 7–2 Judicial Salary Rankings

Salaries and Rankings for Appellate and General-Jurisdiction Judges - *Listed in Order of State Rank*

The tables below list the salaries for associate justices of the courts of last resort, associate judges of intermediate appellate courts, and judges of general jurisdiction trial courts (actual salaries and cost-of-living adjusted salaries) as of January 1, 2013. Where possible, the salary figures are actual salaries. In jurisdictions where some judges receive supplements, the figures are the most representative available—either the base salary, the midpoint of a range between the lowest and highest supplemented salaries, or the median. The listings are in rank order from highest to lowest salary. The mean, median, and salary range for each of the positions are also shown.

				General-Jurisdiction Trial Court			
Highest Court		**Intermediate Appellate Court**		**Salary**		**Adjusted for Cost of Living**	
California	$218,237	California	$204,599	Illinois	$182,429	Illinois	$171,637
Illinois	$211,228	Illinois	$198,805	Alaska	$181,440	Tennessee	$167,694
Pennsylvania	$199,606	Pennsylvania	$188,337	Delaware	$180,233	Delaware	$165,684
Alaska	$196,224	Alaska	$185,388	California	$178,789	Pennsylvania	$159,331
Delaware	$190,639	Alabama	$178,878	District of Columbia	$174,000	Nevada	$149,775
New Jersey	$185,482	New Jersey	$175,534	Pennsylvania	$173,271	Arkansas	$148,073
District of Columbia	$184,500	New York	$168,600	New Jersey	$165,000	Georgia	$147,969
Virginia	$183,839	Virginia	$168,322	Tennessee	$161,808	Virginia	$146,926
Alabama	$180,005	Tennessee	$167,592	Nevada	$160,000	Louisiana	$146,628
New York	$177,000	Georgia	$166,186	New York	$160,000	Alabama	$140,756
Tennessee	$173,352	Washington	$156,328	Virginia	$158,134	Michigan	$140,233
Nevada	$170,000	Connecticut	$152,637	Wyoming	$150,000	Arizona	$139,720
Georgia	$167,210	Maryland	$152,543	Rhode Island	$149,207	Wyoming	$139,221

TABLE 7-2 (Continued)

Highest Court		Intermediate Appellate Court		General-Jurisdiction Trial Court			
				Salary		Adjusted for Cost of Living	
Rhode Island	$165,726	Indiana	$152,293	Georgia	$148,891	Iowa	$138,669
Maryland	$165,600	Michigan	$151,441	Washington	$148,832	Alaska	$138,362
Wyoming	$165,000	Florida	$150,077	Connecticut	$146,780	South Carolina	$137,014
Michigan	$164,610	Arizona	$150,000	Arizona	$145,000	Indiana	$135,677
Washington	$164,221	Iowa	$147,900	Maryland	$143,160	Kentucky	$135,558
Iowa	$163,200	Louisiana	$143,647	Florida	$142,178	Oklahoma	$134,273
Connecticut	$162,520	Arkansas	$140,732	Michigan	$139,919	Nebraska	$134,152
Florida	$157,976	Utah	$140,100	New Hampshire	$137,804	Utah	$133,441
Indiana	$156,667	Hawaii	$139,924	Louisiana	$137,744	West Virginia	$133,219
Arizona	$155,000	Nebraska	$138,334	Iowa	$137,700	California	$133,203
Hawaii	$151,118	South Carolina	$137,753	Arkansas	$136,257	Florida	$132,840
Louisiana	$150,772	Minnesota	$137,552	Hawaii	$136,127	New Jersey	$131,624
Texas	$150,000	Texas	$137,500	Alabama	$134,943	Washington	$128,352
Missouri	$147,591	Wisconsin	$136,316	Nebraska	$134,694	North Dakota	$127,456
New Hampshire	$146,917	Massachusetts	$135,087	South Carolina	$134,221	Wisconsin	$127,124
Utah	$146,800	Missouri	$134,685	Utah	$133,450	Missouri	$127,101
Massachusetts	$145,984	Colorado	$134,128	Indiana	$130,080	North Carolina	$126,571
Minnesota	$145,981	North Carolina	$133,109	Massachusetts	$129,694	Texas	$125,177
Nebraska	$145,615	Ohio	$132,000	Minnesota	$129,124	Minnesota	$124,066
Arkansas	$145,204	Kansas	$131,518	Wisconsin	$128,600	Rhode Island	$122,202
Wisconsin	$144,495	Oklahoma	$130,410	Colorado	$128,598	Ohio	$121,922
Ohio	$141,600	Kentucky	$130,044	Missouri	$127,020	Maryland	$121,864
South Carolina	$141,286	Oregon	$122,820	North Dakota	$126,597	Colorado	$119,089
Colorado	$139,660	Idaho	$120,900	Vermont	$126,369	District of Columbia	$118,367
North Carolina	$138,896	New Mexico	$117,506	West Virginia	$126,000	Mississippi	$118,291
North Dakota	$138,159	Mississippi	$114,994	North Carolina	$125,875	Kansas	$118,091
Oklahoma	$137,655			Texas	$125,000	Idaho	$115,270
West Virginia	$136,000			Kentucky	$124,620	South Dakota	$114,010
Kansas	$135,905			Oklahoma	$124,373	New Hampshire	$112,274
Kentucky	$135,504			Ohio	$121,350	Montana	$111,675
Vermont	$132,928			Kansas	$120,037	New Mexico	$109,028
Oregon	$125,688			Oregon	$114,468	Vermont	$108,353
New Mexico	$123,691			Idaho	$114,300	Connecticut	$106,951
Mississippi	$122,460			Montana	$113,928	New York	$104,726
Idaho	$121,900			South Dakota	$113,688	Oregon	$99,920
South Dakota	$121,718			Mississippi	$112,128	Massachusetts	$98,972
Montana	$121,434			Maine	$111,969	Maine	$96,537
Maine	$119,476			New Mexico	$111,631	Hawaii	$90,463
Mean	$155,143		$148,834		$139,166		
Median	$150,000		$140,732		$134,943		
Range	$119,476 to $218,237		$114,994 to $204,599		$111,631 to $182,429		

Information in this survey is collected from designated representatives in each state. The National Center for State Courts has protocols in place to help ensure the accuracy of the data that are collected, analyzed, and ultimately reported.

Source: National Center for State Courts, *Survey of Judicial Salaries*, available at www.ncsc.org/~/media/Microsites/Files/Judicial%20Salaries/jud_2012.ashx (accessed February 15, 2013).

Retention

Whereas federal judges do not have to worry about retention, many state judges do. Some are elected and must go before the electorate to retain their posts; others who are appointed via a version of the Missouri Plan (see above) sometimes face retention elections. Still other states, regardless of selection mechanism, require judicial performance appraisals and evaluations.

Arizona is the only state with a constitutionally authorized performance evaluation program for its judges, and some other states have adopted judicial retention evaluation programs similar to Arizona's but have stopped short of making them constitutional requirements. Beginning in 2008, the Kansas Commission on Judicial Performance conducted evaluations of all Kansas judges and provided them with the results. The judges then use information from the commission's report to voluntarily take steps to improve themselves.

Commissions such as these perform an important function, but this function may be a largely symbolic one. The norm for selection of trial court judges (as we saw earlier) is election. Absent significant misconduct, the only thing that would ensure that a judge was removed from the bench is election of another candidate in the next election. Other states grant judges life tenure, so removal from the bench can be difficult. We now look at some of the state-level mechanisms for removing judges from the bench.

Retirement and Removal

States adopt different rules for judicial retirement. Age formulas, sliding salary scales, varying levels of part-time work, and other factors result in considerable variation from place to place. As for removal of judges, most states have adopted impeachment procedures that resemble the impeachment process for federal judges, and some states provide more than one mechanism for judicial removal. In Florida, judges can be removed either by recommendation of the Judicial Qualifications Commission or via impeachment in the state's house of representatives (a two-thirds vote) and conviction in the Senate (also a two-thirds vote).[63] Maryland judges can be removed in one of four ways:

1. Judges may be removed by the governor on the address of the general assembly, with the concurrence of two-thirds of the members of each house.
2. Judges may be retired by the general assembly, with a two-thirds vote of each house and the governor's concurrence.
3. Judges may be impeached by a majority of the house of delegates and convicted by two-thirds of the senate.
4. Judges may be removed or retired by the court of appeals on the recommendation of the Commission on Judicial Disabilities.[64]

Learning Objective 4

Summarize judicial ethics and incompetence as well as what constitutes judicial misconduct.

judicial ethics
"[T]he standards and norms that bear on judges and [that] cover such matters as how to maintain independence [and] impartiality and avoid impropriety."[vii]

JUDICIAL ETHICS

Judicial ethics is part of a larger category of legal ethics. According to the Legal Information Institute at Cornell University, **judicial ethics** is defined as "the standards and norms that bear on judges and covers such matters as how to maintain independence, impartiality, and avoid impropriety."[65] Judges who fail to maintain their independence, act impartially, and avoid impropriety run afoul of ethical standards and guidelines spelled out by various authorities:

- Professional associations
- Ethical codes
- Statutes
- State judicial commissions

In this section, we look at the influence of professional associations and state commissions on judicial ethics. We wrap up with a look at federal judicial conduct and some discussion of ethical dilemmas that judges face as well as the characteristics of the ideal judge.

Professional Associations

A number of professional associations are involved in judicial ethics through efforts to promote the independence and integrity of the courts. One such association that judges, lawyers, and concerned citizens can join is the **American Judicature Society**, which collects information from state judicial ethics commissions, conducts research, responds to press inquiries, and holds conferences on judicial ethics each year and also serves as a clearinghouse of useful information for people concerned with possible judicial misconduct. Links on the organization's website provide contact information, state by state, for the "go-to" authority in each state where a complaint of judicial impropriety may be filed. The society also publishes the *Judicial Conduct Reporter*, a quarterly periodical that tracks developments in judicial discipline and changes in judicial codes of conduct.

The ABA is also heavily involved in judicial ethics. The ABA's **Model Code of Judicial Conduct** was adopted in 1972, replacing the so-called Canon of Legal Ethics, which was created some 50 years earlier. The code's five canons emphasize the importance of upholding integrity, minimizing the appearance of impropriety, remaining impartial, and avoiding conflicts of interest. Judges are also encouraged to avoid political activities.[66]

State Commissions

States have adopted their own codes of judicial conduct, not unlike the ABA Model Code of Judicial Conduct. Most states also maintain judicial commissions that monitor the behavior of judges and engage in disciplinary actions when necessary. For example, New York's Commission on Judicial Conduct consists of 11 members; four are appointed by the governor, three by the chief judge of the court of appeals, and one each by the leaders of the state legislature. The commission considers complaints against judges, but only if they are written and signed.

Arizona, like most other states, maintains a similar process. Its Commission on Judicial Conduct also investigates complaints against judges in a number of categories:

- Willful misconduct in office
- Willful and persistent failure to perform duties
- Habitual intemperance (e.g., alcohol or drug abuse)
- Permanent disabilities that interfere with judicial duties
- Violation of the Code of Judicial Conduct
- Conduct that brings the judiciary into disrepute[67]

Complaints about Judicial Conduct

Complaints against federal judges are governed by the **Judicial Conduct and Disability Act of 1980**, which permits any person to file a written complaint alleging that a federal judge has engaged in "conduct prejudicial to the effective and expeditious administration of the business of the courts [or] is unable to discharge all duties of office by reason of mental or physical disability."[68] The act further requires that complaints be filed with the chief judge of the court of appeals in the circuit from which the complaint

American Judicature Society (AJS)
A professional association for judges, lawyers, and concerned citizens that is involved in judicial ethics through efforts to promote the independence and integrity of the courts.

Model Code of Judicial Conduct
A code of judicial conduct, adopted by the American Bar Association in 1972, that replaced the so-called Canon of Legal Ethics, which had been created some 50 years earlier.

Web Extra
7–4 American Bar Association

Web Extra
7–5 National Association of Women Judges

Web Extra
7–6 American Judges Association

Library Extra
7–3 Code of Conduct for U.S. Judges

Judicial Conduct and Disability Act of 1980
The U.S. legislation that permitted any person to file a written complaint alleging that a federal judge has engaged in "conduct prejudicial to the effective and expeditious administration of the business of the courts" or "is unable to discharge all duties of office by reason of mental or physical disability."[viii]

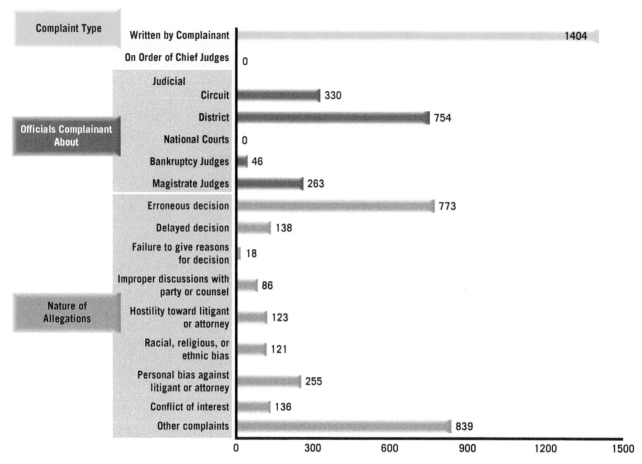

FIGURE 7–1

Complaints Filed and Actions Taken against Federal Judges (2011)

Source: Administrative Office of the U.S. Courts, *2011 Annual Report of the Director: Judicial Business of the United States Courts* (Washington, DC: Administrative Office of the U.S. Courts, 2012), table S-22, available at www.uscourts.gov/uscourts/Statistics/JudicialBusiness/2011/JudicialBusiness2011.pdf (accessed February 15, 2013).

arises. The chief judge then dismisses the complaint, concludes the proceeding if corrective action has been taken, or appoints a special committee to investigate the judge in question. In practice, most complaints are found to be baseless and are promptly dismissed.[69] Why? Most complaints are "directly related to the merits of a decision or procedural ruling," meaning that people who complain tend to be more upset about a judge's decision rather than the judge him- or herself.[70] This, along with other information concerning the nature and disposition of complaints against federal judges, can be seen in Figure 7–1.

If a special committee is appointed, it investigates the case and makes a recommendation to the appropriate federal circuit judicial council (see Chapter 3). The judicial council then chooses from one of several options:

- Dismiss the complaint
- Certify the disability of a judge
- Request that a judge voluntarily retire
- Order that no further cases be assigned to a judge on a temporary basis for a certain time
- Censure or reprimand the judge by private communication
- Censure or reprimand the judge by public announcement
- Order such other action as it considers appropriate under the circumstances[71]

Judicial Ethical Dilemmas

The range of ethical dilemmas judges can face is wide, yet there are some that come up more often than others. Here are a few examples:

- The judge presides over a case in which a relative is related to the counsel of record.
- Some judges work part-time, and if they operate a private practice on the side, this can raise concerns if their cases are heard in the courts in which they serve as judicial officers.
- The judge may be a former prosecutor, and this could compromise his or her objectivity.
- A case coming before a judge may involve a business either with which he or she has an affiliation or of which he or she is a client.
- Appointments of judges to governmental committees and commissions may raise ethical dilemmas, especially if such committees or commissions involve issues related to policy and law.
- Political activities can raise ethical dilemmas, especially in states that maintain partisan judicial elections.

The list goes on. Judicial codes of ethics generally provide guidance on ethical dilemmas of several varieties, including most of those we have listed here. See the accompanying Web Extra (particularly Part 4 of the report it takes you to) for a longer list of ethical dilemmas and prohibited conduct. The following "Courts in the News" feature discusses the removal of judges for egregious violation of judicial ethics.

Web Extra
7–7 Judicial Ethics Handbook

What Makes a Good Judge?

All this discussion about judicial misconduct leaves one asking a question: What makes a good judge? What are the characteristics most sought after in a judge? There are certain minimal qualifications, such as a law degree for certain posts (which we discussed earlier), and there are also many other qualities that aspiring judges should bring to the table. The ABA has gone so far as to identify eight of them: integrity, legal knowledge and ability, professional experience, judicial temperament, diligence, good health, financial responsibility, and public service.[72]

Most of these are self-explanatory. Legal knowledge and ability as well as professional experience are obviously desirable, as is someone who is in good health. We would certainly hope that judges go about their jobs with diligence considering the importance of the role, and our ethics discussion above also reinforces the notion that judges should possess integrity. Financial responsibility is a characteristic that many government employers look for; for example, aspiring police officers undergoing background investigations routinely have their financial histories checked out. Public service is also important—giving of one's time selflessly is a sought-after characteristic for everyone, from college applicants to presidential candidates. But what is judicial temperament? According to the ABA, "Among the qualities which comprise judicial temperament are patience, open-mindedness, courtesy, tact, firmness, understanding, compassion and humility."[73]

JUDICIAL DECISION MAKING

Ideally, judges act in an entirely neutral and detached fashion, but judges are human. They are not immune from making decisions based on emotion, stereotypes, preconceived ideas, and personal experience—in addition to legal considerations. This has come to light after decades of research on factors affecting judicial decisions.[74] Much of the research has focused on Supreme Court justices' decisions, but many of the findings

Learning Objective 5
Describe judicial decision making and limits on judicial decisions.

COURTS IN THE NEWS

Judicial Misconduct

While most judges are honest, hardworking civil servants, there are some who abuse their office for personal gain. Of these corrupt judges, none may be worse than Pennsylvania judges Mark Ciavarella, Jr., and Michael Conahan. Since 2003, the two received millions of dollars in bribes for condemning minors to maximum prison sentences. In one case, Ciavarella sentenced a 10-year-old to two years in a detention facility for accidently bottoming out his mother's car. He also sentenced children to extended stays in juvenile detention for offenses as minimal as mocking a principal on Myspace, trespassing in a vacant building, and shoplifting DVDs from Walmart.

Conahan, the president judge of Luzerne County from 2002 to 2006, closed a county-owned juvenile detention center in December 2002, forcing the county to send juveniles to the for-profit facility when it opened in 2003. He signed a secret agreement to place children in the new facility that the facility's backers used to secure financing for its construction.

According to the Pennsylvania Supreme Court, over 5,000 young men and women were unjustly sentenced to prison and denied their constitutional rights. Many of them have now been released and cleared of their charges. In the private prison industry, longer sentences earn more money from the state.

Ciavarella, known for his harsh and autocratic courtroom manner, was convicted of racketeering, money laundering, mail fraud, and tax evasion and sentenced to 28 years in prison. He was also ordered to pay $1.2 million in restitution. Conahan pleaded guilty for accepting a share of $2.8 million

AP Photo/David Kidwell, File

Former Judge Mark Arthur Ciavarella Jr. (pictured here), along with fellow judge Michael Conahan, was convicted of a felony for selling kids for cash to detention center operators.

from the builder and co-owner of the for-profit detention centers. He received a 17½-year federal prison sentence and a bill for nearly $900,000 in fines and restitution. "Unfortunately, two judges in Luzerne County have caused unimaginable taint to the laudable efforts of many dedicated individuals," Chief Justice Ronald D. Castille commented on the case, "conduct for which those two judges presently are paying dearly." ■

DISCUSSION QUESTIONS

1. Ciavaralla's attorneys requested a reasonable sentencing, arguing that the media attention brought to the case was punishment enough: "He will forever be unjustly branded as the 'Kids For Cash' judge." Would you have been swayed by this argument if you were the sentencing judge?

2. What can be done to eliminate judicial corruption?

Sources: Michael Rubinkam, "Mark Ciavarella Jr., Judge, Gets 28 Years In 'Kids For Cash' Case," *Huffington Post,* August 11, 2011, available at www.huffingtonpost.com/2011/08/11/mark-ciavarella-jr_n_924324.html (accessed May 30, 2013); Michael R. Sisak and Patrick Sweet, "'Boss' Conahan Sentenced to 17 1/2 Years," citizensvoice.com, September 23, 2011, available at http://citizensvoice.com/boss-conahan-sentenced-to-17-years-1.1207996 (accessed May 30, 2013); Zack Needles and Leo Strupczewski, "Judge Convicted in 'Cash for Kids' Scandal, Mother of Dead Teen Confronts Him," February 22, 2011, *The Legal Intelligencer,* available at www.law.com/jsp/pa/PubArticlePA.jsp?id=1202483040912 (accessed May 30, 2013).

generalize to other types of judges.[75] The literature reveals that judges' decisions are affected by many considerations:

- Personal ideology and attitudes
- Election considerations
- Public opinion
- Strategic considerations
- Consensus seeking
- Laws

Personal Ideology and Attitudes

First and foremost, judges' decisions are affected by their ideology and attitudes.[76] In one of the more sophisticated studies to date, a team of researchers found that Supreme Court justices' ideology and beliefs were almost perfectly correlated with their decisions.[77] Justices' attitudes and beliefs may change over time, but most studies report remarkable stability.[78] This may seem a bit disturbing, but it helps explain all the controversy revolving around the confirmation of new Supreme Court justices.

Sentencing research reveals that judges base their decisions on everything from philosophical preferences to demographic characteristics; for example, a judge who favors rehabilitation would sentence differently than one who believes that deterrence is most important. As for demographic characteristics, it appears that gender is important: One study of state supreme court justices found that female justices voted more liberally and that the very presence of a female on the court increased the probability that the male justices would decide liberally.[79] A judge's race appears to matter, too, but only to a limited extent.[80]

Election Considerations

Researchers have found that elected judges who are nearing the end of their terms tend to vote in unexpected ways.[81] It also appears that judges take steps to avoid drawing too much attention to themselves when they are faced with a looming election period. One study of state supreme court justices stated,

> [J]ustices who strongly desire re-election and fear the possibility of electoral sanction will not distinguish themselves from the rest of the court by dissenting on highly salient political questions. Instead, a justice will either vote with the majority or . . . mask his or her disagreement in a concurrence rather than a dissent.[82]

Public Opinion

Public opinion has been shown to influence judges' decisions.[83] One study found that Supreme Court decisions matched up well with public opinion polls 63% of the time.[84] This was echoed by a later study that found strong correlation between people's attitudes on controversial subjects and Supreme Court decisions concerning them.[85] There is some debate, however, over exactly how public opinion shapes justices' decisions. Does it have a direct effect? Do justices listen to popular sentiments and read opinion polls? Conversely, does public opinion affect their decisions indirectly, such as through presidential elections? Public opinion most likely exerts an indirect effect on the justices[86]; one study found that Supreme Court justices reference public opinion in their decisions a scant 2% of the time.[87] This is to be expected, especially when we look at former Justice Robert H. Jackson's argument in *West Virginia Board of Education* v. *Barnette*:

> The very purpose of the Bill of Rights was to withdraw certain subjects from the vicissitudes of political controversy, to place them beyond the reach of majorities and officials and to establish them as legal principles to be applied by the courts. One's right to life, liberty and property, to free speech, free press, freedom of worship and assembly, and other fundamental rights may not be submitted to vote; they depend on the outcome of no elections.[88]

Strategic Considerations

Researchers have also found that judges occasionally make decisions for strategic self-interested reasons. For example, some research suggests that Supreme Court justices who are not well versed in the details of a particular issue will be inclined to switch their votes more readily, perhaps to join with a majority.[89] Recall from Chapter 3 that the justice who authors the Supreme Court's opinion is assigned by the senior justice in the majority, so if the chief justice is in the minority on a particular issue but has a desire to decide who authors the opinion, he may switch sides to control who is assigned to write the opinion, with the switch occurring between the initial conference that follows oral arguments and the point at which the opinion is written. Former Justice William O. Douglass once accused former Chief Justice Warren Burger of switching sides in the famous *Roe* v. *Wade* abortion case in order to control opinion assignment.[90]

Very little of the behind-the-scenes work of the Supreme Court is revealed, but researchers who have studied it have found that strategic maneuvering plays an important role in the process. It is rarely the case that the Court hears oral arguments and then promptly authors an opinion; instead, draft opinions circulate and are revised several times, providing ample opportunity for one justice to try to win over another. One study stated that "to achieve their policy objectives, it may be necessary for majority opinion authors to act strategically, taking the choices of other justices into consideration when crafting opinions of the Court."[91] Former Justice William Brennan once remarked, "Before everyone has finally made up his mind a constant interchange among us . . . continues while we hammer out the final form of the opinion. I had one case during the past Term in which I circulated 10 printed drafts before one was approved as the Court opinion."[92]

What about trial court judges and appellate court judges? There is ample evidence that strategic considerations come into play in these courts as well.[93] Trial court judges may employ different types of strategies than appellate court judges. Whereas the latter occasionally decide cases with profound policy implications, there is less of this at the trial level. For example, a judge who is facing reelection may decide a case in a particular way to garner votes, a form of strategy that meshes with the responsiveness to public opinion that we mentioned in the previous section. Another means by which strategy is employed in trial courts is through the assignment of judges to case types and courtrooms. The chief judge in a particular jurisdiction usually has considerable say in this, so he or she may make assignments to fulfill one or more specific agendas.[94]

Consensus Seeking

norm of consensus
A phrase used by political scientists to refer to unanimity in appellate court decisions that results from a concern for strengthening the authority of the court.

Political scientists have used the phrase **norm of consensus** to refer to unanimity in appellate court decisions—unanimity that occurs out of a concern over strengthening the authority of the court. In the Supreme Court context, the theory is that justices may disagree privately over a particular case but then mask their disagreements from the public by producing consensual opinions and unanimous decisions.[95] If the Court comes across as divided (such as in a 5–4 decision), there is a concern that its authority could be weakened when the nation's highest court could not reach agreement over an important policy issue. By most accounts, consensus has slipped away on the Supreme Court: Between approximately 1930 and 1960, the percentage of cases with at least one dissenting opinion increased from around 10% to approximately 70%.[96]

Laws

All this discussion of how extralegal considerations affect judges leaves one asking, What about the law? Ideally, judges base their decisions on legal considerations and nothing else, but by now we know this is not true. But to what extent do laws matter at all? Researchers are mixed in their answers to this question. Many feel that judicial decision making is based almost entirely on extralegal considerations (individual backgrounds, strategic concerns, and so on), and these people argue that the law has almost no effect on judicial decision making, particularly at the Supreme Court level.[97] Dozens (if not hundreds) of research studies have bought into this perspective hook, line, and sinker. A minority has taken the opposite view, arguing, for example, that "characteristics of the judges or the political party of the judge's appointing president are not significant predictors of judicial decisions."[98] Reality probably lies somewhere in the middle between legal and extralegal considerations.[99]

Limits on Judicial Decisions

While judges are indeed powerful figures within the criminal justice system, their decisions are limited in several key respects.[100] First and foremost, judges must maintain their impartiality. This holds true for *all* judges, from those working in limited jurisdiction courts all the way up to those deciding cases in the U.S. Supreme Court. As we move from the trial court level to the appellate level and beyond, there are some additional restrictions: Decisions must be limited to actual controversies; judges cannot answer political questions; when laws are overturned, they must be overturned on the narrowest of grounds; and judges cannot rule on the wisdom of legislation.

Web Extra
7–8 ABA Standing Committee on Judicial Independence

Importance of Impartiality

Judges need to remain impartial despite the obvious fact that they don't always live up to this expectation (see above). For example, the Supreme Court has held that the Fourteenth Amendment guarantees criminal defendants the right to trial by an impartial judge, so the Fourteenth Amendment is violated if the judge "has a direct, personal, substantial pecuniary interest in reaching a conclusion against him in his case."[101] This decision was reached in *Tumey* v. *Ohio*,[102] a case where the judge of a municipal court was also the city mayor and received the fines and fees that he levied against those convicted in his courtroom.

In another case, *Ward* v. *Monroeville*,[103] a mayor/judge collected fines and fees that went to the town's general fund instead of to him. The Supreme Court held, in part, that "the mayor's executive responsibilities for village finances may make him partisan to maintain the high level of contribution from the mayor's court."[104] But contrast this decision with *Dugan* v. *Ohio*,[105] where the Supreme Court held that due process was *not* violated when the mayor/judge was one of several members of a city commission who did not have substantial control over the city's funding sources.

If there are concerns that a judge is not impartial, in most jurisdictions either the defense or the prosecution can seek to have the judge removed for cause. The party seeking to have the judge removed will argue that the judge is biased against a particular party. Strangely, though, the only party who can remove the impartial judge is the impartial judge himself.

The second method of removing impartial judges is fairly rare. Some jurisdictions allow either party to a case to "peremptorily" remove a judge, meaning that the judge can be removed without any reason whatsoever. The number of peremptory removals, if permitted, is very small (usually one); if the judge is peremptorily removed, then the parties can seek to remove the second judge only with cause.

In most situations, judges do not need to be removed at the request of another party because responsible judges would remove themselves when conflicts of interest exist. Indeed, most judicial codes of ethics require that judges recuse (i.e., disqualify) themselves if they have a personal bias or prejudice concerning a party, have personal knowledge of disputed evidentiary facts concerning the proceeding, or otherwise have some conflict of interest in the case.

Decisions Limited to Actual Controversies

Article III, Section 2, of the U.S. Constitution states that "the judicial Power shall extend to all Cases, in Law and Equity, arising under this Constitution, the Laws of the United States, and Treaties made . . . under their Authority." The most important word in this excerpt is "Cases." The courts have interpreted this to mean that there must be an actual controversy between two parties who have met all the necessary requirements to have their dispute heard in court; moreover, the dispute must involve something nontrivial, and there must be some sort of "wrong" that adversely affects at least one of the parties. If these requirements are not met, there is no case, and without a case, a judge cannot get involved.

A different way to understand this limitation on judicial decision making is to think about who initiates a dispute. When a dispute is brought before the court, the court will hear it if other requirements are met (e.g., standing, a requirement in a civil case that the person bringing suit has suffered a direct and significant injury, physical, monetary, or otherwise). The opposite would occur if a judge initiated the case him- or herself; for example, if a judge disliked a particular statute, he or she would declare it unconstitutional. This cannot occur, however, unless the case is first brought to the court by another party because judges cannot initiate legal disputes or cases on their own, period.

Something of an exception to this general rule is known as a **declaratory judgment**, in which a judge's ruling prevents something from happening. In the civil context, when one party is threatened with a lawsuit but the lawsuit is not yet filed, the party may ask the court to clarify its rights under some statute, will, or contract. An example would be an insurance company seeking clarification as to whether a policy covers a certain type of incident or event. Declaratory judgments are more preventive than reactive. A dispute usually occurs after some right has allegedly been violated, but a declaratory judgment is intended to be made before this occurs to ensure that one party does not violate the law or terms of a contract. In 1934, Congress enacted the Declaratory Judgment Act,[106] which authorizes the federal courts to make declaratory judgments concerning matters of federal law; states have enacted similar legislation.

declaratory judgment
A type of exception to the general rule that judges cannot initiate legal disputes or cases on their own. In the civil context, when one party is threatened with a lawsuit but the lawsuit is not yet filed, the party may ask the court to clarify its rights under some statute, will, or contract. A declaratory judgment is more preventive than reactive. A dispute usually occurs after some right has allegedly been violated, but a declaratory judgment is intended to be made before this occurs to ensure that one party does not violate the law or terms of a contract.

No Involvement with Political Questions

The legislative and executive branches of government are clearly political. As we have shown throughout this book, the courts can also be political, but they are not supposed to be. In other words, the founders did not intend for the courts to serve as a forum for responding to questions involving the public will. As an example, prior to the 1962 Supreme Court case of *Baker* v. *Carr*,[107] the Supreme Court steered clear of cases involving the reapportionment of legislative districts (i.e., drawing geographic boundaries such that equal population size was maintained in each). It has since become heavily involved in such cases, but there was a time when the Court kept its distance due to the political nature of the issue.

Another example involves the state of Oregon's 1902 decision to give its citizens the right to vote on statewide referendums. Shortly after the new law went into effect, the Pacific States Telephone and Telegraph Company objected and claimed that referendums violated the Constitution, particularly the language in Article IV, Section 4, concerning a "republican" form of government. It felt that profits would be threatened if the voters had a say in how business and other affairs were conducted. It also argued that laws should be made only through elected representatives rather than directly by the people themselves. In other words, it was arguing for a specific interpretation of "republican."

Laws Overturned on Narrow Grounds

Courts sometimes overturn laws on the theory that they run counter to the Constitution. This is fairly rare, however. More often, judges engage in one of two actions when a law is considered problematic. First, they may invalidate only that portion of the law that is considered unconstitutional rather than the entire law; for example, in 2004 a federal judge declared part of the PATRIOT Act (the post-9/11 antiterrorism legislation) unconstitutional, namely, that part that barred giving expert advice or assistance to groups labeled as terrorist organizations.[108]

Second, if there is a question about an official's action, the court may hold that the official stepped outside the bounds of his or her authority, which has the effect of preserving the law. An example is found way back in the 1883 case of *Morrill* v. *Jones*.[109] In question in that case was a federal statute that permitted animals that were to be used for breeding purposes to be brought into the United States without duty: "Animals, alive, specially imported for breeding purposes from beyond the seas, shall be admitted free [of duty] upon proof thereof satisfactory to the Secretary of the Treasury and under such regulations as he may prescribe."[110] The secretary of the treasury interpreted the statute to mean that only animals of "superior stock" were exempt from the duty. Rather than ruling on the statute itself, the Supreme Court focused on the secretary's actions, ruling that he had "no authority to prescribe a regulation requiring that before admitting them free, the collector shall 'be satisfied that they are of superior stock, adapted to improving the breed in the United States.'"[111]

No Rulings on the Wisdom of Legislation

Related to the rule that laws can be overturned only on the narrowest grounds is the rule that judges cannot rule on the wisdom of legislation, meaning that they cannot express their personal preferences for or against legislation or use such preferences to influence their decisions. Instead, the only issue that should bear on whether a statute deserves to be overturned is its relationship to the Constitution—if it runs afoul of the Constitution, it can be overturned. It is not enough for a statute to be fiscally irresponsible, offensive, or unfair. It must literally violate a specific constitutional provision; only then can it be overturned. While this rule is a good one in theory, it is difficult to follow to the letter. Judges sometimes express their own views during the course of making their decisions, and the court's "opinion" is, in these instances, just that—opinion. As is clear by now, judges are fallible human beings who do not always base their decisions on the facts and legal questions at hand.

SUMMARY

1. SUMMARIZE THE ROLE AND FUNCTIONS OF JUDGES

- Judges are sometimes called "triers of law," which means that they are tasked generally with resolving any legal matter that comes before the court. A "trier of fact" is one who listens to the evidence and renders a decision of guilty or not guilty (in a criminal trial).
- Judges sometimes serve as triers of law *and* fact. This occurs in a bench trial.

2. DESCRIBE THE QUALIFICATIONS AND APPOINTMENT OF FEDERAL JUDGES

- The most visible federal judges are the Supreme Court justices, the appellate court judges, and the district court judges.
- Both the Constitution and federal law are silent on the subject of qualifications for Supreme Court justices and federal judges.
- A position on the federal bench is largely about informal qualifications, but nearly all federal judges are accomplished attorneys.
- Federal judges are appointed via a complex process that involves the president (nomination), the Justice Department (investigation), interest groups (input), the ABA (input), and the Senate (compensation).
- Federal judges are paid more than state judges. Judicial salaries tend to lag behind those that top attorneys can earn in the private sector.
- Judges are socialized into their positions, usually by working with senior judges. Inappropriate behavior can result in their impeachment.
- Federal judges can retire at full pay and benefits under the Rule of 80. Many judges achieve senior status and work part-time on certain cases.

3. DESCRIBE THE QUALIFICATIONS AND SELECTION OF STATE JUDGES

- Requirements to become a state (or local) judge are more carefully spelled out than are the requirements for federal judges in the Constitution. As a general rule, the qualifications for judges who work in limited jurisdiction courts are less stringent than those for judges who work in general jurisdiction courts, appellate courts, or state supreme courts.

- State judges are selected by election, merit, or appointment. Under merit systems, a nonpartisan commission is typically appointed, and then it evaluates prospective candidates. The commission selects the best and most-qualified candidates and then forwards their names to the appointing authority (typically the governor).

- Some state judges will face retention elections. Methods for their removal and retirement are similar to those for federal judges.

4. SUMMARIZE JUDICIAL ETHICS AND INCOMPETENCE AS WELL AS WHAT CONSTITUTES JUDICIAL MISCONDUCT

- Judges who fail to maintain their independence, act impartially, and avoid impropriety run afoul of ethical standards and guidelines spelled out by various authorities, including professional associations, ethical codes, statutes, and state judicial commissions.

- The ABA has identified eight characteristics of good judges: integrity, legal knowledge and ability, professional experience, judicial temperament, diligence, health, financial responsibility, and public service.

5. DESCRIBE JUDICIAL DECISION MAKING AND LIMITS ON JUDICIAL DECISIONS

- The scientific literature reveals that judges' decisions are affected by many considerations.

- Factors that influence judicial decision making include personal ideology and attitudes, election considerations, public opinion, strategic considerations, consensus seeking, and the law.

- Judicial decisions are limited in several respects.

- Decisions must be limited to actual controversies.

- Judges cannot answer political questions.

- When laws are overturned, they must be overturned on the narrowest of grounds.

- Judges cannot rule on the wisdom of legislation.

KEY TERMS

American Judicature
   Society, 179

anticipatory
   socialization, 170

articles of
   impeachment, 171

declaratory judgment, 186

freshman effects, 171

freshman socialization, 170

impeachment, 171

Judicial Conduct
   and Disability
   Act of 1980, 179

Judicial Councils Reform
   and Judicial Conduct
   and Disability Act of
   1980, 172

judicial ethics, 178

Missouri Plan, 175

Model Code of Judicial
   Conduct, 179

norm of consensus, 184

occupational
   socialization, 170

Rule of 80, 172

senatorial courtesy, 168

senior status, 172

trier of fact, 163

trier of law, 163

REVIEW QUESTIONS

1. What qualifications should judges possess before assuming the bench?

2. Are official qualifications (e.g., degrees, scholarly publications) more important than personal ones (e.g., life experience, personality, values) when it comes to determining the qualities that make a good judge?

3. How are judges socialized into the judiciary? Is judicial socialization necessary and desirable?

4. What judicial selection methods (if any) ensure that judges will be objective and qualified?

5. Should judges be permitted to make decisions based on extralegal factors? If so, what kinds of factors should they consider? If not, why not?

6. What kinds of ethics apply to the activities of a judge? What professional bodies are responsible for the promulgation of judicial ethics?

7. What kinds of limits should be imposed on judicial decision making? Are more limits needed?

WHAT WILL YOU DO?

You are a state court trial judge, and you were elected by voters a little over two years ago. When you ran your campaign, your slogan was "Judges should enforce the law—not make it!"

Today, as you don your judicial robes and prepare to leave your chambers to enter the courtroom, you know that the case you will be hearing presents special challenges. It involves a defendant named Tim DeFoy, who had been the superintendent of public schools in your county until he resigned a few months ago amidst allegations of a financial scandal involving embezzlement of public funds by his office.

The case against DeFoy has been well publicized, with local newspapers carrying at least one story or editorial piece about it each day; local television and radio stations have been equally involved. It is easy to see that DeFoy has already been convicted in the court of public opinion.

DeFoy has opted for a bench trial, something that your state allows in cases like this, and you will be the one to decide his guilt or innocence. You face something of a quandary, however. From what you've heard of the evidence, it seems incriminating, but you're not sure that when all the facts are known, you can be sure beyond a reasonable doubt that DeFoy is guilty. After all, a "trial by media" is not the same as a trial in a court of law.

In the back of your mind, there is the thought that if you find DeFoy not guilty, members of the public will be outraged. You're up for reelection in six months, and you certainly don't want to be seen as the "liberal judge" who let a guilty man go free—especially a man who people think stole their money.

It would be easier, of course, if you lived in a jurisdiction where judges were appointed instead of elected. Although you feel your first duty is following the law and seeing justice done, you'd also like to be reelected.

What will you do?

NOTES

i. M. J. Friedman, Outline of the U.S. Legal System (Washington, DC: U.S. State Department, 2004). Available at http://usinfo.state.gov/products/pubs/legalotln/judges.htm (accessed September 22, 2009).

ii. Friedman, Outline of the U.S. Legal System.

iii. E. V. Heck and M. G. Hall, "Bloc Voting and the Freshman Justice Revisited," Journal of Politics 43 (1981):852–860; A. P. Melone, "Revisiting the Freshman Effect Hypothesis: The First Two Terms of Justice Anthony Kennedy," Judicature 74(1990):6–13.

iv. Black's Law Dictionary, p. 753.

v. Friedman, Outline of the U.S. Legal System.

vi. Friedman, Outline of the U.S. Legal System.

vii. Legal Information Institute, Judicial Ethics: An Overview. Available at http://topics.law.cornell.edu/wex/judicial_ethics (accessed April 21, 2009).

viii. American Judicature Society, Federal Judicial Conduct (Des Moines, IA: American Judicature Society, 2008). Available at http://www.ajs.org/ethics/eth_fed-jud-conduct.asp (accessed August 28, 2009).

1. Jo Mathis, "Judge Honored for Commitment to Reducing Domestic Violence," Legal News, January 16, 2013, available at www.legalnews.com/oakland/1371621 (accessed March 1, 2013).

2. Ibid.

3. Ibid.

4. M. J. Friedman, Outline of the U.S. Legal System (Washington, DC: U.S. State Department, 2004), available at http://photos.state.gov/libraries/korea/49271/dwoa_122709/Outline-of-the-U_S_-Legal-System.pdf (accessed February 15, 2013).

5. Ibid.

6. Ibid.

7. Federal Judicial Center, Biographical Directory of Federal Judges, 1789–present, available at www.fjc.gov/history/home.nsf/page/judges.html (accessed February 15, 2013).

8. Ibid.

9. Ibid.

10. Ibid.

11. Ibid.

12. Ibid.

13. Friedman, Outline of the U.S. Legal System.

14. Ibid.

15. A. Kozinski, "So You Want to Become a Federal Judge by 35?," National Law Journal, Vol. 18 (1996), p. 1.

16. L. Porteus, "Interest Groups Begin Roberts Battle," Fox News, available at www.foxnews.com/story/0,2933,163160,00.htm (accessed February 15, 2013).

17. American Bar Association, Standing Committee on the Federal Judiciary: What It Is and How It Works (Chicago: American Bar Association, 2007).

18. Friedman, Outline of the U.S. Legal System, p. 149.

19. Administrative Office of the U.S. Courts, Judicial Salaries since 1968, available at www.uscourts.gov/Viewer.aspx?doc=/uscourts/JudgesJudgeships/docs/JudicialSalarieschart.pdf (accessed February 15, 2013).

20. Ibid.

21. Ibid.

22. Ibid.

23. Ibid.

24. National Commission on the Public Service, Urgent Business for America: Revitalizing the Federal Government for the 21st Century (January 2003), p. 23, available at www.washingtonpost.com/wp-srv/opinions/documents/Urgent_Business_for_America__Revitalizing_the_Federal_Government_for_the_21st_Century.pdf (accessed February 15, 2013).

25. Administrative Office of the U.S. Courts, Fact Sheet.

26. www.opensecrets.org/news/2011/09/ruth-bader-ginsburg-steven-breyer.html?utm_source=CRP+Mail+List&utm_campaign=303e79ae2d-News_Alert_9_6_119_6_2011&utm_medium=email (accessed February 15, 2013).

27. Friedman, Outline of the U.S. Legal System.

28. Ibid.

29. Available at www.fjc.gov (accessed February 15, 2013).

30. L. Alpert, B. M. Atkins, and R. C. Ziller, "Becoming a Judge: The Transition from Advocate to Arbiter," Judicature, Vol. 62 (1979), pp. 325–335.

31. W. J. Brennan, "The National Court of Appeals: Another Dissent," University of Chicago Law Review, Vol. 40 (1973), p. 484.

32. P. C. Arledge and E. V. Heck, "A Freshman Justice Confronts the Constitution: Justice O'Connor and the First Amendment," Western Political Quarterly, Vol. 45 (1992), pp. 761–772.

33. E. V. Heck and M. G. Hall, "Bloc Voting and the Freshman Justice Revisited," Journal of Politics, Vol. 43 (1981), pp. 852–860; A. P. Melone, "Revisiting the Freshman Effect Hypothesis: The First Two Terms of Justice Anthony Kennedy," Judicature, Vol. 74 (1990), pp. 6–13.

34. Arledge and Heck, "A Freshman Justice Confronts the Constitution," pp. 761–762.

35. Black's Law Dictionary, 6th ed. (St. Paul, MN: West, 1990), p. 753.

36. Legal Information Institute at Cornell Law School, BackGrounder on Impeachment, available at www.law.cornell.edu/background/impeach/impeach.htm (accessed February 15, 2013), reprinted with permission.

37. J. Rutledge, "Judicial Impeachment: History and Current Trends," Justice at Stake Backgrounder, September 18, 2006, available at www.justiceatstake.org/newsroom/press-releases-16824/?judicial_impeachment_history_and_current_trends_a_justice_at_stake_backgrounder&show=news&newsID=6086 (accessed February 15, 2013).

38. Ibid.

39. Ibid.; also see Nixon v. United States, 506 U.S. 224 (1993).

40. Friedman, Outline of the U.S. Legal System.

41. Ibid.

42. J. F. Spriggs II and P. J. Wahlbeck, "Calling It Quits: Strategic Retirement on the Federal Courts of Appeals, 1893–1991," *Political Research Quarterly*, Vol. 48 (1995), pp. 573–597; for a contrasting view, see P. Squire, "Politics and Personal Factors in Retirement from the United States Supreme Court," *Political Behavior*, Vol. 10 (1988), pp. 180–190.

43. D. C. Nixon and J. D. Haskin, "Judicial Retirement Strategies," *American Politics Research*, Vol. 28 (2000), pp. 458–489.

44. Friedman, *Outline of the U.S. Legal System*, p. 153.

45. V. T. C. A., Election Code, Section 141.001; V. T. C. A., Election Code, Section 145.003.

46. Maryland Constitution, Article I, Section 12; Article IV, Section 2.

47. P. A. Garcia, *Judicial Selection: The Process of Choosing Judges* (Chicago: American Bar Association, 1998). For state-by-state specifics, go to www.ajs.org/selection/sel_state-select-map.asp (accessed February 15, 2013).

48. E. A. Larkin, "Judicial Selection Methods: Judicial Independence and Popular Democracy," *Denver University Law Review*, Vol. 79 (2001), pp. 65–89.

49. Ibid., p. 78.

50. Ibid.

51. National Center for State Courts, *Judicial Selection and Retention FAQs*, available at www.ncsc.org/Topics/Judicial-Officers/Judicial-Selection-and-Retention/Resource-Guide.aspx (accessed February 15, 2013).

52. M. R. Dimino, "The Futile Quest for a System of Judicial 'Merit' Selection," *Albany Law Review*, Vol. 67 (2004), pp. 803–819.

53. S. Anderson, "Examining the Decline in Support for Merit Selection in the States," *Albany Law Review*, Vol. 67 (2004), pp. 793–802.

54. Available at www.ajs.org/selection/sel_state-select-map.asp (accessed February 15, 2013).

55. Larkin, "Judicial Selection Methods," p. 72.

56. M. L. Henry, Jr., *The Success of Women and Minorities in Achieving Judicial Office: The Selection Process* (New York: Fund for Modern Courts, 1985).

57. C. Sheldon and L. Maule, *Choosing Justice: The Recruitment of State and Federal Judges* (Pullman: Washington State University Press, 1997).

58. C. F. Epstein, *Women in Law* (Champaign: University of Illinois Press, 1993).

59. K. A. Bratton and R. L. Spill, "Existing Diversity and Judicial Selection: The Role of the Appointment Method in Establishing Gender Diversity in State Supreme Courts," *Social Science Quarterly*, Vol. 83 (2002), pp. 504–518.

60. Past surveys are available at www.ncsc.org/salarytracker (accessed February 15, 2013).

61. National Center for State Courts, *Survey of Judicial Salaries*, available at www.ncsc.org/~/media/Microsites/Files/Judicial%20Salaries/jud_2012.ashx (accessed February 15, 2013).

62. Ibid.

63. American Judicature Society, *Methods of Judicial Selection: Removal of Judges* (Des Moines, IA: American Judicature Society, 2008), available at www.judicialselection.us/judicial_selection/methods/removal_of_judges.cfm?state (accessed February 15, 2013).

64. Ibid.

65. Legal Information Institute at Cornell Law School, *Judicial Ethics: An Overview*, available at www.law.cornell.edu/wex/judicial_ethics (accessed February 15, 2013), reprinted with permission.

66. American Bar Association, *Model Code of Judicial Conduct: Preamble* (Chicago: American Bar Association, 2003).

67. Arizona Commission on Judicial Conduct, *Scope of Authority* (Phoenix: Commission on Judicial Conduct, 2008), available at www.azcourts.gov/ethics/moreinformation/overview.aspx (accessed February 15, 2013).

68. American Judicature Society, *Federal Judicial Conduct* (Des Moines, IA: American Judicature Society, 2008), available at www.ajs.org/ethics/eth_fed-jud-conduct.asp (accessed February 15, 2013).

69. Ibid.

70. Ibid.

71. Ibid.; also see 28 U.S.C., Sections 351–364, for more details.

72. American Bar Association, *Guidelines for Reviewing Qualifications of Candidates for State Judicial Office* (Chicago: American Bar Association, 1984).

73. Ibid.

74. See, e.g., L. Baum, *The Puzzle of Judicial Behavior* (Ann Arbor: University of Michigan Press, 1998); L. Epstein and J. Knight, "Field Essay: Toward a Strategic Revolution in Judicial Politics: A Look Back, a Look Ahead," *Political Research Quarterly*, Vol. 53 (2000), pp. 625–661.

75. For references to studies on decision making in lower courts, particularly intermediate appellate courts and trial courts, see references available at www.bsos.umd.edu/gvpt/mcgrad (accessed February 15, 2013).

76. See, e.g., L. Epstein and C. Mershon, "Measuring Political Preferences," *American Journal of Political Science*, Vol. 40 (1996), pp. 261–294.

77. J. Segal and A. Cover, "Ideological Values and the Votes of U.S. Supreme Court Justices," *American Political Science Review*, Vol. 83 (1989), pp. 557–565.

78. L. Epstein, V. Hoekstra, J. A. Segal, and H. J. Spaeth, "Do Political Preferences Change? A Longitudinal Study of U.S. Supreme Court Justices," *Journal of Politics*, Vol. 60 (1998), pp. 801–818.

79. D. R. Songer and K. A. Crews-Meyer, "Does Judge Gender Matter? Decision Making in State Supreme Courts," *Social Science Inquiry*, Vol. 81 (2000), pp. 750–762.

80. C. Spohn, "Sentencing Decisions of Black and White Judges: Expected and Unexpected Similarities," *Law and Society Review*, Vol. 24 (1990), pp. 1197–1216.

81. M. G. Hall, "Electoral Politics and Strategic Voting in State Supreme Courts," *Journal of Politics*, Vol. 52 (1992), pp. 427–446.

82. M. G. Hall, "Constituent Influence in State Supreme Courts: Conceptual Notes and a Case Study," *Journal of Politics*, Vol. 49 (1987), p. 1119.

83. T. George and L. Epstein, "On the Nature of Supreme Court Decision Making," *American Political Science Review*, Vol. 86 (1992), pp. 323–337.

84. T. R. Marshall, *Public Opinion and the Supreme Court* (Boston: Unwin Hyman, 1989).

85. W. Mishler and R. Sheehan, "The Supreme Court as a Counter-Majoritarian Institution? The Impact of Public Opinion on Supreme Court Decisions," *American Journal of Political Science*, Vol. 41 (1997), pp. 122–149.

86. "Popular Influence on Supreme Court Decisions," *American Political Science Review*, Vol. 88 (1994), pp. 711–724.

87. Marshall, *Public Opinion and the Supreme Court.*

88. *West Virginia Board of Education v. Barnette*, 319 U.S. 624 (1943), p. 638.

89. F. Maltzman and P. J. Wahlbeck, "Policy Considerations and Voting Fluidity on the Burger Court," *American Political Science Review*, Vol. 90 (1996), pp. 581–592.

90. Ibid; also see S. Brenner, "Strategic Choice and Opinion Assignment on the U.S. Supreme Court: A Reexamination," *Western Political Quarterly*, Vol. 35 (1982), pp. 204–211.

91. P. J. Wahlbeck, J. F. Spriggs, and F. Maltzman, "Marshalling the Court: Bargaining and Accommodation on the United States Supreme Court," *American Journal of Political Science*, Vol. 42 (1998), pp. 295–296.

92. W. J. Brennan, "State Court Decisions and the Supreme Court," *Pennsylvania Bar Association Quarterly*, Vol. 31 (1960), p. 405.

93. See, e.g., V. A. Hettinger, S. A. Lindquist, and W. L. Martinek, "Comparing Attitudinal and Strategic Accounts of Dissenting Behavior on the U.S. Courts of Appeal," *American Journal of Political Science*, Vol. 48 (2004), pp. 123–137.

94. H. Jacob, "The Governance of Trial Judges," *Law and Society Review*, Vol. 31 (1997), pp. 3–30.

95. L. Epstein, J. A. Segal, and H. J. Spaeth, "The Norm of Consensus on the U.S. Supreme Court," *American Journal of Political Science*, Vol. 45 (2001), pp. 362–377.

96. Ibid.; also see G. A. Caldeira and C. J. W. Zorn, "Of Time and Consensual Norms in the Supreme Court," *American Journal of Political Science*, Vol. 42 (1998), pp. 874–902.

97. For a detailed review, see H. Gillman, "What's Law Got to Do with It? Judicial Behavioralists Test the 'Legal Model' of Judicial Decision Making," *Law and Social Inquiry*, Vol. 26 (2001), pp. 465–504.

98. O. Ashenfelter, T. Eisenberg, and S. J. Schwab, "Politics and the Judiciary: The Influence of Judicial Background on Case Outcomes," *Journal of Legal Studies*, Vol. 24 (1995), pp. 257–281.

99. Gillman, "What's Law Got to Do with It?," pp. 465–504.

100. Much of the discussion that follows is based on Friedman, *Outline of the U.S. Legal System.*

101. *Tumey v. Ohio*, 273 U.S. 510 (1927), p. 523.

102. Ibid.

103. *Ward v. Monroeville*, 409 U.S. 57 (1972).

104. Ibid., p. 59.

105. *Dugan v. Ohio*, 277 U.S. 61 (1928).

106. 28 U.S.C.A., Section 2201.

107. *Baker v. Carr*, 369 U.S. 186 (1962).

108. L. Deutsch, "U.S. Judge Rules Part of the Patriot Act is Unconstitutional," available at www.globalissues.org/article/458/federal-judge-rules-part-of-patriot-act-unconstitutional (accessed February 15, 2013).

109. *Morrill v. Jones*, 106 U.S. 466 (1883).

110. Ibid, p. 466.

111. Ibid.

Frances Twitty/Getty Images

8

Prosecutors

A prosecutor presents a case against a criminal defendant in court. What is prosecutorial discretion, and why is it important?

bikeriderlondon/Shutterstock

INTRODUCTION

In December 2012, the National Institute of Justice released a report on prosecutorial decision making. The report's key finding said, "While prosecutorial discretion is generally seen as very broad and unconstrained, prosecutors often rely on a fairly limited array of legal and quasi-legal factors to make decisions, and their decision making is further constrained by several contextual factors. These contextual constraints—rules, resources, and relationships—sometimes trump evaluations of the strength of the evidence, the seriousness of the offense, and the defendant's criminal history."[1] Researchers also found that prosecutors were guided by two questions when making decisions about what cases to bring before the court: (1) "Can I prove the case? and (2) "Should I prove the case?"[2] The report concluded that "prosecuting attorneys enjoy broader discretion in making decisions that influence criminal case outcomes than any other actors in the American justice system."[3]

Learning Objective 1

Identify the names and types of prosecutors.

prosecutor

"[A]n attorney who is the elected or appointed chief of a prosecution agency, and whose official duty is to conduct criminal proceedings on behalf of the people against persons accused of committing criminal offenses, also called 'district attorney,' 'DA,' 'state's attorney,' 'county attorney,' and 'U.S. Attorney,' and any attorney deputized to assist the chief prosecutor."[i]

TYPES OF PROSECUTORS

A **prosecutor** is an attorney whose official duty is to conduct criminal proceedings on behalf of the state or the people against those accused of having committed criminal offenses. "Other terms for *prosecutor* are 'district attorney,' 'DA,' 'state's attorney,' 'county attorney,' and 'U.S. Attorney,' and any attorney deputized to assist the chief prosecutor."[4] In other words, the prosecutor is the one who charges criminal suspects in the name of the government.

Recall that crimes are offenses against society, which is why our definition of prosecutor references "on behalf of the people." In fact, criminal cases are often referenced by the parties involved (e.g., *People* v. *John Smith* or *State* v. *John Smith*). The prosecutor represents the people or the state in cases such as these, the "people" or the "state" being the party aggrieved by a criminal act. Of course, there are individuals who are victimized, but giving the impression that crimes are against society ensures that the government rather than a victim is in the business of dispensing justice.

Prosecution is typically organized along four levels of government: federal, state, county, and city. We look at each in the following four subsections.

Web Extra
8-1 National District Attorneys Association

Federal Level

At the federal level, the **attorney general** is the head of the U.S. Department of Justice and the chief law enforcement officer of the federal government (see Figure 8–1 for the Justice Department's organizational chart). He (Eric H. Holder as of this writing) or she represents the United States in legal matters and provides advice both to the president and to the heads of other executive branch agencies. The attorney general rarely appears in court, like federal prosecutors do, but occasionally goes before the U.S. Supreme Court to argue matters of exceptional importance. Most duties of the attorney general are administrative in nature and do not involve firsthand criminal prosecution.

Actual trial work in the federal system is performed by **U.S. attorneys** who fall within the criminal division of the U.S. Justice Department and thus serve under the direction of the attorney general. There are 93 U.S. attorneys serving the 94 federal judicial districts (one person in each district except one person serving both the Guam and Northern Mariana Islands districts). They are appointed by the president to supervise assigned assistant U.S. attorneys and support staff in conducting trial work in which the United States is a party.[5]

The 93 U.S. attorneys are assisted by over 6,000 **assistant U.S. attorneys** and an equal number of support staff. Assistant U.S. attorneys are not appointed but rather serve at the pleasure of the U.S. attorney; they are the workhorses in U.S. attorneys' offices, as it would be unreasonable to expect the appointed U.S. attorney to represent the government in all cases. Together, the U.S. attorneys and their assistants accomplished the following—in terms of criminal prosecutions—during fiscal year 2012 (the most recent year for which data are available as of this writing) alone (see Figure 8–2 for more details):

- Received 163,831 criminal matters
- 63,118 cases filed against 85,621 defendants
- 65,230 cases against 87,709 defendants terminated
- 80,963 defendants convicted
- 90% conviction rate
- 97 percent of all convicted defendants pled guilty prior to or during trial
- 80% of convicted defendants sentenced to prison[6]

Another actor in the federal system is the **solicitor general**, who is in charge of representing the government in suits and appeals in the Supreme Court as well as in all lower federal trial and appellate courts in cases where the interests of the U.S. government are at stake. Like attorneys general, the solicitor general is not considered a prosecutor, but he or she has several duties:

- Supervise and conduct government litigation in the U.S. Supreme Court.
- Determine the cases in which Supreme Court review will be sought by the government and the positions the government will take before the Court.
- Supervise the preparation of the government's Supreme Court briefs, petitions, and other legal documents.
- Conduct oral arguments before the Supreme Court.
- Review all cases decided adversely to the government in the lower courts to determine whether they should be appealed and, if so, what position should be taken.
- Determine whether the government will submit an *amicus curiae* brief or otherwise intervene in any appellate court case.[7]

attorney general
The head of the U.S. Department of Justice and the chief law enforcement officer in the federal government; also, the chief law enforcement officer in each of the state and territorial-level governments.

U.S. attorney
An attorney appointed by the president and serving under the direction of the U.S. attorney general to supervise the attorneys and staff of the U.S. Attorney's Office in each of the federal judicial districts.

Media
Simulation: Prosecutor

assistant U.S. attorney
One of more than 5,600 subordinate attorneys assigned throughout the various offices of the U.S. attorneys in the 94 federal judicial districts to perform the brunt of litigation work involving the federal government.

solicitor general
The federal official charged with representing the government both in suits and appeals in the Supreme Court and in all lower federal trial and appellate courts in cases where the interests of the U.S. government are at stake.

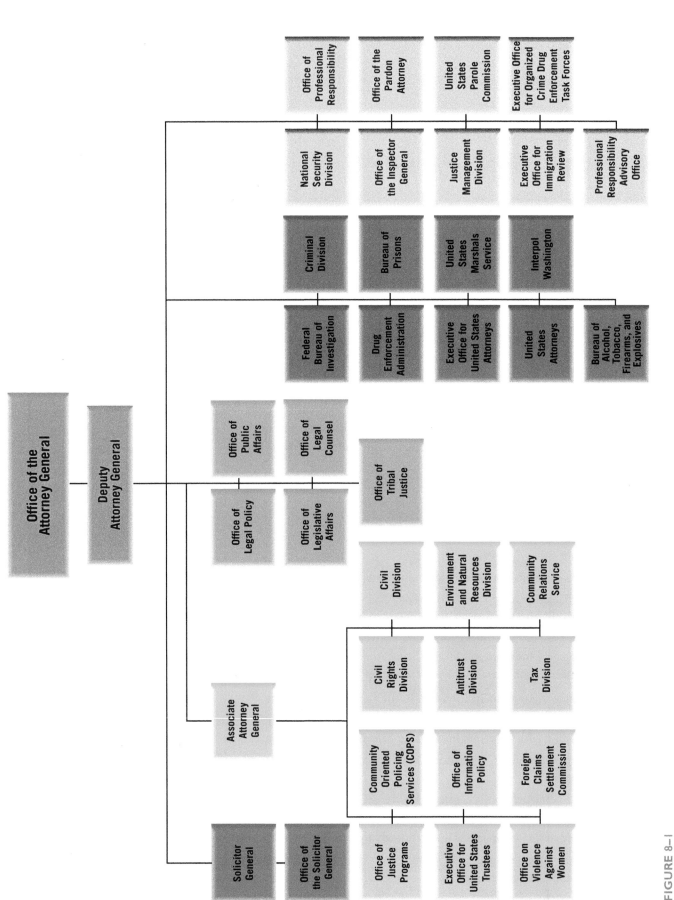

FIGURE 8–1

U.S. Justice Department Organizational Chart

Source: www.justice.gov/agencies/index-org.html (accessed February 18, 2013).

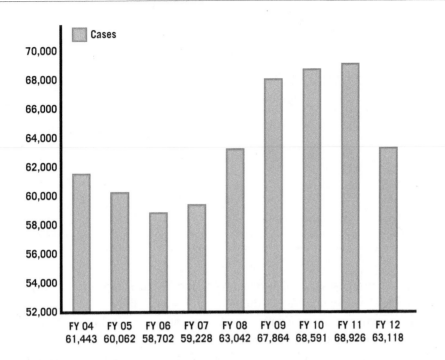

FIGURE 8–2

Criminal Cases Filed by U.S. Attorneys' Offices, 2004–2012

Source: U.S. Department of Justice, Executive Office for U.S. Attorneys, *United States Attorneys' Annual Statistical Report: Fiscal Year 2012* (Washington, DC: U.S. Department of Justice, 2012), p. 7.

State Level

At the state level, the state attorney general is the chief legal officer. According to the National Association of Attorneys General, the typical powers of these officials include authority to do the following:

- Issue formal opinions to state agencies.
- Act as public advocates in areas such as child enforcement, consumer protections, antitrust suits, and utility regulation.
- Propose legislation.
- Enforce federal and state environmental laws.
- Represent the state and state agencies before the state and federal courts.
- Handle criminal appeals and serious statewide criminal prosecutions.
- Institute civil suits on behalf of the state.
- Represent the public's interests in charitable trust and solicitations.
- Operate victim compensation programs.[8]

Since most prosecutions take place at the local level, state attorneys general rarely act as prosecutors. They sometimes do prosecute complex crimes, such as those involving white-collar offenders, but such prosecutions are fairly rare. They may take over for local prosecutors, as happened in the infamous Duke lacrosse scandal after county prosecutor Mike Nifong recused himself[9]; charges against the players were then promptly dropped. Lately, state attorneys general have emphasized their civil authority more than their criminal authority. Litigation, such as that aimed at protecting consumers, is also fairly common.

County Level

Most criminal work is conducted at the county level because this is where common law felonies and misdemeanors are tried. The **district attorney** is the chief local prosecutor and is in charge of bringing murder, rape, and robbery cases to trial. Today, there are more than 2,300 such prosecutor's offices employing approximately 78,000 personnel. Table 8–1 shows how the personnel are allocated on average.

district attorney
The chief local (typically, county-level) prosecutor charged with bringing criminal cases to trial; also called *county attorney, state's attorney, prosecuting attorney, commonwealth attorney, county prosecutor, district attorney general, county and prosecuting attorney, solicitor,* or *circuit attorney.*[ii]

TABLE 8–1 Allocation of Personnel in Prosecutor's Offices, 2007

Estimated number of personnel	77,927
Percent of total personnel in prosecutor's offices	
Support staff	33
Assistant prosecutors	32
Investigators	9
Victim advocates	6
Legal services	5
Supervisory/managing attorneys	7
Chief prosecutor	3
Civil attorneys	2
Other	2

Source: Adapted from S. W. Perry and D. Banks, *Prosecutors in State Courts, 2007* (Washington, DC: U.S. Department of Justice, 2011), p. 4, table 3, available at http://bjs.ojp.usdoj.gov/content/pub/pdf/psc07st.pdf (accessed February 18, 2013).

While district attorney is the most common title for the chief prosecutor, some jurisdictions use different titles: county attorney (Arizona, Iowa, Kansas, Minnesota, Montana, Nebraska, New Hampshire, and Utah), state's attorney (Connecticut, Florida, Illinois, Maryland, North Dakota, South Dakota, and Vermont), prosecuting attorney (Arkansas, Hawaii, Idaho, Indiana, Michigan, Missouri, Ohio, Washington, and West Virginia), commonwealth attorney (Kentucky and Virginia), county prosecutor (New Jersey), district attorney general (Tennessee), county and prosecuting attorney (Wyoming), solicitor (South Carolina), and circuit attorney (Missouri).[10] Some states have no local prosecutors (Alaska, Delaware, and Rhode Island).

In most states, chief prosecutors are elected officials. The exceptions are Alaska, Connecticut, Delaware, the District of Columbia, New Jersey, and Rhode Island.[11] Chief prosecutors in these states either are appointed or are employees of the state attorney general's office.

The fact that most prosecutors are elected raises several interesting issues. First, elections are sometimes intensely partisan. Second, deputy district attorneys often serve at the pleasure of their elected supervisors, meaning that they can be dismissed if there is a sudden change in administration (although there are some civil service protections). This happened in Dallas when Craig Watkins, a Democrat, unseated former prosecutor Craig Shook, a Republican; as soon as Watkins took the reins in the district attorney's office, he promptly dismissed several senior prosecutors. Many elected prosecutors get their political "feet wet" during their tenure and then go on to be elected to higher political offices, including the presidency.[12]

City Level

city attorney
The city-level official charged with providing legal services to other city-level agencies.

Library Extra
8–1 Bureau of Justice Statistics: Prosecutors in State Courts

Just as state attorneys general provide legal services for other state agencies, **city attorneys** provide legal services to other city-level agencies. This is usually the sole responsibility of most city attorney's offices, but larger cities often permit city attorneys to serve as prosecutors for low-level offenses such as misdemeanors. City attorneys in Dallas, Los Angeles, Minneapolis, and several other large cities are often organized into two functions: civil and criminal. The civil division provides a broad range of legal services to the city's elected officials, staff, departments, boards, and commissions, and the criminal division usually prosecutes misdemeanors.

City attorneys are starting to receive more attention than they have in the past. This owes, in part, to the broken windows theory of crime, which holds that serious crime will flourish if minor problems, including misdemeanors, are not taken seriously.[13] Since city attorneys are in a unique position to handle these minor problems, they can assist law enforcement agencies that favor the broken windows approach to policing by aggressively going after low-level offenders, and since their criminal prosecution authority is limited to misdemeanors, city attorneys cannot be readily criticized for neglecting more serious crimes.[14]

PROSECUTION THROUGHOUT HISTORY

Learning Objective 2
Outline how American prosecution has changed and evolved over time.

The American prosecutor is truly unrivaled in the world. First, prosecutors straddle the line that separates courts from politics. As Joan Jacoby has put it, "The prosecutor is established as the representative of the state in criminal litigation, by either constitutional or statutory mandate, and yet is directly answerable to the local electorate at the ballot box."[15] As we discussed in Chapter 2, courts are by no means insulated from political pressures, but we also made the case that since prosecutors represent the executive branch, their regular appearance in courts can certainly exert some degree of influence.

Prosecution in America is also somewhat unique in the sense that prosecutors perform a range of functions. The usual functions are representing the government in court, executing the law, and upholding the federal and state constitutions, but prosecutors can also influence law enforcement activity as a result of their screening function. They can alter both the quality and the nature of law enforcement investigations by deciding not to press charges against offenders; for example, if a prosecutor continually rejects a particular type of case, this may send a message to the police that enforcement of the underlying crime is not important.

Choices Shaping American Prosecution

There were three critical choices that shaped prosecution.[16] First, Americans chose a system of public instead of private prosecution; second, the decision to adopt a democratic form of government led to decentralization, with local prosecutors' offices rather than a single national office; and, third, prosecutors have over time moved from appointed to elected status to be consistent with democratic ideals.

Private to Public Prosecution Prosecution in America is public, which means that all criminal prosecutions are initiated by government officials rather than private parties. What is the advantage of public prosecution? The answer lies with the idea that crimes are offenses against the state, not individual victims per se. This was argued in a famous 1921 Connecticut court decision:

> In all criminal cases in Connecticut, the state is the prosecutor. The offenses are against the state. The victim of the offense is not a party to the prosecution, nor does he occupy any relation to it other than that of a witness, an interested witness may-haps, but none the less, only a witness. . . . It is not necessary for the injured party to make complaint nor is he required to give bond to prosecute. He is in no sense a rela-tor. He cannot in any way control the prosecution and whether reluctant or not, he can be compelled like any other witness to appear and testify.[17]

In 1704, Connecticut became the first colony to use government attorneys as prosecu-tors, effectively abandoning private prosecution.[18] The statute providing for public prosecu-tion stated, "Henceforth there shall be in every county a sober discreet and religious person appointed by the county court to be attorney for the Queen to prosecute and implead (sic) in the law all criminals and to do all other things necessary or convenient as an attorney to suppress vice and immorality."[19]

Centralization to Decentralization Early American colonists vehemently opposed the centralized British government. Their desire to place governmental controls in the hands of locals, together with the great distances between population centers in early America, gave rise to decentralized prosecution.[20] Another historical force that contributed to decentralized prosecution was the relative neglect by the British government of the courts in the early colonies, allowing local courts and prosecutors' offices to evolve on their own.[21]

Appointed to Elected Status The earliest American prosecutors were appointed to their posts, a practice that continued in the postrevolutionary era when the first Congress created—via the Judiciary Act of 1789 (see Chapter 3)—the office of attorney general and the U.S. attorneys.[22] But beginning around 1820, during Andrew Jackson's presidency, there was a strong push for increased democratization, including a push for elected rather than politically appointed prosecutors.[23]

Early prosecutors were often defined as judicial figures; many states had prosecutors listed in the judicial articles of their constitutions. Leading up to and following the Civil War, prosecutors began to find their way, through various amendments, into the executive articles of state constitutions. By 1821, the first prosecutor was elected in Ohio, serving Cuyahoga County; in 1832, Mississippi became the first state to include a constitutional provision providing for the election of prosecutors. "By 1859 the trend was clear and irreversible—the prosecutor was a locally elected position."[24]

Increased Prominence

American prosecutors gained prominence over the years as a result of two distinct forces. First, as they became executive rather than judicial figures, their power increased. Second, as the Supreme Court handed down several important decisions with implications for defendants' constitutional rights, this forced prosecutors into the limelight.

More Power over Time The prosecutor was "in the eyes of the earliest Americans, clearly a minor actor in the court's structure."[25] In contrast, sheriffs and coroners were considered much more powerful. They were also the first judicial officers to gain independence and elective status.[26] As the prosecutorial function shifted to the executive branch and as prosecutors became elected officials, their powers increased. By the early 1900s, the prosecutor was regarded as having significant (if not total) power over enforcement of the criminal law.[27]

Around this time, courts began to take note of the surge in prosecutorial power. For example, in an 1883 decision, the Illinois Court of Appeals noted that the prosecutor "is charged by law with large discretion in prosecuting offenders against the law. He may commence public prosecution in his capacity by information and he may discontinue them when, in his judgment the ends of justice are satisfied."[28] In another case, a court noted that the prosecutor has "absolute control of the criminal prosecution."[29] Yet another declared, "The remedy for the inactivity of the prosecutor is with the executive and ultimately with the people."[30]

By the 1920s, it was clear that the American prosecutor had reached a pinnacle of power in criminal justice, enough to cause some commentators concern: "The people of the United States have traditionally feared concentration of great power in the hands of one person and it is surprising that the power of the prosecuting attorney has been left intact as it is today."[31] Despite such fears, courts routinely uphold prosecutors' control over life and liberty.[32]

Defendants' Rights In 1932, the Supreme Court called attention to the constitutional basis for a defendant's right to counsel.[33] Later on, it decided in *Gideon* v. *Wainwright* that states must honor the Sixth Amendment right to counsel, ensuring that criminal defendants are represented by counsel in state criminal trials, not just federal trials.[34] But since *Gideon* was limited to felonies, the Court later decided that the right to counsel should be extended to all defendants who face prison terms in *Argersinger* v. *Hamlin*.[35] Still other important decisions, such as *Miranda* v. *Arizona*,[36] extended the right to counsel to police interrogation.

Decisions such as these significantly altered the prosecutorial workload, and the result was that prosecutors suddenly needed to be present at many more stages of the criminal process. For example, prosecutors were suddenly compelled to be present at more hearings, such as preliminary hearings, due to the Supreme Court's decisions requiring the presence of counsel at critical stages of the process.

Prosecutors now must prepare themselves to deal with defense attorneys from initial processing all the way through to the appellate stage. This makes the typical criminal case take more time and ensures additional procedural complexity[37]: "Defendants [are] more likely to file motions, to demand rather than waive preliminary hearing, and to institute postconviction proceedings and appeals."[38]

Library Extra
8–2 Bureau of Justice Statistics: Prosecution Statistics

Progressive Era

The Cleveland Survey of Criminal Justice,[39] the Wickersham Commission,[40] and several other early-twentieth-century crime commission reports[41] led to what has been called the **progressive era** in criminal justice. Most members of these commissions were reformers who sought to remove corruption and political favoritism from the criminal process. They studied criminal justice operations and wrote reports that reflected what they learned, and they also presented various recommendations for improvements that would professionalize the justice system. Despite these important services, the crime commissions failed to dig deeply into real-world criminal justice operations; they relied mostly on official data and did not directly observe criminal justice operations, including the actions of prosecutors.[42]

The commissions believed that the criminal justice system was filled with professionals who always applied the law fairly and impersonally. They also felt that the law could—and always should—be strictly adhered to and that anything less was evidence of failure. But historian Sam Walker observed that "this reform strategy seems hopelessly naïve. It shows no awareness of the phenomenon of discretion, or of its underlying dynamics."[43]

The commissions totally ignored the realities of criminal justice and the pressures facing the people who worked in the system. Such realities and pressures included heavy workloads, backlogs of cases, public pressures to prioritize certain problems, turf wars between agencies, and self-serving interests on the part of various individuals. The progressive era view of criminal justice was, quite simply, the "textbook" view, one of a fully functional, competent, and effective system, but, as even the most casual observer knows today, the reality of criminal justice is considerably different.

progressive era
A period in the evolution of the U.S. criminal justice system that occurred in the early twentieth century and was marked by reform efforts aimed at removing corruption and political favoritism from the criminal process.

Discovery of Discretion

The progressive vision of a harmonious criminal justice system quickly fell out of favor as researchers began to observe prosecutors and other officials in action. A new view emerged, one that recognized the importance of discretion.[44] One commentator observed in 1954 that "[t]o a large extent, the administration of criminal justice can be characterized as a series of important decisions from the time a crime is committed until the offender is finally released from supervision."[45] This seems obvious today, but at the time it was revolutionary and flew in the face of the progressives' view of criminal justice officials who enforced the law blindly and evenhandedly.

Researchers began to grasp the complexity of the criminal justice system: "[Studies] revealed a very different picture, in which the criminal process was used routinely to handle a broad range of social problems including alcohol abuse, mental illness, family difficulties, petty financial disputes, and other miscellaneous matters."[46] In addition, decisions appeared to be guided by anything but legal guidelines and predictable procedures. Prosecutors made decisions to charge based on factors besides just an apparent violation of the law—they weighed the consequences of proceeding with criminal charges, considered alternatives to traditional adjudication, and plea-bargained extensively with the defense.[47]

President's Commission of 1967 The new view that prosecutors wielded considerable discretion was somewhat replaced as a result of the 1967 President's Commission on Law Enforcement and the Administration of Justice.[48] The commission identified three prosecutorial functions: "[First the prosecutor can] . . . determine whether an alleged offender should be charged to obtain convictions through guilty plea negotiations. . . . [Second] the prosecutor has the responsibility of presenting [the] government's case in court. . . . [Third] . . . the prosecutor is often an investigator and instigator of the criminal process."[49] Prosecutors once again came to be regarded as case processors, as blind enforcers of the law.

The President's Commission played down the discretion prosecutors enjoyed. Why? One answer is that the commission was appointed during the 1960s, a time when the country saw a surge in crime and felt that improvements to the criminal justice system were necessary. Nearly all the commission's prosecution recommendations were concerned with improving prosecutorial professionalism, performance, and case processing. The American Bar Association (ABA), the National Association of Attorneys General, and the National District Attorneys Association followed this lead by preparing manuals and guides to promote standardization of screening and case management[50]; they also adopted guidelines to improve the control of prosecutors' discretion and to increase efficiency in office operations.

felony case processor model
A model of criminal prosecution that consists of the elements of mission, source of authority, demand, organization, tactics, environment, and outcomes.

The President's Commission gave rise to what has been called the **felony case processor model** of prosecution, which, according to Catherine Coles, meant that the prosecutor's office marketed "itself primarily as a professional organization equipped to hold offenders accountable by obtaining guilty pleas or trial convictions, or in some cases diverting cases for treatment. . . . [The main outcome measures were] the number of trials (particularly involving Part I crimes), convictions, and length of sentences."[51]

New Prosecution Paradigm

During the 1960s and 1970s, prosecutors and other criminal justice officials began to learn that traditional case processing strategies did not work well for all crime types.[52] They became familiar with the "revolving door" concept, and in an effort to close it, they set out to identify effective strategies that would help them target crime effectively. This gave rise to a new prosecution paradigm that included an emphasis on community prosecution and accountability.

community prosecution
An approach intended to improve cooperation and collaboration between prosecutors and individuals outside the criminal justice system (e.g., community members and business leaders). More formally, it is "an organizational response to the grassroots public safety demands of neighborhoods, as expressed in highly concrete terms by the people who live in them. They identify immediate, specific crime problems they want addressed and that the incident-based 911 system is ill suited (sic) to handle."[iii]

Community Prosecution **Community prosecution** is to prosecutors what community policing is to police officers—an approach intended to improve cooperation and collaboration between prosecutors and individuals outside the criminal justice system, such as community members and business leaders: "More than anything else, community prosecution is an organizational response to the grassroots public safety demands of neighborhoods, as expressed in highly concrete terms by the people who live in them."[53]

Some prosecutors are quick to say that they have been doing this type of work for many years and that only recently has the term "community prosecution" been attached to the practice. As we pointed out earlier, many city attorneys, whose jobs often require the prosecution of misdemeanors, claim that community prosecution has been going on for decades[54]; they claim that their job has always consisted of dealing with low-level crime problems.[55] While this is certainly true in some jurisdictions, what makes community prosecution distinctly different from the prosecution of misdemeanors is the two-way relationship between prosecutors and outsiders that has been largely absent in the past.

Also, community prosecution—like certain aspects of community policing—is premised on Wilson and Kelling's now-famous broken windows thesis,[56] particularly its concern with prioritizing low-level problems and "incivilities" like unkempt yards and vandalism.

The Duke Rape Case: *North Carolina State Bar* v. *Michael B. Nifong* (2007)

On March 14, 2006, Crystal Gail Magnum told police in Durham, North Carolina, that she had been beaten, raped, and sodomized the previous evening at a party thrown by Duke University lacrosse players at an off-campus house. Three weeks later, Magnum identified her attackers in a photo lineup, and a grand jury subsequently indicted Duke students Reade Seligmann and Collin Finnerty on rape and other charges on April 17 and David Evans on rape charges on May 15.

With its racial overtones—Magnum is African-American, and the accused rapists are Caucasian—and media-inflamed imagery of white boys of privilege preying on an African-American girl, the case quickly became a cause célèbre. On- and off-campus protest rallies kept tensions high for days, and national print and broadcast commentators joined the fray. Duke fired the lacrosse coach and suspended the team.

Over time, Michael Byron Nifong, the Durham County district attorney, assumed an increasingly prominent role in the case. Although this was not unexpected (he was, after all, the district attorney), Nifong's rapid emergence as a key figure in the case was enhanced by his own aggressive pursuit of a microphone to talk into or a television camera to stand before. Some believed that Nifong's pursuit of both the case against the students and the attendant publicity was designed to bolster his chances in the upcoming primary election, in which his bid for reelection was being strongly challenged from within his own political party.

According to those familiar with the case, there was a lack of physical evidence, the victim's story constantly changed, her character was questioned, and Kim Roberts, another stripper who performed at the party, told authorities that Mangum was not raped or hurt. On March 27, 2006, police investigator Ben Himan told Nifong that the case pretty much was at a dead end, with no real evidence existing of a rape. Nifong replied, 'We're f**ked.' However, instead of packing it in right there, Nifong went out that day and began an out-an[d]-out media barrage in which he would tell one news organization after another that there 'definitely' was a rape, and that it was racially motivated. In other words, after he realized that he did not have a case, Nifong *at that point began his media offensive.*"

Indeed, even as accuser Magnum's story began to unravel, Nifong's media blitz continued. Ethics charges filed against Nifong on December 28, 2006, by the North Carolina State Bar documented more than 150 separate statements he made to various local and national print and broadcast media that he "knew or should have known . . . had a substantial likelihood of prejudicing the criminal adjudicative process."

On January 13, 2007, North Carolina Attorney General Roy Cooper took over the case from Nifong. Just three months later, on April 11, 2007, Cooper dropped all charges and called the original charges against the students a "rush to judgment" that was driven by Nifong's "bravado."[6]

An amendment to the ethics charges filed against Nifong, submitted on January 24, 2007, alleged that Nifong and the president and director of a DNA analysis company, Dr. Brian Meehan, agreed to exclude some of the DNA analysis results from the final report by limiting the report only to the "positive results" and that these actions denied the defendants access to "potentially exculpatory DNA evidence and test results." The complaint further charged that "this resulted in Nifong failing to comply with mandated discovery requirements, and . . . making 'misrepresentations and false statements of material fact to the court.'"

On June 16, 2007, a North Carolina bar disciplinary committee found Nifong guilty of "fraud, dishonesty, deceit or misrepresentation; of making false statements of material fact before a judge; of making false statements of material fact before bar investigators, and of lying about withholding exculpatory DNA evidence, among other violations." Announcing Nifong's disbarment, committee chairman F. Lane Williamson "excoriated the disgraced prosecutor. He said Nifong was driven to prosecute the Duke Lacrosse case out of 'self-interest and self-deception. . . . Sometimes character is called upon . . . and it is found wanting,' Williamson said. 'That is what happened to Mr. Nifong.'"

Soon after Nifong's disbarment, Duke University announced that Finnerty and Seligmann had been invited to return to school and were eligible to rejoin the team (David Evans had already graduated). On August 31, 2007, Nifong was convicted of criminal contempt for knowingly making false statements during the criminal proceedings and was sentenced to a single day in jail. The lacrosse team, reinstated for the 2007 season, reached the NCAA finals as the number one seed. On July 12, 2010, the house at which the party took place, 610 North Buchanan Boulevard, was demolished after it had sat unoccupied for the four years following the Duke lacrosse case. As for Crystal Mangum, she managed to finish college and write a book about her experiences before being charged with killing boyfriend Reginald Daye, 46, in 2011; she is currently out on bail pending trial. At the time of this writing, numerous lawsuits against Duke University, the city of Durham, Nifong, and others involved in the case filed by the three accused students, members of the lacrosse team, and the coach are winding their way through the courts.

Such rushes to judgment, often fueled by false, misleading, or unverified media reports or uncensored rumormongering between private citizens via electronic communications, are a tragic phenomenon in this so-called information age. The rapid passing of rumor and innuendo serves to inflame social passions and evoke social responses that are often proven unwarranted and can do irreparable harm to individuals, institutions, and communities.

(continued)

The steady, almost ceremonial processes of American courts quash the effects of unfettered rumor. Further, the courts' demand for investigatory thoroughness and the introduction of only such evidence as may be substantiated and verified serve to expose and derail just the sort of rush to judgment seen in this case. ■

Sources: "Timeline of Events in Duke Lacrosse 'Rape' Case," Foxnews.com, April 11, 2007, available at www.foxnews.com/story/0,2933,265386,00.html (accessed June 2, 2013); Stuart Taylor, Jr., and K. C. Johnson, (New York: Thomas Dunne Books/St. Martin Press, 2007); William L. Anderson, "Dishonesty, Dishonor, and Duke: Now in a Bookstore Near You," v. , 2007, available at www.wral.com/asset/news/local/2007/01/24/1177454/1186416119-Nifong%20Final%20Order%20Amended.pdf (accessed June 2, 2013); Lara Setrakian, "Charges Dropped in Duke Lacrosse Case," ABC News Law and Justice Unit, April 11, 2007, available at http://abcnews.go.com/US/LegalCenter/Story?id=3028515&page=1 (accessed June 2, 2013); Lara Setrakian and Chris Francescani, "Former Duke Prosecutor Nifong Disbarred," ABC News Law and Justice Unit, June 16, 2007, available at http://abcnews.go.com/TheLaw/story?id=3285862 (accessed June 2, 2013); WTVD News, "Infamous Duke Lacrosse House Demolished," July 12, 2010, available at http://abclocal.go.com/wtvd/story?section=news/local&id=7549729 (accessed June 2, 2013).

DISCUSSION QUESTIONS

1. Should prosecutors listen to public opinion in deciding when to bring charges or in deciding when charges should be dropped?

2. If a prosecutor feels the need for legal or ethical advice, from whom should he or she seek it?

Library Extra
8–3 Community Prosecution

Library Extra
8–4 Prosecution in the Community

Library Extra
8–5 Prosecutors' Programs to Ease Victim Anxiety

Accountability   Throughout criminal justice, there has been an increasing concern with accountability. Prosecutors have responded in a number of ways:

- They have taken steps to promote financial accountability to ensure that tax dollars are well spent on strategies most likely to effectively target crime.[57]

- They have adopted strategies that include improving conviction rates, minimizing dismissals, and speeding up the time to judgment to ensure that offenders are held accountable for their actions.

- They have improved their accountability to the public by acting in a more open fashion, such as by keeping victims informed about the progress of criminal cases: "Traditionally, the line of accountability by assistants has been inward to the organization, although more recently considerable accountability has developed to victims and their families. For example, from 1974 to 1990, the rate at which prosecutors notified police and victims of the outcomes of their cases more than doubled, rising from 44 to 98 percent for police notification, and from 35 to 93 percent for victims."[58]

Learning Objective 3

Explain the factors affecting charging decisions.

CHARGING DECISIONS

Prosecutors' charging decisions have been the focus of plenty of attention. Researchers try to explain why they press charges in some cases and not others, voters respond when prosecutors make controversial decisions, and the press gives its share of attention to prosecutors' decisions, especially those involving high-profile cases. Prosecutors' professional associations have also given plenty of attention over the years to decision making and procedures for ensuring fairness and accountability. Even the courts have dealt with challenges to prosecutorial decision making.[59]

Prosecutorial Discretion

prosecutorial discretion
"[T]he decision of a prosecutor to submit a charging document to a court, or to seek a grand jury indictment, or to decline to prosecute."[iv]

Prosecutorial discretion has been defined as "the decision of a prosecutor to submit a charging document to a court, or to seek a grand jury indictment, or to decline to prosecute."[60] This is an awesome responsibility with no parallel throughout criminal justice. Criminal suspects' lives and liberty can literally hang on a prosecutor's single decision on what to do with a case. This does not mean that criminal charges will lead to a conviction, but once a person has been formally charged with a crime, there are significant restrictions on his or her mobility. There may even be some time spent in jail leading up to the court date; alternatively, the suspect-defendant may be released prior to trial, but he or she will not be allowed to venture very far.

Limitations on Prosecutorial Discretion

While prosecutors have considerable power, this power is not unlimited. Prosecutors often work for elected district attorneys who occasionally order their subordinates to pursue or refrain from filing criminal charges. Likewise, a low-level prosecutor's decision not to charge may be met with an unfavorable reaction by a superior who insists on filing charges. Even the state attorney general can get involved in local prosecution affairs. Many states give the attorney general power to prosecute in cases where the local prosecutor fails to act.[61]

Although higher-ranking prosecutors may influence their subordinates' decisions, the courts are not permitted to do the same: "Such factors as the strength of the case, the prosecution's general deterrence value, [and] the Government's overall enforcement plan are not readily susceptible to the kind of analysis the courts are competent to make."[62]

Prosecutors are also required to follow their office policies and professional standards of conduct, such as those set by state bar associations, and they must always be mindful of constitutional limitations on their charging decisions. For example, if a prosecutor's decision to charge or not charge is unfair and selective (e.g., it targets certain individuals, such as a conspicuous or highly visible offender, unfairly), then it will run afoul of the Constitution. This is quite difficult to prove, however.

Prosecutors who act vindictively also threaten defendants' due process rights. *Blackledge* v. *Perry*[63] involved a defendant convicted in a lower court for misdemeanor assault with a deadly weapon. After Perry filed an appeal with the county superior court, the prosecutor obtained an indictment charging him with *felony* assault for the same conduct. After pleading guilty, Perry was sentenced to five to seven years in prison. Was the extra charge an example of prosecutorial discretion or, as Perry charged, vindictiveness motivated by a defendant exercising his constitutional rights? The Supreme Court agreed with Perry's argument that the prosecutor acted vindictively, stating that "vindictiveness against a defendant for having successfully attacked his first conviction must play no part in the sentence he receives after a new trial."[64]

Factors Affecting Charging Decisions

Prosecutors' charging decisions are motivated by both legal and extralegal factors.[65] Examples of legal factors include the following:

- Strength of the evidence
- Relationship between the defendant and the victim
- Defendant's prior history
- Facts of the case

Unfortunately, legal factors do not tell the whole story. Prosecutors also base their decisions, consciously or not, on a host of other extralegal factors.[66] For example, researchers have shown that prosecutors sometimes base their charging decisions on victim stereotypes: "[T]he character and credibility of the victim [are] a key factor in determining prosecutorial strategies, one at least as important as 'objective' evidence about the crime or characteristics of the defendant."[67] Besides victim stereotypes, several other extralegal factors influence charging decisions:

- *Limited prosecution resources*. For example, there may not be enough resources to charge offenders accused of minor crimes due to an excess of serious crimes.
- *Lack of motivation to pursue a particular case*. This has been true historically in domestic-violence cases, where sometimes there is a hesitancy on the part of the government to intervene in family affairs.[68]

- *Desire to win.* Prosecutors hate to lose, and a burning desire to secure a conviction can certainly influence a charging decision.
- *Case brought to prosecutor's attention by police or crime victim.*[69] Researchers found that "citizen-invoked complaints of domestic violence stand a slim change of producing criminal charges because of their lower legal visibility and because, as critics claim, prosecutors view such cases as more appropriate for social service agencies."[70]
- *Victim/offender race.* In general, prosecution is more likely when the offender is nonwhite and the victim is white.[71]
- *Victim/offender sex.* In domestic-violence cases, charges are more likely to be filed against male rather than female perpetrators.[72]

no-drop prosecution
The practice of not dropping charges against domestic-violence victims that emerged as a response to the high rate of dismissals in domestic-violence cases"; also called *evidence-based prosecution.*

No-Drop Prosecution Some practices, such as no-drop prosecution, have been implemented in response to the problems that can result from prosecutorial discretion. **No-drop prosecution** (also called "evidence-based prosecution") refers to the practice of not dropping charges against domestic-violence victims, which emerged in response to the high rate of dismissals in domestic-violence cases.[73] The problem was that many victims of domestic violence refused to testify in court against their abusers, and that meant that prosecutors would decline to pursue criminal charges.

Some prosecutors' offices have gone so far as to implement policies that *require* prosecutors to charge in domestic-violence cases. Limiting prosecutors' discretion in this fashion has raised a number of questions. Some critics believe that no-drop policies limit the discretion of prosecutors to decide whether charges should be brought against an accused person[74]; others charge that no-drop prosecution may be harmful to victims because they restrict victim input, which may be both accurate and necessary in some domestic-violence cases. An aggressive prosecution strategy may also have implications for future violence if the accused is allowed to return home at some point after being convicted. But at least one author has argued that the benefits of no-drop prosecution outweigh the costs, stating that "no-drop policies can play an important role in combating domestic violence, because they account for victims' realities, counteract long-standing justifications for inaction, and transform the statutory promise of justice for battered women into a credible threat of prosecution for their batterers."[75]

Some researchers have studied no-drop prosecution in an effort to gauge its effectiveness. For example, researchers recently compared 200 domestic-violence court cases during the year prior to implementation of a no-drop policy with 200 cases that began after the new policy went into effect.[76] The cities of Everett, Washington, and Klamath Falls, Oregon, were the research sites. As expected, no-drop prosecution substantially increased guilty pleas and the number of domestic-violence cases going to court—the latter increased tenfold.

While it would seem that no-drop prosecution served its intended purpose in Everett and Klamath Falls, it is not clear whether there was a corresponding decrease in domestic-violence incidents. Why? There are at least two explanations. First, no-drop prosecution policies are expensive, which is not surprising given that they apparently result in more trials. Second, no-drop prosecution may actually deter victims of domestic violence from calling the police because to the extent that they are codependent, a prison sentence could disrupt the home.[77]

Alternatives to Traditional Prosecution

Prosecutors have other options at their disposal besides simply filing charges. Examples include diversion, deferred prosecution, and deferred sentencing. Each of these strategies provides opportunities for offenders to fulfill some obligation in exchange for the prosecutor's decision to avoid or put off formal charges.

Diversion Diversion is a term that refers to any number of informal or programmatic methods of steering offenders out of the criminal justice system. In one sense, diversion has been around since the emergence of community-based corrections. For example, when a judge sentences an offender to probation, the judge may feel that prison would do more harm than good for the offender, so the judge has decided, in essence, that the offender should be diverted out of prison into an environment that fosters reintegration.

Another informal method of diversion could be a police officer's decision not to arrest but instead to encourage a suspect to do something to get on the straight and narrow. This kind of informal diversion basically amounts to the exercise of discretion but still serves as an example of a criminal justice official advocating a different, less enforcement-oriented method of dealing with the crime problem. Our focus here is on programmatic methods of diversion, especially diversion programs for defendants during the pretrial period.

There was a significant push for diversion programs following the recommendations of the 1967 President's Commission on Law Enforcement and the Administration of Justice.[78] The Law Enforcement Assistance Administration, which resulted from the commission's efforts, funded several diversion programs, the rationale being that they would reduce the number of offenders being drawn into the criminal justice system and would prevent the harmful effects of criminal stigmatization that suspects would experience if they went to court, were convicted, and were put in prison. Diversion has several goals:

> [It fosters] (1) avoidance of negative labeling and stigmatization, (2) reduction of unnecessary social control and coercion, (3) reduction of recidivism, (4) provision of service (assistance), and (5) reduction of justice system cost.[79]

Perhaps a more cynical view of diversion programs is that they amount to a "break" for certain offenders. Some people feel that young first-time or low-level offenders should be treated with a measure of leniency. Even if offenders are treated with leniency under diversion programs, the leniency they receive is not the same as traditional sanctions like probation, fines, and community service; instead, diversion programs usually require that offenders complete a specific program as part of their more lenient sentence.

Diversion programs manifest themselves in several forms:[80]

- *Precharge diversion.* When offenders are diverted out of the criminal justice system before they are charged, it is called **precharge diversion.**

- *Deferred prosecution diversion.* **Deferred prosecution diversion** (see next subsection) occurs when an offender has been charged but the actual in-court prosecution is held off until the offender completes treatment or some other program. Then, if the offender completes his or her obligations, the prosecutor will revisit the charges and most likely drop them.

- *Sentencing diversion.* Instead of the offender going straight to jail or prison, he or she may be the object of **sentencing diversion** by being sent to participate in drug treatment, anger management, or some other program. This approach is akin to the hypothetical judge's decision presented earlier and is based on a belief that prison may do more harm than good for some offenders.

- *Postincarceration diversion.* Most programs of **postincarceration diversion** are reserved for chronic low-level offenders and are aimed at getting these offenders who keep ending up incarcerated to stop committing crime.[81]

diversion
An informal or programmatic method of steering an offender out of the criminal justice system.

precharge diversion
The diversion of an offender out of the criminal justice system before he or she is charged.

deferred prosecution diversion
A delay in the actual in-court prosecution of an offender until the offender completes treatment or some other program.

sentencing diversion
The requirement that an offender participate in drug treatment, anger management, or some other program in lieu of going straight to jail or prison.

postincarceration diversion
A structured treatment or program typically reserved for chronic low-level offenders immediately following their release from incarceration that is aimed at getting these offenders to stop committing crimes.[vi]

Deferred Prosecution   Deferred prosecution amounts to putting off or delaying criminal charges against a suspect until he or she fulfills some obligation. The obligation could be participation in a treatment or diversion program, or it could be a probation term. If the suspect completes a period of probation supervision successfully, then the prosecutor will forgo criminal charges. This is the approach that has been taken in several jurisdictions around the country. For example, the Kalamazoo (Michigan) County Citizens' Probation Authority, which operated during the late 1970s, allowed suspected offenders an opportunity to complete a pretrial period of probation supervision[82]; if probation was successfully completed, the person's record of the criminal offense was expunged.

Although it is a useful alternative to traditional prosecution, deferred prosecution raises some concerns. While it may serve the noble purpose of reducing the stigma of a criminal charge on someone's record, some have argued that the practice threatens important constitutional protections.[83] First, the right to counsel may be threatened because deferred prosecution basically amounts to adjudication without trial. Second, deferred prosecution may run counter to the Fifth Amendment's self-incrimination clause because it basically coerces the suspect into admitting a degree of guilt even though neither a guilty verdict was obtained nor a trial was conducted.

deferred sentencing
A twist on deferred prosecution that puts off sentencing instead of putting off charges.

Deferred Sentencing   **Deferred sentencing** represents a twist on deferred prosecution: Instead of putting off charges, it puts off sentencing. Deferred sentencing also requires defendants to plead guilty to a crime; then, if they complete a diversion and/or treatment program, their record will be expunged.

Drug Treatment Alternative to Prison (DTAP) program
The Brooklyn, New York, deferred sentencing program.[vii]

One of the better-known deferred sentencing programs is the popular Brooklyn (New York) **Drug Treatment Alternative to Prison (DTAP) program**, which was started by Charles Hynes, Brooklyn's elected district attorney, in response to an alarming increase in drug arrests in Brooklyn during the late 1980s. According to figures from the Center on Addiction and Substance Abuse at Columbia University, drug arrests there escalated by some 325% between 1981 and 1990.[84] When Hynes assumed his position, 8,182 indictments had been filed against drug felons in Brooklyn in one year, so he developed the DTAP program in order to divert eligible drug offenders into treatment and avoid the traditional "revolving door" method of dealing with chronic drug offenders.

Prior to 1998, the DTAP program was reserved for defendants arrested during "buy-bust" encounters who had been previously convicted of a nonviolent felony. The program provided for deferred prosecution if eligible defendants agreed to participate in 15 to 24 months of intensive drug treatment and vocational training. If a defendant refused to participate, he or she would most likely be convicted and sent to prison. If participants in the DTAP program failed, they would start the process over again—a new prosecution and a new agreement to participate in treatment.

In January 1998, the DTAP program was significantly altered when it changed from a deferred prosecution program to a deferred sentencing program. Instead of holding the charges in abeyance, prosecutors now obtain guilty pleas from DTAP participants, and then sentencing is deferred pending successful completion of the treatment and vocational program, at which point the defendants' guilty plea is withdrawn and the charges are dismissed. Those who fail the DTAP program are brought back to court by the district attorney's special warrant enforcement team, and sentencing takes place.

Learning Objective 4
Summarize the protections and immunity afforded to prosecutors.

PROTECTIONS FOR PROSECUTORS

Due to prosecutors' considerable power, they have been given equally considerable protection from retaliation for their charging decisions. (The same applies to police officers, who can assert any number of defenses when sued.) Prosecutors enjoy even more protection. It is useful to think in terms of two types of immunity: absolute and qualified.

Absolute Immunity

Absolute immunity refers to total immunity from suit; in other words, a prosecutor cannot be sued for his or her charging decision. Prosecutors enjoy absolute immunity when they act as "advocates."[85] By charging offenders, prosecutors serve as advocates for the government, and they are immune from suit for charging suspects with crimes. This is reasonable because imagine what would happen to the criminal process if prosecutors could be sued at every turn for charging offenders.

Prosecutors also act as advocates when they argue the government's case and can do almost anything in this capacity to secure a conviction without fear of being sued. They cannot even be held liable for flagrant misconduct in their charging decisions. This misconduct can include making false statements at pretrial hearings,[86] using false testimony at trial,[87] failing to disclose exculpatory evidence (that which casts doubt on the defendant's involvement in the crime),[88] fabricating evidence,[89] influencing witnesses,[90] and even breaching plea agreements.[91]

Not everyone agrees that prosecutors should enjoy absolute immunity, especially in light of recently publicized incidents of DNA exonerations of wrongfully convicted persons. According to one critic, prosecutors should only enjoy qualified immunity (which we introduce in the next subsection):

> Absolute immunity frustrates the purpose of civil rights legislation by failing to deter frequent and egregious misconduct. It also hinders the development of constitutional standards and the implementation of structural solutions for systemic problems. Prosecutorial liability—with the safeguard of qualified immunity to prevent vexatious litigation—is necessary to ensure the integrity of the criminal justice system.[92]

Despite the controversy, wayward prosecutors can be punished through other means besides being sued. For example, they can receive reprimands from their superiors, face public reprimand, be suspended from law practice, and even be disbarred. These sanctions are the exception, however. A study by the Center for Public Integrity found that in over 11,000 cases of alleged prosecutorial misconduct, only 44 prosecutors were disciplined, and only two were disbarred.[93]

Qualified Immunity

Qualified immunity attaches when prosecutors (1) act as administrators or investigators and (2) make reasonable mistakes. Alternatively, if the plaintiff in a lawsuit can show that a prosecutor acted as an administrator or investigator and violated clearly established constitutional law, the prosecutor can be held liable. Such a case is described in the following "Courts in the News" feature.

What are administrative and investigative functions? Unfortunately, there are no clear answers. The Supreme Court has yet to decide on this question, and there is clearly confusion in the lower courts. For example, in one case the prosecutor intimidated and coerced witnesses, actions that the Washington, D.C., circuit concluded were investigative.[94] It said that the prosecutor's actions were "a misuse of investigative techniques legitimately directed at exploring whether witness testimony is truthful and complete and whether the government has acquired all incriminating evidence."[95] Contrast this with the Fifth Circuit's decision in *Cousin v. Small*.[96] The court held that a prosecutor who was accused of coercing witnesses to testify falsely was acting as an advocate rather than an investigator, so absolute immunity applied. The court said that "the interview was intended to secure evidence that would be used in the presentation of the state's case at the pending trial of an already identified suspect, not to identify a suspect or establish probable cause."[97]

absolute immunity
The total immunity of a prosecutor from a suit.

qualified immunity
The immunity that attaches when a prosecutor acts as an administrator or investigator and makes reasonable mistakes.

Web Extra
8–2 American Prosecutors Research Institute

COURTS IN THE NEWS

Prosecutorial Misconduct

In March 2000, Petros Bedi was convicted of killing a man in an Astoria, Queens, New York, nightclub. At trial, the defense attacked a prosecution witness's credibility on the grounds that he had received nearly $20,000 in exchange for testimony. The witness denied the allegation, but all the while, Queens prosecutors knew that the witness had been given $16,640 for hotel bills and about $3,000 in cash. Based on this testimony, Bedi was convicted and sentenced to 42 years in prison. While in prison Bedi, with the help of a private investigator, battled for ten years to obtain these court records, which Queens prosecutors should have turned over at the trial. In the meantime, with the help of a new lawyer, Bedi filed a lawsuit asking the court to overturn the conviction. "This is," the lawyer said, "a reprehensible case of prosecutorial misconduct."

Bedi was no Boy Scout. He had been convicted in other cases of drug dealing and conspiracy to murder. But as his lawyer claimed, "Just because the prosecution thinks he's a criminal, that doesn't mean they can rig the result."

This type of behavior is not unique. In 2010, the state bar association created a task force that studied 53 cases of wrongful conviction. It found that prosecutorial and police misconduct accounted for over half the cases.

So what happened to Bedi? In 2013, a New York state judge ordered that he get a new trial and faulted Queens prosecutors for not correcting an eyewitness's false testimony that he received no financial benefits from the district attorney's office and failing to turn over all information related to the nearly $20,000 that the witness received for living expenses.

"While the defendant has a deplorable criminal history, an honest application of the reasonable possibility

AP Photo/Mary Altaffer

If you were on a jury, would you believe a witness if you discovered they were paid by the prosecution? Did the Queens prosecutor shown here overstep the boundaries of legal fairness by paying a witness too much money?

standard as defined by appellate courts of this State compels the granting of the motion to vacate the conviction," wrote Queens Acting Supreme Court Justice James Griffin in his decision. The judge added that the "reasonable possibility" standard was satisfied when a defendant—even in the face of overwhelming evidence of guilt—demonstrated that the undisclosed evidence "might have" contributed to the trial result and the error was not "unimportant and insignificant." ■

DISCUSSION QUESTIONS

1. Should the prosecutors in this case be held criminally liable? After all, Bedi spent more than a decade in prison for a crime he may not have committed. Or should he be awarded civil damages?

2. Should a conviction be overturned because a prosecutor forgot to mention that a witness was paid? After all, just because he was paid does not mean he lied at trial.

Sources: Andrew Keshner, "Judge Faults Queens D.A., Vacates Murder Conviction," *New York Law Journal*, March 19, 2013, available at www.newyorklawjournal.com/PubArticleNY .jsp?id=1202592492667&Judge_Faults_Queens_DA_Vacates_ Murder_Conviction&slreturn=20130501110924 (accessed June 2, 2013); Acting Justice James Griffin, "The People v. Petros Bedi, 4107/96," available at www.newyorklawjournal.com/Case DecisionNY.jsp?id=1202592836531 (accessed June 2, 2013); Jessica Dye, "False Testimony Spurs Judge to Vacate 2000 Murder Conviction," Thomson Reuters News and Insight, March 18, 2013, available at http://newsandinsight.thomsonreuters.com/ Legal/News/2013/03_-_March/False_testimony_spurs_judge_to_ vacate_2000_murder_conviction (accessed June 2, 2013).

Learning Objective 5

Describe the rules of conduct and ethics for prosecutors as well as what constitutes prosecutorial misconduct.

ETHICS

All attorneys are bound by elaborate ethical guidelines. These vary by state, but the ABA has adopted some model standards. While all attorneys are bound by similar ethical standards, there are some that apply uniquely to prosecutors because there are some ethical dilemmas that affect prosecutors more than other attorneys.

Rules of Professional Conduct

Nearly every state bar association has adopted its own standards of professional conduct for attorneys, including prosecutors. Rather than making an effort to look at them individually, we summarize the ABA's Model Rules of Professional Conduct for attorneys.[98] In addition to detailing lawyers' responsibilities, the Model Rules also contains a specific set of rules aimed at prosecutors. According to Model Rule 2.8, all prosecutors should do the following:

> [R]efrain from prosecuting a charge that the prosecutor knows is not supported by probable cause.
>
> [M]ake reasonable efforts to assure that the accused has been advised of the right to, and the procedure for obtaining, counsel and has been given reasonable opportunity to obtain counsel.
>
> [N]ot seek to obtain from an unrepresented accused a waiver of important pretrial rights, such as the right to a preliminary hearing.
>
> [M]ake timely disclosure to the defense of all evidence or information known to the prosecutor that tends to negate the guilt of the accused or mitigates the offense, and in connection with sentencing, disclose to the defense and to the tribunal all unprivileged mitigating information known to the prosecutor, except when the prosecutor is relieved of this responsibility by a protective order of the tribunal.
>
> [N]ot subpoena a lawyer in a grand jury or other criminal proceeding to present evidence about a past or present client unless the prosecutor reasonably believes (i) the information sought is not protected from disclosure by any applicable privilege; (ii) the evidence sought is essential to the successful completion of an ongoing investigation or prosecution; and (iii) there is no other feasible alternative to obtain the information.
>
> [E]xcept for statements that are necessary to inform the public of the nature and extent of the prosecutor's action and that serve a legitimate law enforcement purpose, refrain from making extrajudicial comments that have a substantial likelihood of heightening public condemnation of the accused and exercise reasonable care to prevent investigators, law enforcement personnel, employees or other persons assisting or associated with the prosecutor in a criminal case from making an extrajudicial statement that the prosecutor would be prohibited from making.[99]

Key Ethical Dilemmas for Prosecutors

Prosecutors enjoy a great deal of immunity from allegations of impropriety concerning their charging decisions, yet just because prosecutors cannot be sued for acting in an overzealous or improper fashion, they can still run afoul of ethical standards. One area where prosecutors can act improperly and in violation of ethical standards yet remain immune from suit deals with disclosure of exculpatory evidence. In general, prosecutors are constitutionally bound, as a matter of due process, to disclose evidence that is favorable to the accused. We look at this in more detail in Chapter 11.

Web Extra
8–3 Center for Prosecutor Integrity

Many prosecutors are also concerned about conflicts of interest. This is especially apparent in some small jurisdictions where prosecutors work on a part-time basis.[100] The general rule is that part-time prosecutors cannot turn around and defend the same individuals they convict—or even do any defense attorney–related work.[101] But in most jurisdictions, part-time prosecutors are also permitted to practice law and otherwise represent private clients. What if a client wants to sue the government that employs the prosecutor (if only on a part-time basis)? These types of dilemmas are not readily resolved, and the ABA rules are not particularly vocal on this subject.

Prosecutors also have to make difficult decisions about what to reveal to the press concerning specific cases (see Rule 2.8 referred to in the previous subsection). Prosecutors who talk to the press and reveal too much about their opinions on particular cases can get into trouble for trying their cases "in the press."[102] Unfortunately, there are no clear rules in this area. The Supreme Court has said only this much: "Collaboration between counsel and the press as to information affecting the fairness of a criminal trial is not only subject to regulation but . . . highly censurable and worthy of disciplinary measures."[103] Despite the ambiguity of this general rule, judges sometimes issue gag orders in response to attorneys who reveal too much to the press (we look at this more closely in Chapter 13).

No matter what the ethical dilemma is, prosecutors' key responsibility is to seek justice. This is especially true in capital cases where the stakes are very high (a defendant's life). Courts have overturned death penalty convictions due to overzealous prosecution, even if the prosecutors themselves cannot be held liable.[104]

Learning Objective 6
Describe the organization and administration of prosecutors' offices.

PROSECUTORS ON THE JOB

We have looked in some detail at prosecution throughout history and the all-important charging decisions. But what is the job really like? How are prosecutors' offices organized? How does one get promoted? These and other questions concerning the real world of prosecution are answered in this chapter's remaining sections.

Office Structure and Organization

Prosecutors' offices are organized similarly to other public agencies, such as police departments. In the case of a district attorney office, the elected district attorney serves as chief and supervises several division heads or deputies, who in turn supervise other attorneys. There can be several layers of supervision, as is seen in the Essex (Massachusetts) District Attorney's Office (see Figure 8–3).

Other district attorney's offices have simpler organizational structures, such as the one for Collin County (Texas) that appears in Figure 8–4. Indeed, some rural prosecutors' offices (e.g., Pennington County, Minnesota) are so small that they may employ five or fewer persons, and an organizational chart for such agencies is probably unnecessary.[105] Despite differences from one office to the next, most prosecutors' offices are organized into divisions according to case types, such as felonies, misdemeanors, and juvenile cases. The more of a particular type of case a prosecutor's office has, the more likely it is that a separate division may be created to handle it.

Web Extra
8–4 National Association of Prosecutor Coordinators

In some large prosecutors' offices, several attorneys can be involved in a single case: One may handle pretrial matters, another the trial, and still another the posttrial hearings. Critics have claimed that having multiple prosecutors involved in the adjudication process is inefficient. In response, many jurisdictions have implemented a so-called program of **vertical prosecution**, which ensures that one prosecutor handles a given case from beginning to end.[106] The same prosecutor represents the state from the point that criminal charges are filed all the way through sentencing.

vertical prosecution
The practice of having the same prosecutor represent the state from the point that criminal charges are filed all the way through to sentencing.[viii]

Contrasting Goals and Styles

Prosecution in America is decentralized and lacking in uniformity. Goals and styles of prosecution, office culture, relationships with constituents, and interactions vary across and between jurisdictions. This can have interesting implications for employment. If a budding prosecutor favors crime prevention, treatment of criminals, and rehabilitation (the exception), then he or she would probably not fit well in an office that prefers conservative

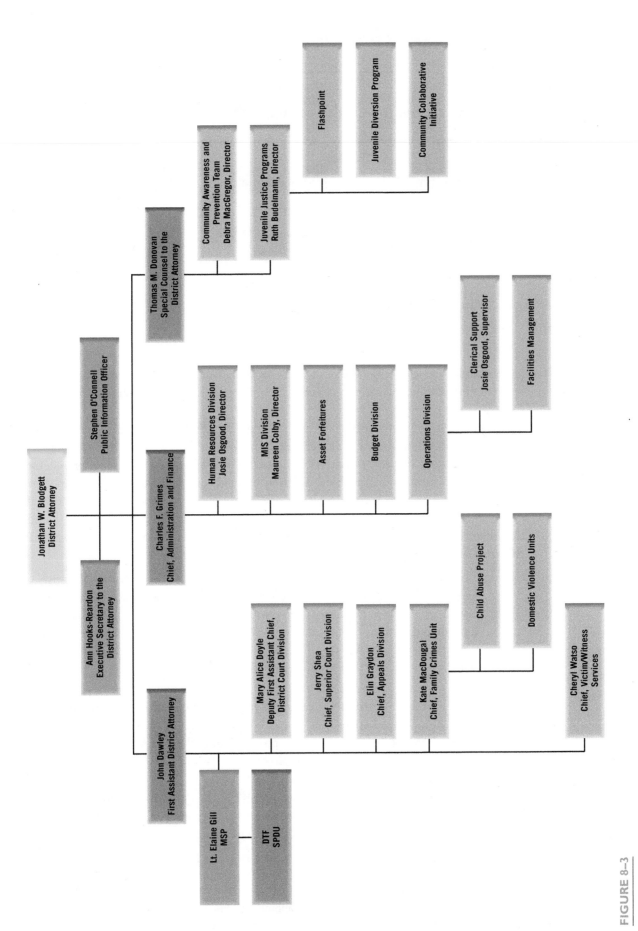

FIGURE 8–3

Essex (Massachusetts) District Attorney's Office Organizational Chart

Source: www.mass.gov/bb/fy2008h1/img08/org/EAS.PDF (accessed February 18, 2013).

FIGURE 8–4

Typically Simpler District Attorney's Office Organizational Chart

law-and-order strategies; likewise, the traditional hard-line prosecutor who buys whole-heartedly into the felony case processor model may not thrive in an office that does not share the same priorities.

In what ways do prosecutors' goals and styles differ? Roy Flemming's landmark examination of prosecution in nine counties across the United States found that two important considerations shaped prosecutors' policies.[107] One was whether the chief prosecutor was dissatisfied with his or her office's relationship with the courts and the bar. Another was whether the chief prosecutor enjoyed conflict: "Some prosecutors disdain the idea of openly challenging the bench or bar while others relish the prospect."[108] Flemming found that these two considerations yielded three political styles: courthouse insurgent, policy reformer, and office conservator:[109]

1. *Courthouse insurgent.* Courthouse insurgents are prosecutors who are dissatisfied with the office's position within the courts and throughout the criminal justice system, and they also disagree with how the office was run beforehand. Returning to Dallas County, mentioned earlier in this chapter, the current district attorney, Craig Watkins, fits the role of courthouse insurgent—he sought the office largely out of frustration with his predecessor's policies.

2. *Policy reformer.* Policy reformers are those prosecutors who change internal practices, such as by restricting the number of plea agreements, but who do so in a way that minimizes opposition. They also "encouraged more assertive attitudes among their assistants, increased the professional caliber of their staff, or tried to develop innovative approaches to prosecutorial work. They also did not shrink from trying to alter their relationships with judges."[110]

3. *Office conservator.* The office conservator is the chief prosecutor who is satisfied with the status quo. One prosecutor who fit the conservator mold made this observation concerning relationships with judges:

   I think half the judges are frustrated district attorneys. They all have opinions on how this office should be run, and at one time or another they're all going to try it. . . . You've gotta be firm. They can't run your office. But it's give and take. . . . If you start a war with a judge, make sure it's an appropriate case because they can slow down the list [docket] and clog up your system. . . . You gotta be nice, but you gotta be firm.[111]

To summarize, if a new chief prosecutor is satisfied with the status of his or her office, a conservator style will be adopted. If the opposite is true, the prosecutor will adopt a policy reformer or courthouse insurgent approach. The choice between each of these hinges on the value the prosecutor sees in conflict. There are two parts to this: "One is what the prosecutor perceives as his or her chances of winning or succeeding. The other is the prosecutor's attitude about conflict."[112]

As you may recall, the concept of the courtroom work group (Chapter 2) suggests that prosecutors, defense attorneys, and judges always enjoy a harmonious, orderly, and collegial working relationship. Flemming's research reveals that reality is much more complex. Prosecutors and the bench occasionally do *not* see eye to eye, and their relationships with defense can often be strained.

Retention and Pay

To become a prosecutor, one first has to attend law school and be admitted to the state bar. Entry-level prosecutors used to be thrust into the position with little or no experience in handling cases.[113] More recently, prosecutors' offices have become more adept at training, with new prosecutors going through orientation programs where they watch various proceedings and ease into their jobs somewhat more gradually.

What can one expect to earn as a prosecutor? Unfortunately, fully updated figures are not available on a national scale, but Table 8–2 shows a number of salary-related figures for prosecutors with varying levels of experience in offices of different sizes. Not surprisingly, the most highly paid prosecutors are those with the most experience and who work in the largest office. The figures in Table 8–2 do not reflect current pay due to the lag between data collection, reporting, and publication of this book, but they likely give a clear estimate of the current situation, in part because of the fiscal crisis that has struck a large number of jurisdictions around the country.

TABLE 8–2 Assistant Prosecutors' Average Minimum and Maximum Salary in State Prosecutors' Offices, by Population Served

| | Full-Time Office Serving a Population of— | | | | | | | | Part-Time | |
| | 1,000,000 or More | | 250,000 to 999,999 | | 100,000 to 249,999 | | 99,999 or Less | | | |
Salary	Mean	Median	Mean	Median	Mean	Median	Mean	Median	Mean	Median
Entry level assistant prosecutor										
Minimum	$51,354	$51,378	$47,580	$46,704	$44,007	$43,000	$42,380	$42,931	$33,460	$34,307
Maximum	$64,517	$58,013	$57,759	$51,707	$55,263	$48,000	$50,050	$46,000	$36,712	$39,000
Assistant prosecutor with 1 to 5 years experience										
Minimum	$59,671	$56,478	$53,542	$51,604	$48,930	$47,000	$45,921	$46,000	$33,645	$37,550
Maximum	$82,227	$79,296	$68,993	$65,000	$62,074	$57,585	$55,248	$53,134	$36,391	$40,691
Assistant prosecutor with 6 or more years experience										
Minimum	$73,010	$68,609	$65,400	$64,000	$57,056	$57,000	$53,113	$54,000	$36,481	$40,000
Maximum	$108,434	$111,987	$94,257	$90,796	$83,139	$79,566	$64,932	$65,000	$42,473	$44,990

Note: Based on data from prosecutors' offices that responded. Salary data were missing for about 50% of offices.

Source: S. W. Perry and D. Banks, *Prosecutors in State Courts, 2007* (Washington, DC: U.S. Department of Justice, 2011), p. 6, available at http://bjs.ojp.usdoj.gov/content/pub/pdf/psc07st.pdf (accessed February 18, 2013).

Library Extra
8–6 National Prosecutors'
Survey Series

Table 8–2 should not be interpreted to mean that prosecutors stay in their posts for some time. In reality, the turnover rate is actually fairly high because private practice can prove especially appealing to underpaid prosecutors.[114] In fact, one study showed that prosecutors in jurisdictions where private lawyer salaries are highest take more cases to trial (as opposed to plea-bargaining them) because trial experience is regarded favorably by private law firms.[115]

To gauge the extent of turnover and pay problems, the American Prosecutors Research Institute recently surveyed a significant number of prosecutors from around the country. They found that almost 90% of the 2,119 prosecutors who responded were still paying off their student loans and that many of them were holding second jobs in order to pay down their debts.[116]

It is not always the case that prosecutors leave their public positions for lucrative private practice. Some private defense attorneys and public defenders (albeit not too many) cross over into the realm of prosecution out of a desire to serve the public. An example is Dallas County's current prosecutor, Craig Watkins, who began his career as a defense attorney and owner of a bail bonds agency in south Dallas.

Threats and Violence against Prosecutors

It is often said that policing is a thankless profession. The same can be said of prosecution, at least based on the frequency with which prosecutors are targeted with work-related threats and assaults. A recent survey revealed, surprisingly, that 47% of prosecutors' offices nationwide received work-related threats against a staff member or had one of their staff assaulted (see Table 8–3 for more details).[117] Assaults and batteries appear to be the exception, but the number of threats is somewhat startling.

TABLE 8–3 Work-Related Threats and Assaults against Prosecutors and Their Staff

Type of Threat/ Staff Carrying Firearm	All Offices		Full-Time Offices Serving a Population of—								Part-Time Offices	
			1,000,000 or More		250,000 to 999,999		100,000 to 249,999		99,999 or Less			
	Number	Percent	Number	Percent	Number	Percent	Number	Percent	Number	Percent	Number	Percent
Any threat*	960	47%	34	89%	132	69%	154	54%	555	45%	85	28%
Written threat	537	26	30	79	93	49	105	37	273	22	36	12
Threatening phone call	646	32	27	71	101	54	107	38	350	28	61	20
Face-to-face verbal threat	602	29	27	71	90	48	101	36	338	28	46	15
Battery/assault	55	3	5	13	13	7	9	3	24	2	4	1
Any staff carry firearm*	971	47%	36	90%	158	82%	189	66%	526	43%	62	20%
Chief prosecutor carries a firearm	421	21	6	15	32	17	59	21	275	22	49	16
Assistant prosecutor carries a firearm	377	18	13	33	64	33	81	29	199	16	20	7
Staff investigator carries a firearm	685	34	35	88	150	78	162	57	324	27	14	5

Note: Based on data from all prosecutors' offices that responded. Data were missing for 12% of offices.

*Details adds to more than total due to multiple responses.

Source: S. W. Perry and D. Banks, *Prosecutors in State Courts, 2007* (Washington, DC: U.S. Department of Justice, 2011), p. 7, available at http://bjs.ojp.usdoj.gov/content/pub/pdf/psc07st.pdf (accessed February 18, 2013).

SUMMARY

1. IDENTIFY THE NAMES AND TYPES OF PROSECUTORS

- Types of prosecutors include U.S. attorneys and their assistants, district attorneys (or their equivalents) and their deputies, and city attorneys.

- Not all city attorneys perform prosecution functions; of those who do, most prosecute misdemeanors.

2. OUTLINE HOW AMERICAN PROSECUTION HAS CHANGED AND EVOLVED OVER TIME

- Throughout history, prosecution has moved from private to public, centralized to decentralized, and appointed to elected.

- Prosecutors' power has increased over time, and they have become busier and more visible due to the emergence of the criminal defense bar and important Supreme Court civil liberties decisions.

- Initially, it was thought that prosecutors processed cases and that they did this for all law violations, neutrally and evenhandedly. Once researchers discovered that the criminal justice system does not always follow a "textbook" pattern, it was never looked at the same again. Prosecutors were seen to have enormous discretion and power.

- Most recently, a new prosecutorial paradigm has emerged, that of community prosecution and its increased emphasis on accountability.

3. EXPLAIN THE FACTORS AFFECTING CHARGING DECISIONS

- Prosecutorial discretion refers to the prosecutor's authority whether to charge. This decision is almost unlimited, but there are some constraints. For example, a prosecutor cannot charge vindictively.

- Prosecutors base their charging decisions on legal (e.g., evidence) and extralegal (e.g., stereotypes) factors.

- No-drop prosecution policies have been adopted in response to the problem of uncooperative domestic-violence victims.

- Alternatives to prosecution include diversion, deferred prosecution, and deferred sentencing.

4. SUMMARIZE THE PROTECTIONS AND IMMUNITY AFFORDED TO PROSECUTORS

- Prosecutors enjoy absolute immunity from suit when they act as advocates, particularly when they choose to charge.

- They enjoy qualified immunity when (1) they act as administrators or investigators and (2) they make reasonable mistakes.

5. DESCRIBE THE RULES OF CONDUCT AND ETHICS FOR PROSECUTORS AS WELL AS WHAT CONSTITUTES PROSECUTORIAL MISCONDUCT

- Prosecutors, like other attorneys, are bound by professional rules of conduct. Key areas where ethical dilemmas for prosecutors arise include disclosure of exculpatory evidence, conflicts of interest (particularly for part-time prosecutors), and relationships with the press.

- Key areas where ethical dilemmas for prosecutors arise include disclosure of exculpatory evidence, conflicts of interest (particularly for part-time prosecutors), and relationships with the press.

- Prosecutors' offices follow a bureaucratic structure, with the chief prosecutor occupying the top post.
- There can be significant differences in the goals and styles of chief prosecutors from one jurisdiction to the next.
- There is a problem of turnover in prosecutors' offices, partly due to the attraction of lucrative private sector jobs.
- Another unfortunate aspect of the job is that prosecutors are sometimes threatened and/or assaulted during the performance of their official duties.

KEY TERMS

absolute immunity, 209
assistant U.S. attorney, 195
attorney general, 195
city attorney, 198
community
    prosecution, 202
deferred prosecution
    diversion, 207
deferred sentencing, 208
district attorney, 197

diversion, 207
Drug Treatment
    Alternative to Prison
    (DTAP) program, 208
felony case processor
    model, 202
no-drop prosecution, 206
postincarceration
    diversion, 207
precharge diversion, 207

progressive era, 201
prosecutor, 194
prosecutorial discretion, 204
qualified immunity, 209
sentencing diversion, 207
solicitor general, 195
U.S. attorney, 195
vertical prosecution, 212

REVIEW QUESTIONS

1. What are the various types of prosecutors that work at federal, state, county, and city levels?

2. How did the American experience shape the prosecution function early in our country's history?

3. How has the prosecutor's role recently evolved?

4. What is prosecutorial discretion? How does it affect charging decisions?

5. What is the workday of a typical prosecutor like?

 WHAT WILL YOU DO?

You are a prosecutor with a background as a police officer. After working for 12 years as a patrol officer in the city where you grew up, you decided to attend law school, then you returned to run for the office of district attorney in the jurisdiction that you had always called home. You were elected in a landslide win, but now you face a serious dilemma.

Weeks ago, the district that you serve was rocked by media headlines describing an alleged terror plot against your small city. The plot came to light when police arrested two men of Arabic descent and confiscated what they described as a weapons cache from the backyard shed of the house where the men lived. The weapons inventory included handguns, hollow-point rounds, AK-47 ammunition, and a number of assault rifles that further investigation revealed had been legally purchased after Congress refused to renew the ban on assault weapons a few years ago. In a box alongside a collection of handguns, investigators found two complete sets of breathing apparatus, such as might be used by firefighters, that had been stockpiled by some people years ago who feared biological or gas attacks in the wake of the terrorist destruction of September 11, 2001.

A search of the suspects' house turned up a box full of pornographic magazines and photographs, some of them showing nude children. A crime laboratory assessment of a computer hard drive taken from the men's house revealed that it contained an assortment of pornographic images, including some of children under the age of 12.

The situation grew much more serious when, following 24 hours of police interrogation, the men admitted to plotting an attack on the city's elementary schools. As details of the plot unfolded, local newspapers, television stations, and radio newscasters reported that the men had planned to seize the city's two elementary schools and lock the children inside by chaining the doors shut. The men, said police, had then planned on setting fire to the buildings and escaping in the initial confusion after the arrival of firefighters. Their escape would be made only after many of the children had succumbed to smoke inhalation and what they had hoped would be a raging inferno. The men, they said, would survive the fire by using the gas masks.

A few hours ago, however, the attorneys appointed to represent the suspects claimed that their confessions had been forced and that the defendants wanted to retract their statements. They refused to enter guilty pleas at arraignment and wanted to go to trial.

That report and a thorough review of the physical evidence gathered from the men's house left you with an uneasy feeling. Although you felt confident that you could bring child pornography charges against at least one of the suspects, you did not think that their possession of weapons and gas masks amounted to a crime. But the signed confessions now in your possession—if valid—provided powerful evidence of a terrorist conspiracy.

When you talk to the two police interrogators who obtained the confessions, their stories appear to differ. One says that the first suspect, a man named Akbar, had confessed almost immediately, while the second man, Khalid, denied any terrorist involvement but admitted his part in the plot only after viewing Akbar's signed confession. The second investigator describes a different scenario, saying that Khalid confessed almost immediately after being shown photos of his own children and then being asked to think about what it would be like if he lost them.

You call the two interrogators into your office and tell them of your concerns. After only a few minutes of talking, the first interrogator, a detective named Steve with whom you had worked for ten years while on the police force, candidly admits that the confessions had been coerced. "Look," said Steve, "you know how it is. We knew these guys were up to something— and it was likely to be big. We just didn't know exactly what it was, and we weren't sure we could prove it."

"That's right," said Bill, the second detective. "We're pretty sure that they were planning some kind of attack, but they wouldn't tell us what it was."

You quickly learn that both suspects had been exhaustively interrogated but that neither one had admitted to any terrorist plans. The detectives, however, had been secretly watching the men accumulate weapons and had seen them drive by the city's elementary schools and linger there on a number of occasions. "We figured that they were planning to hurt the kids," said Steve. "We weren't exactly sure how, and that's when we used the Tasers."

Both detectives admitted to repeatedly shocking the suspects with Tasers during the interrogation session but

(continued)

claimed that the action was necessary. "The confessions are good," said Bill. "They're both signed, and we even Mirandized them before we started talking to them. And the Tasers didn't leave any marks, so they can't prove a thing against us, and who's a jury going to believe—us or them?"

"You mean these guys didn't actually say that they were planning to attack the schools," you ask incredulously, "and that you tortured them, that these confessions are entirely fabricated?"

"Yeah, but so what?" said Steve. "We prevented an attack, didn't we? You let these guys go now, and there's no telling what they'll do."

What will you do?

NOTES

i. U.S. Department of Justice, *Dictionary of Criminal Justice Data Terminology*, p. 176.

ii. S. W. Perry, *Prosecutors in State Courts*, 2005 (Washington, DC: U.S. Department of Justice, 2006), p. 11.

iii. Barbara Boland, "What Is Community Prosecution?" *National Institute of Justice Journal* (August 1996):35–40.

iv. Ibid., p. 177.

v. J. R. C. Davis, B. E. Smith, and H. J. Davies, "Effects of No-Drop Prosecution of Domestic Violence upon Conviction Rates," *Justice Research and Policy* 3(2001):1–13.

vi. See, e.g., S. Fairhead, *Persistent Petty Offenders* (London: HMSO, 1981).

vii. We will discuss other treatment-oriented components in Chapter 8. Treatment is discussed here in the context of law enforcement only insofar as it heavily involves prosecutors.

viii. J. M. Dawson, S. K. Smith, and C. J. DeFrances, *Prosecutors in State Courts*, 1992 (Washington, DC: National Institute of Justice, 1992).

---

1. Bruce Frederick and Don Stemen, *The Anatomy of Discretion: An Analysis of Prosecutorial Decision Making: Technical Report* (Washington, DC: National Institute of Justice, December 2012).

2. Bruce Frederick and Don Stemen, *The Anatomy of Discretion: An Analysis of Prosecutorial Decision Making* (Washington, DC: National Institute of Justice, December 2012), p. iii.

3. Ibid.

4. U.S. Department of Justice, *Dictionary of Criminal Justice Data Terminology*, 2nd ed. (Washington, DC: U.S. Department of Justice, Bureau of Justice Statistics, 1981), p. 176.

5. U.S. Justice Department, available at www.justice.gov/usao/about/mission.html (accessed February 19, 2013).

6. U.S. Department of Justice, Executive Office for U.S. Attorneys, *United States Attorneys' Annual Statistical Report: Fiscal Year 2012* (Washington, DC: U.S. Department of Justice, 2012).

7. Office of the Solicitor General, available at www.justice.gov/osg/about-osg.html (accessed February 19, 2013).

8. National Association of Attorneys General, available at http://www.naag.org/what_does_an_attorney_general_do.php (accessed February 19, 2013).

9. L. Setrakian, "Charges Dropped in Duke Lacrosse Case," *ABC News Law & Justice Unit*, April 11, 2007, available at http://abcnews.go.com/US/story?id=3028515&page=1 (accessed February 19, 2013).

10. S. W. Perry, *Prosecutors in State Courts, 2005* (Washington, DC: U.S. Department of Justice, 2006).

11. Ibid.

12. J. Eisenstein, R. Flemming, and P. Nardulli, *The Contours of Justice: Communities and Their Courts* (Boston: Little, Brown, 1988); J. Schlesinger, *Ambition and Politics: Political Careers in the United States* (Chicago: Rand McNally, 1966).

13. J. Q. Wilson and G. Kelling, "Broken Windows: The Police and Neighborhood Safety," *Atlantic Monthly* (March 1982), pp. 29–38.

14. See, e.g., R. V. Wolf and J. L. Worrall, *Lessons from the Field: Ten Community Prosecution Leadership Profiles* (Alexandria, VA: American Prosecutors Research Institute, 2004).

15. J. Jacoby, *The American Prosecutor: A Search for Identity* (Lexington, MA: Lexington Books, 1980), p. xv.

16. Ibid.

17. *Mallery v. Lane*, 97 Conn. 132 (1921), p. 138.

18. W. S. Van Alstyne, "The District Attorney—A Historical Puzzle," *Wisconsin Law Review* (1952), pp. 125–138.

19. Ibid, p. 28.

20. Jacoby, *The American Prosecutor*.

21. Ibid.

22. 1 Stat. 73.

23. L. Mayers, *The American Legal System* (New York: Harper and Row, 1964).

24. Jacoby, *The American Prosecutor*, p. 38.

25. Ibid., p. 23.

26. Ibid.

27. National Commission on Law Observance and Enforcement, *Report on Prosecution* (Washington, DC: U.S. Government Printing Office, 1931).

28. *People v. Wabash, St. Louis and Pacific Railway*, 12 Ill. App. 263 (1883), p. 263.

29. *Wilson v. County of Marshall*, 257 Ill. App. 220 (1930), p. 220.

30. *Milliken v. Stone*, 7 F.2d 397 (S.D.N.Y. 1925), p. 399.

31. N. Baker, "The Prosecuting Attorney—Provisions of Organizing a Law Office," *Journal of Criminal Law and Criminology*, Vol. 23 (1932), p. 934.

32. See, e.g., *People v. Berlin*, 361 N.Y.S. 2d 114 (1974); *State v. LeVien*, 44 N.J. 323 (1965); *People v. Adams*, 117 Cal. Rptr. 905 (1974).

33. *Powell v. Alabama*, 287 U.S. 45 (1932).

34. *Gideon v. Wainwright*, 372 U.S. 335 (1963).

35. *Arsinger v. Hamlin*, 407 U.S. 25 (1972).

36. *Miranda v. Arizona*, 384 U.S. 436 (1966).

37. Jacoby, *The American Prosecutor*.

38. Ibid., p. 101.

39. Cleveland Survey of Criminal Justice, *Criminal Justice in Cleveland* (Cleveland, OH: Cleveland Foundation, 1922).

40. National Commission on Law Observance and Enforcement, *Reports* (Washington, DC: U.S. Government Printing Office, 1931).

41. Illinois Association for Criminal Justice, *Illinois Crime Survey* (Montclair, NJ: Patterson Smith, 1929); Missouri Crime Survey, *The Missouri Crime Survey* (New York: Macmillan, 1926); S. Walker, *Popular Justice: A History of American Criminal Justice* (New York: Oxford University Press, 1980).

42. S. Walker, "Origins of the Contemporary Criminal Justice Paradigm: The American Bar Foundation Survey, 1953–1969," *Justice Quarterly*, Vol. 9 (1992), pp. 47–76.

43. Ibid., p. 54.

44. See, e.g., R. O. Dawson, *Sentencing: The Decision as to Type, Length, and Conditions of Sentence* (Boston: Little, Brown, 1969); W. R. LaFave, *Arrest: The Decision to Take the Suspect into Custody* (Boston: Little, Brown); D. M. McIntyre, Jr., *Law Enforcement in the Metropolis* (Chicago: American Bar Foundation, 1967); F. Miller, *Prosecution: The Decision to Charge a Suspect with a Crime* (Boston: Little, Brown, 1969); D. J. Newman, *Conviction: The Determination of Guilt or Innocence without Trial* (Boston: Little, Brown, 1966); F. Remington, "Survey of the Administration of Justice," *National Probation and Parole Association Journal*, Vol. 2 (1956), pp. 260–265; F. Remington, D. J. Newman, E. L. Kimball, M. Merci, and H. Goldstein, *Criminal Justice Administration* (Indianapolis, IN: Bobbs-Merrill, 1969).

45. Walker, "Origins of the Contemporary Criminal Justice Paradigm," p. 57.

46. Ibid., p. 67.

47. Ibid.

48. President's Commission on Law Enforcement and the Administration of Justice, *Task Force Report: The Courts* (Washington, DC: U.S. Government Printing Office, 1967).

49. Ibid., p. 72.

50. C. M. Coles, "Evolving Strategies in 20th Century American Prosecution," in J. L. Worrall and M. E. Nugent-Borakove, eds., *The Changing Role of the American Prosecutor* (Albany: State University of New York Press, forthcoming), pp. 177–209; also see National Association of Attorneys General, *The Prosecution Function: Local Prosecutors and the Attorney General* (Raleigh, NC: National Association of Attorneys General, 1974); National District Attorneys Association, *The Prosecutor's Screening Function: Case Evaluation and Control* (Alexandria, VA: National District Attorneys Association, 1973); American Bar Association, *Standards Relating to the Prosecution Function and the Defense Function* (Chicago: American Bar Association, 1970).

51. Coles, "Evolving Strategies in 20th Century American Prosecution," pp. 184–185.

52. J. L. Worrall, "Prosecution in America: A Historical and Comparative Account," in Worrall and Nugent-Borakove, *The Changing Role of the American Prosecutor.*

53. Barbara Boland, "What Is Community Prosecution?," *National Institute of Justice Journal* (August 1996), pp. 35–40.

54. See, e.g., Wolf and Worrall, *Lessons from the Field.*

55. Ibid.

56. Wilson and Kelling, "Broken Windows," pp. 29–38.

57. M. E. Nugent-Borakove, "Performance Measures and Accountability," in Worrall and Nugent-Borakove, *The Changing Role of the American Prosecutor.*

58. C. M. Coles, *Community Prosecution, Problem Solving, and Public Accountability: The Evolving Strategy of the American Prosecutor* (working paper, Harvard University, 2000), p. 11.

59. R. B. Fleming, "The Political Styles and Organizational Strategies of American Prosecutors: Examples from Nine Courthouse Communities," *Law and Policy*, Vol. 12 (1990), pp. 25–50.

60. U.S. Department of Justice, *Dictionary of Criminal Justice Data Terminology*, p. 177.

61. Yale Kamisar, Wayne LaFave, and Jerold Israel, *Modern Criminal Procedure*, 9th ed. (St. Paul, MN: West, 1999).

62. *Wayte v. United States*, 470 U.S. 598 (1985), p. 606.

63. *Blackledge v. Perry*, 417 U.S. 21 (1974).

64. Ibid., p. 33.

65. C. Albonetti, "Criminality, Prosecutorial Screening, and Uncertainty: Toward a Theory of Discretionary Decision Making in Felony Case Processings," *Criminology*, Vol. 24 (1986), pp. 623–644.

66. See, e.g., W. Hepperly, "Women Victims in the Criminal Justice System," in I. Moyer, ed., *The Changing Role of Women in the Criminal Justice System* (Prospect Heights, IL: Waveland, 1985), pp. 165–179; W. Kerstetter, "Gateway to Justice: Police and Prosecutorial Response to Sexual Assaults against Women," *Criminology*, Vol. 81 (1990), pp. 267–313; F. Miller, *Prosecution: The Decision to Charge a Suspect with a Crime* (Boston: Little, Brown, 1969).

67. E. Stanko, "The Impact of Victim Assessment on Prosecutors' Screening Decisions: The Case of the New York City County District Attorney's Office," in G. Cole, ed., *Criminal Justice: Law and Politics* (Pacific Grove, CA: Brooks/Cole, 1988), p. 172.

68. J. Schmidt and E. Steury, "Prosecutorial Discretion in Filing Charges in Domestic Violence Cases," *Criminology*, Vol. 27 (1989), pp. 487–510.

69. D. A. Ford and M. J. Burke, "Victim-Initiated Criminal Complaints for Wife-Battery: An Assessment of Motives," paper presented at the third annual conference for Family Violence, Durham, NC, 1987.

70. Schmidt and Steury, "Prosecutorial Discretion in Filing Charges in Domestic Violence Cases," p. 489.

71. See, e.g., L. Bienen, N. Weiner, D. Denno, P. Allison, and D. Mills, "The Reimposition of Capital Punishment in New Jersey: The Role of Prosecutorial Discretion," *Rutgers Law Review*, Vol. 48 (1988), pp. 386–398; T. Keil and G. Vito, "Race, Homicide, Severity, and Application of the Death Penalty: A Consideration of the Barnett Scale," *Criminology*, Vol. 27 (1989), pp. 511–533; G. LaFree, "The Effect of Sexual Stratification by Race on Official Reactions to Rape," *American Sociological Review*, Vol. 45 (1980), pp. 842–854; R. Paternoster, "Prosecutorial Discretion in Requesting the Death Penalty: A Case of Victim-Based Racial Discrimination," *Law and Society Review*, Vol. 18 (1984), pp. 437–478; M. Radelet and G. Pierce, "Race and Prosecutorial Discretion in Homicide Cases," *Law and Society Review*, Vol. 19 (1985), pp. 587–621; C. Spohn, J. Gruhl, and S. Welch, "The Impact of Ethnicity and Gender of Defendants on the Decision to Reject or Dismiss Felony Charges," *Criminology*, Vol. 25 (1987), pp. 175–191.

72. J. L. Worrall, J. W. Ross, and E. S. McCord, "Modeling Prosecutors' Charging Decisions in Domestic Violence Cases," *Crime and Delinquency*, Vol. 52 (2006), pp. 472–503.

73. R. C. Davis, B. E. Smith, and H. J. Davies, "Effects of No-Drop Prosecution of Domestic Violence upon Conviction Rates," *Justice Research and Policy*, Vol. 3 (2001), pp. 1–13.

74. K. Robbins, "No-Drop Prosecution of Domestic Violence: Just Good Policy, or Equal Protection Mandate?," *Stanford Law Review*, Vol. 52 (1999), pp. 205–233.

75. A. Corsilles, "No-Drop Policies in the Prosecution of Domestic Violence Cases: Guarantee to Action or Dangerous Solution?," *Fordham Law Review*, Vol. 63 (1994), p. 853.

76. For a summary of the research, see Davis et al., "Effects of No-Drop Prosecution of Domestic Violence upon Conviction Rates."

77. Ibid.

78. T. G. Blomberg, "Widening the Net: An Anomaly in the Evaluation of Diversion Programs," in M. Klein and K. Tielman, eds., *Handbook of Criminal Justice Evaluation* (Beverly Hills, CA: Sage, 1980), pp. 572–592.

79. T. Palmer, "Juvenile Diversion: When and for Whom?," *California Youth Authority Quarterly*, Vol. 32 (1979), pp. 14–20.

80. The discussion that follows borrows from J. Nuffield, *Diversion Programs for Adults* (Ottawa: Solicitor General of Canada, 1997), available at http://ww2.ps-sp.gc.ca/publications/corrections/pdf/199705_e.pdf (accessed February 19, 2013).

81. See, e.g., S. Fairhead, *Persistent Petty Offenders* (London: HMSO, 1981).

82. P. C. Friday, K. R. Malzahn-Bass, and D. K. Harrington, "Referral and Selection Criteria in Deferred Prosecution: The Impact on the Criminal Justice System," *British Journal of Criminology*, Vol. 21 (1981), pp. 166–172.

83. K. M. Goetsch, "Deferred Prosecution: A Critical Analysis of Michigan Programs," *Detroit College of Law Review* (Fall 1978), pp. 433–456.

84. Center on Addiction and Substance Abuse, *Crossing the Bridge: An Evaluation of the Drug Treatment Alternative-to-Prison (DTAP) Program* (New York: National Center on Addiction and Substance Abuse at Columbia University, 2003).

85. M. Z. Johns, "Reconsidering Absolute Prosecutorial Immunity," *Brigham Young University Law Review* (2005), pp. 53–154.

86. *Burns v. Reed*, 500 U.S. 478 (1991).

87. *Imbler v. Pachtman*, 424 U.S. 409 (1976).

88. *Kalina v. Fletcher*, 522 U.S. 118 (1997).

89. Ibid.

90. Ibid.

91. Ibid.

92. Johns, "Reconsidering Absolute Prosecutorial Immunity," p. 56.

93. Center for Public Integrity, *Harmful Error: Investigating America's Local Prosecutors*, available at www.publicintegrity.org/pm/ (accessed February 19, 2013).

94. *Moore v. Valder*, 65 F.3d 189 (D.C. Cir. 1995).

95. Ibid., p. 194.

96. *Cousin v. Small*, 325 F.3d 627 (5th Cir. 2003).

97. Ibid., p. 635.

98. From *The ABA Annotated Model Code of Judicial Conduct*, published by the American Bar Association Center for Professional Responsibility Judicial Division, 2004. © 2004 by the American Bar Association. Reprinted with permission. All rights reserved. This information or any portion thereof may not be copied or disseminated in any form or by any means or stored in an electronic database or retrieval system without the express permission of the American Bar Association.

99. Ibid., Rule 2.8.

100. R. H. Underwood, "Part-Time Prosecutors and Conflicts of Interest: A Survey and Some Proposals," *Kentucky Law Journal*, Vol. 81 (1992/1993), pp. 1–104.

101. Ibid.

102. J. Pollock, *Ethical Dilemmas and Decisions in Criminal Justice*, 5th ed. (Belmont, CA: Wadsworth, 2006).

103. *Sheppard v. Maxwell*, 384 U.S. 333 (1966), p. 363.

104. See, e.g., *People v. Cochran*, 313 Ill. 508 (1924), p. 526.

105. Available at http://co.pennington.mn.us/departments/attorney/staff.asp (accessed February 19, 2013).

106. J. M. Dawson, S. K. Smith, and C. J. DeFrances, *Prosecutors in State Courts, 1992* (Washington, DC: National Institute of Justice, 1992).

107. Flemming, "The Political Styles and Organizational Strategies of American Prosecutors," pp. 25–50.

108. Ibid., p. 28.

109. Ibid.

110. Ibid., p. 32.

111. Ibid., p. 37.

112. Ibid., p. 47.

113. See, e.g., M. Heumann, *Plea Bargaining: The Experience of Prosecutors, Judges, and Defense Attorneys* (Chicago: University of Chicago Press, 1978).

114. J. Dixon and C. Seron, "Stratification in the Legal Profession: Sex, Sector, and Salary," *Law and Society Review*, Vol. 29 (1995), pp. 381–412; S. Rosen, "The Market for Lawyers," *Journal of Law and Economics*, Vol. 35 (1992), pp. 215–246.

115. R.T. Boylan and C. X. Long, "Salaries, Plea Rates, and the Career Objectives of Federal Prosecutors," *Journal of Law and Economics*, Vol. 48 (2005), pp. 627–651.

116. T. J. Charron, "Law School Loans and Lawyers in Public Service," The Prosecutor, Vol. 40 (2006), p. 6.

117. S. W. Perry and D. Banks, *Prosecutors in State Courts, 2007* (Washington, DC: U.S. Department of Justice, 2011), p. 7, available at http://bjs.ojp.usdoj.gov/content/pub/pdf/psc07st.pdf (accessed February 18, 2013).

John Neubauer/PhotoEdit

9

Defense Attorneys

LEARNING OBJECTIVES

1. Describe the functions of defense attorneys.
2. Outline the history of criminal defense.
3. Describe the types of defense attorneys.
4. Explain the realities of defense work.
5. Summarize the different ways defense attorneys are perceived.
6. Describe the codes of ethics and conduct for defense attorneys.

INTRODUCTION

In 2013, 56-year-old Miriam Conrad, head of the federal public defender's office in Boston, was appointed to represent surviving Boston Marathon bomber Dzhokhar Tsamaev. Conrad, a graduate of the prestigious Harvard Law School, defended "shoe bomber" Richard Reid in 2001 for attempting to destroy a Paris to Miami jetliner and is one of the most experienced and well respected public defenders in the nation. Conrad was described as "excellent, tough, tenacious and wise," by Tamar R. Birckhead, a University of North Carolina law professor who worked with Conrad for four years.[1] Some people might find it distasteful for a defense lawyer to take on a case involving a young man who killed innocent people and maimed many others, but in our free society even those who set out to destroy it are entitled to a competent and spirited legal defense.

Miriam Conrad, the Boston federal public defender who was appointed to represent Boston Marathon bombing suspect, Dzhokhar Tsamaev. What ethical issues might the defense pose for Conrad?

THE FUNCTION OF DEFENSE ATTORNEYS

While the press and the public hold judges and prosecutors in high esteem, more often than not the wily defense attorney is treated with scorn. Why such derision? It is most likely because defense attorneys have the unenviable job of representing those who wind up on the wrong side of the law—they seem to earn their fees by freeing child molesters and drug dealers using every legal means at their disposal.

It is common for television shows to depict a hard-edged defense lawyer damaging the reputation of a rape victim while she dissolves in tears and the audience grits its collective teeth. Although there are some shady and unscrupulous defense attorneys, the vast majority of criminal defense attorneys perform a valuable and necessary function with professionalism and integrity: They provide an essential check against overreaching state power and ensure that criminal defendants get the assistance they need as they move through the justice system.

The **defense attorney** is "the lawyer who advises, represents, and acts for the defendant (or, in postconviction proceedings, the offender)."[2] There are many varieties of defense attorneys: Some adopt a narrow specialty, such as defending suspected drunk drivers; some represent indigent defendants, whereas others represent only the most affluent clients; some are skilled litigators who have convinced numerous juries that the wrong person has been charged; some have mastered plea bargaining and rarely see the inside of a courtroom; some work in small firms, some work in large firms with hundreds of attorneys, and some work for the government; and some even work for free, perhaps by representing indigent death-row inmates.

All defense attorneys perform essentially the same task—helping criminal defendants navigate the sometimes rough waters of the justice process. The defense attorney serves "as the accused's counselor and advocate with courage and devotion to render effective, quality representation."[3] Good defense attorneys' helping function is multifaceted:

- They provide a knowledgeable, objective perspective on what the defendant's situation is and what is likely to happen should his or her case go to trial.
- They understand the law and legal rules, including court interpretations of federal and state constitutions.
- They are familiar with local court customs and procedures.
- They understand the possible hidden costs of various outcomes, particularly those associated with a plea of guilty.
- They immerse themselves in and spend time on the case.

Learning Objective 1
Describe the functions of defense attorneys.

defense attorney
"[T]he lawyer who advises, represents, and acts for the defendant (or, in post-conviction proceedings, the offender)."[i]

- They gather information from various sources, including the prosecution's witnesses
- They often hire and manage investigators, who assist in building the defense case.
- If their client is found guilty, they can bring the case to the next level on appeal and in doing so help change the content of the law.

The following "Lasting Impact" feature illustrates this concept

LASTING IMPACT

McDonald v. Chicago: The Right to Bear Arms

As you may recall from the Supreme Court's decision in *District of Columbia* v. *Heller* case, the District of Columbia's ban on handgun ownership was shot down. In a 5–4 ruling, the Court declared a constitutional right to keep a loaded handgun at home for self-defense. The Court's ruling cast aside the argument of antigun activists that the Second Amendment tied the right to gun ownership to service in a "well-regulated militia."

Justice Antonin Scalia acknowledged the pressing social problem of handgun violence in the United States but gave priority to the "enshrinement of constitutional rights" over "certain policy choices." He did, however, declare support for "longstanding prohibitions on the possession of firearms by felons and the mentally ill, or laws forbidding the carrying of firearms in sensitive places such as schools and government buildings, or laws imposing conditions and qualifications on the commercial sale of arms."

The opinion further suggested that existing prohibitions against the possession of "dangerous and unusual weapons" (e.g., machine guns or so-called assault weapons) that are not of the type normally associated with recreational or self-defense applications are not set aside by this ruling. Prohibitions against the carrying of concealed weapons are similarly unaffected.

One issue left out by *Heller* was whether this Second Amendment right applies to the states and local governments and not just the District of Columbia, which is under federal jurisdiction. The Court answered this question in *McDonald* v. *Chicago* when it held that an individual's right to keep and bear arms is incorporated and applicable to the states through the Fourteenth Amendment's due process clause. In their arguments, McDonald's defense attorneys claimed that the Chicago laws violate the right to keep and bear arms for two reasons. First, they argued that the right is among the "privileges or immunities of citizens of the United States" and that a narrow interpretation of the privileges or immunities clause be rejected. As a secondary argument, they claimed that the Fourteenth Amendment's due process clause "incorporates" the Second Amendment right to bear arms. Their arguments swayed the justices. Writing for the majority, Justice Alito observed, "It is clear that the Framers and ratifiers of the Fourteenth Amendment counted the right to keep and bear arms among those fundamental rights necessary to our system of ordered liberty." He went on to say, "The Fourteenth Amendment makes the Second Amendment right to keep and bear arms fully applicable to the States."

The Court did not rule on the constitutionality of the gun ban, deciding instead to return the case for additional proceedings. However, the decision makes it clear that banning guns outright is unconstitutional. Nonetheless, the Second Amendment only protects a right to possess a firearm in the home for lawful uses, such as self-defense, and firearm regulation is constitutionally permissible because the right to possess firearms is not unlimited. It does not guarantee a right to possess any firearm, anywhere, and for any purpose.

These decisions may the groundwork for subsequent lawsuits that seek to define—and likely widen—the laws of use and carry, according to Ilya Shapiro, a senior fellow at the Cato Institute in Washington, D.C., and in turn shape reshape the boundaries of the kind of force individuals can use to defend themselves: "In evaluating future gun regulation, self-defense will be a very important part. That's what the right to keep and bear arms is about," says Shapiro. "It's about protecting life, liberty, property. It will be up to the government to justify restrictions to those rights." But while the government sets the laws in courts, it is law enforcement, prosecutors, judges, and juries who ultimately decide when using force is justified and when it is criminal. Therefore, says, Lisa J. Steele, a defense attorney who has written a brief on building a self-defense case for the National Association of Criminal Defense Lawyers, such cases remain "a big gamble for the defendant . . . . You're saying, 'I did this, I meant to do this, and I was justified in doing it.'"

As this feature points out, rulings by the U.S. Supreme Court can trump legislation passed by the states or Congress. With regard to the material discussed in this feature, we might ask ourselves a few questions. ■

Sources: Sour District of Columbia v. Heller, 554 U.S. (2008); McDonald v. Chicago, 561 U.S. 3025 (2010); Linda Greenhouse, "Justices Rule for Individual Gun Rights," New York Times, June 27, 2008; Lisa Riordan Seville, "Killing in Self Defense," The Crime Report, July 19, 2010, available at www.thecrimereport.org/news/inside-criminal-justice/killing-in-self-defense-2 (accessed June 2, 2013).

DISCUSSION QUESTIONS

1. Where did the Court's authority come from in this case? Is it likely that further action by Congress or state legislatures will cause the Court to reconsider its position? Why or why not?

2. Why did the Supreme Court apparently disregard the potential for social harm that its decision might carry?

HISTORY OF CRIMINAL DEFENSE

Learning Objective 2
Outline the history of
criminal defense.

The history of criminal defense can be traced back to ancient Rome when Emperor Claudius legalized the practice of law and allowed the first lawyers to ply their craft for a fee.[4] Most of the early Roman "advocates" were trained in rhetoric and argument, not law, but Rome did go on to create a class of legal specialists known as "jurisconsults." These individuals did not practice law in the sense that lawyers do today; rather, law was more of a hobby, and authorities called on the jurisconsults for their thoughts on complex matters of law.

By the fourth century, "things had changed in the eastern Empire: advocates now were really lawyers."[5] The legal profession became more specialized, regulated, and stratified. In A.D. 460, Emperor Leo required that advocates be endorsed by their teachers before they were allowed to produce testimonials. By the sixth century, legal training lasting approximately four years was necessary.

After the onset of the Dark Ages, whatever legal "profession" was in place quickly disappeared. According to historian James Brundage, "[By 1140], no one in Western Europe could properly be described as a professional lawyer or a professional canonist in anything like the modern sense of the term 'professional.'"[6] Eventual efforts of church and state to regulate the law led to a resurgence of the legal profession, a pattern that continued through the Middle Ages.

Growth of the Criminal Defense Bar

Defendants who faced criminal charges during colonial America enjoyed some rights but not to the level they do today. As historian David Bodenhamer put it, "The good order of society took precedence over the liberty of the individual."[7] A concern with greater societal good meant that judges could reach their verdicts swiftly and that the criminal process was more informal than it is today.

Criminal defense attorneys became significant players in the criminal process around the 1730s,[8] but there were few trained lawyers in the American colonies during that time. By the time of the American Revolution, there were fewer than 100 lawyers in Massachusetts, which had a population of around 200,000, a much smaller ratio than today.[9] Indigent defense was nonexistent, so only the most wealthy defendants were able to hire their own attorneys.

Throughout the nineteenth century, most attorneys were trained in apprenticeships.[10] Some went to England, but most began their work with seasoned attorneys and eventually had to pass oral bar exams before the court. Soon after they first appeared in America in 1771, Blackstone's famous *Commentaries on the Laws of England* became a favorite with aspiring lawyers; given the relative lack of legal texts, Blackstone's provided a convenient source for the comprehensive study of law and legal principles and had a considerable influence on the legal profession.

The number of lawyers surged after the American Revolution, growth prompted by several forces. Increased formalization of law and the legal process was met with a demand for professionals skilled in these areas. At the same time, the rather lax standards for becoming a lawyer encouraged more people to pursue law as a career,[11] prompting the beginning of law schools. Some schools grew out of the law offices that specialized in training apprentices. One such school was the Litchfield School, founded in 1784 and located in Connecticut; the instructors at Litchfield were said to be the first law instructors who broke the study of law into distinct topical areas, further fueling growth in the legal profession.

Harvard University established its own law school in 1817, prompting other universities to take the same road. There were approximately 15 law schools in 1850, but by 1900 more than 100 had been established.[12] They differed considerably from the law schools of today: They did not require previous college education, nor did they take as long to graduate from.[13] At first, legal education could be completed in a single year, but by 1900, a second year was added.

When Harvard instituted stricter entrance requirements in 1870, legal training underwent a dramatic transition.[14] Law students who did not have previous college experience were first required to pass an exam prior to entrance. By 1876, the law school curriculum was increased to a three-year program, and students were required to pass an exam between their first and second years of education in order to continue.

These reforms were relatively minor in comparison to the most dramatic change—the introduction of the case method of teaching at Harvard. Teachers replaced lectures and textbooks with books containing actual cases (referred to as casebooks). Instructors used the Socratic method of teaching, a confrontational approach that is intended to improve students' critical thinking, in order to present the cases. The training forced students to think like lawyers by pitting students against instructor in a (hopefully) spirited argument intended to reveal the truth. Other law schools followed Harvard's lead.

By the 1960s, concern with civil rights, poverty, and other social problems made a legal career highly desirable. High-profile Supreme Court cases further fueled growth in the legal profession due to the new requirement that indigent criminal defendants be provided with representation. Law school admissions became quite selective, and schools introduced strict entrance requirements.

Criminal Defense Bar Today

According to the American Bar Association (ABA), there are now more than 1.1 million licensed attorneys working in the United States, which equates to roughly 1 lawyer per 265 people, the highest ratio of any country in the world.

While estimating the exact number of lawyers who devote themselves to criminal defense work is difficult, the **National Association of Criminal Defense Lawyers** (NACDL), the main professional association for defense attorneys in the United States, boasts nearly 13,000 members and estimates that affiliated organizations at the local, state, and international levels have more than 35,000 additional members.

National Association of Criminal Defense Lawyers (NACDL)
The leading professional organization for defense attorneys in the United States.

Learning Objective 3
Describe the types of defense attorneys.

Web Extra
9–1 National Association of Criminal Defense Lawyers (NACDL), the leading professional organization for defense attorneys in the United States

Library Extra
9–1 Defense Council in Criminal Cases

retainer
An amount paid by a criminal defendant to his or her defense attorney in order to engage the attorney's services; also called *retaining fee*.

TYPES OF DEFENSE ATTORNEYS

Areas of specialty notwithstanding, criminal defense attorneys fall into two general categories: (1) attorneys who are privately retained and (2) attorneys who represent indigent defendants. The Supreme Court's *Gideon* v. *Wainwright*[15] decision (discussed further in Chapter 10, along with several other cases relating to defendants' right to counsel) requires that counsel be provided *all* criminal defendants, not just the wealthy ones, in all courts and for most offenses. In this section, we look first at privately retained counsel. Then we look at three different systems by which counsel is provided to indigent defendants: assigned counsel, contract model, and public defender.

Privately Retained Counsel

Retaining an attorney for a criminal defense is expensive. Legal fees in a typical felony case may cost upwards of $25,000.[16] In cases involving celebrity defendants, fees may run into the millions. At the other extreme, even misdemeanors can cost several thousand dollars to defend, and as a result, many defendants cannot afford to hire their own attorney. This is much truer in the criminal context than the civil context. Attorneys often take civil cases in exchange for a percentage of the award if the plaintiff is successful; in contrast, attorneys in criminal cases typically require their clients to pay a **retainer**, a fee paid in advance for their services.

TABLE 9–1 Type of Counsel for Felony Defendants in Cases Terminated in U.S. District Courts, by Offense

Type of Counsel	Violent	Fraud	Other Property	Drug	Regulatory	Other Public Order
Federal defender organizations[a]	42.4%	26.9%	31.0%	21.7%	16.9%	43.9%
Panel attorney	38.0	29.9	34.3	42.2	19.8	32.4
Private attorney	19.3	42.8	34.2	35.8	63.0	23.4
Self-representation (pro se)	0.3	0.3	0.5	0.2	0.2	0.3
Number of defendants	3,426	10,795	2,487	23,699	1,063	14,476

[a]Includes both federal public defenders and community defender organizations.

Note: Excludes 1,739 defendants with missing data on type of counsel and 494 with missing data on offense.

Source: C.W. Harlow, *Defense Counsel in Criminal Cases* (Washington, DC: Bureau of Justice Statistics, 2000), p. 3, available at http://bjs.ojp.usdoj.gov/content/pub/pdf/dccc.pdf (accessed February 19, 2013).

Just how many defendants can afford to hire their own attorney? One study found that 82% of state defendants received appointed counsel, leaving only 18% who could hire their own attorneys.[17] This percentage shifts considerably upward in federal cases: Roughly 30% of defendants charged with federal law violations retain their own attorneys.[18] The difference between state and federal courts probably owes to the fact that the federal courts often prosecute higher-profile cases with wealthier clients. Table 9–1 shows that private attorneys are the norm in regulatory cases but are very much the exception when the defendant is charged with a violent crime in federal court (the data reported in Table 9–1 are the most recent available at the time of this writing).

Do You Get What You Pay For? In many walks of life, "you get what you pay for," but does this apply in the case of defense attorneys? Is a privately retained attorney more effective than a public defender who represents an indigent defendant? Plenty of research has revealed that wealthier offenders end up better off on the whole than their poorer counterparts,[19] but this does not necessarily hold true when it comes to criminal defense. For the most part, public counsel and privately retained attorneys achieve the same results. A Bureau of Justice Statistics report found no differences between both types of attorneys in terms of guilty pleas, trial verdicts, and case dismissals. The same held true for both state and federal criminal cases, as can be seen in Table 9–2. Below are the report's summary findings:

- Conviction rates for indigent defendants and those with their own lawyers were about the same in federal and state courts. About 90% of the federal defendants and 75% of the defendants in the most populous counties were found guilty regardless of the type of attorney.

- Of those found guilty, however, those represented by publicly financed attorneys were incarcerated at a higher rate than those defendants who paid for their own legal representation: 88% compared to 77% in federal courts and 71% compared to 54% in the most populous counties.

- On average, sentence lengths for defendants sent to jail or prison were shorter for those with publicly financed attorneys than those who hired counsel. In federal district court, those with publicly financed attorneys were given just under five years on average and those with private attorneys just over five years. In large state courts, those with publicly financed attorneys were sentenced to an average of two and a half years and those with private attorneys to three years.[20]

Web Extra
9–2 Association of Federal Defense Attorneys

TABLE 9–2 Case Outcomes for Defendants with Publicly Financed or Private Attorneys

Case Disposition	Public Counsel	Private Counsel
75 largest counties		
Guilty by plea	71.0%	72.8%
Guilty by trial	4.4	4.3
Case dismissal	23.0	21.2
Acquittal	1.3	1.6
U.S. district courts		
Guilty by plea	87.1%	84.6%
Guilty by trial	5.2	6.4
Case dismissal	6.7	7.4
Acquittal	1.0	1.6

Source: C.W. Harlow, *Defense Counsel in Criminal Cases* (Washington, DC: Bureau of Justice Statistics, 2000), p. 1, available at http://bjs.ojp.usdoj.gov/content/pub/pdf/dccc.pdf (accessed February 19, 2013).

While not everyone agrees that public defenders and others in the business of providing defense services to indigents are necessarily as effective as privately retained attorneys,[21] many researchers agree that the two perform similarly.[22] It also appears that the different methods of providing representation to indigent defendants (see below) get roughly the same results.[23]

Indigent Defense Systems

There are three main indigent defense systems in operation throughout the United States: assigned counsel, contract model, and public defender. Each is defined as follows:

- *Assigned counsel.* Appointment from a list of private bar members who accept cases on a judge-by-judge, court-by-court, or case-by-case basis results in **assigned counsel**. This may include an administrative component and a set of rules and guidelines governing the appointment and processing of cases handled by the private bar members.

- *Contract model.* In the **contract model**, nonsalaried individual private attorneys, bar associations, law firms, consortiums or groups of attorneys, or nonprofit corporations that contract with a funding source provide court-appointed representation in a jurisdiction. This does not include public defender programs primarily funded by an awarded contract.

- *Public defender.* A salaried staff of full-time or part-time attorneys, called **public defenders**, render criminal indigent defense services either through a public or private nonprofit organization or as direct government-paid employees.[24]

Who qualifies for these services? Most states rely on statutory definitions to determine indigent status. Under this system, criminal defendants request defense representation and provide evidence of indigency, including income statements, asset reporting, and so on.

Who foots the bill? Again, the answer varies by state. Most indigent defense services are paid completely by the states, which fund their programs at the county level. The norm is for taxpayers to pay, but some states pay for indigent defense through county and municipal fees.[25] Some states have gone so far as to declare some defendants "partially indigent" such that they pay a part of their defense bill. This is in contrast to recognizing only two categories of defendants: the indigent and the nonindigent. No matter what the system, the cost is high. According to one count, the 100 most populous counties in the United States

assigned counsel
Lawyers appointed from a list of private bar members who accept cases on a judge-by-judge, court-by-court, or case-by-case basis.[ii]

contract model
A method of appointing counsel that uses nonsalaried individual private attorneys, bar associations, law firms, consortiums or groups of attorneys, or nonprofit corporations that contract with a funding source to provide court-appointed representation in a jurisdiction, excluding public defender programs primarily funded by an awarded contract.[iii]

public defender
The counsel appointed from a salaried staff of full- or part-time attorneys who renders criminal indigent defense services through either a public or private nonprofit organization or as a direct government-paid employee.[iv]

spent more than $1 billion on indigent defense.[26] The attorneys get paid between $40 and $100 per hour,[27] and the pay varies by location, case type, and legal arrangements. While $100 per hour seems attractive, it does not all go into the attorney's pocket because overhead expenses, staff salaries, and the like can cut into profits.

Despite the cost of indigent defense, some respected authorities continue to lament the state of the system. The ABA describes indigent defense representation as being in a state of crisis because of high caseloads and low productivity.[28] While legal experts recommend a felony caseload of no more than 150 per attorney per year, some attorneys represent upwards of 1,000 indigent defendants in any given year.[29] Noted defense researchers Robert Spangenberg and Tessa Schwartz point out that only 3% of justice expenditures are devoted to the representation of indigent defendants.[30]

Web Extra
9–3 Indigent Legal Services

Assigned Counsel Assigned counsel is selected to represent indigent clients in one of two ways:

- **Ad hoc assigned counsel systems** are those in which the judge chooses a defense attorney on a case-by-case basis. This system has been criticized because it can lead to favoritism and patronage (the judge has discretion who is selected) and does not account for experience levels or qualifications of the attorneys.

- **Coordinated assigned counsel systems** rely on a coordinator who chooses the attorney. This ensures consistency and fairness in terms of who is selected, and it can be structured such that attorneys are required to meet minimal qualification standards.

ad hoc assigned counsel system
A method for appointing legal assistance in which the judge chooses a defense attorney on a case-by-case basis.

coordinated assigned counsel system
A method for appointing legal assistance that relies on a coordinator who chooses the attorney.

To ensure that an assigned counsel system operates as intended, it is important to move away from the *ad hoc* approach in favor of a coordinated strategy. Recall that Louisiana is one of that states that leave it up to a commission to decide which defense representation strategy is best at the local level. The state recommends that its indigent defender boards adopt a number of strategies in order to ensure the integrity of their assigned counsel systems. Box 9–1 summarizes the general duties of defense counsel, according to the state of Louisiana.

Web Extra
9–4 Indigent Defense on the Web

BOX 9–1   Assigned Counsel Guidelines: Louisiana

A. Before agreeing to act as counsel or accepting appointment by a court, counsel has an obligation to make sure that counsel has available sufficient time, resources, knowledge and experience to offer effective representation to a defendant in a particular matter. If it later appears that counsel is unable to offer effective representation in the case, counsel should move to withdraw.

B. Counsel must be alert to all potential and actual conflicts of interest that would impair counsel's ability to represent a client. When appropriate, counsel may be obliged to seek an advisory opinion on any potential conflicts.

C. Counsel has the obligation to keep the client informed of the progress of the case.

D. If a conflict develops during the course of representation, counsel has a duty to notify the client and the court in accordance with the Louisiana Rules of Court and in accordance with the Louisiana Rules of Professional Conduct.

E. When counsel's caseload is so large that counsel is unable to satisfactorily meet these performance standards, counsel shall inform the district defender for counsel's judicial district and, if applicable, the regional director, the court or courts before whom counsel's cases are pending. If the district defender determines that the caseloads for his entire office are so large that counsel is unable to satisfactorily meet these performance standards, the district defender shall inform the court or courts before whom cases are pending and the state public defender. ■

Source: From Title 22. Corrections, Criminal Justice and Law Enforcement, Part XV, Louisiana Public Defender Board. Reprinted by permission of Louisiana Office of the State Register.

Assigned counsel systems are most often used in rural areas where it is not practical to have one or more full-time public defenders on staff. Counsel are paid according to set rates, usually on an hourly basis or on a per-case basis. Assigned counsel rates vary considerably by jurisdiction: Average compensation is somewhere in the neighborhood of $50 per hour but can be as high as $100 per hour.[31]

Contract Model Under the contract model, the state, county, or other jurisdictional authority contracts with private attorneys who provide defense services. These attorneys may work for private firms, bar associations, or nonprofit organizations that specialize in providing defense services to indigent offenders. The contractual arrangements vary from place to place and also specify under what circumstances services are provided. For example, if there is a public defender who has a conflict of interest in a particular case, the contract for defense services may specify that the contracted attorney represents the defendant, or the contract may state that defense services are provided to misdemeanor defendants, juveniles, felony cases, or all three. Many variations are possible.

There are two main types of contracts for defense services: fixed-price contracts and fixed-fee contracts. In a **fixed-price contract**, the firm agrees to accept an unspecified number of cases for a single annual flat fee. The amount the firm gets paid usually covers not only defense services but also the firm's investigative costs, costs of hiring expert witnesses, and support services costs. The problem with this arrangement is that the caseload could exceed that which was originally anticipated, but the firm is required by the terms of the contract to provide equal services for all the defendants. Not surprisingly, fixed-price contracts have been criticized by the likes of the ABA because of the uncertainty involved and the possibly inadequate criminal defenses that can result when caseloads become excessive. Some contracts also fail to place limits on additional cases (apart from those the contract would yield) that the attorneys can take on.

In a **fixed-fee contract**, such problems are minimized because the defense firm contracts to provide defense representation in a fixed number of cases for a fixed fee per case, helping to ensure a manageable workload and equal treatment across cases. The contracting attorney typically submits a monthly bill that specifies the number of cases handled during the billing period; depending on the contract, the attorney may also be able to bill for secretarial services, investigative costs, and expenses associated with hiring expert witnesses. Once the predetermined number of cases has been reached, the contract may be terminated or renegotiated. Fixed-fee contracts are desirable because they help funding authorities predict with near certainty what their defense-related expenses will be for the upcoming year. Several jurisdictions have adopted this model with great success.[32]

Public Defender The first public defender program in the United States opened in Los Angeles in 1913, and since then, the public defender model has become the dominant model for delivery of defense services to indigent defendants. In contrast to contractual and assigned counsel systems, public defender systems rely on full- or part-time attorneys who do nothing but represent indigent defendants. In large jurisdictions, the public defender's office can employ hundreds of attorneys and support staff; for example, today there are more than 600 licensed attorneys in the Los Angeles County Public Defender's Office. Despite the appeal of having a stable defense presence, no jurisdiction can survive with a public defender alone. Invariably, the time will arise when a public defender has a conflict of interest in a particular case that necessitates having assigned or contract counsel available to assist when the need arises. Sometimes this is called a "mixed system" in that it tries to capitalize on the benefits of both the public defender and other systems for assigning defense counsel. Does the type of defense counsel assigned make a difference? To find out read the following "Courts in the News" feature.

fixed-price contract
A fee agreement for appointed defense counsel fees whereby a law firm agrees to accept an unspecified number of cases for a single annual flat fee.

fixed-fee contract
A fee agreement for appointed legal defense fees whereby a law firm contracts to provide defense representation in a fixed number of cases for a fixed fee per case.

COURTS IN THE NEWS

Does Your Lawyer Make a Difference?

What difference does the type of lawyer you get make in a criminal case? Many people believe that getting a private attorney leads to a better outcome, but what about when the private attorney is appointed and paid for by the court (i.e., an assigned counsel)? Are you still better off? To find out, James M. Anderson and Paul Heaton took advantage of the fact that one in five indigent murder defendants in Philadelphia is randomly assigned representation by the Defender Association of Philadelphia, while the remainder receive court-appointed private attorneys. Anderson and Heaton studied a sample of 3,412 defendants charged with murder between 1994 and 2005. Compared to appointed counsel, public defenders reduce their client's murder conviction rate by 19%, lowered the probability that their clients would receive a life sentence by 62%, and reduced overall expected time served in prison by 24%.

How can the vast difference in outcomes for defendants assigned different counsel be explained, especially since their findings flaunt conventional wisdom? The authors found that appointed private counsel have comparatively few resources, face more difficult incentives, and are more isolated than public defenders. The extremely low pay for private counsel in criminal court reduces the pool of attorneys willing to take the appointments and makes doing preparation uneconomical. In contrast, the public defenders' financial and institutional independence from judges, the steady salaries provided to attorneys and investigators, and the team approach they adopt avoid many of these problems.

Another problem is that both judges and defense counsel in Philadelphia face potential conflicts of interest. Appointments in Philadelphia are controlled by the judges of the Philadelphia Court of Common Pleas. When a lawyer is needed, court administration determines whose turn it is to next appoint the attorney and contacts that judge's chambers, and then the judge provides the name of the attorney. Because Pennsylvania is the only state in which each county is solely responsible for funding indigent defense without any assistance from the state, every dollar that is spent on defense comes directly from the court budget. Judges, worried about finances, may be

© ZUMA Press, Inc./Alamy

Despite what the public may think, research shows that having a public defender actually increases a criminal defendants chances of a favorable verdict.

appointing lawyers known not to waste too much judicial time and energy. They may file fewer pretrial motions, ask fewer questions during jury selection (i.e., *voir dire*), raise fewer objections, and present fewer witnesses. This costs the court less and also allows judges to process more cases in less time. It may also encourage lawyers who are paid $185 per hour in capital cases to be more hesitant to request numerous experts or to represent defendants in time-consuming ways because if they do, they may lose favor in the court and receive fewer (if any) cases. In contrast, public defenders, on a fixed salary and not beholden to judges for future appointments, lack these particular incentives.

So if you're accused of murder in Philadelphia and can't afford an attorney, you better hope you are one of the lucky few to get a public defender rather than a court-appointed attorney. ■

DISCUSSION QUESTIONS

1. Does an appointment of a defense attorney by the presiding judge create an insurmountable conflict of interest?

2. Maybe there are other factors influencing the outcome of these cases. For example, public defenders may be trying harder because they are looking for higher-paying jobs, while private attorneys do not have that incentive. What do you think?

Sources: James M. Anderson and Paul Heaton, "How Much Difference Does the Lawyer Make? The Effect of Defense Counsel on Murder Case Outcomes," Rand Corporation, 2012, available at www.rand.org/content/dam/rand/pubs/working_papers/2011/RAND_WR870.pdf (accessed June 2, 2013); Dan Stamm, "Study Finds Public Defenders Best in Homicide Cases," NBC10 Philadelphia, March 3, 2013, available at www.nbcphiladelphia.com/news/politics/Private-Defense-Vs-Public-Defender-Murder-Cases-Philadelphia-195018231.html (accessed June 2, 2013); Peter A. Joy and Kevin Mcmunigal, "Does the Lawyer Make a Difference? Public Defender v. Appointed Counsel," ABA *Criminal Justice* 27 (2012), available at www.americanbar.org/content/dam/aba/publications/criminal_justice_magazine/sp12_ethics.authcheckdam.pdf (accessed June 2, 2013).

Learning Objective 4
Explain the realities of
defense work.

DEFENSE ATTORNEYS ON THE JOB

What is defense work really like? What do defense attorneys do on the job? Do they constantly butt heads with prosecutors in adversarial court settings, or is most of their work done behind the scenes? Do they zealously advocate for their clients, are they overburdened with excessive caseloads, or do they do their best to preserve the status quo and avoid rocking the boat? Are there differences in these dynamics between public and private attorneys? Are there reasons why some attorneys are regulars in the courthouse and some attorneys get hired for a single case and remain unfamiliar to most prosecutors and judges? A number of researchers have tried to answer questions such as these by observing defense attorneys on the job.

Some early studies revealed that defense attorneys, whether public or private, were "economic captives" of the court rather than aggressive adversaries.[33] Others have found that defense attorneys develop a realistic (as opposed to idealistic) approach to their work that rests on their experience, their understanding of the prosecutor's evidence, and their knowledge of the likely sentence to be handed down.[34] This appears to be true from the early stage of a criminal proceeding all the way through to sentencing.

Craft of Defense Attorneys

In the classic study "Elements of the Defense Attorney's Craft," Roy Flemming evaluated defense attorneys' decisions, with their clients' input, to waive preliminary hearings (a hearing where it is decided whether there is probable cause to take a case to trial—see Chapter 11 for more), and he revealed that there is a concern with efficiency in such decisions: "If files are accessible, guilty pleas can be arranged with a measure of certainty, or if time is scarce, attorneys prefer to waive hearings."[35] The prosecutor may offer a concession to the defendant for his or her agreement to waive a preliminary hearing.

At the same time, defense attorneys adopt a professional orientation, suggesting that preliminary hearings should not be waived. After all, if there is no probable cause to take a case to trial, then why wait for a trial? Also, defense attorneys seek to "minimize regrets" in their decisions.[36] For example, if a client insists on a preliminary hearing but the defense attorney waives it, this could come back to haunt the attorney. A concern with efficiency can thus run counter to a concern with professionalism and minimizing of regrets. Flemming decided that criminal defense work is truly a "craft."

Library Extra
9–2 Common Defenses to
Criminal Charges

Insider Justice

Researchers have also looked at the dynamics of "insider justice," possible differences between the regular public defenders who are familiar faces in the courthouse and "outsiders," meaning privately retained counsel.[37] In a classic study, Peter Nardulli sought to determine whether the regular defense attorneys (typically public defenders and their equivalents) were (1) "manipulators of the process," who have close ties to the local court community and use this to their advantage; (2) "cop-out artists," whose main concern is securing guilty pleas; or (3) "creators and protectors of routine," who are concerned more with efficient and consistent court operations than with the interests of their clientele.[38] Unfortunately, drawing lines between each was difficult: On the one hand, the regulars were less likely to obtain dismissals for their clients, translating into higher guilty plea and conviction rates; on the other hand, there was no evidence that regulars did any better with plea agreements than the outsiders. These effects varied across the jurisdictions that Nardulli studied, so the moral of the story is that there is no one best way to describe defense attorneys.

Myth of the Zealous Advocate

In one of the most famous studies of defense attorneys in action, Abraham Blumberg debunked the myth that defense attorneys are "zealous advocates" for their clients and are, instead, "double agents" who function as cogs in the wheel of a largely nonadversarial plea-bargaining process.[39] More recently, Rodney Uphoff added a third possible characterization to the mix—the defense attorney as a "beleaguered dealer."[40]

The view that defense attorneys are zealous advocates for their clients' interests is furthered in the movies, on television, and in fictional courtroom portrayals, and it holds that defense attorneys' main concern is looking out for their clients' interests. Nothing matters more to them than securing favorable plea agreements or (ideally) acquittals. While many private defense attorneys advertise themselves as "zealous advocates" to this day (do a Google search of "zealous advocate" and "defense attorney" to see what we mean), this is a romanticized conception of the defense function. The simple fact that most cases are decided prior to trial should serve as evidence enough that zealous advocacy goes only so far.

Yet it would be inaccurate to state that there are no defense attorneys who are zealous advocates. For example, the wealthy defendant who can afford to hire a team of superstar attorneys surely benefits from more of their attention than would the client of an overburdened public defender. But, as we know by now, the outcome that each type of attorney achieves does not differ significantly according to most available studies.

Double Agent What does it mean for a defense attorney to act as a double agent? The general definition of a **double agent** is one who appears to work for one side but instead works for another. Blumberg applied this definition to defense attorneys when he argued that the formal and informal relationships between the various courtroom actors are often more important than the interests of the client; that is, defense attorneys look out for their own interests more than those of the defendant: "[D]efense counsel utilized her unique role in the organization to persuade or cajole the client to accept a result—a plea bargain—that served the interests of the organization and the lawyer above those of the client."[41]

Blumberg also focused much of his attention on defense attorneys' efforts to con their clients: "To pull off this con, the criminal defense lawyer had to collect a fee, convince the client to accept a guilty plea, and still terminate the litigation as quickly as possible."[42] This was true even of privately retained attorneys. Uphoff came up with a third description of the defense attorney due to dissatisfaction with Blumberg's somewhat cynical view that they are double agents:

> Blumberg painted the portrait of the criminal defense lawyer as a manipulative con artist who succumbs to the pressures of making a living in a closed community by "duping" clients to enter pleas that benefit the system more than the clients.[43]

Put differently, is it really fair to describe defense attorneys as "looking out for number one," or at least looking out for the interests of harmony in the courtroom, more than their clients' interests? The answer may be "no" because if defense attorneys ignore their clients too much, then surely they would find themselves out of a job—no one wants to hire an inept attorney who has never secured an acquittal for his or her client.

"Beleaguered Dealer" Uphoff concluded that the best characterization of defense attorneys today is that of the "beleaguered dealer": "Simply to characterize all criminal defense lawyers as double agents . . . grossly distorts the overall picture of the criminal defense bar."[44] "Beleaguered" basically means struggling against difficulty, and in the defense context, this difficulty can be the demands of having a high caseload or being confronted with a client who cannot afford much more than putting up a retainer for private counsel.[45]

double agent
An attorney who appears to work for one side but instead works for another; also, a defense attorney who looks out for his or her own interests more than the interests of the defendant.

Library Extra
9–3 Developing a Defense
Strategy

Uphoff also found that many defendants *want* to plead guilty, suggesting that high rates of guilty pleas cannot be evidence of acting like a "double agent": "Under such circumstances, defense counsel is not a double agent but a beleaguered dealer negotiating from a position of weakness."[46] He even argued that the very justice system itself is set up to discourage trials, so bargaining cannot be blamed on defense attorneys shirking their duties. Jurisdictional differences also explained variations in how defense attorneys worked. The main point is that defense attorneys may be doing their best within the institutional constraints they face. Some seek to preserve the status quo, and others work tirelessly on behalf of their clients, but most just "muddle through."

Learning Objective 5

Summarize the different ways defense attorneys are perceived.

Defense Attorneys, Their Clients, and the Public

So far, we have examined different types of defense attorneys and what defense attorneys do on the job. In this section, we briefly consider the research on both defense attorneys' perceptions of their clients and perceptions of defense attorneys by defendants and by the public. We end with a look at defense attorneys' satisfaction with their work.

Defense Attorneys' Perceptions of Their Clients

public client
A client who receives a court-appointed attorney.[v]

Roy Flemming studied defense attorneys' perceptions of their clients. In this classic study, he found that attorneys report that **public clients** (those who receive court-appointed attorneys) are less trusting than private clients.[47] This finding is not particularly surprising considering that a defendant who retains his or her own attorney generally can choose who the individual is. There is a general perception among indigent defendants that court-appointed lawyers represent the criminal justice system rather than defendants' interests. Court-appointed attorneys reported these types of interactions with their clients:

- The standard joke around this county is, "Do you want a public defender or a real attorney?"
- Well, I think the general impression is, "I don't have the money to hire a real attorney, so I have you." We get a lot of that.
- A lot of times they don't respect you as an attorney because you accepted this court appointment.
- Because you're part of the system, your indigent client doesn't trust you.[48]

J. D. Casper found that there is a very different dynamic between criminal defendants and their privately retained attorneys compared to public defender–client relationships:

> The nature of the transaction between attorney and client provides a context for *interpreting* the behavior of the attorney. In part because the defendant (or his family) was paying the attorney, the whole tone of the relationship was altered. For example, insistence upon a particular course of action by a street [private] lawyer (e.g., pleading guilty, commitment for observation to a hospital) is interpreted differently by his client. Similar "advice" from a public defender might well be interpreted as giving orders, as telling the client what to do rather than discussing it with him.[49]

Defendants' Perceptions of Their Attorneys

Relatively little research is available concerning defendants' perceptions of their attorneys, but what we do know can be organized into two broad categories. First, researchers focusing on the attorney–client relationship have found that it is important.[50] For example,

S. Feldman and K. Wilson found that the relationship was sometimes more important than the attorney's legal skills.[51] Another researcher observed, "It is a common misconception that litigants let their fates rest entirely upon the machinations of their attorneys. In actuality, the attorney-client relationship and the client's ability to assume an active role within this relationship are critical issues in the American legal system."[52]

A second line of research concerns the trust that defendants display toward their attorneys. One study of 163 convicted male juvenile offenders (ages 12 to 20 years) found that defendants with limited understanding of the court process and of the defense attorney role reported less faith in their attorneys.[53] Another study of 307 male inmates found that specific case circumstances had the most influence on clients' trust of their attorneys: "Low attorney-client trust was associated with having a court-appointed attorney and going to trial . . . . Criminal defendants facing the most serious charges (e.g., those with long-term prison sentences) and being defended by, arguably, the most overburdened attorneys (i.e., court appointed) appear to harbor the lowest amount of trust in their attorneys."[54]

Trust was also influenced by case outcomes. For obvious reasons, defendants who were convicted and sentenced to long prison terms did not harbor favorable sentiments toward their attorneys. Finally, the authors of the same study speculated that those offenders convicted of the most serious crimes were least trusting because of an inherent inability to formulate constructive interpersonal relationships.[55]

Public Perceptions of Defense Attorneys

Public perceptions of attorneys have shifted from overwhelmingly positive to somewhat negative. There was a time when the likes of Perry Mason or *To Kill a Mockingbird*'s Atticus Finch placed attorneys in high regard with the general public. Such attitudes have since waned and been replaced by an unfortunate amount of scorn and ridicule.[56]

Recent advertising media have portrayed attorneys as everything from sharks in a feeding frenzy to rodeo cattle. As one critic of this recent trend observed, "This recurring distortion of lawyers' behavior has contributed to the mistaken impression that zealous advocacy calls for rude, intimidating, aggressive tactics."[57]

It is one thing to joke about lawyers and to portray them unfavorably in the media, but what does the public *really* think? While there appears to be no public opinion research linked specifically to defense attorneys, the ABA has conducted several surveys seeking to gauge public opinions of attorneys in general. One such survey revealed some positives and negatives.[58] Following are factors on the positive side:

- Americans say that lawyers are knowledgeable about the law and can help clients navigate through difficult situations.
- Personal experiences with lawyers substantiate these positive beliefs. The majority of consumers who have hired a lawyer are satisfied with the service their lawyer provided.
- Consumers tell stories of lawyers who apply significant expertise and knowledge to their cases, identify practical solutions, and work hard on behalf of their clients.
- Americans also believe that law is a good and even respectable career.[59]

The negative side reveals these views:

- Americans say that lawyers are greedy, manipulative, and corrupt. Personal experiences with lawyers substantiate these beliefs. Consumers tell stories of lawyers who misrepresent their qualifications, overpromise, are not up front about their fees, charge too much for their services, take too long to resolve matters, and fail to return client phone calls.

- Americans are uncomfortable with the connections that lawyers have with politics, the judiciary, government, big business, and law enforcement. These connections imbue lawyers with a certain degree of power in society, and Americans believe that the central place of lawyers in society enables them not only to play the system but also to shape that very system.

- Americans also believe that lawyers do a poor job of policing themselves. Bar associations are viewed not as protectors of the public or the public interest but as clubs to protect lawyers.[60]

How do lawyers sit relative to other professions? Are they held in higher or lower regard compared to judges? What about doctors? This is where the positive gets overshadowed by the negative: The ABA survey revealed that public opinions of lawyers put them one notch above the media—and far below the medical profession.[61] Clearly there is room for improvement.

Library Extra
9–4 Developing a Defense Strategy

Defense Attorneys' Satisfaction with Their Work

The ABA often commissions studies aimed at gauging attorneys' satisfaction with their professional positions. The results of one such study are depicted in Figure 9–1. In this study, several thousand attorneys were surveyed a few years out of law school and asked to report on several dimensions of job satisfaction, ranging from job security to their level of responsibility; for the most part, the attorneys were quite satisfied with their chosen careers.[62] One interesting finding absent from Figure 9–1 reaffirms the age-old adage that "money can't buy happiness": Attorneys with the highest incomes reported less job satisfaction than those earning far less.[63]

No amount of survey research can capture the satisfaction that accompanies a job well done. Many defense attorneys take great pride in their work, even if their work involves representing unpopular clients. There is no better example than the work of Neal Katyal, lead counsel in the now-famous *Hamdan* v. *Rumsfeld* Supreme Court case.[64] The case involved Salim Hamdan, a Yemeni citizen and Guantanamo Bay detainee who was charged with conspiracy to commit terrorism. The Bush administration sought to try him before a military commission, but Hamdan, with the assistance of Katyal, challenged this decision and prevailed. The Supreme Court held that the commissions did not comply with U.S. military law.

FIGURE 9–1

Attorneys' Job Satisfaction

Source: Based on data from Ronit Dinovitzer, *After the JD: First Results of a National Study of Legal Careers* (Overland Park, KS: NALP Foundation for Law Career Research and Education, 2004).

Job security	5.2
Value of work to society	4.7
Performance evaluation process	4.0
Diversity	4.4
Opportunities to build skills	5.3
Intellectual challenge	5.4
Opportunities for *pro bono*	4.3
Relationships with colleagues	5.7
Control over how you work	5.4
Control over amount of work	4.6
Compensation	4.5
Opportunities for advancement	4.7
Tasks you perform	5.1
Substantive area of work	5.3
Recognition for your work	4.9
Level of responsibility	5.6

1 = highly dissatisfied and 7 = highly satisfied

In early 2009, Katyal was appointed by President Obama to the position of principal deputy solicitor general, the number two solicitor general position in the U.S. Department of Justice. Before that, he was professor of national security law at Georgetown University and was named Lawyer of the Year by *Lawyers USA* in 2006.

While the prospect of defending a suspected terrorist may be disturbing to some current and aspiring defense attorneys, for others it is the best part of the job. The fight for justice and equality for everyone, regardless of their origin or crime, is what gives meaning to the work of many defense attorneys. Several are so passionate about particular cases that they work for free (also called *pro bono*), as Katyal did. In fact, he incurred nearly $40,000 in debt for his work on Hamdan's case.[65] We look at some additional examples toward the end of the book when we consider the problems of wrongful convictions in the rush to judgment.

DEFENSE ETHICS

Learning Objective 6
Describe the codes of ethics and conduct for defense attorneys.

Every attorney is bound by certain ethical principles and guidelines. Every state maintains standards of professional conduct that lawyers must follow, and professional associations, such as the ABA's Center for Professional Responsibility,[66] do the same. Yet because defense attorneys represent people accused of crime, they are sometimes accused of being less ethical than other attorneys. A common question is asked: How can a defense attorney represent someone who he or she *knows* is guilty? While this situation sometimes exists, the defense attorneys' foremost concern as well as their professional responsibility is acting on behalf of their client. Defense attorneys are empowered to put the prosecution's case to the test. It is their job to ensure the prosecution does so—and it is also each defendant's constitutional right.

To further elaborate on the subject of defense ethics, this section looks at some ethical dilemmas, examines the main professional organizations for defense attorneys, and then considers some codes of ethics as well as conduct that defense attorneys are required to adhere to. The section ends with ethical dilemmas that arise in the context of death-row volunteering, cases where death-row inmates waive appeals and essentially "volunteer" to be executed.

Ethical Dilemmas for the Defense

There are several types of ethical dilemmas a defense attorney may face during the course of his or her career:

- *Confidential confession.* What if the defendant confesses to the crime but only to his or her attorney? This is the classic defense ethical dilemma. On the one hand, the attorney must represent his or her client's interest; on the other hand, how can a defense attorney represent a client who he or she knows is guilty?

- *Client perjury.* The attorney–client privilege promotes open communication between client and attorney. A defendant cannot possibly benefit from the assistance of counsel without an assurance that his or her communications will be kept private. But what if the defense attorney knows the defendant lied on the stand? Does this not conflict with a defense attorney's obligation to employ means consistent with the truth?[67]

- *Defense receipt of physical evidence.* While the attorney–client privilege protects communications, it does not protect physical evidence. What if the defendant gives his or her attorney physical evidence related to the crime? What should the defense attorney do? Some have suggested that the defense attorney should deliver the evidence to the prosecutor anonymously.[68]

- *Problems with defendant's prior record.* Ethical guidelines prohibit attorneys from misleading the court, but if a defense attorney is asked about his or her client's prior record, what should the attorney do? The attorney should answer truthfully to comply with ethical guidelines, but open disclosure can have an adverse effect on sentencing. What if the client fails to inform his or her attorney about a prior conviction? What happens then?

Professional Organizations

We introduced some leading professional associations in Chapter 2, and we discussed some of the specific associations that judges and prosecutors belong to in Chapters 7 and 8, respectively. Here we do the same for defense attorneys. Why? There are two reasons. First, professional associations maintain codes of ethics for their members; second (and more important), certain professional associations (e.g., state bar associations) essentially license attorneys. When attorneys fail to follow the rules, they run the risk of losing their authority to practice law.

Bar Associations   The ABA's Model Code of Professional Responsibility[69] (previously called the Canons of Professional Ethics) was first adopted in 1908. Back in 1934, in an important speech, Justice Harlan Fiske (later Chief Justice Fiske) said,

> Before the Bar can function at all as a guardian of the public interests committed to its care, there must be appraisal and comprehension of the new conditions, and the chained relationship of the lawyer to his clients, to his professional brethren and to the public. That appraisal must pass beyond the petty details of form and manners which have been so largely the subject of our Codes of Ethics, to more fundamental consideration of the way in which our professional activities affect the welfare of society as a whole.[70]

Similar codes of professional responsibility are found in each state. Membership in a state bar association affords an attorney the authority to practice law in that state, but part of that privilege entails adhering to that state's ethical codes and principles.

The NACDL   The NACDL is the leading professional organization for defense attorneys in the United States. While its membership is not limited to attorneys, the organization's main thrust is to advance the mission of defense attorneys nationwide. Through its Ethics Advisory Committee, the NACDL seeks to foster integrity, independence, and expertise in the criminal defense profession. For example, the NACDL often publishes ethics opinions concerned with how defense lawyers should act in situations ranging from clients who lie to jail conversations that are monitored.

National Legal Aid and Defender Association   The **National Legal Aid and Defender Association** (NLADA) is roughly equivalent to the NACDL, but its main focus is on defense attorneys who provide aid to indigent defendants. The NLADA has promulgated minimum standards for defense representation in public defense systems throughout the United States.[71] Its Model Public Defender Act, Guidelines for Legal Defense Systems in the United States, and Standards for the Administration of Assigned Counsel, among other documents, set forth important rules and guidelines for the provision of defense services to ensure that indigent defendants receive effective representation in their cases.

National Legal Aid and Defender Association (NLADA)
A professional organization for defense attorneys in the United States that is roughly equivalent to the National Association of Criminal Defense Lawyers but that is mainly focused on defense attorneys who provide aid to indigent defendants.

Codes of Ethics and Conduct

While professional associations maintain their own codes of ethics (some of which were referenced above), the judiciaries also often have their own. For example, the federal government's **Code of Conduct for Federal Public Defender Employees** is a publication of the Administrative Office of the U.S. Courts and appears in abridged form in Box 9–2. An example of a state's code is Nevada's Model Code of Conduct for Judicial Employees, which guides all judicial officers in that state. Together with professional associations' ethical guidelines, lawyers are certainly saddled with a wide range of professional obligations.

Code of Conduct for Federal Public Defender Employees
A publication of the Administrative Office of the U.S. Courts.

Essential Elements of Competent Representation While codes of ethics and professional responsibility vary considerably, they tend to have a number of essential core elements. Defense attorneys must do the following:

- Prepare their cases promptly and work to protect the accused's rights.
- Be thorough in their efforts to research the case and discover evidence that can be used to mount a defense.
- Carefully investigate the facts of the case.
- Build a working professional relationship with their clients.
- Be in regular contact and communication with their clients.
- Retain expert witnesses as circumstances merit.
- Explore alternative dispositions and share these with the client.
- Engage in plea bargaining as needed and share plea offers with the client.
- Competently discharge all responsibilities at all stages of the criminal process.
- Serve as an advocate for the defendant during sentencing, if applicable. This includes being familiar with sentencing guidelines and alternatives to traditional sentencing.
- Represent the client at all stages of the appellate process—if needed. This includes explaining to the client all possible consequences associated with an appeal.
- Continue with legal education as required.[72]

Death-Row Volunteering

Given the political sensitivity of capital punishment, it is no wonder that ethical issues arise when this sanction looms for convicted criminals. Some defense attorneys volunteer their

---

BOX 9–2 Canons of the Code of Conduct for Federal Public Defender Employees

Canon 1. A federal public defender employee should uphold the integrity and independence of the office.
Canon 2. A federal public defender employee should avoid impropriety and the appearance of impropriety in all activities.
Canon 3. A federal public defender employee should adhere to appropriate standards in performing the duties of the office.
Canon 4. A federal public defender employee may engage in activities to improve the law, the legal system, and the administration of justice.
Canon 5. A federal public defender employee should regulate extra-official activities to minimize the risk of conflict with official duties.
Canon 6. A federal public defender employee should regularly file reports of compensation received for all extra-official activities.
Canon 7. A federal public defender employee should refrain from inappropriate political activities. ■

Source: http://www.uscourts.gov/uscourts/FederalCourts/AppointmentOfCounsel/vol7/Vol07A-Ch04-Appx4B.pdf (accessed February 19, 2013).

services by doing *pro bono* work for death-row inmates—often because they are personally opposed to it.[73] (The ABA's Death Penalty Representation Project is but one example.) This is beneficial in the sense that death-row inmates have the most to lose and, as such, should have every chance to ensure that they are not wrongfully executed. On the other hand, some people ask why the worst of the worst should get continued free legal services when it already takes a long time to carry out a sentence of death.

Another problem that is replete with even more ethical dilemmas occurs when a death-row inmate decides to stop appealing and let the sentence be carried out, which has been termed **death-row volunteering**.[74] One defense attorney recounted the experience this way:

death-row volunteering
A phenomenon involving a death-row inmate making a decision to stop appealing and let the sentence be carried out.[vi]

> This is just like if a student of yours walked into your office and said, "I need to talk to you about something. You know, I've had a bad life. It's a wonderful school. You're a wonderful professor. But I don't want to live anymore. Will you help me end my life?" You wouldn't say, "Great. You have the free will to do it. I'll help you." You wouldn't do that. No one would do that. Lawyers shouldn't do that either.[75]

What is a defense attorney to do in such a situation? Professional demands call for zealous representation. But should client demands be ignored? If the inmate wants to give up, should the attorney work against the client's wishes?

C. Lee Harrington's study of death-row volunteering (almost a form of client suicide) offers few answers to these questions because the attorneys themselves are divided. Many of the attorneys she interviewed were against the death penalty and struggled mightily to get their clients to continue the fight, but sometimes the situation demanded a different approach: "Defense attorneys adopt a wide variety of approaches to volunteering, from 're-spect the client's wishes' to 'unavoidable triage' to 'question his competency' to 'withdraw immediately' to 'fight it every step of the way.'"[76] What makes the dilemma even worse is that when death-row volunteering is allowed to occur, defense attorneys are frequently criticized by their colleagues for doing the very job they are charged with doing—serving their client's interest. One attorney reported,

> I made an agreement [with my client not to pursue appeals], and I feel like at the time it was the only thing I could have done, . . . but I've been criticized for it. And the criticism came from within the death penalty community. It came from people I admire very much. It was hard to take.[77]

CHAPTER 9 > SUMMARY

1. DESCRIBE THE FUNCTIONS OF DEFENSE ATTORNEYS

- A defense attorney is a lawyer who advises, represents, and acts for his or her client (the defendant).
- The defense attorney serves as the accused's counselor and advocate.

2. OUTLINE THE HISTORY OF CRIMINAL DEFENSE

- Criminal defense attorneys became significant players in the criminal process around the 1730s. After the American Revolution, the number of lawyers surged.
- There are more than 1.1 million attorneys practicing in the United States today.

3. DESCRIBE THE TYPES OF DEFENSE ATTORNEYS

- Two broad categories of defense counsel exist: attorneys who are privately retained and attorneys who represent indigent defendants (sometimes called "public" attorneys).

- Defendants who can afford to do so may hire their own attorneys, but this does not mean they can hire an attorney of their choosing. A conflict of interest, for example, may require that a different attorney be selected.

- Privately retained attorneys perform essentially the same as public attorneys.

- There are three primary systems for providing defense services to indigent defendants: (1) assigned counsel—the appointment from a list of private bar members who accept cases on a judge-by-judge, court-by-court, or case-by-case basis; (2) contract model—nonsalaried individual private attorneys, bar associations, law firms, consortiums or groups of attorneys, or nonprofit corporations that contract with a funding source to provide court-appointed representation in a jurisdiction; and (3) public defender—a salaried staff of full-time or part-time attorneys who render criminal indigent defense services either through a public or private nonprofit organization or as direct government-paid employees.

4. EXPLAIN THE REALITIES OF DEFENSE WORK

- Researchers have studied defense attorneys on the job and found that rather than "zealous advocates," they tend to act as "double agents" or "beleaguered dealers."

- The "double agent" is an attorney who appears to work for one side but instead works for another.

- A "beleaguered dealer" is an attorney who struggles with the difficulties of his or her job, such as high caseloads.

5. SUMMARIZE THE DIFFERENT WAYS DEFENSE ATTORNEYS ARE PERCEIVED

- In terms of public opinion, defense attorneys tend to report that their clients are less than supportive, especially of public attorneys.

- Researchers have also found that defendants' trust of their attorneys is dictated largely by decisions made throughout the court process.

- Generally speaking, the public is both supportive and unsupportive of attorneys. Contrary to popular perceptions, defense attorneys are not universally scorned.

6. DESCRIBE THE CODES OF ETHICS AND CONDUCT FOR DEFENSE ATTORNEYS

- Ethical guidelines for defense attorneys stem from professional associations (e.g., ABA, NACDL, and NLADA) and codes of professional conduct.

- Death-row volunteering (death-row inmates who decide to stop appealing and go forward with the execution) poses a serious ethical dilemma for defense attorneys.

KEY TERMS

ad hoc assigned counsel system, 231
assigned counsel, 230
Code of Conduct for Federal Public Defender Employees, 241
contract model, 230
coordinated assigned counsel system, 231

death-row volunteering, 242
defense attorney, 225
double agent, 235
fixed-fee contract, 232
fixed-price contract, 232
National Association of Criminal Defense Lawyers, 228

National Legal Aid and Defender Association, 240
public client, 236
public defender, 230
retainer, 228

REVIEW QUESTIONS

1. What is the historical development of the criminal defense bar in the United States? What is the bar like today?

2. What are the various types of defense attorneys working in the criminal courts today? How do they differ?

3. What are the tasks normally undertaken by a defense attorney in the performance of his or her job?

4. How do members of the public view defense attorneys? How do the clients of those attorneys tend to see them?

5. What ethical standards guide defense attorneys today? What are the various sources of those standards?

WHAT WILL YOU DO?

You are attending law school and hope to become a criminal defense attorney. One day, a professor whom you like very much says that she wants to tell you a true story about an attorney who was faced with a serious ethical dilemma and begins her remarks by saying that an attorney has dual obligations that are often in conflict. The first is an obligation to the judicial system as an officer of the court, and the other involves the attorney's duty as a fiduciary representative of his or her client.

The Supreme Court, she says, in the case of *Nix* v. *Whiteside*, held that a trial is essentially a search for the truth. However, she goes on, that does not necessarily mean that a defense attorney must be truthful in everything that he or she says or does. A defense attorney's primary duty, she tells you, is the full and adequate legal representation of the client.

A distinction, your professor continues, must be made between the goal of the judicial system and the duties of a defense attorney in representing his or her client. A defense attorney, she says, must be a zealous advocate for the client, putting that person's interests ahead of all others. She tells you the story of Lord Brougham, an English attorney in the 1820s who uttered a famous phrase that still guides attorneys today: "An advocate in the discharge of his duty knows but one person in all the world, and that person is his client."

Finding the truth, your professor says, may be the goal of the judicial system, but it is not the governing principle of the criminal defense attorney. Instead, she says, the defense lawyer should be concerned with honesty in dealing with clients, opponents, and the system. It is the principle of *honesty* rather than *truth*, she says, that should govern the attorney at all times.

Although truth and honesty are related, she tells you, they are not the same thing. Truth, she says, is concerned with uncovering the existence of a historical fact; honesty focuses on the authenticity of the defense attorney's assertions on behalf of his or her client. For example, a defense attorney should be expected to provide accurate and unaltered documents to the court when presenting written evidence, but he or she is not required to reveal whether he or she knows with certainty whether his or her client is guilty.

The story that I want to tell you about, says your professor, involves a man who was accused of two grisly murders of two five-year-old little girls. The girls' bodies had not been found by the time the trial started, but before the trial ended,

the defendant admitted to his attorney that he had committed the murders and shared with him the location of the bodies. As the trial continued, the defense attorney represented his client as best he could and offered alternative scenarios to the jury about how the girls may have disappeared. Throughout the trial, the girls' parents were extremely distressed and often cried when testimony was offered.

Despite the attorney's efforts, the man was convicted. Prior to sentencing, the defendant was asked whether he would reveal the location of the girls' bodies so that the parents might begin to bring closure to the horrible experience they had been through, but he refused.

At that point, the parents approached the defense attorney and asked him if he knew where their daughters' bodies were. The attorney's understanding of the ethical codes that govern the attorney–client relationship led him to say that even if he knew, he was not at liberty to share any such information. Soon, however, the attorney's conscience bothered him, and he wrote an anonymous letter to the authorities telling them where the bodies could be found. Not long after, it was determined that the anonymous letter had come from the attorney; he was brought before the state bar, was accused of violating attorney–client privilege, and was disbarred. Before entering law school, your professor says, my ethics would have told me that he did the right thing, but now I know that he was wrong in disclosing information that was privileged. Before you answer, you might want to read about the Danielle Van Dam murder case, in which a seven-year-old California girl was abducted from her bedroom and later found dead in a wooded area. Suspicion was soon directed at a neighbor, David Westerfield, who was arrested and charged with the crime. During the trial, Westerfield's defense team of Steven Feldman and Robert Boyce put on a vigorous defense. They pointed a finger at the lifestyle of the seven-year-old's parents, Brenda and Damon van Dam, who were forced to admit on the stand that they engaged in partner swapping and group sex. The defense lawyers told jurors that the couple's sex life brought them in contact with sleazy characters who were much more likely to harm Danielle then Westerfield, a neighbor with no felony record. The defense also told jurors that scientific evidence proved that Westerfield could not have dumped Danielle's body by a remote roadside. Forensic entomologists testified that the insects in her decaying body indicated that her death occurred during a period for which Westerfield could account for his activities. Despite their efforts, physical evidence found in Westerfield's home proved very damaging in court, and he was convicted of the murder and sentenced to death. After the trial was over, the *San Diego Union-Tribune* broke the story that Westerfield's lawyers, Feldman and Boyce, tried to broker a deal before trial in which Westerfield would reveal the location of Danielle's body in exchange for a guarantee that he would not face the death penalty but rather life without parole. Both sides were about to make the deal when volunteer searchers found Danielle's body. In defending the attorneys, defense lawyers and former prosecutors pointed out that plea discussions are never admissible during trial and that Feldman and Boyce would

have been accused of incompetence if they did not try to raise reasonable doubt in the case. A defense attorney's job isn't to decide whether their client committed the offense but to provide them with a vigorous defense and ensure that their client isn't convicted unless the prosecution can prove its case beyond a reasonable doubt. And it's impossible to make the prosecution meet its burden without aggressively challenging the evidence, even if the defender believes the client committed the crime.

Source: J. Harry Jones, "Van Dam Case Shook Nation 10 Years Ago, Case of Girl Snatched from Her Room Shook Nation," *San Diego Union-Tribune*, February 1, 2012, available at www.utsandiego.com/news/2012/Feb/02/tp-van-dam-case-shook-nation-10-years-ago-10 (accessed June 1, 2013).

NOTES

i. U.S. Department of Justice, Dictionary of Criminal Justice Data Terminology, p. 27.

ii. C. J. DeFrances and M. F. X. Litras, Indigent Defense Services in Large Counties, 1999 (Washington, DC: Bureau of Justice Statistics, 2000), p. 2.

iii. C. J. DeFrances and M. F. X. Litras, Indigent Defense Services in Large Counties, 1999 (Washington, DC: Bureau of Justice Statistics, 2000), p. 2.

iv. DeFrances and Litras, Indigent Defense Services in Large Counties, 1999, p. 2.

v. R. B. Flemming, "Client Games: Defense Attorney Perspectives on Their Relations with Criminal Clients," Law and Social Inquiry 11(1986):253–277.

vi. C. L. Harrington, "A Community Divided: Defense Attorneys and the Ethics of Death Row Volunteering," Law and Social Inquiry 25(2000):849–881.

1. Russell Goldman, "Suspected Boston Bomber Receives All-Star Defense Team," ABC News, April 24, 2013, http://abcnews.go.com/US/boston-bomber-receives-star-defense-team/story?id=19025841 (accessed December 3, 2013).

2. U.S. Department of Justice, Dictionary of Criminal Justice Data Terminology, 2nd ed. (Washington, DC: U.S. Department of Justice, Bureau of Justice Statistics, 1981), p. 27.

3. American Bar Association, Criminal Justice Standards, available at www.americanbar.org/publications/criminal_justice_archive/crimjust_standards_dfunc_blk.html (accessed February 19, 2013).

4. Much of this historical discussion draws from Fritz Schulz, History of Roman Legal Science (Oxford: Oxford University Press, 1946).

5. Ibid., p. 113.

6. James A. Brundage, "The Rise of the Professional Jurist in the Thirteenth Century," Syracuse Journal of International Law and Communication, Vol. 20 (1994), p. 185.

7. D. J. Bodenhamer, Fair Trial: Rights of the Accused in American History (New York: Oxford University Press, 1992), p. 28.

8. S. Walker, Popular Justice: A History of American Criminal Justice, 2nd ed. (New York: Oxford University Press, 1998).

9. T. N. Ferdinand, "Criminal Justice: From Colonial Intimacy to Bureaucratic Formality," in D. Street and Associates, eds., Handbook of Contemporary Urban Life (San Francisco: Jossey-Bass, 1978), pp. 261–287.

10. Walker, Popular Justice.

11. M. J. Friedman, Outline of the U.S. Legal System (Washington, DC: U.S. State Department, 2004), available at http://photos.state.gov/libraries/korea/49271/dwoa_122709/Outline-of-the-U_S_-Legal-System.pdf (accessed February 19, 2013).

12. Ibid.

13. Ibid.

14. Ibid.

15. Gideon v. Wainwright, 372 U.S. 335 (1963).

16. Available at www.expertlaw.com/library/criminal/criminal_lawyer.html#Q2 (accessed February 19, 2013).

17. C. W. Harlow, Defense Counsel in Criminal Cases (Washington, DC: Bureau of Justice Statistics, 2000).

18. Ibid.

19. For some details, see J. Reiman, The Rich Get Richer and the Poor Get Prison: Ideology, Class, and Criminal Justice, 8th ed. (Boston: Allyn and Bacon, 2007).

20. Data compiled by the Bureau of Justice Statistics, available at http://bjs.ojp.usdoj.gov/content/pub/pdf/dccc.pdf (accessed February 19, 2013).

21. See, e.g., A. Rattner, H. Turjeman, and G. Fishman, "Public versus Private Defense: Can Money Buy Justice?," Journal of Criminal Justice, Vol. 36 (2008), pp. 43–49.

22. R. Flemming, "If You Pay the Piper, Do You Call the Tune? Public Defenders in America's Criminal Courts," Law and Social Inquiry, Vol. 14 (1989), pp. 393–405; P. Wice, Chaos in the Courthouse: The Inner Workings of the Urban Criminal Courts (New York: Prager, 1985); J. Eisenstein, R. Flemming, and P. Nardulli, The Contours of Justice: Communities and Their Courts (Boston: Little, Brown, 1988).

23. P. Houlden and S. Balkin, "Quality and Cost Comparisons of Private Bar Indigent Defense Systems: Contract vs. Ordered Assigned Counsel," Journal of Criminal Law and Criminology, Vol. 76 (1985), pp. 176–200.

24. C. J. DeFrances and M. F. X. Litras, Indigent Defense Services in Large Counties, 1999 (Washington, DC: Bureau of Justice Statistics, 2000).

25. National Center for State Courts, Who Pays for Indigent Defense?, available at www.ncsc.org/Topics/Access-and-Fairness/Indigent-Defense/Resource-Guide.aspx (accessed February 19, 2013).

26. DeFrances and Litras, Indigent Defense Services in Large Counties, 1999, p. 1.

27. R. A. Desilets, R. L. Spangenberg, and J. W. Riggs, Rates of Compensation Paid to Court-Appointed Counsel in Non-Capital Felony Cases at Trial: A State-by-State Overview (West Newton, MA: Spangenberg Group, 2007).

28. American Bar Association, Gideon's Broken Promise: America's Continuing Quest for Equal Justice (Chicago: American Bar Association, 2004).

29. D. Cauchon, "Indigents' Lawyers: Low Pay Hurts Justice?," USA Today, February 3, 1999, p. 4A.

30. R. Spangenberg and T. J. Schwartz, "The Indigent Defense Crisis Is Chronic," Criminal Justice Journal, Vol. 9 (1994), pp. 13–16.

31. Desilets et al., Rates of Compensation Paid to Court-Appointed Counsel in Non-Capital Felony Cases at Trial.

32. L. Spears, "Contract Counsel: A Different Way to Defend the Poor—How It's Working in North Dakota," American Bar Association Journal on Criminal Justice, Vol. 6 (1991), pp. 24–31.

33. D. Sudnow, "Normal Crimes: Sociological Features of the Penal Code in a Public Defender's Office," Social Problems, Vol. 12 (1965), pp. 255–276; A. Blumberg, "The Practice of

Law as a Confidence Game: Organizational Cooptation of a Profession," *Law and Society Review*, Vol. 1 (1967), pp. 15–40.

34. L. M. Mather, *Plea Bargaining or Trial?* (Lexington, MA: Lexington Books, 1979).

35. R. B. Flemming, "Elements of the Defense Attorney's Craft: An Adaptive Expectations Model of the Preliminary Hearing Decision," *Law and Policy*, Vol. 8 (1986), p. 55.

36. Ibid.

37. P. F. Nardulli, "Insider Justice: Defense Attorneys and the Handling of Felony Cases," *Journal of Criminal Law and Criminology*, Vol. 77 (1986), pp. 379–417.

38. Ibid.

39. Blumberg, "The Practice of Law as a Confidence Game," pp. 15–40.

40. R. J. Uphoff, "The Criminal Defense Lawyer: Zealous Advocate, Double Agent, or Beleaguered Dealer," *Criminal Law Bulletin*, Vol. 28 (1992), pp. 419–456.

41. Blumberg, "The Practice of Law as a Confidence Game," p. 20.

42. Ibid.

43. Uphoff, "The Criminal Defense Lawyer," pp. 425–426.

44. Ibid., p. 427.

45. Ibid.

46. Ibid., p. 443.

47. R. B. Flemming, "Client Games: Defense Attorney Perspectives on Their Relations with Criminal Clients," *Law and Social Inquiry*, Vol. 11 (1986), pp. 253–277.

48. Ibid., p. 257.

49. J. D. Casper, *American Criminal Justice: The Defendant's Perspective* (Englewood Cliffs, NJ: Prentice Hall, 1972), pp. 117–118.

50. A. Sarat and W. L. F. Felstiner, "Vocabularies of Motive in Lawyer/Client Interaction," *Law and Society Review*, Vol. 22 (1988), pp. 737–769.

51. S. Feldman and K. Wilson, "The Value of Interpersonal Skills in Lawyering," *Law and Human Behavior*, Vol. 5 (1981), pp. 311–324.

52. M. T. Boccaccini and S. L. Brodsky, "Attorney-Client Trust among Convicted Criminal Defendants: Preliminary Examination of the Attorney-Client Trust Scale," *Behavioral Sciences and the Law*, Vol. 20 (2002), p. 70.

53. C. Schnyder and S. L. Brodsky, "Trust and Understanding in the Attorney-Juvenile Relationship," *Behavioral Sciences and the Law*, Vol. 20 (2002), pp. 89–107.

54. Boccaccini and Brodsky, "Attorney-Client Trust among Convicted Criminal Defendants," pp. 82–83.

55. Ibid.

56. R. A. Clifford, "Raising the Bar: Opening Statement," *Litigation*, Vol. 27 (Summer 2001), available at http://cliffordlaw.com/aba-illinois-state-delegate/articles-on-public-perceptions-of-lawyers/raising-the-bar (accessed February 19, 2013).

57. Ibid.

58. "Summary of Findings," *Public Perception of Lawyers*, prepared by Leo J. Shapiro & Associates, for and published by the American Bar Association Section of Litigation, 2002, p. 4. © 2002 by the American Bar Association. Reprinted with permission. All rights reserved. This information or any portion thereof may not be copied or disseminated in any form or by any means or stored in an electronic database or retrieval system without the express permission of the American Bar Association.

59. Ibid.

60. Ibid.

61. Ibid.

62. R. Dinovitzer, *After the JD: First Results of a National Study of Legal Careers* (Overland Park, KS: NALP Foundation for Law Career Research and Education, 2004).

63. Ibid.

64. *Hamdan v. Rumsfeld*, 548 U.S. 557 (2006).

65. J. Mahler, *The Challenge: Hamdan v. Rumsfeld and the Fight over Presidential Power* (New York: Farrar, Straus, and Giroux, 2008).

66. Available at www.americanbar.org/groups/professional_responsibility/resources/links_of_interest.html (accessed February 19, 2013).

67. For some sample cases, see *Rock v. Arkansas*, 483 U.S. 44 (1987), p. 29; *People v. Guzman*, 45 C.3d 915 (1988), p. 944; *People v. Johnson*, 62 CA 4th 608 (1998).

68. *State v. Olwell*, 394 P.2d 681 (Wash. 1964).

69. Available at www.law.cornell.edu/ethics/aba/mcpr/MCPR.HTM (accessed February 19, 2013).

70. Ibid.

71. Available at www.nlada.org/Defender/Defender_Standards/Performance_Guidelines (accessed February 19, 2013).

72. J. M. McCauley, "Excessive Workloads Create Ethical Issues for Court-Appointed Counsel and Public Defenders," *Virginia Lawyer*, Vol. 53 (2004), p. 27.

73. A. Sarat and S. Scheingold, Cause Lawyering: *Political Commitments and Professional Responsibilities* (New York: Oxford University Press, 1998).

74. C. L. Harrington, "A Community Divided: Defense Attorneys and the Ethics of Death Row Volunteering," *Law and Social Inquiry*, Vol. 25 (2000), pp. 849–881.

75. Ibid., p. 850.

76. Ibid., p. 877.

77. Ibid.

Dwayne Newton/PhotoEdit

efendants and Victims:
heir Roles and Rights

Jodi Arias, whose 2013 murder trial was nationally televised. Arias was convicted of the brutal murder of her boyfriend, Travis Alexander. What role does the defendant play in a criminal trial?

REUTERS/Tom Tingle/The Arizona Republic/Pool

INTRODUCTION

On May 8, 2013, Arizona jurors found 32-year-old Jodi Arias guilty of first-degree murder in the brutal killing of her former boyfriend, Travis Alexander. Arias, who admitted shooting and stabbing her then-30-year-old lover at his home in 2008, claimed that she had been trying to defend herself from emotional, physical, and sexual abuse. Alexander's throat had been cut from ear to ear, he had been stabbed thirty times, and was shot in the face.

Arias appeared as a petite and demure woman during her trial, and dressed like a school-girl while on the stand. Although her appearance might have been unremarkable, Arias's trial captured the attention of the nation and the world as it wound through five months of testimony, cross-examination, and jury debate. USA Today described it this way, "the Jodi Arias trial, which would ordinarily be a run-of-the-mill domestic murder case," drew a media circus that fed a large following of TV viewers who watched the trial unfold. They were captivated by it's intimate details of "love, lies, sex, and dirty secrets."[1]

Prosecutors showed jurors how Arias had become an obsessed stalker when Alexander told her that he was interested in having only a sexual relationship with her, and didn't love her. At one point, an audio recording was played during the trial in which Alexander said that he wanted to tie Arias to a tree and commit deviant sex acts on her. After Arias was found guilty, she told news reporters that she would rather receive a death sentence than spend the rest of her life in prison.

At the conclusion of trial, Clancy Talbot, a friend of Alexander, said "Looking at Jodi's face, I think this is probably the first time in her life she has ever been held responsible for what she's done, ever, and I think she's in shock."[2]

DEFENDANT CHARACTERISTICS

Some people view the criminal defendant as being "along for the ride" once the trial commences. Their fate is most often put into the hands of a defense attorney who must convince

Learning Objective 1
Characterize typical criminal defendants.

a judge or jury that the accused did not commit the crime and who speaks for the defendant during the trial process.

To say that defendants sit on the sidelines or take on an obscure role in the criminal process is not totally accurate. Some of them commit heinous crimes and thus receive no shortage of press coverage, and celebrities accused of crimes also garner plenty of publicity. But these are not typical offenders. Most criminal defendants are relatively unknown persons accused of committing garden-variety offenses, so their "dirty laundry" is not of interest to most people, and the crimes they commit rarely receive any press attention. The typical defendant is, in many respects, a "nobody."

Who is the typical defendant? The Federal Bureau of Investigation collects data on the characteristics of arrestees, but arrestees are not offenders per se, only suspects, and the Bureau of Justice Statistics collects data on felony defendants but only those tried in the largest U.S. counties. More data are available on sentenced offenders, but we will look at such information in Chapter 15 when we consider the subjects of discrimination and differential treatment.

Most crimes are committed by males. Males are arrested at rates much higher than females, and male defendants far outnumber female defendants. This is especially true of murder, rape, and weapons offenses, as can be seen in Table 10–1. There is much more equality across the sexes for the crimes of fraud and forgery.

A problem with Table 10–1 is that it contains only index crimes and other traditional criminal offenses. We can learn much more by turning our attention to some other offenses not listed in the table. Two violent crimes committed more frequently by women than men

TABLE 10–1 Sex of Felony Defendants, by Most Serious Arrest Charge

Most Serious Arrest Charge	Number of Defendants	Percent of Defendants		
		Total	Male	Female
All offenses	57,980	100%	82	18
Violent offenses	13,264	100%	87	13
Murder	370	100%	97	3
Rape	666	100%	98	2
Robbery	3,446	100%	90	10
Assault	6,381	100%	83	17
Other violent	2,400	100%	85	15
Property offenses	16,907	100%	76	24
Burglary	4,495	100%	88	12
Larceny/theft	5,257	100%	68	32
Motor vehicle theft	1,661	100%	87	13
Forgery	1,414	100%	63	37
Fraud	2,109	100%	62	38
Other property	1,197	100%	84	16
Drug offenses	21,197	100%	83	17
Trafficking	8,474	100%	88	12
Other drug	12,724	100%	80	20
Public-order offenses	6,612	100%	89	11
Weapons	1,953	100%	96	4
Driving-related	1,836	100%	89	11
Other public-order	2,822	100%	84	16

Note: Data on sex of defendants were available for 99.8% of all cases.
Source: T. H. Cohen and T. Kyckelhahn, *Felony Defendants in Large Urban Counties, 2006* (Washington, DC: Bureau of Justice Statistics, 2010), available at http://bjs.ojp.usdoj.gov/content/pub/pdf/fdluc06.pdf (accessed February 20, 2013).

TABLE 10-2 Race and Hispanic Origin of Felony Defendants, by Most Serious Arrest Charge

Most Serious Arrest Charge	Number of Defendants	Total	Percent of Felony Defendants Who Were—			
			Black non-Hispanic	White non-Hispanic	Other non-Hispanic	Hispanic, Any Race
All offenses	56,978	100%	45	29	2	24
Violent offenses	13,035	100%	47	26	2	25
Murder	368	100%	67	10	1	22
Rape	645	100%	39	30	1	30
Robbery	3,407	100%	57	20	3	20
Assault	6,288	100%	47	26	2	26
Other violent	2,329	100%	33	35	3	30
Property offenses	16,545	100%	39	36	2	23
Burglary	4,412	100%	36	36	1	27
Larceny/theft	5,186	100%	44	34	2	20
Motor vehicle theft	1,626	100%	38	26	5	31
Forgery	1,387	100%	37	40	4	20
Fraud	2,021	100%	39	37	3	22
Other property	1,916	100%	36	40	3	21
Drug offenses	20,904	100%	49	26	1	24
Trafficking	8,348	100%	59	16	2	23
Other drug	12,556	100%	43	33	1	24
Public-order offenses	6,494	100%	41	30	2	27
Weapons	1,934	100%	60	14	–	26
Driving-related	1,793	100%	25	39	2	34
Other public-order	2,767	100%	40	37	2	22

Note: Data on both race and Hispanic origin of defendants were available for 99% of all cases.
Detail may not sum to total because of rounding.
– Less than 0.5%
Source: T. H. Cohen and T. Kyckelhahn, *Felony Defendants in Large Urban Counties, 2006* (Washington, DC: Bureau of Justice Statistics, 2010), available at http://bjs.ojp.usdoj.gov/content/pub/pdf/fdluc06.pdf (accessed February 20, 2013).

(and not shown in Table 10–1) are child abuse and infanticide.[3] Why? One answer is that women historically have had more child-care responsibilities than men.

In terms of race, there are more black than white defendants for almost all offenses (see Table 10–2). Offenses involving more white than black defendants include forgery, driving-related offenses, and certain property crimes; on the other hand, there are more black defendants than white defendants for crimes of violence.

The data in Table 10–2 tell only part of the story. It is also important to consider the percentage of each race in the general population. According to U.S. Census figures,[4] blacks made up just over 12% of the population in 2010, yet they accounted for 45% of felony defendants in the most populous counties (as shown in Table 10–2). In contrast, whites made up 29% of the defendants but made up approximately 72% of the population. We look at racial discrepancies such as these more closely in Chapter 15.

Table 10–3 looks at the age distribution of felony defendants. We are often given the impression that crime is committed almost exclusively by young minority males. While it is true that crime is largely a young person's game, whether one group is represented more than the next depends on the offense in question. By and large, though, most crimes are committed overwhelmingly by young people.

Library Extra
10–1 Felony Defendants in Large Urban Counties, 2004

TABLE 10-3 Age at Arrest of Felony Defendants, by Most Serious Arrest Charge

Most Serious Arrest Charge	Number of Defendants	Total	Percent of Felony Defendants Who Were—							Average Age at Arrest (Years)
			Under 18	18–20	21–24	25–29	30–34	35–39	40 or Older	
All offenses	57,948	100%	3	14	17	16	13	12	26	32
Violent offenses	13,246	100%	6	16	17	16	12	10	23	31
Murder	370	100%	7	19	18	24	13	7	11	28
Rape	665	100%	4	15	15	16	16	15	18	30
Robbery	3,451	100%	13	27	17	12	8	8	15	27
Assault	6,376	100%	3	13	17	17	14	11	25	32
Other violent	2,385	100%	2	11	15	15	14	12	31	34
Property offenses	16,882	100%	2	15	15	17	13	13	25	32
Burglary	4,486	100%	3	19	16	15	11	13	23	31
Larceny/theft	5,259	100%	2	14	13	16	12	14	29	33
Motor vehicle theft	1,653	100%	4	23	17	16	14	11	16	29
Forgery	1,416	100%	1	9	18	19	14	11	28	32
Fraud	2,091	100%	1	8	12	19	16	16	29	34
Other property	1,977	100%	2	16	20	18	14	10	20	30
Drug offenses	21,223	100%	2	13	17	15	13	12	28	32
Trafficking	8,482	100%	3	17	22	17	11	10	21	30
Other drug	12,741	100%	2	10	14	14	13	13	33	34
Public-order offenses	6,597	100%	2	12	17	16	14	11	28	32
Weapons	1,958	100%	3	25	27	20	10	4	12	27
Driving-related	1,836	100%	0	3	12	18	16	12	39	36
Other public-order	2,805	100%	2	9	13	13	16	16	31	34

Note: Data on age of defendants were available for 99.7% of all cases. Detail may not sum to total because of rounding.

Source: T. H. Cohen and T. Kyckelhahn, *Felony Defendants in Large Urban Counties, 2006* (Washington, DC: Bureau of Justice Statistics, 2010), available at http://bjs.ojp.usdoj.gov/content/pub/pdf/fdluc06.pdf (accessed February 20, 2013).

Learning Objective 2

Summarize defendants' rights during the court process.

Library Extra

10-2 Criminal Justice Handbook for Defendants

CRIMINAL DEFENDANTS' RIGHTS

All throughout the court process, the accused enjoys a host of different protections from overreaching police, biased judges, and overzealous prosecutors. First, criminal defendants enjoy the right to counsel, whether they can afford it or not (see Chapter 9). Because our justice system is also concerned with giving those charged with a crime a fair shake and a reasonable opportunity to defend themselves against the allegations others make, there are two more rights defendants enjoy: confrontation and compulsory process.

Right to Counsel

Three constitutional provisions govern the defendant's right to counsel. While the Sixth Amendment is the only part of the Constitution that explicitly references a right to counsel, the Supreme Court has over the years recognized that the right to counsel also extends beyond the Sixth Amendment to both the Fifth and Fourteenth Amendments.

Sixth Amendment and the Right to Counsel The Sixth Amendment to the U.S. Constitution states, in part, that "in all criminal prosecutions, the accused shall enjoy the right . . . to have the Assistance of Counsel for his defense." In the 1938

case of *Johnson* v. *Zerbst*,[5] the Supreme Court first recognized the Sixth Amendment right to counsel in *federal* prosecutions. It said that the Sixth Amendment "embodies a realistic recognition of the obvious truth that the average defendant does not have the professional legal skill to protect himself."[6] This decision applied only to federal courts, a restriction that was echoed in the 1942 case of *Betts* v. *Brady*, where the Court said, "The Due Process Clause of the Fourteenth Amendment does not incorporate, as such, the specific guarantees found in the Sixth Amendment."[7] Recall from Chapter 1 that the Bill of Rights (the first ten amendments) applies only to the federal government. The Supreme Court has over the years used the Fourteenth Amendment's due process clause to make some of the protections laid out in the Bill of Rights applicable to the states, but the *Betts* decision did not do this for the right to counsel. That all changed in a 1963 case: *Gideon* v. *Wainwright*.[8]

Gideon held that the Sixth Amendment right to counsel is so fundamental to a fair trial that due process *requires* that every state, as well as the federal government, honor this important part of the Sixth Amendment. The Court said that "lawyers in criminal courts are necessities, not luxuries."[9] Ironically, while the Court concluded that the Sixth Amendment right to counsel is critical, it limited its application to felony cases only. A few years later, in *Argersinger* v. *Hamlin*,[10] the Court extended the right to counsel to misdemeanor cases: "The requirement of counsel may well be necessary for a fair trial even in petty-offense prosecution. We are by no means convinced that legal and constitutional questions involved in a case that actually leads to imprisonment even for a brief period are any less complex than when a person can be sent off for six months or more."[11] The current Sixth Amendment interpretation is that whenever there is a risk of confinement, whether currently or at some point down the line, the right to counsel attaches.[12]

Fifth Amendment and Self-Incrimination How does the Fifth Amendment's provision that no person "shall be compelled in any criminal case to be a witness against himself" relate to the right to counsel? The Supreme Court held in the influential case of *Miranda* v. *Arizona*[13] that "the prosecution may not use statements, whether exculpatory or inculpatory, stemming from *custodial interrogation* of the defendant unless it demonstrates the use of procedural safeguards effective to secure the privilege against self-incrimination."[14]

Miranda applies only during police–citizen encounters that amount to custodial interrogation. Usually this means a person is arrested and then questioned about his or her suspected involvement in a crime, but custody also occurs when a person is "deprived of liberty in any significant way."[15] Interrogation can include the usual questions an officer may ask a criminal suspect, but it can also include actions that amount to the "functional equivalent of a question," including "any words or actions on the part of the police (other than those normally attendant to arrest and custody) that the police should know are reasonably likely to elicit an incriminating response from the suspect."[16] If the police place a bundle of confiscated cash in front of a suspect in order to get a response, this could amount to the functional equivalent of a question.

Miranda requires that police officers make an affirmative and active effort to inform someone of his or her Fifth Amendment rights; they cannot assume that the suspect is aware of his or her constitutional rights. The warnings contain four parts that are now familiar to most Americans:

1. You have the right to remain silent.
2. Anything you say can and will be used against you in court.
3. You have the right to talk with an attorney and to have an attorney present before and during any questioning.
4. If you cannot afford an attorney, one will be appointed free of charge to represent you before and during any questioning.

Gideon v. Wainwright (1963)

In 1961, Clarence Earl Gideon was accused of breaking into and entering the Bay Harbor Poolroom in Panama City, Florida. When brought to trial, Gideon, a penniless drifter too poor to hire a lawyer, asked that the state appoint counsel for him. His request was denied based on the precedent set by the 1942 U.S. Supreme Court ruling in the case of *Betts v. Brady*, which said that the right to a lawyer is not essential to a fair trial.

Gideon was forced to defend himself. One example of damaging testimony came from the taxi driver who picked up Gideon at the pool hall. He quoted Gideon as saying, "Don't tell anyone you picked me up." Gideon, acting in his own defense, did not challenge this statement during the first trial. He was found guilty and sentenced to five years in prison.

From prison, Gideon filed a handwritten petition, *in forma pauperis*, to the U.S. Supreme Court. His "Petition for a Writ of *Certiorari* to the Supreme Court State of Florida" asked the U.S. Supreme Court to hear his case and overrule his conviction on the basis that he was denied a fair trial because he did not have the assistance of counsel at his trial.

In 1963, the Court agreed to hear Gideon's case and ruled that a state must provide legal counsel to anyone charged with a felony who cannot afford a lawyer. The Court found that the Sixth Amendment's guarantee of counsel is a fundamental right, essential to a fair trial.

Gideon was retried and acquitted. His lawyer in the second trial asked the taxi driver—who had given damaging testimony during the first trial—if Gideon had ever asked him before to deny that the driver had picked him up. The taxi driver responded that Gideon said this every time the driver picked him up and suggested that it was because of a problem with his wife.[1]

The Court's landmark ruling in *Gideon v. Wainwright* (1963) has been described as the cause of "the single biggest change in the history of the U.S. criminal justice system."[2] Indeed, former U.S. Attorney General Robert F. Kennedy once said of the case, "If an obscure Florida convict named Clarence Earl Gideon had not sat down in prison with a pencil and paper to write a letter to the Supreme Court; and if the Supreme Court had not taken the trouble to look at the merits in that one crude petition among all the bundles of mail it must receive every day, the vast machinery of American law would have gone on functioning undisturbed. But Gideon did write that letter; the court did look into his case; he was re-tried with the help of competent defense counsel; found not guilty and released from prison after two years of punishment for a crime he did not commit. And the whole course of legal history has been changed."[3]

The effect of *Gideon* has been profound. An eighth-grade dropout, Gideon crafted a plain and simple message that brought to the attention of the nation's highest court an egregious shortcoming in the criminal justice system: Poor and indigent people were not being treated equally under the law because of their inability to obtain legal counsel. The resulting decision ensures that all criminal defendants now have access to counsel, a measure that has certainly prevented uncountable miscarriages of justice such as that which Gideon himself experienced.

The remarkable story of Gideon's successful challenge of the legal system was told in Anthony Lewis's 1964 book *Gideon's Trumpet* and made into a popular 1980 movie of the same title, directed by Robert E. Collins and starring Henry Fonda as Gideon. And what of Clarence Gideon? Following his release in 1963, he resumed his simple life as a laborer and sometime electrician in Florida. On January 18, 1972, at age 61, he died in Fort Lauderdale. His remains were returned to his native Hannibal, Missouri, and interred in an unmarked grave; later, a granite headstone was added to mark the site. ▪

Notes

[1] National Association of Criminal Defense Lawyers, Lesson Plan, *Gideon at 40: Understanding the Right to Counsel* (National Association of Criminal Defense Lawyers: December 2002), pp. 1–2.

[2] Ibid., p. 1.

[3] Clarence Earl Gideon, Wikipedia, available at http://en.wikipedia.org/wiki/Clarence_Earl_Gideon (accessed June 2, 2013).

DISCUSSION QUESTIONS

1. This feature says that "*Gideon* v. *Wainwright* (1963) has been described as the cause of 'the single biggest change in the history of the U.S. criminal justice system.'" What change was that?

2. Which constitutional amendment provides the central focus in *Gideon* v. *Wainwright*? What does that amendment guarantee?

One of three things can occur after the warning is read:

1. The suspect refuses to talk, in which case police questioning must stop.

2. The suspect agrees to talk without the assistance of counsel.

3. The suspect agrees to talk and expresses a desire to have counsel present.

Fourteenth Amendment and Due Process In the 1932 case of *Powell* v. *Alabama*,[17] the Supreme Court reversed the convictions of several poor defendants who were not represented by counsel at their trial. The Court argued, in part, that the defendants' due process rights were violated, not the Sixth Amendment's right to counsel provision. It said that the defendants were "denied due process of law and the equal protection of the laws in contravention of the Fourteenth Amendment."[18]

While a critical milestone in itself, the *Powell* case only applied to "capital case[s], where the defendant is unable to employ counsel, and is incapable adequately of making his own defense because of ignorance, feeble-mindedness, illiteracy, or the like."[19] Because of this limitation, the Supreme Court was forced to return to this issue in a series of cases that relied on the Sixth Amendment.

Effective Assistance of Counsel Over the years, the Supreme Court has paid increasing attention to effective assistance of counsel. In general, defense representation must be effective for the Sixth Amendment to be satisfied. The Sixth Amendment does not explicitly state that effective assistance of counsel is required, but the Supreme Court has interpreted it this way. However, the right to effective assistance applies only where the right to counsel applies. For example, the Supreme Court has held that a defense attorney's failure to file a timely discretionary appeal was not "ineffective" because the right to counsel does not extend to such appeals.[20] Only where counsel is required can an ineffective assistance claim be made.

Ineffective assistance claims can be filed against both retained and appointed counsel. For a time the Supreme Court held that nonindigent defendants who retained their own attorney were bound by that attorney's representation (for better or worse) because there was no "state action" responsible for the ineffective representation. However, in *Cuyler* v. *Sullivan*,[21] the Court held that privately retained counsel can be ineffective in the same way a public defender can.[22]

When Is Counsel Effective? What is effective assistance of counsel? The Supreme Court first tried to answer this question in the 1970 case of *McMann* v. *Richardson*.[23] There, it held that counsel is effective when the legal advice is "within the range of competence demanded of attorneys in criminal cases."[24] This standard was somewhat vague, so the Court offered clarification in *Strickland* v. *Washington*.[25] In that case, the Court created a two-pronged test for determining effective assistance of counsel:

> First, the defendant must show that counsel's performance was deficient. This requires showing that counsel made errors so serious that counsel was not functioning as the "counsel" guaranteed the defendant by the Sixth Amendment. Second, the defendant must show that the deficient performance prejudiced the defense. This requires showing that counsel's errors were so serious as to deprive the defendant of a fair trial, a trial whose result is unreliable.[26]

These two prongs have come to be known as the "performance prong" and the "prejudice prong." Concerning performance, "The proper measure of attorney performance remains simply reasonableness under prevailing professional norms."[27] What are these "norms"? We discuss them further in the "Effective Assistance of Counsel" section that appears in this chapter, but some of the key elements of effective performance include the following:

■ Avoiding conflicts of interest

■ Advocating for the defendant

■ Bringing to bear "such skill and knowledge as will render the trial a reliable adversarial testing process"[28]

■ "[Making] reasonable investigations or . . . [making] a reasonable decision that makes particular investigations unnecessary"[29]

Library Extra
10–3 Defendants in Cases Concluded in U.S. District Court

Library Extra
10–4 Felony Defendants in
Large Urban Counties, 1992:
National Pretrial

As for the prejudice prong of *Strickland*, the defendant must prove that "there is a reasonable probability that, but for counsel's unprofessional errors, the result of the proceeding would have been different."[30] In other words, it is not enough for counsel to be ineffective; if the defendant is to succeed in an argument that his or her Sixth Amendment right to counsel was violated, the defendant must prove that the attorney's ineffectiveness prejudiced the case. This means that little mistakes probably won't matter, but gross incompetence probably does.

When Is Counsel Ineffective?

The *Strickland* performance and prejudice prongs explain somewhat abstractly what could lead counsel to be ineffective. A look at some specific situations will make them clearer.

In *Bell* v. *Cone*,[31] the Supreme Court held that a defense attorney's failure to present any mitigating evidence (factors that may be considered as being extenuating or reducing the defendant's moral culpability) or to make a closing statement at the defendant's capital sentencing hearing did not amount to ineffective assistance. Among the reasons for the Court's decision was that the mitigating evidence that was not presented during the sentencing hearing *was* presented at trial, so the jury did have at least one occasion to review it.

In *Rompilla* v. *Beard*,[32] the Court declared that defense counsel is required to make reasonable efforts to obtain and review material that it knows the prosecution will probably rely on as part of its case, something the defense attorney did not do. Contrast *Beard* with the Court's decision in *Florida* v. *Nixon*.[33] There, the defense attorney acknowledged—in open court—his client's guilt and instead focused his defense on reasons why the defendant's life should be spared; however, the evidence was so clearly indicative of the defendant's guilt that the Supreme Court did not feel that the defense attorney's strategy was ineffective.

There are countless other means by which counsel can be considered ineffective; attorney errors can come in several varieties. Generally, though, the defendant must point to a specific error or set of errors, not the overall performance of his or her counsel. If defense counsel makes a specific error and can offer no explanation for the error, then the defendant will have a good chance in succeeding with a claim of ineffective assistance of counsel, a chance that hinges on the second prong announced in *Strickland*.

Pro Se Defense

Although the Sixth Amendment provides for the right to counsel, accused individuals sometimes prefer to represent themselves. Indeed, according to the Supreme Court, criminal defendants have a constitutional right to represent themselves at trial[34]; this is known as a ***pro se* defense**.

Not every defendant who wishes to proceed without counsel is allowed to do so, however. In *Johnson* v. *Zerbst*,[35] the Supreme Court stated that a defendant may waive counsel only if the waiver is "competent and intelligent." The Court went on to say that "the record must show, or there must be an allegation and evidence must show, that an accused was offered counsel but intelligently and understandingly rejected the offer. Anything less is not a waiver."[36]

What constitutes "intelligently and understandingly" waiving the right to counsel is not always clear. In *Massey* v. *Moore*,[37] the Court offered clarification by stating, "One might not be insane in the sense of being incapable of standing trial and yet lack the capacity to stand trial without benefit of counsel."[38] But in *Godinez* v. *Moran*,[39] a case decided some years later, the Court held that a person who is competent to stand trial is also competent to waive counsel both at trial and for pleading purposes.[40]

In certain circumstances permitting waiver of counsel, the court can require that standby counsel be available to the defendant. **Standby counsel** is simply an attorney who is "standing by" in order to assist the accused when necessary. This was the decision reached in *McKaskle* v. *Wiggins*,[41] where the Court held that judges can appoint standby counsel "to relieve the judge of the need to explain and enforce basic rules of courtroom protocol or to assist the defendant in overcoming routine obstacles that stand in the way of the defendant's achievement of his own clearly indicated goals."[42]

Counsel of the Defendant's Choice? Clearly, defendants who are not indigent can hire counsel of their choosing; unfortunately, indigent defendants do not have such a choice. The Sixth Amendment right to counsel does not guarantee the indigent defendant permission to choose counsel—counsel will be provided. Usually counsel will be a public defender, but if an indigent can show good cause that the attorney appointed to represent him or her is not doing so adequately, another attorney can be appointed. What constitutes inadequate representation was discussed above.

Surprisingly, there are situations where defendants, if they can afford representation, cannot hire counsel of their choice. If, for example, the defendant's choice of an attorney poses serious conflict-of-interest problems, the defendant may be forced to hire another attorney.[43] If the defendant's attorney is not qualified to practice law, then another attorney may also be required.[44] Somewhat controversially, if a defendant's assets are frozen pursuant to a civil forfeiture statute and he or she cannot afford counsel of his or her choosing, then a less expensive attorney may be required or a public defender appointed.[45]

An issue related to counsel of one's choice is whether indigent defendants can retain expert witnesses of their own choosing. In *Ake v. Oklahoma*,[46] the Supreme Court held that an indigent defendant enjoys a constitutional right to an expert witness when the defendant's sanity is at issue; however, the Court limited its holding to provide for one and only one expert, one who is state-employed. Experts in other fields besides psychiatry are generally not provided to indigent defendants. At some point it becomes necessary to assume that the state's experts (e.g., ballistics experts) present objective and accurate testimony that is not prejudicial to the accused.

Right to Confrontation

The Sixth Amendment's provision that accused persons enjoy the right to be "confronted with the witnesses against him" is manifested in three ways. The first method is by allowing the defendant to appear at his or her own trial. In *Illinois v. Allen*, the Supreme Court stated, "One of the most basic of rights guaranteed by the confrontation clause is the accused's right to be present in the courtroom at every stage of his trial."[47] The other two means by which confrontation is manifested include requiring live testimony of witnesses before the defendant and permitting the accused to challenge any witness's statements in open court. Each of these methods of confrontation are considered below.

Defendant's Right to Be Present The defendant would be seriously hampered in his or her ability to confront adverse witnesses if he or she was not allowed to attend the trial. But allowing the defendant to be physically present in the courtroom may not be enough to satisfy the Sixth Amendment's confrontation clause. In particular, if the accused is not competent and is unable to understand what is taking place so as to challenge the opposition, the Sixth Amendment may be violated. This means, then, that the defendant has two rights—to be physically present and to be mentally competent:

1. *Physical presence.* Even though the *Illinois v. Allen* case suggests that the accused enjoys an unqualified right to be present, nothing could be further from the truth. In cases decided after *Allen*, the Court has placed significant restrictions on when the defendant is permitted to be physically present. The Court's decisions indicate that (1) the accused can only be present during "critical"

proceedings[48] and that (2) the defendant's physical presence can be voluntarily waived or forfeited (i.e., given up) by failing to appear or by acting improperly.[49]

2. *Mental competence.* The Supreme Court has held not only that defendants enjoy the right to be present at their own trials (assuming that the right is not waived or forfeited, as discussed above) but also that they must be mentally competent. In other words, the conviction of an incompetent person is unconstitutional.[50] Due process (and, by implication, the right to confrontation) is violated when a defendant cannot understand what is happening to him or her in a criminal trial.

The question of whether a defendant is mentally competent to stand trial is answered by a test announced by the Supreme Court in *Dusky* v. *United States*.[51] The test is whether the defendant "has sufficient present ability to consult with his lawyer with a reasonable degree of rational understanding—and whether he has a rational as well as factual understanding of the proceedings against him."[52] The burden of proving incompetence falls on the defendant.[53]

It is important to understand that this test for competency is different from the insanity defense often discussed in criminal law texts. Competency to stand trial—the type of competency considered here—deals with the defendant's ability to understand what is happening at trial (as well as at pretrial hearings and so on). The insanity defense deals with the defendant's competence at the time of the crime. The issue of competency to stand trial is narrowly concerned with the defendant's ability both to understand what is happening and to communicate with counsel.

The defendant's competency is usually considered in a separate pretrial hearing. This was the rule announced in *Pate* v. *Robinson*,[54] a case dealing with an Illinois trial judge's decision not to hold a hearing on the question of Robinson's mental condition even though he had a long history of mental problems.

Defendant's Right to Hear Live Testimony The Sixth Amendment's mention of confrontation includes, according to the Supreme Court, the defendant's right to **live testimony**. This means that the defendant enjoys the right to have witnesses physically appear in the courtroom to give their testimony. Yet this right is also qualified. Over 100 years ago, the Supreme Court stated, in *Mattox* v. *United States*,[55] that the defendant's right to live testimony is "subject to exceptions, recognized long before the adoption of the Constitution."[56] Consider this example: If a witness is unavailable because he or she is dead, then an exception to the defendant's right to live testimony will be made; similar exceptions are made where witnesses are unavailable for other reasons, such as being in the hospital.

Death and unavailability are considered exceptions to the defendant's right to live testimony. In either situation, the witness's statements are introduced by a third party, which is known as **hearsay**. Hearsay is testimony about what a **declarant** who is not in court has said and is often introduced by someone who hears and then says (hence the term *hearsay*) what the declarant said.

Hearsay is generally not admissible in criminal trials. It is regarded skeptically because if the declarant is not available to be confronted by the defense, then there is no opportunity to question the truthfulness of the declarant's statements. The possibility also exists that the person communicating the declarant's statements may have misunderstood the declarant's intentions or forgot all of what was said out of court.

Even so, there are several exceptions to the so-called **hearsay rule** (the rule that all hearsay is inadmissible) that permit out-of-court statements made by declarants to be admitted at trial. On the surface, these exceptions seem to violate the defendant's right to live testimony, but the Supreme Court nevertheless permits hearsay in limited circumstances.

live testimony
A defendant's constitutional entitlement to have witnesses physically appear in the courtroom to give their testimony.

hearsay
Anything that is not based on the personal knowledge of a witness.

declarant
One who makes a statement or declaration.

hearsay rule
The long-standing practice that hearsay is inadmissible as testimonial evidence in a court of law.

The reader is encouraged to consult an evidence textbook for a full review of specific exceptions to the hearsay rule. The following cases consider only two such exceptions.

One pertinent case is *White v. Illinois*,[57] which dealt with the admissibility at the defendant's trial of out-of-court statements made by a four-year-old girl. The prosecution argued that the statements should be admissible because of the "making a spontaneous declaration" and "seeking medical treatment" exceptions to the hearsay rule (the former admits statements that someone makes in the "heat of the moment," and the latter admits statements that are made while an individual is seeking medical treatment from a doctor). The Court held that the confrontation clause was not violated in this instance.[58]

In the second case, the Court decided on the admissibility of out-of-court statements from a co-conspirator.[59] The Court admitted the statements, claiming that they "derive much of their value from the fact that they are made in a context very different from trial, and therefore are usually irreplaceable as substantive evidence."[60] The Court thought that the out-of-court statements of one co-conspirator to another during a conspiracy should be admitted at trial because it would be difficult to replicate the conversation in a courtroom.

Numerous other hearsay exceptions exist (see Box 10–1). Even if a relevant exception does not exist, a court may still admit the hearsay. Generally, if other "indicia of reliability" exist such that the accuracy and truthfulness of a hearsay statement can be judged, then it may be admissible.[61] These indicia must, according to the Court, be "particularized guarantees of trustworthiness."[62]

BOX 10–1   Common Hearsay Exceptions

- *Present sense impression.* A statement describing or explaining an event or condition made while the declarant [person making the statement] was perceiving the event or condition, or immediately thereafter.

- *Excited utterance.* A statement relating to a startling event or condition made while the declarant was under the stress of excitement caused by the event or condition.

- *Existing mental, emotional, or physical condition.* A statement of the declarant's then existing state of mind, emotion, sensation, or physical condition (such as intent, plan, motive, design, mental feeling, pain, and bodily health) but not including a statement of memory or belief to prove the fact remembered or believed unless it relates to the execution, revocation, identification, or terms of declarant's will.

- *Statements for purposes of medical diagnosis or treatment.* Statements made for purposes of medical diagnosis or treatment and describing medical history or past or present symptoms, pain, or sensations or the inception or general character of the cause or external source thereof insofar as reasonably pertinent to diagnosis or treatment.

- *Recorded recollection.* A memorandum or record concerning a matter about which a witness once had knowledge but now has insufficient recollection to enable the witness to testify fully and accurately, shown to have been made or adopted by the witness when the matter was fresh in the witness's memory and to reflect that knowledge correctly. If admitted, the memorandum or record may be read into evidence but may not itself be received as an exhibit unless offered by an adverse party.

- *Public records and reports.* Records, reports, statements, or data compilations, in any form, of public offices or agencies, setting forth (1) the activities of the office or agency; (2) matters observed pursuant to duty imposed by law as to which matters there was a duty to report, excluding, however, in criminal cases matters observed by police officers and other law enforcement personnel; or (3) in civil actions and proceedings and against the government in criminal cases, factual findings resulting from an investigation made pursuant to authority granted by law, unless the sources of information or other circumstances indicate lack of trustworthiness. ■

Source: "Federal Rules of Evidence," available at www.law.cornell.edu/rules/fre/rules.htm#Rule803 (accessed February 20, 2013).

Defendant's Right to Challenge Witness Testimony Part of the defendant's right to confrontation is the ability to challenge witnesses in the courtroom. The defendant's ability to challenge witnesses is manifested when the witness physically appears in court before the defendant. This type of confrontation permits questioning by the defense and is intended to ensure that the defendant receives a fair shake.

Also, the Court has held that the defendant can be limited in terms of the confrontation—usually accomplished through questioning, specifically **cross-examination**—that he or she can engage in; this cross-examination is conducted by a party other than the party who called the witness. As an example of cross-examination, the state may call a witness in a criminal trial, and once direct examination concludes, the defense has an opportunity to cross-examine the state's witness (see Chapter 13 for more information).

Whereas the scope of questioning in a **direct examination** is broad, the scope of questioning on cross-examination is restricted (i.e., it is limited to matters covered on direct examination), and inquiries into the credibility of the witness are also permissible; together, these two restrictions constitute the **scope of direct rule**. This rule helps ensure that the opposing party (the party conducting the cross-examination or, in our example, the defense) cannot use cross-examination of the witness to direct the jury's attention to other issues not raised by the party calling the witness.

The Supreme Court has had considerably more to say with respect to the defendant's right to challenge witness testimony. It has also addressed cases involving the two issues of whether witnesses must appear in person and whether court-imposed restrictions on the defendant's ability to challenge witness testimony can be sanctioned:

1. *Must witnesses appear in person?* The Supreme Court has identified at least one situation where the defendant's right to challenge witness testimony is not compromised by the absence of a witness. In *Coy v. Iowa*,[63] the Supreme Court considered the constitutionality of a state law that permitted the placement of a large opaque screen between the defendant and two young girls who testified that he sexually assaulted them. It declared that the statute was unconstitutional because "the confrontation clause guarantees the defendant a face-to-face meeting with witnesses appearing before the trier of fact."[64]

   In another case, *Maryland v. Craig*,[65] the Court considered whether a statute permitting a witness's testimony via closed-circuit television was constitutional. The statute provided for such a procedure when the judge determines that face-to-face testimony "will result in the child suffering serious emotional distress such that the child cannot reasonably communicate." The Court upheld the procedure, claiming that it did not violate the confrontation clause. It stated that a "central concern" of the confrontation clause "is to ensure the reliability of the evidence against a criminal defendant by subjecting it to rigorous testing in the context of an adversary proceeding before the trier of fact."[66] Further, it held that the statute in question did "not impinge upon the truth-seeking or symbolic purposes of the confrontation clause."[67]

2. *Are court-imposed restrictions on cross-examination acceptable?* The Supreme Court has more than once considered the constitutionality of state- or court-imposed restrictions on the defendant's right to cross-examine. In *Smith v. Illinois*,[68] the Court considered whether the prosecution can conceal the identity of a witness who is a police informant. The Court held that the witness's identity must be revealed because such information "opens countless avenues of in-court examination and out-of-court investigation."[69]

cross-examination
The questioning of a witness at trial by the opposing counsel.

direct examination
The questioning of a witness by the attorney for the side (prosecution or defense) that originally scheduled that witness to testify. As a general rule, the questions on direct examination must be specific but not leading.

scope of direct rule
A rule that restricts the questions that may be asked on cross-examination to only those matters addressed on direct examination or to inquiries into the credibility of the witness.

COURTS IN THE NEWS

Mental Incompetency Rulings: A Growing Problem for U.S. Courts

James Holmes killed 12 people in a Colorado movie theater. Is it possible that such a bizarre act could be the product of a sound mind?

RJ SANGOSTI/POOL/EPA/Newscom

On July 20, 2012, a heavily armed James Holmes walked into the Century movie theater in Aurora, Colorado, during a midnight screening of the film *The Dark Knight Rises*, set off tear gas grenades, and shot into the audience with a 12-gauge Remington 870 Express Tactical shotgun, a Smith & Wesson M&P15 with a 100-round drum magazine, and a Glock 22 handgun. When he was done, 12 innocent people were dead and 58 more wounded, the highest number of casualties in an American mass shooting Details soon developed about Holmes's mental state. Classmates, teachers, and family all revealed that they knew this was a young man in mental distress. He had sought and received care from a psychiatrist at the University of Colorado, but the relationship was severed when Holmes withdrew from the university. Once he was no longer enrolled, it is unclear to what extent he sought or received further treatment. While in jail awaiting trial, Holmes was hospitalized after making several suicide attempts. Should a person as disturbed as Holmes be tried as a criminal or treated as someone severely mentally ill?

A pressing issue facing America's courts today is that a growing number of defendants are being declared mentally incompetent to stand trial. The U.S. Supreme Court defined *competency to stand trial* as "a sufficient present ability to consult with one's attorney with a reasonable degree of rational understanding, and . . . a rational as well as factual understanding of the legal proceedings against him."

Data from 10 of the 12 largest U.S. states show significant increases in incompetency declarations, with some states reporting as much as a 100% rise in the past five years.[2] The economic impact of these increases is enormous. In Florida alone, for example, the current annual bill for treatment aimed at restoring defendants' mental fitness is about $250 million, and state officials expect that cost to double in the next seven years.

These massive costs are just one problem related to this issue, however. The sheer numbers of claimants place a tremendous burden on already limited public mental health resources. California's Department of Mental Health, for example, reports that occupancy of its 5,000 mental hospital beds has increased from 500 more than a decade ago to 4,500 now. Officials attribute the 900% increase to demands placed on the system by the requirement to provide beds for accused and convicted offenders.

It is also becoming increasingly difficult to plan for the provision of mental health services to defendants. Fluctuations in the inclination of judges to invoke the services, coupled with changes in the laws relating to legal mental competency, create an environment of uncertainty. In a recent 7–2 decision, for example, the U.S. Supreme Court decision ruled that "a defendant can be held to be competent to stand trial but held incompetent to represent himself." George Washington University Law School Professor Jonathan Turley calls the decision "an invitation for judges to make their lives easier by preventing self-representation."

There is an air of certainty, however, about future funding of the increased mental health needs associated with findings of mental incompetency among criminal defendants. In an era of austere (even shrinking) public budgets, officials will be forced to scramble for every economic advantage to meet these growing demands.

Courts and criminal justice officials, meanwhile, face the difficult problem of resolving what to do with defendants found to be mentally incompetent to stand trial. In most jurisdictions, such a finding mandates that the defendants be held in an appropriate mental health facility and provided treatment in an attempt to restore their competency. But they cannot simply be held indefinitely. Thus, if a defendant is unresponsive to treatment, he or she will ultimately be released from the treatment facility without ever having to stand before the bar to answer for the crime(s) that led to his or her placement in the treatment facility to begin with.

Restoration to competency is normally accomplished through the use of psychoactive medications. Interestingly, however, researchers found that in cases where defendants received treatment involving videos and instructions on courtroom procedures in addition to medication, 43% were found more likely to be competent on reevaluation, compared to just 15% of those receiving medication alone.

(continued)

Mental incompetence represents a special challenge for all aspects of the justice system. Courts, in particular, are charged with assessing claims of mental incompetence in order to determine whether a particular defendant can understand the nature of the charges against him or her and whether he or she should be tried on those charges—or perhaps sent to a mental health facility for treatment. Significantly, claims of incompetence may be tied to wrongful convictions, and mental incompetence can increase the likelihood of wrongful convictions if not properly recognized because it increases the chances that a defendant will plead guilty or will be unable to assist in mounting an effective defense. ■

DISCUSSION QUESTIONS

1. Why is the number of cases involving mental incompetence reported to be increasing? What's behind the rise?

2. Competency claims are gaining acceptance among judges, prosecutors, and defense lawyers in part because of growing efforts to identify the wrongfully convicted. What might mental incompetence have to do with wrongful convictions?

Sources: BBC, "Profile: Aurora Cinema Shooting Suspect James Holmes," July 21, 2012, available at www.bbc.co.uk/news/world-us-canada-18937513 (accessed June 2, 2013); *Dusky* v. *United States*, 362 U.S. 402 (1960); Kevin Johnson and Andrew Seaman, "Mentally Incompetent Defendants on Rise," *USA Today*, May 28, 2008, available at http://usatoday30.usatoday.com/news/washington/judicial/2008-05-28-Incompetent_N .htm?csp=34 (accessed June 2, 2013); *Indiana* v. *Edwards*, 554 U.S. 164 (2008); Jonathan Turley, "Court Rules That Mentally Disturbed Defendants Can Be Competent to Stand Trial but Incompetent to Represent Themselves," available at http://jonathanturley.org/2008/06/20/court-rules-that-mentally-disturbed-defendants-can-be-competent-to-stand-trial-but-incompetent-to-represent-themselves (accessed June 2, 2013); A. M. Siegel and A. Elwork, "Treating Incompetence to Stand Trial," *Human Behavior*, Vol. 14, No. 1 (1990), pp. 57–65.

In another case, *Davis* v. *Alaska*,[70] the Court considered whether the identity of juveniles who testify at criminal trials can be disguised. There, the state's lead witness in the defendant's burglary trial was a juvenile witness. The Court held that the juvenile's identity should have been revealed because "the right of confrontation is paramount to the State's policy of protecting a juvenile offender."[71]

In summary, the defense is given wide latitude in terms of its authority to cross-examine. Courts and states cannot conceal the identity of witnesses testifying against the defense, nor can they bar cross-examination simply because the defense is calling the witness it wishes to cross-examine. Finally, the defendant's right to cross-examine rarely is violated if the prosecution fails to produce documentation of a witness's out-of-court statements where they are not at all exculpatory.

The "Dark Side" of Confrontation   Guaranteeing defendants the right to be present at trial could be prejudicial or harmful. First, if the defendant is present but refuses to take the stand and testify, as is guaranteed by the Fifth Amendment, the jury may conclude that the defendant has something to hide. The Supreme Court has been so concerned with this possibility that it has prohibited the prosecution from calling attention to the defendant's refusal to testify[72]; it even required judges to advise jury members that no adverse inferences can be drawn from the defendant's refusal to testify.[73]

The defendant's presence may also be prejudicial because by virtue of being in the courtroom, the defendant may remind jurors about the crime. It is often thought, in fact, that a defendant who is dressed in prison attire is not viewed the same, in the eyes of a jury, as someone who is dressed in street clothes. An illustrative case concerning this matter is *Estelle* v. *Williams*.[74] In that case, the Supreme Court held that a state may not compel the defendant to wear jail attire in the courtroom and concluded that a "constant reminder of the accused's condition implicit in such distinctive, identifiable attire may affect a juror's judgment."[75]

Right to Compulsory Process

The compulsory process clause of the Sixth Amendment mandates the **compulsory process** by providing that the defendant can use subpoenas to obtain witnesses, documents, and other objects that are helpful to his or her defense. This right was made binding on the states in *Washington* v. *Texas*,[76] a case in which the Supreme Court stated that compulsory process protects the "right to offer the testimony of witnesses, and to compel their attendance."[77]

Several state and federal statutes govern compulsory process, as do the Federal Rules of Criminal Procedure. Figure 10–1 contains an example of a subpoena typically used in a criminal case. The Supreme Court has also been vocal on the subject. For example, in *Roviaro* v. *United States*, the prosecution refused to provide the defense with the identity of a police informant.[78] The Court recognized that the government had a significant interest in concealing the identity of the informant—mainly to further its efforts in combating illicit drugs—but it also found that the defendant's right to confrontation was denied by the prosecution's refusal to release the witness's identity. The informant was the only witness to the drug transaction for which Roviaro was charged, so it is clear that the defense would have a difficult time mounting an effective case without this witness.

In another case, *Chambers* v. *Mississippi*, the Supreme Court overturned the conviction of a defendant who was not allowed to put three witnesses on the stand.[79] The defendant had attempted to prove that another person, MacDonald, committed the murder for which he was charged, and the three people he wanted to put on the stand were those to whom MacDonald had allegedly confessed. The Court felt that the witnesses' testimony should have been admissible, even though it would have been considered hearsay, because MacDonald "spontaneously" confessed to each person, making it likely that their testimony would be truthful and accurate. The Court felt that "the exclusion of this critical evidence, coupled with the State's refusal to permit Chambers to cross-examine MacDonald, denied him a trial in accord with traditional and fundamental standards of due process."[80]

compulsory process
A defendant's constitutional entitlement to use subpoenas to obtain witnesses, documents, and other objects that are helpful to his or her defense.

The Defendant's Marginal Role

While the defendant is at the center of the drama that makes up a criminal case and has the rights to counsel, to confrontation, and to a compulsory process, he or she generally sits idly by while the process plays out. Except in rare cases where defendants represent themselves, they are mostly at the mercy of their retained or appointed attorneys. Additionally, since most defendants are undereducated, they often have considerable difficulty even understanding the events occurring before them. As we saw in Chapter 9, many defendants are distrustful of authority figures, even their own attorneys. One classic study put it this way:

> [Most defendants] submit to the painful consequences of conviction but do not know for certain whether they committed any of the crimes of which they are accused. Such defendants are so unschooled in law that they form no firm opinion about their technical innocence or guilt.[81]

Victim Characteristics

The National Crime Victimization Survey tells us a great deal about the characteristics of crime victims. Men are the most frequent victims of violent crime, as shown in Figure 10–2, but not by a large margin. The typical victim of violent crime is also black, American Indian, or multiracial. Only Asians and Pacific Islanders are victimized less than whites. Finally, most victimizations are concentrated in a person's earlier years; the peak periods are the teen years, followed by a leveling off thereafter. The most victimization-prone group ranges from 12 to 17 years of age.

Learning Objective 3
Characterize typical crime victims.

Web Extra
10–1 National Crime Victim Law Institute

Web Extra
10–2 National Organization for Victim Assistance

UNITED STATES DISTRICT COURT
for the

United States of America)
v.)
) Case No.
_____)
Defendant)

SUBPOENA TO TESTIFY AT A HEARING OR TRIAL IN A CRIMINAL CASE

To:

YOU ARE COMMANDED to appear in the United States district court at the time, date, and place shown below to testify in this criminal case. When you arrive, you must remain at the court until the judge or a court officer allows you to leave.

| Place of Appearance: | Courtroom No.: |
| | Date and Time: |

You must also bring with you the following documents, electronically stored information, or objects *(blank if not applicable)*:

Date: _____

CLERK OF COURT

_____
Signature of Clerk or Deputy Clerk

The name, address, e-mail, and telephone number of the attorney representing *(name of party)* _____
_____ , who requests this subpoena, are:

FIGURE 10–1

Sample Subpoena

Source: www.uscourts.gov/uscourts/FormsAndFees/Forms/AO089.pdf (accessed February 20, 2013).

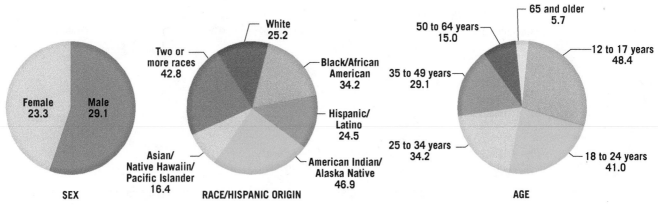

SEX

RACE/HISPANIC ORIGIN

AGE

*Excludes persons of Hispanic origin.

FIGURE 10–2

Violent Victimizations per 1,000 Persons Age 12 or Older

Source: Jennifer Truman, Lynn Langton, and Michael Planty, *Criminal Victimization, 2012* (Washington, DC: Bureau of Justice Statistics, 2013), http://www .bjs.gov/content/pub/pdf/cv12.pdf (accessed December 8, 2013).

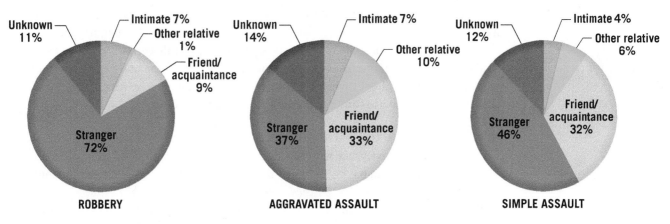

ROBBERY

AGGRAVATED ASSAULT

SIMPLE ASSAULT

FIGURE 10–3

Victim–Offender Relationships for Male Victims in Violent Offenses

Source: J. L. Truman, *Criminal Victimization, 2010* (Washington, DC: Bureau of Justice Statistics, 2011), available at http://bjs.ojp.usdoj.gov/content/pub/pdf/ cv10.pdf (accessed February 20, 2013).

Victim–Offender Relationships

The media give the unfortunate impression that most crimes are random acts of violence, but reality is much more complex. First, violent crimes are the exception; property crime is *far* more common. Second, most crimes are not random. Whether a crime is truly random depends on the offense in question, as revealed in Figure 10–3 (male victims) and Figure 10–4 (female victims). Reported in both figures are percentages of violent victimizations based on victim–offender relationships (intimate partners, acquaintances, and so on).

Figures 10–3 and 10–4 show that many aggravated assaults and simple assaults are committed by acquaintances. In contrast, and not unexpectedly, the majority of robberies occur between parties who do not know each other.

Web Extra
10–3 What You Can Do If You Are a Victim of Crime

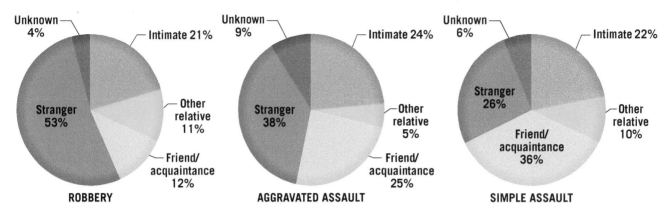

FIGURE 10–4

Victim-Offender Relationships for Female Victims in Violent Offenses

Source: J. L. Truman, *Criminal Victimization, 2010* (Washington, DC: Bureau of Justice Statistics, 2011), available at http://bjs.ojp.usdoj.gov/content/pub/pdf/cv10.pdf (accessed February 20, 2013).

Victim Attitudes and Images

Web Extra
10–4 Office on Violence against Women

Victims once played a prominent role in the court process, that is, until the prosecutor came along. In this day and age, if defendants are said to have a marginal role in the court process, the victims' role lies somewhere off the page altogether. While certain advances have been made to get victims more involved (we look at them toward the end of this chapter), victims still have little direct involvement in the court process—and certainly very little effect on actual case outcomes (other than through giving testimony).

Victim Attitudes toward the Courts Crime victims have repeatedly complained about the difficulties they face while participating in the court process.[82] The problems they face run the gamut from having difficulty finding the courthouse to dealing with long delays and problems securing services, if they are even available.

Researchers have also known for years that criminal victimization leads to psychological problems in victims.[83] For example, victims of physical assaults often display signs of post-traumatic stress.[84] Similar findings have been reported for rape victims who testify.[85] Victims are not always interested in attending the trial of those who victimized them—partly out of fear that the trial will open old wounds.[86] Some researchers have found, in fact, that the trial brings back symptoms of post-traumatic stress.[87]

Web Extra
10–5 National Center for Victims of Crime

Most victims just want to be involved in some capacity. According to a U.S. Justice Department study, "The right to participate in the process of justice, including the right to attend criminal proceedings and to be heard at various points in the criminal justice process, is important to crime victims."[88] Victims' main concerns are with factors such as the following:[89]

- Being informed about whether anyone was arrested
- Being involved in the decision to drop the case
- Being informed about the defendant's release on bond
- Being informed about the date of the defendant's earliest possible release from incarceration
- Being heard in decisions about the defendant's release on bond
- Discussing the case with the prosecutor's office
- Discussing whether the defendant's plea to a lesser charge should be accepted

- Making a victim impact statement during the defendant's parole hearing
- Being present during the grand jury hearing
- Being present during release hearings
- Being informed about postponement of grand jury hearings
- Making a victim impact statement before sentencing
- Being involved in the decision about what sentence should be given

Court Impressions of Victims   Recall from Figures 10–3 and 10–4 that a significant number of violent crimes occur between strangers. This means that once a person is arrested, charged, and put on trial, the prosecution often must rely on witnesses who are known or related to the defendant to build its case. Victims do not always want to cooperate. This has been especially apparent in the domestic-violence context, where prosecutors have frequently been faced with the problem of a victim who refuses to testify against the abuser.[90] In light of such difficulties, some prosecutors have resorted to evidence-based prosecutions or no-drop prosecution policies (see Chapter 8), where they proceed with or without victim cooperation.[91]

Web Extra
10–6 Office for Victims of Crime Online Directory of Crime Victim Services

Victim Involvement in the Court Process

In light of the mind-set that the American system of criminal justice caters too much to criminals, some people have argued that victims need more involvement in the criminal process. There has been a significant push toward more victim involvement in recent years. Victims have called for everything from more involvement in the criminal process to financial assistance to help them recoup their losses. Legislation has even been passed to provide victims with certain rights, and there has also been a movement to alter the Constitution with an amendment concerning victims' rights.

Learning Objective 4
Describe victims' involvement in the court process.

The Movement to Get Victims Involved

Before the nineteenth century, victims did play an important role in the criminal process: Before prosecutors tried criminal cases, victims would represent themselves before judges. But as prosecutors came to try criminal cases and as concerns for the rights of individuals accused of crimes became more pronounced, victims slipped into relative obscurity.

During the 1970s especially, calls were heard for a return to past practices, and a desire was expressed to get victims more involved in the criminal process. Victims groups started to organize themselves and to argue that their lack of involvement in the criminal process was unfair and that the justice system was stacked in favor of criminals.

No single event ushered in the victims' rights movement. Traditionally, police and prosecutors rarely (if ever) informed victims of the status of criminal cases. Victims were left wondering whether criminals were tried and, if they were, whether they were sentenced to prison and when they were released (if they were). Victims also had no say in plea agreements or in the sentences handed down by judges.

Interest groups also gave the victims' rights movement a voice. For example, Mothers Against Drunk Driving (MADD) led a national movement against drunk drivers to protect victims of drunk driving. Certain laws, such as three-strikes laws, have been passed in the wake of outcries over crime victims, and even some groups that have historically opposed victims' rights are now part of the movement.[92]

The victims' rights movement has been responsible for at least two major changes. One is the provision of assistance to victims; this assistance comes in several forms,

Web Extra
10–7 California Department of Justice Office of Victims' Services

Web Extra
10–8 U.S. Office of Sex Offender Sentencing, Monitoring, Apprehending, Registering, and Tracking (SMART)

Payne v. Tennessee (1991)

In *Payne* v. *Tennessee* (1991), the U.S. Supreme Court took the unusual step of overturning two earlier decisions relating to the same question before the Court. In *Booth* v. *Maryland* (1987) and *South Carolina* v. *Gathers* (1989), the Court had declared the *per se* inadmissibility of evidence and argument relating to the victim and the impact of the victim's death on the victim's family at a capital sentencing hearing. *Payne* reversed those rulings, declaring that the "Eighth Amendment erects no *per se* bar prohibiting a capital sentencing jury from considering 'victim impact' evidence relating to the victim's personal characteristics and the emotional impact of the murder on the victim's family, or precluding a prosecutor from arguing such evidence at a capital sentencing hearing."[1]

The facts of the case are clear—and horrifying. On June 27, 1987, following a morning and early afternoon spent injecting cocaine, drinking beer, and reading pornographic magazines, Pervis Tyrone Payne visited the apartment of his girlfriend, Bobbie Thomas. Finding that Thomas was not at home, Payne entered the occupied apartment of 28-year-old Charisse Christopher, whose apartment was located across the hall from Thomas's. Christopher; her two-year-old daughter, Lacie; and her three-year-old son, Nicholas, were in the apartment when Payne entered.

When he began making sexual advances toward Christopher, she resisted, and Payne became violent. A neighbor reported hearing Christopher screaming to the children to "get out, get out." Then, after a brief period of silence, the neighbor stated that he heard a "blood-curdling scream."

Called to the scene, police found blood-covered walls and floors throughout the unit and Charisse and her children lying on the kitchen floor. Charisse and Lacie were dead. Despite several wounds inflicted by a butcher knife that completely penetrated through his body from front to back, Nicholas was still breathing. After undergoing seven hours of surgery and a transfusion of 1,700 cc of blood—400 to 500 cc more than his estimated normal blood volume—Nicholas miraculously survived.

Later that evening, Payne was found hiding in the attic of a former girlfriend's home. Blood on his body and clothes matched the blood of the victims, and he had several scratches across his chest. On arrest, he stated to the arresting officers, "Man, I ain't killed no woman." The overwhelming evidence against him led the jury to quickly and unanimously convict him.

During the sentencing phase, the defense presented testimonial evidence from Payne's mother and father and his girlfriend, Bobbie Thomas, regarding Payne's sterling character. Also offered was the testimony of Dr. John T. Hutson, a privately hired clinical psychologist specializing in criminal court evaluation work. Hutson classified Payne as "mentally handicapped," as evidenced by the low score that Payne achieved on an IQ test. He also stated that Payne was neither psychotic nor schizophrenic and that he was the most polite prisoner Hutson had ever met.

The state countered these character-bolstering witnesses with testimony from Christopher's mother, Mary Zvolanek. The prosecutor elicited an emotion-evoking description from Zvolanek of the effects the crime had on her grandson, Nicholas. Then, during his closing argument for the death penalty, the prosecutor repeatedly hammered home the continuing effects of the crime on Nicholas. Payne was sentenced to death on each of the murder counts.

On appeal to the Tennessee Supreme Court, the defense contended that the grandmother's testimony and the prosecutor's closing argument "constituted prejudicial violations of his rights under the Eighth Amendment as applied in *Booth* v. *Maryland* … and *South Carolina* v. *Gathers*."[2] The Tennessee Supreme Court rejected those contentions, and Payne sought relief from the U.S. Supreme Court.

In its finding, the Court stated that, contrary to its rulings in *Booth* and *Gathers*, "We are now of the view that a State may properly conclude that for the jury to assess meaningfully the defendant's moral culpability and blameworthiness, it should have before it at the sentencing phase evidence of the specific harm caused by the defendant." Further, the Court explained its turn away from its own rulings in *Booth* and *Gathers* thusly: "By turning the victim into a 'faceless stranger at the penalty phase of a capital trial,' . . . *Gathers* . . . *Booth* deprives the State of the full moral force of its evidence and may prevent the jury from having before it all the information necessary to determine the proper punishment for a first-degree murder."[3]

In concluding her compelling study of victims' rights reform, Jennifer K. Wood expressed the following concerns about the Court's ruling in *Payne*: "If the degree of the defendant's guilt is determined in part by a contest with the victim's innocence, those who harm 'guilty' victims have very little to fear. When the legal system relies upon testimony about the victim's characteristics as a basis for determining whether an offender lives or dies, it further entrenches relations of power between races, sexes, ages, sexualities, and economic classes. The discourse of 'innocent victims' the Court uses in *Payne* v. *Tennessee* may benefit some victims like Nicholas Christopher and his family. Unfortunately, it ignores most victims of violent crime by requiring them to establish their innocence—and their worth as human beings—on the basis of their characteristics."[4]

Death penalty proponents hail *Payne* as a balancing of the scales, arguing that if the defense is allowed to present character testimonials for the defendant as mitigating factors at sentencing, the prosecution should be allowed to present extenuating factors, such as the effects of the defendant's crimes on the victims, as a counterbalance. Not surprisingly, opponents of capital punishment see such descriptions merely as efforts to inflame the passions of the jury against the defendant.

It is unlikely that a middle ground will ever be reached. In the meantime, as with all controversial holdings from the

U.S. Supreme Court, the finding in *Payne* holds sway—
for the moment. ■

Notes

1 *Payne v. Tennessee*, 501 U.S. 808 (1991).

2 Ibid.

3 Ibid.

4 Jennifer K. Wood, "Refined Raw: The Symbolic Violence of
Victims' Rights Reforms," *College Literature*, Winter 1999, p. 14.

DISCUSSION QUESTIONS

1. What was the central issue before the Court in *Payne* v.
Tennessee? How did the Court rule?

2. What is meant by "innocent victims"? What other kinds of
victims are there? What difference might a victim's innocence make in a criminal trial?

3. Do you believe that the standards established in *Payne* v.
Tennessee should be retained? Why or why not?

such as shelters for domestic-violence victims and financial assistance. The other major change is the emergence of victims' rights. Victims' rights also come in several
forms: Victims are sometimes given a voice in the sentencing phase of trials, and they
are also being granted the right to be notified of the progress of criminal cases. More
broadly, though, the victims' rights movement has been concerned largely with in-
troducing equity into the criminal process and promoting fairness for all the parties
involved. The movement is about balancing victim and offender interests to the fullest
extent possible.

Victims' Assistance

Victims' assistance was spearheaded by the **Victims of Crime Act** of 1984, which
provided about $50 million each year for victim assistance programs. By 1997, about
one-third of all police departments and sheriff's offices had a unit for providing victim
assistance[93]; prosecutor's offices also provided extensive services to victims.[94] Prosecutor's offices have taken steps to reach out to victims, allowing them to receive updates on
the status of criminal cases. For example, the Hennepin County Attorney's Office, which
serves the city of Minneapolis, provides a community prosecution link on its website
that allows victims and other concerned persons to track the progress of criminal cases
throughout the county.[95]

Victims of Crime Act (1984)
The federal legislation that
spearheaded the establishment
of victims' assistance programs
nationally.

Victims' services are also provided without criminal justice system involvement. For example, shelters for victims of domestic violence are often maintained in communities and
do not necessarily rely on government funding or involvement by police and/or prosecutors.
According to one study, there are some 1,300 domestic-violence shelters in the United
States.[96]

Victim compensation programs are also popping up around the country. For example, in
1965, California voters passed the first crime victims' compensation law. In the 1980s, some
44 states had similar laws, and the 1984 Victims of Crime Act provided financial support for
state and local governments to develop victim compensation programs.

Don't confuse victim compensation programs with restitution. Sometimes judges order restitution, in which case offenders are required to compensate their victims. Victim
compensation programs, in contrast, usually are something of a government-sponsored
insurance program that provides funds (usually limited to a certain amount) to help
people recover their losses experienced as a result of a crime; such losses could include
medical bills, wages, and related expenses. Unfortunately, the research on victim compensation programs has not been particularly encouraging. One study revealed that victim attitudes toward the criminal justice process did not improve in the wake of such
programs.[97] In the following "Courts in the News" feature, another kind of victim's
rights is discussed.

COURTS IN THE NEWS

Helping Victims Who Cannot Help Themselves

© ZUMA Press, Inc./Alamy

For more than 40 years, disabled men were housed in this former school and forced to work in unsanitary and unsafe conditions.

In 2009, 32 men with intellectual disabilities, ages 40 to 60, were emancipated from a century-old schoolhouse in Atalissa, Iowa. For most of their adult lives, they had worked for next to nothing and lived in dangerously unsanitary conditions.

In 2013, the Equal Employment Opportunity Commission (EEOC) won a $240 million judgment against the turkey-processing company at which the men worked. The civil suit involved severe physical and emotional abuse of men with intellectual disabilities. When jurors announced the judgment, Sherri Brown, the sister of one of the 32 men, broke down in tears.

"I totally lost it," she said later. "I wanted the jury to make a statement so that my brother Keith and all of those men would know that someone had heard them. And if this isn't a statement, I don't know what is." The $240 million judgment reflects $2 million in compensatory damages plus $5.5 million in punitive damages for each man.

This case highlights the difficulty of preventing and identifying the abuse of vulnerable workers who are also the least likely to come forward about violations. Robert Canino, prosecutor for the EEOC, said, "[H]opefully we don't ever in the future have to ask the question 'How could this go on for so long and nobody notice?'"

Over a period of 40 years, hundreds of disabled men were sent from Texas to Iowa to work in the turkey-processing plant. When authorities visited the facility, they found that windows were boarded up, allowing little ventilation or light. The cockroaches were overwhelming. A leaky roof, mildew, accumulated grease, and mice droppings contributed to an overwhelming stench. A fire marshal immediately condemned the building, later testifying that it was the worst he had seen in nearly 3,000 inspections.

The men had worked at a nearby processing plant, gutting turkeys. A contractor was paid to oversee the men's work and living arrangements. The supervisors hit, kicked, handcuffed, and verbally abused the men, each of whom were paid $2 per day. This went on for three decades, affecting 32 men. Medical exams later revealed that the men suffered from diabetes, hypertension, malnutrition, festering fungal infections, and severe dental problems that had gone untreated. It went on and on because the men knew nothing better and because no one reported the abuse.

Kenneth Henry, the owner of Hill County Farms, acknowledged paying the men $65 a month but denied knowing about the neglect or abuse. Robert Canino, the prosecuting attorney for the EEOC office that won the verdict, says, "We are always shocked to find out about these extreme cases because we don't believe that they could have happened in our own backyard." The EEOC is making a priority of prosecuting cases involving "vulnerable workers." Examples include migrant farmworkers who are raped by supervisors in the fields or those who are the most likely to be exploited and least able to speak out in their own defense.

Some people criticize lawyers as people interested only in money. But does this case show that they actually perform an important public service, helping those who cannot help themselves? Should criminal charges be brought against the owners in this case? If yes, what would they be? ■

Sources: Yuki Noguchi, "A 'Wake-Up Call' to Protect Vulnerable Workers from Abuse," National Public Radio, May 16, 2013, available at www.npr.org/2013/05/16/184491463/disabled-workers-victory-exposes-risks-to-most-vulnerable (accessed June 2, 2013); Clark Kauffman, "Abused Disabled Iowa Workers Awarded $240M," *USA Today*, May 1, 2013, available at www.usatoday.com/story/money/business/2013/05/01/abused-disabled-iowa-plant-workers-awarded-240m/2126651 (accessed June 2, 2013); Associated Press, "Abused Mentally Disabled Iowa Plant Workers Awarded $240M," Fox News, May 1, 2013, available at www.foxnews.com/us/2013/05/01/abused-mentally-disabled-iowa-plant-workers-awarded-240m/#ixzz2Tewmrfh7 (accessed June 2, 2013).

Victims' Rights

Victims' rights tend to come in two forms. One is giving victims a voice, and the other is granting them the right to notification and participation in the criminal process. See Box 10–2 and Box 10–3 for a listing of victims' rights in two states, Texas and California.

Victims have been granted at least two types of rights by various laws and statutes:

1. *Victims' voice laws.* It has become common to give victims the right to make a statement at an offender's sentencing or parole hearing. These statements, known as victim impact statements, either are made orally before the trial judge or parole board or are provided in writing. Written statements are sometimes preferred because an actual appearance may be traumatic for the victim.

BOX 10–2   Selected Victims' Rights in Texas

A victim, guardian of a victim, or close relative of a deceased victim is entitled to the following rights within the criminal justice system:

- The right to receive from law enforcement agencies adequate protection from harm and threats of harm arising from cooperation with prosecution efforts

- The right to have the magistrate take the safety of the victim or his family into consideration as an element in fixing the amount of bail for the accused

- The right to be informed, when requested, by a peace officer concerning the defendant's right to bail and the procedures in criminal investigations and by the district attorney's office concerning the general procedures in the criminal justice system, including general procedures in guilty plea negotiations and arrangements, restitution, and the appeals and parole process

- The right to provide pertinent information to a probation department conducting a presentencing investigation concerning the impact of the offense on the victim and his family by testimony, written statement, or any other manner prior to any sentencing of the offender

- The right to receive information regarding compensation to victims of crime as provided by Subchapter B including information related to the costs that may be compensated under that subchapter and the amount of compensation, eligibility for compensation and procedures for application for compensation under that subchapter, the payment for a medical examination under Article 56.06 for a victim of a sexual assault, and when requested, to referral to available social service agencies that may offer additional assistance

- The right to be informed, upon request, of parole procedures, to participate in the parole process, to be notified, if requested, of parole proceedings concerning a defendant in the victim's case, to provide to the Board of Pardons and Paroles for inclusion in the defendant's file information to be considered by the board prior to the parole of any defendant convicted of any crime subject to this subchapter, and to be notified, if requested, of the defendant's release

- The right to be provided with a waiting area, separate or secure from other witnesses, including the offender and relatives of the offender, before testifying in any proceeding concerning the offender; if a separate waiting area is not available, other safeguards should be taken to minimize the victim's contact with the offender and the offender's relatives and witnesses, before and during court proceedings

- The right to prompt return of any property of the victim that is held by a law enforcement agency or the attorney for the state as evidence when the property is no longer required for that purpose

- The right to have the attorney for the state notify the employer of the victim, if requested, of the necessity of the victim's cooperation and testimony in a proceeding that may necessitate the absence of the victim from work for good cause ■

Source: Portions of Texas Code of Criminal Procedure, Article 56.02, Crime Victims' Rights, available at www.statutes.legis.state.tx.us/SOTWDocs/CR/htm/CR.56.htm (accessed February 20, 2013).

BOX 10–3   Victims' Bill of Rights, "Marsy's Rights," California Constitution, Article I, Section 28(b)

In order to preserve and protect a victim's rights to justice and due process, a victim shall be entitled to the following rights:

1. To be treated with fairness and respect for his or her privacy and dignity, and to be free from intimidation, harassment, and abuse, throughout the criminal or juvenile justice process.

2. To be reasonably protected from the defendant and persons acting on behalf of the defendant.

3. To have the safety of the victim and the victim's family considered in fixing the amount of bail and release conditions for the defendant.

4. To prevent the disclosure of confidential information or records to the defendant, the defendant's attorney, or any other person acting on behalf of the defendant, which could be used to locate or harass the victim or the victim's family or which disclose confidential communications made in the course of medical or counseling treatment, or which are otherwise privileged or confidential by law.

5. To refuse an interview, deposition, or discovery request by the defendant, the defendant's attorney, or any other person acting on behalf of the defendant, and to set reasonable conditions on the conduct of any such interview to which the victim consents.

6. To reasonable notice of and to reasonably confer with the prosecuting agency, upon request, regarding the arrest of the defendant if known by the prosecutor, the charges filed, the determination whether to extradite the defendant, and, upon request, to be notified of and informed before any pretrial disposition of the case.

7. To reasonable notice of all public proceedings, including delinquency proceedings, upon request, at which the defendant and the prosecutor are entitled to be present and of all parole or other post-conviction release proceedings, and to be present at all such proceedings.

8. To be heard, upon request, at any proceeding, including any delinquency proceeding, involving a post-arrest release decision, plea, sentencing, post-conviction release decision, or any proceeding in which a right of the victim is at issue.

9. To a speedy trial and a prompt and final conclusion of the case and any related post-judgment proceedings.

10. To provide information to a probation department official conducting a pre-sentence investigation concerning the impact of the offense on the victim and the victim's family and any sentencing recommendations before the sentencing of the defendant.

11. To receive, upon request, the pre-sentence report when available to the defendant, except for those portions made confidential by law.

12. To be informed, upon request, of the conviction, sentence, place and time of incarceration, or other disposition of the defendant, the scheduled release date of the defendant, and the release of or the escape by the defendant from custody.

13. To restitution.
    a. It is the unequivocal intention of the People of the State of California that all persons who suffer losses as a result of criminal activity shall have the right to seek and secure restitution from the persons convicted of the crimes causing the losses they suffer.
    b. Restitution shall be ordered from the convicted wrongdoer in every case, regardless of the sentence or disposition imposed, in which a crime victim suffers a loss.
    c. All monetary payments, monies, and property collected from any person who has been ordered to make restitution shall be first applied to pay the amounts ordered as restitution to the victim.

14. To the prompt return of property when no longer needed as evidence.

15. To be informed of all parole procedures, to participate in the parole process, to provide information to the parole authority to be considered before the parole of the offender, and to be notified, upon request, of the parole or other release of the offender.

16. To have the safety of the victim, the victim's family, and the general public considered before any parole or other post-judgment release decision is made.

17. To be informed of the rights enumerated in paragraphs (1) through (16).

A victim, the retained attorney of a victim, a lawful representative of the victim, or the prosecuting attorney upon request of the victim, may enforce the above rights in any trial or appellate court with jurisdiction over the case as a matter of right. The court shall act promptly on such a request. ■

Source: Cal. Const., Art. I, § 28(c)(1).

Researchers have been interested in whether victims' voice laws change the outcome of criminal trials. One study has shown that victims do not participate to the degree the law allows.[98] It revealed, for instance, that only 6% of crime victims exercised their right to speak; moreover, the researchers found that case outcomes were most likely to be influenced by the offender's prior record and the seriousness of the offense.[99] But a later study found that some 60% of crime victims exercised their right to make statements at sentencing,[100] and a study of victim participation in parole hearings revealed that parole was much less likely to be granted when victims argued against it.[101]

2. *Victims' notification and participation.* Laws also provide victims the right to be notified of the status of criminal cases and to participate in the criminal process. One example is California's Proposition 8, which was passed by the state's voters in 1982. It provided that "the victim of any crime, or the next of kin of the victim … has the right to attend all sentencing proceedings . . . [and] to reasonably express his or her views concerning the crime, the person responsible, and the need for restitution."[102] Other states maintain similar laws that grant victims important rights as well as the ability to be involved to varying degrees in the adjudication of criminal cases.

Web Extra
10–9 National Victims' Constitutional Amendment Passage

Should There Be a Victims' Rights Amendment?

In 1979, Wisconsin enacted the nation's first Victim Bill of Rights.[103] Within the following ten years, nearly every other state passed similar bills. More recently still, the state of Rhode Island became the first to amend its constitution to provide for victims' rights, and that led other states to amend their constitutions as well. For example, South Carolina has an amendment to its constitution stating that victims should have rights protected by "[l]aw enforcement agencies, prosecutors, and judges in a manner no less vigorous than the protections afforded criminal defendants."[104] Not long after states amended their constitutions to provide victims rights, calls were heard to amend the federal Constitution in a similar fashion. Such an amendment does not exist yet, but there has been a fervent debate concerning the need for one.

Ronald Reagan was the first president to propose support for victims' rights at the federal level. In 1982, he impaneled the Task Force on Victims' Rights, which ultimately recommended an attachment to the Sixth Amendment as follows: "The victim has the right to be present and to be heard at all critical stages of judicial proceedings."[105] No action was taken, but the task force's recommendation was significant. Thereafter, another organization, known as the National Organization for Victim Assistance, recommended adoption of a stand-alone amendment providing for various victim protections:

> Victims of crime are entitled to certain basic rights, including, but not limited to, the right to be informed, to be present, and to be heard at all critical stages of the federal and state criminal process to the extent that these rights do not interfere with existing Constitutional rights.[106]

Yet another proposed amendment was offered up by the Victims' Constitutional Network:

> Victims of crime are entitled to certain basic rights including the right to be informed of, to be present at and to be heard at all critical stages of the criminal justice process, to the extent that these rights do not interfere with the constitutional rights of the accused. The legislature is authorized to enforce the amendment by appropriate enabling legislation.[107]

Of course, neither of these proposals resulted in a new constitutional amendment, but they made clear the level to which victims' rights advocates were prepared to go to ensure proper protection. The upside of an amendment would be stability because victims would enjoy protections regardless of who is in the White House or which party is dominating Congress.

The prospect of a victims' rights amendment raises several critical questions: Who would be responsible for infringements? Would criminal charges result, or would lawsuits be filed? Also, who could be considered a victim? Immediate family members? Friends? Other relatives? Coworkers? There are no answers because crime can affect a number of people, even in ways that can't be quantified or understood.

Other Victim Remedies   Even in the absence of victims' voice laws and other forms of victim involvement, crime victims can still seek other remedies for their suffering. For example, they can sue for monetary damages, or, in the case of domestic violence and other violent crimes, they can seek restraining orders. There are other avenues of redress besides just those that are a product of the victims' rights movement.

Censorship   Has the victims' rights movement run its course? Some courts have taken steps to put certain "hot-button" words on ice by prohibiting witnesses and victims from uttering them in court. An increasing number of courts across the country are prohibiting words such as "rape," "victim," "homicide," "drunk," "murderer," and "crime scene."[108] Why would a court do this? The intent is to afford the defendant the right to a fair trial— presumably words like "rape" and "victim" can bias a jury in favor of the prosecution. A criminal defense lawyer who has succeeded in having judges bar certain words from court cases said this:

> It only makes sense. You don't want the witnesses and officers of law enforcement talking as if it was a foregone conclusion, almost drumming it into the jurors' minds that a crime was committed by virtue of the fact that there is a victim. . . . I think the courts are more and more open to restricting terminology like this because of the number of wrongful convictions that have been demonstrated to have occurred in the U.S.[109]

But isn't censorship of this sort a slap in the face to crime victims everywhere? It can certainly make the prosecution's case a little more difficult. As one prosecutor said, "It's pretty hard to prosecute a murder case without being able to say the word *murder*."[110] Another district attorney said this about prosecuting a rape case: "You have a woman who's been attacked and she has to say that she had sexual intercourse with the man, rather than calling him her attacker? . . . I think this is going 50 years back in our legal evolution."[111] Some sort of balance will have to be struck.

SUMMARY

1. CHARACTERIZE TYPICAL CRIMINAL DEFENDANTS

- Most defendants are male, black, and young.
- Child abuse and infanticide are two crimes committed more often by women than men.

2. SUMMARIZE DEFENDANTS' RIGHTS DURING THE COURT PROCESS

- Three constitutional provisions relate to the right to counsel. While the Sixth Amendment is the only part of the Constitution that explicitly references a right to counsel, the Fifth and Fourteenth Amendments have also been invoked to provide a right to counsel.
- While the Fourteenth Amendment (due process) approach to counsel has been effectively replaced by the Sixth Amendment right to counsel, a Fifth Amendment–based right to counsel still applies. The Supreme Court decided in *Miranda* v. *Arizona* that criminal suspects enjoy the right to counsel during custodial interrogations.
- Defense attorneys must provide effective assistance. Ineffective assistance occurs when the attorney performs poorly to the extent that his or her poor performance is prejudicial to the defendant's case.
- The right to counsel can be waived. If it is and the defendant represents himself or herself, this is known as a *pro se* defense.
- Defendants also enjoy the rights to confrontation and compulsory process.
- Confrontation is concerned with the defendant's right to challenge witness testimony. Confrontation is manifested in three key ways: (1) the defendant's right to be present, (2) the defendant's right to hear live testimony, and (3) the defendant's right to challenge witness testimony.
- There can be a downside to confrontation—the defendant's presence in the courtroom may remind jurors of the crime.
- Compulsory process means that the defendant has the right to use subpoenas to obtain witnesses, documents, and other objects that are helpful to his or her defense.
- Despite the many protections afforded to criminal defendants, they occupy a fairly marginal role in the criminal process.

3. CHARACTERIZE TYPICAL CRIME VICTIMS

- Victims of crime tend to be male, minority, and young.
- Most victims and offenders know one another.

4. DESCRIBE VICTIMS' INVOLVEMENT IN THE COURT PROCESS

- Victim involvement in the court process has been minimal until recently.
- Victims report difficulties and trauma associated with participation in the court process.
- Many victims, especially those in domestic-violence cases, are uncooperative, making the prosecutor's job difficult.
- In recent years, a victims' rights movement has been started. Victims have gained additional involvement through assistance programs and various rights (some from state constitutions) that provide for their involvement in the process. As yet, there is no crime victims' amendment to the U.S. Constitution.
- Despite the many advances crime victims may have made of late, some courts have begun to censor certain communications in court, even the use of the word "victim," so the defendant can be afforded a fair trial.

KEY TERMS

compulsory process, 263

cross-examination, 260

declarant, 258

direct examination, 260

hearsay, 258

hearsay rule, 258

live testimony, 258

pro se defense, 256

scope of direct rule, 260

standby counsel, 256

Victims of Crime Act, 269

REVIEW QUESTIONS

1. What social characteristics do many criminal defendants who come before American courts share? Is there a typical defendant?

2. What rights do criminal defendants have in American courts?

3. What role do victims play in the courtroom and in the justice process as a whole?

WHAT WILL YOU DO?

You are a victims' advocate and work out of the district attorney's office. At the moment, you are working on a case in which a woman was stalked by a man for five months before he was finally arrested for violating a restraining order that she was successful in having issued against him.

Both you and the victim believe that the man is potentially very dangerous and that she is quite fortunate in having escaped physical harm. Moreover, you have reason to think that the man is a repeat offender and that he has stalked a number of other women in the past.

Unfortunately, however, none of this can be taken into consideration by the judge before whom the stalker is about to appear for sentencing. That's because the offender has chosen to plead guilty in the current case, and other allegations against him remain unproven. You're afraid that the man will receive a mere slap on the wrist and be given only a short probationary sentence.

You realize, however, that an opportunity exists to increase the likelihood of prison time for the offender—but it involves convincing the victim with whom you are working to provide an in-court statement prior to sentencing, telling of the highly negative effects that the stalking experience has had on her.

Your state allows each victim a chance to be heard in open court prior to a sentence being imposed on the victimizer. You have come to believe that your job in this case is to convince the victim to make just such a statement in the hope that it will lead the judge to impose an active prison sentence on the offender.

When you suggest this to the victim, however, she is immediately reluctant to cooperate. For one thing, she says, she's shy and doesn't speak well in public; for another, she's afraid that the perpetrator might receive probation no matter what she says and that he might come after her seeking revenge.

When you question her about how the stalking experience has impacted her life, she quickly admits that it has shaken her to the core and that she no longer feels safe in any environment. Knowing that the man is probably a serial stalker, she agrees with you that he should be locked up in order to prevent him from harassing and harming other women.

She tells you that she will make an in-court statement if you can guarantee her safety after the sentencing hearing concludes.

What will you do?

NOTES

1. "Jodi Arias Attorney Closes with Love, Lies, Sex and Dirty Secrets," USA Today, http://usatoday30.usatoday.com/video/jodi-arias-attorney-closes-with-love-lies-sex-and-dirty-secrets/2351230873001 (accessed October 1, 2013).

2. Catherine E. Shoichet, "Jodi Arias Guilty of First-Degree Murder; Death Penalty Possible," CNN, May 9, 2013, http://www.cnn.com/2013/05/08/justice/arizona-jodi-arias-verdict/index.html (accessed October 1, 2013).

3. R. L. McNeely and G. Robinson-Simpson, "The Truth about Domestic Violence: A Falsely Framed Issue," Social Work, Vol. 32 (1987), pp. 485–490.

4. Available at http://factfinder2.census.gov/faces/tableservices/jsf/pages/productview.xhtml?pid=DEC_10_DP_DPDP1 (accessed February 20, 2013).

5. Johnson v. Zerbst, 304 U.S. 458 (1938).

6. Ibid., pp. 462–463.

7. Betts v. Brady, 316 U.S. 455 (1942), pp. 461–462.

8. Gideon v. Wainwright, 372 U.S. 335 (1963).

9. Ibid., p. 344.

10. Argersinger v. Hamlin, 407 U.S. 25 (1972).

11. Ibid., p. 332.

12. See Scott v. Illinois, 440 U.S. 367 (1979), and Alabama v. Shelton, 535 U.S. 654 (2002).

13. Miranda v. Arizona, 384 U.S. 436 (1966).

14. Ibid., p. 444.

15. Ibid., p. 477.

16. Ibid., p. 302, n. 8.

17. Powell v. Alabama, 287 U.S. 45 (1932).

18. Ibid., p. 50.

19. Ibid., p. 71.

20. Wainwright v. Torna, 455 U.S. 586 (1982).

21. Cuyler v. Sullivan, 446 U.S. 335 (1980).

22. Ibid., p. 344.

23. McMann v. Richardson, 397 U.S. 759 (1970).

24. Ibid., p. 771.

25. Strickland v. Washington, 466 U.S. 668 (1984).

26. Ibid., p. 687.

27. Ibid., p. 688.

28. Ibid.

29. Ibid.

30. Ibid., p. 694.

31. Bell v. Cone, 535 U.S. 685 (2002).

32. Rompilla v. Beard, 545 U.S. 374 (2005).

33. Florida v. Nixon, 543 U.S. 175 (2004).

34. Faretta v. California, 422 U.S. 806 (1975).

35. Johnson v. Zerbst, 304 U.S. 458 (1938).

36. Carnley v. Cochran, 369 U.S. 506 (1962), p. 516.

37. Massey v. Moore, 348 U.S. 105 (1954).

38. Ibid., p. 108.

39. Godinez v. Moran, 509 U.S. 389 (1993).

40. This decision all but reversed an earlier decision where the Court held that competence to stand trial could be interpreted as competence to waive counsel; see Westbrook v. Arizona, 384 U.S. 150 (1966).

41. McKaskle v. Wiggins, 465 U.S. 168 (1984).

42. Ibid., p. 184.

43. See, e.g., Wheat v. United States, 486 U.S. 153 (1988).

44. Cf. Leis v. Flynt, 439 U.S. 438 (1979).

45. Caplin and Drysdale v. United States, 491 U.S. 617 (1989).

46. Ake v. Oklahoma, 470 U.S. 68 (1985).

47. Illinois v. Allen, 397 U.S. 337 (1970), p. 338.

48. United States v. Gagnon, 470 U.S. 522 (1985); Kentucky v. Stincer, 479 U.S. 1028 (1987).

49. Taylor v. Illinois, 484 U.S. 400 (1988); Diaz v. United States, 223 U.S. 442 (1912); Taylor v. United States, 414 U.S. 17 (1973).

50. Pate v. Robinson, 383 U.S. 375 (1966).

51. Dusky v. United States, 362 U.S. 402 (1960).

52. Ibid., p. 402.

53. Medina v. California, 505 U.S. 437 (1992).

54. Pate v. Robinson, 383 U.S. 375 (1966).

55. Mattox v. United States, 156 U.S. 237 (1895).

56. Ibid., p. 243.

57. White v. Illinois, 502 U.S. 346 (1992).

58. Ibid., p. 356.

59. United States v. Inadi, 475 U.S. 387 (1986).

60. Ibid., p. 406.

61. Idaho v. Wright, 497 U.S. 805 (1990).

62. Ibid., p. 816.

63. Coy v. Iowa, 487 U.S. 1012 (1988).

64. Ibid., p. 1016.

65. Maryland v. Craig, 497 U.S. 836 (1990).

66. Ibid., p. 845.

67. Ibid., p. 852.

68. Smith v. Illinois, 390 U.S. 129 (1968).

69. Ibid., p. 131.

70. Davis v. Alaska, 415 U.S. 308 (1974).

71. Ibid., p. 319.

72. Griffin v. California, 380 U.S. 609 (1965).

73. Carter v. Kentucky, 450 U.S. 288 (1981).

74. Estelle v. Williams, 425 U.S. 501 (1976).

75. Ibid., p. 504; also see Portuondo v. Agard, 529 U.S. 61 (2000).

76. Washington v. Texas, 388 U.S. 14 (1967).

77. Ibid., p. 19.

78. Roviaro v. United States, 353 U.S. 53 (1957).

79. Chambers v. Mississippi, 410 U.S. 284 (1973).

80. Ibid., p. 302.

81. A. Rosett and D. Cressey, Justice by Consent: Plea Bargaining in the American Courthouse (Philadelphia: J. B. Lippincott, 1976), p. 146.

82. W. McDonald, *Criminal Justice and the Victim* (Newbury Park, CA: Sage, 1976); F. Cannavale and W. Falcon, *Witness Cooperation* (Lexington, MA: D. C. Heath, 1976).

83. See, e.g., R. C. Davis, B. Taylor, and A. J. Lurigio, "Adjusting to Criminal Victimization: The Correlates of Postcrime Distress," *Violence and Victims*, Vol. 11 (1996), pp. 21–38.

84. See, e.g., R. C. Kessler, A. Sonnega, E. Bromet, M. Hughes, and C. B. Nelson, "Posttraumatic Stress Disorder in the National Comorbidity Survey," *Archives of General Psychiatry*, Vol. 52 (1995), pp. 1048–1060.

85. P. Resick, "The Trauma of Rape and the Criminal Justice System," *Justice System Journal*, Vol. 9 (1984), pp. 52–61; G. Steketee and A. Austin, "Rape Victims and the Justice System: Utilization and Impact," *Social Service Review*, Vol. 63 (1989), pp. 285–303.

86. See, e.g., T. G. Gutheil, H. Bursztajn, A. Brodsky, and L. H. Strasburger, "Preventing 'Critogenic' Harms: Minimizing Emotional Injury from Civil Litigation," *Journal of Psychiatry and Law*, Vol. 28 (2000), pp. 5–18.

87. See, e.g., J. N. Epstein, B. E. Saunders, and D. G. Kirkpatrick, "Predicting PTSD in Women with a History of Childhood Rape," *Journal of Traumatic Stress*, Vol. 10 (1997), pp. 573–588.

88. D. G. Kilpatrick, *The Rights of Crime Victims—Does Legal Protection Make a Difference?* (Washington, DC: National Institute of Justice, 1998), p. 3.

89. Ibid.

90. M. Dawson and R. Dinovitzer, "Victim Cooperation and the Prosecution of Domestic Violence in a Specialized Court," *Justice Quarterly*, Vol. 18 (2001), pp. 593–622.

91. E. L. Claypoole, "Evidence-Based Prosecution: Prosecuting Domestic Violence Cases without a Victim," *The Prosecutor*, Vol. 39 (2005), pp. 18, 20–21, 26, 48.

92. J. H. Stark and H. Goldstein, *The Rights of Crime Victims* (New York: Bantam, 1985), p. 19.

93. Bureau of Justice Statistics, *Law Enforcement Management and Administrative Statistics, 1997* (Washington, DC: U.S. Government Printing Office, 1999), p. xix.

94. Bureau of Justice Statistics, *Prosecutors in State Courts, 1994* (Washington, DC: Department of Justice, 1996), p. 9.

95. See www.hennepinattorney.org (accessed July 24, 2009).

96. A. J. Saathoff and E. A. Stoffel, "Community-Based Domestic Violence Services," *The Future of Children: Domestic Violence and Children*, Vol. 9 (1999), pp. 97–110.

97. W. Doerner, "The Impact of Crime Compensation on Victim Attitudes toward the Criminal Justice System," *Victimology*, Vol. 5 (1980), pp. 61–77.

98. E. Erez and P. Tontodonato, "The Effect of Victim Participation in Sentencing and Sentence Outcome," *Criminology*, Vol. 28 (1990), pp. 451–474.

99. Ibid.

100. A. Walsh, "Placebo Justice: Victim Recommendations and Offenders' Sentences in Sexual Assault Cases," *Journal of Criminal Law and Criminology*, Vol. 77 (Winter 1986), pp. 1126–1141.

101. W. H. Parsonage, F. Bernat, and J. Helfgott, "Victim Impact Testimony and Pennsylvania's Parole Decision Making Process: A Pilot Study," *Criminal Justice Policy Review*, Vol. 6 (1994), pp. 187–206.

102. See, e.g., Candace McCoy, *Politics and Plea Bargaining: Victims' Rights in California* (Philadelphia: University of Pennsylvania Press, 1993).

103. F. Carrington and G. Nicholson, "Victims' Rights: An Idea Whose Time Has Come—Five Years Later: The Maturing of an Idea," *Pepperdine Law Review*, Vol. 17 (1989), pp. 1–19.

104. D. J. Hall, "Victims' Voices in Criminal Court: The Need for Restraint," *American Criminal Law Review*, Vol. 28 (1991), pp. 233–256.

105. D. L. Roland, "Progress in the Victim Reform Movement: No Longer Forgotten Victim," *Pepperdine Law Review*, Vol. 17 (1989), pp. 35–59.

106. L. L. Lambon, "Victim Participation in the Criminal Justice Process," *Wayne Law Review*, Vol. 34 (1987), pp. 125–220.

107. Ibid., p. 132.

108. T. Baldas, "Courts Putting Hot-Button Words on Ice," *National Law Journal*, June 16, 2008, available at www.law.com/jsp/article.jsp?id=1202422274880&slreturn=20130120105555 (accessed February 20, 2013).

109. Ibid.

110. Ibid.

111. Ibid.

John Boykin/PhotoEdit

11

Pretrial Procedures

LEARNING OBJECTIVES

1. Summarize the arrest procedure, including the probable cause requirement.

2. Explain the exclusionary rule, its exceptions, and extensions.

3. Describe the booking process and the initial appearance of suspects.

4. Summarize the various types of pretrial release, including bail.

5. Describe the mechanisms for charging the offender.

6. Summarize the purpose of arraignment and the different defendant pleas.

7. Describe the discovery process and the types of discovery.

INTRODUCTION

In 2013, Dzhokhar Tsamaev, better known as the Boston Marathon Bomber, was captured after an intense police manhunt in which his older brother, Tamerlan, was killed. Authorities said that the Tsamaev brothers had set off two homemade explosive devices at the finish line of the 2013 Boston Marathon, resulting in the deaths of three people and injuring more than 200 others. Dzhokhar, who survived bullet wounds and two gun battles with law enforcement officers, was charged by federal authorities with using and conspiring to use a weapon of mass destruction and malicious destruction of property with an explosive device. Conviction of either charge could result in the death penalty. The Tsamaev case is of special interest not only because it represents the first completed terrorism attack on American soil since the 9/11 attacks on the World Trade Center and the Pentagon but also because police officials announced that they would question Tsamaev under the public safety exception to the *Miranda* rule.[1] The *Miranda* rule, which is discussed elsewhere in this chapter, requires police officers to advise a criminal suspect of his or her constitutional rights prior to any questioning—especially the rights to remain silent and to be afforded an attorney. The public safety exception, however, recognizes that circumstances can arise in which the need for police questioning takes on special urgency. One example might be the arrest of a shooter who has discarded a loaded firearm during a police chase. Officers, fearing that an innocent party might pick up the weapon and discharge it, could, under the exception, ask "where's the gun?" immediately after arrest without advising the suspect of his or her rights.

While the courts have supported the need for urgent questioning in special cases, the announcement by authorities that Dzhokhar would not be advised of his rights prior to questioning—even though he had been hospitalized for hours after arrest and the immediate danger of more bombs seemed to have passed—surprised legal experts. Interrogators, however, argued that the need for urgency still existed, as he might have conspired with collaborators who continued to work on carrying out other attacks as he lay immobilized.

ARREST AND PROBABLE CAUSE

An **arrest** occurs after the police develop probable cause that the suspect committed a crime and/or obtain an arrest warrant issued by a judicial magistrate. The arrest process is one of the most important steps in the criminal justice system for a number of reasons. First, it is the gateway to the entire system, determining who will be formally charged and who will escape the justice process (see Figure 11–1). There is also plenty of opportunity for things to go wrong during the arrest phase, which could result in innocent people losing their freedom and the guilty going free. Next, because a legal arrest must be based on proper justification (i.e., probable cause), police must be vigilant to ensure that they meet constitutional requirements. If they don't, an arrest may be declared invalid by a judge, and a dangerous offender could be released into the community.

The key requirement for an arrest is that it be based on probable cause. **Probable cause** has been defined by the Supreme Court in *Beck* v. *Ohio* as more than mere suspicion; it exists when "the facts and circumstances within [the officers'] knowledge and of which they [have] reasonably trustworthy information [are] sufficient to warrant a prudent man in believing that the [suspect] had committed or was committing an offense."[2] For all intents and purposes, the true measure of probable cause lies somewhere below absolute certainty and proof beyond a reasonable doubt (the latter of which is necessary to obtain a criminal conviction) and somewhere above a hunch or reasonable suspicion.

© FBI Photo/Alamy

Dzhokhar Tsamaev, the surviving Boston Marathon bomber. Tsamaev's interrogation while he was in the hospital after being captured raised questions about the Miranda rule. What were those questions?

arrest
The taking of an adult or juvenile into physical custody by authority of law for the purpose of charging the person with a criminal offense or a delinquent act or status offense, terminating with the recording of a specific offense.[i]

Library Extra
11–1 FindLaw: Arrest

Learning Objective 1

Summarize the arrest procedure, including the probable cause requirement.

probable cause
A cause defined by the U.S. Supreme Court as more than bare suspicion. A probable cause exists when "the facts and circumstances within [the officers'] knowledge and of which they [have] reasonably trustworthy information [are] sufficient to warrant a prudent man in believing that the [suspect] had committed or was committing an offense."[ii] To this the Court added, "The substance of all the definitions of probable cause is a reasonable ground for belief of guilt."[iii]

POLICE	COURTS			CORRECTIONS		
ENTRY INTO THE SYSTEM	PROSECUTION & PRETRIAL SERVICES	ADJUDICATION	SENTENCING & SANCTIONS	PROBATION	PRISON	PAROLE

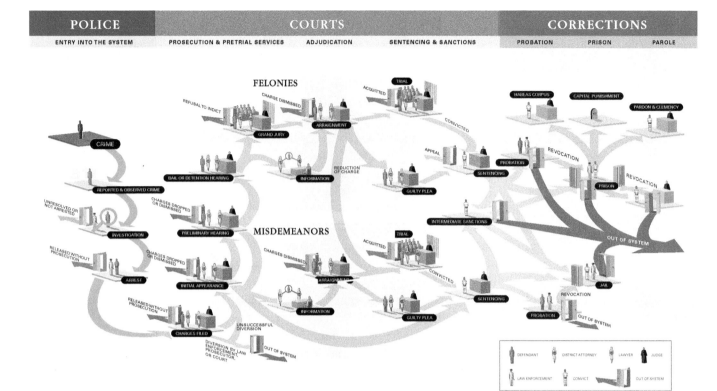

FIGURE 11–1

Criminal Justice Process

BOX 11–1 Factors Used to Distinguish between a Stop and an Arrest

If a police–citizen encounter occurs at a police station, the encounter may not be considered an arrest; however, if the encounter is overly lengthy and the citizen is not free to leave, then it would be considered an arrest. There are four criteria to use when determining whether an arrest has taken place:

1. Purpose
   a. Intent to arrest (arrest)
   b. No intent to arrest (*Terry* stop or consensual encounter)

2. Manner
   a. Person not free to leave (arrest or *Terry* stop)
   b. Person free to leave (consensual encounter)

3. Location
   a. At police station or in private (arrest or *Terry* stop)
   b. In public (arrest, *Terry* stop, or consensual encounter)

4. Duration
   a. Lengthy time (arrest)
   b. Short time (*Terry* stop or consensual encounter) ▪

Source: J. L. Worrall, *Criminal Procedure*, 4th ed. (Upper Saddle River, NJ: Pearson Education, 2012).

For some specific examples of conduct that could give rise to probable cause to arrest, see Box 11–1.

Why do we care about probable cause? Probable cause is important because, without it, an arrest or search would be considered deficient, and a deficient arrest or search can result in a clearly guilty criminal who can go free and/or in evidence that cannot be used. This occurs because of the so-called exclusionary rule, the subject of the next section. When officers make arrests that are unsupported by probable cause and suspects go free, heads generally roll. No one likes the idea of a guilty criminal roaming free because of a police mistake.

Once arrested, the arrestee loses his or her liberty and personal freedom. The arrestee can be held in detention, interrogated, and searched for contraband.[3] Because this experience is psychologically traumatic, the suspect may be scared and susceptible to police interrogation tactics. To protect the suspect from aggressive police tactics, the Supreme Court has issued a number of sweeping decisions granting arrestees legal rights, not the least of which is the right to legal counsel to protect their interests and shield them from psychological and/or physical coercion.[4]

Library Extra
11–2 Arrest

After the arrest, there are several important steps in the criminal process: decision to charge an arrestee with a crime, bail, plea negotiations, indictment, arraignment, trial, and sentencing. Each state and federal jurisdiction has its own method for carrying out the criminal process, sometimes using different names for hearings and events and varying the sequence in which they are carried out. While variations exist, there is enough similarity in events and activities to make a systematic review of these events possible and meaningful. Keeping this diversity in mind, this chapter analyzes some of the most critical events in the criminal process, from arrest through the preliminary **trial** stages of the justice process.

Library Extra
11–3 FindLaw: Probable Cause

trial
A judicial proceeding to decide upon the facts and legal issues between the parties in a civil or criminal case.

EXCLUSIONARY RULE

The **exclusionary rule** is formally defined as the requirement that evidence obtained in violation of the Constitution during an illegal arrest, search, or other process cannot be used in a criminal trial. The tainted evidence cannot be mentioned or referred to; it is as if it did not exist.

Learning Objective 2
Explain the exclusionary rule, its exceptions, and extensions.

exclusionary rule
The requirement that evidence obtained in violation of the Constitution during an illegal arrest, search, or other process cannot be used in a criminal trial.

Somewhat surprisingly, the U.S. Constitution contains no provisions for enforcement of the protections enunciated in the Bill of Rights. For example, even though people enjoy the right to be free from unreasonable searches and seizures, nowhere does the Constitution specify how this right is to be enforced. For a time, then, evidence obtained in flagrant violation of the Constitution was admissible at trial.

This troubling practice began to be remedied as early as 1886 when the U.S. Supreme Court suggested in *Boyd* v. *United States* that improperly obtained evidence be excluded from trial.[5] In *Boyd*, the Court held that business records should have been excluded from trial because "compulsory production of the private books and papers of the owner of goods . . . is compelling him to be a witness against himself, within the meaning of the Fifth Amendment to the Constitution, and is the equivalent of a search and seizure—and an unreasonable search and seizure—within the meaning of the Fourth Amendment."[6]

Then, in *Weeks* v. *United States*,[7] the Court relied solely on the Fourth Amendment as a basis for exclusion; the Court held that papers seized following a search that was in violation of the Fourth Amendment should have been returned rather than used in a criminal trial against the offender. Later, in *Silverthorne Lumber Co.* v. *United States*,[8] Justice Holmes stated that without an enforcement mechanism, "the Fourth Amendment [is reduced] to a form of words" and little else.

It is important to note that *Boyd*, *Weeks*, and *Silverthorne Lumber* were all *federal* cases and that following these decisions the Supreme Court continued for several years to apply the exclusionary rule only in federal cases.[9] In the 1961 case of *Mapp* v. *Ohio*, the Supreme Court decided, in a 5–4 decision, that the exclusionary rule applied to the states.[10] Justice Clark stated that the exclusionary rule is the "imperative of judicial integrity," noting,

> The criminal goes free, if he must, but it is the law that sets him free. Nothing can destroy a government more quickly than its failure to observe its own law, or worse, its disregard of the charter of its own existence.[11]

There is a measure of debate concerning the applicability of the exclusionary rule beyond the Fourth Amendment. On the one hand, some people believe that because the Fourth Amendment itself contains no specific reference to what should happen when improper searches or seizures take place, the purpose of the exclusionary rule is to "enforce" the Fourth Amendment. They argue, furthermore, that because the exclusionary rule operates differently outside the Fourth Amendment context, it was not meant to apply to Fifth and Sixth Amendment violations; for example, just because a confession is improperly obtained does not mean that any subsequently obtained physical evidence will be excluded.

On the other hand, some observers argue that evidence can still be excluded because of Fifth, Sixth, and even Fourteenth Amendment violations. Improperly obtained confessions are not admissible; that is, they will be excluded from a criminal trial. Coercive confessions will be excluded under the Fourteenth Amendment's due process clause, identifications stemming from Sixth Amendment violations will not be admissible, and so on. Their point is that evidence can technically be excluded for several reasons, not just Fourth Amendment violations. For our purposes, it is safe to conclude that the exclusionary rule extends well beyond the Fourth Amendment.

Library Extra
11–4 FindLaw: Arrest Process

Library Extra
11–5 FindLaw: Exclusionary Rule

Arguments For and Against the Exclusionary Rule

There is considerable debate surrounding the exclusionary rule. The debate centers on three important issues: (1) whether the rule deters police misconduct, (2) whether the rule imposes unnecessary costs on society, and (3) whether alternative remedies are effective and should be pursued.

LASTING IMPACT

Mapp v. Ohio (1961)

On May 23, 1957, Cleveland police were searching for a suspect in a recent bombing. When told that the suspect was hiding in Dollree Mapp's house, the police knocked on her door and demanded entrance. Mapp refused to let the police in without a search warrant.

After several hours, when Mapp again rejected their demand for admittance, the police forcibly opened at least one door and entered the house despite the lack of a warrant. They then proceeded to search Mapp's room, her daughter's bedroom, the kitchen, the dinette, the living room, and the basement.

When police found "lewd and lascivious" books, pictures, and photographs in a trunk in the basement, they arrested Mapp for violating Ohio's criminal law prohibiting the possession of obscene materials. She was subsequently convicted based on the evidence presented by the police and sentenced to one to seven years in the Ohio Women's Reformatory. When the Ohio Supreme Court upheld her conviction, Mapp's subsequent appeal to the U.S. Supreme Court led to the Court's application of the exclusionary rule, articulated in *Weeks v. United States* (1914), to the states.

The exclusionary rule remains one of the most controversial elements of American criminal law. It prohibits the introduction of any unconstitutionally obtained evidence against a

defendant at trial. Thus, it imposes on law enforcement the requirement to abide by all legal strictures in the development of a case against a criminal suspect.

Proponents of the exclusionary rule laud its controlling effect on methods used by police to obtain evidence. In the absence of the exclusionary rule, they say, some well-intentioned officers might be tempted to break the law themselves in overexuberant pursuit of convictions by falsifying evidence outright or by obtaining valid evidence by unconstitutional means. Knowing beforehand that such wrongfully obtained evidence will be excluded and knowing that the credibility of the remainder of their case might be tainted serve to prevent such maneuvers. Proponents also contend that the rule has elevated police professionalism by causing the police to become better at their jobs in order to prevent technical investigatory errors.

Opponents claim that the exclusionary rule handcuffs police, makes it unreasonably difficult and costly to build a legally sufficient criminal case, and too often allows suspects to evade charges as a result of technicalities. It is just plain wrong, they say, to let a known criminal walk free because of a relatively minor bureaucratic foul-up.

But isn't that the essence of law? Laws establish the precise limits by which an act or omission is defined as legal or illegal and therefore punishable or not punishable; thus, any act that stays within legal limits—no matter how close it comes to exceeding those limits—is legal.

Suppose, for example, that a law prohibits the manufacture or possession of an assault weapon. Such a law would have to include a clear description of an assault weapon to ensure full understanding of exactly what was prohibited. So let us say that this hypothetical law defines an assault weapon as "any weapon capable of a cyclic rate of fire of 1,000 rounds or more per minute." In this instance, anyone who builds a weapon that can achieve the cited cyclic rate of fire would be violating the law.

But suppose further that one manufacturer devises a way to build an assault weapon with a cyclic rate of fire that is restricted to only 995 rounds. Such a weapon would be completely legal, despite the fact that it was 99.5% as lethal as the banned weapon, because that 0.5% difference in the rate of fire would serve to discriminate the legal weapon from the illegal weapon.

The law also defines the legal limits of investigatory conduct in the building of a criminal case. Thus, any police conduct that exceeds those limits is illegal and, by the Court's ruling, can be rectified only by the exclusion of any evidence obtained as a result of that illegal conduct. If a police officer finds a piece of incriminating evidence while conducting an illegal search and then contrives a way to use that evidence by falsifying the manner in which it is "found," he or she is breaking the law. Our Constitution specifically protects against such search-and-seizure excesses.

From 1914 until the *Mapp* ruling in 1961, the exclusionary rule served to protect only those charged with violating federal laws against excesses by federal law enforcement agents investigating those alleged violations. *Mapp* extended the reach of that constitutional protection to the far greater number of people who stand accused of violating state laws.

Unfortunately, Dollree Mapp herself did not reap any benefit from the case she brought to the U.S. Supreme Court. Although the ruling in *Mapp* v. *Ohio* overturned her conviction and reversed the ruling of the Ohio Supreme Court, by the time the ruling was handed down, she had already been paroled from the confinement she was serving following her conviction. ■

DISCUSSION QUESTIONS

1. According to this feature, "Proponents of the exclusionary rule laud its controlling effect on methods used by police to obtain evidence." Are you a proponent of the exclusionary rule? Why or why not?

2. This feature also says, "Opponents claim the exclusionary rule handcuffs police, makes it unreasonably difficult and costly to build a legally sufficient criminal case, and too often allows suspects to evade charges as a result of technicalities." Are you an opponent of the exclusionary rule? Why or why not?

3. What alternatives to the exclusionary rule can you envision?

4. Many people say that the exclusionary rule serves as an example of judge-made law because it effectively created a restriction on police behavior that had not previously existed in state jurisdictions. Do you agree that the rule is a kind of judge-made law? Why or why not?

Does the exclusionary rule deter police misconduct? Critics argue that the rule does not deter police misconduct and claim that most constitutional rights violations are unintentional and that such mistakes are "undeterrable." Police officers who act in bad faith will commit perjury to mask a constitutional rights violation. Supporters of the deterrence argument, by contrast, state that the rule is not intended to deter individual officers (specific deterrence) but that it is intended to have a broader, systemic deterrent effect (general deterrence).

Does the rule impose unnecessary costs on society? Critics also believe that the exclusionary rule requires omitting some of the most reliable forms of evidence (e.g., confessions); this, they argue, allows guilty people to go free while at the same time increasing the public's cynicism about the effectiveness of the justice system. They believe that the exclusionary rule is too restrictive, limiting police discretion and penalizing even a relatively trivial violation by police officers, a violation that may result in exclusion of significant evidence.

Supporters of the exclusionary rule, by contrast, do not believe that the costs outweigh the benefits. For example, they argue—persuasively—that the exclusionary rule is rarely applied, that motions to exclude evidence are relatively rare, and that those that are filed rarely succeed. For example, one study found that only 21 of 1,355 defendants were allowed to go free because their attorneys filed successful motions to suppress evidence (i.e., successfully invoked the exclusionary rule).[12] For further examples of such research, see Box 11–2.

Are alternative yet effective remedies available? Critics of the rule claim that there are effective alternatives that should be pursued, including civil litigation, criminal prosecution, and internal discipline. Their view is that overzealous law enforcement officers can be

BOX 11–2 Summary of Empirical Research on the Exclusionary Rule

The question of whether the exclusionary rule is beneficial or harmful has been subjected to a fair amount of empirical research. Of particular interest to researchers have been the effects of the rule on police policy and procedure as well as on the outcomes of criminal cases. Thus, most of the research can be organized around two topics: (1) the impact of the rule on the police and prosecutors and (2) the incidence of cases in which the rule resulted in the suppression of evidence and/or the extent to which search-and-seizure concerns dictated the decision to prosecute. The information that follows comprises the main findings of leading studies. Citations are also provided so that readers can examine the findings and research designs in more detail, as desired.

EFFECTS OF THE RULE ON POLICE AND PROSECUTORS

1. Following *Mapp*, arrests declined among detectives in the narcotics bureau but increased for other detectives (Comment, "Effect of *Mapp* v. *Ohio* on Police Search and Seizure Practices in Narcotics Cases," *Columbia Journal of Legal and Social Problems*, Vol. 4 [1968], p. 87).

2. The exclusionary rule has virtually no effect on the arrest behavior of police (Oaks, "Studying the Exclusionary Rule in Search and Seizure," *University of Chicago Law Review*, Vol. 37 [1970], p. 665).

3. The exclusionary rule has no deterrent effect on illegal search practices and exacts a high cost on society because of its potential to free guilty criminals (Spiotto, "Search and Seizure: An Empirical Study of the Exclusionary Rule and Its Alternatives," *Journal of Legal Studies*, Vol. 2 [1973], p. 243).

4. Law enforcement search-and-seizure practices changed significantly following *Mapp*; namely, police officers were more likely to comply with search warrant procedures (Canon, "Is the Exclusionary Rule in Failing Health? Some New Data and a Plea against a Precipitous Conclusion," *Kentucky Law Journal*, Vol. 62 [1974], p. 681).

5. Interviews with narcotics detectives in Chicago led a researcher to conclude that the exclusionary rule had "significant deterrent effects [It] changed police, prosecutorial, and judicial procedures [It] educated police officers in the requirements" (Orfield, "The Exclusionary Rule and Deterrence. An Empirical Study of Chicago Narcotics Officers," *University of Chicago Law Review*, Vol. 54 [1987], p. 1016).

RESEARCH ON THE INCIDENCE OF LOST CASES AND RELATED ISSUES

1. Of 2,804 cases analyzed between July 1 and August 31, 1978, successful motions for the exclusion of evidence were made in only 1.3% of prosecuted cases, that is, 1.3% of the 16% whose cases were accepted for prosecution (General Accounting Office, *Report of the Comptroller General of the United States, Impact of the Exclusionary Rule on Federal Criminal Prosecutions* [Washington, DC: Government Printing Office, 1979]).

2. An estimated 4.8% of cases rejected for prosecution were rejected because of search-and-seizure problems. Approximately half of those individuals released because of the exclusionary rule were rearrested within two years of their release (National Institute of Justice, *The Effects of the Exclusionary Rule: A Study in California* [1982]).

3. In a reanalysis of the previous study, one researcher found that prosecutors rejected only 0.8% of felony arrests because of Fourth Amendment concerns. He concluded further that "only about 2.35% of felony arrests are lost because of illegal searches" (Davies, "A Hard Look at What We Know (and Still Need to Learn) about the 'Costs' of the Exclusionary Rule: The NIJ Study and Other Studies of 'Lost' Arrests," *American Business Foundation Research Journal*, Vol. 3 [1983], p. 611).

4. A nine-county study of 7,500 felony court cases revealed that motions to suppress were filed in less than 5% of all cases, and the success rate of such motions was reported to be 0.69%. The study concluded that less than 0.6% of all cases were lost due to the exclusion of evidence (Nardulle, "The Societal Cost of the Exclusionary Rule: An Empirical Assessment," *American Business Foundation Research Journal*, Vol. 3 [1983], p. 585).

5. "[M]otions to suppress were successful in only 0.9% of the primary warrants (15 of 1,748). Judges sustained motions for 2% of all defendants (27 of 1.355) in our warrant based sample.

Few cases were 'lost' as a result of the exclusionary rule in seven jurisdictions when police used search warrants. Twenty-one of 1,355 defendants (1.5%) were allowed to go free as a result of a successful motion to suppress physical evidence" (Uchida and Bynum, "Search Warrants, Motions to Suppress, and 'Lost Cases': The Effects of the Exclusionary Rule in Seven Jurisdictions." *Journal of Criminal Law and Criminology*, Vol. 81 [1991], p. 1034). ■

Source: J. L. Worrall, *Criminal Procedure*, 2nd ed. (Boston: Allyn and Bacon, 2007), p. 58, fig. 2.6.

deterred from violating the Constitution by these enforcement mechanisms. Other legal experts doubt the efficiency of alternatives, claiming, for example, that juries are more likely to favor police officers in civil trials, that immunity is often extended to police officers in civil litigation cases, and that internal police discipline is something of a sham (e.g., disciplinary decisions tend to favor the officer, not the citizen filing the complaint).

Both sides to the exclusionary rule debate make interesting points. However, given the relatively rare number of celebrated cases where serious criminals have gone free, the exclusionary rule is probably more beneficial than harmful. In addition, just because evidence may be excluded because of police misconduct does not mean that the defendant "walks"; often, the prosecutor possesses other evidence. For example, if a defendant's confession is excluded but several witnesses are still willing to testify that the defendant committed the crime, he or she will, in all likelihood, be convicted.

Exceptions to the Exclusionary Rule

The Supreme Court has tinkered with the exclusionary rule considerably over the years. On the one hand, it has created certain exceptions to the rule, exceptions that help the police in their investigations. On the other hand, the Court has extended the reach of the rule through creation of the so-called fruit of the poisonous tree doctrine—but the Court has also created exceptions to fruit of the poisonous tree.

There are two exceptions to the exclusionary rule: the good-faith exception and the impeachment exception. With respect to the **good-faith exception**, the Supreme Court has ruled that when police officers make an honest and "good-faith" mistake during the course of certain searches or seizures, any subsequently obtained evidence may be considered admissible. Two cases, *United States* v. *Leon*[13] and *Massachusetts* v. *Sheppard*,[14] created the good-faith exception, but it has been curtailed and restricted over time. The good-faith exception is limited in four respects:

1. If a warrant is "so lacking in indicia of probable cause as to render official belief in its existence entirely unreasonable,"[15] then evidence obtained following its service will not be admissible.

2. If a warrant is "so facially deficient—that is, in failing to particularize the place to be searched or things to be seized—that the executing officers cannot reasonably presume it to be valid,"[16] then the exception does not apply.

3. If the judge issuing the warrant is deliberately misled by information in the affidavit, that is, when a police officer acts in *bad* faith, the good-faith exception will not apply.[17]

4. If the judge "rubber-stamps" a search warrant, good faith cannot later be asserted.

Together, these four restrictions make it clear that good faith is a narrowly drawn exception to the exclusionary rule and that it does not mean that any good-faith search that turned out to be in violation of the Fourth Amendment will be sanctioned.

As for the **impeachment exception**, if the prosecution seeks to use such evidence for the purpose of impeaching (i.e., attacking the credibility of) a witness, then it will be considered admissible for that purpose. In *Walder* v. *United States*,[18] a narcotics case, the Supreme

good-faith exception An exception to the exclusionary rule. Law enforcement officers who conduct a search or who seize evidence on the basis of good faith (that is, when they believe they are operating according to the dictates of the law) and who later discover that a mistake was made (perhaps in the format of the application for a search warrant) may still provide evidence that can be used in court.

impeachment exception An exception to the exclusionary rule that renders otherwise inadmissible evidence admissible if the prosecution seeks to use such evidence for the purpose of impeaching (i.e., attacking the credibility of) a witness.

Court permitted the introduction of heroin that had been illegally seized from the defendant two years earlier to attack the defendant's statement that he had never purchased, used, or sold drugs; importantly, this evidence was introduced at a *later* trial where Walder was once again charged with narcotics violations.

Extensions of the Exclusionary Rule

fruit of the poisonous tree doctrine
A legal principle that excludes from introduction at trial any evidence later developed as a result of an illegal search or seizure.

In *Silverthorne Lumber Co.* v. *United States*,[19] the Supreme Court created the **fruit of the poisonous tree doctrine**, which refers to the use of evidence that is tainted. In that case, Silverthorne Lumber Company was convicted on contempt charges for failing to produce documents that were discovered during the course of an illegal search. The Court reversed the conviction; the company was not required to produce documents that were uncovered during an illegal search. The courts often speak in terms of "derivative evidence" in the same breath as fruit of the poisonous tree. The term *derivative evidence* refers to evidence *derived* from a previous unconstitutional search or seizure. The exclusionary rule applies not only to evidence obtained as a direct result of a constitutional rights violation but also to evidence *indirectly* derived from the constitutional rights violation. In many ways, the fruit of the poisonous tree doctrine resembles a "but for" test, where courts have to ask, "But for the unconstitutional police conduct, would the evidence have been obtained regardless?" If the answer is no, then the evidence will be excluded, but if the answer is yes, then the issue becomes more complicated. To deal with "yes" answers to the "but for" question, the Supreme Court has carved out important exceptions to the fruit of the poisonous tree doctrine. While the fruit of the poisonous tree doctrine extends the exclusionary rule, the Supreme Court has also taken at least three steps to limit it:

independent source exception
A limitation on the fruit of the poisonous tree doctrine that renders admissible any witness testimony that had been offered totally independent of an illegal search.

1. In *United States* v. *Ceccolini*,[20] the Court created the so-called **independent source exception** when they observed that witnesses "can, and often do, come forward and offer evidence entirely of their own volition"; had this occurred in that case, the independent source exception would have applied. In other words, had the witness testimony been offered totally independent of the illegal search, it would have been admissible.

inevitable-discovery exception
A limitation on the fruit of the poisonous tree doctrine that renders admissible evidence that would be found regardless of unconstitutional police conduct.

2. The Court has articulated an **inevitable-discovery exception**, which means that if evidence would be found regardless of unconstitutional police conduct, then it will be admissible. This exception was first recognized by the Supreme Court in *Nix* v. *Williams*.[21] In that case, the "fruit" was the body of a young girl that was discovered after the police had illegally questioned the defendant concerning the body's whereabouts. Under ordinary circumstances, the body would not be considered admissible, but the prosecution was able to prove that at the time of the illegal questioning, a search party looking for the girl's body was narrowing in on its target and would have "inevitably discovered" the body.

purged taint exception
A limitation on the fruit of the poisonous tree doctrine that may permit, when sufficient time elapses between an initial unconstitutional search and later seizure of derivative evidence, the admissibility of such derivative evidence at trial.

3. In *Wong Sun* v. *United States*, the Court created the "attenuation" or **purged taint exception** to the fruit of the poisonous tree doctrine,[22] ruling that statements provided by a defendant who was illegally arrested and released but later returned to the police station house on his own initiative were admissible because the statements did not result from the illegal arrest when the defendant decided to come back *later*, following his release. The Court noted that his statement had become attenuated to the extent that it dissipated the taint of the initial unconstitutional act.

Despite all these cases and appeals, the exclusionary rule remains a highly controversial aspect of the law. The following "Courts in the News" feature addresses the current state of the rule.

COURTS IN THE NEWS

The Exclusionary Rule in Flux

The exclusionary rule has been under attack as the Supreme Court has placed restrictions and limitations on its scope. In an important 2009 case, *Arizona v. Gant*, the Court placed limits on police searches. The case involved Rodney J. Gant, who was arrested by Tucson, Arizona, police and charged with driving on a suspended license. Police arrested Gant in a friend's yard after he had parked his vehicle and was walking away. Gant and all other suspects on the scene were then secured in a patrol car. The officers then searched Gant's vehicle. After finding a weapon and a bag of cocaine, Gant was charged with possession of a narcotic for sale and possession of drug paraphernalia. The Court disallowed the search, ruling,

> Police may search a vehicle incident to a recent occupant's arrest only if the arrestee is within reaching distance of the passenger compartment at the time of the search or it is reasonable to believe the vehicle contains evidence of the offense of arrest. When these justifications are absent, a search of an arrestee's vehicle will be unreasonable unless police obtain a warrant or show that another exception to the warrant requirement applies.

While the Court expanded the exclusionary rule in *Gant*, it later backtracked in *Davis v. United States*. On an April evening in 2007, police officers in Greenville, Alabama, conducted a routine traffic stop that eventually resulted in the arrests of driver Stella Owens (for driving while intoxicated) and passenger Willie Davis (for giving a false name to police). The police handcuffed both Owens and Davis and placed them in the back of separate patrol cars. The police then searched the passenger compartment of Owens's vehicle and found a revolver inside Davis's jacket pocket. Clearly, this search violated the *Gant* doctrine. Unless the officers could state a reasonable belief that there was evidence in the automobile related to the charges being brought (i.e., evidence of driving while intoxicated or giving a false name), the search at issue violated the rule, which was announced two years later in *Gant*. The officers in *Davis* did not have any reason to believe that they would find contraband after the suspects were incapacitated and out of the car. However, the search in *Davis* was common law enforcement practice and consistent with the practices in their jurisdiction.

© ZUMA Press, Inc./Alamy

In the *Davis* case, the Supreme Court ruled that a search was reasonable if it was conducted under the rules that existed at the time the search took place, even if they were later overturned in another case.

Davis argued that the gun should be excluded based on the *Gant* ruling. At the outset of its analysis, the Court noted that the sole purpose of the exclusionary rule was to deter law enforcement misconduct. The Court then identified when the exclusionary rule should apply and when the evidence should be allowed. Citing prior cases, the Court asserted,

> The basic insight of the . . . cases is that the deterrence benefits of exclusion "vary with the culpability of the law enforcement conduct" at issue. When the police exhibit "deliberate," "reckless," or "grossly negligent" disregard for Fourth Amendment rights, the deterrent value of exclusion is strong and tends to outweigh the resulting costs. But when the police act with an objectively "reasonable good-faith belief" that their conduct is lawful, or when their conduct involves only simple, "isolated" negligence, the "'deterrence rationale loses much of its force,'" and exclusion cannot "pay its way."

The Court outlined a number of different instances where its prior decisions had applied the good faith of the officers to overcome exclusion of evidence. In doing so, the majority framed the issue as follows: "The question in this case was whether to apply the exclusionary rule when the police conduct a search in objectively reasonable reliance on binding judicial precedent."

At the time of the search at issue here, they had not yet decided *Arizona v. Gant*.

In looking at the officer's conduct in this case, the Court noted that the U.S. Court of Appeal for the Eleventh Circuit, which was controlling court for the officers, allowed the very type of search undertaken by the officers. As such, the officers had no culpability with respect to a violation of the Fourth Amendment. Thus, the officers' actions at the time of the search were objectively reasonable and declined Davis's appeal. Because Davis's conviction had not become final when *Gant* was announced, Davis was correct when he invoked the newly announced rule as a basis for seeking relief. But retroactive application of a new rule does not determine the question of what remedy the defendant should obtain. The remedy of exclusion does not automatically follow from a Fourth Amendment violation. In sum, they held that searches conducted in objectively reasonable reliance on binding appellate precedent are not subject to the exclusionary rule. ∎

(continued)

Learning Objective 3

Describe the booking process and the initial appearance of suspects.

booking
A law enforcement or correctional administrative process officially recording an entry into detention after arrest and identifying the person, the place, the time, the reason for the arrest, and the arresting authority.

initial appearance
An appearance before a magistrate during which the legality of the defendant's arrest is initially assessed and the defendant is informed of the charges on which he or she is being held; also called *first appearance* or *presentment.* At this stage in the criminal justice process, bail may be set or pretrial release arranged.

Web Extra
11–1 Booking Mug Shots

Web Extra
11–2 Daily Arrest Cards

INITIAL APPEARANCE

Once a person is arrested, be it with or without a warrant, the arrestee is booked at the arresting officer's police station. **Booking** consists of recording the identity of the arrestee, the time of the arrest, the offense involved, and other relevant information. At one time, the information was stored in ledger books held at the police station (hence the term *booking*), but now the arrest data are stored electronically in most departments.

Next, the suspect's personal items are inventoried, and depending on the offense and the jurisdiction involved, the suspect's photograph and fingerprints may also be taken. Finally, the arrestee is placed in a holding cell, jail cell, or similar confinement facility and is allowed to contact counsel, family, friends, or other individuals as needed. Contrary to Hollywood depictions, more than one phone call is typically allowed.

Once arrested and booked, suspects are brought before a magistrate in what is known as the **initial appearance**, which is designed to serve a number of purposes. In misdemeanor cases (e.g., a minor in possession of alcohol), a trial may take place at this stage. In more serious cases, the accused will be advised of (1) the reasons he or she is being detained (notification of formal charges often comes later at arraignment), (2) the various protections he or she has against self-incrimination, and (3) the right to appointed counsel he or she has if need be. The judge may also set bail at the initial appearance, but bail determinations often require a separate hearing. The initial appearance is usually swift and subject to few procedural constraints.

In *Gerstein v. Pugh,* the Supreme Court held that the Fourth Amendment also requires a so-called probable cause hearing either before or promptly after arrest.[23] A probable cause hearing *before* an arrest usually results in an arrest warrant being issued (recall that an arrest warrant is issued based on a judge's determination as to whether probable cause is in place); no hearing to determine probable cause after such an arrest is necessary because it would be redundant. However, when an arrest is made *without* a warrant, a probable cause determination must often be made. The purpose of the probable cause hearing is, in essence, to determine whether there is probable cause to keep a person detained, and sometimes the probable cause hearing is folded into the initial appearance.

Learning Objective 4

Summarize the various types of pretrial release, including bail.

PRETRIAL RELEASE

If the arrestee does not pose a significant risk of flight and has been arrested for a relatively minor offense, he or she is eligible for pretrial release. Conversely, if the arrestee is likely to fail to appear in later proceedings, he or she will probably be jailed pending additional court proceedings.

The Eighth Amendment states, "Excessive bail shall not be required." This means that bail must be reasonable, but it does *not* mean that that everyone enjoys a constitutional right to bail. For example, bail is almost always denied in capital cases.

One could argue that because our criminal justice system presumes innocence, everyone should be eligible for pretrial release. However, the Supreme Court has stated that the presumption of innocence is merely "a doctrine that allocates the burden of proof in criminal trials."[24] Also, it is important to note that the protection against excessive bail does not apply to the states, so states can basically set bail at any level.

Pretrial Release Hearing

The Constitution does not specify whether bail should be set in a separate hearing, but numerous Court decisions seem to suggest that a separate hearing is warranted. In *Stack* v. *Boyle*, the Court stated that as part of the bail determination, judges should consider "the nature and circumstances of the offense charged, the weight of the evidence against [the accused], the financial ability of the defendant to give bail and the character of the defendant."[25]

Library Extra
11–6 Purpose of Bail or Pretrial Release

It is also not clear, assuming that a bail hearing is required, whether a more adversarial proceeding is necessary. Since bail is set once charges have already been filed, it would seem that, at a minimum, counsel should be provided. In fact, in *United States* v. *Salerno*,[26] the Court concluded that a federal preventive detention (see below for more on preventive detention) statute that provided for counsel, evidence presentation, and cross-examination was acceptable, but it did not state whether such rights should be afforded to the accused in every bail hearing. Thus, the question of what type of bail hearing is required, if any, remains unanswered. In some situations and in certain jurisdictions, the bail decision is made during another hearing.

Mechanisms for Release (or Continued Detention)

There are three accepted methods for either releasing defendants prior to their trial or keeping them locked up. The first is bail, which occurs when the court collects a deposit from the individual being released in order to ensure that he or she appears for later scheduled hearings. Next, some arrestees are released on their own recognizance, which means that they simply promise to show up when required. Finally, in recent years, the courts have adopted a policy of what is called "preventive detention" for certain individuals; this involves a calculation as to the arrestee's level of dangerousness and flight risk, denying release to those individuals who are likely to pose a threat to others or who are likely not to appear at their scheduled hearings. Preventive detention is a mechanism for continued detention, in contrast to bail or release on recognizance.

bail
"To effect the release of an accused person from custody, in return for a promise that he or she will appear at a place and time specified and submit to the jurisdiction and judgment of the court, guaranteed by a pledge to pay to the court a specified sum of money or property if the person does not appear."[iv] It is the money or property pledged to the court or actually deposited with the court to effect the release of a person from legal custody.

Bail **Bail** has been defined formally as follows: "To effect the release of an accused person from custody, in return for a promise that he or she will appear at a place and time specified and submit to the jurisdiction and judgment of the court, guaranteed by a pledge to pay to the court a specified sum of money or property if the person does not appear."[27] Some common types of bail are described in Box 11–3.

Federal law provides that "upon all arrests in criminal cases, bail shall be admitted, except where the punishment may be death."[28] Most states have adopted similar language in their constitutions; California's constitution, for example, provides that "all persons shall be bailable by sufficient sureties, unless for capital offenses when the proof is evidence or the presumption great."[29]

The bail decision is sometimes problematic because more often than not, judges set bail according to the nature of the offense in question, not according to the accused's ability to pay.[30] A frequent result is that indigent defendants languish in jail cells until their court dates if they cannot afford to pay.

If the defendant cannot afford to post bail, he or she may turn to the services of a professional **bail bondsman**, who collects a fee (usually a percentage of bail) and then posts a

bail bondsman
A person, usually licensed, whose business it is to effect release on bail for people charged with offenses and held in custody by pledging to pay a sum of money if the defendants fail to appear in court as required.

BOX 11–3 Common Types of Bail and Alternatives to Bail

- *Cash bail.* The defendant or someone else on the defendant's behalf pays the full bail amount out of pocket.
- *Secured bail.* The defendant must pay a specified amount or post security in order to be released. Security can include property.
- *Unsecured bail.* The defendant is not required to pay money but must sign a bond guaranteeing that he or she will return for future court appearances. A fine is imposed if the defendant fails to appear.
- *Conditional bail.* In lieu of paying cash, the defendant is ordered to satisfy some specific condition (e.g., complete drug treatment) in exchange for being released before trial.
- *Release on recognizance.* The defendant is not required to pay money but must sign a bond guaranteeing that he or she will return for future court appearances. ■

bond so that the accused can be released. If, for instance, bail is set at $20,000, the bond agent might charge a fee of $2,000 and post the rest. If the accused shows up at trial, the bondsman keeps the fee and gets his money back from the court; if the accused fails to show up, then the bondsman loses the amount posted. In order to avoid such an eventuality, bondsmen employ bounty hunters, whose job it is to catch the accused and bring him or her before the court. Many bondsmen also maintain third-party insurance to protect them from loss.

There is a misperception that bail bonds agents can, with impunity, do whatever it takes to apprehend those who skip bail, a perception that has been fueled by popular "bounty hunter" programs on cable television. In response to concerns that bail bondsmen have been given too much authority, some states have adopted legislation to restrict their activities.

The bondsman system gives power to private citizens to determine who gets released or who stays in jail. It discriminates against the poor because the decision is based on the accused's ability to pay a fee in order to get a bond: Those who can pay the fee effectively buy their freedom, even if only temporarily; those who cannot pay stay in jail. The courts sit on the sidelines while the whole bail bond process plays out.[31]

Because of these problems, a number of alternative bail release mechanisms have been developed. One example is called "deposit bail," a system in which the defendant pays a percentage of the bail amount to the court. When the defendant appears in court, the fee is returned, less a percentage of that which covers administrative costs.

Library Extra
11–7 Pretrial Release: Key Policy Issues and Research

release on recognizance
The unsecured pretrial release of an accused person with the assumption that he or she will show up for subsequently scheduled court hearings.

Release on Recognizance Courts have also experimented with releasing people on their own recognizance. **Release on recognizance** means that the accused is released with the assumption that he or she will show up for scheduled court hearings. For obvious reasons, this method of pretrial release is reserved for those individuals posing a minimal risk of flight.

New York City's Manhattan Bail Project was the first significant effort to explore the possibilities of release on recognizance. This program, administered by the Vera Institute, focused on indigent defendants who, according to carefully set criteria, posed a minimal flight risk. Among the criteria considered were what the previous convictions were, what the nature of the offense was, whether the accused was employed, and whether the accused had roots in the community (e.g., a family to go back to). The program was a resounding success; only 1.6% of those individuals recommended for release intentionally failed to appear at court.

The results of the Manhattan Bail Project prompted other cities around the country to adopt similar programs. In 1996, Congress passed the Federal Bail Reform Act, which provided that any person charged with a noncapital offense "be ordered released pending trial on his personal recognizance or upon the execution of an unsecured appearance bond in an amount specified by the judicial officer, unless the officer determines . . . that such a release will not reasonably assure the appearance of the person as required."[32]

An important feature of the new legislation is that bail was to be considered as only one of many options to ensure the accused's appearance at trial. Among the other options were restrictions on travel and association as well as other conditions that would ensure the appearance of the accused.[33] The Bail Reform Act also provided that when bail was to be used, the money should be deposited with the court, not with a bail bondsman.

The Bail Reform Act further provided that "the judge shall . . . take into account the available information concerning: the nature and the circumstances of the offense charged, the weight of evidence against the accused, the accused's family ties, employment, financial resources, character and mental condition, the length of his residence in the community, his record of convictions, and his record of appearances at court proceedings or of flight to avoid prosecution or failure to appear at court proceedings."[34]

Preventive Detention Growing concern over crimes committed by defendants out on pretrial release prompted some reforms. In 1970, for example, the District of Columbia passed the first statute regarding **preventive detention**, which authorized denial of bail to "dangerous" persons charged with certain offenses for up to 60 days.[35] Then Congress passed the **Federal Bail Reform Act** of 1984,[36] which authorized judges to revoke pretrial release for firearm possession, failure to comply with curfew, or failure to comply with other conditions of release. The act also permitted detention for up to ten days for an individual who "may flee or pose a danger to any other person or the community."[37] The Bail Reform Act of 1984 permits pretrial detention for *more than* ten days with certain individuals; if it is deemed that no pretrial release condition "will reasonably assure the appearance of the person as required and the safety of any other person and the community," then indefinite detention is acceptable. For a detention of this nature to conform to Fourth and Eighth Amendment restrictions, a hearing must be held to determine whether the case "involves a serious risk that the person will flee; [or] a serious risk that the person will obstruct or attempt to obstruct justice, or threaten, injure, or intimidate, a prospective witness or jury."[38]

preventive detention
A statutory authorization to deny bail to dangerous persons charged with certain offenses for up to 60 days.

Federal Bail Reform Act
The U.S. legislation that authorized judges to revoke pretrial release for firearm possession, failure to comply with curfew, or failure to comply with other conditions of release and that permitted detention for up to ten days of an individual who "may flee or pose a danger to any other person or the community."[v]

Bail Decision

As indicated already, the Constitution does not guarantee the right to bail. Some people are denied bail, and others are granted bail. What criteria influence the judge's decision? Three factors are typically considered: the accused's flight risk, the accused's level of dangerousness, and the accused's financial status.

Flight Risk In *Stack* v. *Boyle*, the Supreme Court declared that the purpose of bail is to ensure the accused's appearance at trial:

> Like [the] ancient practice of securing the oaths of responsible persons to stand as sureties for the accused, the modern practice of requiring a bail bond or the deposit of a sum of money subject to forfeiture serves as additional assurance of the presence of an accused. . . . Since the function of bail is limited, the fixing of bail for any individual defendant must be based upon standards relevant to the purpose of assuring the presence of that defendant.[39]

COURTS IN THE NEWS

Bounty Hunters

Every now and then, some news report or television crime drama will bring bounty hunters into the public eye, invariably in a less-than-favorable light. The public then becomes upset about the sweeping rights bounty hunters enjoy in their pursuit of an absconder (i.e., one who has skipped out on a bail bond). With seemingly unfettered freedom of movement, these agents are allowed to make warrantless entries of private homes and seizures of individuals, to hold such individuals in custody, and to transport them across state lines without their consent.

How is that possible in a society so tightly bound by civil rights protections that murderers are sometimes untouchable because of law enforcement's inability to build a case sufficiently strong enough to support an arrest warrant? Bounty hunters seem to have far greater latitude than law enforcement officers.

Well, it's possible because it's the law, found specifically in the U.S. Supreme Court's holding in *Taylor* v. *Taintor, Treasurer*, 83 U.S. 366 (1872). That's the case in which the Court articulated those sweeping rights. The language in *Taylor* is clear and unambiguous: "When bail is given, the principal [i.e., the person being bailed out] is regarded as delivered to the custody of his sureties [i.e., the person or persons paying the money]. Their dominion is a continuance of the original imprisonment. Whenever they choose to do so, they may seize him and deliver him up in their discharge; and if that cannot be done at once, they may imprison him until it can be done. They may exercise their rights in person or by agent. They may pursue him into another State; may arrest him on the Sabbath; and, if necessary, may break and enter his house for that purpose. The seizure is not made by virtue of new process. None is needed. It is likened to the rearrest by the sheriff of an escaping prisoner. . . . The rights of the bail in civil and criminal cases are the same."[1]

Basically, in half of the 50 states, a person—such as a bail bondsman—into whose custody another person accused of a crime is remanded as part of the accused's bail has almost unlimited entitlement to pursue and recover that accused person. In the remaining half of the states, the bounty hunter or bail agent's freedom of movement is banned or is

A&E/The Everett Collection

Dog the Bounty Hunter, shown here, became a media favorite for his exploits in tracking down bail jumpers.

restricted in some fashion.[2] Following are those states that have restrictions:

- Four states (Illinois, Kentucky, Oregon, and Wisconsin) have outlawed commercial bonding, use of public bail systems, and bounty hunting.
- Three states (Florida, North Carolina, and South Carolina) have eliminated freelance bounty hunting, but all full-time "runners" who work for one bond agent at a time may operate freely.
- Eleven states (Arizona, California, Connecticut, Indiana, Iowa, Louisiana, Mississippi, Nevada, South Dakota, Utah, and West Virginia) require licensing that can be obtained only on meeting various conditions, such as psychological examinations, training, or possession of a high school diploma.
- Seven states (Arkansas, Colorado, Georgia, New Hampshire, Oklahoma, Tennessee, and Texas) impose unique legal rules, including, among others, the requirement for a bounty hunter to be accompanied by a local law enforcement officer to obtain a warrant from a local court and to notify the local police of his or her presence as well as the defendant's name, the charges he or she faces, and his or her suspected location. ■

To some, the practice of bounty hunting seems like something from another century, yet as television shows like *Dog the Bounty Hunter* demonstrate, the practice is still very much alive and well in most of the United States. It's a practice about which we might ask a couple of questions.

DISCUSSION QUESTIONS

1. Should bounty hunting be further regulated, especially in those states where it is subject to few regulations at present? If so, what kinds of regulations should be imposed?

2. What purpose does bounty hunting serve? Could the same purpose be served by other agencies like police or sheriff's departments? What would be the advantages and disadvantages of charging law enforcement agencies with bounty hunting?

Notes

1 *Taylor* v. *Taintor*, 83 U.S. 366 (1872).

2 http://fugitiverecovery.com/bail-bond-laws/directory (accessed June 2, 2013).

In short, a delicate balance needs to be struck in ensuring the accused's appearance at trial. Bail should be set at an amount designed to minimize the risk of flight; at the same time, however, the amount set should not be so excessive that the accused cannot reasonably afford to pay it, either by cash or by bond.

Dangerousness Aside from the obvious risk of flight, some defendants are particularly dangerous individuals, so courts sometimes see fit to either deny bail or set the amount relatively high because of perceived dangerousness. For example, in *Schall* v. *Martin*, the Supreme Court upheld a statute that provided for detention of juveniles who posed a "serious risk" of committing a crime while on release.[40] The statute was criticized as essentially amounting to punishment without trial, but the Court decided that punishment exists only where the government's *intent* is to punish. And since the purpose of the state's detention policy was not to punish but rather to protect the community from a dangerous individual, it was declared constitutional.

Financial Status Courts often take into account the accused's financial status in making a bail decision. For example, in *Schilb* v. *Kuebel*,[41] the Supreme Court decided on the constitutionality of a state statute that provided that a criminal defendant who was not released on his own recognizance could (1) deposit 10% of the amount of set bail with the court, 10% of which would be forfeited to the court as "bail bond costs," or (2) pay the full amount of bail, all of which would be refunded if the accused showed up at court. The defendant argued that the statute unfairly targeted indigent individuals because the poor were forced to choose the first option. Interestingly, the Supreme Court upheld the statute, noting that "it is by no means clear that [the second option, paying the full amount,] is more attractive to the affluent defendant."[42]

Library Extra
11–8 Pretrial Release of Felony Defendants in State Courts

CHARGING OF THE OFFENDER

Learning Objective 5
Describe the mechanisms for charging the offender.

The decision to charge someone with a crime is an important one. In Chapter 8, we looked at some of the issues surrounding prosecutorial charging, including means of avoiding charges altogether, so we will not revisit them here. Our concern in this chapter is with the legal issues surrounding prosecutorial charging and the differences between charging decisions between jurisdictions that do and do not require grand jury indictment.

Charging in Grand Jury Jurisdictions

According to the Fifth Amendment, "No person shall be held to answer for a capital, or otherwise infamous crime, unless on a presentment or indictment of a grand jury." At its creation in 1791, the framers of the Fifth Amendment favored grand jury indictments for fear that the prosecutor, a representative of government, could become too powerful in terms of making charging decisions. Indeed, there was a clear sentiment among the framers that government should be kept in check; the grand jury was one method of ensuring prosecutorial restraint.

As time has passed, the grand jury has become highly dependent on the actions of the prosecutor. Grand juries still perform important investigative functions, and they are able to subpoena witnesses and records, but their role today is tied closely to the prosecutor. In fact, almost every state makes the prosecutor the main legal adviser of the grand jury and requires him or her to be present during all grand jury sessions. However, in some states the grand jury functions independently of the prosecutor.

The Fifth Amendment has been interpreted to require grand jury indictment for federal felonies, but this right has not been applied to the states. In the 1884 decision of

Hurtado v. California, the Supreme Court stated that indictment by a grand jury is not a right guaranteed by the due process clause of the Fourteenth Amendment.[43]

grand jury
"[A] body of persons who have been selected according to law and sworn to hear the evidence against accused persons and determine whether there is sufficient evidence to bring those persons to trial, to investigate criminal activity generally, and to investigate the conduct of public agencies and officials."[vi]

Grand Jury Composition The **grand jury** is "a body of persons who have been selected according to law and sworn to hear the evidence against accused persons and determine whether there is sufficient evidence to bring those persons to trial, to investigate criminal activity generally, and to investigate the conduct of public agencies and officials."[44] Who serves on grand juries? How are they composed? How long do they serve? There are some common practices in place throughout the United States.

People are selected for grand juries in the same way people are selected for ordinary trial (i.e., petit) juries: They are subpoenaed. In some states, grand jury members are selected from a list of eligible voters; in others, they are selected from a list of licensed drivers; and still other states select grand jury members from a list of tax returns, telephone directories, and other lists. Most people do not get the opportunity to serve on a grand jury because, compared to ordinary juries, they are not convened that frequently.

The grand jury selection process usually unfolds in two stages. First, a list of potential grand jury members is compiled by any of the methods (or others) described above; this list of grand jury members is known as the "venire." Next, people are selected from the list to serve on the grand jury. At both stages, constitutional complications can arise. For example, special steps need to be taken to ensure that the list of potential grand jurors, like that for the typical petit jury, is fair and impartial because defendants can raise constitutional challenges to the grand jury selection process if it is not fair and impartial.[45]

Library Extra
11–9 Constitutional Rights Foundation: Grand Jury Lesson Plan

Library Extra
11–10 Frequently Asked Questions about the Grand Jury System

Once a grand jury is convened, the members serve for a specified period of time. Terms can last from one month to as much as a year, but grand jurors may work for only a few days during this period. Under the Federal Rules of Criminal Procedure, a "regular" grand jury cannot serve for a period longer than 18 months, unless the court extends the service "upon a determination that such extension is in the public interest."[46]

Grand juries are larger than ordinary trial juries. In the past, grand juries consisting of 24 people or so were not uncommon, but today grand juries can be smaller, usually in the neighborhood of 16 to 20 people. Tennessee, for example, permits a grand jury of 13 individuals, but the voting requirements in that state are fairly restrictive. See Figure 11–2 for a list of grand jury size requirements by state. Finally, grand jury voting requirements vary by state as well as by size. The most common voting requirement is that 12 grand jury members

FIGURE 11–2

Grand Jury Sizes by State

Source: Available at http://campus.udayton.edu/~grandjur/stategj/sizegjtx.htm.

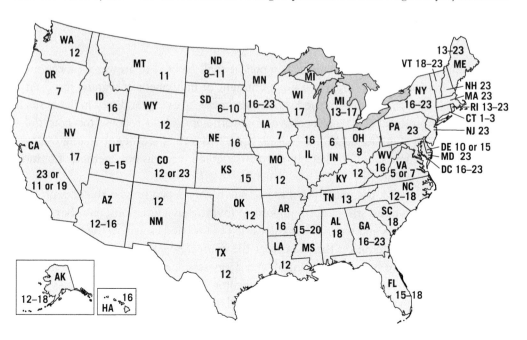

agree on an indictment. However, Virginia requires only 4 votes for a charge, and Louisiana requires 9 of 12 jurors to agree on an indictment.

Grand Jury Proceedings Grand jury proceedings are intensely secretive. In *United States* v. *Rose*, the Third Circuit Court of Appeals announced several reasons for this:

> (1) [T]o prevent the escape of those whose indictment may be contemplated; (2) to insure the utmost freedom to the grand jury in its deliberations, and to prevent persons subject to indictment or their friends from importuning the grand jurors; (3) to prevent subornation of perjury or tampering with the witnesses who may testify before the grand jury and later appear at the trial of those indicted by it; (4) to encourage free and untrammeled disclosures by persons who have information with respect to the commission of crimes; [and] (5) to protect the innocent accused who is exonerated from disclosure of the fact that he has been under investigation, and from the expense of standing trial where there was no probability of guilt.[47]

According to the Federal Rules of Criminal Procedure, grand jury proceedings can be shared with the defense when the defendant makes "a showing that grounds may exist for a motion to dismiss the indictment because of matters occurring before the grand jury."[48] This type of disclosure is exceedingly rare and is generally limited to situations where there is evidence of prosecutorial misconduct occurring before the grand jury proceedings commenced.

Grand juries have significant investigative authority: They can subpoena witnesses and documents, and they can hold uncooperative witnesses in contempt. Even though witnesses appearing before the grand jury enjoy the Fifth Amendment privilege against self-incrimination, the grand jury can get around this; for example, the grand jury can extend *grants of immunity* to witnesses in exchange for their testimony.

Library Extra
11–11 U.S. District Court: Handbook for Federal Grand Jurors

Grand Jury Indictment An **indictment** is "a formal, written accusation submitted to the court by a grand jury, alleging that a specified person(s) has committed a specified offense(s), usually a felony."[49] In other words, the indictment is the grand jury's charging document. The procedure is for the prosecutor to first present the government's case to the grand jury members (sometimes called a "bill of indictment"), and then the members will take a vote if they agree with the prosecutor that there is enough evidence to merit a criminal charge. With a sufficient number of votes, the grand jury will sustain the accusations and return an indictment, which is also known as a **true bill**. When it is delivered to the court, the indictment summarizes the facts about the case in question, discusses the proof in the government's possession, and names specific penal code provisions that have been violated. Indictments are sometimes sealed, meaning that the prosecutor will not alert the defendant of the charges, perhaps to leverage the defendant into testifying against a "bigger fish."

indictment
"[A] formal, written accusation submitted to the court by a grand jury, alleging that a specified person(s) has committed a specified offense(s), usually a felony"[vii]; also called *true bill*.

true bill
The grand jury's endorsement that it found sufficient evidence to warrant a criminal charge.

information
The prosecutor's formal charging document, and the alternative to a grand jury indictment, that informs the defendant of what crime he or she is charged with.

Preliminary Hearing

In lieu of an indictment, prosecutors may opt to charge by information. An **information** has been defined as the "written accusation submitted to the court by a prosecutor, alleging that a specified person(s) has committed a specified offense."[50] An information is one type of charging document (an indictment is another). If the prosecutor charges via an information, a preliminary hearing may be necessary. On the other hand, there are advantages to charging via grand jury. Because of the secrecy of grand jury proceedings, prosecutors can present evidence without the defense present, thus ensuring that the defense will not know much about the prosecution's case until trial. This occurred in the O. J. Simpson case.

The **preliminary hearing** is "the proceeding before a judicial officer in which three matters must be decided: whether a crime was committed; whether the crime occurred within the territorial jurisdiction of the court; and whether there are reasonable grounds to believe

preliminary hearing
"[T]he proceeding before a judicial officer in which three matters must be decided: whether a crime was committed; whether the crime occurred within the territorial jurisdiction of the court; and whether there are reasonable grounds to believe that the defendant committed the crime."[viii]

that the defendant committed the crime."[51] The preliminary hearing is intended to prevent "hasty, malicious, improvident, and oppressive prosecutions" and to ensure that "there are substantial grounds upon which a prosecution may be based."[52]

The Constitution does not require a preliminary hearing.[53] It is thus up to the states to determine whether such a hearing is warranted. Whether a preliminary hearing is required typically depends on a jurisdiction's method of filing criminal charges. In grand jury indictment jurisdictions (those that require that charges be filed in the form of a grand jury indictment), if the prosecutor secures an indictment within a specified time period, no preliminary hearing is required; however, if a prosecutor proceeds by information, then the defendant will usually be entitled to a preliminary hearing before the charges are filed.

Whether a jurisdiction proceeds by indictment or information has important implications concerning the defendant's rights. For example, the targets of grand jury investigations neither enjoy the right to counsel nor enjoy the right to challenge the state's case, but in preliminary hearings, both rights exist. Thus, a zealous prosecutor in a jurisdiction that provides for either an indictment or information charging decision may opt for indictment because the accused enjoys fewer rights. This issue may be moot, however, because accused individuals can and often do waive their preliminary hearings.

Probable Cause Requirement Assuming that a preliminary hearing is required, the prosecutor has the burden of proving that the case be bound over (i.e., handed over to) to a grand jury or go to trial, with the standard of proof being probable cause. Invariably, this is confused with the probable cause hearing. Distinguishing between the two types of hearings is based on the following: Probable cause hearings dwell on the justification to arrest, whereas the preliminary hearing dwells on whether probable cause exists to proceed with a trial. This is a critical distinction and is often responsible for separate probable cause and preliminary hearings in certain states.

The reason for setting probable cause as the appropriate standard for a preliminary hearing is that setting a higher standard would essentially make a trial pointless. Proof beyond a reasonable doubt, for example, would make a later criminal trial redundant. On the other hand, some people favor more proof than probable cause because the preliminary hearing seems somewhat redundant once a probable cause hearing has taken place. To minimize some of the confusion, one court observed that "probable cause to arrest does not automatically mean that the Commonwealth has sufficient competent legal evidence to justify the costs both to the defendant and to the Commonwealth of a full trial."[54]

Basically, the prosecutor needs to convince the judge that there is enough evidence to proceed with a trial. More specifically, there must be enough evidence to proceed such that the judge or jury has to contemplate whose case is more convincing. If it is clear that the state has no case but perhaps had probable cause for arrest, the court will order that the would-be defendant be released.

Procedural Issues Since preliminary hearings are adversarial in nature, it seems sensible that the right to counsel should apply. It does, and the state must provide counsel if the accused is indigent. This is because the preliminary hearing is a critical stage of the criminal process: "Plainly the guiding hand of counsel at the preliminary hearing is essential to protect the indigent accused against an erroneous and improper prosecution."[55]

Evidence procedures in a preliminary hearing are markedly different than in a criminal trial. First, the Federal Rules of Evidence states, "The finding of probable cause [in a preliminary hearing] may be based upon hearsay evidence in whole or in part."[56] By contrast, hearsay evidence (i.e., what one person previously heard and then says while testifying in court) is restricted in a criminal trial. Also, the exclusionary rule does not technically apply in preliminary hearings—actually, it's not so much that the rule does not apply but rather that the preliminary hearing is an inappropriate stage of the criminal process in which to object to evidence.

Another procedural matter in the preliminary hearing concerns the right to cross-examine witnesses as well as use the compulsory process to require their appearance. While these rights exist at criminal trials, preliminary hearings restrict them somewhat. In fact, the Supreme Court has held that there is no constitutional right to cross-examine witnesses at the preliminary hearing.[57]

Double Jeopardy

The constitutionally guaranteed protection against **double jeopardy** is designed to ensure that a person who has been convicted or acquitted of a crime is not tried or punished for the same offense twice. Double jeopardy occurs when a person is (1) reprosecuted for the same offense after acquittal, (2) reprosecuted after conviction, or (3) subjected to separate punishments for the same offense. Since two of these deal with prosecution, we discuss double jeopardy in this chapter, but it is also relevant at the sentencing phase.

Early English common law contains the foundations of the modern-day protection against double jeopardy. The rule of *autrefois acquit* prohibited the retrial of a defendant who was found not guilty; *autrefois convict*, on the other hand, prohibited the retrial of a defendant who was found guilty. These rules were adopted by the American colonies. Today, every state provides double jeopardy protection because of the Supreme Court's decision in *Benton v. Maryland* (395 U.S. 784 [1969]), where the Court declared that the Fifth Amendment's protection against double jeopardy is a fundamental right.

Double jeopardy does not apply in separate sovereigns, such as state and federal governments. This is important because charging someone for the same offense at both the federal and the state level does not violate double jeopardy.

Blockburger Rule   A rather complicated issue in double jeopardy jurisprudence concerns the definition of "same offense." In *Blockburger* v. *United States*, the Supreme Court developed a test that states, "Where the same act or transaction constitutes a violation of two distinct statutory provisions, the test to be applied to determine whether there are two offenses or only one is whether each requires proof of an additional fact which the other does not,"[58] a test that came to be known as the **Blockburger rule**.

According to the Blockburger rule, an offense is considered the same offense if two separate statutes contain elements A, B, and C. Likewise, if one crime contains elements A, B, and C and the other has elements A and B, both are considered the same offense because each statute does not require proof of a fact that the other does not. For example, assume that the offense of first-degree murder contains elements A (premeditated), B (deliberate), and C (killing) and that second-degree murder contains elements B (deliberate) and C (killing). Both offenses are considered the same for double jeopardy purposes because second-degree murder does not require proof of another element that first-degree murder does not. If a person is convicted of first-degree murder, then according to this example, the person cannot also be charged with second-degree murder.

Separate offenses can be identified. For example, one crime contains elements A, B, and C, and the other contains elements A, B, and D; both crimes require proof of an additional element that the other does not. For example, assume that the offense of joy-riding contains elements A (unlawful taking), B (of an automobile), and C (the intent to *temporarily* deprive the owner of possession). Assume also that the offense of car theft contains elements A (unlawful taking), B (of an automobile), and D (the intent to *permanently* deprive the owner of possession). These are considered separate offenses because each offense requires

double jeopardy
The Fifth Amendment requirement that a person cannot be reprosecuted after acquittal, reprosecuted after conviction, or subjected to separate punishments for the same offense.

Library Extra
11–12 Double Jeopardy

Blockburger rule
A complicated issue in double jeopardy jurisprudence concerning the definition of "same offense," resolved by the U.S. Supreme Court's development of a test that states, "Where the same act or transaction constitutes a violation of two distinct statutory provisions, the test to be applied to determine whether there are two offenses or only one is whether each requires proof of an additional fact which the other does not."[ix]

proof of an element that the other does not, so a person who is found guilty of joy-riding can also be charged with the crime of car theft, although from a practical standpoint this almost never occurs.[59]

Learning Objective 6

Summarize the purpose of arraignment and the different defendant pleas.

Web Extra
11–3 Electronic Discovery Blog

nolo contendere
A plea to a criminal charge that means "I do not desire to contest the action." While it resembles a guilty plea, it is different in the sense that it may not be used against the defendant in any later civil litigation arising from the act that gave rise to the criminal charges.

allocution
The defendant's explanation to the judge, usually in open court, of exactly what he or she did and why. An allocution is documented in court records and can be used against the defendant in related civil proceedings.

Learning Objective 7

Describe the discovery process and the types of discovery.

discovery
The process whereby both parties to a case learn of the evidence that the opposition will present.

Arraignment

Once a person has been formally charged, he or she will be arraigned. The purpose of arraignment is to formally notify the defendant of the charge lodged against him or her. At arraignment, the defendant enters one of three pleas: guilty, not guilty, or *nolo contendere*. A plea of guilty, which can be entered for a number of reasons, is an admission by the defendant of every allegation in the indictment or information. For example, the defendant could simply elect to "fess up" and admit responsibility, or the defendant may plead guilty because of a plea agreement with the prosecution.

A plea of not guilty is fairly self-explanatory—the defendant formally contends that he or she did not commit the crime in question. A plea of not guilty will result, especially for serious crimes, in a full-blown criminal trial. Finally, a plea of **nolo contendere**, which means "I do not desire to contest the action," resembles a guilty plea but is different in the sense that it may not be used against the defendant in any later civil litigation arising from the acts that gave rise to the criminal charges. Also, in some jurisdictions, if the defendant enters a plea of *nolo contendere*, the court may not ask the defendant whether he or she committed the crime in question, whereas with a guilty plea, the defendant is required to allocute. **Allocution** is the act of the defendant explaining to the judge exactly what he or she did and why; it is documented in court records and can be used against the defendant in related civil proceedings.

Discovery

Discovery is the process whereby both parties to a case learn of the evidence that the opposition will present. Rule 16 of the Federal Rules of Evidence provides that the defendant may, on request, "discover" the following from the prosecution: (1) any written statements or transcriptions of oral statements made by the defendant that are in the prosecution's possession, (2) the defendant's prior criminal record, and (3) any documents, photographs, tangible items, results from physical and mental evaluations, and other forms of real evidence considered material to the prosecution's case. The term *materiality* refers to whether evidence is consequential to the case, that is, whether it is capable of influencing the outcome of the case. If the defense requests items in the second or third category, then the prosecution will be granted "reciprocal discovery," where it learns of the defense's evidence. Relevant portions of Rule 16 that govern the prosecution's disclosure of evidence are reprinted in Box 11–4.

Federal Rule 16 is actually restrictive. Several states permit even more discovery, such as the names and addresses of all persons known to have any information concerning the case. This means that the prosecution must provide the defense (and vice versa) with a list of all individuals likely to give testimony at trial.

Discovery ends where strategy begins; that is, while both sides are given great latitude in terms of learning what evidence the opposition intends to use, strategy does not need to be shared. For example, the method of argument that the prosecution wishes to use in order to convince the jury of a particular fact is not subject to discovery, and neither is the order in which the defense seeks to call witnesses. Strategy is also referred to as "work product," and work product is off limits and not part of the discovery process.

BOX 11–4 Examples of Prosecution Discovery

INFORMATION SUBJECT TO DISCLOSURE

- *Defendant's oral statement.* Upon a defendant's request, the government must disclose to the defendant the substance of any relevant oral statement made by the defendant, before or after arrest, in response to interrogation by a person the defendant knew was a government agent if the government intends to use the statement at trial.

- *Defendant's written or recorded statement.* Upon a defendant's request, the government must disclose to the defendant, and make available for inspection, copying, or photographing, all of the following.

- *Defendant's prior record.* Upon a defendant's request, the government must furnish the defendant with a copy of the defendant's prior criminal record that is within the government's possession, custody, or control if the attorney for the government knows—or through due diligence could know—that the record exists.

- *Documents and objects.* Upon a defendant's request, the government must permit the defendant to inspect and to copy or photograph books, papers, documents, data, photographs, tangible objects, buildings or places, or copies or portions of any of these items.

- *Reports of examinations and tests.* Upon a defendant's request, the government must permit a defendant to inspect and to copy or photograph the results or reports of any physical or mental examination and of any scientific test or experiment. ■

Source: Rule 16, Federal Rules of Evidence.

Forms of Discovery

Discovery is part of the pretrial process and takes place in the hours and days leading up to the criminal trial. However, if a new witness becomes available during the course of a trial, then discovery can take place later in the criminal process. There are three types of discovery: discovery by the defense, discovery by the prosecution, and nonreciprocal discovery.

Discovery by the Defense Discovery should benefit the defense more than the prosecution. After all, the prosecution presents the state's case against the defendant, so it's only sensible that the defense learn the nature of the prosecution's case. Generally, though, the prosecution has more information because it has to prove beyond a reasonable doubt that the defendant committed the crime; the defense, by contrast, needs only to raise reasonable doubt in the minds of the jurors. As an example of defense discovery, the Supreme Court has held that the prosecution must provide the defense with a list of witnesses who will testify in rebuttal to the defendant's alibi or defense.[60]

Discovery by the Prosecution Discovery by the prosecution is relatively limited because of the constitutional rights enjoyed by criminal defendants. For example, the defense cannot be compelled to provide the prosecution with incriminating information, particularly in the form of statements and admissions.

What if the defense wishes to present an alibi at trial or assert a defense to criminal liability? Should the prosecutor be permitted to discover this information? The Supreme Court faced the alibi issue in *Williams* v. *Florida*.[61] Florida had a "notice of alibi" statute that provided that the defendant had to permit discovery of alibi defenses coupled with a list of witnesses who support it. The Court found that this type of discovery does not violate the Fifth Amendment because it is not self-incriminating.

The *Williams* decision extends to other defenses as well. For example, if the defense intends to argue that the defendant is not guilty by reason of insanity, then the prosecutor needs to be notified in advance of this intention. Alternatively, if the defense intends to

Library Extra
11–13 Discovery

argue that the defendant acted in self-defense, then the prosecution should be notified. The reason for requiring this notification is that it provides the prosecutor with an opportunity to plan its argument to the contrary.

One item concerning witnesses that the defense is *not* required to share with the prosecutor is whether the defendant will testify. In one case, the Supreme Court declared unconstitutional a state statute that required defendants, if they were to testify, to do so immediately after the prosecution rested its case.[62] The Court held that the statute violated the Fifth Amendment's privilege against self-incrimination and diminished the role of defense counsel's ability to make such determinations as to when witnesses will testify.

In another prosecution discovery case,[63] the defense attempted to call to the stand a private investigator whose testimony would have cast doubt on the prosecution's case. The trial judge ruled that the investigator could not testify until the prosecution received portions of the investigator's pretrial investigative report, and the Supreme Court upheld this decision. Plaintiff Nobles argued that this decision infringed on his right to compulsory process, namely, to call the investigator to the stand, but according to the Court, "The Sixth Amendment does not confer the right to present testimony free from the legitimate demands of the adversarial system; one cannot invoke the Sixth Amendment as a justification for presenting what might have been a half-truth."[64] The defense argued that being forced to supply information from the investigator's report violated attorney–client privilege, but the Court countered by concluding that attorney–client privilege was basically waived when the defense decided to have the investigator testify about the contents of his report.

Another prosecution discovery issue concerns whether the testimony of a witness about whom the defense does not inform the prosecution can be excluded. In *Taylor v. Illinois*,[65] the defense called a witness who had not been on a witness list supplied to the prosecution before trial, and the trial court excluded the witness's testimony, citing a violation of discovery procedure. The defendant appealed, arguing that exclusion of the witness's testimony violated the compulsory process clause of the Sixth Amendment. The Supreme Court sided with the trial court's decision.

Nonreciprocal Discovery With few exceptions, discovery is a two-way street: The defense must supply the prosecution with certain information and vice versa. For example, when the defense wants to assert an alibi, it must supply the prosecution with that alibi, and the prosecution must in turn supply the defense with a list of witnesses who will testify in rebuttal to the alibi. On the other hand, there are some circumstances where the prosecution is required to supply information to the defense but the reverse is *not* required. Examples of nonreciprocal discovery include the prosecutor's duty to disclose exculpatory evidence and to preserve evidence.

First, if the prosecution obtains evidence suggesting that the defendant is not guilty, it needs to inform the defense of this fact either before or well into the trial.[66] In *Brady v. Maryland*,[67] the Supreme Court held that "the suppression by the prosecution of evidence favorable to an accused upon request violates due process where the evidence is *material either to guilt or to punishment*, irrespective of the good faith or bad faith of the prosecution."[68] Later cases have interpreted this to mean that the prosecution's constitutional duty to disclose exculpatory evidence hinges on whether such evidence would have a "reasonable probability" of changing the outcome of the case.[69] If the evidence would not have a reasonable probability of changing the outcome of the case, failure to disclose it will not violate due process.

As for preserving evidence, the prosecution cannot destroy exculpatory evidence in an effort to gain a conviction, and to do so would be a violation of due process. For the defense to convince the court that the prosecution destroyed exculpatory evidence, it must demonstrate three facts: (1) that the evidence was expected to "play a significant role in the suspect's defense," (2) that the evidence was of "such a nature that the defendant would be unable to obtain comparable evidence by other reasonably available means," and (3) that the destruction of the evidence was a result of "official animus toward [the defendant] or . . . a conscious effort to suppress exculpatory evidence."[70] Note that the third requirement departs from the *Brady* decision discussed in the previous subsection because *Brady* did not consider the prosecution's state of mind as relevant.

A case that offers some clarification concerning these three requirements is *Arizona* v. *Youngblood.*[71] The Supreme Court stated that "unless a criminal defendant can show bad faith on the part of the police [or prosecution], failure to preserve potentially useful evidence does not constitute due process of law."[72]

In addition to prosecutors, the police must also preserve evidence. Without proper documentation of how the evidence was acquired and who handled it, which is called the **chain of custody**, the defense will allege that the evidence was tampered with or tainted in such a way that it cannot prove the defendant's involvement in a crime. Because of this, prosecutors' offices and police departments are very concerned with maintaining a proper chain of custody.

chain of custody
A documented record of custodial preservation of evidence in the original condition in which it was discovered during an investigation.

SUMMARY

CHAPTER 11

1. SUMMARIZE THE ARREST PROCEDURE, INCLUDING THE PROBABLE CAUSE REQUIREMENT

- The arrest is the gateway to the formal criminal justice process.
- Arrests must be supported by probable cause.
- A practical measure of probable cause is somewhere below proof beyond a reasonable doubt but above a hunch or reasonable suspicion.

2. EXPLAIN THE EXCLUSIONARY RULE, ITS EXCEPTIONS, AND EXTENSIONS

- The exclusionary rule provides that evidence obtained in violation of the Constitution (usually the Fourth Amendment) cannot be admitted in a criminal trial to prove guilt.
- The exclusionary rule extends beyond the Fourth Amendment to include, for example, improperly secured confessions.
- The exclusionary rule is controversial. Critics feel that it is a loophole; supporters feel that it is not and that it promotes police integrity.
- Exceptions to the exclusionary rule include good faith and impeachment.
- The exclusionary rule's reach was extended with the fruit of the poisonous tree doctrine, which covers "derivative evidence."
- Exceptions to the fruit of the poisonous tree doctrine include purged taint, independent source, and inevitable discovery.

3. DESCRIBE THE BOOKING PROCESS AND THE INITIAL APPEARANCE OF SUSPECTS

- Booking follows arrest.
- The initial appearance follows booking and serves to notify the accused of (1) the reasons for his or her detention (notification of formal charges often comes later at arraignment), (2) his or her protections against self-incrimination, and (3) his or her right to appointed counsel if need be.

- Pretrial release is concerned with whether an accused person should be released back into the community pending trial.
- There is no requirement that there be a dedicated pretrial release hearing.
- Bail and release on recognizance are methods of pretrial release, and preventive detention is a means of detaining the accused in jail prior to trial.
- Judges' bail decisions are based on the accused's flight risk, dangerousness, and financial status.

- The Fifth Amendment's grand jury indictment provision has not been applied to the states, so the charging mechanisms (grand jury indictment or prosecutor's information) vary from state to state and from offense to offense.
- Grand juries are similar to ordinary trial juries, but they are larger and serve longer terms. Unanimous votes are rarely required to return an indictment. Grand jury proceedings are also intensely secretive.
- If the prosecutor proceeds by information, a preliminary hearing may be necessary.
- The preliminary hearing serves as a "check" on the prosecutor's charging decision, is adversarial in nature, and ensures that there is sufficient evidence to take the case to trial.
- Prosecutors must ensure defendants are not twice charged for the same offense. Two separate statutory provisions, each of which contains at least one similar element, can be considered the same offense (e.g., first- and second-degree murder are considered the same offense because each contains the elements of intentional killing).

- The purpose of arraignment is to formally notify the defendant of the charge lodged against him or her.
- At arraignment, the defendant enters one of three pleas: guilty, not guilty, or *nolo contendere* (the latter translates into "I do not desire to contest the action").

- Discovery is the process by which both parties to a case learn of the evidence that the opposition will present.
- There are three forms of discovery: discovery by the defense, discovery by the prosecution, and nonreciprocal discovery (i.e., discovery that does not go both ways).
- An example of defense discovery is learning of witnesses the prosecution will call.
- An example of prosecution discovery is learning which defenses the defense will assert (e.g., insanity).
- An example of nonreciprocal discovery is the prosecution's constitutional duty to share exculpatory evidence.

KEY TERMS

allocution, 300

arrest, 281

bail, 291

bail bondsman, 291

Blockburger rule, 299

booking, 290

chain of custody, 303

discovery, 300

double jeopardy, 299

exclusionary rule, 283

Federal Bail Reform
    Act, 293

fruit of the poisonous tree
    doctrine, 288

good-faith exception, 287

grand jury, 296

impeachment
    exception, 287

independent source
    exception, 288

indictment, 297

inevitable-discovery
    exception, 288

information, 297

initial appearance, 290

nolo contendere, 300

preliminary hearing, 297

preventive detention, 293

probable cause, 281

purged taint exception, 288

release on recognizance, 292

trial, 283

true bill, 297

REVIEW QUESTIONS

1. What constitutes a lawful arrest? What legal issues surround the arrest process?

2. What's the purpose of an initial court appearance? What takes place during the initial appearance?

3. What's the purpose of pretrial release? What mechanisms are available to effect release?

4. What is the purpose of a grand jury? How does indictment by a grand jury differ from charging by a prosecutor?

5. What is the purpose of arraignment? What are the various types of pleas available to defendants at arraignment?

6. What is discovery? To what extent is discovery helpful? To what extent is it a hindrance?

WHAT WILL YOU DO?

You are a rookie police officer and have just made your first arrest. The police academy that you attended taught you many things: how to handle violent confrontations, how to be skilled at interpersonal communications, how to write reports, how to effectively use hand-to-hand tactics, how to use firearms safely, how to make an arrest, how to question suspects, and how to properly respond to numerous ethical issues.

The arrest happened a few days ago when you and your partner were called to respond to the scene of a reported domestic-violence incident. When you arrived, you found the apartment door open and a middle-aged man and woman yelling at each other. The man had his hand on her wrist and was twisting the woman's arm. She was vigorously hitting him with a big Yellow Pages phone book.

You attempted to quickly gain control of the situation and forcefully removed the man's hand from the woman's wrist. What surprised you the most, however, was the woman's reaction. Instead of continuing to hurl verbal abuse at the man, whom you soon learned was her husband, she started flailing away at you with the phone book, yelling for you to turn her husband loose.

Your partner moved in and made the woman retreat to a corner, where he told her to sit in a chair. As she had the beginnings of a black eye as well as welts and bruises on her arms, you decided that it would be best to arrest the man in order to remove him from the home to ensure the woman's safety. The smell of liquor on the man's breath and his slurred speech quickly told you that he was intoxicated, but you knew from your training that it would be necessary for you to read him his *Miranda* rights before you asked him to admit his guilt.

You had been given a number of *Miranda* warning cards when you were in the academy, and you pulled one from your shirt pocket and dutifully began reading the suspect his rights. Unfortunately, in the midst of your recitation, the man lurched forward. You weren't sure if he was trying to get away or if he had merely lost his balance as a result of being intoxicated. As you moved to restrain him, you dropped the *Miranda* warning card from which you had been reading. Feeling that you knew the warnings by heart and knowing that you wanted to put this incident behind you as quickly as you could, you continued to recite the *Miranda* warnings from memory.

When you finished, you asked the man a few questions. He essentially admitted to assaulting his wife, so you arrested him on the charge of battery. In your notebook, you duly noted the man's responses to your questions and jotted down that he had admitted his guilt. You thought yourself pretty clever when you got the man to affix his initials to your notebook page after you read it to him.

Since that night, things have quickly become more complicated. Today, you find yourself seated on the witness stand in a special domestic-violence court. The court sees many cases like the one in which you made an arrest, and it likes to process them quickly.

You have been told by other officers that one of the things the public defender will likely ask you during your testimony is whether you read the defendant his *Miranda* rights—with an emphasis on the word *read*. Those officers reminded you (as you had been taught at the academy) that reading those rights is considered essential in being sure that the suspect has been properly advised. A recitation of the *Miranda* rights from memory could be regarded by the judge as insufficient for purposes of advisement. If that happened, of course, the suspect's admission of guilt—which you have already related to the court—could be thrown out. You're pretty sure that no one but you (probably not even your partner) knows that the *Miranda* warning card from which you were reading fell to the floor and that you didn't live up to your academy training by failing to retrieve it.

When the prosecutor asks you if you read the defendant his rights, what will you say?

NOTES

i. Adapted from U.S. Department of Justice, *Dictionary of Criminal Justice Data Terminology*, p. 22.

ii. *Beck v. Ohio*, 379 U.S. 89 (1964), p. 91.

iii. *Brinegar v. United States*, 338 U.S. 160 (1949), p. 175.

iv. U.S. Department of Justice, *Dictionary of Criminal Justice Data Terminology*, p. 28.

v. 18 U.S.C., Sections 3141–3150.

vi. U.S. Department of Justice, *Dictionary of Criminal Justice Data Terminology*, p. 99.

vii. U.S. Department of Justice, *Dictionary of Criminal Justice Data Terminology*, p. 108.

viii. U.S. Department of Justice, *Dictionary of Criminal Justice Data Terminology*, p. 161.

ix. *Blockburger v. United States*, 284 U.S. 299 (1932), p. 304.

1. ABC News, "No Miranda Rights for Boston Jihadi Bomber—Public Safety Exception," April 19, 2013, available at http://patdollard.com/2013/04/abcnews-no-miranda-rights-for-boston-jihadi-bomber-public-safety-exception (accessed May 5, 2013).

2. *Beck v. Ohio*, 379 U.S. 89 (1964), p. 91.

3. *Chimel v. California*, 395 U.S. 752 (1969).

4. *Miranda v. Arizona*, 384 U.S. 436 (1966).

5. *Boyd v. United States*, 116 U.S. 616 (1886).

6. Ibid., p. 634.

7. *Weeks v. United States*, 232 U.S. 383 (1914).

8. *Silverthorne Lumber Co. v. United States*, 251 U.S. 385 (1920), p. 392.

9. See, e.g., *Agnello v. United States*, 269 U.S. 20 (1925).

10. *Mapp v. Ohio*, 367 U.S. 643 (1961).

11. *Elkins v. United States*, 364 U.S. 206 (1960), p. 222.

12. C. D. Uchida and T. S. Bynum, "Search Warrants, Motions to Suppress and 'Lost Cases': The Effects of the Exclusionary Rule in Seven Jurisdictions," *Journal of Criminal Law and Criminology*, Vol. 81 (1991), pp. 1034–1066.

13. *United States v. Leon*, 468 U.S. 897 (1984).

14. *Massachusetts v. Sheppard*, 468 U.S. 981 (1984).

15. *United States v. Hove*, 848 F.2d 137 (9th Cir. 1988), p. 139.

16. *United States v. Leary*, 846 F.2d 592 (10th Cir. 1988), p. 607.

17. *Lo-Ji v. State of New York*, 442 U.S. 319 (1979).

18. *Walder v. United States*, 347 U.S. 62 (1954).

19. *Silverthorne Lumber Co. v. United States*, 251 U.S. 385 (1920).

20. *United States v. Ceccolini*, 435 U.S. 268 (1978), p. 276.

21. *Nix v. Williams*, 467 U.S. 431 (1984).

22. *Wong Sun v. United States*, 371 U.S. 471 (1963).

23. *Gerstein v. Pugh*, 420 U.S. 103 (1975).

24. *Bell v. Wolfish*, 441 U.S. 520 (1979), p. 533.

25. *Stack v. Boyle*, 342 U.S. 1 (1951), p. 6, n. 3.

26. *United States v. Salerno*, 481 U.S. 739 (1987).

27. U.S. Department of Justice, *Dictionary of Criminal Justice Data Terminology*, 2nd ed. (Washington, DC: U.S. Department of Justice, Bureau of Justice Statistics, 1981), p. 28.

28. 18 U.S.C.A., Section 3142.

29. Cal. Const. Art. I, Section 6.

30. See, e.g., M. Paulsen, "Pre-Trial Release in the United States," *Columbia Law Review*, Vol. 66 (1966), pp. 109, 113.

31. *Pannell v. United States*, 320 F.2d 698 (D.C. Cir. 1963), p. 699.

32. 18 U.S.C., Sections 3146–3152.

33. See, e.g., 18 U.S.C., Section 3146(a).

34. Ibid., Section 3146(b).

35. D.C. Code (1970), Section 23–1322.

36. 18 U.S.C., Sections 3141–3150.

37. Ibid., Section 3142(d).

38. Ibid., Section 3142(f).

39. *Stack v. Boyle*, 342 U.S. 1 (1951), p. 5.

40. *Schall v. Martin*, 467 U.S. 253 (1984).

41. *Schilb v. Kuebel*, 404 U.S. 357 (1971).

42. Ibid., p. 370.

43. *Hurtado v. California*, 110 U.S. 516 (1884), p. 538.

44. U.S. Department of Justice, *Dictionary of Criminal Justice Data Terminology*, p. 99.

45. See, e.g., *Casteneda v. Partida*, 430 U.S. 482 (1977); also see *Taylor v. Louisiana*, 419 U.S. 522 (1975).

46. Federal Rules of Criminal Procedure, 6(g).

47. *United States v. Rose*, 215 F.2d 617 (1954), pp. 628–629.

48. Federal Rules of Criminal Procedure, 6(e)(3)(c)(ii).

49. U.S. Department of Justice, *Dictionary of Criminal Justice Data Terminology*, p. 108.

50. Ibid.

51. Ibid., p. 161.

52. *Thies v. State*, 178 Wis. 98, 103 (1922).

53. See *Lem Woon v. Oregon*, 229 U.S. 586 (1913), and *Gerstein v. Pugh*, 420 U.S. 103 (1975).

54. *Myers v. Commonwealth*, 363 Mass. 843 (1973), p. 849.

55. *Coleman v. Alabama*, 399 U.S. 1 (1970), p. 9.

56. Federal Rules of Evidence, 5.1.

57. *Goldsby v. United States*, 160 U.S. 70 (1895).

58. *Blockburger v. United States*, 284 U.S. 299 (1932), p. 304.

59. *Brown v. Ohio*, 432 U.S. 161 (1977).

60. *Wardius v. Oregon*, 412 U.S. 470 (1973), pp. 475–476.

61. *Williams v. Florida*, 399 U.S. 78 (1970).

62. *Brooks v. Tennessee*, 406 U.S. 605 (1972).

63. *United States v. Nobles*, 422 U.S. 225 (1975).

64. Ibid., p. 241.

65. *Taylor v. Illinois*, 484 U.S. 400 (1988).

66. *United States v. Baxter*, 492 F.2d 150 (9th Cir. 1973), and *United States v. Harris*, 498 F.2d 1164 (3rd Cir. 1974).

67. *Brady v. Maryland*, 373 U.S. 83 (1963).

68. Ibid., p. 87, emphasis added.

69. *United States v. Bagley*, 473 U.S. 667 (1985).

70. *California v. Trombetta*, 467 U.S. 479 (1984).

71. *Arizona v. Youngblood*, 488 U.S. 51 (1988).

72. Ibid., p. 58.

TIMOTHY A. CLARY/Getty Images

12

Plea Bargaining and Guilty Pleas

LEARNING OBJECTIVES

1. Summarize the history and development of plea bargaining.

2. Explain the plea bargaining process.

3. Describe the elements of guilty pleas and how guilty pleas are contested.

Kenneth Kassab stands in front of the building housing the United States District Court for the Western District of Michigan. Kassab's case was tried there in 2012. What made the case unusual?

Gary Fields/The Wall Street Journal

INTRODUCTION

In 2012, 53-year-old Kenneth Kassab of Marquette, Michigan, was on the verge of pleading guilty to federal charges of illegally transporting thousands of pounds of explosives but changed his mind at the last minute and decided to go to trial.[1] Kassab, who always maintained his innocence, was arrested after his employer had ordered him to use a truck to move a large number of 50-pound bags of fertilizer similar to those that had been used in the 1995 bombing of the Alfred P. Murrah federal building in Oklahoma City, Oklahoma. Kassab had thought of accepting a plea deal offered by prosecutors in order to avoid what might have been a lengthy prison sentence—which a judge could have imposed had he been convicted at trial. Instead, a week after deciding to reject the plea arrangement, a federal jury found him not guilty, and he was set free. Kassab's case is unusual because 97% of all federal criminal defendants agree to plead guilty rather than going to trial—a significant increase from the 84% who made that choice in 1990.[2]

PLEA BARGAINING

The overwhelming majority of all criminal convictions in the United States result from guilty pleas rather than trials. These guilty pleas are usually the result of some bargaining between the defense attorney and the prosecutor. Both parties stand to gain something from a guilty plea: The prosecutor obtains a conviction, and the defense attorney usually succeeds in getting a lesser conviction for his or her client.

Plea bargaining is essential to the administration of justice. If every defendant demanded his or her right to a jury trial and succeeded in such a demand, the criminal justice system would literally collapse. Nonetheless, plea bargains take the administration of justice out of the hands of judges and juries and turn it over to prosecutors and defense attorneys. Plea bargaining essentially permits the attorneys to decide the outcome of a case without the need to go to trial, and it is well known that when two defendants face the same charge, the one who plea bargains invariably receives a lesser sentence than the one who does not.

Learning Objective 1

Summarize the history and development of plea bargaining.

Definition of Plea Bargaining

plea bargaining
The process by which the prosecution and defense reach an agreement resulting in a guilty plea from the defendant that results in a reduced charge, reduced sentence, or some other concession favorable to the defendant.

charge bargaining
The prosecutor's ability to negotiate with the defendant in terms of the charges that could be filed.

sentence bargaining
A defendant agreement to plead guilty in exchange for a less serious sentence.

There is no agreed-on definition of **plea bargaining**. At the risk of simplification, it is the process by which the prosecution and defense reach an agreement resulting in a guilty plea from the defendant that results in a reduced charge, reduced sentence, or some other concession favorable to the defendant.

It is useful to distinguish between two types of plea bargaining: charge bargaining and sentence bargaining. **Charge bargaining** refers to the prosecutor's ability to negotiate with the defendant in terms of the charges that could be filed; **sentence bargaining** occurs when a defendant agrees to plead guilty in exchange for a less serious sentence.

The definition of plea bargaining first implies that plea bargains result in a mutually satisfactory disposition. It is true (as we will see later) that plea bargains must be intelligent and voluntary, but it is not always the case that a bargain is satisfactory to both parties to the agreement. For example, the prosecutor may simply be forced to present a favorable offer to the defendant because of procedural errors that would make it difficult to prove the state's case; on the other hand, the prosecutor may present the defendant with equally unfavorable choices.

All plea bargaining is "subject to court approval." While this is usually true, the plea bargaining process is mostly carried on between the defense and the prosecution, with little judicial review. For example, prosecutors can do a great deal to drop or alter charges against an individual prior to bringing any subsequent agreement to the attention of the trial judge.

Many plea bargaining concessions—besides a lighter sentence or a reduced charge—can be offered to the defendant in exchange for a guilty plea. For example, some defendants have received unique probation conditions and/or have been permitted to serve time at certain institutions in exchange for pleading guilty.[3]

Web Extra
12–1 The Plea

History and Rise of Plea Bargaining

Library Extra
12–1 Development of Plea Bargaining

Plea bargaining has a long history.[4] Cases referencing plea agreements go all the way back to the nineteenth century. One of the earliest reported court decisions addressing plea bargaining was *Commonwealth* v. *Battis*.[5] In that case, a court was hesitant to permit a guilty plea by a defendant charged with a capital crime, so the court gave the defendant time to contemplate his plea and even "examined, under oath, the sheriff, the jailer and justice . . . , as to the sanity of the prisoner; and whether there had been tampering with him, either by promises, persuasions, or hopes of pardon if he would plead guilty."[6] This portion of the court's decision suggests that, perhaps, some degree of plea bargaining took place in the early 1800s.

Following *Battis*, other cases involving some degree of plea bargaining began to be reported. *Edwards* v. *People* focused on a Michigan statute that set forth specific requirements necessary for a valid guilty plea in which the court expressed concern that some of what could be called plea bargaining was taking place without the approval of the courts.[7] The court observed that Michigan passed the statute "for the protection of prisoners and of the public" in response "to serious abuses caused by [prosecutors] procuring prisoners to plead guilty when a fair trial might show they were not guilty, or might show other facts important to be known."[8] The court also found it "easy to see that the Legislature thought there was danger that prosecuting attorneys . . . would procure prisoners to plead guilty by assurances [that] they have no power to make of influence in lowering the sentence, or by bringing some other unjust influence to bear on them."[9] These claims suggest that plea bargaining was a somewhat common practice by the second half of the nineteenth century.

Plea bargaining became even more common in the early to middle 1900s. Many states had by then impaneled commissions to study the workings of their criminal justice systems, and the studies published by these commissions reported an increase in the practice of plea bargaining. For example, the Georgia Department of Public Welfare reported that guilty plea rates increased 70% from 1916 to 1921;[10] similarly, statistics in New York revealed that between 1839 and 1920, the guilty plea rate rose to some 90% of all cases.[11]

Why the apparent rise in plea bargaining? Historical accounts show that in the early days of English criminal justice, juries would hear 12 to 20 felony cases in a single day,[12] and trials played out in a similar fashion in American courts during the 1800s. One historian pointed out that many early American trials were carried out without lawyers for the defendant or, in some cases, for the government.[13] But as the American legal system began to mature and lawyers entered the fray, trials slowed down, and guilty plea rates increased out of necessity. One legal scholar stated that "plea bargaining should be viewed as a natural outgrowth of a progressively adversarial criminal justice system."[14]

Despite its apparent necessity, plea bargaining was criticized extensively by early commentators: Some called it an "incompetent, inefficient, and lazy method of administering justice"[15]; others suggested that plea bargaining was just a means to avoid trials for individuals charged with committing criminal acts. The following section considers some of these criticisms—and responses to them—in further depth.

Arguments For and Against Plea Bargaining

There are several arguments in support of plea bargaining, and these have clearly won out because plea bargaining is a widely accepted practice in today's justice system. It is widely accepted because, despite certain drawbacks, plea bargaining benefits all members of the courtroom work group—the judge, the prosecutor, and the defense attorney (not to mention the defendant). Thus, the arguments in support of plea bargaining are really arguments concerning the benefits of reaching plea agreements, but each of these arguments needs to be viewed in context. In some situations—such as in highly celebrated cases—the costs of plea bargaining may outweigh the benefits.

Benefits Plea bargaining benefits the prosecution because it provides an increased ability to deal with a busy caseload. District attorneys are often faced with limited resources and, as such, cannot prosecute every case that comes before them. Specifically, the district attorney may opt to pursue charges on cases that have a highly public element and/or are likely to result in guilty convictions, and cases that don't look promising may be prime candidates for a plea bargain. According to one observer, plea bargaining may be favored by the prosecution simply because it allows the courtroom work group to further its "mutual interest in avoiding conflict, reducing uncertainty, and maintaining group cohesion."[16]

Defense attorneys also benefit from plea bargaining. Public defenders—the most common type of counsel in criminal trials—face resource constraints similar to those of prosecutors, and plea bargaining benefits them both by allowing quick disposition of cases and by allowing them to focus on cases that they perceive as being more worthy of trial. Bargaining also benefits privately retained counsel because it speeds up the process, which translates into more money for less work. This is not to suggest, however, that defense attorneys are goldbrickers; many jealously guard the interests of their clients. Defendants may also benefit because bargaining gives them the opportunity to receive a favorable sentencing outcome.

The court also benefits from plea bargaining. The prompt disposition of cases saves judicial resources. The reason for this should be clear: Plea bargaining takes less time than a full-blown trial.

To the chagrin of many, victims may also benefit from plea bargaining. A quickly reached plea bargain may give victims the satisfaction of having the case closed quickly; in addition, victims may not want to testify or risk the possibility that the prosecution will not succeed in obtaining a conviction.[17]

Costs   While actors in the criminal process seem to benefit from plea bargaining, there are also drawbacks to this procedure. For one thing, criminal defendants lose their chance at an acquittal and, sometimes, lose important rights, including the right to a trial by jury (though the Supreme Court has said that these costs may be outweighed by the benefits of "avoiding the anxieties and uncertainties of trial"[18]). This issue is addressed in the following "Courts in the News" feature.

In some cases, the procedure can hamper prosecutors. In an effort to secure a conviction, the prosecutor will start with the most serious charge and work down from there; that is, prosecutors may "overcharge" as a first step in the plea bargaining process. This negotiation process is much like that associated with buying a used car at a dealership, where the dealer usually starts with a ridiculously high price but is willing to negotiate; in the end, however, few "negotiators" end up purchasing a car for its fair market value. The concern with plea bargaining, then, is that defendants will be encouraged to plead guilty to an offense that is more serious than that which they would be convicted of at trial.

Some critics of plea bargaining claim that the practice actually contributes to inefficiency in the justice process. One researcher observed that "defense attorneys commonly devise strategies whose only utility lies in the threat they pose to the court's and prosecutor's

COURTS IN THE NEWS

Bargaining for Life

In a brutal 2002 murder, Patrick Bearup, Sean Gaines, Jeremy Johnson, and Jessica Nelson beat and shot Mark Mathes. It seems that Mathes and Nelson were living together and that Nelson suspected Mathes of stealing money. She asked Gaines, Bearup, and Johnson for help, and the four plotted to take care of the matter. After he was killed, Mathes's body was thrown off a cliff in the remote Crown King area north of Phoenix.

JOSHUA LOTT/The New York Times/Redux Pictures

Bearup was convicted of one count of kidnapping and one count of first-degree murder, and a jury sentenced him to death. On automatic appeal, the court found sufficient evidence supporting the jury's findings that Bearup was a major participant in the crime. Armed with a knife, Bearup joined two others who encircled the victim as he was savagely beaten. The court concluded that Bearup acted with reckless indifference to human life. After the beating, Bearup helped confine the victim to a car trunk, cut off his

Patrick Bearup, shown here in his prison cell, was the only one of 4 conspirators sentenced to death for their part in a murder plot. The reason: the other three brokered plea deals.

finger while he might have still been alive, and helped throw his body into a ravine. Those acts, the appellate court found, supported a finding that Bearup acted with reckless indifference to human life. The court found that the victim suffered both physical pain and mental anguish and that Bearup knew of his suffering. The victim attempted to stand and shield himself while screaming, "No. Leave me alone," as he was attacked with a baseball bat. The assault lasted between 60 and 90 seconds, and the victim suffered visible facial fractures and substantial blood loss.

The evidence showed that Bearup relished his crime when he was overheard laughing while talking about cutting off a person's finger and was amused when he told his ex-girlfriend about the crime. The court found the aggravating circumstances substantial and upheld the death penalty.

(continued)

What makes this case unusual was that the other three brokered plea deals, avoiding a trial. The roommate, Jessica Nelson, 37, who instigated the beating, and a skinhead recruit named Jeremy Johnson, 30, who pummeled Mathes with a baseball bat, were eligible to be out of prison in four years. Sean Gaines, who shot Mathes as he was thrown naked from a car onto a county road, is scheduled for release in 2028 at the age of 47.

Is the Bearup case unique? Are people able to avoid death by pleading while those who ask for trial risk death? Such cases, in which a defendant with lesser responsibility draws the harshest sentence, are not uncommon in Arizona and elsewhere. Of the six inmates executed in Arizona in 2012, four were equally or less culpable than co-defendants implicated in the same crimes; prison records show that three of those four co-defendants had been released before the executions were carried out. In Ohio, Jason Getsy was convicted in a murder-for-hire plot, and despite a clemency recommendation by the state parole board, he was executed in 2009 despite the fact that other participants in the crime, including its architect, were given prison sentences.

One reason for this phenomenon is cost: Prosecutors, when deciding whom to charge, weigh the cost of mounting a capital trial, which can reach $1 million, against the likelihood of a conviction. Richard Dieter, the executive director of the Death Penalty Information Center in Washington, said about the Bearup case, "In an ideal world, the prosecution would have ironclad proof against all the co-defendants to be able to pick the worst for the death penalty, but we have an inequitable system, a bargaining system. If you give the prosecution some help, you'll get something out of it."

Sometimes, money determines whether a defendant's life is on the line. Greg McPhillips, the deputy attorney in Mohave County in northwestern Arizona, said in a motion that because of a "budgetary crisis," the county could not afford to try more than one death penalty case at a time. He gave up on seeking the death penalty against a man facing charges of first-degree murder in the 2010 death of his infant son, choosing instead to pursue a capital case against a man accused of killing a teenage girl and injuring her mother.

From death row, Bearup has been studying to become a pastor, while he awaits his sentence to be carried out. ■

DISCUSSION QUESTIONS

1. While giving benefits to people who admit guilt and punishing those who ask for a trial seems unfair on its face, how else would you get people to cooperate and testify against co-conspirators at trial?

2. If you could, would you abolish the plea bargaining system now in place?

Sources: Fernanda Santos, "Less Culpable, but with Longer Sentences," *New York Times*, April 5, 2013, available at www.nytimes .com/2013/04/06/us/in-many-capital-cases-less-culpable-defendants-receive-death-penalty.html?hp&_r=0 (accessed June 2, 2013); Terry Carter, "Pending Death Penalty Cases Weigh against Maricopa County," *ABA Journal*, April 1, 2010, available at www.abajournal .com/magazine/article/pending_death_penalty_cases_weigh_against_maricopa_county (accessed June 2, 2013); *State v. Bearup*, 2009 WL 2060231 (2009), available at www.supreme.state.az.us/ courtserv/crtproj/capsentguid/page76.htm (accessed June 2, 2013).

time."[19] Critics also believe not only that plea bargaining is inefficient but also that it wastes time. Bargaining is, after all, not necessary to obtain guilty pleas, and most defendants would plead guilty anyway if they thought there were a high degree of probability that a trial would result in a verdict of guilty.[20]

Perhaps one of the most well-known criticisms of plea bargaining is that it undermines the integrity of the criminal justice system. Critics of plea bargaining claim that the practice circumvents the "rigorous standards of due process and proof imposed during trials" by the courts and the Constitution.[21]

Another reason that plea bargaining may undermine the criminal process is that it effectively decides the defendant's guilt without a trial, an exhaustive investigation, or the presentation of evidence and witness testimony:

> One mark of a just legal system is that it minimizes the effect of tactical choices upon the outcome of its processes. In criminal cases, the extent of an offender's punishment ought to turn primarily upon what he did and, perhaps, upon his personal characteristics rather than upon a postcrime, postarrest decision to exercise or not to exercise some procedural option.[22]

Critics of plea bargaining also argue that the practice allows criminals to get away with their crimes—or at least get more lenient sentences; further, critics claim that lesser sentences may reduce the deterrent effect of harsh punishment. In both cases, plea bargaining may give the impression that defendants can negotiate their way out of being adequately punished for their crimes.

At the other extreme, critics of plea bargaining also claim that innocent individuals may be coerced to plead guilty. In such situations, a plea bargain amounts to an admission of legal guilt when in fact the defendant may not be factually guilty. An example of the pressure for innocent defendants to plead guilty was seen in *North Carolina* v. *Alford.*[23] There, the Court reprinted a statement made by the defendant:

> I pleaded guilty on second degree murder because they said there is too much evidence, but I ain't shot no man, but I take the fault for the other man. We never had an argument in our life and I just pleaded guilty because they said if I didn't they would gas me for it, and that is all.[24]

This quote illustrates that with the right amount of pressure and intimidation, authorities can coerce certain suspects to plead guilty to crimes they didn't commit. It also ushered in what is now called the **Alford plea**, or "best-interests plea." An *Alford* plea is one in which the defendant pleads guilty but maintains his or her innocence. Also, an *Alford* plea does not require the defendant to "allocate," or explain the details surround the offense to the judge. It is basically a claim of neither guilt nor innocence. Table 12–1 summarizes the arguments for and against plea bargaining.

Attempts to Restrict Plea Bargaining

Concerns over plea bargaining have even led some jurisdictions to abandon the practice. In fact, at one point the whole state of Alaska banned plea bargaining, but some researchers concluded that Alaska's criminal justice system could function efficiently without it.[25]

Several other jurisdictions have experimented with restricting the practice of plea bargaining, and the experiences of these jurisdictions are perhaps more illustrative than the Alaska experience (Alaska is not exactly the epicenter of America's crime problem). Methods of restricting plea bargaining have ranged from outright bans to bans on certain types of crimes.

One method by which some jurisdictions have restricted plea bargaining is to impose cutoff dates. These cutoff dates prohibit plea bargaining after a case has been in process for a certain amount of time. For example, the Brooklyn district attorney has adopted a cutoff date of 74 days after indictment.[26] Prior to the deadline, plea bargaining is acceptable, and if a case goes all the way to trial within the cutoff period, plea bargaining could conceivably take place all the way through jury deliberations.

Alford plea
The defendant pleads guilty but maintains his or her innocence. It is basically a claim of neither guilt nor innocence.

Library Extra
12–2 *Time*: Is Plea Bargaining a Cop-Out?

TABLE 12–1 Arguments For and Against Plea Bargaining

Arguments For	Arguments Against
Helps the prosecutor dispose of a busy caseload	Behooves the prosecutor to choose the most serious charge from which to begin bargaining
Helps the public defender dispose of a busy caseload	Contributes to inefficiency
Benefits the defendant by providing a reduction in charges and/or a favorable sentencing recommendation	Wastes time because most defendants plead guilty anyway
Saves on judicial resources by avoiding the costs of going to trial	Undermines the integrity of the justice system
Gives the victim the satisfaction of having a prompt resolution of the case	Decides the defendant's guilt without having a trial
Benefits the victim who does not wish to testify at trial	Allows the criminal to get away with his or her crime
Contributes to cohesion in the courtroom workgroup	Can coerce an innocent individual to plead guilty (i.e., legal vs. factual guilt)

Another method of restricting plea bargaining has been to ban pleas. These bans prohibit either some or all types of plea agreements. Alaska is the most notable example of a total ban; in 1975, Alaska's attorney general banned all forms of plea bargaining. This was done in an effort to increase convictions and restore public confidence in the justice system.[27] In a study on the ban, Alaska's Judicial Council stated,

> Plea bargaining as an institution was clearly curtailed. The routine expectation of a negotiated settlement was removed; for most practitioners justifiable reliance on negotiation to settle criminal cases greatly diminished in importance. There is less face-to-face discussion between adversaries, and when meetings do occur, they are not usually as productive as they used to be.[28]

It is important to understand that Alaska banned plea bargaining but not guilty pleas, so defendants could still plead guilty to the crimes for which they were charged. In fact, the Judicial Council also found that the rate of guilty pleas remained essentially the same in the wake of the ban, suggesting that perhaps some degree of behind-the-scenes plea bargaining was still taking place. Also, in Alaska the attorney general could hire and fire the district attorneys, which gave him substantial leverage to ban plea bargaining. In most jurisdictions around the country, district attorneys are elected officials and do not serve at the whim of the state attorney general.

Some jurisdictions have also experimented with banning plea bargaining for certain offenses. For example, the Bronx County district attorney enacted a ban on plea bargaining whenever a grand jury returned a felony indictment. This move was seriously criticized—as are most attempts to restrict plea bargaining—but the district attorney stated that the ban "means that society has ceded control to those it has accused of violating its laws; and it means that our system is running us, instead of the other way around."[29] Critics challenged the Bronx County district attorney's ban on post–felony indictment plea bargaining for at least two reasons: (1) It did not eliminate plea bargaining, and (2) the policy encouraged plea bargaining prior to indictment.[30]

Another approach tried in Philadelphia was the jury waiver, which gives defendants the opportunity to engage in plea negotiations in exchange for giving up their right to a jury trial. Actually, this approach is not plea bargaining in the traditional sense; instead, the defendant gets his or her day in court, but to receive concessions from the state, he or she must not demand a jury trial. This process has come to be known as the "slow plea of guilty" insofar as it does not result in the disposition of a case prior to trial. One researcher described the process in more detail:

> Slow pleas are informal and abbreviated and consist largely of the defense's presentation of statements concerning the defendant's allegedly favorable personal characteristics. . . . The defense presentation is not concerned with guilt or innocence since it usually is implicitly assumed by all parties involved in the process that the defendant is guilty of at least some wrongdoing.[31]

California attempted to abandon plea bargaining by popular referendum in 1982. The voters passed the referendum, and the resulting statute (California Penal Code, Section 1192.7) imposes the following restrictions: no plea bargaining in any case involving (1) a serious felony, (2) a felony where a firearm was used, or (3) the offense of driving under the influence. Plea bargaining is permissible, however, if the prosecution's evidence is weak, witnesses are unavailable, or a plea agreement does not result in a significantly reduced sentence. Despite the statute, plea bargaining continues almost unabated in the state of California.[32]

El Paso (Texas) also experimented with plea bargaining restrictions. There, two state district judges adopted a policy of prohibiting all plea negotiations in their courts as a method of ensuring equal treatment for similarly situated defendants.[33] Maricopa County (Arizona)

Library Extra
12–3 Cato Institute: The Case against Plea Bargaining

adopted a similar approach: Five Maricopa County Superior Court judges adopted a policy that prohibited plea agreements based on "stipulated" (i.e., agreed-on) sentences; in other words, the judges refused to accept plea agreements that included a negotiated sentence because they felt that sentencing should be a decision left to the trial courts.

Supreme Court's View on Plea Bargaining

The Supreme Court has sanctioned plea bargaining. It stated in *Brady* v. *United States* that "we cannot hold that it is unconstitutional for the State to extend a benefit to a defendant who in turn extends a substantial benefit to the State."[34] In the later case of *Santobello* v. *New York*, the Court offered the following argument in support of plea bargaining:

> The disposition of criminal charges by agreement between the prosecutor and the accused, sometimes loosely called "plea bargaining," is an essential component of the administration of justice. Properly administered, it is to be encouraged.[35]

Library Extra
12–4 *Encyclopedia of Everyday Law*: Plea Bargaining

How, then, is plea bargaining to be properly administered? The following sections seek to answer this question. Let's begin by describing the plea bargaining process, then discuss the effect of plea bargaining, the rules concerning plea bargaining, and situations where guilty pleas can be challenged. As before, the reader will develop an understanding of the complex practice of plea bargaining as it has been interpreted through the courts, most notably the U.S. Supreme Court.

Learning Objective 2

Explain the plea bargaining process.

THE PLEA BARGAINING PROCESS

There are several different offers the prosecutor can make in an effort to secure a guilty plea. The most straightforward and common is to reduce the charge against the defendant; other alternatives include the dismissal of other pending charges, a promise to recommend a particular sentence, or a promise not to contest a point made by the defense. Assuming that what is offered by the prosecution is acceptable to the defendant, he or she can make one of two pleas. One is a simple plea of guilty, and the other is a plea of *nolo contendere*. The former is akin to the defendant saying, "I am guilty." The latter (as we saw in the previous chapter) amounts to the defendant saying, "I do not contest this." Both pleas are effectively the same, the only difference being that the *nolo contendere* plea cannot be used as an admission of guilt in a subsequent civil case. An actual plea form is presented in Figure 12–1.

Constitutional Rights during Plea Bargaining

Plea bargaining is a method of circumventing a criminal trial, so, not surprisingly, the rights available to a defendant during bargaining are not the same as those available at trial. There are, however, important rights that the defendant still enjoys during the plea bargaining process.

First, the Sixth Amendment right to counsel applies during plea bargaining because charges have already been filed before bargaining commences. According to the Supreme Court, the right to counsel attaches when, after charges have been filed, the "defendant finds himself faced with the prosecutorial forces of organized society, and immersed in the intricacies of substantive and procedural criminal law."[36] This means that the prosecutor cannot bargain directly with the defendant unless counsel has been waived.

The Sixth Amendment also requires that defense counsel be effective during the plea negotiation process. This means that the defense attorney must, at a minimum, investigate the case so as to make an informed decision with regard to what sentences and charges are

PLEA FORM: IN PERSON

CAUSE NUMBER: _____

STATE OF TEXAS	§	IN THE MUNICIPAL COURT
VS.	§	CITY OF _____
_____	§	_____COUNTY, TEXAS

PLEA OF NOLO CONTENDERE

I, the undersigned, do hereby enter my appearance on the complaint of the offense, to wit:_____, charged in Municipal Court Cause Number _____. I have been informed of my right to a jury trial and that my signature on this plea of nolo contendere (meaning "no contest") will have the same force and effect as a plea of guilty on the judgment of the Court. I do hereby plead nolo contendere to said offense as charged, waive my right to a jury trial or hearing by the Court, and agree to pay the fine and costs the judge assesses. I understand that payment of the fine and costs constitutes satisfaction of the judgment and waiver of the right to appeal. I understand that my plea may result in a conviction appearing on either a criminal record or a driver's license record.

_____
Defendant's Signature   Date

_____
Address

PLEA OF GUILTY

I, the undersigned, do hereby enter my appearance on the complaint of the offense, to wit: _____, charged in Municipal Court Cause Number _____. I understand that I have a right to a jury trial. I do hereby plead guilty to the offense as charged, waive my right to a jury trial or hearing by the Court, and agree to pay the fine and costs the judge assesses. I understand that payment of the fine and costs constitutes satisfaction of the judgment and waiver of the right to appeal. I understand that my plea may result in a conviction appearing on either a criminal record or a driver's license record.

_____
Defendant's Signature   Date

_____
Address

PLEA OF NOT GUILTY

I, the undersigned, do hereby enter my appearance on the complaint of the offense, to wit: _____. charged in Municipal Court Cause Number _____. I plead not guilty.

Initial One:

_____   I want a jury trial.

_____   I waive my right to a jury trial and request a trial before the Court.

I promise to appear, in person, in the _____ Municipal Court on any date for which this case is scheduled before this Court. I understand that if I do not appear anytime I am required to appear for this case, a Failure to Appear charge may be filed and warrants may be issued for my arrest.

_____
Defendant's Signature   Date

_____
Address

Plea accepted on this _____ day of _____, 20___.

_____
Judge, Municipal Court

City of _____

(municipal court seal)

FIGURE 12–1

Sample Plea Form

LASTING IMPACT

Santobello v. New York (1971)

Rudolph Santobello, facing significant jail time if convicted on two felony counts related to gambling, negotiated an agreement with the prosecutor whereby he would plead guilty to one count of a lesser included offense. A proviso of the agreement was that the prosecutor would make no sentencing recommendation.

At the sentencing hearing many months later, a new prosecutor (who had replaced the prosecutor with whom Santobello had reached the agreement) recommended the maximum allowable sentence, which the judge subsequently imposed. Santobello, after an unsuccessful effort to withdraw his guilty plea, appealed the sentence. When the sentence was affirmed on appeal to the New York Supreme Court, Santobello petitioned the U.S. Supreme Court, which vacated the judgment and remanded the case for reconsideration.

The Court's ruling in Santobello is significant because it is the first case wherein the Court specifically recognized plea bargaining as being "important in the administration of justice both at the state and at the federal levels and . . . [as serving] an important role in the disposition of today's heavy calendars."[1]

The far-reaching effects of Santobello are profound. Through its holding, the Court served notice to every prosecutor in every jurisdiction that every agreement reached with every defendant must be honored. In rejecting a change of prosecutorial staff as justification for reneging on an agreement, Justice Douglas stated that there "is no excuse for the default merely because a member of the prosecutor's staff who was not a party to the 'plea bargain' was in charge of the case when it came before the New York court. The staff of the prosecution is a unit and each

member must be presumed to know the commitments made by any other member. If responsibility could be evaded that way, the prosecution would have designed another deceptive 'contrivance,'" such as those condemned by the Court in Mooney v. Holohan (1935) and Napue v. Illinois (1959).

Today, Santobello serves to protect even the lowest-level offender from corrupt or manipulative practices by overzealous prosecutors. It also preserves the integrity of the plea bargaining process that is so essential to the efficient functioning of a criminal justice system that is almost overwhelmed with pending cases. ■

Note
[1] Santobello v. New York, 404 U.S. 257 (1971), from the concurring opinion of Justice Douglas.

DISCUSSION QUESTIONS

1. As this feature points out, the U.S. Supreme Court has held that plea bargaining is "important in the administration of justice both at the state and at the federal levels." What is its importance?

2. What would the American system of justice be like without plea bargaining?

3. How would American criminal courts have to change if plea bargaining could not be employed?

4. What do you see as the future of plea bargaining in criminal courts?

offered by the prosecution; counsel must also ensure that his or her client understands the consequences of the plea bargaining process. However, this is not to suggest that defendants can easily succeed in claiming ineffective assistance of counsel during negotiation. According to the Supreme Court, the defendant must show "a reasonable probability that, but for counsel's errors, he would not have pleaded guilty and would have insisted on going to trial."[37]

Second, defendants enjoy the right to be informed of exculpatory evidence possessed by the prosecution; that is, if the prosecutor has evidence that casts doubt on the accused's guilt, he or she must inform the defense of that evidence. For evidence to be considered exculpatory, it must have a reasonable probability of affecting the outcome of the case, so exculpatory evidence that is inconsequential (hard to imagine) to the question of guilt need not be provided to the defense.[38]

Finally (as we will see in Chapter 13), defendants enjoy a right to be present at their own trial. However, this right does not apply in the context of plea bargaining, which means that no court has required that criminal defendants enjoy a constitutional right to be present during plea bargaining. This could change, but for now all that is required is that the defense effectively communicate to his or her client the nature of the sentence or charges proffered by the prosecution.

Acceptable Inducements

The Constitution places few restrictions on offers that the prosecution (i.e., prosecutorial inducements) may make during the plea bargaining process. Since *Brady* v. *United States*[39] was the first Supreme Court case to condone plea bargaining, it is a fitting point of departure before considering the offers prosecutors can make. The defendant in *Brady* was charged with kidnapping under a statute that permitted (1) a jury to recommend the death penalty if it saw fit *or* (2) a judge to sentence the defendant to life in prison if guilt was determined via a bench trial. The defendant opted for a jury trial but then changed his plea to guilty and was sentenced to 30 years. He then argued that the statute effectively "compelled" him to plead guilty because of fear of the death penalty. The Supreme Court rejected this claim.

The reasoning the Court offered for its decision is somewhat complicated but important. Justice White emphasized that the statute in the *Brady* case *caused* the guilty plea but did not *coerce* it. He then emphasized that coercion is possible only where physical force or mental pressures are applied, which means that if "Brady was so gripped by fear of the death penalty or hope of leniency that he did not or could not, with the help of counsel, rationally weigh the advantages of going to trial against the advantages of pleading guilty," then his argument would have succeeded.[40] However, White found that the statute at most *influenced* Brady and that the coercion argument was a stretch. In further support of his opinion, Justice White quoted an appellate court decision dealing with plea bargaining:

> [A] plea of guilty entered by one fully aware of the direct consequences, including the actual value of any commitments made to him by the court, prosecutor, or his own counsel, must stand unless induced by threats (or promises to discontinue improper harassment), misrepresentation (including unfulfilled or unfulfillable promises), or perhaps by promises that are by their nature improper as having no proper relationship to the prosecutor's business (e.g., bribes).[41]

In short, guilty pleas resulting from inducements from the prosecution, like confessions in police interrogation rooms, cannot be involuntary. A guilty plea will be considered involuntary where it results from prosecutorial coercion (e.g., physical force or strong psychological pressuring). If, by contrast, the prosecutor causes a guilty plea simply because the accused thinks that it is his or her best chance of avoiding a long prison term, then the defendant cannot succeed by claiming that such a plea is involuntary.

What, then, are proper offers or inducements that the prosecution can make? *Brady* answered this question only insofar as the Court held that the prosecutor cannot coerce a guilty plea. In *Bordenkircher* v. *Hayes*,[42] the Court attempted to offer a clearer answer. In that case, the defendant was indicted by a grand jury for forging a check for $88.30, and the range of punishment was two to ten years in prison. The prosecutor offered to recommend a five-year sentence but threatened to seek an indictment under a habitual criminal statute if the defendant did not accept his offer. Since the defendant had two prior felony convictions, a conviction under the habitual criminal statute could result in life in prison.

Somewhat controversially, in a 5–4 decision, the Supreme Court upheld the defendant's conviction under the habitual criminal statute on the theory that it resulted from a choice among known alternatives. Basically, the Court said that the defendant "had the choice" to accept five years in prison and neglected to take the opportunity. The defendant argued that his second conviction was vindictive, but the Court countered by stating that "the imposition of these difficult choices [is] an inevitable—'and permissible'—attribute of any legitimate system which tolerates and encourages the negotiation of pleas."[43]

Reduced to its most fundamental elements, the Court's opinion in *Bordenkircher* thus implies that the prosecution has great latitude in terms of being able to persuade the defendant to accept a plea as long as the higher charges are authorized by law and are openly presented to the defense. This suggests as well that the prosecution may offer a charge or sentencing concession in exchange for the defendant agreeing not to appeal or claim that some constitutional right has been violated.

In a related case, *United States* v. *Goodwin*,[44] the Court reached a similar decision. There, the defendant was indicted on additional charges after plea negotiations broke down. The Court held that the prosecutor may file additional charges if an initial expectation that the defendant would plead guilty to a lesser charge proved unfounded. The Court refused to accept the defendant's argument that this prosecution was vindictive and, once again, gave broad authority to prosecutors in the plea bargaining process.

There are, however, certain prosecutorial inducements that are *not* permissible. For example, the Supreme Court has stated that "a prosecutor's offer during plea bargaining of adverse or lenient treatment for some person *other* than the accused . . . might pose a greater danger of inducing a false guilty plea by skewing the assessment of the risks a defendant must consider."[45] Also, if the prosecutor flagrantly deceives the accused, fabricates evidence, or starts rumors concerning the accused's level of involvement in the offense, resulting guilty pleas will be deemed unconstitutional.

Questionable Inducements

ad hoc plea bargaining
A term coined by one legal scholar that refers to some strange concessions defendants agree to make as part of the prosecutor's decision to secure a guilty plea.[i]

Law professor Joseph Colquitt used the term **ad hoc plea bargaining** to refer to some strange concessions defendants agree to make as part of the prosecutor's decision to secure a guilty plea.[46] He also stated that *ad hoc* plea bargaining "may involve neither a plea nor a sentence. For example, if a defendant charged with public intoxication seeks to avoid a statutorily mandated minimum sentence of ten days in the county jail, the prosecutor might agree to dismiss the charges if the defendant agrees to make a monetary contribution to a local driver's education program."[47]

Judges can also get involved in *ad hoc* plea bargaining. One case involved a woman who was required to participate in a drug-treatment program as a result of several narcotics convictions. Her probation officer asked to have the woman removed from the program because she supposedly failed to follow program guidelines. At a hearing to decide the matter, the woman, "who was wearing a low-cut sweater, bent over several times to remove documents from her purse. Thereafter the judge dismissed all criminal charges against her. When his clerk asked why the charges had been dropped, [the judge] replied [that] 'she showed me her boobs.'"[48] The judge was subsequently removed from the bench. Some additional (and less extreme) examples of *ad hoc* plea concessions (and some relevant cases) are described in Box 12–1.

Judicial and Statutory Inducements

So far we have only considered what the prosecution can and cannot do as far as inducing the defendant to plead guilty. There have also been some interesting cases dealing with statutory and judicial inducements. Statutory inducements refer to laws that provide lenient sentences in exchange for guilty pleas, and judicial inducements include actions by judges that influence the bargaining process.

With regard to statutory inducements, an illustrative case is *Corbitt* v. *New Jersey*.[49] In that case, the defendant was convicted of first-degree murder and sentenced to life in prison, as required by the state statute with which he was charged; however, the statute provided that if he decided to plead guilty to the crime, he could be sentenced to either life imprisonment or a term of 30 years. The defendant claimed that the statute violated due process, but the Supreme Court upheld it in the spirit of consistency:

> It cannot be said that defendants found guilty by a jury are "penalized" for exercising the right to a jury trial any more than defendants who plead guilty are penalized

BOX 12–1   Examples of *Ad Hoc* Plea Bargaining Concessions

- Charitable contributions in lieu of fines or jail terms: *State v. Stellato*, 523 A.2d 1345 (Conn. App. Ct. 1987); *Ratliff v. State*, 596 N.E. 2d 241 (Ind. Ct. App. 1992).

- Relinquished property ownership: *United States v. Thao Dinh Lee*, 173 F.3d 1258 (10th Cir. 1999).

- Agreement to surrender a professional license or to not work in a particular profession: *United States v. Hoffer*, 129 F.3d 1196 (11th Cir. 1997).

- Voluntary agreement to undergo sterilization: *State v. Pasicznyk*, 197 W.L. 79501 (Wash. Ct. App. 1997).

- Voluntary agreement to undergo surgical castration: *ACLU v. State*, 5 S.W. 2d 418 (Ark. 1999).

- Agreement to enter the army on a four-year enlistment: *State v. Hamrick*, 595 N.W. 2d 492 (Iowa 1999).

- Agreement not to appeal: *People v. Collier*, 641 N.Y.S. 2d 181 (App. Div. 1996).

- Use of shaming punishments, such as bumper stickers for convicted drunk-driving offenders: *Ballenger v. State*, 436 S.E. 2d 793 (Ga. Ct. App. 1993).

- Agreement to seal the records of a case: *State v. Campbell*, 21 Media. L. Rep. 1895 (Wash. Super. Ct. 1993).

- Order to offenders to surrender profits, such as from books written about their crimes: *Rolling v. State ex rel. Butterworth*, 741 So. 2d 627 (Fla. Dist. Ct. App. 1999).

- Banishment to another location: *State v. Culp*, 226 S.E. 2d 841 (N.C. Ct. App. 1976); *Phillips v. State*, 512 S.E. 2d 32 (Ga. Ct. App. 1999).

- Plea of guilty to nonexistent crimes (i.e., crimes that are not prohibited by law): *Bassin v. Isreal*, 335 N.E. 2d 53 (Ill. App. Ct. 1975). ■

Source: Based on J. A. Colquitt, "*Ad Hoc* Plea Bargaining," *Tulane Law Review*, Vol. 75 (2001), pp. 695–776.

because they give up the chance of acquittal at trial. In each instance, the defendant faces a multitude of possible outcomes and freely makes his choice. Equal protection does not free those who made a bad assessment of risks or a bad choice from the consequences of their decision.[50]

The Court also noted, though, that plea bargaining should be an executive as opposed to legislative function; legislatures should not be permitted to decide "that the penalty for every criminal offense to which a defendant pleads guilty is to be one-half the penalty to be imposed upon a defendant convicted of the same offense after a not guilty plea."[51]

Traditionally, plea bargaining results from the prosecution and the defense reaching an agreement; judges are usually not part of the negotiation process. Today, however, certain jurisdictions permit a degree of judicial involvement in the plea bargaining process. For example, the standards of the American Bar Association regarding guilty pleas permit judicial participation where it is requested but only for the purpose of clarifying acceptable charges and sentences. The judge cannot at any point "either directly or indirectly [communicate] to the defendant or defense counsel that a plea agreement should be accepted or that a guilty plea should be entered."[52]

Steps Following a Plea Agreement

Once a plea agreement is reached, the court, the prosecutor, and the defense attorney must perform certain functions. In general, the court must approve, the prosecutor must follow through, and the defense attorney should inform his or her client of the consequences of entering into a plea agreement.

Court Approval The court is not directly bound by a plea agreement. The federal courts permit a plea "only after due consideration of the views of the parties *and* the interest of the public in the effective administration of justice."[53] Thus, if a plea agreement poses significant risk to the public (perhaps because a dangerous criminal will be spared prison and placed on probation—an unlikely event), then the court has the discretion to deny it.

An illustrative case is *United States* v. *Bean*.[54] Bean was charged on October 22, 1976, with theft of property (an automobile) and with burglary of a habitation, in violation of state law. At the initial arraignment, Bean pleaded not guilty to both counts. On November 30, another arraignment was held at Bean's request. At this time the court was informed that a plea bargain had been reached between the government prosecutor, Bean, and his counsel: Bean would plead guilty to the theft count and cooperate with the prosecutor in investigating others involved in the burglary; in return, the prosecutor would move for a dismissal of the burglary charge. Judge Spears rejected the plea because the offense of entering a home at night where people were sleeping was a much more serious offense than the theft of an automobile. The Fifth Circuit Court of Appeals upheld Judge Spears's decision.[55]

Prosecutor's Responsibility

Prosecutors have an important role in the plea bargaining process. After the court accepts a plea bargain (whether it is a charge or a sentence reduction), it is the prosecutor's turn to fulfill his or her end of the bargain. In contrast, the prosecutor is not bound by the plea bargain prior to the point at which it is accepted by the court. Let us look at these requirements in more detail.

Prosecutors have a considerable amount of latitude with regard to fulfilling a plea bargain before it is accepted by the court. This should not be particularly surprising because before the court accepts (or rejects) the plea bargain, it is not formalized, but when the court accepts the plea bargain, it becomes formalized, at which point the prosecutor must fulfill his or her promises.

A case dealing with the extent to which a prosecutor must uphold his or her end of the bargain prior to the point when the court accepts the bargain is *Mabry* v. *Johnson*.[56] In that case, the defense attorney called the prosecutor to accept a plea offer, but the prosecutor told him that the offer was a mistake and withdrew it. The prosecutor then offered a harsher offer in its place, one that would have resulted in a longer prison term. Surprisingly, the Supreme Court upheld this practice, arguing that the plea agreement was reached with full awareness on the part of the defendant and "was thus in no sense the product of governmental deception; it rested on no 'unfulfilled promise' and fully satisfied the test for voluntariness and intelligence."[57]

As for the period after the court accepts the bargain, the prosecution is generally bound to carry out its promises. Consider the case of *Santobello* v. *New York*.[58] The defendant was indicted for two felonies. He first entered a plea of not guilty on both counts, but after subsequent negotiations, the prosecutor agreed to allow the defendant to plead guilty to a lesser offense, so the defendant then withdrew his plea of not guilty and agreed to plead guilty to the lesser offense. The court accepted the plea. At sentencing, however, a new prosecutor who was unaware of what transpired earlier requested the maximum sentence, and the defense objected on the ground that the previous prosecutor promised not to make any particular sentencing recommendation. The judge then stated that he was not influenced by the second prosecutor's sentencing recommendation and imposed the maximum sentence.

In response to this turn of events, the Supreme Court declared that the sentence should be declared unconstitutional as a matter of due process. The Court stated that "when a plea rests in any significant degree on a promise or agreement of the prosecutor, so that it can be said to be part of the inducement or consideration, such promise must be fulfilled."[59]

Unfortunately, though, the Court was not altogether clear in terms of what remedy is preferable when the prosecutor breaches his or her agreement. In *Santobello*, the Court voided the defendant's conviction, but the justices seemed mixed on the appropriate remedy for future cases: Some agreed that if the prosecution breaches its promise after the court has accepted the bargain, it must then be forced to uphold the bargain, or the defendant should be able to withdraw the guilty plea if the prosecution fails to uphold its end of the bargain; others felt that the trial court should decide what remedy is necessary. The issue remains unresolved.

Later, in the case of *United States* v. *Benchimol*, the Supreme Court revisited a prosecutor's breach of a plea agreement.[60] In *Benchimol*, the prosecutor agreed to recommend a sentence of probation with restitution, but the presentence report mentioned nothing of the agreement. The defense attorney pointed out the error, and the prosecution agreed that an agreement had been reached. Even so, the court sentenced the defendant to six years. The defendant then sought to have his sentence vacated, and the court of appeals agreed; however, the Supreme Court reversed, holding that unless the prosecution supports a recommendation "enthusiastically" or sets forth its reasons for a lenient recommendation, the court is under no obligation to honor the agreement. According to the Supreme Court,

> It may well be that the Government in a particular case might commit itself to "enthusiastically" make a particular recommendation to the court, and it may be that the Government in a particular case might agree to explain to the court the reasons for the Government's making a particular recommendation. But respondent does not contend, nor did the Court of Appeals find, that the Government had in fact undertaken to do either of these things here. The Court of Appeals simply held that as a matter of law such an undertaking was to be implied from the Government's agreement to recommend a particular sentence. But our view of Rule 11(e) [of the Federal Rules of Criminal Procedure, which sets forth procedures for plea bargaining] is that it speaks in terms of what the parties in fact agree to, and does not suggest that such implied-in-law terms as were read into this agreement by the Court of Appeals have any place under the Rule.[61]

Effects on the Defendant Defendants who accept offers to plead guilty often face consequences besides a reduced sentence or charge. For instance, the defendant can be required to waive his or her right to appeal a guilty plea. Also, if the defendant supplies inaccurate information during the course of plea negotiations, he or she may not benefit from lenient treatment. Furthermore, in exchange for pleading guilty, the prosecution may require that the defendant testify against a codefendant.

Consider the case of *Ricketts* v. *Adamson*, one in which a defendant (Ricketts) testified against both of his codefendants in exchange for a reduction in the charge he was facing.[62] His codefendants were convicted. After Ricketts was sentenced on the reduced charge, his codefendants' convictions were overturned on appeal. The prosecution then retried the codefendants, but Ricketts refused to testify at the second trial, claiming that his duty had been fulfilled. The prosecution then filed an information charging him with first-degree murder. The Supreme Court did not bar the first-degree murder prosecution because the original agreement contained a clause to the effect that the agreement would be void if the defendant refused to testify against his codefendants. Justice Brennan did acknowledge, however, that the defendant could have construed the plea agreement to only require his testimony at the first trial. The Court noted that the proper procedure if such a situation arises in the future would be to submit a disagreement over the plea to the court that accepted the plea; that way, the expense of another trial and appeals could be avoided.

conditional guilty plea
A negotiated arrangement whereby a defendant can sometimes preserve certain rights following a plea agreement.

At the other extreme, the defendant can sometimes preserve certain rights following a plea agreement, a type of arrangement known as a **conditional guilty plea**. For example, New York law provides that an order denying a motion to suppress evidence alleged to have been obtained as a result of unlawful search and seizure "may be reviewed on appeal from a judgment of conviction notwithstanding the fact that such judgment of conviction is predicated upon a plea of guilty."[63] These types of agreements are rare, however, because the Supreme Court has stated,

> When a criminal defendant has solemnly admitted in open court that he is in fact guilty of the offense with which he is charged, he may not thereafter raise independent claims relating to the deprivation of constitutional rights that occurred prior to the entry of the guilty plea.[64]

Factors Affecting Plea Agreements

Researchers have identified four sets of factors that influence prosecutors' decisions to offer plea bargains.[65] The first is the strength of the state's case: If the physical evidence is limited and/or the witnesses are weak, a prosecutor will be more inclined to offer a negotiated plea. Second, the seriousness of the offense dictates whether the prosecutor will offer a reduced charge or recommend a lenient sentence. For obvious reasons, the prosecutor would not want to be lenient in cases involving particularly serious or heinous crimes. Third, the defendant's prior record is important, meaning that those who have extensive criminal histories will be less likely to benefit from plea agreements. Fourth, researchers have identified several extralegal factors that influence bargaining: age, sex, attitudes, marital status, and employment. For example, a defendant who is gainfully employed may be more likely to benefit from a plea agreement than one who is not.

Learning Objective 3
Describe the elements of guilty pleas and how guilty pleas are contested.

GUILTY PLEAS

Plea bargaining always precedes a guilty plea to a lesser offense, but a guilty plea need not be preceded by plea bargaining. In the former case, the prosecution and the defense reach an agreement, and the defendant pleads guilty to a lesser offense or gets a favorable sentencing recommendation. In the latter case, none of this need occur. It could be that a person who has committed a crime feels overcome with remorse and simply pleads guilty in the absence of bargaining. This section thus describes the requirements of a valid guilty plea. It can be read without any understanding or background in plea bargaining; in other words, the requirements for a valid guilty plea apply regardless of whether plea bargaining actually took place.

Elements of a Valid Guilty Plea

Even if the prosecutor offers an acceptable inducement to the defendant and the defendant agrees to plead guilty in exchange for leniency, the judge still must determine that the defendant understands the plea. This is in addition to the need to determine that the plea conforms to statutory and other requirements (as discussed above). In *Boykin* v. *Alabama*, the Supreme Court held that it would be unconstitutional "for the trial judge to accept [a] guilty plea without an affirmative showing that it is intelligent and voluntary."[66] This has been construed to mean that the plea must be intelligent and understood, be voluntary, and have a factual basis. The judge usually questions the defendant as to each of these elements (see Figure 12–2 for a sample guilty plea form).

STATE OF NEBRASKA FORM NO. CC 2:1 08/2007 Rev.	**WAIVER AND PLEA OF GUILTY**	CASE NUMBER

Instructions for Completing Waiver and Plea

Please be advised that you are accused of violating a statute or city ordinance under the laws of Nebraska. The waiver and plea system has been established for your convenience. You are under no compulsion to use it. Should you desire to appear in Court and contest the matter, you may do so. The waiver and plea may be used only by persons who wish to waive all available rights and to enter a plea of guilty.

If you sign this form, you will waive the following rights: (1) To have an attorney assist you in preparation of your defense and to represent you in Court; you may be entitled to an attorney at public expense if you cannot afford one. (2) To have the complaint read to you and to be informed of the possible penalties in the event of your conviction. (3) To have a trial before a judge, and in certain cases, a jury. (4) To confront and cross-examine witnesses against you. (5) To require witnesses to attend Court and testify on your behalf. (6) To remain silent and not make any statement concerning the circumstances surrounding this violation. (7) To testify in your own behalf. (8) To require the prosecution to prove you guilty beyond a reasonable doubt and to appeal any final decision or order of the Court. (9) To have sufficient time to prepare your defense.

> **Out-of-state residents may be required to post bond should a court appearance be desired. Only cash, certified check, or money order will be accepted in payment of any fine and costs. If you would like a receipt, a pre-addressed stamped envelope must be sent to this court requesting such receipt.**

Waiver and Plea

❑You have until _____
_____ at _____ _____.M. to return this plea of guilty form or to appear in County Court in person. **Failure to do either may result in the issuance of a warrant for your arrest or suspension of your driver's license by your home state.**

STATE OF NEBRASKA _____

vs.

_____
                                        Defendant

Having read and understood the instructions and my rights, I, the undersigned, do hereby enter my appearance on the complaint of violation(s) of _____

As a matter of convenience to me, I request the Court to accept this plea of guilty and waiver of my statutory and constitutional rights and the payment at this time of the scheduled fine. I have been informed that if this plea of guilty and waiver of appearances are accepted, the Court will enter a judgment of conviction finding me guilty as charged, and where applicable, points may be assessed against my driving record. I also realize that this plea admits the fault of my violation(s), which may be used against me in any later proceeding.

DATE: _____ DEFENDANT'S SIGNATURE: _____
THE COUNTY COURT HEREBY ACCEPTS the plea of guilty and enters judgment of conviction finding the defendant guilty as charged.

DATE: _____

BY THE COURT: _____ (Seal)

COUNT 1: $_____
COUNT 2: $_____
COUNT 3: $_____
COUNT 4: $_____
COSTS: $_____
TOTAL: $_____

RETURN TO THIS COURT:

CITATION NO. _____

FIGURE 12–2

Sample Guilty Plea Form (Nebraska)

Source: http://www.supremecourt.ne.gov/sites/supremecourt.ne.gov/files/forms/CC-2-1.pdf (accessed February 25, 2013).

Intelligence and Understanding In general, for a plea to be intelligent (i.e., understood), it must conform to specific requirements. The defendant must understand (1) the nature of the charges of which he or she is accused, (2) the possible sentences that are associated with the charges, and (3) the rights that he or she may waive if a guilty plea is entered.

With respect to the nature of the charges, consider the case of *Henderson v. Morgan*.[67] After being charged with first-degree murder, Henderson pleaded guilty to second-degree murder. Several years later, he sought to have his conviction voided on the ground that he did not understand at the time he entered his plea that one of the elements of second-degree murder was "intent" to cause death. The Supreme Court held that "since respondent did not receive adequate notice of the offense to which he pleaded guilty, his plea was involuntary and the judgment of conviction was entered without due process of law."[68] The element of "intent" in second-degree murder (the *mens rea*) was viewed as "critical," which meant that it should have been explained to the defendant.

It is not clear based on *Henderson* whether the judge must explain the elements of the offense to the defendant or whether this is the job of counsel. The Court intimated that if defense counsel explains the offense to the accused, then little else is needed, stating that "it may be appropriate to presume that in most cases defense counsel routinely explain the nature of the offense in sufficient detail to give the accused notice of what he is being asked to admit."[69] Nevertheless, the judge should at least inquire as to whether the defendant understands the charge.

As for possible sentences, there are virtually no Supreme Court cases dealing with the defendant's understanding of possible sentences resulting from a plea bargain. However, the Federal Rules of Criminal Procedure requires that the defendant understand the consequences of the plea, which includes an understanding of the minimum and maximum sentences as well as applicable sentencing guidelines that the judge might be required to abide by.

Other consequences attendant to plea bargaining sentencing do not have to be explained, however. For instance, at least one lower court has held that the defendant does not need to be informed of the loss of the right to vote.[70] Whether failure to inform the defendant of the consequences associated with sentencing rises to the level of a constitutional violation has yet to be determined.

Finally, rights *waived* as a result of plea bargaining are different from rights *denied* as a result of plea bargaining. For example, loss of the right to vote is not a loss due to voluntary waiver; it is a consequence tied to being convicted (even if by a guilty plea) for certain serious crimes. Rights waived are those rights that the defendant would otherwise be granted by the Constitution but that are essentially given up in exchange for lenient treatment.

Constitutional rights typically waived through plea bargaining are the right to trial by jury, the privilege against self-incrimination, and the right to confront adverse witnesses. By pleading guilty, the defendant forgoes a trial where these rights are frequently applicable. The privilege against self-incrimination, however, still applies outside the trial context, such as in pretrial custodial interrogations. Regardless, the defendant must be clearly informed of constitutional rights that are waived as a result of plea bargaining. According to the Supreme Court, there can be no presumption of "a waiver of these three important federal rights from a silent record."[71]

Voluntariness In addition to the requirement that a plea be understood, it also must be voluntary. Even though a plea is understood, it could have resulted from coercion, threats, physical abuse, or the like. The Federal Rules of Criminal Procedure requires that a plea be "voluntary and not the result of force or threats or of promises apart from a plea agreement."[72]

Factual Basis   For a plea bargain to be valid, the plea must result from conduct that has a basis in fact; in other words, someone cannot plead guilty to a crime he or she hasn't committed (according to the courts anyway). This means that the court should inquire about the crime in question, perhaps by having the accused describe the conduct giving rise to the guilty plea. This does not always occur, but according to the Supreme Court,

> Requiring this examination of the relation between the law and the acts the defendant admits having committed is designed to "protect a defendant who is in the position of pleading voluntarily with an understanding of the nature of the charge but without realizing that his conduct does not actually fall within the charge."[73]

Importantly, the Court in *McCarthy* did not state that a factual basis for the plea bargain is a constitutional requirement, only that there should be one.

The Court elaborated on this matter in a similar case where the defendant pleaded guilty but insisted on his innocence. The Court stated that "an express admission of guilt . . . is not a constitutional requisite to the imposition of a prison sentence even if he is unwilling or unable to admit his participation in the acts constituting the crime."[74] The Court upheld the man's plea but also stated,

> Because of the importance of protecting the innocent and of insuring that guilty pleas are a product of free and intelligent choice, various state and federal court decisions properly caution that pleas coupled with claims of innocence should not be accepted unless there is a factual basis for the plea . . . and until the judge taking the plea has inquired into and sought to resolve the conflict between the waiver of trial and the claim of innocence.[75]

Thus, while there appears to be no constitutional basis for requiring that a guilty plea be tied to specific criminal acts, the courts (including the Supreme Court) prefer to avoid guilty pleas accepted by otherwise innocent defendants. Unfortunately, we can only guess how many innocent criminal defendants plead guilty in order to "play the odds" and potentially avoid a lengthy prison term.

In summary, a valid guilty plea must consist of several elements: intelligence and understanding, voluntariness, and factual basis. Box 12–2 presents relevant portions of Rule 11 of the Federal Rules of Criminal Procedure and succinctly summarizes the elements of a valid guilty plea through some eyes other than those of the Supreme Court.

Contesting a Guilty Plea

For several reasons, a defendant may wish to contest the guilty plea he or she enters: (1) if the plea is the product of coercion by the prosecution, (2) if the prosecution fails to fulfill its end of the bargain, and (3) if other problems exist such as unconstitutional conduct on the part of law enforcement officials. Defendants who challenge their guilty pleas do so in two ways: withdrawal of the guilty plea and appeal of the guilty plea.[76] Each mechanism is considered in the following subsections.

Withdrawal of a Guilty Plea   Anytime the court refuses to accept a plea agreement reached by the prosecution and defense, the defendant can usually withdraw the plea. Similarly, if the defendant pleads guilty even when there has been no plea bargaining, he or she can seek to withdraw the plea. However, if the prosecution disagrees with the court's decision to refuse the plea, then the defendant might *not* be able to withdraw his or her plea.

Once a plea is accepted by the court, it can be withdrawn only in limited circumstances. The Federal Rules of Criminal Procedure provides that a plea can be withdrawn prior to sentencing if the defendant shows a "fair and just" reason for overturning the plea. Fair and just reasons are the same as those mentioned at the outset of this section, meaning involuntary pleas, prosecutorial breaches, or lack of evidence or similar deficiency. Once a sentence

BOX 12–2   Relevant Portions of Rule 11 of the Federal Rules of Criminal Procedure Relating to Guilty Pleas

ADVISING AND QUESTIONING THE DEFENDANT

Before the court accepts a plea of guilty or *nolo contendere*, the defendant may be placed under oath, and the court must address the defendant personally in open court. During this address, the court must inform the defendant of, and determine that the defendant understands, the following:

* the government's right, in a prosecution for perjury or false statement, to use against the defendant any statement that the defendant gives under oath;

* the right to plead not guilty, or having already so pleaded, to persist in that plea;

* the right to a jury trial;

* the right to be represented by counsel—and if necessary have the court appoint counsel— at trial and at every other stage of the proceeding;

* the right at trial to confront and cross-examine adverse witnesses, to be protected from compelled self-incrimination, to testify and present evidence, and to compel the attendance of witnesses;

* the defendant's waiver of these trial rights if the court accepts a plea of guilty or *nolo contendere*;

* the nature of each charge to which the defendant is pleading;

* any maximum possible penalty, including imprisonment, fine, and term of supervised release;

* any mandatory minimum penalty;

* any applicable forfeiture;

* the court's authority to order restitution . . .

ENSURING THAT THE PLEA IS VOLUNTARY

Before accepting a plea of guilty or *nolo contendere*, the court must address the defendant personally in open court and determine that the plea is voluntary and did not result from force, threats, or promises (other than promises in a plea agreement).

DETERMINING THE FACTUAL BASIS FOR THE PLEA

Before entering judgment on a guilty plea, the court must determine that there is a factual basis for the plea. ■

Source: Rule 11, Federal Rules of Criminal Procedure (2009), available at www.law.cornell.edu/rules/frcrmp (accessed February 25, 2013).

has been entered, however, the only methods to challenge a plea are appeal (and, to a lesser extent, *habeas* review). Also, many jurisdictions place a time limit on plea withdrawals; usually withdrawal is not permitted once a sentence has been imposed.

One of the most famous examples of seeking withdrawal of a guilty plea is the recent incident involving former Idaho Senator Larry Craig, who was arrested in the Minneapolis–St. Paul Airport in June 2007 on suspicion of lewd conduct. He quickly pleaded guilty to a misdemeanor charge of disorderly conduct (for allegedly soliciting sex in the airport bathroom) but later sought to withdraw his guilty plea, arguing that it was not knowing and intelligent. A judge denied his motion, the Minnesota Court of Appeals affirmed, and Craig did not seek reelection.

Appeal of a Guilty Plea   If a defendant moves to withdraw his or her plea and is denied this request, then an appeal is appropriate. However, if the withdrawal period has passed, then the only method of appealing a guilty plea is through what is called "direct appeal." This creates something of a difficult situation for the defense. Since appeals are mostly considered based on the trial court record, the defendant has limited resources with which to prepare an argument; no trial court transcript limits the scope of potential appeals because a guilty plea means the defendant elects to forgo a trial. Thus, the only record left may be that from arraignment or a similar pretrial proceeding. All this means that it is *very* difficult to succeed with a direct appeal of a guilty plea.

Fortunately, some states as well as the federal government permit appeals based on specific pretrial motions, such as motions to exclude evidence on constitutional grounds; for example, New York and some other jurisdictions maintain conditional plea mechanisms. These issues aside, there are few Supreme Court precedents addressing appeals of guilty pleas. In *McCarthy v. United States*,[77] the Supreme Court held that the trial court's failure to abide by proper arraignment procedure requires reversal of a guilty plea on appeal. This is because the arraignment procedure—especially when there is no trial—"is designed to assist the district judge in making the constitutionally required determination that a defendant's guilty plea is truly voluntary."[78]

Note that the decision to appeal a court's denial of a motion to withdraw a guilty plea is not necessarily the same as an appeal of a conviction. The former may be based on the voluntariness of the plea, whereas the latter may concern some other procedural matter, such as an improper search or seizure, and may be appealable, provided the defendant hasn't waived his or her right to appeal as a result of plea bargaining.

Finally, remember that engaging in plea bargaining and pleading guilty are not the same thing. Regardless of how the guilty plea is arrived at, the defendant can still seek to withdraw the plea. By contrast, guilty pleas that are entered without plea bargaining are more subject to appeal than pleas reached as a result of bargaining because in the latter instance the accused often gives up important rights, such as the right to appeal.

SUMMARY

CHAPTER
12

1. SUMMARIZE THE HISTORY AND DEVELOPMENT OF PLEA BARGAINING

- Plea bargaining usually comes in two forms: charge bargaining (there is an agreement to plead guilty to a lesser charge) and sentencing bargaining (the prosecutor offers a favorable sentencing recommendation in exchange for a guilty plea).
- Plea bargaining has expanded to include more concessions than lesser charges or favorable sentencing recommendations.
- Plea bargaining was first recognized during the nineteenth century.
- Plea bargaining became more common as more trials were held and lawyers became involved in criminal justice.
- Arguments in favor of plea bargaining cite that it is efficient; arguments against plea bargaining claim that it is a loophole and that it undermines the integrity of the justice system.
- Several jurisdictions have experimented with limitations on plea bargaining. Some still have restrictions in place, but the practice proceeds more or less unabated.
- The Supreme Court condoned plea bargaining in *Brady v. United States*.

2. EXPLAIN THE PLEA BARGAINING PROCESS

- Defendants enjoy the rights to have effective assistance of counsel and to be informed of exculpatory evidence but not to be present at important stages of the plea bargaining process.

- The Constitution places no limitations on the concessions prosecutors can offer as part of plea agreements, meaning that there are many concessions the prosecutor can offer.

- *Ad hoc* plea bargaining refers to the practice of offering questionable inducements (e.g., getting the defendant to enter the army in exchange for leniency) to a criminal defendant.

- Statutory inducements (a law instead of the prosecutor offers leniency in exchange for a guilty plea) to plead guilty are acceptable; judicial inducements (the judge offers leniency) are not.

- Once a plea agreement is reached between the prosecution and the defense, the court must approve it for it to become official.

- The prosecution is not bound to fulfill its end of the bargain *before* the court accepts the plea bargain, but the prosecution is bound to follow through on the agreement *after* the court accepts the agreement.

- The defendant can be required to waive his or her right to appeal a guilty plea. The defendant must be truthful during the process and may also be required, as part of a plea agreement, to testify against a codefendant.

3 DESCRIBE THE ELEMENTS OF GUILTY PLEAS AND HOW GUILTY PLEAS ARE CONTESTED

- Plea bargaining always precedes a guilty plea, but a guilty plea need not be preceded by plea bargaining; that is, someone can plead guilty in the absence of plea bargaining.

- Elements of a valid guilty plea include (1) intelligence and understanding, (2) voluntariness, and (3) factual basis.

- An intelligent understanding of a guilty plea is one in which the defendant understands (1) the nature of the charges of which he or she is accused, (2) the possible sentences that are associated with the charges, and (3) the rights that he or she may waive if a guilty plea is entered.

- A voluntary guilty plea is one that has not been coerced.

- A guilty plea has a factual basis if the defendant actually committed the crime in question.

- Guilty pleas can be contested via withdrawal and/or appeal.

- A guilty plea can be withdrawn prior to the point at which the court accepts the agreement, but doing so becomes considerably more difficult after the court accepts the plea bargain.

- Guilty pleas that are entered without plea bargaining are more subject to appeal than pleas reached as a result of bargaining.

KEY TERMS

ad hoc plea bargaining, 320

Alford plea, 314

charge bargaining, 310

conditional guilty plea, 324

plea bargaining, 310

sentence bargaining, 310

REVIEW QUESTIONS

1. What is plea bargaining? How did plea bargaining develop? How is it used in courts today?

2. What is involved in entering a guilty plea? What are the consequences of such a plea?

WHAT WILL YOU DO?

You are a public defender, and today you find yourself representing a 54-year-old African-American man named Winfred who was arrested the night before and charged with illegal possession of methamphetamine. Your caseload is high, and you expect to see at least another dozen defendants before you can go home for the night. You only have about ten minutes before you and Winfred will be called before the judge to enter a plea.

You learn that your client had some prescription diet pills in his possession when he was stopped by the police for driving the wrong way on a one-way street. Winfred, however, says that he wasn't drunk and that he wasn't under the influence of any drugs but that he was confused after leaving his new construction job and was driving in a part of the city that he was not familiar with.

He tells you that he is not as young as he used to be and that he suffers from arthritis. He says that he bought the pills from a friend who told him that they would give him the energy he needed to stay alert and keep working throughout the day. He didn't know what they were, and he didn't think about the possibility that they were illegal or that they could result in his arrest. He has since learned of the potential legal consequences, however, and is now afraid of losing his job

if he is convicted of a drug crime. He says that he needs the money his job pays to support himself and his wife and that she has no one else to care for her.

As your ten-minute consultation draws to a close, you wonder how you should advise Winfred. You know that, technically speaking, he has broken the law, but you also know that if he pleads guilty to possession of a small quantity of this kind of controlled substance, he is likely to be found guilty and put on probation. With a probationary sentence, he could continue working and earning an income. Even better, a simple plea deal would allow you to move on to your next client.

On the other hand, you believe that you might be able to convince the judge that Winfred did not know that he was in possession of a controlled substance and that therefore he did not possess the necessary *mens rea* to support a finding of guilty.

However, a plea of not guilty could mean that this case could go to trial—and that could take a lot of time. If Winfred ended up being found guilty of possession of a controlled substance, he could conceivably be sentenced to serve time behind bars. After you lay out the possibilities, Winfred tells you that he wants to plead guilty.

Do you agree with his decision?

NOTES

i. J. A. Colquitt, "Ad Hoc Plea Bargaining," *Tulane Law Review* 75(2001):695–776.

1. Gary Fields and John R. Emshwiller, "Federal Guilty Pleas Soar as Bargains Trump Trials," *Wall Street Journal*, September 23, 2012, available at http://online.wsj.com/article/SB10000872396390443589304577637610097206808.html (accessed April 1, 2013).

2. Ibid.

3. See H. S. Miller, W. F. McDonald, and J. A. Cramer, *Plea Bargaining in the United States* (Washington, DC: Government Printing Office, 1978), for a review of other such concessions.

4. Much of the discussion that follows is adapted from D. D. Guidorizzi, "Should We Really 'Ban' Plea Bargaining? The Core Concerns of Plea Bargaining Critics," *Emory Law Journal*, Vol. 47 (1998), pp. 753–783.

5. *Commonwealth v. Battis*, 1 Mass. 95 (1804).

6. Ibid., p. 96.

7. *Edwards v. People*, 39 Mich. 760 (1878).

8. Ibid., p. 761.

9. Ibid., p. 762.

10. See B. M. Edens, "Crime and the Georgia Courts: A Statistical Analysis," *Journal of the American Institute of Criminal Law and Criminology*, Vol. 16 (1924), pp. 169–218.

11. R. Moley, "The Vanishing Jury," *University of Southern California Law Review*, Vol. 97 (1928), p. 107.

12. J. H. Langbein, "The Criminal Trial before Lawyers," *University of Chicago Law Review*, Vol. 45 (1978), p. 277.

13. L. M. Friedman, *Crime and Punishment in American History* (New York: Basic Books, 1993), p. 235.

14. Guidorizzi, "Should We Really 'Ban' Plea Bargaining?," p. 756.

15. A. W. Alschuler, "Plea Bargaining and Its History," *Law and Society Review*, Vol. 13 (1979), pp. 211–245, quoting *Chicago Tribune*, April 27, 1928, p. 1.

16. R. A. Weninger, "The Abolition of Plea Bargaining: A Case Study of El Paso County, Texas," *University of California Los Angeles Law Review*, Vol. 35 (1987), p. 267, n. 5.

17. C. E. Demarest, "Plea Bargaining Can Often Protect the Victim," *New York Times*, April 15, 1994, p. A30.

18. *Blackledge v. Allison*, 431 U.S. 63 (1977), p. 71.

19. A. Alschuler, "The Prosecutor's Role in Plea Bargaining," *Chicago Law Review*, Vol. 36 (1968), p. 54.

20. P. Arenella, "Rethinking the Functions of Criminal Procedure: The Warren and Burger Courts' Competing Ideologies," *Georgia Law Journal*, Vol. 72 (1983), pp. 185–248, esp. pp. 216–219.

21. A. P. Worden, "Policymaking by Prosecutors: The Uses of Discretion in Regulating Plea Bargaining," *Judicature*, Vol. 73 (1990), p. 336.

22. A.W. Alschuler, "The Changing Plea Bargaining Debate," *California Law Review*, Vol. 69 (1981), p. 652.

23. *North Carolina v. Alford*, 400 U.S. 25 (1970).

24. Ibid., p. 28.

25. M. L. Rubenstein and T. J. White, "Alaska's Ban on Plea Bargaining," *Law and Society Review*, Vol. 13 (1979), pp. 367–383.

26. C. Mirsky, "Plea Reform Is No Bargain," *New York Newsday*, March 4, 1994, p. 70.

27. T. D. Carns and J. A. Kruse, "Alaska's Ban on Plea Bargaining Reevaluated," *Judicature*, Vol. 7 (1992), pp. 310–317, esp. p. 317.

28. Cited in Guidorizzi, "Should We Really 'Ban' Plea Bargaining?," p. 775.

29. See statement of Robert T. Johnson, district attorney, Office of the District Attorney of Bronx County, press release, November 24, 1992.

30. Guidorizzi, "Should We Really 'Ban' Plea Bargaining?," p. 778.

31. M. A. Levin, *Urban Politics and the Criminal Courts* (Chicago: University of Chicago Press, 1977), p. 80.

32. *People v. Brown*, 223 Cal. Rptr. 66 (Ct. App. 1986), p. 72, n. 11.

33. See Weninger, "The Abolition of Plea Bargaining," p. 275.

34. *Brady v. United States*, 397 U.S. 742 (1970), pp. 752–753.

35. *Santobello v. New York*, 404 U.S. 257 (1971), p. 260.

36. *Kirby v. Illinois*, 406 U.S. 682 (1972), p. 689.

37. *Hill v. Lockhart*, 474 U.S. 52 (1985), p. 58.

38. See, e.g., *United States v. Bagley*, 473 U.S. 667 (1985).

39. *Brady v. United States*, 397 U.S. 742 (1970).

40. Ibid., p. 750.

41. *Shelton v. United States*, 246 F. 2d 571 (5th Cir. 1957), p. 572.

42. *Bordenkircher v. Hayes*, 434 U.S. 357 (1978).

43. Ibid., p. 364.

44. *United States v. Goodwin*, 457 U.S. 368 (1982).

45. *Bordenkircher v. Hayes*, 434 U.S. 357 (1978), p. 365, n. 8.

46. J. A. Colquitt, "Ad Hoc Plea Bargaining," *Tulane Law Review*, Vol. 75 (2001), pp. 695–776.

47. Ibid., p. 711.

48. *Ryan v. Comm'n on Judicial Performance*, 754 P.2d 724 (Cal. 1988), p. 734.

49. *Corbitt v. New Jersey*, 439 U.S. 212 (1978).

50. Ibid., p. 226.

51. Ibid., p. 227.

52. American Bar Association Criminal Justice Standard 14-3.3(d).

53. Federal Rules of Criminal Procedure, 11(b).

54. *United States v. Bean*, 564 F.2d 700 (5th Cir. 1977).

55. Ibid., p. 704.

56. *Mabry v. Johnson*, 467 U.S. 504 (1984).

57. Ibid., p. 510.

58. *Santobello v. New York*, 404 U.S. 257 (1971).

59. Ibid., p. 262.

60. *United States* v. *Benchimol*, 471 U.S. 453 (1985).

61. Ibid., p. 455.

62. *Ricketts* v. *Adamson*, 483 U.S. 1 (1987).

63. New York Criminal Procedure Law, Sections 710.20(1), 710.70(2).

64. *Tollett* v. *Henderson*, 411 U.S. 258 (1973), p. 267.

65. R. A. Harris and J. F. Springer, "Plea Bargaining as a Game: An Empirical Analysis of Negotiated Sentencing Decisions," *Review of Policy Research*, Vol. 4 (1984), pp. 245–258.

66. *Boykin* v. *Alabama*, 395 U.S. 238 (1969), p. 242.

67. *Henderson* v. *Morgan*, 426 U.S. 637 (1976).

68. Ibid., p. 647.

69. Ibid.

70. See, e.g., *People* v. *Thomas*, 41 Ill.2d 122 (1968).

71. *Boykin* v. *Alabama*, 395 U.S. 238 (1969), p. 243.

72. Federal Rules of Criminal Procedure, 11(d).

73. *McCarthy* v. *United States*, 394 U.S. 459 (1969), p. 467.

74. *North Carolina* v. *Alford*, 400 U.S. 25 (1970).

75. Ibid., p. 38, n. 10.

76. *Habeas corpus* review of guilty pleas is also possible.

77. *McCarthy* v. *United States*, 394 U.S. 459 (1969).

78. Ibid., p. 465.

Ron Chapple/Taxi/Getty Images

13

The Jury and the Trial

LEARNING OBJECTIVES

1. Summarize the history and development of juries and jury trials.

2. Explain the jury selection process, including *voir dire*.

3. Describe the jury decision-making process and factors that affect jurors' decisions.

4. Explain the right to speedy trial and the problem of delays.

5. Explain the right to a public trial.

6. Outline the trial process from pretrial motions and opening statements through jury deliberations and verdict.

The Palm Beach County, Florida, courthouse in West Palm Beach. What is the role of a juror in a criminal trial?

Thinkstock

INTRODUCTION

In 2013, Palm Beach Circuit Court Judge Jeffrey Colbath voided the conviction and 16-year prison sentence of 49-year-old billionaire polo mogul John B. Goodman for causing a traffic accident in which a 23-year-old college student died. Goodman had been convicted in 2012 of manslaughter after driving his Bentley through a stop sign on a back road after a night of drinking and striking a car driven by Scott Patrick Wilson, who was on his way home from college. Wilson drowned when his Hyundai went off the road and overturned in a water-filled canal. Following Goodman's conviction and pending appeal, he was allowed to remain under house arrest at his multi-million-dollar residence after posting a $7 million bond. Although the facts of the case seemed clear and a jury rejected Goodman's defense of faulty brakes in the late-model luxury car, Judge Colbath tossed Goodman's conviction after he learned that one of the jurors in the case, Dennis DeMartin, a 69-year-old retired accountant, had failed to reveal in pretrial questioning that his wife had received a DUI years earlier that he may have blamed for the end of his marriage. DeMartin had also failed to disclose that his daughter had been the victim of a violent crime and, as the trial was nearing its conclusion, conducted a secret drinking experiment to personally assess the impact of alcohol on reaction time and judgment. In overturning Goodman's conviction, Judge Colbath said that DeMartin had a "reckless indifference" to the truth and added that allowing Goodman's conviction to stand in light of DeMartin's action "would erode the integrity of the judicial system."[1] DeMartin faced contempt of court charges and pled not guilty.

THE JURY

In **bench trials**, the judge is both the trier of law and the trier of fact (sometimes called "finder of law" and "finder of fact"). This means that the judge decides on issues of law but also decides whether the defendant should be found guilty. Bench trials generally outnumber jury trials even in felony cases, as can be seen in Figure 13–1. They are sometimes preferred to jury trials so that the parties can focus closely on the issues at hand, such as when a case deals with highly sensitive or possibly disturbing conduct, but they also place a

Learning Objective 1

Summarize the history and development of juries and jury trials.

bench trial
A trial in which the judge is both the trier of law *and* the trier of fact; also called *finder of law* or *finder of fact.*

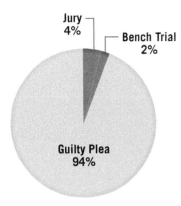

FIGURE 13-1

Felony convictions in state courts by method of conviction

Source: http://bjs.ojp.usdoj.gov/content/pub/pdf/fssc06st.pdf (accessed February 25, 2013).

trial jury
"[A] statutorily defined number of persons selected according to law and sworn to determine, in accordance with the law as instructed by the court, certain matters of fact based on evidence presented in a trial, and to render a verdict"; also called *petit jury* (in contrast to a grand jury).

defendant's fate in one person's hands. (For more information on bench trials, also see the beginning of Chapter 7.)

In contrast, a jury trial puts the defendant's fate in the hands of several individuals, which may or may not be desirable, as we will see shortly. Having said that, when are jury trials required? Why are juries important? How are they assembled? What constitutional issues come into play? How do jury members make decisions? Are jurors truthful and honest? Where does the right to a jury trial hail from? The following sections offer answers.

History of the Jury Trial

The **trial jury**, or "petit jury" (in contrast to a grand jury), has been explained as "a statutorily defined number of persons selected according to law and sworn to determine, in accordance with the law as instructed by the court, certain matters of fact based on evidence presented in a trial, and to render a verdict."[2] An important element of this definition is "persons . . . instructed by the court." Jurors are independent from the court, meaning that persons other than the judge decide factual matters. This helps prevent excess meddling by the government. Having a jury decide on factual matters provides the defendant with a "safeguard against the corrupt or overzealous prosecutor and against the compliant, biased, or eccentric judge."[3]

The concern with having impartial individuals engage in fact-finding goes all the way back to the period when Anglo-Saxon kings ruled England between the sixth and eleventh centuries. The Normans who conquered England in 1066 also used procedures that set the stage for modern juries. One of the most influential figures was King Henry II, who reigned from 1154 to 1189. In the twelfth century, Henry II set up a system to resolve land disputes using a jury of 12 free men; unlike the modern jury, these men investigated the case (as opposed to listening to arguments by the complainants, as is typical today). These panels of 12 "free and lawful men" were required to state who was a true property owner.[4] Henry II also introduced the concept of the "presenting jury"—panels of "lawful men" who were also asked to report under oath whether they knew of anyone engaged in criminal activity. This became one of the precursors to the grand jury system.

In 1215, England's King John signed the Magna Carta. Its Article 39 also provides some basis for modern juries:

> No Freeman shall be taken, or imprisoned, or be disseised of his Freehold, or Liberties, or free Customs, or be outlawed, or exiled, or any otherwise destroyed; nor will we pass upon him, nor condemn him, but by lawful Judgment of his Peers, or by the Law of the Land.

Early juries often made determinations of guilt and innocence based on preconceived ideas and knowledge of the case going into the trial; in other words, the juries were "self-informing." Over the centuries, though, juries gradually assumed the more modern role of listening to evidence without preconceived ideas or preexisting knowledge of the details of a case. Additionally, juries came to be seen as helping to protect the individual liberties of accused persons.

Eventually, early American colonists used juries as a means of rallying against unpopular British laws. For example, colonists disagreed with the so-called Navigation Acts, which tried to ensure British control over trading by requiring that goods going from one colony to another be carried on British ships. Colonial juries often refused to convict individuals charged with violations of the Navigation Acts, so in response the British fell back on the practice of trying offenders without juries, one of many factors that prompted the American Revolution. Indeed, the Declaration of Independence even contained language to the effect that colonists were angry with the British king "for depriving us, in many cases, of the benefits of trial by jury." This solidified a place in the U.S. Constitution for trial by jury.

JURY PROCESS

The Sixth Amendment states, in part, that the "accused shall enjoy the right to a speedy and public trial, by an impartial jury of the state." This provision seems straightforward on its face, but like other constitutional provisions, it has been subjected to intense scrutiny over the years. This is especially true of the Sixth Amendment's reference to jury trials. When does the right apply? If it does apply, what steps must be taken to ensure that a jury is impartial? When is the Sixth Amendment right to jury trial violated? We answer these questions in the subsections that follow.

Situations When the Right to a Jury Trial Applies

The right to a jury trial has always been recognized in the federal courts, but this right was not extended to the states until 1968 in the case of *Duncan* v. *Louisiana*.[5] The Court noted in that case that the right to a jury trial is "an inestimable safeguard against the corrupt or overzealous prosecutor and against the compliant, biased, or eccentric judge."[6] The right to a jury trial has therefore been incorporated, but subsequent decisions have restricted this right.

First, there is no Sixth Amendment constitutional right to a jury in noncriminal proceedings, which has come to be known as the **noncriminal proceeding rule**. The reason for this should be fairly obvious: The Sixth Amendment states, "In all *criminal prosecutions*, the accused shall enjoy the right to a . . . trial, by an impartial jury" (emphasis added). Unfortunately, it is not always clear what constitutes a noncriminal proceeding. One example is a juvenile delinquency hearing because in *McKeiver* v. *Pennsylvania*,[7] the Court held that juveniles charged with delinquent acts do not enjoy a right to a jury trial; also, civil commitment hearings do not need to be conducted before a jury.[8]

noncriminal proceeding rule
A rule recognizing that there is no Sixth Amendment constitutional right to a jury in noncriminal proceedings, based on the amendment's wording which states, "In all *criminal prosecutions*, the accused shall enjoy the right to a . . . trial, by an impartial jury" (emphasis added).

The Supreme Court has also carved out a "petty crime" exception to the Sixth Amendment right to a jury trial. In *Duncan* v. *Louisiana*, the Court expressly forbade jury trials for petty offenses, and in *Baldwin* v. *New York*, the Court announced its reason for this: The "disadvantages, onerous though they may be," of denying a jury trial for petty crimes are "outweighed by the benefits that result from speedy and inexpensive nonjury adjudication."[9]

What exactly is a "petty crime"? Unfortunately, there are no easy answers to this question. *Duncan* failed to define a "petty offense," but in *Baldwin* the Court concluded that crime that can bring punishment of more than six months is no longer a petty one. This has come to be known as the six-month imprisonment rule or the six-month rule—defendants do not enjoy a right to jury trial when the punishment they face is less than six months in jail or prison.

What if a person is charged with several crimes whose individual imprisonment terms do not exceed six months? The Court has decided that a defendant charged in a single proceeding with several petty crimes does not have a right to jury trial even if the maximum penalty for all offenses could exceed six months in prison.[10]

Waiving of the Right to a Jury Trial

It is clear that despite concerns with defendants' civil liberties, the Supreme Court has chipped away at the Sixth Amendment right to a jury trial. Nevertheless, there are occasions where a defendant may even wish to waive his or her right to a jury trial. If the case is particularly inflammatory or is one with which the community is intimately familiar, then obtaining a fair jury may be difficult, so in such a situation the defendant may opt for a bench trial.

The leading case dealing with waiver of the right to a jury trial is *Patton v. United States*.[11] In that case, the defendants argued that their decision to waive the right to a jury trial was invalid because they lacked the authority to waive the right, but the Supreme Court disagreed and stated that the right to a jury trial can be waived at the request of the defendant. The waiver must, however, be "express and intelligent." The waiver must also be voluntary, not a product of government coercion.[12]

Interestingly, the waiver of the right to a jury trial can be vetoed by the trial judge; that is, the judge can require a jury trial even if the defendant desires otherwise; often, such a veto comes at the request of the prosecutor. Indeed, the Supreme Court has upheld at least one federal statute permitting vetoes of this nature.[13] In its words, refusal to grant the defendant a waiver merely subjects the defendant to "the very thing that the Constitution guarantees him,"[14] namely, a jury trial. What are some reasons for a veto? The Court explains,

> The Constitution recognizes an adversary system as the proper method of determining guilt, and the Government, as a litigant, has a legitimate interest in seeing that cases in which it believes a conviction is warranted are tried before the tribunal which the Constitution regards as most likely to produce a fair result.[15]

Thus, if the government feels that a jury trial is preferable in the sense that it will produce a fairer result than a bench trial, a veto of the defendant's waiver of a jury trial is constitutionally permissible.

Selection of Impartial Jurors

voir dire
A term that literally means "to see what is said." It refers to the jury selection process whereby the prosecutor and the defense attorney question members of the jury panel in an effort to seat a jury that achieves the Sixth Amendment goal of impartiality.

The process behind selecting an impartial jury is rather complicated. Before **voir dire** (the process of examining potential jurors for bias) commences, a list of potential or prospective jurors must be compiled, and the creation of this list is critical; without an impartial list, the final jury will not reflect a fair cross section of the community. Once a list is put together, a panel of jurors is selected. This is where individuals are selected, usually randomly, for jury duty.

Think of jury selection as a three-stage process: A list of potential jurors must be compiled, potential jurors are selected from that list, and the jury itself is chosen from the potential jurors who are selected. This section addresses the first and second stages, and we turn to jury selection and *voir dire* later.

jury list
The list of potential jury members; also called *jury pool* or *master jury wheel*.

The list of potential jury members is usually called the "jury pool," "master jury wheel," or **jury list**; for simplicity, we will use the latter term. This jury list can be compiled from a number of sources, one of the more common being voter registration lists. The federal courts, the state of Washington, and several other states rely on this method. Another method of compiling the list is via driver's license registration lists, a method that California currently uses. Some states use telephone directory lists, and still other states rely on jury commissioners, individuals appointed by a judge who are responsible for compiling jury lists.

To be on the jury list, potential jurors usually have to possess important traits. For example, they must be of a certain age (usually older than 18 years), they must be U.S. citizens, and they have to have their civil rights restored if they have been convicted of a felony. The requirements to serve on a jury vary considerably from one state to the next.

Once the jury list is compiled, people are selected from the list for service. Individuals selected from the jury lists are called a "panel" or "venire," and we will use the term **jury panel** to reference these individuals.

jury panel
The people selected from the jury list for service as members of a jury in a trial; also called *panel* or *venire*.

Everyone who has been called on for jury duty has, at one time, been part of a jury panel. As most people know, there are several means by which someone can be excused from the jury panel. Examples of people typically exempted from jury service are those who are nonresident aliens, individuals who are unable to speak English, persons who are under age 18, those who are charged with a felony or who are serving a sentence, individuals for whom jury service could cause severe hardship, and those who are sworn law enforcement officers.

Once the jury panel is chosen, then *voir dire* commences. First, though, it is important to note that many defendants have appealed their convictions on the grounds that the jury list or panel was biased in some fashion, an appeal requiring that the defendant prove three facts:

> [The defendant must prove] (1) that the group alleged to be excluded is a "*distinctive*" group in the community; (2) that the representation of this group in venires from which juries are selected is not fair and reasonable in relation to the number of such persons in the community; and (3) that this *underrepresentation* is due to *systematic exclusion* of the group in the jury-selection process.[16]

If recognized "distinctive" groups include women and minorities, how does someone detect "underrepresentation" because of "systematic exclusion"? There is no easy answer to this question. On the one hand, the Supreme Court has decided that federal defendants have the right to inspect and copy jury lists in order to mount fair cross-section challenges.[17] On the other hand, the jury list generally provides little more than individuals' names, so sex and race must be inferred from the names found on the list.

Library Extra
13-1 Juror Selection

***Voir Dire* Process** Once *voir dire* commences, the concern is not to ensure that the jury represents a fair cross section of the community; instead, *voir dire* is concerned with the selection of jury members who can be impartial, as the Sixth Amendment requires. The term "*voir dire*" literally means "to see what is said." Thus, at this stage the judge, prosecutor, and defense have an opportunity to examine potential jurors for evidence of bias.

There is an important point to stress here: An unbiased jury list or panel and an unbiased jury are *not* always one in the same. While the jury list or panel may be unbiased and highly representative of the community at large, the final jury may not be because it is difficult to represent the community with 12 or fewer people. It is much easier to represent the community via the jury panel, however.

In some jurisdictions, judges question prospective jurors, and the prosecution and defense merely suggest questions to the judge in these jurisdictions. This speeds the process up and helps ensure that jurors do not develop preconceived ideas about the case in question. Usually, however, it is the attorneys who do the questioning in a process that can last for a few hours or can take several weeks in high-profile trials. *Voir dire* can take some time because nothing precludes the attorneys from investigating jurors' backgrounds, interviewing their acquaintances, or hiring social scientists who are experts in anticipating prospective jurors' probable decisions. There are three main steps to the *voir dire* process:

1. *Questioning by the judge.* *Voir dire* usually begins with the judge asking questions concerning potential jurors' familiarity with the case, attitudes toward one or other party to the case, demographic information, and so on. This is often done to guide the attorneys in their *voir dire* questioning. The Supreme Court has upheld this type of questioning, noting that it is perfectly acceptable for the judge to question jurors about their knowledge and opinions concerning the case.[18]

   Note that the reverse is also true—the judge is not required to ask any questions in certain types of cases. In an obscenity case, the Supreme Court noted that the judge is not required to ask questions as to "whether the jurors' educational, political, and religious beliefs might affect their views on the question of obscenity."[19] In contrast, the Supreme Court, in *Ham v. South Carolina*, required that in certain types of cases, notably those dealing with racial prejudice and capital punishment, the judges ask certain types of questions. For instance, the

Court noted that questions about racial prejudice must be asked if racial issues are closely tied to the criminal conduct at issue.[20]

In *Ristaino* v. *Ross*,[21] a black defendant was convicted of a violent crime committed against a white security guard. The trial judge denied the defendant's motion that specific questions about racial prejudice be asked of potential jurors; instead, the judge just asked basic questions about general prejudice, not any directed at the facts of the case in question. Surprisingly, the Supreme Court upheld the trial judge's decision. This decision seems contradictory to *Ham*, but the Court noted that racial issues did not permeate in this case because the facts that the defendant was black and that the victim was white were secondary to the question of guilt. There is only one case where the Supreme Court has sanctioned exclusion of a potential juror because of alleged bias: In *Leonard* v. *United States*,[22] the Court held that jury panel members who had heard the guilty verdict at the defendant's previous trial should have been excluded from serving on the jury in the present trial because the Court believed that the previous verdict may have influenced jurors in the second trial.

In summary, there are few constitutional restrictions on judges' questioning of potential jurors. With the exceptions of capital cases and cases where racial matters permeate the trial, judges are under no obligation to ask questions of potential jurors. By the same token, they are also given considerable latitude in terms of asking almost any question they desire.

The Supreme Court has decided that judges should ask detailed questions of potential jurors who serve on "death certified" juries, that is, juries that recommend a death sentence. It has stated that the judge *must*—at the request of either party and only in cases where capital punishment is a possible outcome—ask specific questions of jurors determined to assess their attitudes toward capital punishment.[23] The Court held that defendants in capital cases may require potential jurors to state whether they automatically impose the death penalty on conviction.

challenge for cause
A prosecutor's or defense attorney's call for removal of a potential juror from service on a jury based on bias or a similar reason demonstrated by the potential juror.

2. *Challenges for cause.* During *voir dire*, both the defense and the prosecution have an unlimited number of so-called **challenges for cause**, which are used to exclude potential jurors from service on the jury because of bias or a similar reason. For example, if a member of the jury panel is related to the defendant, a challenge for cause will almost certainly succeed, or if the potential juror served on a past jury in a case dealing with a similar crime, a challenge for cause could probably succeed. If a potential juror stands to benefit financially from the outcome of the case, he or she will probably be excused based on a challenge for cause. The list goes on, but the only challenges dealt with by the Supreme Court include those based on bias and attitudes toward capital punishment.

Generally, if a juror is unable or unwilling to hear the case fairly and impartially, he or she may be excluded in a challenge for cause. However, as Supreme Court precedent seems to attest, challenges for cause dealing with alleged bias rarely succeed; that is, in situations where a person appears to be biased but does not state anything to this effect, it is difficult to succeed with a challenge for cause.

Defendants in capital trials have the right to exclude jurors with certain preconceived ideas about the death penalty. In *Witherspoon* v. *Illinois*,[24] the Court decided on the constitutionality of a statute that provided for exclusion of all potential jurors who "expressed scruples" against the death penalty. The Court held that a death sentence returned from such a jury would be unconstitutional because the jury resulting from the statute would be "organized to return a verdict of death."[25] Importantly, in *Witherspoon* it was only the defendant's death sentence that was invalidated, not his conviction. Also, note that nothing prohibits prosecutors from excluding jurors who would *never* return a verdict of death.

In short, challenges for cause in death penalty cases usually come in two varieties. If the defendant can show that a potential juror is predisposed to return a verdict of death, such a juror will probably be excluded. Similarly, if the prosecution can show that a potential juror is all but certain to oppose capital punishment in the case at hand, that person will probably be excluded.

3. *Peremptory challenges*. In contrast to challenges for cause, **peremptory challenges** call for removal of potential jurors without any type of argument. Think of the peremptory challenge as a fallback measure. If, say, the defense fails with a challenge for cause to exclude a potential juror whom it believes will be biased against the defendant, a peremptory challenge can be used—in fact, peremptory challenges can be used to exclude potential jurors for any reason whatsoever.

> **peremptory challenge**
> The right to challenge a potential juror without disclosing the reason for the challenge. Prosecutors and defense attorneys routinely use peremptory challenges to eliminate from juries individuals who, although they express no obvious bias, are thought to be capable of swaying the jury in an undesirable direction.

It is generally unacceptable for the prosecution or the defense to exclude a juror based on race. A challenge for cause arguing that a person's race will cause him or her to be biased will *never* succeed. But what if a peremptory challenge is used to exclude a juror based on race? This question was first addressed in *Swain* v. *Alabama*[26]; in that case, the defendant argued that the prosecutor excluded all minority jurors through peremptory challenges and, as such, violated the equal protection clause of the Fourteenth Amendment. The Court rejected this argument:

> [The peremptory challenge] is often exercised upon the "sudden impressions and unaccountable prejudices we are apt to conceive upon the bare looks and gestures of another," . . . upon a juror's "habits and associations," . . . or upon the feeling that "the bare questioning [a juror's] indifference may sometimes provoke a resentment." . . . It is no less frequently exercised on grounds normally thought irrelevant to legal proceedings or official action, namely, the race, religion, nationality, occupation or affiliations of people summoned for jury duty. For the question a prosecutor or defense counsel must decide is not whether a juror of a particular race or nationality is in fact partial, but whether one from a different group is less likely to be.[27]

Several years after *Swain*, the Supreme Court revisited the issue of using peremptory challenges for excluding racial minorities. In *Batson* v. *Kentucky*,[28] the Court decided that prosecutors can be called on to explain their use of peremptory challenges to exclude minorities but only if the defense shows that the challenges were used for this purpose. This showing requires that the people excluded through the peremptory challenges constitute a distinct group, that these people were excluded by the prosecution through the use of peremptory challenges, and that "these facts and any other relevant circumstances raise an inference that the prosecutor used [peremptory challenges] to exclude the veniremen from the petit jury on account of their race."[29]

If the defense makes the showing, then the prosecution will be required to explain his or her reasons for excluding jurors based on their race. However, this explanation does not need to be as convincing as one that would accompany a challenge for cause but simply needs to be what the Court calls "race neutral."

> **Library Extra**
> 13-2 Juror Qualifications

What is an explanation that is "race neutral"? In *Hernandez* v. *New York*,[30] the prosecutor sought to use peremptory challenges to exclude four potential jurors of Hispanic descent. They were the only four people on the panel with apparent Hispanic origins. The prosecutor argued that the jurors were excluded for two reasons: that two of the panel members were involved in criminal activity and that the other two "looked away" from him during questioning, an apparently suspicious gesture. The Court declared that this explanation was race neutral. Had the prosecution argued that the excluded jurors would be likely to decide in a certain way given their Hispanic descent, the Court would have decided differently. Thus, a race-neutral argument is one that really has nothing to do with race.

In summary, peremptory challenges used to exclude racial minorities (and, by extension, women or members of other "protected" groups) are constitutionally valid only when (1) the prosecutor offers a race-neutral explanation for doing so and (2) the judge believes the reason is genuine. These two requirements matter, however, only if the defendant raises the argument that race was a motivating factor behind the prosecutor's use of peremptory challenges; in other words, the defense has the initial burden of showing racial bias in the peremptory challenge stage.

The defense also cannot exclude potential jurors through its peremptory challenges based on race. For example, the Supreme Court has refused to support the exclusion of African-American panel members in the trial of white defendants charged with assaulting African-Americans.[31] Other cases concerning peremptory challenges by the defense have revolved around the question of how many (if any) peremptory challenges are constitutionally permissible. Peremptory challenges are generally limited because the Supreme Court has stated that peremptory challenges are not constitutionally guaranteed (see Table 13–1 for the number of peremptory challenges in criminal cases by state).[32]

Jury Consultants: Useful?

jury consultant
An individual who claims the ability to determine, based on various demographic and behavioral characteristics, how prospective jurors will decide.

To assist in their decisions to excuse prospective jurors via challenges, some attorneys hire professional **jury consultants**, individuals who may assist in juror questioning (such as by designing questionnaires for the attorneys to use in selecting from prospective jurors) and/or claim to be able to identify how prospective jurors (based on their various demographic and behavioral characteristics) will decide a case and who use social science research on juror decision making to back up their recommendations. Jury consultants are controversial, however, because the research community is far from unanimous on factors that influence jurors' decision making.

Jury consulting became popular during the famous case of the "Harrisburg Seven," a group of Vietnam War protesters who in 1971 were tried for several acts of civil disobedience.[33] The defense attorneys in that case hired a team of social scientists to assist in jury selection; these social scientists sought to identify a set of demographic characteristics that would be consistent with the defendants' antiwar views. The defendants were eventually acquitted even though the government spent millions on the case. The jury consultant profession took off from that point forward.

There are arguments for and against professional jury consulting. On the one hand, experts can help take some of the guesswork out of play. Presumably, these consultants can make more objective decisions (as opposed to gut decisions) concerning which prospective jurors should be excused, and they can also help attorneys protect against allegations of unfair dismissals, such as dismissals of all minority prospective jury members. On the other hand, jury consultants are expensive and now benefit only the well-to-do. Moreover, some have questioned the "science" behind jury consulting, claiming that it is somewhat lacking.[34]

Learning Objective 3
Describe the jury decision-making process and factors that affect jurors' decisions.

JURY DECISION MAKING

Jury decision making is a complex process. There are formal requirements that vary from one jurisdiction to the next concerning jury sizes and voting requirements. Because jurors are human beings, various factors affect their decisions, they sometimes act strangely

TABLE 13–1 *Voir Dire* Processes by State for Courts of General Jurisdiction

Number of Peremptory Challenges

State	Criminal					
	Capital		Felony		Misdemeanor	
	State	Defense	State	Defense	State	Defense
Alabama	12	12	6	6	3	3
Alaska	N/A	N/A	10	10	3	3
Arizona	10	10	6	6	6	6
Arkansas	10	12	6	8	3	3
California	20	20	20/10	20/10	10/6	10/6
Colorado	10	10	5	5	3	3
Connecticut	25	25	15/6	15/6	3	3
Delaware	12	20	6	6	6	6
District of Columbia	N/A	N/A	10	10	3	3
Florida	10	10	10/6	10/6	3	3
Georgia	10	20	6	12	2	4
Hawaii	N/A	N/A	12/3	12/3	3	3
Idaho	10	10	10/6	10/6	4	4
Illinois	14	14	7	7	5	5
Indiana	20	20	10	10	5	5
Iowa	N/A	N/A	10/6	10/6	4	4
Kansas	12	12	12/8/6	12/8/6	3	3
Kentucky	8	8	8	8	3	3
Louisiana	12	12	12/6	12/6	6	6
Maine	N/A	N/A	10/8	10/8	4	4
Maryland	10	20	5	10	4	4
Massachusetts	N/A	N/A	12/4	12/4	4	4
Michigan	N/A	N/A	12/5	12/5	5	5
Minnesota	N/A	N/A	9/3	15/3	3	5
Mississippi	12	12	6	6	6	6
Missouri	9	9	6	6	2	2
Montana	8	8	6/3	6/3	6/3	6/3
Nebraska	12	12	6	6	3	3
Nevada	8	8	4	4	4	4
New Hampshire	10	20	15/3	15/3	3	3
New Jersey	12	20	12	20	10	10
New Mexico	8	12	3	5	3	5
New York	20	20	20/15	20/15/10	10	10
North Carolina	14	14	6	6	6	6
North Dakota	N/A	N/A	6/4	6/4	6/4	6/4
Ohio	6	6	4	4	3	3
Oklahoma	9	9	5	5	3	3
Oregon	12	12	6	6	6/3	6/3
Pennsylvania	20	20	7	7	5	5
Puerto Rico	N/A	N/A	10/5	10/5	5	5
Rhode Island	N/A	N/A	6	6	3	3
South Carolina	5	10	5	10	5	5
South Dakota	20	20	20/10	20/10	3	3
Tennessee	15	15	8	8	3	3
Texas	15	15	10	10	5	5
Utah	10	10	4	4	3	3
Vermont	N/A	N/A	6	6	6	6
Virginia	4	4	4	4	3	3
Washington	12	12	6	6	3	3
West Virginia	N/A	N/A	2	6	4	4
Wisconsin	N/A	N/A	6/4	6/4	4	4
Wyoming	12	12	8	8	4	4

Note: The following states do not have a death penalty statute: Alaska, District of Columbia, Hawaii, Iowa, Maine, Massachusetts, Michigan, Minnesota, North Dakota, Puerto Rico, Rhode Island, Vermont, West Virginia, and Wisconsin.

Source: D. B. Rottman and S. M. Strickland, *State Court Organization, 2004* (Washington, DC: Bureau of Justice Statistics, 2006), available at http://bjs.ojp.usdoj.gov/content/pub/pdf/sco04.pdf (accessed February 25, 2013).

(such as by returning guilty verdicts when the evidence would suggest otherwise), and they do not always tell the truth during the selection process. This has prompted some critics of America's jury system to suggest alternatives like professional jurors.

Jury Size and Voting Requirements

The media always seem to portray juries as consisting of 12 people, yet the Supreme Court has stated that a 12-person jury is not a constitutional requirement. In *Williams* v. *Florida*, for example, the Court stated that the 12-member jury was a "historical accident" and "unnecessary to effect the purposes of the jury system."[35] The Court noted that a six-member jury would even provide "a fair possibility for obtaining a representative cross-section of the community, . . . [a]s long as arbitrary exclusions of a particular class from the jury rolls are forbidden."[36]

However, in *Ballew* v. *Georgia*,[37] the Court concluded that a five-member jury was unconstitutional and found it unlikely that such a small group could engage "in meaningful deliberation, . . . remember all the facts and arguments, and truly represent the common sense of the entire community."[38] Thus, the appropriate size for a jury is anywhere between six and 12 members. See Table 13–2 for a listing of jury sizes and voting requirements by state and case type, specifically for courts of general jurisdiction (those with jurisdiction to try several types of cases, including more serious criminal cases).

Another popular misconception is that juries must return unanimous verdicts. In two companion cases,[39] the Supreme Court upheld a Louisiana statute that permitted 9–3 jury verdicts as well as an Oregon statute permitting 10–2 decisions. According to the Court,

> In our view, disagreement of three jurors does not alone establish reasonable doubt, particularly when such a heavy majority of the jury, after having considered the dissenters' views, remained convinced of guilt. . . . That want of jury unanimity is not to be equated with the existence of reasonable doubt emerges even more clearly from the fact that when a jury in a federal court, which operates under the unanimity rule and is instructed to acquit a defendant if it has a reasonable doubt . . . cannot agree unanimously upon a verdict, the defendant is not acquitted, but is merely given a new trial.[40]

TABLE 13–2 Jury Sizes and Voting Requirements by State for Courts of General Jurisdiction

State	Felony		Misdemeanor	
	Size	Voting Requirements	Size	Voting Requirements
Alabama	12	Unanimous	12	Unanimous
Alaska	12	Unanimous	12	Unanimous
Arizona	12/8[a]	Unanimous	8	Unanimous
Arkansas	12	Unanimous	12[b]	Unanimous
California	12	Unanimous	12[c]	Unanimous
Colorado	12	Unanimous	6	Unanimous
Connecticut	6[d]	Unanimous	6	Unanimous
Delaware	12	Unanimous	12	Unanimous
District of Columbia	12	Unanimous	12	Unanimous
Florida	6[e]	Unanimous	6	Unanimous
Georgia	12	Unanimous	6	Unanimous
Hawaii	12	Unanimous	12[f]	Unanimous
Idaho	12	Unanimous	6	Unanimous
Illinois	12	Unanimous	12	Unanimous
Indiana	12/6[g]	Unanimous	6	Unanimous
Iowa	12	Unanimous	12/6[h]	Unanimous
Kansas	12	Unanimous	6	Unanimous
Kentucky	12	Unanimous	12	Unanimous
Louisiana	12[i]	Unanimous[j]	6	Unanimous

State	Felony Size	Felony Voting Requirements	Misdemeanor Size	Misdemeanor Voting Requirements
Maine	12	Unanimous	12	Unanimous
Maryland	12	Unanimous	12	Unanimous
Massachusetts	12	Unanimous	12	Unanimous
Michigan	12	Unanimous	12	Unanimous
Minnesota	12	Unanimous	6	Unanimous
Mississippi	12	Unanimous	6	Unanimous
Missouri	12	Unanimous	12[k]	Unanimous
Montana	12	Unanimous	12	Unanimous
Nebraska	12	Unanimous	12	Unanimous
Nevada	12	Unanimous	12	Unanimous
New Hampshire	12	Unanimous	6	Unanimous
New Jersey	12[l]	Unanimous	12[m]	Unanimous
New Mexico	12	Unanimous	12	Unanimous
New York	12	Unanimous	12	Unanimous
North Carolina	12	Unanimous	12	Unanimous
North Dakota	12	Unanimous	12/6[n]	Unanimous
Ohio	12	Unanimous	8	Unanimous
Oklahoma	12	Unanimous	6[o]	Unanimous
Oregon	12	10/12[p]	6	Unanimous
Pennsylvania	12[q]	Unanimous	12[r]	Unanimous
Puerto Rico	12	9	12	9
Rhode Island	12	Unanimous	12	Unanimous
South Carolina	12	Unanimous	12	Unanimous
South Dakota	12	Unanimous	12	Unanimous
Tennessee	12	Unanimous	12	Unanimous
Texas	12	Unanimous	6	Unanimous
Utah	12/8[s]	Unanimous	6/4[t]	Unanimous
Vermont	12	Unanimous	12	Unanimous
Virginia	12	Unanimous	7	Unanimous
Washington	12[u]	Unanimous	12[v]	Unanimous
West Virginia	12	Unanimous	12	Unanimous
Wisconsin	12	Unanimous	6	Unanimous
Wyoming	12	Unanimous	6	Unanimous

[a]A 12-member jury is required if the death penalty or a sentence of 30 years or more is being sought.

[b]The number of jurors may be fewer if the parties agree.

[c]The number of jurors may be fewer if the parties agree.

[d]A 12-member jury is used in capital cases, but the defendant may elect otherwise.

[e]Capital and eminent domain cases require a 12-member jury (unanimous verdict).

[f]This applies to crimes punishable by six months or more.

[g]Twelve for Class A, B, and C felonies or enhanced penalty; six for other felonies.

[h]In misdemeanor trials, 12-member jury if "serious" or "aggravated," six if "simple."

[i]Capital cases and cases where punishment necessarily is confinement at hard labor—12 jurors. Cases where punishment may be confinement at hard labor—six jurors.

[j]Capital cases and cases where punishment necessarily is confinement at hard labor—unanimous; cases where punishment may be confinement at hard labor—10/12.

[k]In practice, juries consist of 12 members. However, if the case is tried before an associate judge, the parties agree on a number of jurors.

[l]Juries in criminal cases consist of 12 persons. Except in trials for crimes punishable by death, parties may stipulate in writing that the jury shall consist of fewer than 12 persons.

[m]Ibid.

[n]In class A misdemeanor, defendant may make motion for 12 jurors.

[o]In cases where imprisonment is authorized for more than six months, all jurors must concur in the verdict.

[p]In murder or aggravated murder trials, verdict must be at least 11 or 12 jurors.

[q]On consent, jury may be fewer than 12 but not fewer than six.

[r]Ibid.

[s]A 12-member jury is required for a capital offense.

[t]For misdemeanors: If potential sentence is over six months, then six jurors; if shorter than six months, then four jurors.

[u]In noncapital cases, a defendant may elect trial before a six-member jury.

[v]Ibid.

Source: http://bjs.ojp.usdoj.gov/content/pub/pdf/sco04.pdf (accessed February 25, 2013).

In short, guilt can be determined by less than a unanimous jury in certain jurisdictions. This is somewhat controversial—permitting less-than-unanimous decisions diminishes reliability because jurors will not debate as fully as they might if a unanimous decision were required; that is, people can succumb to group pressures.

Factors Affecting Jurors' Decisions

It would be nice if jurors based their decisions solely on the facts of the case, but thanks to hundreds of studies of juror decision making, we know that jurors are often swayed by factors outside the legal realm. Unfortunately, because jury deliberations are generally secret, researchers rarely have access to real jurors, so most have been forced to study juror decision making in the context of so-called mock juries.[41] The mock jury process works like this: A simulated trial is held, usually in a university classroom, and the professor(s) will study the decisions of the jurors, often with attention to demographic factors like race, sex, employment background, and marital status.

Capital Jury Project
An ongoing research program in which in-depth post-trial interviews are conducted with members of capital juries.

An exception to the mock jury exercise is found in the work of the **Capital Jury Project**, an ongoing research program in which in-depth post-trial interviews are conducted with members of capital juries. Since the program began, over 1,000 jurors have been interviewed from over 300 capital trials in 14 states,[42] and the work of the Capital Jury Project has factored into what we know about juror decision making.

Researchers have looked at four main sets of factors that affect juror decision making: (1) procedural characteristics, (2) juror characteristics, (3) case characteristics, and (4) deliberation characteristics.[43] Procedural characteristics include everything from jury size and juror involvement during the trial to jury instructions and jury voting requirements, whereas juror characteristics refer to all manner of individual demographic factors, such as age, race, and employment status. Case characteristics refer to the case at hand, such as to the strength (or weakness) of the evidence, and deliberation characteristics include everything that happens behind closed doors once the jury is deliberating.

Which of the four is most influential? All four are important to varying degrees. Case characteristics and the evidence are important, but jurors' personal beliefs and past experiences weigh in quite heavily.[44]

liberation hypothesis
The tendency for jurors to fall back on their own gut instincts when presented with evidence that is vague.[ii] The term derives from the phenomenon of jurors feeling "liberated" when the meaning or application of evidence is unclear.

In summary, jurors do not always act objectively, and their own personal beliefs and biases affect their decisions. When the evidence is vague, jurors tend to fall back on their gut instincts, which has been termed the **liberation hypothesis**,[45] a phenomenon occurring when jurors are "liberated" from the evidence when it is vague.

Jury Nullification and Vilification

jury nullification
The practice, exercised by some juries, of either ignoring or misapplying the law in a certain situation.

Sometimes juries act strangely and run amok, returning decisions that are altogether opposite of what would be expected by tradition, process, or law. They sometimes return a guilty verdict in cases where the defendant is clearly not guilty and/or return a not-guilty verdict in cases where the defendant is guilty. This practice of either ignoring or misapplying the law in a certain situation is known as **jury nullification**. Jury nullification sounds counter to the way the jury system should operate, but there can be an upside to it. Back in 1997, an Aurora (Illinois) bar owner, Jessie Ingram, booby-trapped his bar after it was burglarized three times. He put warning signs outside the windows that had been broken during previous burglaries announcing that anyone entering the premises without permission would be subject to electric shock. One burglar ignored the signs and broke a window; on climbing through it, he was shocked to death by a piece of electrified steel that Ingram had adhered to the windowsill. The grand jury refused to indict Ingram on homicide charges (interestingly, though, he was later held civilly liable for the burglar's death). This was a grand jury case, not a trial jury case, but the same logic applies—sometimes justice can be served (or so the grand jurors felt) by going somewhat counter to what the law requires.

There is precedent for jurors ignoring the law and deciding what they feel is best. During Prohibition, for example, jurors routinely refused to convict people charged with liquor-law violations.[46] But jury nullification can also live up to its negative connotations. Historically, southern juries often refused to convict white defendants who were charged with offenses against black victims despite the presence of evidence that would warrant conviction.[47] Some have argued that jury nullification can also be used for political purposes and has little to do with the facts of the case at hand or even with juror characteristics. For example, the acquittal of O. J. Simpson may have been little more than an effort on jurors' part to show that the Los Angeles Police Department was racist.[48]

Is jury nullification really a problem? One study showed, for example, that as penalties become more severe, jurors become less likely to convict, possibly suggesting nullification.[49] In another study, researchers used mock jurors to decide the fate of a hypothetical physician who was accused of knowingly transfusing a patient with blood he knew hadn't been screened for HIV; the researchers found that the jurors were less likely to convict if the penalty was severe (e.g., prison instead of a fine).[50] These studies do not provide clear evidence of jury nullification, but they at least illustrate that there can be apprehension on jurors' part to apply the law to the letter, meaning that jurors sometimes do what *they* think will best serve the ends of justice.

The flip side of jury nullification has been called **jury vilification**:[51] "Juries may return verdicts that reflect prejudiced or bigoted community standards and convict when the evidence does not warrant a conviction."[52] Jury vilification is exceptionally rare; more often, if a person is unjustifiably convicted, the decision is more likely due to jurors' failure to understand important dimensions of the case.

jury vilification
"The return of a jury verdict that reflects prejudiced or bigoted community standards and convicts when the evidence does not warrant a conviction."[iii]

Do Jurors Tell the Truth?

When the subject of truth telling comes up in the trial context, usually the concern is with defendants and witnesses not being honest during their testimony. But jurors have been known to stretch the truth as well, particularly during the *voir dire* phase. For example, the author of one early study found that one in three jurors lied under oath during the selection process.[53] In a similar study, a researcher found that nearly three-quarters of jurors harbored preconceived opinions concerning the defendant's guilt, but only 15 percent of them admitted as much during *voir dire*.[54] Whether this is due to actual dishonesty or simply the intimidation factor is unclear.[55] Either way, these study numbers are interesting:

> If they are representative of juror honesty generally, they suggest that questions put to jurors in certain formats are more likely to elicit a false response. This lack of candor by jurors can have a significant effect in trial strategy and in the verdicts rendered, because juror honesty during open voir dire in the courtroom is now the critical method for exposing juror bias and impartiality.[56]

If jurors are not truthful, what can be done about it? They are often told of the consequences of lying—namely, perjury and possible criminal conviction—but obviously this hasn't stopped the problem. Some have called for written *voir dire* questioning instead of questioning in open court. The logic is that the anonymity of a written instrument may encourage jurors to be more truthful than answering questions in front of court personnel and other prospective jurors. Indeed, research suggests that people are more truthful in their written—as opposed to verbal—responses when it comes to describing their past experiences with drug use,[57] sexual practices,[58] and other sensitive activities.[59]

Time for Professional Jurors?

One of the hallmarks of the American criminal justice system is that jurors are ordinary citizens, not government or other official actors. This is advantageous because it helps protect against overreaching government, but there can be a downside to having ordinary persons serve as jurors as well. First, laypersons may not have the knowledge or wherewithal to pay attention to—much less understand—what they are presented with. Mark Twain once lamented that the jury system "puts a ban upon intelligence and honesty, and a premium upon ignorance, stupidity, and perjury."[60] "I desire to tamper with jury law," he said, "to so alter it as to put a premium on intelligence and character, and close the jury box against idiots, blacklegs, and people who do not read newspapers."[61]

Also, the so-called *CSI* effect has distorted many jurors' image of how criminal justice actually operates because it has been said that programs like *CSI* foster "the mistaken notion that criminal science is fast and infallible and always gets its man. That's affecting the way lawyers prepare their cases, as well as the expectations that police and the public place on real crime labs."[62] Jurors thus may fancy themselves as experts when in reality the process of crime investigation is more tedious.

Another problem is that many jurisdictions throughout the country have been hit hard by the problem of people failing to show up for jury duty after being summoned,[63] and of those who do show up, many individuals are excused due to hardships and other factors that would not permit them to serve on juries; the result has been juries composed of a certain demographic. One study states that "jurors that are able to serve on lengthier trials are more likely to be unemployed or retired, female, or unmarried and are less likely to have a college education."[64]

When considering each of these problems together, one wonders whether it is simply time to install or employ professional jurors in America's criminal justice system.[65] Such individuals would be court employees, not unlike court clerks or court reporters, whose full-time job would consist of rendering verdicts in civil and criminal trials. There are several advantages to this approach. First, making jury service a career would ensure a more robust demographic mix; second, professional jurors would presumably be trained in how best to decide cases, and although they would not need training to the extent that lawyers do, they would have sufficient training to make impartial decisions, and these literate, educated individuals would render fairer decisions; and, third, there would be no serious constitutional issues because the Sixth Amendment only references an "impartial jury of the state."

While this is an intriguing idea, several experts have been critical of the prospect of professional jurors:

> Jurors selected from the community constitute the most independent power in government as they judge the facts unconstrained by whether someone may challenge them in a manner that threatens their livelihood and status. Professional jurors would be part of the system rather than of the community. They would not then operate as the conscience of the community to counterbalance overreaching by institutional governmental agencies. Moreover, we need people involved judging these cases who are experts in what happens every day in the communities, in the streets and in the lives of everyday Americans; not simply experts on what happens in court or in a laboratory, not second hand experts, who as professional jurors may lack "healthy skepticism," discounting that "experts" are potentially afflicted with common human defects, who may jump to conclusions, make mistakes, even lie.[66]

Library Extra
13-3 Juror Pay

THE TRIAL

Once a jury is selected, the case proceeds to trial, but some of the constitutional protections we have discussed carry on. Recall that the Sixth Amendment mentions a "speedy and public trial." While there is no constitutional reference to it, defendants also benefit from

COURTS IN THE NEWS

For Some, Serving on a Jury Can Be Traumatic

In a remarkable display of compassion and personal strength, the mother of a Texas murder victim has asked her state legislator to introduce a bill that would provide counseling for jurors who have to consider cases like her daughter's. Sharon Cave's 21-year-old daughter, Jennifer, was horribly murdered in an Austin, Texas, apartment in August 2005. Her killer, 24-year-old Colton Pitonyak, attempted to conceal his crime by butchering her body in an effort to reduce the body to parts that could be easily transported and disposed of in garbage bags.

At Pitonyak's trial, the prosecution, of necessity, introduced graphic testimony regarding her injuries and displayed vivid photographs of her slaughtered remains. One, a photo of her headless corpse, drove one witness to jump up and run from the courtroom. Cave related that "[t]he medical examiner told me that nobody ever should have seen those pictures. The jurors looked like they had seen something horrific."

The stress is exacerbated because jurors are prohibited from discussing the case during the trial. They ultimately show symptoms of post-traumatic stress and depression and even thoughts of suicide. Texas State Representative Juan Garcia of Corpus Christi believes it is completely understandable. "We ask jurors, from businessmen to soccer moms, to . . . step aside from their everyday duties and go mete out justice in sometimes gruesome cases. Then we ask them to make a transparent transition back to normal life overnight."

The Jennifer Cave murder case is but one of numerous notorious cases that have traumatized jurors. For example, in 2007 in Chesire, Connecticut, Steven Hayes and his partner Joshua Komisarjevsky invaded the home of the Petit family, severely beat Dr. William Petit, raped and strangled his wife Jennifer Hawke-Petit, and then killed the couple's two daughters, Hayley, 17, and Michaela, 11. Hayes, hoping to destroy evidence, poured gasoline on the girls and set fire to the home; the two young girls, still alive, died from smoke inhalation before they could be rescued. The evidence presented at trial was so gruesome that jurors were offered postdecision counseling. Similarly, the infamous Caylee Anthony murder trial took a toll on jurors who found her mother not guilty of killing the two-year-old in 2008.

Michelle Christenson/Corpus Christi Caller-Times

Sharon Cave's daughter Jennifer was brutally murdered. Graphic photographs shown at trial caused jurors to suffer PTSD. She believes the jurors should be eligible to receive counseling after serving on trials involving the use of graphic evidence and photographs.

According to Sonia Chopra, a consultant for the National Jury Project in Oakland, California, one problem is that jurors are prohibited from sharing their thoughts about the case or the experience with anyone until after the trial. "One of the best ways to alleviate stress and anxiety is to talk it through with somebody else," she says. "While the jurors are in trial, that's problematic, because they're not technically supposed to talk about anything that happens in the courtroom with anyone. For the length of the trial, they're having to just internalize everything that they're hearing and they're seeing." Nadine Kaslow, a psychologist at Emory University, suggests that the images that jurors see can be overwhelming. Speaking of the jurors in the Caylee Anthony case, she says, "Everyone's going to have a reason to be impacted by this case. Whether or not you have children of your own, there's no way out of being profoundly influenced. . . . To cope, to survive, actually, you form these new families. It's a very good survival technique," she said. "The problem is, when you start getting things like hung juries, and all the challenges around that, you can end up in a very problematic situation."

Although there are currently no national or state standards regarding post-trial juror counseling, many jurisdictions are developing programs to provide the service. Washington's King County established its program in 1998. The offer of counseling is made at the discretion of the trial judge, and the counseling is provided through contracted local mental health centers. Florida, Georgia, Michigan, Minnesota, New York, and other states are also investigating the need for such counseling and methods for providing it.

Sharon Cave is enthused by the reception her proposal has received in the Texas legislature. She has widened her focus, however, as she now promotes efforts throughout the nation to find ways to help jurors. She recognizes, though, that the biggest obstacle is funding. "Personally," she says, "I think funding should come from the Crime Victim's Compensation Fund. When criminals are fined, . . . they need to do more than just do the time; they need to pay for everything."

Jury service can sometimes be boring, but it can also be stressful—as the story in this feature illustrates. Most jurors

(continued)

are ill-prepared to witness the kinds of evidence presented in trials involving grisly crimes, including homicide, child rape, and terrorism. ■

DISCUSSION QUESTIONS

1. Can jurors be better prepared for participation in trials where defendants are accused of especially spectacular crimes and in which upsetting evidence is likely to be presented? If so, what kind of preparation might be offered?

2. Should professional courtroom participants, such as prosecutors, make an effort to tone down the evidence they present in order to lessen its impact on jurors? Might doing so decrease the likelihood of a conviction?

3. Might it be feasible to allow jurors the option of seeing some evidence but choosing to avoid other evidence that they might find upsetting? How might such a choice impact the outcome of a criminal trial?

Sources: Elizabeth Landau, "Murder Trial Jurors Can Be Overwhelmed, Traumatized," CNN, June 28, 2011, available at www.cnn.com/2011/HEALTH/06/28/jury.stress.ptsd/index.html (accessed June 2, 2013); Maria Sprow, "Post-Traumatic Juror Stress," undated article at the Texas Association of Counties website, available at www.county.org/resources/library/county_mag/county/193/2.html (accessed June 2, 2013); Ben Schmitt, "Victim's Mom Pushes Counseling for Jurors," *USA Today*, November 25, 2007, available at www.usatoday.com/news/nation/2007-11-25-Jurorstress_N.htm (accessed June 2, 2013); Hillary Hylton/Austin, "Putting Jurors on the Couch," *Time*, April 10, 2007, available at www.time.com/time/nation/article/0,8599,1608660,00.html (accessed June 2, 2013).

trials by impartial judges. Finally, there are various steps in the trial process, a carefully choreographed order of events that must be followed to ensure that the accused's constitutional rights are carefully guarded.

Learning Objective 4

Explain the right to speedy trial and the problem of delays.

SPEEDY TRIAL

The Sixth Amendment provides, in part, "In all criminal prosecutions, the accused shall enjoy the right to a *speedy* . . . trial" (emphasis added). What constitutes a "speedy" trial? Unfortunately, there is no set standard either by law or by practice.

Somewhat surprisingly, it was not until 1966 that the Supreme Court addressed the Sixth Amendment's speedy trial provision. In *United States* v. *Ewell*,[67] the Court identified three advantages associated with a speedy trial. First, it prevents excessive incarceration; second, it minimizes anxiety experienced by the accused as a result of a publicized accusation; and, third, it prevents damage to the defendant's case resulting from too much delay.

The Court elaborated on these points in a case we will look at in more detail shortly, *Barker* v. *Wingo*:[68]

> If an accused cannot make bail, he is generally confined, as was Barker for 10 months, in a local jail. This contributes to the overcrowding and generally deplorable state of those institutions. Lengthy exposure to these conditions "has a destructive effect on human character and makes the rehabilitation of the individual offender much more difficult." At times the result may even be violent rioting. Finally, lengthy pretrial detention is costly. The cost of maintaining a prisoner in jail varies from $3 to $9 per day, and this amounts to millions across the Nation. In addition, society loses wages which might have been earned, and it must often support families of incarcerated breadwinners.[69]

Not only does the defense benefit from a speedy trial, but so does the prosecution. First, speedy trials provide the opportunity for a guilty verdict to be secured quickly (assuming, of course, that the defendant is guilty). Also, speedy trials minimize the opportunity for individuals out on bail to commit additional crimes while awaiting trial. However, if the accused is kept in detention prior to trial, too much delay can take a financial toll on the government.

While seemingly advantageous, a speedy trial can be a double-edged sword. Such a trial promotes efficiency, but too much efficiency may damage the defense's case; that is, if the defense is not given adequate time to prepare, then a needless guilty verdict could result. On this point, the Supreme Court has stated, "The essential ingredient is orderly expedition and not mere speed."[70]

Web Extra

13-1 Fair Trial Initiative

Problem of Delays

While a speedy trial is a constitutional privilege, there are significant delays in the trial process. A number of factors, including an excess of crime, an underfunded criminal justice system, and not enough judges, prosecutors, and other court personnel, contribute to delay. Table 13–3 illustrates the median time in days for processing felons from arrest to conviction; the median time for felonies, for example, was over 200 days. Note that the median means that half of all jurisdictions fell below this mark and that the other half fell above.

The time to disposition reported in Table 13–3 may seem like cause for concern, but it appears that courts are moving as quickly as they can and within acceptable guidelines, for the most part.[71]

Many states have enacted speedy trial laws to help ensure cases are quickly disposed of. There is also federal legislation, namely, the Federal Speedy Trial Act, which was signed into law in 1974.[72] Box 13–1 contains some of the key provisions of the Federal Speedy Trial Act.

Situations When the Right to a Speedy Trial Applies In *United States* v. *Marion*,[73] the defendants sought to dismiss the indictment against them by arguing that the government had known of their identities for three years prior to the indictment; more specifically, they argued that their Sixth Amendment right to a speedy trial was violated because the government knew of them prior to the point at which they were indicted. Their argument failed because the Court held that the Sixth Amendment's guarantee to a speedy trial attaches only *after* the person has been accused of a crime. The Court further stated that being "accused" of a crime didn't have to mean that formal charges had to be filed because "the actual restraints imposed by arrest and holding to answer on a criminal charge"[74] can be sufficient to amount to an accusation, something that has since come to be known as the **accusation rule**.

accusation rule
The U.S. Supreme Court holding that the Sixth Amendment's guarantee of a right to a speedy trial attaches only *after* a person has been accused of a crime.

TABLE 13–3 Time to Disposition in Criminal Cases

Most Serious Conviction Offense	Median Time (in days)	Following Arrest, Cumulative Percent Sentenced Within—			
		1 Month	3 Months	6 Months	1 Year
All offenses	265	4 %	14 %	33 %	67 %
Violent offenses	295	2 %	9 %	26 %	62 %
Murder/Nonnegligent manslaughter	505	1	3	8	31
Sexual assault[a]	346	1	5	19	54
Robbery	282	1	7	25	65
Aggravated assault	279	2	10	29	65
Other violent[b]	244	4	14	35	72
Property offenses	237	3 %	15 %	38 %	70 %
Burglary	234	3	15	39	71
Larceny	220	5	18	41	71
Fraud/Forgery[c]	261	2	12	33	66
Drug offenses	271	6 %	15 %	32 %	66 %
Possession	257	9	20	35	68
Trafficking	282	3	12	30	64
Weapon offenses	253	4 %	15 %	34 %	69 %
Other specified offenses[d]	253	3 %	14 %	34 %	69 %

[a]Includes rape.
[b]Includes offenses such as negligent manslaughter and kidnapping.
[c]Includes embezzlement.
[d]Comprises nonviolent offenses such as vandalism and receiving stolen property.
Note: Data on time to dispose of felonies were reported for 33% of convicted felons.
Source: http://bjs.ojp.usdoj.gov/content/pub/pdf/fssc06st.pdf (accessed February 25, 2013).

BOX 13-1   Portions of the Federal Speedy Trial Act

CHARGING AND TRIAL

1. Charges must be filed within 30 days from arrest or service of summons. If no grand jury is in session, a delay can be granted. Also, according to the legislation, the right to a speedy trial only applies once charges have been filed, not at the time of arrest.

2. Trial must take place within 70 days from the point at which charges are filed, or from the date on which the defendant appears before a judge, whichever is later. And in jury trials, the Act provides that trial is said to have commenced once the *voir dire* process is set in motion.

3. Trial cannot take place *less* than 30 days from when the defendant first appears, unless the defendant agrees to an earlier trial. This restriction exists so that the defense can build an adequate case.

SANCTIONED DELAYS

1. Delays caused by the defendant. Examples of such delay are competency hearings, hearings on motions, trials on other charges and interlocutory appeals (i.e., appeals filed before final adjudication).

2. Delays resulting from deferred (i.e., delayed) prosecution, but only with agreement of all parties involved (defense, prosecution, and court).

3. Delays caused by the unavailability of the defendant or important witnesses for either the prosecution or defense.

4. Delays resulting from the defendant's mental incompetence or physical unfitness to stand trial.

5. Delays resulting from treatment of the defendant pursuant to the Narcotics Addict Rehabilitation Act.

6. Delays between dropping charges and filing of new charges for the same or a related offense.

7. Reasonable periods of delay because of joinder of defendants (i.e., because two defendants are tried in the same trial).

8. Any other delay granted by the court with justice cited as the main reason. This is the catchall category. For example, the defense can agree with the prosecution to set a trial date beyond the specified limit (e.g., *New York* v. *Hill*, 528 U.S. 110 [2000]).

FACTORS TO CONSIDER BEFORE A CONTINUANCE WILL BE GRANTED

1. Whether failure to grant a delay would result in a miscarriage of justice.

2. Whether the case is so "unusual or complex" that it is unreasonable to expect adequate preparation during the time limits established by the Act.

3. Whether, when a defendant is arrested and later indicted, the grand jury would have a difficult time determining whether charges should be filed (e.g., because, again, the case is so "unusual or complex").

4. Whether delay would deny the defendant (or either party) the ability to mount an effective case.

5. Whether the continuance was granted for an "inappropriate" reason, such as court backlog or government negligence. ▪

Source: Federal Speedy Trial Act, 18 U.S.C.A., Section 3161.

Situations When the Right to a Speedy Trial Is Violated If the right to a speedy trial applies when someone has been accused of a crime, then when is the right *violated*? The Supreme Court sought to answer this question in *Barker* v. *Wingo*.[75] In that case, the defendant did not assert his Sixth Amendment right until after the prosecution sought 16 continuances over a period of five years. The Supreme Court announced a four-element test to assist in determining when the right to a speedy trial is violated: "(1) Length of delay; (2) the reason for the delay; (3) the defendant's assertion of his right; and (4) prejudice to the defendant."[76] According to the Court, one of these four criteria by itself is not necessarily

COURTS IN THE NEWS

Speedy Trial?

FRANZ JANTZEN KRT/Newscom

It took the state 7 years before it tried accused murderer Jonathan Boyer. Is that too long? The Supreme Court did not think so and failed to uphold his appeal.

How much time can go by before a trial is declared "not speedy"? It depends. Take the case of Jonathan Boyer, who killed Bradlee Marsh in 2002 but whose case did not go to trial until 2009, seven years later. In 2013 the U.S. Supreme Court failed to uphold Boyer's speedy trial appeal even though he claimed that most of the seven-year delay between his arrest and murder trial was the result of inadequate funding to pay for his court-appointed defense attorneys. For the first five years after he was arrested, the state did not have the money to pay for the two defense attorneys required in a death penalty case. The trial went forward only after the prosecutor decided to reduce the first-degree murder charge in favor of a lesser charge, which made Boyer's case less expensive to defend. Boyer argued that the delay violated his Sixth Amendment right to a speedy trial. But the state appeals court ruled that the delay was mainly because of a factor "beyond the control of the state"—naming a "funding crisis"—and therefore that there was no constitutional violation. The state also claimed that it was Boyer's own attorneys who caused the delay with numerous continuances.

The Supreme Court agreed with the prosecutors and stated that other delays before the trial occurred (like Hurricane Rita) were out of anyone's control. The Supreme Court also noted, "If the defense had not sought and obtained continuances, the trial might well have commenced at a much earlier date and might have reached a conclusion far less favorable to the defense."

Justice Sonia Sotomayor, who, in a dissent was joined by three other more liberal judges, said that states are ultimately responsible for providing adequate counsel, whatever their excuses, and that the state appeals court made "a fundamental error" that the justices should have corrected. She further noted that the Boyer case was not isolated and that it illustrated "larger, systemic problems in Louisiana."

After the decision, the *New York Times* published an editorial claiming that the Supreme Court failed to support an "essential American right." It claimed that the Court "should have said that every state has the duty to pay for counsel for indigent criminal defendants and ensure them a speedy trial." ■

DISCUSSION QUESTIONS

1. Would you have granted Boyer freedom? Spending seven years behind bars before a trial begins seems like a speedy trial violation. Do you agree?

2. How can a trial be fair after seven years? Can witnesses give factual testimony? Do you clearly remember things that happened seven years ago?

Sources: Lee Peck, "Supreme Court Dismisses Boyer Murder Conviction Appeal," KPLC.com April 30, 2013, available at www.kplctv.com/story/22113068/supreme-court-dismisses-boyer-murder-conviction-appeal (accessed June 2, 2013); *Boyer* v. *Louisiana*, 569 U.S. ___ (2013); "A State's Duty to Indigent Defendants," *New York Times*, April 29, 2013, available at www.nytimes.com/2013/04/30/opinion/the-supreme-court-rules-on-a-states-duty-to-indigent-defendants.html (accessed June 2, 2013).

determinative; instead, courts must balance one against the others in deciding whether a Sixth Amendment violation has taken place. The following "Courts in the News" feature discusses a recent case which tests the limits of the speedy trial rule

PUBLIC TRIAL

Learning Objective 5
Explain the right to a public trial.

In *In re Oliver*, the Supreme Court stated, "The knowledge that every criminal trial is subject to contemporaneous review in the forum of public opinion is an effective restraint on possible abuse of power. . . . Without publicity, all other checks are insufficient; in comparison of publicity, all other checks are of small account."[77] Furthermore, the Court said that "the presence of interested spectators may keep [the defendant's] triers keenly alive to a sense of their responsibility and to the importance of their functions."[78] This is what is meant by a public trial—it is one that is open to the public.

Oliver dealt expressly with criminal trials, but the Supreme Court has suggested that openness applies to other hearings as well. For example, suppression hearings should be open to the public.[79] By extension, most other hearings—with the exception of grand jury proceedings, which are traditionally carried out in secret—should be considered public as well.

Closing Trials

Most trials are open to the public, but in some situations the judge may bar spectators from the proceedings. Indeed, the defendant, whose interest is frequently served by openness, may want the trial closed to the public, possibly in an effort to minimize negative publicity, especially when the trial is for a heinous crime. In this way, the defendant's Sixth Amendment rights can be waived, just like many other constitutional rights can.

The government can also seek to close trials to the public. In *Waller* v. *Georgia*,[80] the Supreme Court created a three-part test for determining when the government can succeed in closing a trial to the public: (1) There must be an overriding interest, such as protection to certain witnesses; (2) the closure is no broader than absolutely necessary; and (3) reasonable alternatives are considered. *Waller* dealt with the closure of a suppression hearing where a video of people not yet indicted was played. The Court held that closure of the hearing was unconstitutional because the government did not identify "whose privacy interests might be infringed, how they would be infringed, what portions of the tape might infringe on them, and what portion of the evidence consisted of the tapes."[81]

In *Estes* v. *Texas*,[82] the Court reversed the defendant's conviction, noting that the presence of television cameras distracted parties to the case in addition to the witnesses who gave testimony. This does not provide a blanket prohibition of television cameras in courtrooms, however; in another case, the Supreme Court upheld Florida's rule of permitting the use of still photography and television cameras in court.[83] Cameras are impermissible only if the defendant can show that "the media's coverage of his case—be it printed or broadcast—[compromises] the ability of the . . . jury . . . to adjudicate fairly."[84]

Alternatives to Trial Closure

There are several alternatives to closing trials to the public, and each is aimed at ensuring a fair trial for the accused. The alternatives are (1) special *voir dire*, with particular attention paid to pretrial publicity; (2) change of venue; (3) jury sequestration; (4) gag order on the media; and (5) gag order. Each is briefly considered in the following paragraphs:

1. *Special voir dire.* When media coverage of a crime is extensive and presumed to have influenced members of the jury panel, *voir dire* can be used to detect bias that can result from media coverage. In *Marshall* v. *United States*,[85] the Supreme Court held that potential jurors who have learned from news coverage of a defendant's prior record are presumed to be prejudiced. In a similar case,[86] the Court decided that pretrial publicity can be so influential that jurors' statements that they will make impartial decisions can be discounted. But in two later cases,[87] the Court indicated that unless a juror candidly admits bias due to pretrial publicity, a defendant's constitutional challenge to jury impartiality is unlikely to succeed.

2. *Change of venue.* In *Rideau* v. *Louisiana*,[88] the Court overturned a defendant's death sentence because the trial court refused to grant the defendant's motion for a **change of venue** (motion to move the trial to another jurisdiction). In that case, Rideau's confession was broadcast all over local television. The Court

change of venue
A motion to move a trial to another jurisdiction.

stated that "due process of law in this case required a trial before a jury drawn from a community of people who had not seen and heard Rideau's interview."[89] Of course, changes of venue are not a realistic option when pretrial publicity influences potential jurors in multiple jurisdictions. Changes of venue rarely succeed, then, in trials of individuals whose crimes are well known over a wide geographic area.

3. *Jury sequestration.* A method used mostly to minimize the influence of press coverage *during* the trial, sequestration is basically jury isolation. Members are usually put up in a hotel and denied access to television and print media coverage of the trial so they can remain impartial. Sequestration is an extreme method, but judges' warnings to jury members to avoid media accounts while at home are probably naive. The Supreme Court has recognized that jury sequestration is a valid option in certain extreme circumstances.[90]

4. *Gag order on the media.* **Gag orders** are judges' orders to keep the media quiet concerning a particular matter. For example, in one case the trial judge prohibited the media from reporting information regarding the defendant.[91] The Supreme Court disagreed but did indicate that gag orders would be permissible given three factors: "(a) the nature and extent of pretrial coverage; (b) whether other measures [i.e., changes of venue, continuances, *voir dire*, sequestration, and/or instructions to jury to ignore press coverage] would be likely to mitigate the effects of unrestrained pretrial publicity; and (c) how effectively a restraining order would operate to prevent the threatened danger."[92]

5. *Gag order on trial participants.* Courts have experimented with gag orders on trial participants. This is an indirect method of reducing media coverage of a trial because it seeks to quiet the media's sources, and it appears to have met with greater approval by the Supreme Court. In *Sheppard* v. *Maxwell*,[93] for instance, the Court suggested that under certain circumstances the judge has a constitutional obligation "to control the release of leads, information, and gossip to the press by police officers, witnesses and the counsel for both sides." For a gag order of this nature to succeed, it should be clear that the absence of a gag order presents a "clear and present danger" to the impartiality of the trial.

Professional codes of ethics also restrict certain statements. For example, the American Bar Association's Rules of Professional Responsibility prohibits lawyers from making "extrajudicial statements [that] will have a substantial likelihood of materially prejudicing an adjudicative proceeding," including statements as to "the character, credibility, reputation or criminal record of a party, suspect . . . or witness, . . . the expected testimony of a party or witness . . . [or the] . . . possibility of a plea of guilty, . . . the performance or results of any examination or test, [and] . . . any opinion as to . . . guilt or innocence."[94] State bar associations can also reprimand attorneys for making statements that cause a substantial likelihood of material prejudice to the case.[95]

THE TRIAL PROCESS

Once the jury has been selected, the trial date set, and a judge selected, the trial begins. There may be pretrial motions, such as motions by the defense to exclude evidence (see Box 13–2 for a list of common pretrial motions). Throughout the pretrial process and beyond, there may also be what is known as a sidebar, which occurs when the attorneys and judge discuss matters out of earshot of the jury. During the pretrial phase, this could occur during *voir dire*; after the trial has started, the attorneys may discuss in private one or the other's questions, issues concerning particular witnesses, and so on.

gag order
A judge's order to keep the media quiet concerning a particular matter.

Library Extra
13-4 Nolo Law Center: Criminal Trial Procedures—An Overview

Learning Objective 6
Outline the trial process from pretrial motions and opening statements through jury deliberations and verdict.

BOX 13–2   Common Pretrial Motions

Motion for review of conditions of release (if successful, pretrial release conditions could be changed)

Motion for removal of judge (if successful, new judge presides over case)

Motion to suppress evidence (if successful, evidence is excluded from trial)

Motion for continuance (if successful, trial is postponed for period of time)

Motion to dismiss indictment or complaint (if successful, charges are dropped)

Motion to sever offenses (if successful, separate trials are held for separate offenses)

Motion to sever codefendants (if successful, separate trials are held for multiple defendants)

Motion to evaluate defendant competency (if successful, trial may not be held until defendant regains competency)

Motion for change of venue (if successful, trial moves to different jurisdiction)

Motion to exclude public (if successful, trial is closed to public) ■

The following subsections briefly elaborate on each of several critical stages during the process. Depending on the crime in question, some or all of these steps may be taken. As a general rule, the more serious the crime, the more likely it is that all will occur, but some of the following steps, such as redirect examination, may not be taken if there is no need.

Opening Statements

opening statement
The initial statement of the prosecutor or the defense attorney, made in a court of law to a judge or jury, describing the facts that he or she intends to present during a trial to prove the case.

Trials begin with **opening statements**. In their opening statements, both of the attorneys in a case lay out for the jury, in overview form, what they will prove throughout the trial. Opening statements are not unlike the introductory section of a book chapter: A well-written one spells out for readers what lies ahead, provides context and perspective, and offers something for readers to fall back on if they become lost in the details as they read on.

Opening statements are a crucial part of the trial. They give the attorneys a chance to bond with the jury. Studies reveal, indeed, that jurors frequently decide in favor of the party they are most impressed with during the opening statements phase of the trial;[96] they also give attorneys an early shot at summarizing the whole argument that lies ahead. This may resonate better with the jury than a long, arduous process of rolling out exhibit after exhibit and witness after witness.

Prosecutor's Evidence

proof beyond a reasonable doubt
The standard of proof in a criminal case.

preponderance of evidence
The standard of proof in a civil trial.

direct evidence
"[E]vidence that proves a fact without the need for the juror to infer anything from it."[iv]

circumstantial evidence
"[E]vidence that *indirectly* proves a fact."[v]

Once opening statements have concluded, the government (via the prosecutor) has the opportunity to present its case. The prosecutor goes first because the burden of proof in our criminal justice system falls on the government. In a criminal case, the prosecutor must present **proof beyond a reasonable doubt** that the defendant committed the crime, which is roughly the same as 95% certainty.[97] In the civil context, the burden of proof falls on the plaintiff, the party bringing suit; the standard of proof, however, is lower. It is generally the **preponderance of evidence**, roughly akin to "more certain than not."

If proof beyond a reasonable doubt amounts to 95% certainty, then reasonable doubt is that other 5%. It is in the defense's interest to exploit that 5%, to get members of the jury thinking that there is a *chance* the defendant did not commit the crime. In many cases, though, the prosecution exceeds the standard of proof it is required to adhere to and presents a practically airtight case against the defendant.

As prosecutors make their case, they present evidence. Evidence can be thought of in several different ways. **Direct evidence** is "evidence that proves a fact without the need for the juror to infer anything from it,"[98] an example of direct evidence being testimony by a witness that the accused committed the crime. By contrast, **circumstantial evidence** is "evidence that *indirectly* proves a fact."[99] An example of circumstantial evidence is evidence of the defendant's ability to commit the crime or his or her possible motives; for instance, the prospect of receiving a life insurance settlement could serve as someone's motive to kill.

It is also useful to think in terms of real, testimonial, and demonstrative evidence. **Real evidence** refers to "any tangible item that can be perceived with the five senses."[100] Real evidence can consist of everything from clothing and footprints to weapons and drugs as well as documents, contracts, letters, and the like, and it can include scientific evidence, such as blood samples, fingerprints, and lab test results. **Testimonial evidence** refers to what someone says, usually someone who is under oath and giving testimony in a trial. Finally, **demonstrative evidence** is evidence that seeks to demonstrate a certain point, such as drawings, diagrams, illustrations, and computer simulations that are used to help jurors understand how a crime was likely committed.

Not just any of these forms of evidence will do. In the case of real evidence, what is introduced must be relevant, and evidence is relevant when it sheds light on a matter that is in dispute. Real evidence also has to be competent, meaning it was not secured illegally or in violation of the Constitution. Finally, real evidence must be material. **Material evidence** is "that which is relevant and goes to substantial matters in dispute, or has legitimate influence or bearing on the decision of the case."[101] Distinguish between relevant and material evidence in this way: The former relates to the issue in question; the latter is concerned with how significant the evidence is.

With testimonial evidence, the use of witnesses comes into play. There are specific evidentiary requirements for witness testimony. First, witnesses must demonstrate **competency**, which means they must possess certain characteristics that render them legally qualified to testify (e.g., they must be of age). Witnesses also need to be credible. **Credibility** is concerned with whether the witness's testimony should be believed. Attorneys routinely attack the credibility of the other side's witnesses, a process known as impeachment. Witness testimony requirements also differ depending on the types of witnesses, with the requirements generally more stringent for so-called expert witnesses than for lay witnesses.

When the prosecution questions its own witnesses, this is known as direct examination. As a general rule, on direct examination, the questions must be specific but not leading. A **specific question** is one that does not call for a narrative. If the party calling the witness says, "Tell us what happened on the day of the incident," the opposing side will probably object. Instead, it is proper to ask something along the lines of, "Were you the victim of a burglary on August 6 of this year?"

At the other extreme, it is possible to be too specific such that a question becomes leading. According to the California Evidence Code, a **leading question** is one "that suggests to the witness the answer that the examining party desires."[102] Leading questions are generally impermissible on direct examination (subject to some exceptions described below) but are permissible on cross-examination. Further, leading questions are permissible on redirect examination but not on re-cross-examination.

After a question is asked and before a witness gives an answer, the opposition may object to the question; for example, the defense may challenge a question as being leading. The attorneys must remain alert and vigilant in order to avoid the possibility of having the jury hear evidence it should not hear.

Cross-Examination

During cross-examination, the opposing attorney questions the witnesses. In the criminal trial context, then, once the prosecution presents its case, the defense will be given an opportunity to question the prosecution's witnesses, which presents the defense with an opportunity to challenge the prosecution witnesses' credibility.

real evidence
"[A]ny tangible item that can be perceived with the five senses."[vi]

testimonial evidence
The information that someone supplies, usually referring to someone who is under oath and giving testimony in a trial.

demonstrative evidence
Any evidence that seeks to demonstrate a certain point (e.g., drawings, diagrams, illustrations, and computer simulations) to help jurors understand how a crime was likely committed.

material evidence
"[T]hat which is relevant and goes to substantial matters in dispute or has legitimate influence or bearing on the decision of the case."[vii]

competency
A specific evidentiary requirement for witness testimony that requires witnesses to possess certain characteristics (e.g., be "of age") that render them legally qualified to testify.

credibility
A specific evidentiary requirement for witness testimony that is concerned with whether the witness's testimony should be believed.

specific question
A question that does not call for a narrative.

leading question
A question "that suggests to the witness the answer that the examining party desires."[viii]

Web Extra
13-2 Brightcove. TV: How Does a Criminal Jury Trial Work?

Redirect and Re-Cross-Examination Redirect and re-cross-examination can sometimes occur. In our example, the prosecution may then seek to bolster his or her witness's credibility if the defense persuaded the jury that a witness was not to be believed. If issues come up during redirect examination, then the defense may ask the witness about such issues. This process can go on as long as necessary.

Defense Response

Once the prosecution rests its case, the defense gets its turn. The main concern is with establishing reasonable doubt to ensure that the prosecution fails to meet its burden. The defense can use all manner of creative strategies to sway the jury: One may be to challenge the prosecution's scientific evidence, and another may be to put on one of many affirmative defenses. **Affirmative defenses** are those that go beyond simply denying that a crime took place or that the defendant committed it; examples include everything from alibi defenses and self-defense to duress and entrapment.

Interestingly, a defendant in a criminal trial cannot be compelled to testify under *any* circumstances because defendants enjoy absolute Fifth Amendment protection from self-incrimination during criminal proceedings. However, once a defendant takes the stand, he or she can be compelled to answer questions related to the facts of the case at hand.[103]

Rebuttal Once the defense is finished with its case, the prosecution may call one or more **rebuttal witnesses**, those whose testimony is intended to attack the credibility of the previous witnesses. For example, a rebuttal witness may challenge a defense witness's testimony that he or she observed some action relevant to the case.

Final Motions and Closing Arguments

Just as opening arguments lay out the case to be made, closing arguments wrap everything up. Some final motions may be filed at this stage, too, but generally most of these are cleared up earlier. During closing arguments, the parties have one last chance to convince the jury that their story is the accurate one. In a criminal case, the prosecutor goes first and informs jurors of their duty to punish the defendant; the defense goes second and pleads with the jury for a verdict of not guilty.

Judge's Instructions to the Jury Once final motions and closing arguments have been made, the judge will give his or her instructions to the jurors before they head off to deliberate. First, the judge gives the jurors something of a crash course in basic legal principles, discussing burdens and standards of proof. Second, the judge discusses the specific offenses in question and the particular elements of each. Third, if an affirmative defense was raised, the judge will advise the jury of the standards or tests that need to be used to determine whether such a defense is meritorious. Finally, the judge will inform jurors of the verdicts that can be selected and may also discuss the prospect of a guilty verdict for a lesser included offense. In the homicide context, for example, jurors may find the defendant guilty of second- instead of first-degree murder. Second-degree murder is less serious than first-degree murder, but its elements are the same as first-degree murder (deliberate killing); first-degree murder just adds premeditation.

All of this is usually preceded by a charging conference. In a criminal case, this is where the prosecutor, defense attorney, and judge meet out of earshot of the jury to decide on what the instructions to the jurors will be. Jury instructions are important insofar as they can serve as the basis for an appeal; that is, if what the judge tells the jury is wrong, then the defendant may have a basis for challenging a conviction. Unfortunately, even if the judge's instructions to jurors are flawless, getting jurors to understand them is a different matter

affirmative defense
A defense that goes *beyond* simply denying that a crime took place (e.g., alibi, duress, entrapment, or self-defense); also, an answer to a criminal charge in which a defendant takes the offense and responds to the allegations with his or her own assertions based on legal principles. Affirmative defenses must be raised and supported by the defendant independently of any claims made by the prosecutor.

rebuttal witness
A witness whose testimony is intended to attack the credibility of the previous witness.

Library Extra
13-5 The Trial Juror's Handbook

entirely—researchers have found that many jurors, even well-educated ones, have difficulty comprehending the instructions they are given.[104]

Library Extra
13-6 Florida Standard Jury Instructions

Juror Deliberations

Once the jury leaves the courtroom to deliberate, this becomes the "black box" phase of the criminal process. Jury deliberations, as we mentioned earlier, are secretive. If jurors need anything (such as to view an exhibit a second time), they will ask the bailiff; otherwise, jurors are more or less shut off from the rest of the courtroom actors. The reason for this should be obvious: Preserving the jury's neutrality and objectivity is of paramount concern. As we saw earlier, though, it is somewhat naive to think of jurors as entirely objective and concerned solely with the facts as presented.

Researchers have examined not only juror decision making (as discussed earlier in this chapter) but also the dynamics of deliberation. For example, they have found that men are more vocal than women and that people with strong professional and/or educational backgrounds are more likely to be chosen as forepersons.[105] Researchers have also looked at deliberation times: In general, deliberations are over in short order, and jurors tend to stick by their initial votes[106] (if one is taken shortly after entering the deliberation room).

Hung Jury If the jury cannot reach a verdict and becomes hopelessly deadlocked, this is known as a **hung jury**. If this occurs, the result is generally a **mistrial**, and a new trial will then be held. Mistrials can occur for various reasons, not just deadlocked juries, as this explanation illustrates: "[A mistrial is] a trial which has been terminated and declared invalid by the court because of some circumstance which creates a substantial and uncorrectable prejudice to the conduct of a fair trial, or which makes it impossible to continue the trial in accordance with prescribed procedures."[107]

Juries rarely become deadlocked in their deliberations, meaning that rates of hung juries are exceptionally low.[108] Even so, in the event that a jury cannot reach an agreement, one result may be an **Allen charge** (named after the Supreme Court's decision in *Allen* v. *United States*[109]), which is a set of instructions given to jurors after they become deadlocked that instructs them to reexamine their opinions in an effort to reach a verdict. The text of the Allen charge for use in the federal courts appears in Box 13–3.

hung jury
A jury that is so irreconcilably divided in opinion after long deliberation that it is unable to reach any verdict.

mistrial
A trial that has been terminated and declared invalid by the court because of some circumstance that created a substantial and uncorrectable prejudice to the conduct of a fair trial or that made it impossible to continue the trial in accordance with prescribed procedures.

Allen charge
A set of instructions given to jurors after they become deadlocked that instructs them to reexamine their opinions in an effort to reach a verdict.

Verdict

Once the jury informs the judge that a verdict has been reached, they reenter the courtroom and the verdict is read, usually by the foreperson. Verdicts available are "guilty" or "not guilty." Do defendants have a good chance of securing not-guilty verdicts in their criminal trials? In general, the answer is no. Convictions are much more common than findings of not guilty, as shown in Table 13–4. For example, violent felons are convicted 4.6 times as often as they are found not guilty—and that does not include guilty pleas. When added with guilty pleas, 91% of violent felons are convicted in federal district courts.

Postverdict Motions

If the defendant is found not guilty (i.e., is acquitted), the trial ends. In contrast, following a guilty verdict, there will be other hearings. Sentencing occurs in a separate post-trial hearing (see Chapter 14). Prior to sentencing, the defense may also make any number of postverdict motions. One of the more popular is a motion for a new trial, another is a motion to vacate the judgment, and a third is a motion to disregard the jury findings. Few postverdict motions are granted. The next step, then, is sentencing. Due to its complexity, we devoted a whole chapter (Chapter 14) to sentencing. See Figure 13–2 for a summary of the main stages in a criminal trial.

Library Extra
13-7 Offender Race and Case Outcomes

BOX 13-3 **Text of the Allen Charge**

You have informed the Court of your inability to reach a verdict in this case.

At the outset, the Court wishes you to know that although you have a duty to reach a verdict, if that is not possible, the Court has neither the power nor the desire to compel agreement upon a verdict.

The purpose of these remarks is to point out to you the importance and the desirability of reaching a verdict in this case, provided, however, that you as individual jurors can do so without surrendering or sacrificing your conscientious scruples or personal convictions.

You will recall that upon assuming your duties in this case each of you took an oath. The oath places upon each of you as individuals the responsibility of arriving at a true verdict upon the basis of your opinion and not merely upon acquiescence in the conclusions of your fellow jurors.

However, it by no means follows that opinions may not be changed by conference in the jury room. The very object of the jury system is to reach a verdict by a comparison of views and by consideration of the proofs with your fellow jurors.

During your deliberations you should be open-minded and consider the issues with proper deference to and respect for the opinions of each other and you should not hesitate to re-examine your own views in the light of such discussions.

You should consider also that this case must at some time be terminated; that you are selected in the same manner and from the same source from which any future jury must be selected; that there is no reason to suppose that the case will ever be submitted to twelve persons more intelligent, more impartial or more competent to decide it, or that more or clearer evidence will ever be produced on one side or the other.

You may retire now, taking as much time as is necessary for further deliberations upon the issues submitted to you for determination. ■

Source: www.courtswv.gov/supreme-court/docs/fall2005/32693.htm (accessed February 25, 2013).

TABLE 13-4 Disposition of Cases Terminated in U.S. District Courts, 2009

Most Serious Offense at Termination	Total Cases Terminated		Percent Convicted		Percent Not Convicted	
	Number	Percent	Guilty Plea	Bench/ Jury Trial	Bench/ Jury Trial	Dismissed
All offenses	95,891	100%	87.9%	2.8%	0.5%	8.8%
Felonies	84,767	100%	90.2	3.0	0.5	6.3
Violent	2,591	100%	84.3	7.0	1.5	7.2
Property	12,411	100%	86.4	3.3	0.7	9.6
Fraud	10,863	100%	86.5	3.4	0.7	9.4
Other	1,548	100%	86.2	2.5	0.6	10.7
Drug	27,955	100%	89.3	3.2	0.4	7.1
Public order	7,166	100%	84.5	5.7	1.2	8.7
Regulatory	904	100%	82.5	5.6	2.4	9.4
Other	6,262	100%	84.8	5.7	1.0	8.6
Weapons	8,794	100%	86.9	5.3	1.0	6.9
Immigration	25,587	100%	96.4	0.5	0.1	3.0
Misdemeanors	11,124	100%	70.7	1.2	0.6	27.5

Note: Percentages are based on available data. Offense missing in 272 records. District populations are divided into small (17 districts with fewer than 1 million U.S. residents), medium (54 districts with between 1 and 5 million), and large (23 districts with more than 5 million). To improve comparability, percentages for district population have been adjusted for differences in the offense distribution of the three district populations. See appendix table 4 for confidence intervals and *Methodology* for calculation details.

Source: Mark Motivans, *Federal Justice Statistics, 2009* (Washington, DC: Bureau of Justice Statistics, 2009), available at http://bjs.ojp.usdoj .gov/content/pub/pdf/fjs09.pdf (accessed February 25, 2013).

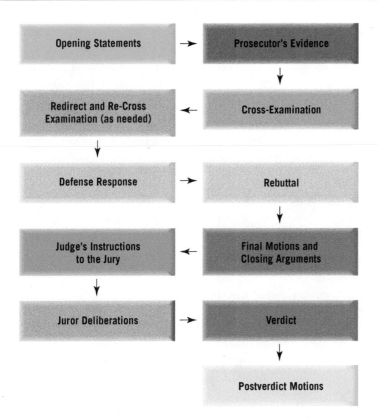

FIGURE 13–2

Summary of Steps in a Criminal Trial

SUMMARY

1. SUMMARIZE THE HISTORY AND DEVELOPMENT OF JURIES AND JURY TRIALS

- The right to a jury trial (found in Article III, Section 2, and the Sixth Amendment) has been restricted by the Supreme Court. There is no right to a jury trial when the punishment is less than six months in prison.
- The American jury system traces its roots as far back as the eleventh century. The Constitution requires jury trials due to fear of overreaching government.
- The right to a jury trial can be waived, but the judge can require a jury trial if need be.

2. EXPLAIN THE JURY SELECTION PROCESS, INCLUDING VOIR DIRE

- Juror selection proceeds through three steps. First, a list of potential jurors must be compiled; second, potential jurors are selected from that list; and, third, once potential jurors are selected, the jury itself is chosen. The last of these steps is known as voir dire.
- Voir dire proceeds through two steps. First, the judge asks questions of prospective jurors, and then the attorneys exercise their challenges for cause (a reason is given) and peremptory challenges (no reason is given).
- Peremptory challenges cannot be used to excuse jurors based on race.
- Some wealthy defendants hire jury consultants, but the evidence is mixed concerning consultants' effectiveness in securing favorable juries.
- Jury sizes and voting requirements vary by state and by offense.

- Jurors' decisions are affected by several factors, such as personal beliefs, not just the facts of the case. In general, when the evidence is vague, jurors tend to fall back on their gut instincts, where they are most susceptible to bias. This has been called the "liberation hypothesis."

- Jury nullification is the jury's practice of either ignoring or misapplying the law in a certain situation. Jury vilification is the opposite, that is, convicting when the evidence does not support a conviction.

- Researchers have found that a significant percentage of jurors are not honest during *voir dire* questioning.

- Some have argued that professional jurors should be used, and there are arguments for and against this proposed reform.

- The right to a speedy trial applies once a person has been formally accused of a crime.

- Four factors are considered in order to determine when the right to a speedy trial is violated: (1) the length of the delay, (2) the reason for the delay, (3) the defendant's assertion of his or her right, and (4) the possibility of prejudice to the defendant.

- A public trial is one that is open to the public, but it is difficult to close a trial to the public.

- Efforts to close trials to the public raise First Amendment concerns. Several alternatives are available in lieu of outright closure: (1) *voir dire*, with special attention to pretrial publicity; (2) changes of venue; (3) jury sequestration; (4) gag orders on the media; and (5) gag orders.

- The criminal trial progresses in several steps: (1) opening statements, where the prosecution and defense summarize the arguments they will present; (2) prosecutor's evidence, where the state puts on its case by presenting real, demonstrative, and testimonial evidence; (3) defense cross-examination, where the defense attorney challenges the prosecution's witnesses in an effort to attack their credibility (i.e., impeach them); (4) redirect and re-cross-examination, where the attorneys use additional questioning as needed; (5) defense's case, where affirmative defenses (e.g., insanity) may be presented; (6) rebuttal witnesses, who are called as needed; (7) final motions and closing arguments, where the attorneys summarize their arguments; (8) judge's instructions, where the judge addresses the jury; (9) jury deliberations, where the jurors discuss the case; (10) verdict, where jurors reach a consensus, or, if none is reached, a hung jury results; and (11) postverdict motions, which are filed as needed.

KEY TERMS

accusation rule, 351

affirmative defense, 358

Allen charge, 359

bench trial, 335

Capital Jury Project, 346

challenge for cause, 340

change of venue, 354

circumstantial evidence, 356

competency, 357

credibility, 357

demonstrative evidence, 357

direct evidence, 356

gag order, 355

hung jury, 359

jury consultant, 342

jury list, 338

jury nullification, 346

jury panel, 338

jury vilification, 347

leading question, 357

liberation hypothesis, 346

material evidence, 357

mistrial, 359

noncriminal proceeding rule, 337

opening statement, 356

peremptory challenge, 341

preponderance of evidence, 356

proof beyond a reasonable doubt, 356

real evidence, 357

rebuttal witness, 358

specific question, 357

testimonial evidence, 357

trial jury, 336

voir dire, 338

REVIEW QUESTIONS

1. How did the right to a jury trial develop?

2. What are the implications of a right to a jury trial for the American system of justice?

3. What takes place during the jury decision-making process? How effective is the process in accurately determining guilt or innocence?

4. What constitutional rights do criminal defendants have at trial? If you were in a position to do so, would you increase or decrease the rights available to defendants at trial? Specifically, what might you do, and why?

5. What is the order of events in a criminal trial? Why are trials described as "highly choreographed"? Is such rigid structure a help or a hindrance in seeing justice done?

WHAT WILL YOU DO?

You have just been called to jury duty and now find yourself about to be questioned by attorneys in preparation for the trial of a young woman who is charged with shoplifting. This is the start of a new semester at your college, and you really don't want to miss a day of class in order to serve on a jury. On the one hand, you'd like to fulfill your civic duty by making yourself available for jury service. On the other hand, class is pretty important, and you want to do well.

You know that there are some things that you can say when questioned by the attorneys before trial that would be sure to get you out of having to serve. Chuckling to yourself, you think that you might blurt out that you believe that shoplifters are the lowest of the low and that no punishment would be too severe for anyone who steals from a retail establishment. *That* should get you removed from the jury pool.

Of course, if you do actually get to serve on a jury, not only will you have done your civic duty, but you will have gotten to observe the workings of a criminal trial court, and you will have been able to participate in jury deliberations—all of which seem like valuable experiences for anyone studying the subject matter of criminal justice.

What will you do?

NOTES

i. U.S. Department of Justice, *Dictionary of Criminal Justice Data Terminology*, p. 176.

ii. H. Kalven and H. Zeisel, *The American Jury* (Chicago: University of Chicago Press, 1966).

iii. I. A. Horowitz, N. L. Kerr, and K. E. Niedermeier, "Jury Nullification: Legal and Psychological Perspectives," *Brooklyn Law Review* 66(2001):1210.

iv. Worrall and Hemmens, *Criminal Evidence*, p. 71.

v. J. L. Worrall and C. Hemmens, *Criminal Evidence: An Introduction* (Los Angeles: Roxbury, 2005), p. 71.

vi. Worrall and Hemmens, *Criminal Evidence*, p. 71.

vii. Kalven and Zeisel, The American Jury, p. 407.

viii. California Evidence Code, Section 764.

---

1. Daphne Duret, "In Scathing Order, Judge Grants John Goodman a New Trial Based on Allegations of Juror Misconduct," *Palm Beach Post*, May 3, 2013, available at www.mypalmbeachpost.com/news/news/breaking-news/sources-goodman-gets-new-trial/nXgWm (accessed May 6, 2013).

2. U.S. Department of Justice, *Dictionary of Criminal Justice Data Terminology*, 2nd ed. (Washington, DC: U.S. Department of Justice, Bureau of Justice Statistics, 1981), p. 208.

3. *Williams v. Florida*, 399 U.S. 78 (1970), p. 100.

4. American Bar Association, *Part I: The History of Trial by Jury*, available at www.americanbar.org/content/dam/aba/migrated/jury/moreinfo/dialoguepart1.authcheckdam.pdf (accessed February 25, 2013).

5. *Duncan v. Louisiana*, 391 U.S. 145 (1968).

6. Ibid., p. 156.

7. *McKeiver v. Pennsylvania*, 403 U.S. 528 (1971).

8. See, e.g., *Lynch v. Baxley*, 386 F. Supp. 378 (M.D. Ala. 1974).

9. *Baldwin v. New York*, 399 U.S. 66 (1970), p. 73.

10. *Lewis v. United States*, 518 U.S. 322 (1996).

11. *Patton v. United States*, 281 U.S. 276 (1930).

12. Also see *United States v. Jackson*, 390 U.S. 570 (1968).

13. *Singer v. United States*, 380 U.S. 24 (1965).

14. Ibid., p. 36.

15. Ibid.

16. *Duren v. Missouri*, 439 U.S. 357 (1979), p. 364.

17. *Test v. United States*, 420 U.S. 28 (1975).

18. *Mu'Min v. Virginia*, 500 U.S. 415 (1991).

19. *Hamling v. United States*, 418 U.S. 87 (1974), p. 139.

20. *Ham v. South Carolina*, 409 U.S. 524 (1973).

21. *Ristaino v. Ross*, 424 U.S. 589 (1976).

22. *Leonard v. United States*, 378 U.S. 544 (1964).

23. *Morgan v. Illinois*, 504 U.S. 719 (1992).

24. *Witherspoon v. Illinois*, 391 U.S. 510 (1968).

25. Ibid., p. 521.

26. *Swain v. Alabama*, 380 U.S. 202 (1965).

27. Ibid., pp. 220–221.

28. *Batson v. Kentucky*, 476 U.S. 79 (1986).

29. Ibid., p. 124.

30. *Hernandez v. New York*, 500 U.S. 352 (1991).

31. *Georgia v. McCollum*, 502 U.S. 1056 (1992).

32. *Gray v. Mississippi*, 481 U.S. 648 (1987).

33. F. Strier and D. Shestowsky, "Profiling the Profilers: A Study of the Trial Consulting Profession, Its Impact on Trial Justice and What, If Anything, to Do about It," *Wisconsin Law Review*, Vol. 441 (1999), pp. 441–499.

34. R. Hartje, "A Jury of Your Peers? How Jury Consulting May Actually Help Trial Lawyers Resolve Constitutional Limitations Imposed on the Selection of Juries," *California Western Law Review* 41(2005): 479–506, p. 493.

35. *Williams v. Florida*, 399 U.S. 78 (1970), p. 102.

36. Ibid.

37. *Ballew v. Georgia*, 435 U.S. 223 (1978).

38. Ibid., p. 241.

39. See *Johnson v. Louisiana*, 406 U.S. 356 (1972), and *Apodaca v. Oregon*, 406 U.S. 404 (1972).

40. Ibid, p. 363.

41. D. R. Cahoy and M. Ding, "Using Experimental Economics to Peek into the 'Black Box' of Jury Behavior: A Proposal for Jury Research Reform," *Southern California Interdisciplinary Law Journal*, Vol. 14 (2004), pp. 31–66.

42. Capital Jury Project, available at www.albany.edu/scj/13192.php (accessed February 25, 2013).

43. D. J. Devine, L. D. Clayton, B. B. Dunford, R. Seying, and J. Pryce, "Jury Decision Making: 45 Years of Empirical Research on Deliberating Groups," *Psychology, Public Policy, and the Law*, Vol. 7 (2001), pp. 622–725. Reprinted with permission.

44. Ibid., pp. 700–701.

45. H. Kalven and H. Zeisel, *The American Jury* (Chicago: University of Chicago Press, 1966).

46. A. Scheflin and J. Van Dyke, "Jury Nullification: The Contours of Controversy," *Law and Contemporary Problems*, Vol. 43 (1980), pp. 51–115.

47. See, e.g., W. W. Hodes, "Lord Brougham, the Dream Team, and Jury Nullification of the Third Kind," *University of Colorado Law Review*, Vol. 67 (1996), pp. 1075–1108.

48. J. Rosen, "The Bloods and the Crits: O.J. Simpson, Critical Race Theory, and the Law and the Triumph of Color in America," *New Republic*, December 9, 1996, pp. 27–42.

49. N. L. Kerr, "Severity of Penalty and Mock Jurors' Verdicts," *Journal of Personality and Social Psychology*, Vol. 36 (1978), pp. 1431–1442.

50. K. E. Niedermeier, I. A. Horowitz, and N. L. Kerr, "Informing Jurors of Their Nullification Power: A Route to a Just Verdict or Judicial Chaos," *Law and Human Behavior*, Vol. 23 (1999), pp. 331–351.

51. I. A. Horowitz, N. L. Kerr, and K. E. Niedermeier, "Jury Nullification: Legal and Psychological Perspectives," *Brooklyn Law Review*, Vol. 66 (2001), pp. 1207–1249.

52. Ibid., p. 1210.
53. N. Bush, "The Case for Expansive Voir Dire," *Law and Psychology Review*, Vol. 2 (1976), pp. 9–25.
54. J. M. Spaeth, "Swearing with Crossed Fingers: Juror Honesty during *Voir Dire*," *Arizona Attorney*, January 2001 © State Bar of Arizona. Reprinted by permission.
55. D. Suggs and B. D. Sales, "Juror Self-Selection in the Voir Dire: A Social Science Analysis," *Indiana Law Review*, Vol. 2 (1980–1981), pp. 245–271.
56. Spaeth, "Swearing with Crossed Fingers."
57. See, e.g., W. Aquilino, "Interviewer Mode Effects in Surveys of Drug and Alcohol Use," *Public Opinion Quarterly*, Vol. 54 (1990), pp. 362–395.
58. See, e.g., M. Acree, M. Ekstrand, T. Coates, and R. Stall, "Mode Effects in Surveys of Gay Men: A Within-Individual Comparison of Responses by Mail and by Telephone," *Journal of Sex Research*, Vol. 36 (1999), pp. 65–75.
59. K. Rasinski, G. Willis, A. Baldwin, W. Yeh, and L. Lee, "Methods of Data Collection, Perceptions of Risks and Losses, and Motivation to Give Truthful Answers to Sensitive Survey Questions," *Applied Cognitive Psychology*, Vol. 13 (1999), pp. 465–484.
60. Cited in R. N. Jonakait, *The American Jury System* (New Haven, CT: Yale University Press, 2003), pp. 57–58.
61. Ibid.
62. See, e.g., K. Podlas, "Please Adjust Your Signal: How Television's Syndicated Courtrooms Bias Our Juror Citizenry," *American Business Law Journal*, Vol. 39 (2001), pp. 1–24; also see R. Willing, "CSI Effect Has Juries Wanting More Evidence," *USA Today*, available at http://usatoday30.usatoday.com/news/nation/2004-08-05-csi-effect_x.htm (accessed February 25, 2013).
63. D. Williams, "Realistic Jury Service: One Small Step towards Improving the Civil Justice System," *Arkansas Lawyer*, Summer 2000, p. 16.
64. D. G. Smith, "Structural and Functional Aspects of the Jury: Comparative Analysis and Proposals for Reform," *Alabama Law Review*, Vol. 48 (1997), p. 491.
65. A. Blum, "Jury System Undergoes Patchwork Remodeling," *National Law Journal*, January 22, 1996, p. A1.
66. M. P. Judge, "Keynote Address, Commencement Ceremony, University of West Los Angeles Law School, June 9, 1996," *University of West Los Angeles Law Review*, Vol. 29 (1998), p. 220.
67. *United States* v. *Ewell*, 383 U.S. 116 (1966).
68. *Barker* v. *Wingo*, 407 U.S. 514 (1972).
69. Ibid., pp. 520–521.
70. *United States* v. *Ewell*, 383 U.S. 116 (1966), p. 120.
71. J. Goerdt, C. Lomvardias, G. Gallas, and B. Mahoney, *Examining Court Delay: The Pace of Litigation in 26 Urban Trial Courts, 1987* (Arlington, VA: National Center for State Courts, 1989), p. xiii. Reprinted with permission.
72. 18 U.S.C.A., Section 3161.
73. *United States* v. *Marion*, 404 U.S. 307 (1971).
74. Ibid., pp. 327–328.
75. *Barker* v. *Wingo*, 407 U.S. 514 (1972).
76. Ibid., p. 530.
77. *In re Oliver*, 333 U.S. 257 (1948), p. 271.
78. Ibid., p. 271, n. 25.
79. *Waller* v. *Georgia*, 467 U.S. 39 (1984).
80. Ibid.
81. Ibid., p. 40.
82. *Estes* v. *Texas*, 381 U.S. 532 (1965).
83. *Chandler* v. *Florida*, 449 U.S. 560 (1981).
84. Ibid., p. 575.
85. *Marshall* v. *United States*, 360 U.S. 310 (1959).
86. *Irvin* v. *Dowd*, 366 U.S. 717 (1961).
87. *Murphy* v. *Florida*, 421 U.S. 794 (1975), and *Patton* v. *Yount*, 467 U.S. 1025 (1984).
88. *Rideau* v. *Louisiana*, 373 U.S. 723 (1963).
89. Ibid., p. 727.
90. *Sheppard* v. *Maxwell*, 384 U.S. 333 (1966).
91. *Nebraska Press Ass'n* v. *Stuart*, 427 U.S. 539 (1976).
92. Ibid., p. 562.
93. *Sheppard* v. *Maxwell*, 384 U.S. 333 (1966), p. 359.
94. ABA Rule 3.6.[a][b].
95. *Gentile* v. *Nevada State Bar*, 501 U.S. 1030 (1991).
96. J. J. Eannace, "Art—Not a Science: A Prosecutor's Perspective on Opening Statements," *The Prosecutor*, Vol. 31 (1997), pp. 32–37.
97. J. L. Worrall, *Criminal Procedure: From First Contact to Appeal*, 2nd ed. (Boston: Allyn and Bacon, 2007), p. 82.
98. J. L. Worrall and C. Hemmens, *Criminal Evidence: An Introduction* (Los Angeles: Roxbury, 2005), p. 71.
99. Ibid.
100. Ibid.
101. Ibid., p. 407.
102. California Evidence Code, Section 764.
103. See, e.g., *Brown* v. *United States*, 356 U.S. 148 (1958), and *Rogers* v. *United States*, 340 U.S. 367 (1951).
104. See, e.g., G. P. Kramer and D. M. Koenig, "Do Jurors Understand Criminal Jury Instructions? Analyzing the Results of the Michigan Juror Comprehension Project," *Journal of Law Reform*, Vol. 23 (1990), pp. 401–437; also see D. Strawn and R. Buchanan, "Jury Confusion: A Threat to Justice," *Judicature*, Vol. 59 (1976), pp. 478–483.
105. See, e.g., R. J. Simon, *The Jury and the Defense of Insanity* (Boston: Little, Brown, 1967).
106. D. W. Broeder, "The University of Chicago Jury Project," *Nebraska Law Review*, Vol. 38 (1959), pp. 744–760.
107. U.S. Department of Justice, *Dictionary of Criminal Justice Data Terminology*, p. 132.
108. P. L. Hannaford, V. P. Hans, and G. T. Munsterman, "How Much Justice Hangs in the Balance? A New Look at Hung Jury Rates," *Judicature*, Vol. 83 (1999), pp. 59–67.
109. *Allen* v. *United States*, 164 U.S. 492 (1896).

Michael Newman/PhotoEdit

Sentencing, Appeals, and *Habeas Corpus*

14

LEARNING OBJECTIVES

1. Summarize the goals of sentencing.
2. Describe the different types of sentences that can be imposed.
3. Summarize the sentencing process and the factors that influence sentencing.
4. Describe the purposes and types of appeals, and the appeals process.
5. Explain *habeas corpus* and the *habeas corpus* process.

INTRODUCTION

In 2008, Iowa Governor Chet Culver signed the nation's first piece of legislation[1] that requires policymakers to conduct racial-impact studies and to prepare racial-impact statements for any proposed policy changes affecting criminal sentencing, probation, or parole. The action came after research showed that Iowa led the nation in racial disparity in its prison population. A few months later, a similar piece of legislation[2] was signed into law by Connecticut Governor M. Jodi Rell, and the Illinois General Assembly passed a law[3] creating the state's Commission to Study Disproportionate Justice Impact, a body charged with investigating the extent to which the structure of criminal sentencing in Illinois affects communities of color.

Marc Mauer, head of the Washington, D.C.–based Sentencing Project says, "The premise behind racial impact statements is that policies often have unintended consequences that would be best addressed prior to adoption of new initiatives."[4] One example Mauer gives is that of enhanced criminal penalties associated with drug sales near school grounds—a law, he says, more likely to be violated by minorities because they tend to live in areas with greater proximity to schools. Studies of the racial impact of sentencing practices, Mauer says, force us to examine twin problems in the justice system: (1) the need for policies and practices that can work effectively to promote public safety and (2) the need to reduce disproportionate rates of minority incarceration when feasible. "These are not competing goals," says Mauer. "If we are successful in addressing crime in a proactive way, we will be able to reduce high imprisonment rates; conversely, by promoting racial justice we will increase confidence in the criminal justice system and thereby aid public safety efforts."

This line of male inmates at the Darrington Unit near Houston, Texas, illustrates the racial disparities that characterize American prison populations today. Can racial-impact studies, like those discussed at the start of this chapter, be effective in addressing such disparities?

© Marjorie Kamys Coteral/Bob Daemmrich Photography/Alamy

AFTER TRIAL

After a felony conviction, defendants are typically granted a separate sentencing or dispositional hearing during which all relevant evidence is considered. A great deal of this information is provided in a presentence report, which is most often prepared by a probation officer. This report provides the judge with information concerning the defendant's pretrial record, financial characteristics, family status, employment status, and other factors that can be relevant in deciding on the appropriate sentence. The time needed to complete this report is the main reason that there is a time lapse between trial and sentencing. A great deal of work goes into preparation of the presentence report, as the requirements listed in Box 14–1 make clear.

Several sentencing options are available to judges. The judge may impose a sentence and then suspend it pending good behavior on the part of the defendant. The judge may also require the defendant to pay a fine or, in more extreme cases, serve a term in prison; probation or a similar method of supervised release is another possibility. The sentence that is finally chosen reflects legislative intent, the judge's personal preferences, and the views of the probation/treatment staff.

Web Extra
14–1   The Sentencing Project

BOX 14–1   Components of a Presentence Report (Michigan)

REQUIRED COMPONENTS

* Evaluation of and prognosis for the defendant's adjustment in the community based on factual information contained in the report

* Any written impact statement submitted by a victim (if requested by a victim)

* Specific written recommendation for disposition based on the evaluation and other information as prescribed by the court

* Statement prepared by the prosecuting attorney as to whether any consecutive sentencing is required by law

* Statement that the defendant is licensed or registered if he or she is to be sentenced for a misdemeanor involving the illegal delivery, possession, or use of alcohol or a controlled substance

* Diagnostic opinions that are available and not exempt from disclosure by state law

* Objective description of the offense

* Defendant's version of the offense

* Full description of the defendant's prior criminal record

* Status of all criminal charges pending against the defendant

* Personal profile of the defendant

OPTIONAL COMPONENTS

* Defendant's juvenile record if the record has not been expunged

* Conclusions or opinions of the probation officer

* Defendant's pending charges and prior arrests without convictions (if any)

SENTENCING RECOMMENDATION

* The presentence report must contain a specific sentence recommendation. A simple recommendation that the defendant be incarcerated or that the defendant not be placed on probation is sufficient. ▪

Source: Adapted from http://jthomasniu.org/PDF/MI_present_invest.pdf (accessed February 28, 2013).

GOALS OF SENTENCING

Four main goals of sentencing have been identified: (1) rehabilitation or reformation, (2) retribution, (3) incapacitation and (4) deterrence. Other goals may include reintegration, restitution, restorative justice, equity, and justice, but these four (summarized in Table 14–1) have been most influential throughout history.[5]

Rehabilitation

Rehabilitation consists of a planned intervention intended to change behavior.[6] The key assumption that underlies rehabilitation is that people can change through a planned intervention. Examples of rehabilitation-oriented sentences include probation, drug treatment, and anger management.

Retribution

Retributive sentencing is designed to punish criminals solely for what they did based on the severity of their crimes. Revenge is an action undertaken simply to satisfy the anger and pain experienced by crime victims, whereas retribution is based on the belief that criminals need to be punished fairly and justly for the crimes they commit. Retribution is based on past rather than future conduct: Criminals should get their "just deserts" for what they have already done, not what they may do in the future.[7]

Incapacitation

Sentencing for the purpose of incapacitation amounts to removing criminals from society, usually through incarceration (or sometimes through home confinement, electronic monitoring, or a similar method of restraint) so that they cannot repeat their criminal activity. The focus here is on potential victims who will be protected by removing the criminal element. Like rehabilitation, incapacitation relies on future considerations: Criminals are punished because of what they may do in the future based on what they did in the past.

Deterrence

Sentencing for the purposes of deterrence is designed to discourage would-be criminals from committing crime. Rather than punishing people for what they have done or what they might do, deterrence strategies are often employed to discourage *others* from committing crime. For example, if a convicted killer is given a death sentence, those contemplating murder might have second thoughts about committing the same crime.

TABLE 14–1 Goals of Sentencing

Goal	Definition/Purpose
Rehabilitation	This planned intervention is intended to change defendants' behavior.
Retribution	This view implies that offenders must be punished fairly and justly for the crimes they commit.
Incapacitation	The goal is to remove offenders from society, most often through incarceration.
Deterrence	General deterrence aims to discourage others from committing similar acts. Specific deterrence uses punishment to discourage/prevent defendants from reoffending or committing other crimes.

General deterrence strategies are designed to eliminate crime by convincing others who might become criminals that "crime does not pay." For instance, when a state government passes a mandatory sentencing policy requiring that all people convicted of drug trafficking be sent to prison, it is sending a strong message: Do not sell drugs, or you will be punished severely.

Specific deterrence is a goal of sentencing aimed at reducing the chances of recidivism—if a person is punished harshly, he or she is unlikely to repeat criminal acts. When a person is locked away after being convicted of a crime, it drives home the point that the pain of punishment is greater than the benefits of crime. Specific deterrence need not be accompanied by a prison term, however; a first-time offender could be placed on probation, and that sanction alone could lead the offender to steer clear of crime for the duration of his or her lifetime.

general deterrence
When others besides the sentenced offender are discouraged from committing additional crimes due to sentencing practices.

specific deterrence
When a sentenced offender is discouraged from committing additional crimes due to his or her sentence.

Library Extra
14–1 Felony Disenfranchisement

TYPES OF SENTENCES

Judges can impose many types of sentences, including monetary penalties, probation, intermediate sanctions (such as boot camp), shaming, forfeiture, prison sentences, and the death penalty, to name a few. These sentences range from modestly punitive, such as probation or fines, to extremely harsh, such as life imprisonment or the death penalty.

Learning Objective 2
Describe the different types of sentences that can be imposed.

Monetary Penalties

A **fine** (money paid to the state for a criminal offense) is the most common punishment used by the criminal justice system today.[8] Fines are used primarily in cases involving minor offenses. If a fine is imposed, the offender will be ordered to pay a certain amount of money, usually in accordance with the seriousness of the offense. Fines can be imposed in lieu of other punishments or in conjunction with other punishments; for example, a convicted criminal may be forced to pay a certain amount as well as serve a period of time in prison.

Despite their popularity, fines are also not without their problems. First, in most jurisdictions, the fine to be imposed is defined by law, regardless of the offender's financial position. If a poor offender is convicted of a serious crime, the fine is likely to be high, meaning that he or she will probably have difficulty paying the required amount.[9] Many fines go uncollected not only because some offenders cannot pay but also because many of the collection systems in place across the country are inadequate.[10]

In light of the difficulty of collecting fines, some jurisdictions across the United States have experimented with a system of day fines. **Day fines** attach unit values to the seriousness of given offenses, and these unit values are then multiplied by a fixed percentage of the offender's income; the result is a proportional fine, one that is not unnecessarily burdensome on an offender but is still enough money to serve a punitive purpose. Day fines were introduced in Sweden in the 1920s and were quickly adopted by other Scandinavian countries. The concept was also adopted in West Germany in the 1970s and throughout other European nations more recently.

A study of a day fine program in Maricopa County (Arizona) found that the fines were successful in diverting offenders from routine supervision (e.g., probation) and in encouraging greater financial payments.[11] Another study showed that day fines resulted in fewer technical violations and rearrests than traditional sentencing.[12] However, other research suggests that it is difficult to implement day fine programs and that outcomes may depart from intentions.[13] For example, some offenders may not be able to afford their day fine. Also, it can be difficult to assign dollar values to certain crimes as well as rank-order their seriousness.

fine
The most common punishment used by the criminal justice system today.[i] Primarily used in cases involving minor offenses, fines involve the assessment of a monetary amount to be forfeited as a punishment for commission of an offense.

day fine
A system for determining monetary fines that involves attaching a "unit value" to the seriousness of a given offense that is then multiplied by a fixed percentage of the offender's income. The result is a proportional fine that is not unnecessarily burdensome on an offender but is still sufficient to serve a punitive purpose.

Probation

probation
A sentence of imprisonment that is suspended; also, the conditional freedom granted by a judicial officer to a convicted offender as long as the person meets certain conditions of behavior.

Probation is one of the most frequent sentences handed down by judges—there are now nearly 5 million people on probation.[14] This represents roughly 70% of all adult criminals under sentence.[15] Criminals can be sentenced to probation in the community at a substantially lower cost than sending them to prison.[16]

Probation involves supervision in the community. Typically, the probationer lives in the community and obeys a set of rules or conditions set down by the sentencing judge while being monitored by probation officers.

reform conditions
Probation or parole conditions that are intended to facilitate a probationer's or parolee's rehabilitation.

There are two general types of conditions that are imposed on probationers. **Reform conditions** are intended to facilitate the offender's rehabilitation; drug treatment is a common reform condition. **Control conditions**, by contrast, are intended to ensure adequate monitoring and supervision of the probationer or parolee. Reform and control conditions help serve the two common goals of probation and parole in America: rehabilitation and the protection of public safety.

control conditions
Probation or parole conditions that are intended to ensure adequate monitoring and supervision of a probationer or parolee.

Some jurisdictions use the terminology "general conditions" and "specific conditions." The former consist of conditions that all probationers must abide by, whereas the latter are tailored to each probationer's individual needs. Specific conditions could include both conditions of control (e.g., home confinement) and reform (e.g., job training program).

Conditions attached to probation are almost too numerous to list (several appear in Box 14–2), but standard conditions exist across most jurisdictions. These conditions usually include requiring that the probationer commit no additional crimes, work regularly, support dependents, submit to random drug testing, continue to reside in the same location, report to the probation/parole officer on a consistent basis, allow the supervising officer to visit at any time, and discontinue associations with other criminals.

In addition to standard conditions, probationers can be required to comply with any number of special conditions. Such conditions are usually tailored to specific offenders on a case-by-case basis and can include requiring them to do any of the following: attend drug treatment, participate in anger management, obtain additional education, refrain from going to particular locations, seek counseling, perform community service, pay restitution, and remain under house arrest. Many of these probation conditions have proven remarkably effective.[17]

Intermediate Sanctions

intermediate sanctions
Punitive measures (e.g., intensive supervision probation, shock probation, boot camps, electronic monitoring, and home confinement) that are tougher than probation but less harsh than a prison sentence.

Intermediate sanctions are tougher than probation but less harsh than a prison sentence. Examples include intensive supervision probation, shock probation, boot camps, electronic monitoring, and home confinement. Intermediate sanctions constitute a relatively new development in the history of criminal justice; although they are more punitive than probation, they are intended to be an improvement over traditional corrections.

net widening
The expanding control that is exercised over the lives of more and more people who find themselves on the wrong side of the law, often seen as an unfortunate side effect of intermediate sanctions.

An unfortunate side effect of intermediate sanction is known as the problem of **net widening**, which is a metaphorical representation of the control that is exercised over the lives of more and more people who find themselves on the wrong side of the law. Intermediate sanctions have brought more offenders under correctional supervision who may not have been under such supervision before. Consider electronic monitoring. It affords authorities the opportunity to keep close tabs on low-level offenders, but before the advent of such technology, these individuals may not have been subjected to such controls. Net widening has been explained as political risk aversion—no one, especially any politician, wants to take a risk (such as releasing an offender into the community) that may reflect poorly on them.[18] Intermediate sanctions give the appearance that something is being done to deal with criminals.

BOX 14–2 Common Probation Conditions (Federal)

1. (Policy Statement) The following "standard" conditions are recommended for probation. Several of the conditions are expansions of the conditions required by statute:
   a. the defendant shall not leave the judicial district or other specified geographic area without the permission of the court or probation officer;
   b. the defendant shall report to the probation officer as directed by the court or probation officer and shall submit a truthful and complete written report within the first five days of each month;
   c. the defendant shall answer truthfully all inquiries by the probation officer and follow the instructions of the probation officer;
   d. the defendant shall support the defendant's dependents and meet other family responsibilities (including, but not limited to, complying with the terms of any court order or administrative process pursuant to the law of a state, the District of Columbia, or any other possession or territory of the United States requiring payments by the defendant for the support and maintenance of any child or of a child and the parent with whom the child is living);
   e. the defendant shall work regularly at a lawful occupation unless excused by the probation officer for schooling, training, or other acceptable reasons;
   f. the defendant shall notify the probation officer at least ten days prior to any change of residence or employment;
   g. the defendant shall refrain from excessive use of alcohol and shall not purchase, possess, use, distribute, or administer any controlled substance, or any paraphernalia related to any controlled substance, except as prescribed by a physician;
   h. the defendant shall not frequent places where controlled substances are illegally sold, used, distributed, or administered, or other places specified by the court;
   i. the defendant shall not associate with any persons engaged in criminal activity, and shall not associate with any person convicted of a felony unless granted permission to do so by the probation officer;
   j. the defendant shall permit a probation officer to visit the defendant at any time at home or elsewhere and shall permit confiscation of any contraband observed in plain view by the probation officer;
   k. the defendant shall notify the probation officer within seventy-two hours of being arrested or questioned by a law enforcement officer;
   l. the defendant shall not enter into any agreement to act as an informer or a special agent of a law enforcement agency without the permission of the court;
   m. as directed by the probation officer, the defendant shall notify third parties of risks that may be occasioned by the defendant's criminal record or personal history or characteristics, and shall permit the probation officer to make such notifications and to confirm the defendant's compliance with such notification requirement;
   n. the defendant shall pay the special assessment imposed or adhere to a court-ordered installment schedule for the payment of the special assessment. ■

Source: Adapted from http://www.ussc.gov/Guidelines/2011Guidelines/Manual_HTML/5b1_3.htm (accessed November 13, 2013).

Shaming

The punishment of **shaming** has also gained popularity in recent years. Instead of capitalizing on recent technologies, it breathes new life into punishments dating to the prebiblical era. In those early times, people lived in tight-knit tribes, and banishment from one's community was one of the most shameful forms of punishment known.[19] Shaming penalties later evolved throughout Europe with the development of public torture that would often end in the death of the accused. Similar but less lethal methods of punishment were then transported to America, where offenders often faced time in the pillory or stocks. Serious offenders were branded and mutilated, thus "fixing on [the offenders] an indelible 'mark of infamy' to warn the community of their criminal propensities."[20] As an example of one such

shaming
A creative judicially imposed punishment that seeks to deter crime by imposing embarrassment or disgrace on an offender.[ii]

punishment, an offender in Williamsburg, Virginia, had his ear nailed to a wooden brace of the pillory, and after he served his sentence, authorities tore him away from the pillory without first removing the nail.[21] He became "earmarked" as a criminal.

As America matured and became a more progressive nation, shaming and other brutal forms of punishment fell out of popularity, and punishment moved away from physical to more psychological methods. Authorities began to favor institutional forms of punishment that would affect offenders' mental state more than their physical being. At the same time, people were becoming more mobile, making certain shaming punishments—especially banishment—less attractive because being forcibly removed from their surroundings no longer carried with it the same permanency and stigmatization; criminals who were shamed in one community could simply move away and start a new life elsewhere. Throughout the twentieth century, shaming punishments fell out of favor, but recently they have reemerged.

Shaming penalties come in three forms: public exposure, debasement, and apology penalties.[22] **Public-exposure penalties** occur when a criminal's conviction is made visible to several people. Such penalties point the offender out to the public so that the public can respond with disapproval, thereby heightening the offender's sense of shame. **Debasement penalties**, though closely related to public-exposure penalties, serve the additional goal of lowering offenders' social status because they tend to require offenders to perform humiliating acts. **Apology penalties** are straightforward—they require offenders to express remorse, usually publicly, for committing a particular crime.

Forfeiture

It is also possible to require that an individual convicted of a crime relinquish ownership of property, most often property that was derived from or used to facilitate the crime; this process is called **forfeiture**. There are two types of forfeiture: criminal and civil. **Criminal forfeiture** follows a criminal conviction. If criminal forfeiture is sought, the prosecutor must prove beyond a reasonable doubt that the offender is guilty *and* that the property is subject to forfeiture. For example, in addition to securing a criminal conviction, if the prosecutor can prove beyond a reasonable doubt that the defendant bought his or her house with the proceeds of the offense for which he or she is convicted, the house can be forfeited. Such penalties clearly minimize the financial gain associated with crime.

Civil forfeiture does not require a criminal proceeding, as is the case with criminal forfeiture, but can be pursued independently of a criminal proceeding. Civil forfeiture is controversial for two key reasons. First, depending on state law, forfeiture proceeds can go back to the law enforcement agency that launched the investigation, meaning that local police agencies that are responsible for the seizure of large quantities of cash can receive that cash (to be used for law enforcement purposes) if ownership to it is forfeited. Critics of this practice have claimed that it encourages "policing for profit"; in other words, forfeiture may put police budgeting ahead of crime control.

A second criticism relates to the standard of proof. The standard of proof in a civil forfeiture case is the "preponderance of evidence," a lower standard than "proof beyond a reasonable doubt." Civil forfeiture critics argue that it is easier to succeed with civil forfeiture when there is not enough evidence to support a criminal conviction.[23] The very fact that preponderance of the evidence is lower than proof beyond a reasonable doubt reinforces this concern.

Prison Sentences

After considering all the facts, if community and alternative sentences are not sufficient, the criminal defendant may be forced to spend time in a secure facility such as a jail or

public-exposure penalty
A form of shaming penalty that seeks to make a criminal's conviction publicly visible so that the public can respond with disapproval, thereby heightening the offender's sense of shame.

debasement penalty
A form of shaming penalty that seeks to lower an offender's social status by requiring him or her to perform humiliating acts.

apology penalty
A form of shaming penalty that requires offenders to express remorse, usually publicly, for committing a particular crime.

forfeiture
The authorized seizure of money, negotiable instruments, securities, property, or other things of value.

criminal forfeiture
A seizure, resulting from a criminal court proceeding, of money, negotiable instruments, securities, property, or other things of value that derived from or was used to facilitate a crime or criminal activity.

civil forfeiture
A seizure, resulting from a civil court proceeding, of money, negotiable instruments, securities, property, or other things of value.

prison. At least four types of prison sentences can be identified (some of which are closely related to others):

1. *Indeterminate sentencing.* The judge has the authority to set the length of incarceration for an **indeterminate sentence**. This form of sentencing empowers the judge to set a maximum sentence (up to what the legislature will allow) and often a minimum sentence as well for the offender to serve in prison. Under this system, parole boards usually end up deciding the actual amount of time the offender will spend in prison.

2. *Determinate sentencing.* When the judge hands down a fixed sentence that cannot later be altered by a parole board, it is called a **determinate sentence**. Determinate sentencing has the effects both of treating all offenders similarly and of ensuring that criminals are incarcerated for longer periods of time than may be permissible under indeterminate sentencing.

3. *Mandatory sentencing.* A **mandatory sentence** is also a form of determinate sentencing, but it differs in that it takes discretion away from judges by requiring a certain length of incarceration. Three-strikes laws require mandatory sentences. For example, under California's three-strikes law, if a person who has two felonies ("strikes") on his or her record commits a third felony of any type, he or she goes to prison for life. Critics of mandatory sentencing say that such laws transfer discretion from judges to prosecutors.

4. *Sentencing guidelines.* The **U.S. Sentencing Commission** was created in 1984 to deal with sentencing problems in the federal courts. The commission put together a sentencing grid that federal judges use to determine the appropriate sentence; this grid is reprinted in Table 14–2. Both criminal history (horizontal axis) and offense levels (vertical axis) are taken into account so that judges can set the appropriate sentence (in months). These **sentencing guidelines** are used to determine the appropriate sentence and serve to reduce disparities between sentences by recommending a specific term of imprisonment for certain types of offenders. In 2005, the Supreme Court ruled, in *United States* v. *Booker*, that the federal guidelines were unconstitutional if they were mandatory, and while judges could still refer to the guideline ranges, they were free to consider other factors in their decision making; sentences could then be subject to appellate review if they were unreasonable.[24] The practical result of this decision is that guidelines are now advisory rather than mandatory.

Sentencing guidelines were always unpopular with some judges because of a perception that they strip courts of their sentencing discretion. Advocates felt that they were necessary to reduce racial disparity in sentencing. Now that guidelines are voluntary rather than mandatory, some critics believe that the effect will be greater racial disparity in sentencing. Is there racism in the sentencing process? This topic is addressed in the following "Courts in the News" feature.

Death Penalty

The most serious punishment that can be imposed is capital punishment. Prior to the 1970s, executions were relatively common. In 1972, however, the Supreme Court decided the landmark case of *Furman* v. *Georgia*,[25] where it ruled that the death penalty was carried out in the United States in ways that amounted to cruel and unusual punishment, in violation of the Eighth Amendment. Then, in 1976, the Court reinstated the death penalty in *Gregg* v. *Georgia*,[26] when it held that death was an acceptable sentence, provided the sentencing process is reasonable. Today, the death penalty remains intact in most states; some do not

---

indeterminate sentence
A type of sentence imposed on a convicted criminal that is meant to encourage rehabilitation through the use of relatively unspecific punishments (e.g., a term of imprisonment of from one to ten years).

determinate sentence
A model of criminal punishment in which an offender is given a fixed term of imprisonment that may be reduced by good time or gain time. Under the model, for example, all offenders convicted of the same degree of burglary would be sentenced to the same length of time behind bars.

mandatory sentence
A statutorily required penalty that must be set and carried out in all cases upon conviction for a specified offense or series of offenses.

U.S. Sentencing Commission
A federal agency created in 1984 to deal with sentencing problems in the federal courts. The commission devised a "sentencing grid" used by federal judges to determine appropriate sentences.

sentencing guidelines
Voluntary or involuntary (depending on state or federal law) sentencing policies that are used to determine appropriate sentences and that serve to reduce disparities between sentences by recommending a certain term of imprisonment for certain types of offenders.

Library Extra
14–2 Felony Sentences in State Courts

COURTS IN THE NEWS

Guidelines and Racial Disparity

One of the biggest sentencing issues facing the nation is racial disparity. According to the nonprofit Sentencing Project, more than 60% of the people in prison are now racial and ethnic minorities. For black males in their thirties, one in every ten is in prison or jail on any given day. These trends have been intensified by the disproportionate impact of the "war on drugs," in which two-thirds of all persons in prison for drug offenses are people of color.

One reason for this disparity, according to the U.S. Sentencing Commission, is that prison sentences of black men are nearly 20% longer than those of white men for similar crimes. The racial gap has widened since the Supreme Court, in *United States* v. *Booker*, mandated that sentencing guidelines be advisory rather than mandatory. While the commission did not suggest that federal judges are racist, it acknowledged that they "make sentencing decisions based on many legitimate considerations that are not or cannot be measured."

Still, the findings drew criticism from advocacy groups and researchers who said that the commission's focus on the very end of the criminal justice process ignored possible bias at earlier stages, such as when a person is arrested and charged or enters into a plea deal with prosecutors. "They've only got data on this final slice of the process, but they are still missing crucial parts of the criminal-justice process," said Sonja Starr, a law professor at the University of Michigan who has analyzed sentencing and arrest data and found no marked increase in racial disparity since 2005.

In the years after the *Booker* ruling, sentences of blacks were on average 15.2% longer than the sentences of similarly situated whites. Between December 2007 and September 2011, sentences of black males were 19.5% longer than those for whites. The analysis also found that black males were 25% less likely than whites in the same

iStockphoto/Thinkstock

African American men are still receiving much longer sentences than white males despite years of effort to reduce racial disparity in sentencing.

period to receive a sentence below the guidelines' range.

The Sentencing Commission also conducted a separate analysis that excluded sentences of probation. It yielded the same pattern, but the racial disparity was less pronounced. Sentences of black males were 14.5% longer than whites rather than nearly 20%.

These findings are troubling because they indicate that despite years of effort to reduce racial bias in the justice system, sentencing disparity still exists and remains a stain on the court system. Because this issue is so important, we will revisit it in Chapter 15. ■

DISCUSSION QUESTIONS

1. Considering this turn of events, would you argue that guidelines should be reinstated as being mandatory in order to reduce racial disparity?

2. What factors other than judicial discretion influence sentencing? For example, people who cannot make bail are more likely to be sent to prison so that indigent defendants who are detained in jail before trial are more likely to receive an incarceration sentence.

Sources: United States Sentencing Commission, "Report on the Continuing Impact of *United States* v. *Booker* on Federal Sentencing," 2012, available at www.ussc.gov/Legislative_and_Public_Affairs/Congressional_Testimony_and_Reports/Booker_Reports/2012_Booker/index.cfm (accessed June 2, 2013); Sentencing Project, "Racial Disparity," available at www.sentencingproject.org/template/page.cfm?id=122 (accessed June 2, 2013); Marisa Taylor, "Racial Disparities in Sentencing Rise after Guidelines Loosened," McClatchy Newspapers, March 12, 2013, available at www.mcclatchydc.com/2010/03/12/90316/racial-disparities-in-sentencing.html#storylink=cpy (accessed June 2, 2013); Joe Palazzolo, "Racial Gap in Men's Sentencing," *Wall Street Journal*, February 14, 2013, available at http://online.wsj.com/article/SB10001424127887324432004578304463789858002.html#printMode (accessed June 2, 2013).

TABLE 14–2 Federal Sentencing Guidelines, 2011

SENTENCING TABLE

(in months of imprisonment)

	Offense Level	Criminal History Category (Criminal History Points)					
		I (0 or 1)	II (2 or 3)	III (4, 5, 6)	IV (7, 8, 9)	V (10, 11, 12)	VI (13 or more)
Zone A	1	0-6	0-6	0-6	0-6	0-6	0-6
	2	0-6	0-6	0-6	0-6	0-6	1-7
	3	0-6	0-6	0-6	0-6	2-8	3-9
	4	0-6	0-6	0-6	2-8	4-10	6-12
	5	0-6	0-6	1-7	4-10	6-12	9-15
	6	0-6	1-7	2-8	6-12	9-15	12-18
	7	0-6	2-8	4-10	8-14	12-18	15-21
	8	0-6	4-10	6-12	10-16	15-21	18-24
Zone B	9	4-10	6-12	8-14	12-18	18-24	21-27
	10	6-12	8-14	10-16	15-21	21-27	24-30
Zone C	11	8-14	10-16	12-18	18-24	24-30	27-33
	12	10-16	12-18	15-21	21-27	27-33	30-37
Zone D	13	12-18	15-21	18-24	24-30	30-37	33-41
	14	15-21	18-24	21-27	27-33	33-41	37-46
	15	18-24	21-27	24-30	30-37	37-46	41-51
	16	21-27	24-30	27-33	33-41	41-51	46-57
	17	24-30	27-33	30-37	37-46	46-57	51-63
	18	27-33	30-37	33-41	41-51	51-63	57-71
	19	30-37	33-41	37-46	46-57	57-71	63-78
	20	33-41	37-46	41-51	51-63	63-78	70-87
	21	37-46	41-51	46-57	57-71	70-87	77-96
	22	41-51	46-57	51-63	63-78	77-96	84-105
	23	46-57	51-63	57-71	70-87	84-105	92-115
	24	51-63	57-71	63-78	77-96	92-115	100-125
	25	57-71	63-78	70-87	84-105	100-125	110-137
	26	63-78	70-87	78-97	92-115	110-137	120-150
	27	70-87	78-97	87-108	100-125	120-150	130-162
	28	78-97	87-108	97-121	110-137	130-162	140-175
	29	87-108	97-121	108-135	121-151	140-175	151-188
	30	97-121	108-135	121-151	135-168	151-188	168-210
	31	108-135	121-151	135-168	151-188	168-210	188-235
	32	121-151	135-168	151-188	168-210	188-235	210-262
	33	135-168	151-188	168-210	188-235	210-262	235-293
	34	151-188	168-210	188-235	210-262	235-293	262-327
	35	168-210	188-235	210-262	235-293	262-327	292-365
	36	188-235	210-262	235-293	262-327	292-365	324-405
	37	210-262	235-293	262-327	292-365	324-405	360-life
	38	235-293	262-327	292-365	324-405	360-life	360-life
	39	262-327	292-365	324-405	360-life	360-life	360-life
	40	292-365	324-405	360-life	360-life	360-life	360-life
	41	324-105	360-life	360-life	360-life	360-life	360-life
	42	360-life	360-life	360-life	360-life	360-life	360-life
	43	life	life	life	life	life	life

Source: www.ussc.gov/Guidelines/2011_Guidelines/Manual_PDF/Sentencing_Table.pdf (accessed February 28, 2013).

use it, and even in those states that do, some offenders are not eligible for a death sentence (more on this shortly).

Determining whether the death penalty should be imposed is now frequently in the hands of a jury. Most state statutes call for essentially two trials, which in legal parlance is called a **bifurcated trial**. In the first trial, the defendant's guilt or lack of involvement in the crime is determined, then the jury sits for what is basically another trial, which is used to determine whether a death sentence should be handed down. The importance of such a procedure is that it allows a jury of the defendant's peers—not just a judge—to determine

bifurcated trial
A criminal trial in which issues relevant to the case (e.g., guilt and punishment, guilt and sanity) are tried separately.

LASTING IMPACT

Furman v. Georgia

Furman v. *Georgia*, *Jackson* v. *Georgia*, and *Branch* v. *Texas*—known collectively as the landmark case *Furman* v. *Georgia* (1972)—"set the standard that a punishment would be 'cruel and unusual' if it was too severe for the crime, if it was arbitrary, if it offended society's sense of justice, or if it was not more effective than a less severe penalty."[1]

While burglarizing a private home, Furman was discovered by a member of the family who lived in the home. While attempting to flee, Furman tripped, and the gun he was carrying discharged, striking and killing the family member. Convicted of murder and sentenced to death, Furman petitioned the U.S. Supreme Court on grounds that the arbitrary manner in which the death penalty was imposed and carried out constituted cruel and unusual punishment under the Eighth Amendment. (Jackson and Branch argued similarly regarding the death penalty sentences they received for rape and murder, respectively.)

In a one-page *per curiam* opinion, the Court held that the imposition of the death penalty in these cases constituted cruel and unusual punishment and violated the Constitution. In over 200 pages of concurrence and dissents, the justices articulated their views on this controversial subject. Only Justices Brennan and Marshall believed the death penalty to be unconstitutional in all instances. Other concurrences focused on the arbitrary nature with which death sentences have been imposed, often indicating a racial bias against black defendants. The Court's decision forced states and the national legislature to rethink their statutes for capital offenses to ensure that the death penalty would not be administered in a capricious or discriminatory manner.[2] The ruling thus "effectively voided 40 death penalty statutes, thereby commuting the sentences of 629 death-row inmates around the country and suspending the death penalty because existing statutes were no longer valid."[3]

But the ruling did not prohibit the various states from rewriting their death penalty statutes to eliminate capricious and discriminatory administration. The state of Georgia, for example, developed guidelines for jurors: After a person is convicted in a capital trial, the trial moves to a penalty phase, during which the jury must determine whether any unique aggravating and mitigating circumstances should be considered before the court decides whether to impose a death sentence. The U.S. Supreme

Court upheld these jury guidelines in *Gregg* v. *Georgia* (1976), thus ending the four-year national moratorium on the death penalty.

This bifurcated trial model is intended to defuse jurors' postconviction emotions and to eliminate capricious and discriminatory decisions regarding the sentence. The ritual of closing out the guilt or innocence phase of the trial and formally moving into the sentencing phase serves as a catalyst for a fresh consideration of the circumstances of the crime, thus permitting a more clinical, less impassioned determination of the appropriate sentence.

After Furman's sentence was overturned by the U.S. Supreme Court, he was resentenced to 20 years in prison. Paroled in April 1984, he later pleaded guilty to a 2004 burglary charge in Bibb County Superior Court. At age 64, he was again sentenced to 20 years in prison. ■

Notes

1. "Constitutionality of the Death Penalty in America," *History of the Death Penalty*, Death Penalty Information Center online, copyright 2008, available at www.deathpenaltyinfo.org/article .php?did=410&scid (accessed June 2, 2013).
2. *Furman* v. *Georgia*, 408 U.S. 238 (1972).
3. "Constitutionality of the Death Penalty in America," available at http://deathpenaltycurriculum.org/student/c/about/history/history-5 .htm (accessed June 2, 2013).

DISCUSSION QUESTIONS

Search the Web for examples of various kinds of real-life criminal offenses and gather as much information on each crime as you can. Then ask yourself the following questions about *each* of those offenses:

1. What kinds of punishments might be too severe for the crime in question?
2. What kinds of punishments might offend society's sense of justice for the crime in question?
3. What kinds of punishments might not be more effective than a less severe penalty for the crime under consideration?

whether capital punishment is appropriate. Further, juries must take into account aggravating and mitigating circumstances. **Aggravating circumstances** are those that increase the seriousness or the outrageousness of a given crime (e.g., a homicide preceded by a period of prolonged torture); **mitigating circumstances** are those that reduce the seriousness or outrageousness of a given crime (e.g., stealing to feed one's family). It is unconstitutional for death penalty juries to ignore aggravating and mitigating circumstances.[27]

While juries should take aggravating and mitigating factors into consideration when determining whether a death sentence is appropriate, it is not appropriate for judges to do so, based on the decision in *Ring v. Arizona*.[28] In that case, the Supreme Court held that allowing a sentencing judge (without a jury) to find aggravating circumstances necessary for imposition of the death penalty violated the defendant's Sixth Amendment right to a jury trial.

aggravating circumstances
Factors that increase the seriousness or the outrageousness of a given crime (e.g., a homicide preceded by a period of prolonged torture).

mitigating circumstances
Factors that reduce the seriousness or outrageousness of a given crime (e.g., stealing to feed one's family).

Web Extra
14–2 Death Penalty Information Center

LASTING IMPACT

Gregg v. Georgia

Following the U.S. Supreme Court's decision in *Furman v. Georgia* (1972), a four-year moratorium on the death penalty existed in the United States. That moratorium ended when the Court upheld the death sentence of Troy Leon Gregg. In *Gregg v. Georgia* (1976), the Court embraced the bifurcated capital trial process instituted by the state of Georgia in response to *Furman* as being constitutionally sufficient to avoid the systemic arbitrariness and capriciousness that had led to its decision in *Furman*.

On November 21, 1973, 25-year-old Gregg and his 16-year-old traveling companion, Floyd Allen, were hitchhiking in northern Florida when they were given a ride by Fred Simmons and Bob Moore. When the bodies of Simmons and Moore were subsequently found at a Georgia rest stop, investigation quickly led to the apprehension of Gregg and Allen in Simmons's car in Asheville, North Carolina, the following afternoon.

In Gregg's presence, Allen stated to a police detective that at the intersection of Georgia Highway 20 and Interstate 85 in Gwinnett County, Georgia, they took a travel break at a rest stop, and Simmons and Moore got out; that Gregg turned around and told Allen to get out because "we're going to rob them"; that Gregg lay up on the car with a gun in his hand to get good aim, and as Simmons and Moore were coming back up the bank, he fired three shots; that one of the men fell, and the other staggered; that Gregg then circled around the back of the car and approached the two men, both of whom were then lying in a drainage ditch; that Gregg placed the gun to one man's head and pulled the trigger and then went quickly to the other one and placed the gun at his head and pulled the trigger again; that he took their money and whatever contents were in their pockets; and that he then told Allen to get in the car, and they drove away.

Following Gregg's conviction at trial, the judge followed the post-*Furman* guidelines crafted by the Georgia legislature to ensure that the jury, as the sentencing authority, was given "adequate information and guidance" by being "apprised of the information relevant to the imposition of sentence and provided

with standards to guide its use of the information."[1] The jury sentenced Gregg to be executed.

When the sentence was affirmed by the Georgia Supreme Court, Gregg petitioned the U.S. Supreme Court, which held that "the statutory system under which Gregg was sentenced to death does not violate the Constitution"[2] and which affirmed the judgment of the Georgia Supreme Court. That ruling made Gregg the first person in the United States whose death sentence was upheld at all appellate levels since the *de facto* abolition of the death penalty that had resulted from *Furman*.

On December 13, 2007, New Jersey repealed its capital punishment law, thereby reducing the number of death penalty states to 36; additionally, the U.S. government and the U.S. military have the death penalty. Courts (and courts-martial) in all 38 death penalty jurisdictions currently operate under statutes adopted after *Furman*.

Despite being the first person sentenced to death after the moratorium, Gregg did not die by legal execution. On July 29, 1980, the night before his scheduled execution, Gregg and three other death-row inmates escaped from the Georgia State Prison in Reidsville—the first death-row breakout in Georgia history. Later that night, Gregg was beaten to death in a bar fight in North Carolina. ■

Notes
1. *Gregg v. Georgia*, 428 U.S. 153 (1976).
2. Ibid.

DISCUSSION QUESTIONS

1. What is a "bifurcated capital trial process"? What is the alternative to such a process?

2. Why did the U.S. Supreme Court uphold the use of such a bifurcated trial process in the case discussed in this feature?

3. Can you think of any ways in which the death penalty decision-making process could be improved? If so, what would they be?

Library Extra
14–3 Capital Punishment in the United States

Library Extra
14–4 Massachusetts Recidivism Study

Death is generally not acceptable for less serious forms of homicide. For example, in *Coker* v. *Georgia*,[29] the Court held that a sentence of death for the crime of rape against an adult woman was grossly disproportionate and was in violation of the Eighth and Fourteenth Amendments to the U.S. Constitution. The Court has also since ruled that it is unconstitutional to execute mentally retarded individuals,[30] offenders who committed their capital crime under the age of 18,[31] and offenders convicted of child rape.[32]

Several other important death penalty decisions issued by the Supreme Court over the years include the following (this is not an exhaustive list):

Woodson v. *North Carolina*:[33] In *Woodson*, decided on the same day as *Gregg*, the Court held that mandatory death penalty laws—those that do not take aggravating and mitigating circumstances into account—are unconstitutional.

Thompson v. *Oklahoma*:[34] According to *Thompson*, the Eighth Amendment is violated when a juvenile who is 15 years old or younger when he or she commits murder is sentenced to death.

Ford v. *Wainwright*:[35] The ruling in *Ford* held that the wording of the Eighth Amendment prevents the state from inflicting the death penalty on someone who is insane at the time of execution.

Cabana v. *Bullock*:[36] Based on *Cabana*, the death penalty cannot be imposed on a mere accomplice unless there is a clear finding that the accomplice killed, attempted to kill, or intended to kill the victim.

Tison v. *Arizona*:[37] It was ruled in *Tison* that the death penalty can legally be imposed in the absence of an intent to kill if the defendant substantially participates in a felony that is likely to result in a loss of life.

Enmund v. *Florida*:[38] According to *Enmund*, it is unconstitutional to impose death on a person who participates in a felony that results in murder without considering the participant's level of intent.

Roper v. *Simmons*:[39] It is a violation of the Eighth Amendment to sentence to death a defendant who committed a capital crime while under the age of 18.

Kennedy v. *Louisiana*:[40] The death penalty cannot be imposed when the victim's life was not taken.

Learning Objective 3
Summarize the sentencing process and the factors that influence sentencing.

concurrent sentence
One of two or more sentences imposed at the same time, after conviction for more than one offense, and served at the same time; also, a new sentence for a new conviction, imposed on a person already under sentence for a previous offense, and served at the same time as the previous sentence.

consecutive sentence
One of two or more sentences imposed at the same time, after conviction for more than one offense, and served in sequence with the other sentence; also, a new sentence for a new conviction, imposed on a person already under sentence for a previous offense, and added to the previous sentence, thus increasing the maximum time the offender may be confined or under supervision.

DETERMINATION OF THE APPROPRIATE SENTENCE

A number of factors, including the seriousness of the crime, the defendant's prior record, the defendant's possible threat to the community, and the defendant's degree of remorse for committing the crime, influence the final sentencing decision. Even age, family ties, employment status, and other demographic factors can come into play. A guilty plea may result in a different sentence than a finding of guilty in a trial court because it suggests that the defendant is willing to admit what he or she did, so he or she should be treated more leniently.

Sentencing can also be determined by the number of separate crimes growing out of a single criminal act. If a defendant is convicted of killing another person with a handgun, he or she may be sentenced for the killing as well as unlawful possession of a handgun if the law prohibits the latter. In such a situation, the judge may sentence the defendant to consecutive or concurrent imprisonment. With a **concurrent sentence**, the defendant would serve time for both crimes at the same time; by contrast, **consecutive sentences** are served back-to-back. In our example, the defendant would be sentenced to prison for the killing; when that term is completed, the sentence for possession will begin.

Sentencing can be influenced by the defendant's degree of cooperation with the police. For example, the Supreme Court has held that the sentencing judge is permitted to consider the defendant's refusal to cooperate with the police in investigating his or her crime.[41] Still other factors, such as the offender's mental status, can also be considered; for example, it has been held that mentally ill individuals can be held in custody (such as in a mental institution) for a longer term than a traditional prison sentence for the crime charged,[42] something that often happens following insanity pleas.

Most jurisdictions have what is known as the **going rate** for a criminal offense,[43] which is an unwritten, informal agreement between members of the courtroom work group (judge, defense attorney, and prosecutor) as to what a typical case is worth. Usually, if the seriousness of the offense and the offender's background characteristics are known, one can predict, with a fair degree of accuracy, what type of sentence will be imposed. The going rate is a by-product of interactions of the courtroom work group (introduced back in Chapter 2).

Judges' sentencing decisions can also be influenced by **victim impact statements**, statements made by victims to the court regarding the effects that the crime had on them (and on other victims). For example, Proposition 8, adopted by California voters in 1982, provides that "the victim of any crime, or the next kin of the victim . . . has the right to attend all sentencing proceedings . . . [and] to reasonably express his or her views concerning the crime, the person responsible, and the need for restitution."[44] The judge is then required to take the victim's statement into account when deciding on a sentence for the offender.

going rate
An unwritten informal agreement between members of the courtroom workgroup (judge, defense attorney, and prosecutor) as to what the appropriate punishment should be for a particular type of case.[iii]

victim impact statement
The in-court use of victim- or survivor-supplied information by sentencing authorities seeking to make an informed sentencing decision.

Constitutional Rights during Sentencing

Convicted criminals enjoy several important constitutional rights during the sentencing process. First, the double jeopardy provision of the Fifth Amendment applies. Further, defendants are entitled to a reasonable punishment for their crimes; that is, punishment should reflect the seriousness of the crime. For example, in *Solem v. Helm*,[45] the Court held that a life sentence for the defendant's seventh nonviolent offense was unconstitutional and prohibited the sentence, stating that the defendant "received the penultimate sentence for relatively minor criminal conduct."[46] Yet the Court has sanctioned life sentences for possessing cocaine[47] and even petty theft with a prior conviction,[48] so it is not entirely clear what "reasonable" really means. Other rights for convicted criminals include the following:

- The defendant has the right to participate in the sentencing process.[49]
- The defendant should be advised of his or her right to appeal.[50]
- The defendant has the right to have counsel present at the sentencing hearing to argue on his or her behalf. The Sixth Amendment right to counsel operates essentially the same way at sentencing as it does at trial.[51]
- The defendant also has the right to ask the sentencing judge to ignore past convictions that were obtained in violation of the right to counsel. For example, in *United States v. Tucker*,[52] the Supreme Court invalidated an individual's 25-year sentence because the sentencing judge arrived at the sentence by considering the defendant's past convictions where he was not afforded counsel.

APPEALS

An appeal occurs when an appellate court (such as one of the federal courts of appeal) examines a lower court's decision in order to determine whether the proper procedure was followed or the law was correctly applied. When a defendant appeals, he or she is claiming that the court made an error. Appeals guarantee that a defendant who is found guilty can challenge his or her conviction; they also guarantee that another judge or panel of judges, disconnected from the initial trial, will review the lower court's decision.

Learning Objective 4
Describe the purposes and types of appeals, and the appeals process.

Web Extra
14–3 Center on Wrongful Convictions

Although the prospect of an appeal is important, the Constitution is silent—nowhere does it state that appeals are warranted, and it certainly does not specify that a certain number of appeals will be granted to each convicted criminal. As the Supreme Court has stated, "A review by an appellate court of the final judgment in a criminal case, however grave the offense of which the accused is convicted, was not at common law, and is not now, a necessary element of due process of law."[53]

Web Extra
14-4 The Innocence Project

Types of Appeals

Despite the Supreme Court's view that appeals are not constitutionally guaranteed, every state as well as the federal government have rules providing a certain number of appeals to convicted criminals. At each of these levels, convicted criminals are usually granted at least one appeal of right as well as at least one discretionary appeal.

appeal of right
An appeal that is automatically granted to the defendant by law (i.e., one that *must* be heard by an appellate court); also called *direct appeal.*

discretionary appeal
An appeal that the appellate courts can decide—based on their own discretion—whether to grant a hearing.

An **appeal of right**, or direct appeal, is one automatically granted to the defendant by law, meaning that an appeal of right *must* be heard by an appellate court; it is not up to the appellate court to decide whether to hear an appeal of right. By contrast, a **discretionary appeal** is an appeal that the appellate courts can decide—based on their own discretion—whether to grant a hearing for. Appeals of right are limited, but discretionary appeals can be filed several times, provided that each appeal is not redundant.

Consequences of Appeals

When a defendant appeals a decision, there are a number of possible consequences of that choice. In the typical appeal, the defendant seeks to correct a decision by the lower court that he or she perceives to be in error. In such instances, the appellate court will either affirm or reverse the lower court's decision. It may also remand the case for further proceedings consistent with its opinion.

trial *de novo*
A term that literally means "a new trial." The term is applied to cases that are retried on appeal, as opposed to those that are simply reviewed on the record.

Another consequence of an appeal can be a **trial *de novo***, in which a defendant is essentially requesting a new independent trial at the appellate level. Trials *de novo* are rare, and they are usually limited to appeals of decisions arising from misdemeanor courts of limited jurisdiction. By contrast, rarely—if ever—will a convicted felon succeed in obtaining a trial *de novo* in an appellate court, primarily because the appellate court interprets the law, not the facts. It is the job of the trial court to determine guilt based on the facts.

Whether the defendant seeks a new trial or simply seeks a review of the trial court's decision on some matter, it is not the case that the defendant will always go free if a decision is returned in his or her favor. If the appellate court considers a lower court's decision not to exclude evidence and decides that the lower court's decision should be reversed, this means that the evidence should have been excluded, not that the defendant should be acquitted. For example, in the famous *Miranda* v. *Arizona*[54] case, where the *Miranda* rights came from, the Supreme Court did not free Ernesto Miranda; instead, it remanded his case for a new trial, and he was subsequently found guilty and sentenced to more than 20 years in prison.

People sometimes wonder what happens to convicted defendants while they are appealing. In almost all cases, they serve out the conditions of their sentence. For instance, assume that a defendant appeals his guilty conviction on the grounds that he was denied counsel at trial and also assume that the defendant's appeal has merit. If he was sentenced to prison following trial, this is where he will remain until the appeal is heard, if it ever is. For a select few convicts, the judge will issue a *stay*, which means the convicted individuals will not serve time in prison prior to the time their appeal is heard. If they are granted at all, stays of this nature are reserved for individuals who pose a low flight risk, but most convicted criminals are considered flight risks, which is why stays of imprisonment are rarely granted.

Appellate Process

Even though the Supreme Court has held that appeals are not constitutionally required, it has held on a number of occasions that when appeals are permissible, the government must follow certain procedures. Subsequent decisions dealing with the defendant can be placed in three categories: (1) the defendant's access to trial transcripts, (2) the defendant's right to counsel, and (3) the defendant's right to be free from government retaliation for successful appeals. Before these procedural issues can be considered, the appellant (the defendant who has been convicted and is now appealing) must file notice of an appeal; an example of such a notice from the U.S. District Court for the Western District of Wisconsin is presented in Figure 14–1.

Access to Trial Transcripts In *Griffin v. Illinois*,[55] the Supreme Court considered whether an Illinois appellate procedure that required the defendant to produce transcripts of the trial—even if the defendant could not afford to do so—violated the Constitution. It struck down the procedure, claiming that the government cannot impose a restriction on the right to appeal "in a way that discriminates against some convicted defendants on account of their poverty."[56] In a related case, decided sometime later, the Court invalidated a state procedure that allowed defense counsel rather than an indigent defendant to decide whether an appeal could continue with an incomplete trial transcript.[57] An actual "transcript order form," from the Tenth Circuit Court of Appeals, is presented in Figure 14–2.

APPENDIX OF FORMS TO FEDERAL
RULES OF APPELLATE PROCEDURE

FORM 1.
NOTICE OF APPEAL TO A COURT OF APPEALS
FROM A JUDGMENT OR ORDER OF A DISTRICT COURT

United States District Court for the Western District of Wisconsin

---

A.B.,

        Plaintiff(s),

    v.

C.D.,

        Defendant(s)

File Number _____

Notice of Appeal

Notice is hereby given that (here name all parties taking the appeal) (plaintiffs) (defendants) in the above named case* hereby appeal to the United States Court of Appeals for the
_____ Circuit (from the final judgment) (from an order (describing it)) entered in this action on the ____ day of _____, _____.

(s) _____
Attorney for _____
Address: _____

* See Rule 3(c) for permissible ways of identifying appellants.

FIGURE 14–1

Notice of Appeal

Source: www.wiwd
.uscourts.gov/assets/pdf/
form-1-1999-09-29.pdf.
(accessed September, 9,
2013.)

NOTICE OF TRANSCRIPT ORDER FORM

PART I—TO BE COMPLETED BY APPELLANT WITHIN TEN DAYS OF FILING OF NOTICE OF APPEAL.
TO BE COMPLETED BY APPELLEE WITHIN TEN DAYS AFTER SERVICE.

Short Title: _____

Bankruptcy Court Number: _____

Name of Attorney: _____Name of Law Firm: _____

Address of Firm: _____Telephone of Firm: _____

Attorneys for: _____

Name of Court Reporter: _____Telephone of Reporter: _____

PART II—COMPLETE SECTION A OR SECTION B.
SECTION A—I HAVE NOT ORDERED A TRANSCRIPT BECAUSE:

☐ A transcript is not necessary for this appeal, or

☐ The necessary transcript is already on file in Bankruptcy Court, or

☐ The necessary transcript was ordered previously in appeal number_____.

SECTION B—I HEREBY ORDER THE FOLLOWING TRANSCRIPT:
(Specify the date and proceeding in the space below)

☐ Opening Statements: _____

☐ Trial Proceedings: _____

☐ Closing Arguments: _____

☐ Other Proceedings: _____

(Attach additional pages if necessary)

☐ **Appellant**   ☐ **Appellee**   **will pay the cost of the transcript.**

CERTIFICATE OF COMPLIANCE

My signature on this form constitutes my agreement to pay for the transcript ordered on this form. I also certify that I have read the instructions on this form and that copies of this transcript order form have been served on the court reporter (if transcript ordered), the Clerk of the United States Bankruptcy Court, and all parties. I further certify that satisfactory arrangements for payment for any transcript ordered have been made with the court reporter(s).

Signature of Ordering Party: _____ Date: _____

PART III—TO BE COMPLETED BY THE REPORTER

Upon completion, please file original with the Clerk of the United States Bankruptcy Court. and one copy with the Clerk of the Tenth Circuit Bankruptcy Appellate Panel.
Date arrangements for payment completed: _____
Estimated completion date: _____Estimated number of pages: _____
I certify that I have read the instructions and that adequate arrangements for payment have been made.
Signature of Court Reporter: _____ Date: _____

FIGURE 14–2

Example of a Trial Transcript Order Form (Eleventh Circuit)

Source: www.flnd.uscourts.gov/forms/Attorney/ECCA_transcript_form_fillable.pdf (accessed February 28, 2013).

Right to Counsel Criminal defendants enjoy their Sixth Amendment right to counsel under a number of circumstances, yet the Sixth Amendment expressly states that this right applies only in "criminal prosecutions." Despite this limitation, the Supreme Court has required that counsel be provided to indigent defendants on appeal.

In *Douglas v. California*,[58] the Court concluded that the government must provide indigent defendants with counsel to assist in their appeals of right, stating that "where the merits of the *one and only* appeal an indigent has as of right are decided without benefit of counsel, . . . an unconstitutional line has been drawn between rich and poor."[59] The Court has also held that the Constitution requires counsel—particularly effective counsel—for nonindigent defendants in their appeals of right.[60]

The Supreme Court has held that counsel is *not* constitutionally guaranteed in *discretionary* appeals:

> A defendant in respondent's circumstances is not denied meaningful access to the State Supreme Court simply because the State does not appoint counsel to aid him in seeking review in that court, since at that stage, under North Carolina's multitiered appellate system, he will have, at the very least, a transcript or other record of the trial proceedings, a brief in the Court of Appeals setting forth his claims of error, and frequently an opinion by that court disposing of his case, materials which, when supplemented by any *pro se* submission that might be made, would provide the Supreme Court with an adequate basis for its decision to grant or deny review under its standards of whether the case has "significant public interest," involves "legal principles of major significance," or likely conflicts with a previous Supreme Court decision.[61]

Government Retaliation Several times the Supreme Court has dealt with retaliation by the prosecution for successful defense appeals. The first noteworthy case in this regard was *North Carolina v. Pierce*,[62] where a defendant was reconvicted after a successful appeal and was actually punished more harshly the second time around. The Court concluded that due process required that the "defendant be freed of apprehension of such a retaliatory motivation on the part of the sentencing judge."[63] In a related case, *Blackledge v. Perry*,[64] the Court ruled against a prosecutor's decision to increase the charge against a defendant who was convicted but who appealed to a higher court for a trial *de novo*; the Court held that "upping the ante" in this fashion, simply because the defendant exercised his right to appeal, was unconstitutional.

By contrast, there have been a few cases where the Supreme Court has held that vindictiveness cannot be inferred from the judge's or jury's decision to increase a defendant's sentence following appeal. For instance, in *Colten v. Kentucky*,[65] the Court held that a judge did not act vindictively by increasing the defendant's sentence following his trial *de novo*, and in a similar case (*Chaffin v. Stynchcombe*),[66] the Court held that a jury's decision to increase the defendant's sentence in his trial *de novo* was constitutional.

In these cases, the sentencing authority was disconnected from the first trial. For example, a different judge sentenced Colten the second time around, and a second jury convicted the defendant in the other case following his trial *de novo*. What if, by contrast, the same judge who presided over the defendant's first trial then decides the defendant's sentence following an appeal? This question was answered in yet another case—*Texas v. McCullough*—where the Court held that the trial judge had no motivation to be vindictive.[67] Importantly, the defendant's first sentence was decided by a jury, and the judge only *presided* over the first trial. Had the judge actually handed down the defendant's sentence in both trials, the second increased sentence probably would have been considered vindictive.

Timing of Appeals The defense can appeal at one of two stages. An appeal can be filed prior to the reading of the verdict, that is, prior to adjudication; an appeal can also be filed following adjudication. The image of the typical appeal is one filed after adjudication, but there can be reasons to appeal before adjudication:

1. *Appeals before adjudication.* Appeals filed prior to adjudication are known as **interlocutory appeals**. In general, these appeals will succeed only if they are important and unrelated to the cause of action; that is, appeals prior to adjudication must deal with critical constitutional questions and have nothing to do with determining the defendant's guilt. Otherwise, defendants face what is known as the **final judgment rule**, which generally limits appeals until the court hands down its final judgment as to the defendant's guilt.

   In *Stack* v. *Boyle*,[68] the Court held that the defendant could appeal a judge's decision rejecting his argument that bail was excessive, in apparent violation of the Eighth Amendment. The Court believed that the trial judge's decision on this matter was more or less independent of deciding the defendant's guilt. It also felt that delaying appeal until after adjudication would make it pointless; a bail determination after a guilty verdict would have virtually no bearing on anything.

   In *Abney* v. *United States*,[69] the Court held that a defendant's appeal of a preadjudication order denying him dismissal of his indictment on double jeopardy grounds was permissible. The reason for this decision should be fairly obvious: If the protection against double jeopardy is to have any meaning, then defendants who claim double jeopardy ought to be able to appeal before the second conviction is handed down; otherwise, the appellate courts would be considering whether a defendant's Fifth Amendment protection was denied in hindsight, not exactly a preferable approach.

   An example of a preadjudication appeal that did *not* succeed can be found in *Carroll* v. *United States*.[70] There, the Court held that a defendant cannot appeal a decision on preadjudication search-and-seizure motions until after final adjudication takes place; in other words, the Court felt that appeals of a decision addressing evidence critical to the defendant's case are not sufficiently "independent" of the trial.

   In *DiBella* v. *United States*,[71] the Court held that a judge's preadjudication decision not to suppress evidence following the defendant's assertion that his Fourth Amendment rights were violated was not appealable until after trial. It felt that "appellate intervention makes for truncated presentation of the issue of admissibility, because the legality of the search too often cannot truly be determined until the evidence at the trial has brought all circumstances to light."[72]

   Despite the obvious time- and resource-saving benefits of restricting preadjudication appeals, requiring that most appeals be filed after trial can have serious consequences for the defendant. Many defendants who are found guilty on serious charges go to prison and are forced to pursue their appeals there. Given that most appeals—especially those that raise constitutional questions and ultimately reach the Supreme Court—can take several years, people who are wrongfully convicted can languish in prison for several years.

2. *Appeals after adjudication.* Appeals filed after adjudication are subject to few restrictions, and there appear to be few Supreme Court cases addressing postadjudication appeals. However, postadjudication appeals are almost limitless in terms of their possible substance—anything from the trial (based on the transcripts that the defense must be given in order to mount its appeal) that the defense perceives to be in error can be appealed. See Box 14–3 for a list of the constitutional rights violations that can serve as the basis for an appeal.

BOX 14–3 Frequently Used Grounds for Appeals and *Habeas Corpus* Petitions

1. Conviction obtained by plea of guilty that was unlawfully induced or not made voluntarily with understanding of the nature of the charge and the consequences of the plea

2. Conviction obtained by use of coerced confession

3. Conviction obtained by use of evidence gained pursuant to an unconstitutional search and seizure

4. Conviction obtained by use of evidence obtained pursuant to an unlawful arrest

5. Conviction obtained by a violation of the privilege against self-incrimination

6. Conviction obtained by the unconstitutional failure of the prosecution to disclose to the defendant evidence favorable to the defendant

7. Conviction obtained by a violation of the protection against double jeopardy

8. Conviction obtained by action of a grand or petit jury that was unconstitutionally selected and impaneled

9. Denial of effective assistance of counsel

10. Denial of right of appeal ■

Source: Adapted from www.courtswv.gov/legal-community/court-rules/habeas/WRIT_HC.PDF (accessed February 28, 2013).

Prosecutorial Appeals The prosecution is usually barred from appealing a defendant's conviction because of the double jeopardy clause of the Fifth Amendment, but other trial court rulings besides those bearing on the question of guilt can sometimes be appealed by the prosecution:

> [A]ppeals by the government in criminal cases are something unusual, exceptional, not favored. The history shows resistance of the Court to the opening of an appellate route for the Government until it was plainly provided by the Congress, and after that a close restriction of its uses to those authorized by statute.[73]

In other words, appeals by the prosecution are possible in certain situations but only as authorized by state or federal law.

Section 18 U.S.C.A., Section 3731, of the Federal Criminal Code provides for interlocutory prosecution appeals of a district court's decision to suppress or exclude evidence from trial. These types of appeals are permissible according to law because if the defendant is acquitted following trial, it will be unlikely that the prosecution could appeal the defendant's conviction because of the double jeopardy clause. Defendants cannot assert double jeopardy protection at preadjudication hearings, which is why it behooves the prosecution to appeal before the end of the trial. Indeed, many of the Supreme Court cases encountered in this book and elsewhere arrived before the Court because the prosecution disagreed with a trial judge's decision to exclude or suppress evidence.

Other prosecutorial appeals besides those addressing decisions to exclude or suppress evidence are severely restricted because of double jeopardy. The most common type of prosecution appeal is one addressing a judge's decision on whether to permit or exclude evidence the prosecution wishes to use against the accused. In criminal procedure, when judges exclude or suppress evidence, it is because the police acted in violation of some constitutional provision.

Harmless Error An appeal may not succeed simply because the appellate court is unwilling to hear it, as is the case with many discretionary appeals. However, even when the appellate court agrees to hear an appeal and even if it agrees with the defendant's position, it may decide that the defendant should remain in prison or otherwise receive the same

harmless error
A mistake at the trial court level that has little practical consequences in terms of deciding whether the defendant is guilty or innocent.

sentence. In such a situation, the appellate court is saying that the trial court's decision was a **harmless error**, a mistake at the trial level that has little practical consequence in terms of deciding whether the defendant is guilty or innocent.

Deciding what constitutes a harmless error requires first determining what type of error is alleged. Two types of errors can be discerned: constitutional and nonconstitutional. Constitutional errors result from constitutional rights violations, such as denying the accused the right to confront adverse witnesses at trial; nonconstitutional errors refer to errors not of a constitutional magnitude, such as a trial court deciding to admit hearsay evidence. The latter decision would be nonconstitutional because there is no constitutional prohibition against hearsay evidence in the courtroom.

Once one decides the type of error alleged, the appropriate test for determining whether the error is harmless must be used. Two Supreme Court cases are helpful in this regard: *Kotteakos* v. *United States*,[74] which set the test for deciding what constitutes nonconstitutional harmless error, and *Chapman* v. *California*,[75] which set the test for constitutional error. Let us consider each case briefly.

In *Kotteakos*, the Supreme Court held that nonconstitutional harmless error occurs when it does not influence the jury but instead has a "very slight effect" on the outcome of the trial. The Court stated that "if one cannot say, with fair assurance, after pondering all that happened without stripping the erroneous action from the whole, that the judgment was not substantially swayed by the error, it is impossible to conclude that substantial rights were not affected."[76]

In *Chapman*, the Court concluded that the test for constitutional harmless error is requiring the prosecution to prove "beyond a reasonable doubt that the error complained of did not contribute to the verdict obtained."[77] This test is reserved for what could be termed "modest" violations of constitutional rights; however, in situations where fundamental constitutional rights are violated, no harmless error test is required.

The *Chapman* decision provides a clear example of what can be considered a harmful error. At issue is what the prosecutor said during closing arguments, such as when he repeatedly referred to the defendant's refusal to take the stand and testify. The Court reversed the defendant's conviction, reasoning that "though the case in which this occurred presented a reasonably strong 'circumstantial web of evidence' against petitioners, it was also a case in which, absent the constitutionally forbidden comments, honest fair-minded jurors might very well have brought in not-guilty verdicts."[78]

Learning Objective 5

Explain *habeas corpus* and the *habeas corpus* process.

habeas corpus
A term that literally means "you have the body." It is a form of collateral attack that allows someone to challenge the constitutionality of his or her confinement.[iv]

collateral attack
An attempt to avoid or invalidate a judicial determination. *Habeas corpus*, a form of collateral attack, seeks to invalidate a criminal conviction by declaring one's confinement unconstitutional.

HABEAS CORPUS

According to the Constitution, convictions can also be challenged via a writ of **habeas corpus**, which is term that literally means "you have the body" and which is a form of **collateral attack**, allowing one to challenge the constitutionality of one's confinement.[79] Note that this is different from an appeal because if the convicted person appeals, he or she is claiming that the trial court made an error. *Habeas corpus* occurs farther down the road, once appeals have been exhausted and the individual is incarcerated.

Habeas corpus plays out as follows. First, the accused petitions one of the federal district courts (or the U.S. Supreme Court) and asks the court (or Court) to issue a "writ of *habeas corpus*." The most common grounds for *habeas corpus* petitions appear in Box 14–3. Then, if the court (or Court) decides to issue the writ, the petitioner is brought before the court (Court) so that the constitutionality of his or her confinement can be reviewed.

Given that the Supreme Court and the federal appellate courts can hear only so many cases, most *habeas corpus* petitions are filed with the federal district courts. *Habeas corpus* petitions are limited to constitutional claims, and it is totally within the discretion of the court that is petitioned to decide whether the writ will be issued. The Constitution provides that the "privilege of the Writ of Habeas Corpus shall not be suspended," but this has been interpreted to mean that defendants can submit *habeas* petitions, not that the accused will get his or her day in court.

Is *Habeas Corpus* Important?

On several occasions, the Supreme Court has emphasized the importance of the writ of *habeas corpus*. In *Sanders v. United States*, the Court stated, "Conventional notions of finality of litigation have no place where life or liberty is at stake and infringement of constitutional rights is alleged."[80] The Court has also ruled that the writ is necessary to provide "adequate protection of constitutional rights."[81]

More recently, the Court has intimated that *habeas* review should be qualified. In particular, it has held that writs should not be liberally issued for claims arising from state courts: "Despite differences in institutional environment and the unsympathetic attitude to federal constitutional claims of some state judges in years past, we are unwilling to assume that there now exists a general lack of appropriate sensitivity to constitutional rights in the trial and appellate courts of the several States."[82]

These conflicting perspectives have influenced a number of important Supreme Court cases addressing the constitutional right to *habeas corpus*. Recently, the Court has placed limitations on the scope of the writ, and the Antiterrorism and Effective Death Penalty Act of 1996 has also had important effects on *habeas corpus*.

Limitations on *Habeas Corpus*

The Supreme Court has restricted the right to *habeas corpus* in at least four ways:

1. The Court has limited the types of claims that can succeed.
2. The Court has held that *habeas* review may not be granted if the petitioner fails to submit a claim within the time frame specified by state law.
3. It is generally necessary for convicted individuals to exhaust all state remedies before federal *habeas* review will be granted.
4. Restrictions have been imposed in situations where prisoners file multiple *habeas* petitions.

Ineligible Petitions Several types of *habeas corpus* petitions will not succeed. Here is one example: "Where the State has provided an opportunity for full and fair litigation of a Fourth Amendment claim," a federal court should not issue a writ of *habeas corpus*.[83] Another is that *habeas* review will be granted only if it raises a federal constitutional question[84]; claims involving harmless errors will not be granted review.[85] There are other types of ineligible petitions, but they get rather tedious and are beyond the scope of an introductory text of this nature.

Importance of Timing *Habeas corpus* petitions must generally be filed within a certain specified time period after the trial or the sentencing hearing. When a defendant fails to appeal or file a *habeas* petition within the specified time period, he or she is said to have "defaulted," that is, given up his or her right to appeal or petition for *habeas* review. At one time, when it was trying to decide whether *habeas* review should be granted following default, the Supreme Court focused on the state rule or statute that imposed time restrictions.[86] If the statute was problematic, then review could be granted.

The current standard for determining whether *habeas* review should be granted is known as the "actual innocence" standard[87]: "[T]he prisoner must show a fair probability that, in light of all the evidence, including that alleged to have been illegally admitted (but with due regard to any unreliability of it) and evidence tenably claimed to have been wrongly excluded or to have become available only after the trial, the trier of the facts would have entertained a reasonable doubt of his guilt."[88] In other words, when a prisoner has failed to file a *habeas* petition in a timely manner, he or she may still succeed in doing so provided that the petition sets forth sufficient facts as to the prisoner's "actual innocence."

Importantly, the appropriate standard of proof for granting review under this new rule is a "fair probability" of the prisoner's innocence. A different standard has been imposed in death penalty cases, however. In *Schlup* v. *Delo*,[89] the Court held that in order to be granted *habeas* review, individuals convicted of capital crimes must show that "it is more likely than not that no reasonable juror would have convicted [the petitioners]."[90]

Exhaustion of State Remedies Before *habeas corpus* becomes an option, convicted criminals typically must exhaust all available state-level appeals. The Supreme Court has stated that "ordinarily an application for *habeas corpus* by one detained under a state court judgment of conviction will be entertained . . . only after all state remedies available, including all appellate remedies in the state courts and in this Court by appeal or writ of certiorari, have been exhausted."[91] Most prisoners are denied *habeas* review until they have exhausted state-level remedies because imposing such a restriction ensures that the states can correct federal constitutional violations. If a federal court sees fit to grant a *habeas* petition before a prisoner has exhausted all available state-level appeals, that is its prerogative.[92]

There is even a federal statute addressing *habeas corpus*, stating that *habeas corpus* is not available to state prisoners "unless it appears that the applicant has exhausted the remedies available in the courts of the State, or that there is either an absence of available State corrective process or the existence of circumstances rendering such process ineffective to protect the rights of the prisoner."[93]

Multiple Petitions The Supreme Court has permitted successive petitions—those raising the same issues—but the petitioner must show that he or she was not given a "full or fair" hearing on the petition the first time around or that there has been "an intervening change in the law or some other justification for having failed to raise a crucial point or argument in the prior application."[94] Later, the Court held that successive petitions raising the same issues must be supplemented with a "colorable showing of factual innocence,"[95] that is, a fairly clear indication that the petitioner is possibly innocent.

The Supreme Court has also held that successive petitions making *different* claims each time are seriously restricted. For instance, if a prisoner accidentally fails to raise a claim the first time around, it will probably not be permitted the second time. Also, a successive petition raising different issues should be dismissed if "the applicant has . . . on the earlier application deliberately withheld the newly asserted ground *or* otherwise abused the writ."[96]

Antiterrorism and Effective Death Penalty Act (AEDPA)
The U.S. legislation that was passed in the wake of the bombings at the World Trade Center in 1993 and the Oklahoma City federal building in 1995 that sought to toughen federal antiterrorism capabilities.

Antiterrorism and Effective Death Penalty Act of 1996

Habeas corpus has become even more clouded in light of the **Antiterrorism and Effective Death Penalty Act** (AEDPA) of 1996, which was passed in the wake of the infamous Oklahoma City bombing. The bombing was arguably America's first real run-in with terrorism. Even though it was *domestic* terrorism (as opposed to international terrorism, as on 9/11), it alerted policy makers to the fact that people can inflict catastrophic damage with relatively crude weaponry. The bombing led to numerous proposals in Congress for how to address terrorism. Early proposals called for drastic and controversial measures designed to curb the new terrorist threat. Several months after the bombing, however, the legislation agreed to by both the House and the Senate was significantly watered down; it was signed into law by President Clinton in April 1996.

AEDPA's supporters heralded it as a significant bipartisan achievement that would help root out terrorism, but critics of the new law claimed that it was so watered down that it had virtually nothing to do with terrorism. To an extent, the critics are correct because one of the most significant components of AEDPA places restrictions on *habeas corpus* petitions for death-row inmates. The reader can draw his or her own conclusion as to the relationship between *habeas corpus* and domestic terrorism, but it is worth considering AEDPA's effects at this point because it has altered the *habeas corpus* landscape in several unmistakable ways.

AEDPA's first change to *habeas corpus* procedure is that it permits review only when the state-level decision "(1) resulted in a decision that was contrary to, or involved an unreasonable application of, clearly established Federal law, as determined by the Supreme Court of the United States", or (2) "resulted in a decision that was based on an unreasonable determination of the facts in light of the evidence presented in the State court proceeding."[97] Perhaps the most significant AEDPA-related Supreme Court case to date, *Williams v. Taylor*,[98] sought to clarify this language, but it fell short. One critic stated that "the Supreme Court's *Williams* decision left many important questions unanswered and left an incoherent pattern of precedent, leaving the lower courts to fend for themselves in interpreting the meaning of [AEDPA]."[99]

Second, AEDPA alters *habeas* review in capital cases, that is, in cases where the accused is on death row. It provides that if a prisoner "defaults" and fails to submit a petition in a timely fashion, then review will be granted only when the prisoner's failure to file a petition is "(1) the result of State action in violation of the Constitution or laws of the United States," (2) "the result of the Supreme Court's recognition of a new Federal right that is made retroactively applicable," or (3) "based on a factual predicate that could not have been discovered through the exercise of due diligence in time to present the claim for State or Federal post-conviction review."[100]

AEDPA also places restrictions on successive *habeas corpus* petitions by stating that a "claim presented in a second or successive habeas corpus application shall be dismissed."[101] AEDPA further restricts successive petitions that raise different claims, a provision that was unsuccessfully challenged in the case of *Felker v. Turpin*.[102]

Third, AEDPA imposes strict filing deadlines for *habeas corpus* petitions: It requires that most *habeas corpus* petitions be filed within one year from the date of the final state-level appellate judgment. For death penalty cases, the legislation is even more restrictive: It requires that death-row petitions be filed within six months from the "final state court affirmance of the conviction and sentence on direct review or the expiration of the time for seeking review."[103] Both restrictions are intended to reduce the opportunities prisoners have to challenge their confinement and, in the case of death-row inmates, speed up execution. The Supreme Court has decided a number of AEDPA cases in recent years, but so far the legislation has not been overturned or significantly altered.[104] In fact, the Supreme Court has routinely denied *habeas corpus* petitions in light of AEDPA, including one filed by an offender who received a 50-year prison sentence for stealing $150 worth of videotapes and another by a 17-year-old who confessed to a murder following an interrogation in which no *Miranda* warnings were issued.[105]

CHAPTER 14 SUMMARY

1. SUMMARIZE THE GOALS OF SENTENCING

- Goals of sentencing include rehabilitation, retribution, incapacitation, and deterrence.
- General deterrence is intended to discourage others from committing crime. Specific deterrence is concerned with discouraging the individual offender from recidivating.

2. DESCRIBE THE DIFFERENT TYPES OF SENTENCES THAT CAN BE IMPOSED

- Types of sentences include monetary penalties (e.g., fines), probation, intermediate sanctions, shaming, forfeiture, prison sentences, and the death penalty.
- Fines are the most common form of punishment used in the criminal justice system today.

3. SUMMARIZE THE SENTENCING PROCESS AND THE FACTORS THAT INFLUENCE SENTENCING

- The appropriate sentence is determined based on several factors, most notably offense seriousness and the offender's prior record.
- Key constitutional rights during sentencing include (1) the right to not be put in jeopardy twice, (2) the right to a sentence conforming to the Eighth Amendment's proscription against cruel and unusual punishment, and (3) the right to counsel at sentencing-related hearings regardless of the defendant's ability to afford representation. There is scant scientific evidence that suggests that harsh sentences deter or prevent crime.

4. DESCRIBE THE PURPOSES AND TYPES OF APPEALS, AND THE APPEALS PROCESS

- There are two types of appeals. Direct appeals are authorized by law; discretionary appeals are heard only if the reviewing court grants a hearing.
- Appeals are concerned with lower courts' legal decisions, not questions of guilt or innocence. Consequently, offenders do not always go free as a result of successful appeals.
- Appeals can be filed by the defense and the prosecution, but the prosecution cannot appeal after adjudication.
- Appeals filed prior to adjudication are known as interlocutory appeals.
- Appellants must be given access to trial transcripts, they must have counsel to assist with their direct appeals, and they must be free from prosecution retaliation for successful appeals. Harmless errors will not result in successful appeals.

5. EXPLAIN HABEAS CORPUS AND THE HABEAS CORPUS PROCESS

- *Habeas corpus* is a constitutional right and provides a means of challenging the constitutionality of one's confinement, and it is the last resort for a prisoner after appeals fail. There are limitations on the types of petitions that can be filed, there are timing constraints, and multiple petitions are restricted. Moreover, petitioners must exhaust state remedies. The Antiterrorism and Effective Death Penalty Act of 1996 has also restricted *habeas corpus*.

KEY TERMS

aggravating
    circumstances, 379
Antiterrorism and Effective
    Death Penalty Act, 390
apology penalty, 374
appeal of right, 382
bifurcated trial, 378
civil forfeiture, 374
collateral attack, 388
concurrent sentence, 380
consecutive sentence, 380
control conditions, 372
criminal forfeiture, 374
day fine, 371

debasement penalty, 374
determinate sentence, 375
discretionary appeal, 382
final judgment rule, 386
fine, 371
forfeiture, 374
general deterrence, 371
going rate, 381
habeas corpus, 388
harmless error, 388
indeterminate sentence, 375
interlocutory appeal, 386
intermediate sanctions, 372
mandatory sentence, 375

mitigating circumstances, 379
net widening, 372
probation, 372
public-exposure
    penalty, 374
reform conditions, 372
sentencing guidelines, 375
shaming, 373
specific deterrence, 371
trial *de novo*, 382
U.S. Sentencing
    Commission, 375
victim impact
    statement, 381

REVIEW QUESTIONS

1. What sentencing goals does this chapter describe? How would you prioritize the goals of sentencing identified in this chapter?

2. Describe the process of criminal appeals. Can the government appeal the decision of a trial court? If so, under what circumstances?

3. What is *habeas corpus*? What are its consequences for the American system of justice? What are the limitations on *habeas corpus* described in this chapter?

WHAT WILL YOU DO?

You are a judge presiding over a criminal trial of a 30-year-old man who has just been convicted of robbery in the third degree (unarmed). Although a jury found him guilty, it is your responsibility under state law to impose sentence.

Your state uses a set of advisory guidelines that suggests a range of sentences appropriate for a wide variety of offenses. If the defendant had been convicted of armed robbery, state law would have specified that he serve a prison term of at least three years, but since his conviction was for strong-arm robbery in which no weapon was used, the sentencing guidelines allow a probationary term but include the possibility of imprisonment.

You feel obligated to follow the guidelines' recommendations, but you know that you will have to consider many things in deciding on an appropriate sentence. Although robbery is a serious offense, it is the first time that this defendant has been convicted of a crime; up until now, it seems that he has lived a fairly mundane existence.

A presentence report prepared by a probation and parole officer at your request examined the defendant's background and his current living arrangements. The report reveals, among other things, that the man has only a high school education but that he has worked at a number of different jobs over the past ten years and always had a good employment record. He appears to have strong family ties, and his wife spoke highly of him to the officer preparing the report, saying she hopes that "nothing bad happens to him."

At trial, you learned that the defendant's motivation in committing the robbery was apparently the need that he felt to take care of his wife and three children. A few weeks before the robbery, he had lost his most recent job, stocking shelves at a local supermarket. Although he had been a good employee and was always punctual (as was the case in his other jobs), the store for which he worked was experiencing financial hardship and had to let him and a number of other employees go.

You know from personal observation that the defendant is industrious, as you have occasionally witnessed him working in your own neighborhood doing odd jobs such as mowing lawns, repairing fences, and painting wood trim. On the other hand, although it was unusual in a case like this, the victim—a young mother—asked to make a victim impact statement prior to sentencing. Such a statement is permitted under a law in your state that supports a crime victim's right of allocution (or the right to be heard) following a defendant's conviction in felony cases.

In her statement, the female victim explained that she had been terrified by the incident and that she is now afraid to walk alone in public places, even in broad daylight. At the time of the robbery (which took place during the day), she had been carrying her infant daughter and feared that the defendant might somehow hurt the child—or even abduct her.

She tells you that although the defendant now seems meek and apologetic, he acted totally different during the incident, gruffly demanding her money and her credit cards. At one point, she became afraid that he would kidnap both her and her child and steal her car. Although she suffered no injury during the incident, she believed that both she and her child would be killed.

It is necessary to protect the community, she says. To personally give her peace of mind, she asks you to send this man to prison. Otherwise, she states, how can she or anyone else feel safe?

What will you do?

NOTES

i. S. T. Hillsman, "Fines and Day Fines," in M. Tonry and N. Morris, eds., *Crime and Justice: A Review of Research*, Vol. 12 (Chicago: University of Chicago Press, 1990); S. T. Hillsman, J. L. Sichel, and B. Mahoney, *Fines and Sentencing: A Study of the Use of the Fine as a Criminal Sanction* (New York: Vera Institute of Justice, 1984); S. G. Casale and S. T. Hillsman, *The Enforcement of Fines as Criminal Sanctions: The English Experience and Its Relevance to American Practice* (New York: Vera Institute of Justice, 1986).

ii. D. R. Karp, "The Judicial and Judicious Use of Shame Penalties," *Crime and Delinquency* 44(1998):277–294, 280–283.

iii. S. Walker, *Sense and Nonsense about Crime and Drugs*, 5th ed. (Belmont, CA: Wadsworth, 2001).

iv. U.S. Constitution, Article I, Section 9, clause 2.

1. House Bill 2393.
2. House Bill 5933.
3. Senate Bill 2476.
4. Marc Mauer, "Racial Impact Statements: Changing Policies to Address Disparities," *Criminal Justice*, Vol. 23, No. 4 (Winter 2009).
5. For more on other possible goals of sentencing, see L. J. Siegel and J. J. Senna, *Introduction to Criminal Justice*, 11th ed. (Belmont, CA: Cengage, 2008), pp. 23–29.
6. See, e.g., J. L. Worrall, *Crime Control in America: What Works?* (Boston: Allyn and Bacon, 2008), chap. 11.
7. A. von Hirsch, *Doing Justice: The Choice of Punishments* (New York: Hill and Wang, 1976), p. 46.
8. S. T. Hillsman, "Fines and Day Fines," in M. Tonry and N. Morris, eds., *Crime and Justice: A Review of Research*, Vol. 12 (Chicago: University of Chicago Press, 1990); S. T. Hillsman, J. L. Sichel, and B. Mahoney, *Fines and Sentencing: A Study of the Use of the Fine as a Criminal Sanction* (New York: Vera Institute of Justice, 1984); S. G. Casale and S. T. Hillsman, *The Enforcement of Fines as Criminal Sanctions: The English Experience and Its Relevance to American Practice* (New York: Vera Institute of Justice, 1986).
9. Sally T. Hillsman, Barry Mahoney, George Cole, and Bernard Auchter, *Fines as Criminal Sanctions* (Washington, DC: National Institute of Justice, 1987).
10. George F. Cole, *Innovations in Collecting and Enforcing Fines* (Washington, DC: National Institute of Justice, 1989).
11. Susan Turner and Judith Greene, "The FARE Probation Experiment: Implementation and Outcomes of Day Fines for Felony Offenders in Maricopa County," *Justice System Journal*, No. 1 (1999), pp. 1–22.
12. S. Turner and J. Petersilia, "Work Release in Washington: Effects on Recidivism and Corrections Costs," *Prison Journal*, Vol. 76 (1996), pp. 138–164.
13. Susan Turner and Joan Petersilia, *Day Fines in Four U.S. Jurisdictions* (Washington, DC: National Institute of Justice, 1996).

14. Laura M. Maruschak, *Probation and Parole in the United States, 2011* (Washington, DC: Bureau of Justice Statistics, 2012).
15. Ibid.
16. C. Camp and G. Camp, *The Corrections Yearbook 1998* (Middletown, CT: Criminal Justice Institute, Inc., 1999).
17. For a detailed review, see Worrall, *Crime Control in America*, chap. 10.
18. M. Tonry and M. Lynch, "Intermediate Sanctions," in M. Tonry, ed., *Crime and Justice: A Review of Research*, Vol. 20 (Chicago: University of Chicago Press, 1996), pp. 99–144.
19. H. E. Barnes, *The Story of Punishment: A Record of Man's Inhumanity to Man* (Boston: The Stratford Company, 1930).
20. A. Wooler, "Shame as Punishment: Common in Early America, It's Making a Comeback," *Fulton County Daily Reporter*, October 6, 1997, p. 5.
21. D. Y. Paschall, "Crime and Its Punishment in Colonial Virginia 1607–1776" (MA thesis, College of William and Mary).
22. D. R. Karp, "The Judicial and Judicious Use of Shame Penalties," *Crime and Delinquency*, Vol. 44 (1998), pp. 280–283.
23. H. Hyde, *Forfeiting Our Property Rights: Is Your Property Safe From Seizure?* (Washington, DC: Cato Institute, 1995).
24. *United States v. Booker*, No. 04-104 (2005).
25. *Furman v. Georgia*, 408 U.S. 238 (1972).
26. *Gregg v. Georgia*, 428 U.S. 153 (1976).
27. *Roberts v. Louisiana*, 97 S.Ct. 1993 (1977).
28. *Ring v. Arizona*, 122 S.Ct. 2428 (2002).
29. *Coker v. Georgia*, 433 U.S. 584 (1977).
30. *Atkins v. Virginia*, 122 S.Ct. 2242 (2002).
31. *Roper v. Simmons*, 543 U.S. 551 (2005).
32. *Kennedy v. Louisiana*, 07-343 (2008).
33. *Woodson v. North Carolina*, 428 U.S. 280 (1976).
34. *Thompson v. Oklahoma*, 108 S.Ct. 2687 (1988).
35. *Ford v. Wainwright*, 477 U.S. 399 (1986).
36. *Cabana v. Bullock*, 474 U.S. 376 (1986).
37. *Tison v. Arizona*, 107 S.Ct. 1714 (1987).
38. *Enmund v. Florida*, 458 U.S. 782 (1982).
39. *Roper v. Simmons*, 543 U.S. 551 (2005).
40. *Kennedy v. Louisiana*, 554 U.S. 407 (2008).
41. *Roberts v. United States*, 445 U.S. 552 (1980).
42. See, e.g., *Jones v. United States*, 103 S.Ct. 3043 (1983).
43. S. Walker, *Sense and Nonsense about Crime and Drugs*, 5th ed. (Belmont, CA: Wadsworth, 2001).
44. California Penal Code Section 1191.1.
45. *Solem v. Helm*, 463 U.S. 277 (1983).
46. Ibid., p. 305.
47. *Harmelin v. Michigan*, 501 U.S. 957 (1991).
48. *Lockyer v. Andrade*, 538 U.S. 63 (2003).

49. J. L. Worrall, *Criminal Procedure: From First Contact to Appeal*, 2nd ed. (Boston: Allyn and Bacon, 2007), p. 442.

50. Ibid.

51. Ibid.

52. *United States v. Tucker*, 404 U.S. 443 (1972).

53. *McKane v. Durston*, 153 U.S. 684 (1894), p. 687.

54. *Miranda v. Arizona*, 384 U.S. 436 (1966).

55. *Griffin v. Illinois*, 351 U.S. 12 (1956).

56. Ibid., p. 18.

57. *Entsminger v. Iowa*, 386 U.S. 748 (1967).

58. *Douglas v. California*, 372 U.S. 353 (1963).

59. Ibid., p. 357.

60. *Evitts v. Lucey*, 469 U.S. 387 (1985).

61. *Ross v. Moffitt*, 417 U.S. 600 (1974), pp. 614–615.

62. *North Carolina v. Pierce*, 395 U.S. 711 (1969).

63. Ibid., p. 725.

64. *Blackledge v. Perry*, 417 U.S. 21 (1974).

65. *Colten v. Kentucky*, 407 U.S. 104 (1972).

66. *Chaffin v. Stynchcombe*, 412 U.S. 17 (1973).

67. *Texas v. McCullough*, 475 U.S. 134 (1986).

68. *Stack v. Boyle*, 342 U.S. 1 (1951).

69. *Abney v. United States*, 431 U.S. 651 (1977).

70. *Carroll v. United States*, 354 U.S. 394 (1957).

71. *DiBella v. United States*, 369 U.S. 121 (1962).

72. Ibid., p. 129.

73. *Carroll v. United States*, 354 U.S. 394 (1957), p. 400.

74. *Kotteakos v. United States*, 328 U.S. 750 (1946).

75. *Chapman v. California*, 386 U.S. 18 (1967).

76. *Kotteakos v. United States*, 328 U.S. 750 (1946), p. 765.

77. *Chapman v. California*, 386 U.S. 18 (1967), p. 24.

78. Ibid., pp. 25–26.

79. U.S. Constitution, Article I, Section 9, clause 2.

80. *Sanders v. United States*, 373 U.S. 1 (1963), p. 8.

81. *Kaufman v. United States*, 394 U.S. 217 (1969), p. 226.

82. *Stone v. Powell*, 428 U.S. 465 (1976), p. 494, n. 35.

83. Ibid, p. 465.

84. *Herrera v. Collins*, 506 U.S. 390 (1993).

85. See, e.g., Worrall, *Criminal Procedure*, p. 461.

86. See, e.g., *Daniels v. Allen*, 344 U.S. 443 (1953).

87. See, e.g., *Murray v. Carrier*, 477 U.S. 478 (1986), and *Sawyer v. Whitley*, 505 U.S. 333 (1992).

88. *Kuhlmann v. Wilson*, 477 U.S. 436 (1986), p. 454, n. 17.

89. *Schlup v. Delo*, 513 U.S. 298 (1995).

90. Ibid., p. 327.

91. *Ex parte Hawk*, 321 U.S. 114 (1944), pp. 116–117.

92. *Granberry v. Greer*, 481 U.S. 129 (1987).

93. 28 U.S.C., Section 2254(b).

94. *Sanders v. United States*, 373 U.S. 1 (1963), p. 17.

95. *Kuhlmann v. Wilson*, 477 U.S. 436 (1986), p. 454.

96. *McCleskey v. Zant*, 499 U.S. 467 (1991), p. 486; also see *Slack v. McDaniel*, 529 U.S. 473 (2000).

97. 28 U.S.C.A., Section 2254(d).

98. *Williams v. Taylor*, 529 U.S. 420 (2000).

99. J. Park, "Supreme Court Review: *Yarborough v. Alvarado*: At the Crossroads of the 'Unreasonable Application' Provision of the Antiterrorism and Effective Death Penalty Act of 1996 and the Consideration of Juvenile Status in Custodial Determinations," *Journal of Criminal Law and Criminology*, Vol. 95 (2005), p. 875.

100. 28 U.S.C.S., Section 2264(a).

101. 28 U.S.C.A., Section 2244(b)(1).

102. *Felker v. Turpin*, 518 U.S. 651 (1996).

103. 28 U.S.C.S., Sections 2244(d)(1)(A) and 2263.

104. Examples include but are not limited to *Artuz v. Bennett*, 531 U.S. 4 (2000); *Slack v. McDaniel*, 529 U.S. 473 (2000); *INS v. St. CYR*, 533 U.S. 289 (2001); *Tyler v. Cain*, 533 U.S. 656 (2001); *Woodford v. Garceau*, 538 U.S. 202 (2003); *Plilier v. Ford*, 542 U.S. 225 (2004); *Rhines v. Weber*, 544 U.S. 269 (2005); *Johnson v. United States*, 544 U.S. 295 (2005); *Gonzalez v. Crosby*, 545 U.S. 524 (2005); *Mayle v. Felix*, 545 U.S. 644 (2005); *Brown v. Payton*, 544 U.S. 133 (2005); *Pace v. Diguglielmo*, 544 U.S. 408 (2005); *Evans v. Chavis*, 546 U.S. 189 (2006); and *Rice v. Collins*, 546 U.S. 333 (2006).

105. P. Foran, "Unreasonably Wrong: The Supreme Court's Supremacy, the AEDPA Standard, and *Carey v. Musladin*," *Southern California Law Review*, Vol. 81 (2008), pp. 571–629.

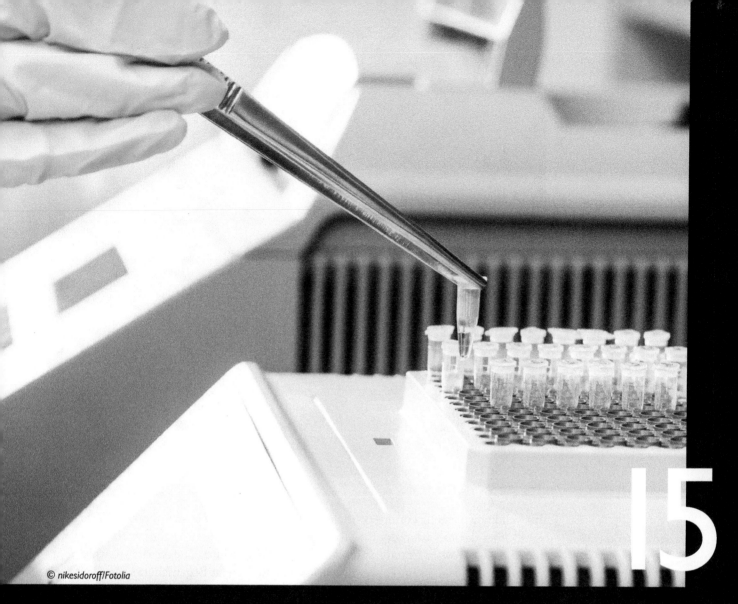

© nikesidoroff/Fotolia

Differential Treatment and Wrongful Convictions

15

LEARNING OBJECTIVES

1. Summarize how various factors may cause the differential treatment of individuals during the criminal justice process.

2. Describe racial and ethnic disparities in the criminal process.

3. Describe gender disparities in the criminal process.

4. Explain the issues surrounding wrongful convictions and the means for exoneration.

A tranquil South Florida waterscape. Can the personal qualities of attorneys sway the decision of jurors or of a judge? Should they?

Pola Damonte/Shutterstock

INTRODUCTION

It's well known among corrupt politicians, drug dealers, crime bosses in South Florida, and even other defense attorneys that the best legal representative anyone with money can hire is famed Broward County counselor J. David Bogenschutz. The area's most widely read newspaper, the *Sun-Sentinel*, recently carried an article about Bogenschutz saying that "he's the lawyer judges, politicians, the wealthy and well-connected in Broward County often call upon in times of legal trouble."[1] Bogenschutz has defended former New York Yankees star Jim Leyritz, former Broward County Sheriff Ken Jenne, the son of billionaire and former Miami Dolphins owner Wayne Huizenga, and Eleanor Adderly, the wife of former Fort Lauderdale Police Chief Frank Adderly, among others.[2] The *Sun-Sentinel* also noted that for some, the high-profile Bogenschutz represents a two-tiered system of justice "that often metes out softer punishment to the well-connected, the powerful or anyone with the means to hire a very talented advocate." Patrick Gudgridge, vice dean of the University of Miami School of Law, notes that "it's being savvy about how the system works, and not just about what the law books say, that makes for a highly effective lawyer."

Learning Objective 1

Summarize how various factors may cause the differential treatment of individuals during the criminal justice process.

DIFFERENTIAL TREATMENT

All criminal cases are not treated the same. Factors ranging from offense seriousness to the defendant's race affect a range of outcomes, including seriousness of the charge, granting of bail, plea negotiations, sentencing, and aftercare. Sometimes it is advantageous to provide individualized justice; for example, it would be time-consuming and costly to hold jury trials for minor misdemeanors. However, differential treatment of criminal defendants can have its drawbacks.

There are six key reasons for which cases are treated differently from one another: (1) offense seriousness, (2) celebrated cases, (3) race/ethnicity, (4) the offender's sex, (5) attorney competence, and (6) financial resources of the defendant. Sometimes more than one of these factors can be combined in a case.

Offense Seriousness

By now it should come as no surprise that offense seriousness matters. We saw in Chapter 13 that jury trials are allowed only when the punishment the defendant faces exceeds six months' incarceration. This differential treatment ensures that it takes longer to hold trials for serious offenses than it does for less serious cases. For example, in his 1992 book *The Process Is the Punishment: Handling Cases in a Lower Criminal Court*, Malcolm Feeley found that the *lengthier* misdemeanor trials took a little over a minute; most were handled in mere seconds.[3]

While it may not seem fair to treat cases differently simply because of the offense involved, there is a logical argument in favor of this approach. To do otherwise would cause the criminal process to be slower than it already is. Thus, if there is such a thing as acceptable differential treatment, this is probably it.

Celebrated Cases

Celebrated cases come in two varieties. The first consists of the high-profile, disturbing, possibly grizzly cases that capture the headlines. Graphic killings, mass murders, and other infamous cases tend to run the full gamut of the criminal process, and the defendants who are charged for such crimes rarely plea-bargain; most face lengthy and highly publicized trials.

The second category of celebrated cases involves celebrities, including Hollywood personalities, star athletes, and politicians. Their trials tend to take a fair amount of time, and all the while they receive plenty of press attention. Even relatively minor cases involving celebrities often lead to full-blown criminal trials. For example, eight prosecutors were involved in the 2001 Winona Ryder shoplifting case when she was accused of stealing over $5,000 in merchandise from a Beverly Hills department store. Would an ordinary person be treated in the same fashion? Certainly not.

Race/Ethnicity

The most well-known and unfortunate form of differential treatment is based on race or ethnicity. **Race** refers to the "major biological divisions of mankind, . . . [particularly those that are] distinguished by color of skin, color and texture of hair, bodily proportions, and other physical features."[4] **Ethnicity** "refers to differences between groups of people based on cultural customs, such as language, religion, foodways, family patterns, and other characteristics."[5] While it is not always easy to determine ethnicity, race is a much more visible characteristic. It is easier for one to ascertain the difference between people of white and black races than it is to determine whether someone's ancestors can be traced to Botswana or Namibia.

There is considerable consensus that race matters in criminal justice, but there is disagreement over how. To understand why there is disagreement, we must first distinguish between discrimination and disparity. **Discrimination** refers to unfair treatment of a person or group because of prejudice about race, sex, age, or other distinguishing characteristics; in contrast, **disparity** "refers to a difference but one that does not necessarily involve discrimination."[6] A discrimination-based criminal justice example would be more death sentences for black defendants simply because they are black, whereas a disparity-based explanation would be that blacks are sentenced to death more than whites because they commit more capital offenses. You may recall (Chapter 14) that sentencing guidelines were created in part to reduce racial disparity in sentencing and that race differences have persisted since guidelines were made advisory rather than mandatory.

race
"[The] major biological divisions of mankind, [particularly those that are] distinguished by color of skin, color and texture of hair, bodily proportions, and other physical features."[i]

ethnicity
"[D]ifferences between groups of people based on cultural customs, such as language, religion, foodways, family patterns, and other characteristics."[ii]

discrimination
The unfair treatment of a person or group because of prejudice about race, sex, age, sexual orientation, religion, or other distinguishing characteristics.

disparity
"[A] difference [in how a person or group is treated] . . . that does not necessarily involve discrimination."[iii]

There are major disparities throughout criminal justice. Crime peaks in younger years, so young people are arrested at higher rates than older people. Also, more men than women are arrested. Yet it is unclear just how much discrimination there is: Some scholars feel it is rampant[7]; others feel it is a myth.[8] Reality probably falls somewhere in the middle of a continuum of discrimination. Sam Walker and his colleagues have developed just such a continuum consisting of five elements:

1. *Systematic discrimination.* Systematic discrimination occurs at all stages of the criminal justice system as well as at all times and all places.
2. *Institutional discrimination.* Racial and ethnic disparities in outcomes that are the result of the application of racially neutral factors, such as prior criminal record, employment status, and demeanor, fall into the category of institutional discrimination.
3. *Contextual discrimination.* Discrimination found in particular contexts or circumstances (e.g., certain regions, particular crimes, or special victim–offender relationships) is called contextual discrimination.
4. *Individual acts of discrimination.* Discrimination that results from the acts of particular individuals but that is not characteristic of entire agencies or the criminal justice system as a whole consists simply of individual acts of discrimination.
5. *Pure justice.* There is no racial or ethnic discrimination at all in pure justice.[9]

Which best characterizes the day-to-day operations of the criminal justice system? Walker and his colleagues reviewed hundreds of studies on the subject and concluded that contextual discrimination is more likely than either pure justice or systematic discrimination: "We suggest that the U.S. criminal justice system falls between the two ends of the continuum. . . . Racial minorities are treated more harshly than whites at some stages of the criminal justice process . . . but no differently than whites at other stages of the process."[10] We will see just how this happens later in this chapter.

Gender

Just as there is differential treatment based on race, there is differential treatment by sex. Throughout history, men and women have not been treated alike, both in criminal justice and beyond. These differences owe in part to the fact that men and women often commit different types of crime (see the discussion in Chapter 10). Other times, the differences owe simply to the fact that one defendant is male and the other is female.

Attorney Competence

Although we sometimes hear about attorney incompetence, especially when convicted defendants claim that they lacked adequate representation, very little is said about the opposite—attorney competence and its effect on criminal trials. In fact, law schools graduate persons with "technical competency," meaning that law school graduates have mastered substantive legal principles and can "think like a lawyer."[11] Truly good attorneys, however, also have the ability to bring their knowledge and skills to bear effectively in a particular case. A good attorney can often persuade jurors to listen to them, even in the face of what might otherwise be regarded as overwhelming odds against their client.

The Defendant's Financial Resources

A generation ago, in what is still a well-remembered criminal case, football star O. J. Simpson was acquitted of charges that he savagely murdered his wife, Nicole Simpson, and her friend, Ronald Goldman. Although much of the evidence that was presented to a California trial jury clearly implicated Simpson, his highly vaunted "dream team" of defenders— F. Lee Bailey, Johnnie Cochran, and Robert Shapiro—managed to convince a trial jury that reasonable doubt existed as to Simpson's guilt. The defense cost Simpson around $6 million, which was a lot of money in 1995 when the trial took place. Had Simpson been unable to afford the defense tab, some think that it is likely that he would have been convicted of two counts of first-degree murder. Many of today's defendants, however, are destitute and depend on public defenders appointed by the court to manage their defense.

RACIAL AND ETHNIC DISPARITIES

Researchers have examined racial and ethnic disparities at various stages of the criminal justice process:

- Police–citizen encounters
- Pretrial period
- Trial
- Sentencing
- Imprisonment and corrections
- Capital punishment[12]

What does it mean to talk about racial and ethnic disparities? While it may be tempting to treat them as one and the same, they are not. The term *race* generally refers to distinct physical characteristics, such as the color of someone's skin; in contrast, the term *ethnicity* refers more to a shared national, religious, linguistic, or cultural heritage.[13] We draw the distinction because researchers have examined both racial and ethnic disparities in criminal justice. More often than not, racial disparities are concerned with unequal treatment between whites (Caucasian) and African-Americans. Researchers have also compared the treatment of whites with that of Hispanics, in which case it may be better to think about ethnic disparities. Keep these distinctions in mind as you read through the coming pages. When you see reference to the term *minorities*, keep in mind that we mean all other groups besides Caucasians.

Police–Citizen Encounters

Why be concerned with racial or ethnic disparities in police–citizen encounters? Why does this matter in a book on courts? The answer to both questions is that arrests and traffic stops are the gateway to the criminal process: Arrests mark the point where a person formally enters the criminal process; although this is not always true with traffic stops, many stops do lead to searches, which in turn lead to arrests. If there is evidence of disparity at either of these early steps, then by definition those suspects who enter the criminal process do not adequately represent the population at large; that is, the criminal justice system could be stacked against one racial or ethnic group at the outset. So, do such disparities exist at the arrest stage or during traffic stops? A number of researchers have tried to answer this important question, as the following subsections attest.

Arrests Minorities (as a percentage of their representation in the general population) are arrested more than whites. Such findings have been confirmed in a number of studies. One that analyzed California data found that 66% of all African-American men in that state were likely to be arrested by age 30.[14] Others, however, have found that a suspect's race is not predictive of his or her likelihood of arrest[15]; instead, evidence factors, crime seriousness, and suspect cooperation are more important. Still other researchers have concluded that

Learning Objective 2
Describe racial and ethnic disparities in the criminal process.

Library Extra
15–1 Reduction of Racial Disparity in the Criminal Justice System

"race does matter," but it depends on both victim and suspect characteristics. One analysis of nearly 6,000 police–citizen encounters revealed that police officers were more likely to arrest when the victim was white and the suspect was black.[16] Researchers have also found that officers may relax the evidentiary standards they use when arresting minorities.[17]

Traffic Stops   Amidst allegations of racial profiling (racial influence on police officer decision making, especially in traffic stops), researchers have in recent years sought to determine whether an individual's race or ethnicity influences an officer's decision to stop him or her. The findings run the gamut from rampant discrimination to none at all. An example of the latter is Geoffrey Alpert, Roger Dunham, and Michael Smith's investigation of the Miami Police Department—they found no evidence of discriminatory activity toward minorities during traffic stops.[18] Moving in the opposite direction, some researchers have found that race matters in traffic stops but not as much as the motorist's age and gender.[19] Others have found that while race or ethnicity may not influence the decision to stop a motorist, it does influence the decision to search.[20] Still others have found fairly clear evidence of discriminatory decision making.[21]

What can we make of these conflicting findings? At the least, the literature offers some evidence of contextual discrimination. It appears that race/ethnicity is important at least some of the time. Add this to findings from the literature on race and arrests, and it becomes clear that the gateway to the criminal justice system may not be open to everyone in quite the same way.

Pretrial Period

As we just saw, it is not entirely clear whether there are racial/ethnic disparities in police–citizen encounters. Researchers have reached essentially the same conclusion when they have looked at the pretrial period: There does not appear to be a clear relationship between race/ethnicity, case outcomes, and (1) defense representation, (2) bail decisions, or (3) plea bargaining. In other words, racial/ethnic disparities do not seem to be a serious problem.

Defense Representation   The median family income for white families tends to be roughly 60% higher than it is for black families and approximately 35% higher than it is for Hispanic families.[22] It should come as no surprise, then, that minority offenders tend to be less financially secure than their white counterparts, meaning that many of them have to settle for appointed counsel because they cannot afford to retain their own attorneys.[23]

In Chapter 9 (covering defense attorneys), we concluded that the clients of public defenders generally fare no worse than those of private attorneys, but what happens when we add race to the mix? There is not much research in this area, and the results are inconclusive. One study found that African-American and Hispanic defendants were less likely to be represented by retained counsel and thus received more punitive sentences than whites.[24] Another study reached the opposite conclusion, namely, that race and representation type had no clear impact on case outcomes.[25]

Bail Decisions   Critics of money bail argue that the poor cannot afford to pay and thus sit in jail until their trial dates, which is *prima facie* evidence of a system that discriminates against minorities. Are their concerns warranted? Researchers have pursued two lines of research in their efforts to answer this question. First, they have looked at the effects of race/ethnicity on bail decision making in general; second, they have looked at the relationship between bail decisions and case outcomes:

   1. *Effects of race/ethnicity on bail decisions.* There is no clear effect of race/ethnicity on bail. Some studies have found that judges base their bail decisions on legitimate criteria, such as offense seriousness and prior record.[26] Others have argued

LASTING IMPACT

Terry v. Ohio (1968)

"A Cleveland detective [named] McFadden, on a downtown beat which he had been patrolling for many years, observed two strangers ([Terry] and another man, [Chilton]) on a street corner. He watched them proceed alternately back and forth along an identical route, pausing to stare in the same store window, which they did for a total of about 24 times. Each completion of the route was followed by a conference between the two on a corner, at one of which they were joined by a third man [Katz] who left swiftly.

"Suspecting the two men of 'casing a job, a stick-up,' the officer followed them and saw them rejoin the third man a couple of blocks away in front of a store. The officer approached the three, identified himself as a policeman, and asked their names. The men 'mumbled something,' whereupon McFadden spun [Terry] around, patted down his outside clothing, and found a pistol in his overcoat pocket that he was unable to remove.

"The officer ordered the three into the store. He removed [Terry's] overcoat, took [a revolver from it], and ordered the three to face the wall with their hands raised. He patted down the outer clothing of Chilton and Katz and seized a revolver from Chilton's outside overcoat pocket. He did not put his hands under the outer garments of Katz (since he discovered nothing in his pat-down which might have been a weapon), or under [Terry's] or Chilton's outer garments until he felt the guns. The three were then taken to the police station, where [Terry] and Chilton were charged with carrying concealed weapons.

"The defense moved to suppress the weapons. Though the trial court rejected the prosecution theory that the guns had been seized during a search incident to a lawful arrest, the court denied the motion to suppress and admitted the weapons into evidence on [grounds] that the officer had cause to believe that [Terry] and Chilton were acting suspiciously, that their interrogation was warranted, and that the officer, for his own protection, had the right to pat down their outer clothing based on reasonable cause to believe that they might be armed. The court distinguished between an investigatory 'stop' and an arrest, and between a 'frisk' of the outer clothing for weapons and a full-blown search for evidence of crime."[1]

The seized weapons, as well as testimony as to the circumstances of the seizure, were introduced at trial. Terry and Chilton were subsequently found guilty, and an intermediate appellate court affirmed the verdict. When the Ohio Supreme Court dismissed the appeal on the ground that "no substantial constitutional question" was involved, Terry petitioned the U.S. Supreme Court, alleging violation of Fourth Amendment protections against unreasonable search and seizure.[2]

In a multipart holding, the Court (1) acknowledged that because it "protects people, not places," the Fourth Amendment "applies as much to the citizen on the streets as well as at home or elsewhere";[3] (2) declared the issue in this case to be the admissibility of the evidence uncovered by the search and seizure, not the propriety of the police behavior;[4] (3) rejected invocation of the exclusionary rule to exclude the products of legitimate

and restrained police investigative techniques;[5] (4) declared the applicability of the Fourth Amendment to "stop and frisk" procedures such as those followed in this case;[6] (5) permitted a reasonable search for weapons when a reasonably prudent officer has cause to believe that his safety or the safety of others is at risk "regardless of whether he has probable cause to arrest [the individual to be searched] for [a] crime or the absolute certainty that the individual is armed";[7] (6) found "[t]he officer's protective seizure of [Terry] and his companions and the limited search which he made were reasonable, both at their inception and as conducted";[8] and (7) upheld admittance of the revolver seized from Terry "into evidence against him, since the search which led to its seizure was reasonable under the Fourth Amendment."[9]

Terry exemplifies the direct impact that court decisions can have on daily law enforcement practices. *Miranda*, for example, introduced a rights warning into the arrest process. *Terry* now defines articulable standards for the conduct of warrantless stop-and-frisk searches. The establishment of such clear guidelines thus informs the development of training and operational policies within law enforcement agencies. ■

Notes

1 Adapted from Syllabus, *Terry* v. *Ohio* (1968).
2 Ibid.
3 *Terry* v. *Ohio* (1968), pp. 8–9.
4 Ibid., p. 12.
5 Ibid., pp. 13–15.
6 Ibid., pp. 16–20.
7 Ibid., pp. 20–27.
8 Ibid., pp. 27–30.
9 Ibid., pp. 30–31.

DISCUSSION QUESTIONS

1. In this case, the U.S. Supreme Court permitted a reasonable search for weapons when a reasonably prudent officer has cause to believe that his or her safety or the safety of others is at risk, regardless of whether the officer has probable cause to arrest the individual to be searched. What would the consequences have been for policing had the Court ruled otherwise?

2. Even though this case was heard in a number of courts, it was never determined whether Terry and his companions were actually planning a robbery or a "smash and grab" type of burglary. Do you think they were? Is this a question the courts should have examined more closely? Why or why not?

3. Some claim that the relatively low standard set for *Terry*-type stops by the Court prompts cavalier behavior on the part of law enforcement officers, thus increasing the potential for discrimination. Do you agree? Why or why not?

that it is the defendant's financial status, not his or her race/ethnicity, that is directly linked to the bail amounts.[27] This means that if there is any racial/ethnic disparity, it is indirect. Still other studies have revealed evidence of direct racial/ethnic discrimination in bail decisions.[28] For example, the author of a Washington State study found that minorities were less likely than whites to be released on their own recognizance[29]; moreover, whites fared better by spending less time in pretrial detention. The author concluded that the findings are "a serious concern for the courts in Washington [as it] implies that, despite efforts of judges and others dedicated to fairness in the administration of justice, justice is not administered fairly."[30] Another study revealed that while race did not have a direct effect on bail, it interacted with other variables in such a way as to suggest discrimination.[31] These authors found, for example, that having a prior felony conviction had a greater negative effect on the bail decision for black defendants than it did for white defendants.

Library Extra
15–2 Racial Disparities in the Criminal Justice System

Library Extra
15–3 Racial Discrimination in Washington State's Criminal Justice System

2. *Bail decisions and case outcomes.* The Bureau of Justice Statistics compared the conviction rates between defendants released prior to trial and those detained until their court dates. It found, not surprisingly, that defendants detained prior to trial were more likely to be convicted than those who were released.[32] This finding offers some indirect support of the discrimination argument: Since the poor cannot afford to post bail, they sit in jail prior to trial and are thus more likely to be convicted. Other researchers have focused more directly on the issue of race in this context. One study of judges' sentences in Chicago and Kansas City found that African-American males were more likely than any other class of offender to be sentenced to prison if they were first detained prior to trial.[33] In summary, while there may be racial/ethnic disparities in the bail context, it is not clear that race has a direct effect on either the decision to set bail or case outcomes.

Plea Bargaining As you may recall from Chapter 8, race/ethnicity is sometimes influential in the charging context. This is especially true when the defendant is a minority and the victim is white.[34] It is less clear that the race of the defendant alone is important.[35] What about plea bargaining? Does race affect plea agreements? Most research suggests plea agreements are affected mostly by (1) the offense seriousness, (2) the defendant's prior record, and (3) the strength of the evidence.[36] Some researchers have found either that race/ethnicity does not affect plea bargains[37] or that minorities fare better than whites, a somewhat counterintuitive finding.[38] Yet a few researchers have found that whites tend to receive better plea deals on the whole than minorities do. The authors of a California study concluded, "Whites were more successful in getting charges reduced or dropped, in avoiding 'enhancements' or extra charges, and in getting diversion, probation, or fines instead of incarceration."[39] The U.S. Sentencing Commission conducted a study that reached almost the same conclusion, namely, that whites receive better deals than minorities.[40]

Trial

Is race/ethnicity relevant at the trial stage? A reading of Harper Lee's *To Kill a Mockingbird* would certainly give the impression that the answer is yes:

> In our courts, when it's a white man's word against a black man's, the white man always wins. They're ugly but those are the facts of life. The one place where a man ought to get a square deal is a courtroom, be he any color of the rainbow, but people have a way of carrying their resentments right into the jury box.[41]

Lee's book, published in 1960, recounted some events that were observed in her childhood some 30 years before that. Most people agree that minorities have made great strides since then, but to what extent? Is race as influential in court today as it was back then? Most efforts to answer these questions have been concentrated in the areas of both jury selection and conviction.

Jury Selection Sadly, there is a wealth of evidence that prosecutors have used their peremptory challenges to screen out prospective minority jurors from the trials of minority

LASTING IMPACT

Chicago v. Morales (1999)

Chicago's Gang Congregation Ordinance prohibited "criminal street gang members" from loitering in public places. Under the ordinance, if a police officer observed a person whom he or she reasonably believed to be a gang member loitering in a public place with one or more persons, he or she was required to order them to disperse. Anyone who did not promptly obey such an order was deemed to have violated the ordinance. The police department's General Order 92-4 purported to limit officers' enforcement discretion by confining arrest authority to designated officers, establishing detailed criteria for defining street gangs and membership therein, and providing for designated (but publicly undisclosed) enforcement areas.

Although two trial judges upheld the ordinance's constitutionality, 11 others ruled it invalid. The Illinois Appellate Court affirmed the latter cases and reversed the convictions in the former. The Illinois State Supreme Court affirmed, holding that the ordinance violates due process in that it is impermissibly vague on its face and places an arbitrary restriction on personal liberties.[1]

The city of Chicago petitioned the U.S. Supreme Court, arguing that three features of the ordinance serve to limit the officer's discretion: (1) It does not permit issuance of a dispersal order to anyone who is moving along or who has an apparent purpose, (2) it does not permit an arrest if individuals obey a dispersal order, and (3) no order can issue unless the officer reasonably believes that one of the loiterers is a gang member. The Court rejected that argument.

Interpreting the ordinance as being in violation of the requirement that a legislature establish minimal guidelines to govern law enforcement, the Court upheld the Illinois Supreme Court's ruling that the definition of loitering contained in the ordinance—"to remain in any one place with no apparent purpose"—gave officers absolute discretion to determine what activities constitute loitering. The Court thus concurred with the Illinois Supreme Court that General Order 92-4 did not sufficiently limit police discretion.[2]

The Court went on to say that such an ordinance must establish standards for the police and public that are sufficient to guard against the arbitrary deprivation of liberty. The vagueness of the Chicago ordinance, said the Court, threatens the

freedom to loiter for innocent purposes—which the Court cited as being part of such "liberty"—thus constituting "a criminal law that contains no *mens rea* requirement . . . and infringes on constitutionally protected rights."[3] Addressing the city's principal response to the adequate notice concern—that loiterers are not subject to criminal sanction until after they have disobeyed a dispersal order—the Court found the response unpersuasive because it fails to "enable the ordinary citizen to conform his or her conduct to the law" and because its terms "compound the inadequacy of the notice afforded by the ordinance."[4]

Of particular note is the fact that the U.S. Supreme Court's holding in *Morales* specifically expressed the Court's unwillingness to adopt a narrower or more limiting interpretation of Illinois law than did the Illinois Supreme Court.[5] This is a clear demonstration of the Court's adherence to the federalist principle of noninterference in the mechanisms of the various states except in such egregious constitutional deviations as may warrant intervention. In turn, this shows that it is the role of courts at all levels to scrutinize government actions and issue rectifying orders only when constitutionality is found lacking. ■

Notes

1. *Chicago v. Morales*, 527 U.S. 41 (1999).
2. Ibid., pp. 16–20.
3. Ibid., pp. 7–12.
4. Ibid., pp. 12–16.
5. Ibid., pp. 1–5.

DISCUSSION QUESTIONS

1. Was the Chicago ordinance a form of discrimination? If so, who was being discriminated against?

2. How likely was it that members of the Chicago Police Department who were trying to enforce the ordinance could have mistaken innocent citizens for gang members?

3. Might it be possible to write an antigang ordinance that prohibits the gathering of suspected gang members in public places without running afoul of constitutional guarantees? If so, how might such an ordinance read?

defendants. The authors of a study in Louisiana found that prosecutors excused African-American jurors at a disproportionately high rate.[42] As we saw in Chapter 13, prosecutors are prohibited from using peremptory challenges to excuse minority jurors, but this does not mean the practice has ceased. In many cases, it can go undetected. How? The authors of the Louisiana jury study offered this answer:

> Because black prospective jurors are a minority in many jurisdictions, the exclusion of most black prospective jurors by [the] prosecution can be accomplished more easily than the similar exclusion of Caucasian prospective jurors by [the] defense.[43]

This practice has not disappeared. More recent Supreme Court cases have dealt with the problem of prosecutors using peremptory challenges to excuse prospective jurors based on race.[44]

If juries can be surreptitiously "stacked" by the prosecutor, then what bearing does this have on conviction? For example, are all-white juries more likely than mixed juries to convict African-American defendants? Mock jury studies suggest the answer to the second question is yes. As one author remarked, "Mock jury studies provide the strongest evidence that racial/ethnic bias frequently affects the determination of guilt."[45] In another study, white college students were presented with case transcripts in which the race of the defendant and victim were mixed up (e.g., white offender, African-American victim).[46] In cases with African-American offenders and white victims, the students voted for conviction 70% of the time; in cases with white offenders and African-American victims, they voted for conviction only 33% of the time. It bears mentioning that several of these studies are dated, but their findings have been echoed in a number of more recent studies.[47]

Conviction In sheer numbers, African-Americans are convicted less often than whites. In fact, for nearly all offense types, whites are convicted more often than African-Americans—or any other minority group.[48] The same holds for convictions in federal and state courts, although the differences are more pronounced in federal courts.[49] While whites are convicted more often, this should not be taken as evidence of a lack of discrimination. In order to gain a more accurate understanding, we need to account for the percentage of each group in the population—whites are convicted more often than African-Americans simply because there are more whites.

If we are to understand how (if at all) race affects conviction, it is critically important to control for other factors besides just race/ethnicity that could affect conviction rates. Examples of such factors include the method of representation, the granting of pretrial release, the strength of the evidence, and the seriousness of the crime. Researchers who have controlled for these factors have reached a fair degree of consensus that race does not matter in the conviction context.[50] As the authors of one study remarked, "Race has no independent effect upon case dispositions."[51] But as Robert Sampson and Janet Lauritsen remarked in their review of this literature, "We have no empirical basis from which to draw conclusions about convictions among Hispanic, Asian, and Native Americans"[52]; most of the studies they reviewed compared only whites and African-Americans.

Sentencing

Hundreds of researchers have for decades focused their attention on racial/ethnic disparities in criminal sentencing, and much has been learned. Some of the simplest studies have examined racial/ethnic differences in sentencing outcomes, whereas others have taken to comparing incarceration rates of African-Americans and Hispanics with those of whites.

Some researchers have looked at sentencing decisions in an effort to detect whether judges are biased against minorities, and still others have looked at how a combination of

Library Extra
15–4 Racial Discrimination in the Administration of Justice

factors, such as gender, age, employment, and race/ethnicity, affects sentencing in concert. The result is a bewildering mix of findings and much conflicting evidence. On the whole, though, the evidence suggests that African-American and Hispanic offenders are more likely to be sent to prison than whites—and for longer periods.

Race/Ethnicity and Sentencing As far back as 1935, researchers began to explore possible racial/ethnic bias in sentencing. The author of one study remarked that "equality before the law is a social fiction."[53] Most such studies were fairly simple in their methodologies, however, limiting the conclusions that could be drawn; for example, most looked solely at race and sentencing outcomes without any effort to control for such key considerations as the offender's prior record or the seriousness of the crime.[54] In 1983, the National Research Council's Panel on Sentencing Research concluded that sentencing practices in the United States did *not* exhibit "a widespread systematic pattern of discrimination."[55] Instead, "some pockets of discrimination are found for particular judges, [for] particular crime types, and in particular settings."[56]

Since 1983, not too many researchers have agreed with the National Research Council. One review of previous research conducted by Marjorie Zatz revealed that "it would be misleading to suggest that race/ethnicity is *the* major determinant of sanctioning, [but] race/ethnicity is *a* determinant of sanctioning, and a potent one at that."[57] More recent studies agree with that of Zatz. One of them, a review of 38 prior sentencing studies published between 1979 and 1991, found "significant evidence of a *direct* impact of race on imprisonment."[58] Another review of 40 earlier sentencing studies found that at both the federal and the state level, African-Americans and Hispanics were more likely to be sentenced to prison than whites—and for longer periods of time.[59] Importantly, these studies controlled for crime seriousness and prior record, yet they still found evidence of a racial/ethnic disparity.

Most recent studies of race and sentencing have examined complex interactions among multiple variables, they have controlled for multiple factors (besides race) that could affect sentencing, and they have looked at indirect effects of race on sentencing outcomes, such as how race influences sentencing of those who were detained prior to trial. Victim–offender pairs, offense type, and other considerations have crept into this research as well. How do we make sense of the findings? Noted sentencing authority Cassia Spohn summarized the findings from dozens of studies on race and sentencing as follows:

- Minorities are sentenced more harshly than whites if they

  Are young and male

  Are unemployed

  Are male and unemployed

  Are young, male, and unemployed

  Have lower incomes

  Have less education

  Are detained in jail prior to trial

  Are represented by a public defender rather than a private attorney

  Are convicted at trial rather than by plea bargain

  Have more serious prior criminal records

- Minorities who victimize whites are sentenced more harshly than other race or offender/race combinations.

- Minorities are sentenced more harshly than whites if they

  Are convicted of less serious crimes

  Are convicted of drug offenses or more serious drug offenses[60]

These findings have led one team of researchers to conclude, "Although the contemporary sentencing process may not be characterized by 'a widespread systematic pattern of discrimination,' it is not racially neutral."[61] In other words, it is risky to assert that rampant discrimination exists in sentencing. What discrimination exists is best described as contextual—it occurs some of the time and in certain situations.

Drug Sentencing Many people are in agreement that drug sentencing has adversely affected African Americans.[62] In its report titled *Punishment and Prejudice*, Human Rights Watch reported the following:

- Of all drug offenders admitted to state prisons during the study period, approximately 63 percent were black. Only 37 percent were white.

- Two out of five black offenders sentenced to prison were put there for drug offenses. The proportion of drug offenders among black inmates was between 30 and 40 percent, compared to 24 percent for whites.

- Blacks were sent to prison more for drug charges than violent crime charges. Approximately 25 percent of black prison admissions were for crimes of violence, compared to 38 percent for whites. [63]

Human Rights Watch is often criticized for its lack of neutrality, with some calling it a liberal interest group. In any case, the findings in its report are not isolated. A number of research reports (including some recent studies) have found racial/ethnic disparities in sentencing outcomes for drug offenders.[64]

Researchers have also paid considerable attention to disparities in sentences for powder cocaine versus crack cocaine offenders. Federal Sentencing Guidelines once provided much harsher sentences for crack, and since crack tends to be found and used in poorer minority-dominated inner-city areas, some interpreted this as evidence of a discriminatory criminal justice system.[65] The Supreme Court has since decided that the use of the Federal Sentencing Guidelines is optional, thus reducing the problem of whites who were caught with powdered cocaine going to prison for far shorter periods than blacks caught with crack cocaine.[66] The U.S. Sentencing Commission has also revised the crack sentencing provisions of the Federal Sentencing Guidelines.[67]

Imprisonment and Corrections

The sentencing research we just looked at revealed that minorities are often sentenced to prison more often—and for longer periods of time—than whites. It should come as no surprise, then, that these findings show up in the imprisonment and corrections contexts. We look first at racial/ethnic disparities in prisons and jails, then we shift our attention to community corrections, particularly probation and parole.

Prisons Table 15–1 presents the racial composition of sentenced prisoners under state and federal correctional supervision (males only). Importantly, the data are reported as rates per 100,000 people in each racial/ethnic group, making it possible to see how one group fares relative to the next while accounting for how many people (prisoners and nonprisoners alike) fall into that group. Note how the rate of imprisoned African-American offenders far exceeds the rate for whites—they are sentenced to prison at a rate more than six times higher than whites. Hispanics are imprisoned three times as much as whites.

Despite the message it tells, Table 15–1 should be interpreted with caution. One possible explanation for the large numbers of black and Hispanic inmates relative to whites is that minorities offend at higher rates.[68] Another is that the association is indirect: Minority group members are more likely to be poor, and being poor is linked

TABLE 15–1 Race/Ethnicity of Male Prisoners Sentenced to State and Federal Correctional Facilities

White, non-Hispanic: 478 per 100,000
African-American, non-Hispanic: 3,023 per 100,000
Hispanic: 1,238 per 100,000

Source: E. Ann Carson and William J. Sabol, *Prisoners in 2011* (Washington, DC: Bureau of Justice Statistics, 2012), p. 8, table 8.

with more pretrial detention and more guilty verdicts, factors that are associated with harsher sentences.[69]

Jails A similar story can be told for America's jails. While African-Americans constitute approximately 12% of the total population, they make up nearly 40% of the jail population.[70] Although minority representation in the jail population has actually declined, the overrepresentation of African-American inmates is still troubling.

It is difficult to determine whether minorities are disproportionately incarcerated in jails because of the constant turnover in jail inmates. According to the Bureau of Justice Statistics, somewhere between half and two-thirds of all jail inmates are awaiting their trials.[71] Even so, minorities are consistently overrepresented in America's jails, an outcome that points to the possibility of racial/ethnic discrimination in setting bail. If most jail inmates are awaiting trial, this means many of them could not post bail. Walker and his colleagues stated that "there is evidence that judges impose higher bail—or are more likely to deny bail altogether—if the defendant is a racial minority."[72] Recall from the discussion on bail earlier in this chapter that not all researchers are in agreement with this statement, but a few have found evidence of discrimination in judges' bail-setting decisions.

Community Corrections More than 4 million people are on probation, and the parole population is approximately 800,000.[73] Figures 15–1 and 15–2 present racial/ethnic data for probationers and parolees, respectively. In general, there is a clear discrepancy between the percentage of African-Americans and whites in the population compared to their representation among the population of probationers and parolees. Also note that far more whites are put on probation, whereas the parole percentages are roughly similar between African-Americans and whites (and similar to the jail and prison data discussed earlier).

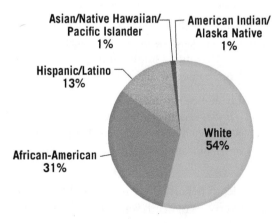

FIGURE 15–1

Racial/Ethnic Breakdown of Probationers

Source: L.M. Maruschak and E. Parks, *Probation and Parole in the United States, 2011* (Washington, DC: Bureau of Justice Statistics, 2012), p. 17.

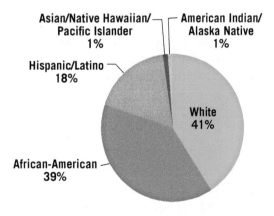

FIGURE 15–2

Racial/Ethnic Breakdown of Parolees

Source: L.M. Maruschak and E. Parks, *Probation and Parole in the United States, 2011* (Washington, DC: Bureau of Justice Statistics, 2012), p. 20.

Walker and his colleagues explained the discrepancy in this way: "Given that probation is a less severe sentence than prison, this difference may indicate that the advantage of receiving the less severe sentence of probation is more likely to be reserved for whites."[74]

Capital Punishment

The U.S. Constitution's Eighth Amendment expressly prohibits "cruel and unusual punishment." What punishment is cruel and unusual? The answer has been left to the courts. The Supreme Court remarked in an 1890 case,

> Punishments are cruel when they involve torture or lingering death; but the punishment of death is not cruel, within the meaning of that word as used in the Constitution. It implies there is something inhuman and barbarous, something more than the mere extinguishment of life.[75]

While the Supreme Court has never held that the death penalty constitutes cruel and unusual punishment, in a 1972 case, *Furman* v. *Georgia*,[76] the Court decided that the death penalty, as it was being carried out at the time, was unconstitutional. Each of the Court's nine justices authored separate opinions in this 5–4 decision. Three of them raised discrimination concerns: Justice Douglas argued that death penalty procedures were "pregnant with discrimination,"[77] Justice Stewart pointed out that the death penalty was "so wantonly and so freakishly imposed,"[78] and Justice White found "no meaningful basis for distinguishing the few cases in which [the death penalty] is imposed from the many cases in which it is not."[79]

The *Furman* decision was far reaching. It brought executions to a halt and "emptied death rows across the country."[80] It also invalidated death penalty statutes in 39 states. Most of the states responded by enacting new laws aimed at curbing the discretion of judges and jurors in death penalty cases to ensure fairness and evenhandedness in the process.[81] The new laws were of two varieties—some provided for the death penalty in cases of first-degree murder, and others provided for the death penalty in several offenses based on the presence of aggravating or mitigating circumstances,[82] which are now called **guided-discretion laws**. This latter type of law required both that a second trial be held in which a jury deliberated whether the convicted should be sentenced to death and that there would be an automatic appellate review of every death penalty sentence.

In the wake of *Furman*, the Court decided a few more death penalty cases. In *Woodson* v. *North Carolina*[83] and *Roberts* v. *Louisiana*,[84] the Court held that North Carolina's and Louisiana's mandatory death penalty statutes were unconstitutional—both states' laws gave jurors no opportunity to consider aggravating and mitigating circumstances. In contrast, the Court looked favorably on the guided-discretion laws in the states of Florida, Georgia, and Texas.[85] For example, in *Gregg* v. *Georgia*, the Court held that Georgia's statute limited the jury's discretion and thus minimized the chances that the death penalty would be arbitrarily imposed[86]:

> No longer can a jury wantonly and freakishly impose the death sentence; it is always circumscribed by the legislative guidelines. In addition, the review function of the Supreme Court of Georgia affords additional assurance that the concerns that prompted our decision in *Furman* are not present to any significant degree in the Georgia procedure applied here.[87]

Was the Supreme Court right to declare the death penalty unconstitutional for a time? Did *Furman* or *Gregg* alter the nature and characteristics of death sentences and eliminate discrimination? Has anything really changed? We organize the research into studies conducted before and after *Furman*.

Evidence before Furman A number of studies found that African-Americans, especially those who killed whites, were more likely than whites to be executed in the pre-*Furman* era.[88]

guided-discretion laws
Laws enacted after *Furman* v. *Georgia* (1972) aimed at curbing the discretion of judges and jurors in death penalty cases to ensure fairness and evenhandedness in the process.[iv]

Garfinkel's study of capital punishment in North Carolina during the 1930s revealed just how important the races of the offender and victim were in deciding who would be sentenced to death: Of those offenders charged with first-degree murder, the conviction rate for African-Americans who killed whites was 43%, compared to 5% for African-Americans who killed blacks and 0% for whites who killed blacks. The likelihood that someone would be sentenced to death was comparable.

Since rapists could be executed in the pre-*Furman* era, researchers also looked at racial/ethnic discrimination in the rape context. Studies revealed that "the death penalty for rape was largely used for punishing blacks who had raped whites."[89] Wolfgang and Reidel's study of pre-*Furman* executions in 12 southern states yielded a similar conclusion, finding that 13% of African-American offenders in their sample were sentenced to death, compared to 2% of white offenders.[90] They also controlled for other factors that would have been likely to influence death sentences and concluded that "all the nonracial factors in each of the states analyzed 'wash out,' that is, they have no bearing on the imposition of the death penalty in disproportionate numbers upon blacks. The only variable of statistical significance that remains is race."[91]

Evidence after Furman It is not particularly surprising that pre-*Furman* research revealed evidence of disparity in death sentences. After all, part of the Supreme Court's logic for declaring the death penalty unconstitutional was that it was applied in an arbitrary—and even discriminatory—fashion. So what happened after the Court reinstated the death penalty in *Gregg*? Did discrimination magically disappear? Is the death penalty applied evenly across all races today?

The Court said in *Gregg* that "the concerns that prompted our decision in *Furman* are not present to any significant degree in the Georgia procedure applied here."[92] Researchers were not so optimistic. Wolfgang and Reidel argued that "it is unlikely that the death penalty will be applied with greater equity when substantial discretion remains in these post-*Furman* statutes."[93] Another team of researchers argued that "under post-*Furman* capital statutes, the extent of arbitrariness and discrimination, if not their distribution over stages of the criminal justice process, might be expected to remain essentially unchanged."[94] Noted legal scholar Austin Sarat argued that "the post-*Furman* effort to rationalize death sentences has utterly failed; it has been replaced by a policy that favors execution while trimming away procedural protection for capital defendants. This situation only exacerbates the incompatibility of capital punishment and legality."[95]

These critics' conclusions have been borne out in several studies published in the decades since *Furman*.[96] The U.S. Government Accountability Office also found "a pattern of evidence indicating racial/ethnic disparities in the charging, sentencing, and imposition of the death penalty after the *Furman* decision."[97] Walker and his colleagues summarize three decades of post-*Furman* research as follows:

> The results of the death penalty studies conducted in the post-*Gregg* era provide compelling evidence that the issues raised by the Supreme Court in *Furman* have not been resolved. The Supreme Court's assurances in *Gregg* notwithstanding, racial discrimination in the capital sentencing process did not disappear as a result of the guided-discretion statutes enacted in the wake of the *Furman* decision. Methodologically sophisticated studies conducted in Southern and non-Southern jurisdictions and in the 1990s as well as the 1970s and 1980s consistently conclude that the race of the victim affects death sentencing decisions. Many of these studies also conclude that the race of the defendant, or the racial makeup of the offender-victim pair, influences the capital sentencing process.[98]

McCleskey v. Kemp One of the post-*Furman* studies was so influential that it was partly responsible for the Supreme Court's decision in the 1987 case of *McCleskey* v. *Kemp*.[99]

A death-row inmate sought *habeas corpus* relief by challenging his sentence on the grounds that defendants in Georgia were four times more likely to be sentenced to death for killing whites than African-Americans, an argument based on findings reported in a study conducted by professors David Baldus, George Woodworth, and Charles Pulaski.[100] The Court called the study "sophisticated," but it nevertheless held, in part,

> There is no merit to the contention that the Baldus study shows that Georgia's capital punishment system is arbitrary and capricious in *application*. The statistics do not *prove* that race enters into any capital sentencing decisions or that race was a factor in petitioner's case. The likelihood of racial prejudice allegedly shown by the study does not constitute the constitutional measure of an unacceptable risk of racial prejudice. The inherent lack of predictability of jury decisions does not justify their condemnation. On the contrary, it is the jury's function to make the difficult and uniquely human judgments that defy codification and that build discretion, equity, and flexibility into the legal system.[101]

The *McCleskey* case was influential not only because it showed the Supreme Court's support for capital punishment but also because it eventually had an influence on claims other than those challenging the death penalty. For example, if someone feels he or she was denied "equal protection of the laws" under the Fourteenth Amendment, that person must now show both a discriminatory effect *and* a discriminatory purpose.[102] The Baldus study showed a discriminatory effect in the application of the death penalty (more minorities were executed than whites) but not a discriminatory purpose (the data could not reveal judges' or jurors' intentions). As a result of the *McCleskey* decision, the Court has also became less inclined to let social science research influence its decisions.[103] None of this came as welcome news to Warren McCleskey; he was executed in Jacksonville, Georgia, on September 26, 1991.

Learning Objective 3

Describe gender disparities in the criminal process.

GENDER DISCRIMINATION

The vast majority of research on differential treatment in criminal justice has focused on racial/ethnic disparities, but we would be remiss to ignore differential treatment across the sexes. Women have historically been treated quite differently than males have. Start with convicted criminals. Approximately 80% of convicted offenders in state courts are males (Figure 15–3).

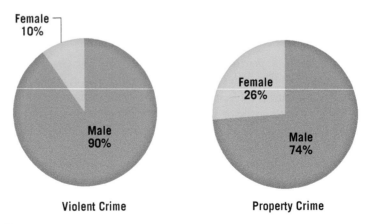

FIGURE 15–3

Gender of Defendants Convicted in State Courts

Source: http://www.albany.edu/sourcebook/pdf/t5452004.pdf (accessed December 11, 2013).

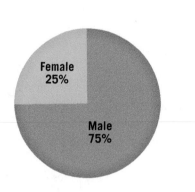

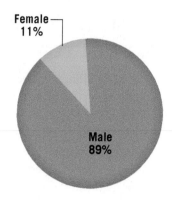

FIGURE 15–4

Gender of Probationers

Source: L.M. Maruschak and E. Parks, *Probation and Parole in the United States, 2011* (Washington, DC: Bureau of Justice Statistics, 2012), p. 17.

FIGURE 15–5

Gender of Parolees

Source: L.M. Maruschak and E. Parks, *Probation and Parole in the United States, 2011* (Washington, DC: Bureau of Justice Statistics, 2012), p. 17.

Since so many convicted criminals are male, it should come as no surprise that the vastmajority of prison inmates are also male. At the federal level, well over 90% of inmates are male,[104] and for prison inmates at both the state and the federal level, there are nearly 14 times as many men in prison as women.[105] Looking at jail inmates, more than 90% are also male.[106] The sexes move closer to parity when it comes to probation: Roughly one in four probationers is female(Figure 15–4), but only about one in ten parolees is female (Figure 15–5).

Is Gender Discrimination a Problem?

The fact that there are vastly more male than female offenders, inmates, probationers, and parolees is probably indicative of the fact that men offend more often than women—at least for most crimes.[107] Could something else be responsible? Clearly there is evidence of racial/ethnic discrimination in certain contexts. Are women discriminated against? Comparatively fewer studies have sought to answer this question; in those that have, it appears female defendants receive more lenient sentences than white males, as evidenced, for example, by the ratio of female to male probationers (see Figure 15–5).[108] These studies reveal that gender effects are most pronounced in the decision whether to imprison (as opposed to decisions on conviction and sentence length).[109]

Researchers have also looked at the interactive effects of race and sex. Some have found that African-American female defendants were treated more leniently than African-American male defendants[110]; others have found that race and ethnicity affect males' sentences but not females' sentences and that gender alone influences sentences across all racial/ethnic groups.[111] D. Steffensmeier and S. Demuth drew four main conclusions from this line of research:

1. [W]omen defendants receive more lenient treatment in court decisions than similarly situated male defendants. . . .

2. [B]lack males are sentenced more severely than white males and black females are sentenced *slightly* more severely than white females. . . .

3. [A] consistent gender effect of more lenient sentencing of female offenders persists not only across race (i.e., white and black) groups but also across any race [by] age combination. . . .

4. [T]he overall race effect is smaller for female defendants than male defendants and is due to the relatively harsher sentencing of young black males.[112]

Learning Objective 4
Explain the issues surrounding wrongful convictions and the means for exoneration.

THE RUSH TO JUDGMENT: WRONGFUL CONVICTIONS

In 2003, outgoing Illinois Governor George Ryan commuted the death sentences of 156 death-row inmates in that state. In his words, "I cannot support a system which, in its administration, has proven to be so fraught with error and has come so close to the ultimate nightmare, the state's taking of innocent life. Thirteen people have been found to have been wrongfully convicted."[113] Ryan's observations reflected a growing sentiment that our criminal justice system is imperfect.

error of justice
A term coined by Forst to describe the many types of mistakes the criminal justice system can make. It is further described as "any departure from an optimal outcome of justice for a criminal case."[v]

Brian Forst used the term **error of justice** to describe the many types of mistakes the criminal justice system can make: "[A]n error of justice occurs when an innocent person (i.e., innocent of the crime in question) is harassed, detained or sanctioned, or when a culpable offender receives a sanction that is either more or less than optimal—one that minimizes social cost—or escapes sanctioning altogether. . . . An error of justice is any departure from an optimal outcome of justice for a criminal case."[114] In Forst's view, an error of justice can be one that favors the accused (e.g., by allowing him or her to escape apprehension) or that goes against him or her (e.g., by carrying out a wrongful execution).

Most people can agree that it is as reprehensible to wrongfully execute a person as it is to fail to prosecute and convict a clearly guilty criminal.[115] But both types of mistakes are made, and both are costly. How costly are they? That question is all but impossible to answer. What, for instance, is the "cost" of wrongfully executing someone? In a similar vein, just how often do errors of justice occur? Again, it is nearly impossible to tell. As Forst has observed, "Accurate counts of the extent of justice errors require knowledge of factual guilt and innocence, and such knowledge is unattainable."[116]

Even given the difficulty of accurately discerning factual guilt, it is possible to arrive at some crude estimates of the incidence of errors of justice. Forst pointed out that the failure to arrest certain individuals is an error; he called this an error of impunity and estimated that around 10 million people escape conviction each year. Examining the other extreme (in particular, wrongful executions), estimates are that between 0.5% and 1.3% of people sentenced to death row since 1976 have been sent there in error.[117] Still other errors, such as "errors of due process,"[118] which refer to the mishandling and/or improper processing of certain suspects by criminal justice officials, occur on a regular basis.

Library Extra
15–5 Race, the Death Penalty, and Wrongful Convictions

The problem of wrongful convictions has become such a visible one, in fact, that an entire movement has been set in motion in response to them. This, coupled with increased popularity of DNA testing, has uncovered some of the most significant errors of justice of our time. We begin this section with a look at the innocence movement, then we turn our attention to the fruits of this movement's labor: exonerations of convicted criminals based on DNA evidence.

Innocence Movement

Web Extra
15–1 The Innocence Project

In the 1980s, DNA testing (also called DNA typing) entered the mainstream. Through the analysis of bodily materials, such as fluids or hair samples, specific individuals could be linked to crimes. Prosecutors began to use the results from DNA tests to strengthen their cases, and defense attorneys also quickly applied the technology to benefit their clients. For example, DNA testing could allow a defense attorney to prove that a rape defendant was wrongfully targeted for prosecution; if the defendant's DNA was not found anywhere on the victim or at the crime scene, it was known with near certainty that someone else was responsible.

If DNA testing follows proper procedures, today it can provide as close to certain evidence of guilt or innocence as anything, but that was not always the case. When DNA testing caught on, its introduction in court was hotly contested because certain tests had higher margins for error than others. For example, mitochondrial sequence testing could yield errors in approximately 1 of 100 cases[119]; in contrast, the short tandem repeat (STR) method could lead to mistaken identification in barely 1 of 1,000,000 cases.[120] See Box 15–1 for a discussion of this process. Below are listed some other reasons that mistakes could be made and the wrong person targeted:

- *Sample mix-up.* Probably the most common source of false matches is that people in the lab mixed up the samples. Sample mix-up is understandable simply because the technologies involve use of standardized tubes and other plasticware, so unless someone is absolutely rigorous, it is very easy to accidentally grab the wrong tube or load the wrong well with a sample. Ultimately, every sample is handled by at least one person before it gets processed, and this step of human handling is a vulnerable one.

- *Sample contamination.* Some cases of sample contamination are similar to sample mix-ups, but in other cases, sample contamination may occur because an officer touches the material with his or her hands or the sample is incorrectly deposited (e.g., when a blood stain gets bacteria in it).

- *DNA degradation.* DNA degrades if it is not kept cold or dry. Thus, by the time the police arrive at a crime scene, the DNA in some of the samples may already be bad. Improper storage of samples also contributes to degradation. Degradation may lead

BOX 15–1 DNA Typing Process

1. Obtain a tissue sample and extract the DNA.
2. "Xerox" the DNA with a technique known as polymerase chain reaction.
3. Determine the DNA type with either of two methods:
   a. *Short tandem repeat (STR).* This method generates the typical DNA bar code and is based on variable regions of DNA from your chromosomes. Chromosome regions have been found that are highly variable among us (even the two chromosome sets you have differ in these regions). Typing involves the assessment of about five of these regions. The method measures the length of the DNA on your chromosomes at those regions but does not determine the actual sequence.
   b. *Mitochondrial sequence.* Each of your cells (except red blood cells) contains hundreds to thousands of organelles known as mitochondria. Mitochondria ultimately evolved from bacteria, and they have their own miniature chromosome. Unlike the case with your (nuclear) chromosomes, all of the mitochondria in your body are inherited from your mother—so you have a single type. The sequence of your mitochondrial DNA matches that of your mother's mitochondrial DNA and can be used as one form of a DNA type.
4. Observe whether one sample has the same DNA type as the other sample (e.g., suspect). If so, calculate the odds of obtaining a match at random (as if the suspect had no association with the crime). The "random match probability" is typically less than 1 in 1,000,000 for STR types, but it is much greater for mitochondrial DNA types (e.g., 1 in 100). For example, two brothers (who aren't identical twins) will certainly have different STR types, but they will also certainly have the same mitochondrial DNA sequence as each other, as will their mother, her mother, any other siblings, any siblings of their mother, and so on. Even so, mitochondrial types are often useful, and they can be determined from samples whose DNA is too degraded for STR determination (because mitochondrial DNA is present in so many more copies than nuclear DNA). ■

Source: Adapted from www.utexas.edu/courses/bio301d/Topics/DNA/text.html (accessed March 1, 2013). Courtesy of James Bull, University of Texas and Craig Pease, Vermont Law School.

to inaccurate DNA typing, although more so for the STR method than for mitochondrial sequence testing.

- *Bad data analysis.* The calculation of random match probability may be straightforward in many cases, and some software automatically calculates it for each STR. However, unusual cases require a deep understanding of probabilities and statistics, which is often lacking.[121]

Innocence Projects In 1992, Barry Scheck (who gained notoriety by serving on O. J. Simpson's defense team) and Peter Neufeld, two attorneys, formed the **Innocence Project**[122] in response to their familiarity with both DNA testing and the prospect of wrongful convictions. In collaboration with the Cardozo Law School in New York, the Innocence Project's mission is to exonerate wrongfully convicted persons through DNA testing.

The Innocence Project receives in excess of 200 letters per month from convicted individuals who claim their innocence, with almost 3,000 letters being received in 2007 alone. Yet the organization has only a handful of attorneys and can take on around 160 cases at a time. To date, more than 240 innocent persons have been freed through DNA testing in the United States. The Innocence Project provided direct representation or critical assistance in most of these cases.

Since the Innocence Project was formed, similar efforts have been spawned in nearly every state. Today, their efforts are coordinated by the **Innocence Network**, which is a series of organizations that provide free legal and investigation services to individuals seeking to prove their innocence and overturn wrongful convictions.[123] The University of Texas at Austin's Tarlton Law Library also maintains the **Actual Innocence Awareness Database**, which contains a wealth of information on the subject of wrongful convictions, including some of the reasons for them.[124] These organizations' efforts have led to a number of reforms:

- State-by-state innocence commissions
- Crime lab oversight committees
- Improved witness identification procedures (to minimize the possibility of mistaken identifications)
- Separation of crime labs from law enforcement organizations
- Compensation for those wrongfully convicted
- Improved evidence preservation
- Recording of police interrogations
- State laws permitting postconviction access to DNA testing (the vast majority of states have one, but seven—Alabama, Alaska, Massachusetts, Mississippi, Oklahoma, South Carolina, and South Dakota—do not)[125]

Progressive Prosecutors Prosecutors are usually in the business of convicting criminals, but some have taken a strong position that wrongful convictions must be avoided at all costs. Craig Watkins, the first African-American district attorney elected in Dallas County (Texas) in 2006, inherited an office with what some have called a "convict at all costs policy."[126] After taking office, Watkins dismissed nine top prosecutors in his office, established a "Conviction Integrity Unit" that ensures that proper policies and procedures are followed in all prosecutions, and opened his office's doors to the Texas Innocence Project.

Innocence Project
An organization that, in collaboration with the Cardozo Law School in New York, seeks to exonerate wrongfully convicted persons through DNA testing.[vi]

Innocence Network
A series of organizations that provide free legal and investigation services to individuals seeking to prove their innocence and overturn wrongful convictions. [vii]

Actual Innocence Awareness Database
A computer-based resource maintained by the University of Texas at Austin's Tarlton Law Library that contains a wealth of information on the subject of wrongful convictions.[viii]

Web Extra
15–2 Wrongful Conviction and Innocence Resources on the Internet

Right about the time Watkins was elected, Dallas County assumed the dubious distinction of having freed the greatest number of wrongfully convicted persons of any county in the country, with almost 20 wrongfully convicted individuals released to date. While aggressive prosecution policies prior to Watkins's election may have been responsible, Dallas County may have exonerated more wrongfully convicted individuals simply because the Dallas County Crime Lab has for years preserved DNA evidence in all cases in which it was available. Charles Chatman was exonerated in 2008 after a DNA test was performed on a rape kit sample collected more than 26 years earlier; until Chatman was exonerated, he was serving a nine-year prison term for a rape he did not commit.

Exonerations

An **exoneration** occurs when a person is wrongfully convicted and later declared not guilty.[127] Exonerations occur through one of four means:

1. A governor issues a pardon based on new evidence of the convicted's innocence.
2. Charges are dismissed by the court after new evidence of innocence is discovered.
3. There is an acquittal at a retrial.
4. There is a posthumous (i.e., after death) acknowledgment of innocence.[128]

In most exoneration cases, there is no dispute over guilt or innocence. In some cases, DNA evidence makes it very certain that the wrong person was convicted; in other cases, some authorities have a problem with the release of someone who has already been convicted even if the evidence is clear.

exoneration
A subsequent declaration by the appropriate legal authority that a person who was wrongfully convicted of a crime is not guilty of having committed that crime.[ix]

Exoneration Trends
The number of exonerations has increased considerably in recent years. According to one study, there were 12 per year in 1989 and an average of 42 each year since 2000.[129] According to the National Registry of Exonerations, 1,067 individuals were exonerated as of this writing.[130] Three explanations have been offered for the trend: One is the growing availability of sophisticated DNA testing technology, another is the newsworthy nature of exoneration cases (e.g., the publicity of one case often prompts interested persons to search for more), and more resources have also been devoted to the problem.[131] The work of people associated with the Innocence Project (mentioned earlier) has had a significant role in seeing hundreds of wrongfully convicted persons exonerated.

Crimes of Exonerees
The vast majority of exonerated persons were convicted of murder, rape, or sexual assault. Samuel Gross (professor of law at the University of Michigan) and his colleagues examined 340 exoneration cases. The offense-by-offense breakdown was as follows:

Murder: 205 cases
Rape: 121 cases
Other crimes of violence: 11 cases
Drug and property crime: 3 cases[132]

Reasons for Wrongful Convictions
Figure 15–6 shows the five leading causes of exonerations. According to the Innocence Project, eyewitness misidentification is the main reason behind wrongful convictions. It is said to play a role in three out of four convictions

overturned after DNA testing.[133] False confessions run a distant second. Why would a person confess to a crime he or she did not commit? There are several possibilities:

- Duress
- Coercion
- Intoxication
- Diminished capacity
- Mental impairment
- Ignorance of the law
- Fear of violence
- Actual infliction of harm
- Threat of a harsh sentence
- Misunderstanding of the situation[134]

Other reasons for exonerations not included in Figure 15–6 include government misconduct (e.g., an overzealous prosecutor) or inadequate legal representation (an ineffective defense attorney may have a hand in his or her client's conviction). The combination of an inadequate defense and an overzealous prosecutor can be especially volatile.

Tip of the Iceberg?   It is impossible to accurately estimate the number of wrongful convictions that have occurred in the United States, but DNA testing and recent exoneration cases may provide a glimpse of the true extent of the problem. Innocence Project efforts do not focus their energies on cases of "mass exonerations," such as those that occurred in the wake of the Los Angeles Police Department Rampart scandal (or those mentioned above). These increase the numbers. Gross and his colleagues offered this estimate: "Any plausible guess at the total number of miscarriages of justice in America in the last fifteen years must be in the thousands, perhaps tens of thousands."[135] The cases we are familiar with may thus represent the tip of the proverbial iceberg. The topic of wrongful convictions is covered in the following "Courts in the News" feature.

FIGURE 15–6

Contributing Causes of Wrongful Convictions (first 225 DNA exonerations)

Note: Total is more than 100% because wrongful convictions can have more than one cause.

Source: "Contributing Causes of Wrongful Convictions," http://www .innocenceproject.org/understand/, accessed December 11, 2013. Courtesy of the Innocence Project.

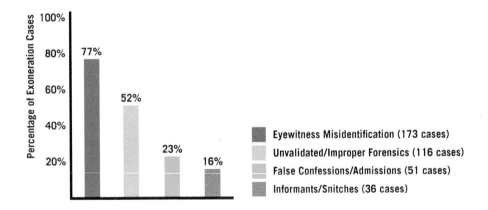

COURTS IN THE NEWS

Wrongful Convictions and Near Misses

Will Seberger/ZUMA Press/Newscom

Damon Thibodeaux was released from prison a free man after DNA evidence was used to prove his innocence. He had served 16 years on death row for a murder he did not commit. Should he be rewarded damages for his ordeal?

When Damon Thibodeaux stepped out of Angola jail in Louisiana in 2012, several guards were at the gate to wish him well, addressing him for the first time in 16 years as "Mr. Thibodeaux." "No offense," he said, "but I hope I never see you again." He walked out as the 300th prisoner in the United States to be freed as a result of DNA testing and one of 18 exonerated from death row. With the help of science, he has been proved innocent of a crime for which the state of Louisiana spent 15 years trying to put him to death. His case was certainly not the last involving an innocent man freed after new evidence emerged. In 2013, Louis Taylor broke down in tears as he described how he spent his first hours of freedom after more than 40 years in prison for a hotel fire that killed 29 people: an evening hike and some fast food. Taylor was released after doubts about his conviction surfaced and he agreed to a deal with prosecutors that set him free. He pleaded no contest to each of the nearly 30 counts of murder against him in an agreement that allowed the judge to sentence him to time served.

Wrongful or erroneous convictions are certainly a significant problem for the nation's court system. At a recent seminar, Jon Gould, professor of law, justice, and society and director of the Washington Institute for Public and International Affairs Research, American University, and John Firman, director, Research Division, International Association of Chiefs of Police, presented findings from their study of the factors that produce wrongful convictions. Focusing on cases of violent felonies where the person was convicted or indicted by a state and later found to be innocent of all charges, Gould and Firman located 460 cases, 260 in which an erroneous conviction took place and 200 similar cases where the defendant was found not guilty.

Among their most important findings was the surprising fact that some of the circumstances widely believed to create false convictions actually had little effect on case outcomes. These suspect factors included the effects of false confessions, the suspect's race, police abuse to elicit confessions (beating a confession out of someone), gang membership, and, finally, whether the defense uses experts in their case. Despite popular belief, these conditions actually had little influence over why one innocent people was convicted, while another was freed.

If these factors do not explain erroneous convictions, what does? Gould and Firman found that the accused's age matters the most: younger defendants are the ones most likely to be falsely convicted. Why is that? First, younger defendants are not as sophisticated as more mature and experienced defendants and were unable to be as helpful to their attorneys in preparing a defense as their older more mature peers. Second, younger defendants are less likely to be employed and thus don't have the kind of corroborating evidence enjoyed by older defendants: They clock into work at a particular time, and there is corroborating evidence that proves they could not have been at the crime scene because "Look, here—I was at work", hence, less false convictions.

A second important factor is having any prior criminal record. Being known to the police or having your photo in a mug shot book means that you are more likely—even if you are innocent—to be erroneously identified and thereafter wrongly convicted.

Forensic errors also lead to false convictions. These occur when a scientific test is simply done wrong or, more likely, when a forensic analyst over testifies at trial. Take hair analysis. Rather that testify that, the only thing that can be said is that the defendant's hair is consistent with the hair found at the crime scene, a forensic scientist at trial may claim that the hair found at the crime scene had to have come from the defendant.

Wrongful convictions are also likely to occur when the prosecution withholds important exculpatory evidence.

Honest eyewitness mistakes are another problem. Cases in which an eyewitness intentionally misidentifies the defendant are usually easier for police to figure out because they can determine that the eyewitness had a motive to lie. The eyewitness simply made a mistake: "Look, I was there, this is what I saw. I have no motive to lie." Eyewitness identification is beset by many problems, including insufficient lighting, the inability to do cross-racial identification, and the emotional anxiety people develop when they find themselves in the midst of a crime. All these factors are related to honest eyewitness errors and associated with a wrongful conviction.

(continued)

Surprisingly, those cases in which the prosecution's evidence is weakest are the ones more likely to end in a wrongful conviction. For example, police may focus on a suspect and ignore other leads. In so doing, they may overlook exculpatory evidence, or it's not turned over to the prosecution, and in turn the exculpatory evidence doesn't make its way to the defense. Then the defense cannot investigate those facts (and in many cases doesn't investigate them anyway).

Lying by a non-eyewitness is also associated with wrongful conviction. A final factor is a death penalty culture or state punitiveness: In states that end up executing a larger percentage of the population than other states, the cases are more likely to go to wrongful conviction than near miss.

The study found that no single factor can explain wrongful convictions alone. When a young, unemployed suspect, living in a punitive environment, is the target of sloppy police work, false eyewitness identification, poorly gathered scientific evidence the chances of wrongful conviction will skyrocket. ■

DISCUSSION QUESTIONS

1. Does the chance of wrongful conviction influence your feelings about the death penalty?

2. Should prosecutors and judges be held personally liable for the effects of wrongful convictions, for example, if someone spends 15 years behind bars and it can be shown that the prosecutor withheld evidence from the defense?

Sources: Brian Skoloff, "Louis Taylor Set Free in Arizona after 40 Years in Prison, Enjoys First Day of Freedom," *Huffington Post*, April 3, 2013, www.huffingtonpost.com/2013/04/03/louis-taylor-set-free-after-forty-year (accessed June 2, 2013); Ed Pilkington, "Louisiana Death Row Inmate Freed after 15 Years—With a Little Help from DNA," *The Guardian*, December 6, 2012, www.guardian.co.uk/world/2012/dec/07/dna-testing-frees-man-death-row (accessed June 2, 2013); Jon Gould and John Firman, "Wrongful Convictions: The Latest Scientific Research and Implications for Law Enforcement," presentation at an National Institute of Justice Seminar, March 25, 2013, http://nij.gov/multimedia/presenter/presenter-gould-firman/data/resources/presenter-gould-firman-transcript.htm (accessed June 2, 2013).

CHAPTER SUMMARY

15

1. SUMMARIZE HOW VARIOUS FACTORS MAY CAUSE THE DIFFERENTIAL TREATMENT OF INDIVIDUALS DURING THE CRIMINAL JUSTICE PROCESS

- Differential treatment refers to the fact that one case may be treated differently than the next for both legitimate and illegitimate reasons.

- There are six key reasons for which cases are treated differently from one another: (1) offense seriousness, (2) celebrated cases, (3) race/ethnicity, (4) the offender's sex, (5) attorney competence, and (6) financial resources of the defendant. Sometimes these factors are combined in various ways.

2. DESCRIBE RACIAL AND ETHNIC DISPARITIES IN THE CRIMINAL PROCESS

- Researchers have uncovered some racial/ethnic disparities during police–citizen encounters (arrests and traffic stops) and during the pretrial period (methods of defense representation, bail decisions, and plea bargaining).

- There is much more evidence of racial/ethnic disparities at trial (this is particularly true in jury selection), during sentencing (minorities tend to receive harsher sentences), and in imprisonment and corrections contexts (minorities go to prison more often than whites, but whites go on probation more often than minorities).

- There is almost no evidence of racial/ethnic disparities in convictions; on the whole, whites are convicted more often than African-Americans.

- Many studies reveal significant racial/ethnic disparities in capital punishment. This prompted the Supreme Court, in the 1972 case of *Furman* v. *Georgia*, to declare the death penalty unconstitutional. The death penalty was reinstated in 1976 in *Gregg* v. *Georgia*.

3. DESCRIBE GENDER DISPARITIES IN THE CRIMINAL PROCESS

- Women are treated differently (generally, more leniently) than men.
- Research reveals that gender effects are most pronounced in the decision whether to imprison as opposed to decisions on convictions and sentence lengths.

4. EXPLAIN THE ISSUES SURROUNDING WRONGFUL CONVICTIONS AND THE MEANS FOR EXONERATION

- The problem of wrongful convictions has become so significant that an entire movement has been set in motion in response to them. Various Innocence Projects have been formed, and some progressive prosecutors have opened the doors of their offices to defense attorneys who are affiliated with Innocence Projects.
- An exoneration occurs when a person is wrongfully convicted and later declared not guilty. The number of exonerations has increased considerably in recent years, averaging 42 each year since 2000. Most exonerations have been for murder or rape/sexual assault.
- Reasons for wrongful convictions include duress, coercion, intoxication, diminished capacity, mental impairment, ignorance of the law, fear of violence, actual infliction of harm, threat of a harsh sentence, and misunderstanding of the situation.

KEY TERMS

Actual Innocence
  Awareness Database, 416
discrimination, 399
disparity, 399

error of justice, 414
ethnicity, 399
exoneration, 417
guided-discretion laws, 410

Innocence Network, 416
Innocence Project, 416
race, 399

REVIEW QUESTIONS

1. What is differential treatment, and why are some cases and some defendants treated differently than others?

2. How might racial and ethnic disparities affect the treatment of suspects and defendants within the justice system and in our country's courts?

3. How might gender discrimination within the justice system impact criminal case processing?

4. Why are some defendants wrongfully convicted? What methods might be used to avoid wrongful convictions and exonerate those who have been wrongfully convicted?

WHAT WILL YOU DO?

You are in your final year of studies in a criminal justice program that requires an internship. The internship supervisor was able to offer you a wide variety of possible field placements. You could have chosen to work for the local police department, the sheriff's department, various offices within the courthouse, or correctional personnel in the local prison. You opted, instead, to join a newly formed Innocence Project, put together by a small team of defense attorneys from the county in which your college is located. Four other students selected the same internship placement and are now working with you in efforts to identify inmates in the state's central prison who may have been wrongfully convicted.

The process involves one-on-one interviews with inmates who have been convicted of serious crimes by juries but are claiming innocence. An initial screening process weeds out those whose convictions are strongly supported by the evidence as well as those who have vacillated in their claims of innocence. Eventually, you hope to be able to identify a small cadre of convicts whose claims of innocence can be successfully demonstrated using technologies that are widely regarded as ironclad—especially those that lend themselves to DNA analysis.

Lately you have found yourself devoting most of your time to the case of one inmate in particular. His name is Willie Johnson, and you have come to believe that Willie provides a textbook case of wrongful conviction. Willie was convicted 15 years ago of the crime of forcible rape. The crime was alleged to have occurred when Willie was 18 years old, but the victim in the crime—a 16-year-old female who was attacked in the parking lot following a high school dance—was never able to identify Willie as her attacker with absolute certainty. Witnesses who heard the girl's screams, however, told responding officers that they had seen Willie running from the parking lot after the attack. Some of them knew Willie quite well and were certain that he was the person they had seen, and, to make matters worse, Willie's fingerprints were found all over the driver's side door of the girl's car.

Willie's story was that he had been trying to break into the car but that he had been frightened off by a large man waiting nearby in the shadows of the parking lot. Willie's target, he said, had been a CD player that he spied lying on the front seat of the car.

The rape victim had been taken to a hospital for examination immediately after the incident, and semen had been retrieved and preserved on a cotton swab. DNA tests conducted before trial were inconclusive. From your studies, however, you know that DNA technology has advanced considerably in the last 15 years, and you are hopeful that a retesting of the evidence could conclusively prove Willie's innocence. Willie's protestations of innocence are strong,

and you have come to feel that, on the strength of his personality, he is likely telling the truth.

Willie, of course, is not the only defendant with whom your team is working. Each of the other students has similarly identified inmates whose stories would seem to indicate their innocence. Moreover, the project's leaders—the defense attorneys under whose supervision you're working—have other clients in mind whose cases they would like to bring before the court for reconsideration. Almost all of the cases depend on a reanalysis of DNA samples gathered at crime scenes, all of which are more than a decade old.

Unfortunately, the Innocence Project has not been very successful in garnering donations and has only a few thousand dollars in its "war chest." Although you've heard rumors that state funding might one day be made available through the legislature to help support efforts like your own, the recent economic downturn has made that less likely.

You've learned that the laboratory selected to analyze the DNA evidence in Willie's case wants $2,500 to complete the test. The project's budget can't afford to foot the bill, and Willie has no relatives or supporters who are able to come up with that kind of money. Consequently, Willie has asked if you would be able to raise the needed money.

Your parents have just sent you a check for $5,500, which is intended to cover your tuition for the coming semester and to pay some of your living expenses. Although they previously sent tuition payments directly to the school, they now funnel them through you, knowing that it will help you to appreciate just how costly your education is and will allow you to increase your skills at managing money. You have begun to think, however, that a man's life hangs in the balance and that you could pay for the needed DNA analysis using part of the money that your parents have sent. You think that if you could prove Willie's innocence, your parents would surely understand.

When you discuss the idea with your roommate, however, he reminds you of the case of Roger Coleman, a Virginia coal miner who was executed in 1992 for the rape and murder of his sister-in-law. Coleman went to his death declaring his innocence and said that one day he would be proven innocent. After Coleman's execution, death penalty opponents lobbied the governor of Virginia, asking him to order new DNA tests that could prove Coleman's innocence. To the surprise of many, retests showed that Coleman had, in fact, been guilty. You remember that at the time a representative of the National District Attorneys Association said to the media that Coleman's guilt "gives the lie to the urban myth that there is an epidemic of wrongful convictions."

What will you do?

NOTES

i. Walker, Spohn, and DeLone, *The Color of Justice*, p. 6.

ii. Walker, Spohn, and DeLone, *The Color of Justice*, p. 10.

iii. S. Walker, C. Spohn, and M. DeLone, *The Color of Justice: Race, Ethnicity, and Crime in America*, 4th ed. (Belmont, CA: Wadsworth, 2007), p. 18.

iv. Walker, Spohn, and DeLone, *The Color of Justice*, p. 293.

v. B. Forst, *Errors of Justice* (New York: Cambridge University Press, 2004), pp. 3–4.

vi. Ibid.

vii. Innocence Network home page. Available at http://www.innocencenetwork.org (accessed July 15, 2009).

viii. Actual Innocence Awareness Database, Jamail Center for Legal Research. Available at http://web.austin.utexas.edu/law_library/innocence/index.cfm (accessed July 15, 2008).

ix. S. R. Gross, K. Jacoby, D. J. Matheson, N. Montgomery, and S. Patil, "Exonerations in the United States 1989 through 2003," *Journal of Criminal Law and Criminology* 95(2005):523–560.

1. Tonya Alanez, "Need a Lawyer? To Wealthy or Famous, Bogenschutz Is the Guy in Broward for Criminal Defense," *Sun-Sentinel*, June 19, 2010, available at http://articles.sun-sentinel.com/2010-06-19/news/fl-bogenschutz-profile-20100619_1_criminal-defense-bogenschutz-criminal-defense (accessed May 10, 2013).

2. Matthew Hendley, "Did Ryan LeVin Buy His Way Out of Prison?," *Broward-Palm Beach New Times*, June 4, 2011. http://blogs.browardpalmbeach.com/pulp/2011/06/ryan_levin_bogenschutz_prison.php (accessed September 10, 2013).

3. M. Feeley, *The Process Is the Punishment: Handling Cases in a Lower Criminal Court* (New York: Russell Sage, 1979).

4. S. Walker, C. Spohn, and M. DeLone, *The Color of Justice: Race, Ethnicity, and Crime in America*, 4th ed. (Belmont, CA: Wadsworth, 2007), p. 6. Wadsworth, a part of Cengage Learning, Inc. Reproduced by permission. www.cengage.com/permissions.

5. Ibid., p. 10.

6. Ibid., p. 18.

7. C. R. Mann, *Unequal Justice* (Bloomington: Indiana University Press, 1988).

8. W. Wilbanks, *The Myth of a Racist Criminal Justice System* (Monterey, CA: Brooks/Cole, 1987).

9. Walker et al., *The Color of Justice*, p. 19.

10. Ibid., p. 420.

11. J. R. Phelps, "What Does 'Competent Representation' Really Mean?" Florida Bar News, available at http://www.floridabar.org/DIVCOM/JN/jnnews01.nsf/Articles/7AAB34D8B89C242385256B6B0051B64E (accessed May 8, 2013).

12. This classification scheme borrows from Walker et al., *The Color of Justice*. Much of the discussion that follows draws from their book; much of the discussion was also drawn from R. J. Sampson and J. L. Lauritsen, "Racial and Ethnic Disparities in Crime and Criminal Justice in the United States," *Crime and Justice: A Review of Research*, Vol. 21 (1997), pp. 311–374.

13. See, e.g., www.merriam-webster.com/dictionary/ethnic (accessed March 1, 2013).

14. R. Tillman, "The Size of the Criminal Population: The Prevalence and Incidence of Adult Arrest," *Criminology*, Vol. 25 (1987), pp. 561–579.

15. D. Black, "The Social Organization of Arrest," *Stanford Law Review*, Vol. 23 (1971), pp. 1087–1111.

16. D. A. Smith, C. Visher, and L. A. Davidson, "Equity and Discretionary Justice: The Influence of Race on Police Arrest Decisions," *Journal of Criminal Law and Criminology*, Vol. 75 (1984), pp. 234–249.

17. J. R. Hepburn, "Race and the Decision to Arrest: An Analysis of Warrants Issued," *Journal of Research in Crime and Delinquency*, Vol. 15 (1978), pp. 54–73.

18. G. P. Alpert, R. G. Dunham, and M. R. Smith, "Investigating Racial Profiling by the Miami-Dade Police Department: A Multimethod Approach," *Criminology and Public Policy*, Vol. 6 (2007), pp. 25–56.

19. J. Schafer, D. Carter, and A. Katz-Bannister, "Studying Traffic Stop Encounters," *Journal of Criminal Justice*, Vol. 32 (2004), pp. 159–170.

20. M. Smith and G. Alpert, "Explaining Police Bias: A Theory of Social Conditioning and Illusory Correlation," *Criminal Justice and Behavior*, Vol. 34 (2007), pp. 1262–1283.

21. B. Withrow, "Race-Based Policing: A Descriptive Analysis of the Wichita Stop Study," *Police Practice and Research*, Vol. 5 (2004), pp. 223–240; B. Withrow, "A Comparative Analysis of Commonly Used Benchmarks in Racial Profiling: A Research Note," *Justice Research and Policy*, Vol. 6 (2004), pp. 71–92.

22. www.census.gov/prod/2007pubs/p60-233.pdf (accessed March 1, 2013). See table 1, p. 5.

23. Bureau of Justice Statistics, *Defense Counsel in Criminal Cases* (Washington, DC: U.S. Department of Justice, 2000), table 5.

24. M. D. Holmes, H. M. Hosch, H. C. Daudistel, D. A. Perez, and J. B. Graves, "Ethnicity, Legal Resources, and Felony Dispositions in Two Southwestern Jurisdictions," *Justice Quarterly*, Vol. 13 (1996), pp. 11–30.

25. C. Spohn and M. DeLone, "When Does Race Matter? An Examination of the Conditions under Which Race Affects Sentence Severity," *Sociology of Crime, Law, and Deviance*, Vol. 2 (2000), pp. 3–37.

26. R. Stryker, I. Nagel, and J. Hagan, "Methodology Issues in Court Research: Pretrial Release Decisions for Federal Defendants," *Sociological Methods and Research*, Vol. 11 (1983), pp. 460–500; also see C. M. Katz and C. Spohn, "The Effect of Race and Gender on Bail Outcomes: A Test of an Interactive Model," *American Journal of Criminal Justice*, Vol. 19 (1995), pp. 161–184.

27. S. H. Clarke and G. C. Koch, "The Influence of Income and Other Factors on Whether Criminal Defendants Go to Prison," *Law and Society Review*, Vol. 11 (1976), pp. 57–92.

28. S. Demuth and D. Steffensmeier, "The Impact of Gender and Race-Ethnicity in the Pretrial Release Process," *Social Problems*, Vol. 51 (2004), pp. 222–242.

29. G. S. Bridges, *A Study on Racial and Ethnic Disparities in Superior Court Bail and Pre-Trial Detention Practices in Washington* (Olympia: Washington State Minority and Justice Commission, 1997).

30. Ibid., p. 98.

31. C. A. Albonetti, R. M. Hauser, J. Hagan, and I. H. Nagel, "Criminal Justice Decision Making as a Stratification Process: The Role of Race and Stratification Resources in Pretrial Release," *Journal of Quantitative Criminology*, Vol. 5 (1989), pp. 57–82.

32. Bureau of Justice Statistics, *Felony Defendants in Large Urban Counties, 2000* (Washington, DC: U.S. Department of Justice, 2003), table 24.

33. Spohn and DeLone, "When Does Race Matter?," pp. 3–37; also see Walker et al., *The Color of Justice*, pp. 182–183.

34. See, e.g., L. Bienen, N. Weiner, D. Denno, P. Allison, and D. Mills, "The Reimposition of Capital Punishment in New Jersey: The Role of Prosecutorial Discretion," *Rutgers Law Review*, Vol. 48 (1988), pp. 386–398; T. Keil and G. Vito, "Race, Homicide, Severity, and Application of the Death Penalty: A Consideration of the Barnett Scale," *Criminology*, Vol. 27 (1989), pp. 511–533; G. LaFree, "The Effect of Sexual Stratification by Race on Official Reactions to Rape," *American Sociological Review*, Vol. 45 (1980), pp. 842–854; R. Paternoster, "Prosecutorial Discretion in Requesting the Death Penalty: A Case of Victim-Based Racial Discrimination," *Law and Society Review*, Vol. 18 (1984), pp. 437–478; M. Radelet and G. Pierce, "Race and Prosecutorial Discretion in Homicide Cases," *Law and Society Review*, Vol. 19 (1985), pp. 587–621; C. Spohn, J. Gruhl, and S. Welch, "The Impact of Ethnicity and Gender of Defendants on the Decision to Reject or Dismiss Felony Charges," *Criminology*, Vol. 25 (1987), pp. 175–191.

35. For a review of this literature, see Walker et al., *The Color of Justice*, pp. 185–186.

36. L. M. Mather, *Plea Bargaining or Trial?* (Washington, DC: Heath, 1979).

37. P. F. Nardulli, J. Eisenstein, and R. B. Flemming, *The Tenor of Justice: Criminal Courts and the Guilty Plea* (Chicago: University of Chicago Press, 1988).

38. M. D. Holmes, H. C. Daudistel, and R. A. Farrell, "Determinants of Charge Reductions and Final Dispositions in Cases of Burglary and Robbery," *Journal of Research in Crime and Delinquency*, Vol. 24 (1987), pp. 233–254.

39. R. Weitzer, "Racial Discrimination in the Criminal Justice System: Findings and Problems in the Literature," *Journal of Criminal Justice*, Vol. 24 (1996), p. 313.

40. L. D. Maxfield and J. H. Kramer, *Substantial Assistance: An Empirical Yardstick Gauging Equity in Current Federal Policy and Practice* (Washington, DC: U.S. Sentencing Commission, 1998).

41. H. Lee, *To Kill a Mockingbird* (New York: Warner Books, 1960), p. 220.

42. B. M. Turner, R. D. Lovell, J. C. Young, and W. F. Denny, "Race and Peremptory Challenges during Voir Dire: Do Prosecution and Defense Agree?," *Journal of Criminal Justice*, Vol. 14 (1986), pp. 61–69.

43. Ibid., p. 68.

44. *Johnson v. California*, 543 U.S. 499 (2005); *Miller El v. Dretke*, 545 U.S. 231 (2005).

45. S. L. Johnson, "Black Innocence and the White Jury," *University of Michigan Law Review*, Vol. 83 (1985), pp. 16–26.

46. K. Klein and B. Creech, "Race, Rape, and Bias: Distortion of Prior Odds and Meaning Changes," *Basic and Applied Social Psychology*, Vol. 3 (1982), pp. 21–33.

47. See, e.g., M. R. Williams and M. W. Burek, "Justice, Juries, and Convictions: The Relevance of Race in Jury Verdicts," *Journal of Crime and Justice*, Vol. 31 (2008), pp. 149–169; M. R. Williams, S. Demuth, and J. E. Holcomb, "Understanding the Influence of Victim Gender in Death Penalty Cases: The Importance of Victim Race, Sex-Related Victimization, and Jury Decision Making," *Criminology*, Vol. 45 (2007), pp. 865–892.

48. U.S. Department of Justice, Bureau of Justice Statistics, *Compendium of Federal Justice Statistics, 2003*, NCJ 210299 (Washington, DC: U.S. Department of Justice, 2005), p. 65.

49. Ibid. Also see U.S. Department of Justice, Bureau of Justice Statistics, *State Court Sentencing of Convicted Felons, 2004 Statistical Tables*, NCJ 217995, tables 2.1 and 2.3, available at http://bjs.ojp.usdoj.gov/index.cfm?ty=pbdetail&iid=1533 (accessed March 1, 2013).

50. P. Burke and A. Turk, "Factors Affecting Post Arrest Decisions: A Model for Analysis," *Social Problems*, Vol. 22 (1975), pp. 313–332; J. Petersilia, *Racial Disparities in the Criminal Justice System* (Santa Monica, CA: RAND, 1983); W. Wilbanks, *The Myth of a Racist Criminal Justice System* (Monterey, CA: Brooks/Cole, 1987).

51. Burke and Turk, "Factors Affecting Post Arrest Decisions," pp. 328–329.

52. Sampson and Lauritsen, "Racial and Ethnic Disparities in Crime and Criminal Justice in the United States," p. 346.

53. T. Sellin, "Race Prejudice in the Administration of Justice," *American Journal of Sociology*, Vol. 41 (1935), p. 217.

54. J. Hagan, "Extra-Legal Attributes and Criminal Sentencing: An Assessment of a Sociological Viewpoint," *Law and Society Review*, Vol. 8 (1974), pp. 357–383; G. Kleck, "Racial Discrimination in Sentencing: A Critical Evaluation of the Evidence with Additional Evidence on the Death Penalty," *American Sociological Review*, Vol. 43 (1981), pp. 783–805.

55. J. Hagan and K. Bumiller, "Making Sense of Sentencing: A Review and Critique of Sentencing Research," in A. Blumstein, J. Cohen, S. Martin, and M. Tonry, eds., *Research on Sentencing: The Search for Reform* (Washington, DC: National Academy Press, 1983), p. 93.

56. A. Blumstein, J. Cohen, S. Martin, and M. Tonry, eds., *Research on Sentencing: The Search for Reform* (Washington, DC: National Academy Press, 1983), p. 93.

57. M. Zatz, "The Changing Forms of Racial/Ethnic Biases in Sentencing," *Journal of Research in Crime and Delinquency*, Vol. 25 (1987), p. 87.

58. T. Chiricos and C. Crawford, "Race and Imprisonment: A Contextual Assessment of the Evidence," in D. F. Hawkins, ed., *Ethnicity, Race, and Crime: Perspectives across Time and Place* (Albany: State University of New York Press, 1995), p. 300.

59. C. Spohn, "Thirty Years of Sentencing Reform: A Quest for a Racially Neutral Sentencing Process, in *Policies, Processes, and Decisions of the Criminal Justice System*, Vol. 3, *Criminal Justice 2000* (Washington, DC: U.S. Department of Justice, 2000), pp. 455–456.

60. Ibid., pp. 462–463 (citations omitted).

61. Walker et al., *The Color of Justice*, p. 239.

62. Abridgement of Section VI. Racially Disproportionate Incarceration of Drug Offenders, *Punishment and Prejudice*, Human Rights Watch, May 2000. © 2000 Human Rights Watch. Reprinted by permission.

63. Ibid.

64. C. Spohn and J. Spears, "Sentencing of Drug Offenders in Three Cities: Does Race/Ethnicity Make a Difference?," in D. F. Hawkins, S. L. Meyers, Jr., and R. N. Stone, eds., *Crime Control and Criminal Justice: The Delicate Balance* (Westport, CT: Greenwood Press, 2002), pp. 197–231; S. Steen, R. L. Engen, and R. R. Gainey, "Images of Danger and Culpability: Racial Stereotyping, Case Processing, and Criminal Sentencing," *Criminology*, Vol. 45 (2005), pp. 435–468; C. A. Albonetti, "Sentencing under the Federal Guidelines: Effects of Defendant Characteristics, Guilty Pleas, and Departures on Sentence Outcomes for Drug Offenses, 1991–1992," *Law and Society Review*, Vol. 31 (1997), pp. 789–822.

65. U.S. Sentencing Commission, *Report to Congress: Cocaine and Federal Sentencing Policy* (Washington, DC: U.S. Sentencing Commission, 2002), p. viii.

66. *United States v. Booker*, 543 U.S. 220 (2005); *Kimbrough v. United States*, 06-6330 (2007).

67. For a discussion of the crack cocaine amendments, go to www.fd.org/ods-other/crack-cocaine-sentencing (accessed March 1, 2013).

68. Walker et al., *The Color of Justice*, p. 235.

69. Ibid.

70. U.S. Department of Justice, Bureau of Justice Statistics, *Prison and Jail Inmates at Midyear 1998*, Bulletin NCJ 173414, p. 6 (table 7), p. 7; *2000*, Bulletin NCJ 185989, p. 7, table 9; *2002*, Bulletin NCJ 198877, p. 8, Table 10; *2003*, Bulletin NCJ 203947, p. 8, Table 10; *2005*, Bulletin NCJ 213133, p. 8, Table 10; *Jail Inmates at Midyear 2007*, Bulletin NCJ 221945, p. 5, Table 6 (Washington, DC: U.S. Department of Justice).

71. W. J. Sabol and T. D. Minton, *Jail Inmates at Midyear 2007* (Washington, DC: Bureau of Justice Statistics, 2008), p. 5.

72. Walker et al., *The Color of Justice*, p. 352.

73. L. E. Glaze, *Probation and Parole in the United States, 2006* (Washington, DC: Bureau of Justice Statistics, 2007).

74. Walker et al., *The Color of Justice*, pp. 355–356.

75. *In re Kemmler*, 136 U.S. 436 (1890), p. 447.

76. *Furman v. Georgia*, 408 U.S. 238 (1972).

77. Ibid., p. 257.

78. Ibid., p. 310.

79. Ibid., p. 313.

80. S. R. Gross and R. Mauro, *Death and Discrimination: Racial Disparities in Capital Sentencing* (Boston: Northeastern University Press, 1989), p. 215.

81. Walker et al., *The Color of Justice*, p. 293.

82. Ibid.

83. *Woodson v. North Carolina*, 428 U.S. 280 (1976).

84. *Roberts v. Louisiana*, 428 U.S. 280 (1976).

85. *Proffitt v. Florida*, 428 U.S. 242 (1976); *Gregg v. Georgia*, 428 U.S. 153 (1976); *Jurek v. Texas*, 428 U.S. 262 (1976).

86. *Gregg v. Georgia*, 428 U.S. 153 (1976).

87. Ibid., pp. 206–207.

88. See, e.g., H. Garfinkel, "Research Note on Inter- and Intra-Racial Homicides," *Social Forces*, Vol. 217 (1949), pp. 369–381; P. H. Ralph, J. R. Sorenson, and J. W. Marquart, "A Comparison of Death-Sentenced and Incarcerated Murderers in Pre-*Furman* Texas," *Justice Quarterly*, Vol. 9 (1992), pp. 185–209; M. E. Wolfgang and M. Reidel, "Race, Judicial Discretion, and the Death Penalty," *Annals of the American Academy*, Vol. 407 (1973), pp. 119–133; D. C. Baldus, G. Woodworth, and C. A. Pulaski, *Equal Justice and the Death Penalty: A Legal and Empirical Analysis* (Boston: Northeastern University Press, 1990).

89. Kleck, "Racial Discrimination in Sentencing," p. 788.

90. Wolfgang and Reidel, "Race, Judicial Discretion, and the Death Penalty," pp. 119–133, tables 1 and 2.

91. Ibid., p. 133.

92. *Gregg v. Georgia*, 428 U.S. 153 (1976), p. 206.

93. Wolfgang and Reidel, "Rape, Race, and the Death Penalty in Georgia," p. 667.

94. W. J. Bowers and G. L. Pierce, "Arbitrariness and Discrimination under Post-*Furman* Capital Cases," *Crime and Delinquency*, Vol. 26 (1980), p. 587.

95. A. Sarat, "Recapturing the Spirit of '*Furman*': The American Bar Association and the New Abolitionist Politics," *Law and Contemporary Problems*, Vol. 61 (1998), p. 27.

96. For a list of studies, see Walker et al., *The Color of Justice*, pp. 336–337, n. 87.

97. U.S. Government Accountability Office, *Death Penalty Sentencing: Research Indicates Pattern of Racial Disparities* (Washington, DC: Government Accountability Office, 1990), p. 5.

98. Walker et al., *The Color of Justice*, p. 313.

99. *McCleskey v. Kemp*, 481 U.S. 279 (1987).

100. It was published in book form in 1990: D. C. Baldus, G. Woodworth, and C. A. Pulaski, *Equal Justice and the Death Penalty: A Legal and Empirical Analysis* (Boston: Northeastern University Press, 1990).

101. *McCleskey v. Kemp*, 481 U.S. 279 (1987), p. 281.

102. See, e.g., *Washington v. Davis*, 426 U.S. 229 (1976), or *Personnel Administrator of Massachusetts v. Feeney*, 442 U.S. 256 (1979); *Palmer v. Thomas*, 403 U.S. 217 (1971).

103. J. Acker, "A Different Agenda: The Supreme Court, Empirical Evidence, and Capital Punishment Decisions, 1986–1989," *Law and Society Review*, Vol. 27 (1993), pp. 65–86.

104. www.albany.edu/sourcebook/pdf/t654.pdf (accessed March 1, 2013).

105. U.S. Department of Justice, Bureau of Justice Statistics, *Prisoners in 2006*, Bulletin NCJ 219416, p. 23, appendix table 8.

106. U.S. Department of Justice, Bureau of Justice Statistics, *Prison and Jail Inmates at Midyear 1998*, Bulletin NCJ 173414, p. 6 (table 7), 7; *2000*, Bulletin NCJ 185989, p. 7, Table 9; *2002*, Bulletin NCJ 198877, p. 8, Table 10; *2003*, Bulletin NCJ 203947, p. 8, Table 10; *2005*, Bulletin NCJ 213133, p. 8, Table 10; *Jail Inmates at Midyear 2007*, Bulletin NCJ 221945, p. 5, table 6.

107. Kathleen Daly found just this in K. Daly, *Gender, Crime, and Punishment* (New Haven, CT: Yale University Press, 1994).

108. See, e.g., G. S. Bickle and R. D. Peterson, "The Impact of Gender-Based Family Roles on Criminal Sentencing," *Social Problems*, Vol. 38 (1991), pp. 372–394; K. Daly and R. L. Bordt, "Sex Effects and Sentencing: An Analysis of the Statistics Literature," *Justice Quarterly*, Vol. 12 (1995), pp. 143–177; C. Spohn, *How Do Judges Decide? The Search for Fairness and Justice in Punishment* (Thousand Oaks, CA: Sage, 2002); D. Steffensmeier, J. Kramer, and C. Streifel, "Gender and Imprisonment Decisions," *Criminology*, Vol. 31 (1993), pp. 411–446.

109. Ibid.

110. C. Spohn, S. Welch, and J. Gruhl, "Women Defendants in Court: The Interaction between Sex and Race in Convicting and Sentencing," *Social Science Quarterly*, Vol. 66 (1985), pp. 178–185.

111. With kind permission from Springer Science+Business Media, D. Steffensmeier and S. Demuth, "Does Gender Modify the Effects of Race-Ethnicity on Criminal Sanctioning? Sentences for Male and Female White, Black, and Hispanic Defendants," *Journal of Quantitative Criminology*, Vol. 22 (2006), pp. 241–261.

112. Ibid., p. 244; also see D. Steffensmeir, J. Ulmer, and J. Kramer, "The Interaction of Race, Gender, and Age in Criminal Sentencing: The Punishment Cost of Being Young, Black, and Male," *Criminology*, Vol. 36 (1998), pp. 763–798.

113. G. H. Ryan, press release, January 31, 2000, available at www3.illinois.gov/PressReleases/ShowPressRelease.cfm?SubjectID=3&RecNum=359 (accessed March 1, 2013).

114. B. Forst, *Errors of Justice* (New York: Cambridge University Press, 2004), pp. 3–4.

115. For some classic works in this area, see E. M. Borchard, *Convicting the Innocent: Sixty-Five Actual Errors of Criminal Justice* (Garden City, NY: Garden City Publishing Company, 1932); H. A. Bedau, *The Death Penalty in America* (Chicago: Aldine, 1964); M. L. Radalet, H. A. Bedau, and C. E. Putnam, *In Spite of Innocence: Erroneous Convictions in Capital Cases* (Boston: Northeastern University Press, 1992); B. Scheck, P. Neufeld, and J. Dwyer, *Actual Innocence and Other Dispatches from the Wrongfully Convicted* (New York: Doubleday, 2000).

116. Forst, *Errors of Justice*, p. 5.

117. A. Berlow, "A Jury of Your Peers? Only If You're Clueless," *Washington Post*, August 11, 2002, pp. B1–B2; C. R. Huff, A. Rattner, and E. Sagarin, *Convicted but Innocent: Wrongful Conviction and Public Policy* (Thousand Oaks, CA: Sage, 1996).

118. Forst, *Errors of Justice*, p. 16.

119. www.utexas.edu/courses/bio301d/Topics/DNA/text.html (March 1, 2013). Courtesy of James Bull, University of Texas and Craig Pease, Vermont Law School.

120. Ibid.

121. Ibid.

122. "About the Innocence Project" and "The Innocence Network," www.innocenceproject.org, © 2009. Courtesy of the Innocence Project..

123. Ibid.

124. http://tarlton.law.utexas.edu/current_awareness/actual_innocence (accessed March 1, 2013).

125. www.innocenceproject.org/fix/Priority-Issues.php (accessed March 1, 2013).

126. R. Balko, "Is This America's Best Prosecutor?." *Reason Magazine*, available at http://reason.com/archives/2008/04/07/is-this-americas-best-prosecut (accessed March 1, 2013).

127. S. R. Gross, K. Jacoby, D. J. Matheson, N. Montgomery, and S. Patil, "Exonerations in the United States 1989 through 2003," *Journal of Criminal Law and Criminology*, Vol. 95 (2005), pp. 523–560.

128. Ibid., p. 524.

129. Gross et al., "Exonerations in the United States 1989 through 2003," pp. 523–560.

130. www.law.umich.edu/special/exoneration/Pages/detaillist.aspx (accessed March 1, 2013).

131. Ibid., p. 528.

132. Ibid., p. 529.

133. "Eyewitness Misidentification," www.innocenceproject.org, © 2009. Courtesy of the Innocence Project.

134. Ibid.

135. Gross et al., "Exonerations in the United States 1989 through 2003," p. 551.

© Guy Cali/Corbis

Technology, Alternatives, and the Future

16

Theodora Dallas, 34, a British juror who was jailed for six months for researching the criminal history of a defendant while sitting on a jury. She was found guilty of contempt of court for ignoring a judge's order to avoid Internet-based research concerning the case that she was hearing. Do you think jurors should be able to take the initiative to learn more about the defendants whose fate they will be deciding? Why do most judges oppose such research?

National News/ZUMAPRESS/Newscom

INTRODUCTION

Library Extra
16–1 Virtual Court Prototype

Advances in technology have made today's courtrooms into far different places than courtrooms of the recent past. As this chapter will show, courts in many parts of the country and throughout the world have embraced high-technology—seeking to improve efficiency, reduce waste, and improve communications between all of the parties involved. The ubiquitous nature of personal technology, however, poses both questions and challenges for today's professional courtroom personnel, including judges, attorneys, and bailiffs. In an interesting case from London, juror Theodora Dallas was jailed for six months for researching the criminal history of a defendant while sitting on a jury. Dallas, 34, a professor of psychology at the University of Bedfordshire, was found guilty of contempt of court after ignoring a judge's order to avoid Internet-based research concerning the case that she was hearing. The chief justice who sent Dallas to jail told reporters that "the damage to the administration of justice is obvious." People less informed than the justice, however, were left to wonder how a juror's desire to be as informed as possible about a defendant would lead to a less-than-effective verdict.

Learning Objective 1
Explain how courts are affected by new technologies.

Library Extra
16–2 E-Courts: Developing a Virtual Court—Clark County (Nevada) Regional Justice Center Experience

TECHNOLOGY IN THE COURTS

Courts are making use of software advances, new hardware, the Internet, communications improvements, database integration, and other technologies, all in the name of improving efficiency. Some courts are "wired," meaning that they employ a variety of technologies in one setting; others use technology on a piecemeal basis; and some barely use it at all and remain mired in the past, clinging to outmoded devices like audiotape players and VCRs (this is the norm, unfortunately). At the other extreme, a handful of jurisdictions have developed courtrooms of the future that, it is hoped, will serve as models for other courts to follow in time. We begin with wired courts.

Wired Courts

wired court
A court that employs one or more technologies to improve its operations; also called *technology-enabled court.*

A **wired court** is one that employs one or more technologies to improve its operations. Wired courts have also been called *technology-enabled courts.* Wired courts use a range of technologies:

- Computers
- Trial presentation software and litigation support software

- Evidence presentation systems
- Evidence displays
- Sound systems
- Reporting/recording systems
- Videoconferencing
- Internet access
- Document cameras
- DVD players[1]

The Federal Judicial Center has identified three levels of courtroom technology[2]:

- *Level 1 technologies.* The technologies at the first level are relatively simple, cost effective, and easily accessible. An example is an evidence camera that displays evidence on a screen for jurors to see.
- *Level 2 technologies.* At the next level, the technologies are more sophisticated and include such devices as integrated lecterns and electronic whiteboards.
- *Level 3 technologies.* The highest-level technologies are the most advanced and include immersive imaging technology (IPIX) and virtual reality displays. Such technologies are not used nearly as often as those in the first or second level.

See Box 16–1 for more examples of technologies from each of the three levels.

Courtroom Hardware   A number of courts contain the hardware necessary for attorneys to present complex arguments using technology. Examples include wireless networks, flat-panel monitors, integrated lecterns (rolling presentation stations outfitted with computers

---

BOX 16–1   Levels of Technology and Examples

LEVEL 1 TECHNOLOGIES

Evidence camera
Laptop computer with retrieval and presentation software
Monitors outside the jury box
Digital projector and projection screen
Annotation equipment
Color video printer
Audio system
Telephone interpreting system
System controls
Legacy equipment

LEVEL 2 TECHNOLOGIES

Small monitors built into the jury box
Electronic whiteboard
Integrated lectern
Videoconferencing equipment
Real-time reporting
Digital audio reporting
Internet connections

LEVEL 3 TECHNOLOGIES

IPIX displays
Virtual reality displays
Holograms
Large-scale video ■

Source: Federal Judicial Center, *Effective Use of Technology: A Judge's Guide to Pretrial and Trial,* available at www.fjc.gov/public/pdf.nsf/lookup/CTtech16.pdf/$file/CTtech16.pdf (accessed March 4, 2013).

and other gadgets), color video printers, light pens, touch screens to control displays, closed-circuit television for some witness testimony, projectors, electronic whiteboards, DVD players, and so on.

Many of these devices have been available for years but have been slow to catch on. A recent American Bar Association (ABA) survey revealed that most attorneys still do not use laptops or notebooks in the courtroom.[3] Courts themselves are also lean on hardware; many courts lag behind and have not integrated information technology into their daily routines.

Litigation Support Software Litigation support software is designed to assist attorneys in organizing and presenting their cases and is useful for managing transcripts and documents, accessing evidence, and providing document imaging. Less than half of practicing attorneys, however, have access to the proper software[4]; of those who do, most work for large legal firms that have the resources necessary for acquiring expensive programs.

There are several dedicated litigation support software programs, including Sanction II (www.sanction.com), Trial Director (www.indatacorp.com), Trial Pro II (www.ideaview .com), and Visionary (www.freevisionary.com). These litigation support programs help attorneys perform a number of tasks:

- Organizing trial exhibits
- Organizing, presenting, and viewing deposition testimony (mainly for civil trials)

Web Extra
16–1 Center for Court Innovation

- Searching witness testimony electronically (as opposed to reading it all)
- Viewing linked exhibits
- Creating video clips for use at trial
- Annotating documents with arrows, stamps, and highlights
- Displaying sections of the trial transcript, such as to emphasize a witness's contradictory testimony
- Overlaying exhibits, such as to compare the authenticity of a signature

Additional computer programs that have proven useful in a trial setting and with which many of us are familiar include the following:

- Microsoft PowerPoint
- Macromedia Director (graphics software)
- SmartDraw (drawing program)
- Microsoft Visio (drawing program)
- TimeMap (timeline program)

Web Extra
16–2 Center for Court Innovation—YouTube Channel

- ACDSee Power Pack (program combining picture viewer, photo editor, and multi-media slide show and screen-saver creator)
- TechSmith Snagit (program for computer screen shots)
- Adobe Photoshop and Corel PhotoPaint (program used for cropping, touching up, and editing digital photos)

Uses for Technology

The courts have begun to use technology for a number of purposes. We look at a few such purposes, including electronic filing, database integration, electronic discovery, online depositions, high-tech evidence presentation, and court Web logs (i.e., blogs), in the subsections that follow.

Electronic Filing **Electronic filing**, or e-filing, is "the process of transmitting documents and other court information to the court through an electronic medium, rather than on paper. Electronic filing lets people get more of their work done with their PCs, . . . send and receive documents, pay filing fees, notify other parties, receive court notices, and retrieve court information."[5] Most attorneys prepare documents with word processing software, print them off, and submit them in hard-copy format. Documents may eventually be archived, but most often they circulate to the various parties in print form. Electronic filing eliminates all this needless paperwork.

Database Integration Public agencies are frequently criticized for their lack of information sharing and communications problems. Integrated databases (also called "justice information systems") help solve some of these problems. In the criminal justice context, these can be set up such that the various branches of the criminal justice system share information with one another. An example is Washington State's Justice Information Network, which provides extensive criminal history and case information for sharing among the various organizations tasked with enforcing the criminal law. Another example is Indiana's Electronic Citation and Warning System (eCWS), which "lets officers electronically record citation information in the field, eliminating the need for redundant manual data entry, drastically reducing administrative work."[6] Data are then transmitted to appropriate law enforcement personnel, courts, and state and federal agencies.

Electronic Discovery In this era of electronic communications, much can be discovered electronically. E-discovery refers to the process of securing and/or using electronic data as evidence in a civil or criminal case. This form of discovery is useful because of the increasing role of electronic communication, both in the criminal world and throughout the criminal justice system.

Online Depositions A **deposition** is the testimony of a witness given under oath and recorded for use in court at a later date. A problem with depositions is that they can be difficult to schedule at a time when all parties are readily available. **Online depositions** (testimony recorded electronically) provide an alternative. According to one source, "An Internet deposition is a deposition in which a videographer and a court reporter are synchronized during depositions. The video and audio signal is fed live through the Internet to a location other than where the deposition is currently taking place."[7]

High-Tech Evidence Presentation Technology is especially useful for presenting evidence to juries in complex cases. However, one expert observed that "most trial lawyers still present exhibits to juries the old-fashioned way: holding up pictures, passing documents to jurors, and using blow-ups on easels that the jury can barely see. That is no longer the best way to present evidence, particularly in document-intensive cases, and is certainly an inefficient use of courtroom time."[8]

Court Web Logs A number of courts publish their own Web logs, or blogs, that contain pertinent information such as hearing dates and decisions. Web logs are attractive both because they are inexpensive to organize and because they improve public access to the goings-on of the court. Some jurisdictions have moved beyond the blog approach and provide links on their websites to case status reports.

Demonstration Projects

Some courts, such as Courtroom 21, a project of the Center for Legal and Court Technology at the College of William and Mary Law School, integrate a variety of technologies.

---

electronic filing
"[T]he process of transmitting documents and other court information to the court through an electronic medium, rather than on paper"[i]; also called e-*filing*.

Library Extra
16–3 Ohio Court Futures Commission—Final Report

Library Extra
16–4 Emerging Trends for Courts

electronic discovery
The process of securing and/or using electronic data as evidence in a civil or criminal case.

deposition
The testimony of a witness given under oath and recorded for use in court at a later date. A problem with depositions is that they can be difficult to schedule at a time when all parties are readily available.

online deposition
An alternative to the conventional process of deposing a witness in person that employs communications technology to depose the witness from a remote location.

Web Extra
16–3 The Center for Legal and Court Technology's Courtroom 21 Project

According to Courtroom 21, "[T]he Courtroom has a wide variety of differing technologies, including all available major court record systems, evidence presentation technologies, assistive and foreign language interpretation technologies and critical infrastructure technologies."[9]

While Courtroom 21 is mostly a demonstration project, some courts throughout the country have created their own version of this high-tech facility. For example, the Roger A. Barker Courtroom in Florida's Ninth Judicial Circuit (Orange County), also called Courtroom 23, has implemented a range of technologies:

- Evidence presentation system
- Internet and remote broadcasting
- Real-time court reporting
- Desktop technology
- Plasma display monitors
- Video annotation
- Videoconferencing
- Digital court reporting
- Computerized legal research
- Advanced audio
- Touch-screen integration
- Wireless network[10]

Technology can also be used to improve courtroom security. To read more about this, see the following "Courts in the News" feature.

ALTERNATIVES TO TRADITIONAL ADJUDICATION

Learning Objective 2

Describe alternatives to criminal prosecutions, including alternative dispute resolution, mediation, and diversion.

Web Extra

16–4 National Council for State Courts—Future Trends in State Courts

Not only is the information technology movement revolutionizing the court process, so too are alternatives to the traditional trial process. Two concerns have led to alternative methods of adjudication. The first concern is that of crowded court dockets; given resource constraints, it is impractical and costly to resolve all disputes in court. The result is a recent surge in alternative dispute resolution. The second concern is the divisive nature of the criminal law, which pits victims and the state against a suspected criminal and often seeks to punish guilty offenders rather than strengthen community bonds. Restorative justice has emerged as a means of addressing this problem. We look at both alternative dispute resolution and restorative justice in the pages that follow.

Alternative Dispute Resolution

alternative dispute resolution (ADR)
"[A]ny means of settling disputes outside of the courtroom."[iii]

arbitration
A simplified version of a trial without discovery and with modified rules of evidence.

arbitrator
A private, neutral person, typically trained in alternative dispute resolution, chosen to arbitrate a disagreement and empowered to impose a binding judgment or decision.

According to the Legal Information Institute at Cornell University, **alternative dispute resolution** (ADR) "refers to any means of settling disputes outside of the courtroom."[11] ADR has gained popularity due to growing court caseloads, expensive litigation, and time delays faced by litigants. Many ADR programs are voluntary, but an increasing number have become mandatory. For example, home buyers often agree to ADR in the event a legal dispute arises between them and the seller. Examples of ADR include arbitration, mediation, neutral evaluation, and conciliation.

Arbitration **Arbitration** is a simplified version of a trial without discovery and with modified rules of evidence. Arbitration hearings are also brief in duration, and their opinions are not made available to the public. Hearings are presided over by an **arbitrator**, a private,

COURTS IN THE NEWS

Improving Courtroom Security with Technology

© ZUMA Press, Inc./Alamy

The threat posed by armed intruders in the courtroom has prompted some jurisdictions to install elaborate security systems for protections.

Courtroom security is becoming a significant issue. For example, three people were killed, including the gunman Thomas F. Matusiewicz, 68, who opened fire in the New Castle County, Delaware, courthouse on February 12, 2013. Among the victims was his former daughter-in-law and her friend; two police officers were wounded in the attack. Matusiewicz was fatally shot and died outside the revolving doors of the courthouse. His motive: One of the victims, Christine Belford, was once married to Matusiewicz's son, David, and the couple had battled for custody of their kids after they divorced. David absconded with the girls and, with his mother Lenore, fled to Central America for 18 months. On their return, both mother and son went to jail; the shooting was an act of revenge by an angry father and husband.

In response to such incidents, the federal government has been supporting the development of devices and systems to detect forbidden items hidden on a person's body in or under clothes. Contraband can be hidden in a person's clothes or baggage or on or in their bodies, or they can be hidden in the surrounding environment, such as on the underside of a chair or in a book on a shelf.

Detection technologies need to be able to locate both metallic and nonmetallic items, including large items, such as guns or bombs, and small items, such as baggies of drugs or razor blades. Some of these devices and systems use millimeter-wave (mmW) radar, which penetrates clothing but is reflected from the body. It can detect both metallic and nonmetallic objects and display them as images on a video screen. For example, the ProVision Active Millimeter-Wave Whole Body Imager is a security screening portal that detects metallic and nonmetallic threats and contraband. Subjects are directed to stand inside the booth and lift their arms over their head for a two-second scan that generates an image in about eight seconds.

Assisted by computer analysis, the operator examines the image to find forbidden items or objects that require further investigation. This technology is also being used by the Transportation Security Administration for airport screening.

Another concept for detecting items hidden on a person involves combining metal detection with ultrasound detection of nonmetallic objects: a prototype handheld, battery-operated Weapons and Non-Permitted Devices Detector (WANDD). The WANDD detects metallic and nonmetallic contraband objects hidden on a clothed person, including plastic knives, wadded money, guns, cell phones, cigarette lighters, and keys. This is an improvement over current handheld detectors that detect only metal. ∎

DISCUSSION QUESTIONS

1. Should lawyers and judges be encouraged to carry guns for self-protection?

2. Does the application of these security devices intrude on personal privacy, or are they worth the cost?

3. Should students be searched with a WANDD before they enter school? After all, school shootings have become all too common.

Sources: Ashley Fantz, "2 Women, Gunman Killed in Delaware Courthouse Shooting, CNN Justice, February 12, 2013, available at www.cnn.com/2013/02/11/justice/delaware-court-shooting (accessed June 2, 2013); Cris Barrish and Melissa Nann Burke, "3 Dead, 2 Wounded in Del. Courthouse Shooting, *USA Today*, February 12, 2013, available at www.usatoday.com/story/news/nation/2013/02/11/delaware-courthouse-shooting/1909075 (accessed June 2, 2013); National Institute of Justice, "Detection and Surveillance Technologies," August 29, 2012, available at www .nij.gov/nij/topics/technology/detection-surveillance/welcome.htm (accessed June 2, 2013).

neutral person who is typically trained in alternative dispute resolution and is chosen to arbitrate a disagreement. Either both sides agree to a single arbitrator or each side selects one arbitrator and the two select a third to comprise a panel of arbitrators.

Arbitration has long been popular with certain types of disputes, but it continues to catch on as a means of dealing with many different types of disputes. Arbitration is often binding, meaning that each side must abide by the arbitrator's decision.

Arbitration is governed by both federal and state laws. Title 9 of the U.S. Code contains federal arbitration law, and nearly every state has adopted its own version of the 1956 Uniform Arbitration Act. (The act was revised in 2000 and adopted by 12 states.) Such laws make arbitration agreements and arbitrators' decisions enforceable by law.

mediation
An alternative dispute resolution process that is less formal than arbitration.

mediator
A person (similar to an arbitrator) who is trained to help disputing parties come together and reach an agreement that is satisfactory to both. However, unlike an arbitrator, a mediator has no power to impose a decision on the parties.

neutral evaluation
A method of alternative dispute resolution in which the parties make informal presentations to a neutral party who then examines the strengths and weaknesses of each side's case and informs the parties of them.

conciliation
An alternative dispute resolution (ADR) process that seeks to reach agreement between parties to a dispute but differs from other techniques discussed in that the conciliator plays a relatively direct role in the actual resolution of a dispute and even advises the parties on certain solutions by making proposals for settlement.[iv]

restorative justice
A term that has been used interchangeably with related approaches such as community justice, peacemaking, relational justice, and therapeutic jurisprudence.[v] It is "a process whereby all the parties with a stake in a particular offence [sic] come together to resolve collectively how to deal with the aftermath of the offence [sic] and its implications for the future"[vi]; it includes "every action that is primarily oriented toward doing justice by repairing the harm that has been caused by a crime."[vii]

Mediation **Mediation** is a less formal dispute-settling process than arbitration. **Mediators**, like arbitrators, are trained to help disputing parties come together to reach an agreement that is satisfactory to both; however, unlike an arbitrator, a mediator has no power to impose a decision on the parties. The practical result of this is that mediation is often used before arbitration. If an agreement cannot be reached in mediation, the parties may elect to pursue arbitration.

Neutral Evaluation **Neutral evaluation** "uses a neutral or impartial third party to provide an objective evaluation (sometimes in writing) of the strengths and weaknesses of a case (see Box 16–2). Under this method, the parties will usually make informal presentations to the neutral party to highlight their respective cases or positions."[12] Its goals include the following:

- Enhance direct communication between the parties about their claims and supporting evidence.
- Provide an assessment of the merits of the case by a neutral expert.
- Provide a reality check for clients and lawyers.
- Identify and clarify the central issues in the dispute.
- Assist with discovery and motion planning or with an informal exchange of key information.
- Facilitate settlement discussions (when requested by the parties).[13]

Neutral evaluation is different from mediation and arbitration. In mediation and arbitration, solutions often emerge from the parties themselves with the help of the arbitrator or mediator, but with neutral evaluation, the evaluator examines the strengths and weaknesses of each side's case and then informs the parties of them. This nonbinding evaluation is intended to serve as a reality check for the parties so they can begin communicating and reaching some measure of resolution.

Conciliation **Conciliation** is another ADR process that seeks to reach agreement between parties to a dispute, but it differs from the other techniques discussed thus far. The conciliator is viewed not so much as an authority figure, but as one who advises the parties on the best solution. It is the conciliator who usually proposes settlement terms. He or she provides guidance to the parties, which is distinct from the role of mediator. Conciliation is usually reserved as a preventive measure early on, once a dispute or misunderstanding develops.[14]

Restorative Justice

Restorative justice is difficult to define because the term has been used interchangeably with related approaches such as community justice, peacemaking, relational justice, and therapeutic jurisprudence, among others[15]; however, one author has offered up a fairly

BOX 16–2 Early Neutral Evaluation Process

The evaluator, an experienced attorney with expertise in the case's subject matter, hosts an informal meeting of clients and counsel at which the following occurs:

1. Each side—through counsel, clients, or witnesses—presents the evidence and arguments supporting its case (without regard to the rules of evidence and without direct or cross-examination of witnesses).

2. The evaluator identifies areas of agreement, clarifies and focuses the issues, and encourages the parties to enter procedural and substantive stipulations.

3. The evaluator writes an evaluation in private that includes the following:
   - An estimate (where feasible) of the likelihood of liability and the dollar range of damages
   - An assessment of the relative strengths and weaknesses of each party's case
   - The reasoning that supports these assessments

4. The evaluator offers to present the evaluation to the parties, who may then choose from the following options:
   - Hear the evaluation (which must be presented if any party requests it)
   - Postpone hearing the evaluation
   - Engage in settlement discussions facilitated by the evaluator, often in separate meetings with each side
   - Conduct focused discovery or make additional disclosures

5. If settlement discussions do not occur or do not resolve the case, the evaluator may do the following:
   - Help the parties devise a plan for sharing additional information and/or conducting the key discovery that will expeditiously equip them to enter meaningful settlement discussions or position the case for resolution by motion or trial
   - Help the parties realistically assess litigation costs
   - Determine whether some form of follow-up to the session would contribute to case development or settlement ■

Source: Adapted from U.S. District Court for the Northern District of California, available at www.cand .uscourts.gov/ene (accessed March 4, 2013).

---

all-encompassing definition: "Restorative justice is a process whereby all the parties with a stake in a particular offence come together to resolve collectively how to deal with the aftermath of the offence and its implications for the future."[16] Another writer describes restorative justice as "every action that is primarily oriented toward doing justice by repairing the harm that has been caused by a crime."[17] For some people, restorative justice is viewed as a "return to tribal justice and a rejection of retributive Western legal practice. For others, it is a response to the needs of crime victims, who typically are ignored in current practice. For others still, it is an infusion of religious doctrine into secular jurisprudence."[18] See Box 16–3 for a listing of several restorative justice concepts.

At the core of restorative justice are two concepts: harm and repair. It is thought that crime causes several types of **harm**[19]: One is material harm, particularly the damage to property and lost wages that are associated with crime, and another is personal or relational harm, which can include physical injury, emotional damage, damaged relationships, increased fear, and a reduced sense of community—all of which can occur following a criminal act. It is also useful to distinguish between public and private harms, the latter being the harm shouldered by individual victims of crime and the former being harm to public places and community cohesiveness. The concern with harm distinguishes restorative justice from other traditional responses to the crime problem, such as rehabilitation and retribution. A focus on the harm caused by crime—as opposed to other concerns—is what places restorative justice in a category by itself.

The second key restorative justice concept is **repair**; that is, those who practice restorative justice are concerned not just with the harm that crime causes but with the repair of

harm
One of two restorative justice concepts (the other term being *repair*).[viii] The term refers to material damage to property, lost wages, physical injury, emotional damage, damaged relationships, increased fear, and a reduced sense of community experienced by victims of a crime. It is also a characteristic that distinguishes damage to public places and community cohesiveness (public harm) from damage or injury shouldered by individual victims of crime (private harm).

repair
One of two restorative justice concepts (the other term being *harm*).[ix] The term refers to measures taken by an offender to repair damage incurred by his or her victim or the community during a crime so as to restore the victim or the community (as closely as possible) to a pre-victimization state.

BOX 16–3   Restorative Justice Principles

1. Crime is primarily an offense against human relationships, and secondarily a violation of a law (since laws are written to protect safety and fairness in human relationships).

2. Restorative Justice recognizes that crime (violation of persons and relationships) is wrong and should not occur, and [it] also recognizes that after it does there are dangers and opportunities. The danger is that the community, victim(s), and/or offender emerge from the response further alienated, more damaged, disrespected, disempowered, feeling less safe, and less cooperative with society. The opportunity is that injustice is recognized, the equity is restored (restitution and grace), and the future is clarified so that participants are safer, more respectful, and more empowered and cooperative with each other and society.

3. Restorative Justice is a process to "make things as right as possible" which includes: attending to needs created by the offense such as safety and repair of injuries to relationships and physical damage resulting from the offense; and attending to needs related to the cause of the offense (addictions, lack of social or employment skills or resources, lack of moral or ethical base, etc.).

4. The primary victim(s) of a crime is/are the one(s) most impacted by the offense. The secondary victims are others impacted by the crime and might include family members, friends, witnesses, criminal justice officials, community, etc.

5. As soon as immediate victim, community, and offender safety concerns are satisfied, Restorative Justice views the situation as a teachable moment for the offender; an opportunity to encourage the offender to learn new ways of acting and being in community.

6. Restorative Justice prefers responding to the crime at the earliest point possible and with the maximum amount of voluntary cooperation and minimum coercion, since healing in relationships and new learning are voluntary and cooperative processes.

7. Restorative Justice prefers that most crimes are handled using a cooperative structure including those impacted by the offense as a community to provide support and accountability. This might include primary and secondary victims and family (or substitutes if they choose not to participate), the offender and family, community representatives, government representatives, faith community representatives, school representatives, etc.

8. Restorative Justice recognizes that not all offenders will choose to be cooperative. Therefore there is a need for outside authority to make decisions for the offender who is not cooperative. The actions of the authorities and the consequences imposed should be tested by whether they are reasonable, restorative, and respectful (for victim(s), offender, and community).

9. Restorative Justice prefers that offenders who pose significant safety risks and are not yet cooperative be placed in settings where the emphasis is on safety, values, ethics, responsibility, accountability, and civility. They should be exposed to the impact of their crime(s) on victims, invited to learn empathy, and offered learning opportunities to become better equipped with skills to be a productive member of society. They should continually be invited (not coerced) to become cooperative with the community and be given the opportunity to demonstrate this in appropriate settings as soon as possible.

10. Restorative Justice requires follow-up and accountability structures utilizing the natural community as much as possible, since keeping agreements is the key to building a trusting community.

11. Restorative Justice recognizes and encourages the role of community institutions, including the religious/faith community, in teaching and establishing the moral and ethical standards which build up the community. ■

Source: From "Restorative Justice-Fundamental Principles" by Ron Claassen. © 1996 Ron Claassen. Reprinted by permission.

that harm and restoring a sense of community. For example, such repair can include having the perpetrator fix property he or she damaged; it can also include a larger-scale response aimed at improving relationships among people in a given area. As one author puts it, repair "may involve restoring offenders by creating social support, integrative opportunities, and competencies."[20] It may also "involve rebuilding communities by renewing respect for and commitment to the criminal justice system; by fostering new social ties among community members; by enriching the deliberative democratic process; and by focusing attention on community problems so that broader institutional weaknesses, such as in schools or families, can be addressed."[21]

Some people are intrigued by the possibilities for restorative justice, whereas others are highly skeptical. On the one hand, restorative justice seems eminently sensible: The practice seeks more involvement on the part of crime victims who have historically been left out of the criminal process and also seeks to reduce the division between criminals and victims that can lead to awkward and tense future relationships (or no relationships at all). On the other hand, restorative justice has no chance of succeeding in areas where there is no defined sense of community. Likewise, it is highly unlikely that victims of serious crimes, especially sex crimes, violent assaults, and the like, would be willing to confront the criminal responsible for the harm they suffered. It seems that restorative justice is probably best relegated to tight-knit rural communities and most feasible for first-time offenders who are accused of committing relatively minor offenses.[22] But this has not stopped some researchers from advocating a restorative justice approach for dealing with serious crime—even homicide![23]

Victim–Offender Mediation **Victim–offender mediation** is basically a version of the mediation approach to alternative dispute resolution consisting of a meeting between victim and offender that is facilitated by a trained mediator. This approach differs from traditional mediation, however, because of the underlying goals of restorative justice—the concern is not so much with resolving a dispute as it is with repairing the harm done by the crime. There are four steps to the process: case referral and intake, preparation for mediation, mediation, and follow-up.[24] When mediation is used, cases are typically referred after an offender admits guilt or a court decides as much. The mediator then contacts the victim and the offender to determine whether both are interested in participation:

> The parties then meet to identify the injustice, [to] rectify the harm (to make things right or restore equity), and to establish payment/monitoring schedules. . . . Both parties present their version of the events leading up to and the circumstances surrounding the crime. . . . The victim has a chance to speak about the personal dimensions of victimization and loss, while the offender has a chance to express remorse and to explain circumstances surrounding his/her behavior. . . . Then the parties agree on the particular nature and extent of the harm caused by the crime in order to identify the acts necessary to repair the injury to the victim. The terms of the agreed reparation (e.g., restitution, in-kind services, etc.) are reduced to writing . . . , along with payment and monitoring schedules.[25]

Conferencing **Conferencing** occurs when the victim and the offender, usually with the assistance of a mediator or arbitrator, have an extended conversation about the crime and its consequences. Conferencing differs from victim–offender mediation because other parties, such as family members and community support groups, may also be involved. Conferencing is ideal when the offender admits guilt. There are three steps to the process: the preparation, the conference, and the postconference monitoring:

1. During preparation, a trained facilitator receives a referral report and consults with juvenile justice officials to become familiar with the case. This gives the facilitator the opportunity to become acquainted with the parties and to identify and discuss any needs of the parties and some purposes of the conference.

2. During the conference, the offender begins by telling his or her side of the story, with the victim then subsequently doing likewise. Both then have a chance to

victim–offender mediation
A version of the mediation approach to alternative dispute resolution that involves a meeting between victim and offender facilitated by a trained mediator. This approach differs from traditional mediation in that it carries underlying goals of restorative justice.

conferencing
An extended conversation between the victim and the offender, usually with the assistance of a mediator or arbitrator, about the crime and its consequences. This approach differs from victim–offender mediation by inclusion of other parties, such as family members and community support groups.

express their feelings about the events and circumstances surrounding the crime. Each may then direct questions to one another, followed by questions posed by their respective families. The offender and his or her family then meet privately to discuss reparation, thereafter presenting an offer to the victim and others in attendance; negotiations continue in the group until consensus is reached. The agreement is put in writing, with payment/monitoring schedules included.

3. During the postconference monitoring, the facilitator oversees the completion of the agreement and locates needed resources for victims, offenders, and family members when needed. If the agreement cannot be successfully completed with the facilitator's intervention, the case is returned to the courts for further action.[26]

Sentencing Circles Circles are used in Native American cultures in the United States and Canada for a number of purposes. They were introduced to the criminal justice system in the 1980s by the First Nations peoples of the Yukon as a means to build closer ties between the community and the criminal justice system.[27] In 1991, Judge Barry Stuart of the Yukon Territorial Court introduced the concept of the sentencing circle (sometimes called *peacemaking circles*).[28] Like mediation and conferencing, **sentencing circles** provide an opportunity for the victim and offender to interact, but they move beyond mediation and conferencing by involving the community in the decision. Community participants may include justice system officials or anyone affected by or impacted by the crime. Family members are often present, as well. A "talking piece" is passed around in the meeting so that everyone is given an opportunity to speak.[29]

The goals of the sentencing circle include the following:

- Promote healing for all affected parties.
- Provide an opportunity for the offender to make amends.
- Empower victims, community members, families, and offenders by giving them a voice and a shared responsibility in finding constructive resolutions.
- Address the underlying causes of criminal behavior.
- Build a sense of community and its capacity for resolving conflict.
- Promote and share community values.[30]

Other Restorative Justice Examples Given the somewhat loose definition of restorative justice presented earlier, it is worth noting there are other approaches besides mediation, sentencing circles, and conferencing. Examples include the following: (1) restitution, (2) community service, (3) victim impact statements, (4) victim impact panels, (5) victim impact classes, and (6) community reparative boards. Most readers are familiar with the concepts of restitution and community service. Victim impact statements and panels are concerned with allowing victims to explain how the crime affected them and/or to have input in sentencing. Victim impact classes take a similar approach: Offenders learn from victims how their actions affected the victims. As for community reparative boards, one in the state of Vermont has been described this way:

> Upon conviction of a minor offense—burglary, drunk driving, for example—the judge will sentence the offender to probation with the condition that he or she must appear before the local reparative board. The board meets with the offender and attempts to work out a solution to the problem created by the offense. Victims and other affected parties, such as parents of a youthful offender, are invited to attend. Board meetings vary in length but average between 35 and 40 minutes. The outcome of the meeting is a negotiated agreement signed by the offender, specifying a set of tasks to be

sentencing circle
A type of victim–offender interaction that moves beyond mediation and conferencing by involving the community in the decision[x]; also called *peacemaking circle.*[xi]

accomplished during a 90-day probationary period. Typically, offenders return to the board for a mid-term review and a final closure meeting before discharge. Offenders who refuse to sign the agreement or fail to comply are returned to the court.[31]

COURTROOMS OF THE FUTURE

Learning Objective 3
Summarize how courts and individual courtroom players' roles may change in the future.

Technology and alternatives to traditional dispute resolution will continue to have an influence on the courts. The changes they will bring about, however, will be somewhat superficial. Technology leads to efficiency improvements, but it leaves the court's mission more or less unaltered; in a similar vein, alternative dispute resolution is also concerned with efficiency and helps to avoid the need for a costly, drawn-out trial. Restorative justice could lead to considerable changes, but it is unlikely to take hold in areas where community bonds are strained or when serious offenses are at issue.

There are three areas in which we are seeing considerable change in the nature of courts themselves.[32] First, recent developments in problem-solving justice are leading to changes in the traditional roles of court personnel. Second, there is some evidence that juvenile courts are looking more and more like adult courts, which means the future of juvenile courts is somewhat uncertain. Finally, increased pressure for public access and involvement in the courts is likely to lead to considerable changes in the future. The following three sections look briefly at each of these developments.

Redefinition of Courts and Roles

Criminal courts will continue their business of adjudicating offenders—but not necessarily in the traditional fashion. There are two reasons for this: First, trials are becoming less common due to resource constraints; second, role distinctions are changing in some respects, meaning that prosecutors, defense attorneys, and judges do not always perform the same functions they once did. These trends will surely continue.

Web Extra
16–5 Michigan Virtual Courtroom

Vanishing Trials?
According to the National Center for State Courts (NCSC), jury trials are much less common than they once were. In the past few decades, juries in criminal trials have decreased by around 15%,[33] a phenomenon that has come to be known as the **vanishing trial**.[34] Unfortunately, current data on disposition type are not readily available, but it is likely the trend is continuing:

> The nature of dispositional activity in state courts is changing. Trials, though never a substantial proportion of dispositions, are being held even less frequently than 10 years ago. . . . While guilty pleas remain the most common form of disposition for criminal cases, courts seem to be disposing of more cases by means of dispositions such as *nolle prosequi* and deferred judgments.[35]

vanishing trial
The phenomenon of a 15 percent decrease in criminal jury trials and a more than 30 percent decrease in civil jury trials[xii] that occurred between 1976 and 2002.[xiii]

The economic downturn of the past few years has also led to fears over the vanishing trial. To the extent that it is expensive to take cases to trial, charges may not be pursued, or plea bargains may be reached more frequently to save resources. As one recent report remarked, "The economic storm has come to this: Justice is being delayed or disrupted in state courtrooms across the country."[36] A number of states have slashed courts' budgets, making it even more difficult to adjudicate cases at previous levels.

Web Extra
16–6 Sonoma County (California) Superior Court Virtual Courthouse

Changing Role Distinctions
By now the traditional roles and functions of prosecutors, defense attorneys, and judges are fairly clear, but these roles and functions are changing in some key respects. First, prosecutors are becoming ever more engaged in problem solving.[37] Many of them are less concerned with securing convictions than they are with addressing the underlying circumstances that lead people to break the law because they are realizing

Web Extra
16–7 Virtual Courthouse.com

that seeing the same offenders over and over again is not helping anyone. Some new prosecution programs seek to avoid a trial altogether. For example, some prosecutors' offices have launched homeless courts whose concern is not adjudicating new offenses but rather helping people in need (see Chapter 6).

There is also some evidence that judges are assuming nontraditional roles. Consider drug courts (also in Chapter 6). Drug court judges tend to be much more involved in offenders' lives once they are sentenced—judges follow up on offenders to ensure their compliance with court orders, and there is genuine concern on their part that offenders are rehabilitated, not just held accountable. This is somewhat contrary to the somewhat detached nature of traditional criminal sentencing wherein judges give out sentences without much attention to helping people who are addicted; instead, judges act almost like probation officers.

Even defense attorneys have become less adversarial in certain contexts. Let's return to the example of homeless courts (see Chapter 6). These courts work best when prosecutors, defense attorneys, and judges collaborate to address the needs of people down on their luck.

Certainly there will continue to be a need for hard-line prosecutors, zealous defense attorneys, and thoroughly detached judges, yet people are beginning to realize that the traditional "fight" for justice is not always the most helpful approach. Many offenders can be rehabilitated but may need individualized attention more than aggressive advocacy. Since there is a need to lighten workloads, more offenders being helped and rehabilitated means that the revolving door problem could be minimized.

Withering of the Juvenile Justice System?

A number of reforms are making the juvenile justice system look more like the adult system and have also prompted some scholars to argue for the abandonment of juvenile justice altogether. Barry Feld's "The Honest Politician's Guide to Juvenile Justice in the Twenty-First Century" is perhaps the best example.[38] He argues that the juvenile justice system is increasingly resembling the adult system.[39] As an example, he points to the increased popularity of juvenile waivers. In his view, people's beliefs and politicians' responses have been based on a view of juveniles being like adults.

While Feld feels that traditional justice is fading in some respects, he does not feel a person's juvenile status should be ignored in determining criminal liability. Instead of having a dedicated juvenile court, Feld feels that juvenile status could be considered one of many possible mitigating factors in an ordinary criminal trial.[40]

Feld's proposals have drawn sharp criticism.[41] First, the sudden abolishment of the juvenile court is unlikely because it is a staple of the justice system. Second, there is the question of status offenses—if juvenile delinquents are to be tried in adult court (or in a criminal court), what becomes of status offenses? These have traditionally been handled by juvenile courts, and they probably won't go away, meaning that some court will need to be available to process status offenders.

Customer Service

Customer service, historically reserved for private sector businesses, is becoming the bread and butter of our nations' courts. One report puts it this way:

> The public is replacing lawyers as the primary constituency in the minds of state court judges and staff. A new consumer orientation is taking hold, evident in provisions by the state courts to assist litigants without lawyers through user-friendly print material, simplified processes, and computer guided Web-based assistance. Some courts are going further, taking steps to make legal advice available in the courthouse, previously considered unfeasible.[42]

LASTING IMPACT

Daubert et al. v. Merrell Dow Pharmaceuticals, Inc. (1993)

The petitioners in this case were two minor children and their parents. In a California state district court suit against respondent Merrell Dow Pharmaceuticals, Inc. (MDP), the Dauberts alleged that the children's serious birth defects had been caused by the mother's prenatal ingestion of Bendectin, a prescription drug marketed by MDP.

The district court granted MDP summary judgment based on a well-credentialed expert's affidavit. On reviewing the extensive published scientific literature on the subject, the expert concluded that maternal use of Bendectin had not been shown to be a risk factor for human birth defects. The Dauberts' attorneys responded to the MDP expert's affidavit by presenting the testimony of eight other well-credentialed experts who based their conclusion that Bendectin can cause birth defects on animal studies, chemical structure analyses, and the unpublished "reanalysis" of previously published human statistical studies. In granting the summary judgment, the district court determined that this evidence did not meet the applicable "general acceptance" standard for the admission of expert testimony.[1]

The U.S. Court of Appeals for the Ninth District agreed and affirmed, citing *Frye v. United States* (1923) for the rule that expert opinion based on a scientific technique is inadmissible unless the technique is "generally accepted" as reliable in the relevant scientific community.[2] The Dauberts petitioned the U.S. Supreme Court, which granted *certiorari* based on "sharp divisions among the courts regarding the proper standard for the admission of expert testimony."[3]

In a unanimous decision, the Court held that *Frye's* "general acceptance" test was superseded by adoption of the Federal Rules of Evidence[4]; thus, the rules provide the standard for admitting expert scientific testimony in a federal trial, not *Frye*.[5] The Court further found that "the Rules—especially Rule 702—place appropriate limits on the admissibility of purportedly scientific evidence by assigning to the trial judge the task of ensuring that an expert's testimony both rests on a reliable foundation and is relevant to the task at hand."[6] This requires the trial judge to "make a preliminary assessment of whether the testimony's underlying reasoning or methodology is scientifically valid and properly can be applied to the facts at issue."[7] Finally, the Court determined that "the appropriate means by which evidence based on valid principles may be challenged [must be]

cross-examination, presentation of contrary evidence, and careful instruction on the burden of proof, [not] wholesale exclusion under an uncompromising 'general acceptance' standard."[8]

Daubert exhibits the shining strength of the American court system: its power to set aside a 70-year-old standard it finds to be lacking in its ability to support a fair ruling. This power enables the courts to continuously adjust to accommodate evolving technologies and social standards, once again demonstrating that the courts serve to preserve the notion of the Constitution as a living document. ■

Notes

1. Adapted from Syllabus, *Daubert et ux., individually and as guardians ad litem for Daubert, et al.* v. *Merrell Dow Pharmaceuticals, Inc.* (1993), available at http://supct.law.cornell.edu/supct/html/92-102.ZS.html (accessed August 30, 2009).

2. Ibid.

3. *Daubert et ux., individually and as guardians ad litem for Daubert, et al.* v. *Merrell Dow Pharmaceuticals, Inc.* (1993), p. 2, available at http://supct.law.cornell.edu/supct/html/92-102.ZO.html (accessed July 28, 2009).

4. Ibid., pp. 4–8.

5. Ibid., pp. 4–17.

6. Ibid., pp. 9–12.

7. Ibid., pp. 12–15.

8. Ibid., pp. 15–17.

DISCUSSION QUESTIONS

1. What rule of expert testimony was established by the 1923 U.S. Supreme Court case of *Frye v. United States*? Is it still in effect today?

2. How does the *Daubert* ruling differ from that in *Frye*? What problems did the Court find with its earlier *Frye* ruling?

3. What is the significance of the Court's ruling in *Daubert* for in-court expert testimony today?

4. Might the Court's holding in *Daubert* be overturned in the future? If so, what might be the basis for such a decision?

Web-based assistance is an important development in this area. For example, the Hennepin County (Minnesota) Attorney's Office allows anyone to search its website for updates on criminal cases, including the dates of key hearings.[43] This gives people access to the courts from remote locations, further promoting transparency and openness. Reforms such as these are not accidental but are direct responses to public demands for improved governmental responsiveness.

Public access to the courts will also continue to be important as technology continues its relentless advance, but such improvements can act like a double-edged sword. One report states that "traditional concepts of public access to court records have been eroded, largely because of new technology, namely, the Internet, and the outcry of special-interest groups to protect personal information in court records from public Internet access."[44] Legislatures and law enforcement agencies are scrambling to protect privacy while at the same time preserving openness and accountability.

Learning Objective 4

Summarize problems that courts will likely face in the future.

EMERGING PROBLEMS AND PRESSING ISSUES[45]

Courts will be impacted by two separate but interrelated changes. First, the demographic composition of the United States is changing. Second, emerging problems such as human trafficking and elder abuse will become increasingly relevant. In terms of demographics, a few changes can be discerned:

1. *The population is aging.* According to the NCSC, this will lead to several issues the courts will be faced with: "more probate and guardianship cases for the elderly . . . , identity theft and fraud . . . , elder abuse . . . , traffic accidents involving the elderly, [and] elderly cases of substance abuse and mental-health problems."[46]

2. *The population is getting more diverse.* "The increase in racial, ethnic, and cultural diversity is likely to raise issues in two areas . . . : access to justice, and equality, fairness, and integrity in the justice system. Courts will continue to face rising demands for qualified interpreter services, translated forms, and culturally competent judges and staff."[47]

3. *Religious controversies and conflict are on the rise.* The NCSC identified several examples, including one case in which a state supreme court ruled that a prosecutor violated the state's constitution by removing two prospective jurors from the jury pool for wearing Muslim religious clothing.[48]

4. *Globalization is becoming increasingly important.* "As international trade increases and more litigants have not merely interstate but international presences, state courts may find themselves with jurisdiction over more disputes involving non-U.S. litigants (both individual and corporate) or requiring the application of unfamiliar laws."[49]

It is also clear that political changes, social trends, and economic conditions will take a toll on the courts. Here are some examples:

1. There will be a widening gap between society's expectations of courts and courts' capacity to meet those expectations.

2. Court users increasingly will be more diverse and have a wide range of changing and evolving needs.

3. Case composition will change, and the complexity of some types of cases will continue to increase.

4. Pressure will continue to mount to achieve better case outcomes and appropriately supervise and monitor offenders.

5. There will be an increasing demand for culturally appropriate and therapeutic approaches to court and justice services.

6. Courts will have a difficult time keeping pace with and using existing and emerging technologies.

7. It will become increasingly difficult to recruit, hire, and retain highly skilled executives, managers, and staff.

8. Court facilities and infrastructure will continue to decline.

9. Ideology-driven politics and issues will continue to threaten judicial independence, influence perceptions of fairness, and affect the public's trust and confidence in courts.

10. Challenging times could create the right conditions for implementing new innovations and revolutionizing how courts do business and provide services.[50]

Human Trafficking

The Victims of Trafficking and Violence Protection Act[51] defines **human trafficking** as follows:

> a) Sex trafficking in which a commercial sex act is induced by force, fraud, coercion, or in which the person induced to perform such act has not attained 18 years of age; or
> b) the recruitment, harboring, transportation, provision or obtaining of a person for labor or services, through the use of force, fraud, or coercion for the purpose of subjection to involuntary servitude, peonage, debt bondage or slavery.[52]

How serious is the human trafficking problem? The U.S. government estimates that no fewer than 700,000 people, mostly women and children, are trafficked *each year* into the United States.[53] Of those, some 50,000 of them are trafficked for purposes of sexual exploitation.[54] One study in the late 1990s estimated that there were over 250 brothels operating in at least 25 cities within U.S. borders.[55] Part b of the definition above includes trafficking of agricultural migrant workers and sweatshop workers.

Impact on the Courts According to the NCSC, the courts will face considerable challenges in addressing the problem of human trafficking:

> [The challenges include] identification of cases, information-sharing difficulties, investigative challenges, low penalties for traffickers, lack of trafficking laws, and overlooking of smaller trafficking cases. Currently, the greatest challenge to the justice system is the identification of human-trafficking cases. Many trafficking victims are isolated, held under debt bondage (with confiscated documents), and told they have no legal recourse. Additionally, fear, cultural [factors], and linguistic factors, as well as the emotional and psychological harm caused to victims, may inhibit them from testifying against the perpetrators.[56]

Elder Abuse and Neglect

Charles Cullen appeared to most observers to be an experienced nursing home employee. Perceptions changed, though, when he admitted that he intentionally administered fatal doses to almost 40 patients in a number of nursing homes over a 16-year period. Unfortunately, toxicology tests were not performed on several of his victims, and criminal investigations were not launched for several years, making it difficult to obtain evidence that could be used against him. Fortunately, on March 2, 2006, Cullen was sentenced to 11 consecutive life sentences after pleading guilty to 22 murders and the attempted murders of three other elderly individuals.

Cullen's story is a celebrated one. It represents perhaps the most serious form of a problem that has only recently come into the limelight: elder abuse. What is elder abuse? According to the National Center on Elder Abuse, **elder abuse** "is a term referring to any knowing, intentional, or negligent act by a caregiver or any other person that causes harm or a serious risk of harm to a vulnerable adult."[57] Below are some examples of elder abuse:

Physical abuse. Inflicting or threatening to inflict physical pain or injury on a vulnerable elder or depriving him or her of a basic need results in **physical abuse**.

---

human trafficking
A term used to refer to "sex trafficking in which a commercial sex act is induced by force, fraud, [or] coercion or in which the person induced to perform such act has not attained 18 years of age"[xiv]; also, the recruitment, harboring, transportation, provision, or obtaining of a person for labor or services through the use of force, fraud, or coercion for the purpose of subjection to involuntary servitude, peonage, debt bondage, or slavery.[xv]

elder abuse
"[A]ny knowing, intentional, or negligent act by a caregiver or any other person that causes harm or a serious risk of harm to a vulnerable adult."[xvi]

physical abuse
The infliction, or the threat to inflict, physical pain or injury on a vulnerable elder or the act of depriving him or her of a basic need.[xvii]

emotional abuse
The infliction of mental pain, anguish, or distress on an elder person through verbal or nonverbal acts.[xviii]

sexual abuse
Any kind of nonconsensual sexual contact.[xix]

exploitation
The illegal taking, misuse, or concealment of funds, property, or assets of a vulnerable elder.[xx]

neglect
The refusal or failure by those responsible to provide food, shelter, health care, or protection for a vulnerable elder.[xxi]

abandonment
The desertion of a vulnerable elder by anyone who has assumed the responsibility for care or custody of that person.[xxii]

Emotional abuse. Inflicting mental pain, anguish, or distress on an elder person through verbal or nonverbal acts is **emotional abuse**.

Sexual abuse. Nonconsensual sexual contact of any kind equals **sexual abuse**.

Exploitation. Illegally taking, misusing, or concealing funds, property, or assets of a vulnerable elder is **exploitation**.

Neglect. Refusal or failure by those responsible to provide food, shelter, health care, or protection for a vulnerable elder results in **neglect**.

Abandonment. Desertion of a vulnerable elder by anyone who has assumed the responsibility for care or custody of that person results in **abandonment**.[58]

Approximately 1.5 million Americans live in long-term care or nursing homes.[59] Several of these people have multiple illnesses, mental problems, and other impairments, conditions that make them almost totally dependent on caregivers for their continued well-being. Unfortunately, there is a pattern of abuse, neglect, and even theft in some of these facilities. A study of 80 nursing homes in Georgia, for instance, found that nearly half the residents reported being abused.[60] This number is startling to say the least, but a possible problem is that the findings were based only on residents' reports. A 1987 survey of 577 nursing home staff members from 31 facilities around the nation found that more than one-third of the respondents had witnessed at least one incident of physical abuse in the past 12 months[61]; others have reached similar conclusions.[62]

Nursing homes in Arkansas are required by law to report all deaths to the local coroner, who then investigates the deaths. Researchers who observed the coroners' investigations over a one-year period identified the following markers as possible signs that elder abuse could be occurring[63]:

Physical condition/quality of care. Specific physical markers include documented but untreated injuries; undocumented injuries and fractures; multiple, untreated, and/or undocumented pressure sores; medical orders not followed; poor oral care, poor hygiene, and lack of cleanliness of residents; malnourished residents with no documentation for low weight; bruising on nonambulatory residents; bruising in unusual locations; statements from family concerning inadequacy of care; and observations about level of care for residents with nonattentive family members.

Facility characteristics. Specific facility markers include unchanged linens, strong odors (urine, feces), unemptied trash cans, food issues (unclean cafeteria), and documented facility problems in the past.

Inconsistencies. Specific markers include inconsistencies in medical records, statements made by staff members, and/or observations of investigators; inconsistencies in statements among groups interviewed; and inconsistencies between reported time of death and condition of the body.

Staff behaviors. Specific behavioral markers include staff members who follow an investigator too closely; staff members who lack knowledge and/or concern about a resident; staff members who are unintentionally or purposefully evasive, either verbally or nonverbally; and a facility that is unwilling to release medical records.[64]

Impact on the Courts   The problem of elder abuse continues to come to the attention of the courts. In 1997, the ABA published a curriculum for judges and court staff.[65]

In 1999, Florida's 13th Judicial Circuit Court created the first Elder Justice Center.[66] In 2002, Judge Julie Conger of the Alameda County Superior Court created the first specialized court docket for elders.[67] Such developments are continuing, according to Judge Conger:

> One of the major challenges is the lack of coordination within the court system itself, so that elder abuse cases are filed in numerous different locations within the court, such as probate, criminal, family law, restraining orders, and civil filings. Additionally, the red tape and bureaucracy of the court can be a daunting barrier to elder access to the courts and should be streamlined or eliminated. Training of both guardians . . . and judicial officers to recognize signs and symptoms of elder abuse remains a major challenge to most courts.[68]

Identity Theft

Identity theft has been defined as "the unlawful use of another's personal identifying information."[69] There is perhaps no other fear-inspiring form of fraudulent activity than this. It need not necessarily rely on computers, but they certainly make the task easier. See Box 16–4 for descriptions of various types of identity theft.

identity theft
"[T]he unlawful use of another's personal identifying information."[xxiii]

The losses that go along with identity theft are quite staggering. According to the General Accounting Office, $745 million was lost to identity theft in the fiscal year 1997.[70] Recent estimates are even more startling, pointing to possible losses of $2.3 billion or more in a given year.[71] Costs aside, there were 86,198 reported cases of identity theft in 2001 and 161,819 in 2002[72]; by comparison, the number of other fraud-related complaints went from 107,890 in 2000 to 133,891 in 2001.[73] Cleary, identity theft is a growing problem that requires further attention, enforcement, and study.

Impact on the Courts   The rise in identity theft, coupled with legislative changes aimed at curbing the problem, will present real challenges for the courts. Courts will also be called on to decide cases involving privacy policies and procedures: "Not only will these cases be brought against the actual thief, identity theft victims will increasingly argue negligence on the part of businesses that do not protect customer information."[74]

Immigration

Immigration—legal and illegal—continues to grow. The U.S. Census Bureau estimates that between 850,000 and 1.2 million people immigrate to the United States each year,[75] with states like California and Texas seeing the largest surge in foreign-born populations. The sheer influx of immigrants will affect the courts in the same way that increased diversity will. There is also a concern, particularly regarding illegal immigrants, that an increase in crime could result.

Impact on the Courts   The question remains whether the increase in immigration (legal and illegal) will affect the U.S. court system. Academics have either found little relationship between immigration and crime or point out that not enough data are currently available.[76] In any case, the courts will be presented with cases involving all aspects of immigration.

BOX 16–4 Identity Theft Terminology

Account takeover. An imposter uses personal information to gain access to another's existing accounts.

Check washing. Someone dips a check in acetone, which washes the ink off so it can be rewritten for a higher amount.

Crimeware. A computer program or set of programs is designed expressly to facilitate illegal activity online.

Dumpster diving. Someone retrieves other people's personal paperwork and discarded mail from trash dumpsters.

Hacker. A person uses a computer to break into other computer systems to steal, change, or destroy information.

Identity fraud. This differs from identity theft in that the thief uses personal information that is fabricated rather than information stolen from a real person.

Identity theft. This fraud is committed or attempted by using a person's identifying information without authority.

Mail fraud. Often used with identity theft, mail fraud is the act of stealing mail to obtain preapproved credit card applications or to obtain sufficient personal identifiers to assume another's identity.

Pharming crimeware. This software misdirects users to fraudulent sites or proxy servers, typically through domain name system (DNS) hijacking or poisoning.

Phishing. In this type of identity theft, someone sends spam e-mail that looks like it came from a bank or a business asking for personal information, such as credit card and Social Security numbers. By hijacking brand names of banks, e-retailers, and credit card companies, phishers often convince recipients to respond.

Shoulder surfing. An identity thief simply stands next to someone in a public place, such as the Department of Motor Vehicles, and watches the person fill out personal information on a form.

Skimming. This type of theft is usually done by an employee of a restaurant, a gas station, or any other establishment where you swipe your card. Skimmers have little swiping tools of their own, which they use to quickly swipe a customer's card.

Social engineering. This practice involves obtaining confidential information by manipulation of legitimate users—often by using the telephone or Internet to trick people into revealing sensitive information or getting them to do something that is against typical policies.

Spam. Sometimes companies or individuals purchase e-mail address lists to send bogus ads for products and services. The unsolicited e-mail is termed *spam*, and it fills up e-mail files and could add additional pop-up windows on computer screens.

Spoof websites. Spoof websites are designed to look like legitimate sites and are used to defraud customers by asking them to enter personal or security details, and fraudsters use these details to access people's accounts. E-mail scams asking people to update their personal information will often contain links to spoof websites.

Spyware. This type of software collects information about Internet use. It is often installed without a user's knowledge while he or she is downloading software.

Technical subterfuge. Someone plants crimeware (often Trojan keylogger spyware) in personal computers to steal credentials directly.

Trojan. Trojan spyware is named after the wooden horse of Troy and is a type of software program created by fraudsters to deliver a virus or sinister code to computers to gain computer access. Trojans are often part of a suspicious opened e-mail or a file that may have been downloaded from an untrustworthy or unknown source.

True-name identity theft. A thief uses personal information to open *new* accounts. ▪

Source: Adapted from T. Peters, N. Kauder, C. Campbell, and C. Flango, *Future Trends in State Courts, 2005* (Williamsburg, VA: National Center for State Courts, 2005).

SUMMARY

1. EXPLAIN HOW COURTS ARE AFFECTED BY NEW TECHNOLOGIES

- Technology is finding its way into the courts in the form of hardware (flat-screen monitors, laptops, and so on) and software (litigation support software and other programs used by attorneys in presenting their cases).

- Uses for technology in the courts include electronic filing of court documents, database integration for information sharing, electronic discovery, online depositions, high-tech evidence presentation, and court Web logs.

- Some courts, such as Courtroom 21 (in the College of William and Mary Law School) and Courtroom 23 (in Florida's Ninth Judicial Circuit), incorporate a range of technologies and are supposedly the courtrooms of the future.

2. DESCRIBE ALTERNATIVES TO CRIMINAL PROSECUTIONS, INCLUDING ALTERNATIVE DISPUTE RESOLUTION, MEDIATION, AND DIVERSION

- Alternatives to traditional adjudication, such as alternative dispute resolution (ADR) and restorative justice, have become popular in recent years.

- ADR includes arbitration, mediation, neutral evaluation, and conciliation.

- Restorative justice emphasizes the harm caused by crime and seeks to repair it. Examples of restorative justice include victim–offender mediation, conferencing, and sentencing circles, among others.

3. SUMMARIZE HOW COURTS AND INDIVIDUAL COURTROOM PLAYERS' ROLES MAY CHANGE IN THE FUTURE

- The future of American courts is changing.

- There is some evidence that trials are "vanishing" due to the smaller percentage of cases that go to trial now compared to in the past.

- Professional role distinctions are also changing; for example, judges supervise drug court offenders, not just probation officers.

- Another change is that the juvenile justice system is starting to look more like the adult criminal justice system.

- The public is also demanding that courts adopt a focus on customer service.

4. SUMMARIZE PROBLEMS THAT THE COURTS WILL LIKELY FACE IN THE FUTURE

- Courts will face a number of challenges in the coming years.

- Challenges the courts will need to face include an aging population, increased diversity, and budget shortfalls.

- Problems the courts will be forced to address include human trafficking, elder abuse and neglect, identity theft, and issues related to both legal and illegal immigration, to name a few.

KEY TERMS

abandonment, 444

alternative dispute
    resolution, 432

arbitration, 432

arbitrator, 432

conciliation, 434

conferencing, 437

deposition, 431

elder abuse, 443

electronic discovery, 431

electronic filing, 431

emotional abuse, 444

exploitation, 444

harm, 435

human trafficking, 443

identity theft, 445

mediation, 434

mediator, 434

neglect, 444

neutral evaluation, 434

online deposition, 431

physical abuse, 443

repair, 435

restorative justice, 434

sentencing circle, 438

sexual abuse, 444

vanishing trial, 439

victim–offender
    mediation, 437

wired court, 428

REVIEW QUESTIONS

1. What various kinds of contemporary technologies are being used in today's courtrooms? What practical applications do they have?

2. What alternative sentencing options are available in many of our nation's criminal courts today? Describe alternative dispute resolution and restorative justice mechanisms.

3. How are courts being redefined? Is this likely to be a benefit or a hindrance?

4. What will courtrooms of the future be like? How will they differ from today's courtrooms? In what ways will they be the same?

5. What are some of the new and pressing issues impacting American courts today that this chapter identifies?

WHAT WILL YOU DO?

A few months ago, you woke up to discover that you had become a victim of auto theft. Looking back at that morning, you can almost laugh at yourself. You stepped out of your apartment, nicely dressed and car keys in hand, and were hurrying to keep an appointment. You were thinking about your appointment as you walked quickly to your car. That's when you noticed that your car was gone. Your mind did a kind of double-take because you knew that you had parked right in front of your apartment the night before. When you didn't see your car, you started thinking that you might have parked somewhere else instead of in your usual place. As you walked around your building searching for your car, it dawned on you that it had been stolen.

That's when you got angry and felt the experience of victimization set in. Although you're not normally prone to anger and always espouse turning the other cheek—especially when giving advice to other people—this was different. You felt as if you had somehow been personally violated. Not only had your car been stolen, it had been taken in the middle of the night right in front of your door. If the offender had been standing in front of you just then, you couldn't imagine a punishment that would be too harsh for him or her.

You had bought the vehicle only a few months earlier; although it was a used car, it was pretty much your pride and joy. You had immediately replaced its worn tires with the best new tires you could afford, bought a new battery, had the hoses and belts redone, and added a satellite radio system with expensive new speakers.

To make matters worse, you had been planning to go on a working vacation with your new girlfriend and had packed the trunk with some of your best clothes. You also had all of your tools in the trunk because she had asked you to come help her restore an older house she had inherited from a family member, and you had been determined to show her how handy you could be with a hammer and saw.

That was months ago. Only a few days ago, you received a call from the police department impound lot saying that they had your car and that you should come pick it up. When you went to get it, the desk sergeant treated you more like a criminal than a victim. Your car, he said, had been found

blocking the driveway at a nearby fire department and had to be towed away to clear a path for the fire engines. He told you that you would have to pay a fine for illegal parking and added hundreds of dollars on top of that for an impound fee.

When you explained to him that your car had been stolen and that you hadn't seen it in months, he almost sneered at you, and you knew that he was thinking, "Everyone tells me that!" Soon, however, he looked at his computer records and saw that you were telling the truth. He then turned you over to another officer, who walked you through the lot in search of your vehicle. You were close to a car you didn't recognize when the officer pointed at it, asking, "Is that it?"

"No," you said, "that's not my car!"

"Well," he said, "it sure looks like it from these records."

At that, you walked over to the car and looked at it more closely. Sure enough, it was your car, but it was hardly recognizable. It looked as though it had been beaten by a gang wielding sledgehammers and baseball bats. The windows were all broken, the headlights and taillights were shattered, and even the dashboard had been beaten into oblivion. Cigarette holes were burned into the seats, your new tires were gone, and the satellite radio was missing; on further inspection, you saw that the trunk had been forced open and that all your clothes and tools were gone.

"Yeah," said the officer, "I guess it doesn't look much like it did when you last saw it, but we matched up the serial numbers—and that's it!"

Two 18-year-olds have been arrested and charged with stealing your car. Witnesses had seen them park the car in front of the fire station and had watched them walk into a McDonald's restaurant only a block away. Firemen had immediately called the police, and the thieves were taken into custody within minutes.

Less than an hour ago, you began meeting with a restorative justice counselor, who told you that many cases like this were resolved informally and that such informal resolutions were typically in the best interests of everyone involved. He was here, he said, to mediate a solution that would be acceptable to you, the court, the offenders, and the community in general. What good would it do, he asked, to haul the two

(continued)

young offenders into court and process them as though they were hardened offenders? After all, he said, this was their first offense, and conviction could result not only in prison time but also in stigmatization that could lead the two young men into further crime.

Restorative justice, he explained, was intended to make the victim feel whole again while at the same time preventing further victimization. If you would agree to mediation, he told you, the offenders would likely be ordered to make restitution directly to you and would be placed on probation. The mediation process, he explained, would likely involve face-to-face meetings between you and the two young offenders in which he would serve as mediator. The boys and their families would agree to give you $20,000 to pay for all the damage to your car, which you had actually bought for $17,000.

At first, you were taken aback by what the mediator was saying. Hadn't you been the victim of a crime? Didn't you deserve justice? After your car had been stolen, not only had you missed your scheduled meeting, but you were unable to make the trip to visit with your new girlfriend, and the relationship had fallen apart. Since you were no longer able to get around, you had to buy another used car with the last of your savings while you waited for the insurance company to pay for the one that had been stolen. And while $20,000 in restitution was tempting, it almost seemed like a bribe in order to get your compliance in the case.

These guys were criminals, you thought, and they had victimized *you*. You were not at all sure that you wanted to participate in the mediation process.

What will you do?

NOTES

i. J. E. McMillan, *A Guidebook for Electronic Court Filing* (Alexandria, VA: National Center for State Courts, 1999), p. 2.

ii. *Definitions*, SearchFinancialSecurity.com. Available at http://searchfinancialsecurity.techtarget.com/sDefinition /0,,sid185_gci1150017,00.html (accessed August 8, 2009).

iii. Legal Information Institute. Available at http://topics.law .cornell.edu/wex/ADR (accessed August 3, 2009).

iv. Alessandra Sgubini, Mara Prieditis, and Andrea Marighetto, *Arbitration, Mediation and Conciliation: Differences and Similarities from an International and Italian Business Perspective*. Available at http://www.mediate.com/ articles/ sgubiniA2.cfm (accessed August 8, 2008).

v. G. Bazemore and L. Walgrave, "Restorative Juvenile Justice: In Search of Fundamentals and an Outline for Systematic Reform," in G. Bazemore and L. Walgrave, eds., *Restorative Juvenile Justice* (Monsey, NY: Criminal Justice Press, 1999).

vi. Tony Marshall, "Criminal Mediation in Great Britain 1980–1996," *European Journal on Criminal Policy and Research* 4(1996):21.

vii. Bazemore and Walgrave, *Restorative Juvenile Justice*, p. 48.

viii. The discussion in this paragraph borrows liberally from D. R. Karp, "Harm and Repair: Observing Restorative Justice in Vermont," *Justice Quarterly* 18(2001): 727–757.

ix. The discussion in this paragraph borrows liberally from D. R. Karp, "Harm and Repair," pp. 727–757.

x. The discussion in this paragraph borrows liberally from Karp, "Harm and Repair," pp. 727–757.

xi. Ibid.

xii. See *Journal of Empirical Legal Studies*, Vol. 1, No. 3 (November 2004), for articles presented at the American Bar Association Section of Litigation's "Vanishing Trials" symposium.

xiii. S. M. Strickland, "Beyond the Vanishing Trial: A Look at the Composition of State Court Dispositions," in T. Peters, N. Kauder, C. Campbell, and C. Flango, eds., *Future Trends in State Courts, 2005* (Williamsburg, VA: National Center for State Courts, 2005), pp. 89–92.

xiv. 22 U.S.C. Section 7102.

xv. S. M. Strickland, "Beyond the Vanishing Trial: A Look at the Composition of State Court Dispositions," in T. Peters, N. Kauder, C. Campbell, and C. Flango, *Future Trends in State Courts, 2005* (Williamsburg, VA: National Center for State Courts, 2005), pp. 89–92.

xvi. National Center for Elder Abuse. Available at http:// www.elderabusecenter.org/default.cfm?p=faqs.cfm (accessed August 8, 2008).

xvii. National Center for Elder Abuse. Available at http:// www.elderabusecenter.org/default.cfm?p=faqs.cfm (accessed August 8, 2008).

xviii. National Center for Elder Abuse. Available at http://www .elderabusecenter.org/default.cfm?p=faqs.cfm (accessed August 8, 2009).

xix. National Center for Elder Abuse. Available at http:// www.elderabusecenter.org/default.cfm?p=faqs.cfm (accessed August 8, 2008).

xx. National Center for Elder Abuse. Available at http:// www.elderabusecenter.org/default.cfm?p=faqs.cfm (accessed August 8, 2009).

xxi. National Center for Elder Abuse. Available at http:// www.elderabusecenter.org/default.cfm?p=faqs.cfm (accessed August 8, 2008).

xxii. National Center for Elder Abuse. Available at http://www .elderabusecenter.org/default.cfm?p=faqs.cfm (accessed August 8, 2009).

xxiii. J. Bellah, "Training: Identity Theft," *Law and Order* 49(2001):222–226.

1. D. G. Ries, "Computer Presentations by Lawyers in the Conference Room, Classroom, and Courts," *Pennsylvania Bar Association Quarterly*, Vol. 78 (2007), pp. 56–67.

2. Federal Judicial Center, *Effective Use of Technology: A Judge's Guide to Pretrial and Trial*, available at www.fjc .gov/public/pdf.nsf/lookup/CTtech16.pdf/$file/CTtech16 .pdf (accessed March 4, 2013).

3. Excerpts from "Special Report: The 2006 ABA Tech Report," by Laura Ikens, 2007, as published in the Law Journal Legal Technology Newsletter. © 2006 by the American Bar Association. Reprinted with permission. All rights reserved. This information or any portion thereof may not be copied or disseminated in any form or by any means or stored in an electronic database or retrieval system without the express permission of the American Bar Association.

4. Ibid.

5. J. E. McMillan, *A Guidebook for Electronic Court Filing* (Alexandria, VA: National Center for State Courts, 1999), p. 2.

6. Indiana Courts, *Electronic Citation and Warning System*, available at www.in.gov/judiciary/jtac/2655.htm (accessed March 4, 2013).

7. www.orangelegal.com/legal-services/internet-depositions (accessed March 3, 2013).

8. C. D. Bos, *Presenting Evidence with Courtroom Technology*, available at www.bosglazier.com/courttech.shtml (accessed March 4, 2013).

9. Center for Legal and Court Technology, available at www .legaltechcenter.net (accessed March 4, 2013).

10. For a full online tour, go to www.ninja9.org/courtadmin/ mis/courtroom_23.htm (accessed March 4, 2013).

11. Legal Information Institute, *Alternative Dispute Resolution: An Overview*, available at www.law.cornell.edu/wex/ alternative_dispute_resolution (accessed March 4, 2013).

12. Equal Employment Opportunity Commission, *Early Neutral Evaluation*, available at www.eeoc.gov/federal/adr/ neutralevaluation.cfm (accessed March 4, 2013).

13. U.S. District Court for the Northern District of California, *Alternative Dispute Resolution Program*, available at www.cand.uscourts.gov/localrules/ADR (accessed March 4, 2013).

14. From "Arbitration, Mediation and Conciliation: Differences and Similarities from an International and Italian Business Perspective" by Alessandra Sgubini, Mara Prieditis, and Andrea Marighetto. Reprinted with permission of Mediate.com.

15. G. Bazemore and L. Walgrave, "Restorative Juvenile Justice: In Search of Fundamentals and an Outline for Systematic Reform," in G. Bazemore and L. Walgrave, eds., *Restorative Juvenile Justice* (Monsey, NY: Criminal Justice Press, 1999), pp. 45–74.

16. Cited in J. Braithwaite, "Restorative Justice: Assessing Optimistic and Pessimistic Accounts," in M. Tonry, ed., *Crime and Justice: Review of Research* (Chicago: University of Chicago Press, 1999), p. 5.

17. Bazemore and Walgrave, "Restorative Juvenile Justice," p. 48.

18. D. R. Karp, "Harm and Repair: Observing Restorative Justice in Vermont," *Justice Quarterly*, Vol. 18 (2001), p. 728.

19. The discussion in this paragraph borrows liberally from D. R. Karp, "Harm and Repair," pp. 727–757. Copyright © Taylor & Francis Group. Reprinted by permission.

20. Ibid., p. 730.

21. Ibid.

22. For other criticisms of restorative justice, see S. Levrant, F. T. Cullen, and B. Fulton, "Reconsidering Restorative Justice: The Corruption of Benevolence Revisited?," *Crime and Delinquency*, Vol. 45 (1999), pp. 3–27.

23. S. Eschholz, M. D. Reed, and E. Beck, "Offenders' Family Members' Responses to Capital Crimes: The Need for Restorative Justice Initiatives," *Homicide Studies*, Vol. 7 (2003), pp. 154–181; M. S. Umbreit and B. Vos, "Homicide Survivors Meet the Offender Prior to Execution: Restorative Justice through Dialogue," *Homicide Studies*, Vol. 4 (2000), pp. 63–87.

24. From "Introduction to Restorative Justice Tutorial," Centre for Justice and Reconciliation, available at www.Restorativejustice.org. Reprinted by permission.

25. Ibid.

26. Ibid.

27. Ibid.

28. Ibid.

29. Ibid.

30. California Administrative Office of the Courts, *Sentencing Circles*, available at www.courts.ca.gov/documents/BARJManual3.pdf (accessed March 4, 2013).

31. Karp, "Harm and Repair," p. 732.

32. For more on the future of courts, see T. Peters, N. Kauder, C. Campbell, and C. Flango, *Future Trends in State Courts, 2005* (Williamsburg, VA: National Center for State Courts, 2005).

33. S. M. Strickland, "Beyond the Vanishing Trial: A Look at the Composition of State Court Dispositions," in Peters et al., *Future Trends in State Courts, 2005*, pp. 89–92.

34. See *Journal of Empirical Legal Studies*, Vol. 1, No. 3 (November 2004), for articles presented at the American Bar Association Section of Litigation's "Vanishing Trials" symposium.

35. Ibid., p. 91.

36. Bob Drogin, "Trials Halted to Save Money," *Los Angeles Times*, available at http://articles.latimes.com/2008/dec/22/nation/na-courts22 (accessed March 4, 2013).

37. J. L. Worrall and M. E. Nugent-Borakove, *The Changing Role of the American Prosecutor* (Albany: State University of New York Press, 2008).

38. B. C. Feld, "The Honest Politician's Guide to Juvenile Justice in the Twenty-First Century," *Annals of the American Academy of Political and Social Science*, Vol. 564 (1999), pp. 10–27. Copyright © 1999 by the Academy of Political and Social Science. Reprinted by Permission of SAGE Publications.

39. Ibid., p. 10.

40. Ibid., pp. 21–22.

41. K. H. Federle, "Will the Juvenile Court System Survive? Is There a Jurisprudential Future for the Juvenile Court?," *Annals of the American Academy of Political and Social Science*, Vol. 564 (1999), pp. 28–35.

42. D. B. Rottman, *Trends and Issues in the State Courts: Challenges and Achievements* (Williamsburg, VA: National Center for State Courts, 2004), p. 236. Reprinted by permission.

43. www.hennepinattorney.org/CommunityProsecution/tabid/56/Default.aspx (accessed March 4, 2013).

44. S. J. Larson, "Public Access and the National Landscape of Data Regulation," in Peters et al., *Future Trends in State Courts, 2005*, pp. 74–76. Reprinted by permission.

45. Much of the discussion in this section comes from the "Future Trends" series of the National Center for State Courts. See, e.g., C. Flango, A. McDowell, D. Saunders, N. Sydow, C. Campbell, and N. Kauder, Future Trends in State Courts, 2012 (Williamsburg, VA: National Center for State Courts, 2012).

46. T. Peters, N. Kauder, C. Campbell, and C. Flango, "Population Demographics," in Peters et al., Future Trends in State Courts, 2005, pp. 2–10. Reprinted by permission.

47. Ibid., pp. 6–7.

48. Ibid., p. 9.

49. Ibid., p. 10.

50. These are drawn from Flango et al., *Future Trends in State Courts, 2011*, pp. 136–137.

51. Public Law 106-386.

52. Ibid.

53. U.S. Department of State, International Information Programs, *Fact Sheet: State Department Programs to Combat Trafficking in Persons* (Washington, DC: U.S. Department of State, 2001).

54. J. G. Raymond, D. M. Hughes, and C. J. Gomez, *Sex Trafficking of Women in the United States: International and Domestic Trends*, Report to Coalition against Trafficking in Women (Washington, DC: National Institute of Justice, 2001).

55. A. O. Richard, *International Trafficking in Women to the United States: A Contemporary Manifestation of Slavery and Organized Crime* (Washington, DC: U.S. State Department, Bureau of Intelligence and Research, 1999).

56. T. Peters, N. Kauder, C. Campbell, and C. Flango, "Human Trafficking: A Growing Crime to Hit the State Courts," in Peters et al., Future Trends in State Courts, 2005, pp. 105–107. Reprinted by permission.

57. National Center for Elder Abuse, available at www.ncea.aoa.gov (accessed March 4, 2013).

58. Ibid.

59. E. Lindbloom, J. Brandt, C. Hawes, C. Phillips, D. Zimmerman, J. Robinson, B. Bowers, and P. McFeeley, *The Role of Forensic Science in Identification of Mistreatment Deaths in Long-Term Care Facilities* (Washington, DC: National Institute of Justice, April 2005), p. 1.

60. Atlanta Long Term Care Ombudsman Program, *The Silenced Voice Speaks Out: A Study of Abuse and Neglect of Nursing Home Residents* (Atlanta: Atlanta Legal Aid Society, 2000).

61. K. Pillemer and D. W. Moore, "Abuse of Patients in Nursing Homes: Findings from a Survey of Staff," *Gerontologist*, Vol. 29 (1989), pp. 314–320.

62. See, e.g., K. Pillemer and B. Hudson, "A Model Abuse Prevention Program for Nursing Assistants," *Gerontologist*, Vol. 33 (1993), pp. 128–131.

63. Lindbloom et al., *The Role of Forensic Science in Identification of Mistreatment Deaths in Long-Term Care Facilities*.

64. This list is reprinted from C. C. McNamee and M. B. Murphy, "Elder Abuse in the United States," *National Institute of Justice Journal*, No. 255, November 2006. Available at: http://www.nij.gov/journals/255/elder_abuse.html

65. From Brenda Uekert, "Elder Abuse and Neglect," Peters et al., Future Trends in State Courts, 2005, pp. 102–104. Reprinted by permission.

66. Ibid.

67. Ibid.

68. Ibid., p. 103.

69. J. Bellah, "Training: Identity Theft," *Law and Order*, Vol. 49 (2001), p. 222.

70. U.S. General Accounting Office, *Identity Fraud: Prevalence and Cost Appear to Be Growing* (Washington, DC: U.S. General Accounting Office, 2002).

71. P. Fichtman, "Preventing Credit Card Fraud and Identity Theft: A Primer for Online Merchants," *Information Systems Security*, Vol. 10 (2001), pp. 52–59.

72. Federal Trade Commission, *Fraud Complaint and Identity Theft Victims by State* (Washington, DC: Federal Trade Commission, 2003).

73. Ibid.

74. A. L. Keith, "Trends in Identity Theft," in Peters et al., *Future Trends in State Courts*, 2005. Reprinted with permission.

75. V. Suveiu, "Immigration and Its Impact on the State Courts," in Peters et al., *Future Trends in State Courts*, 2005. Reprinted by permission.

76. For examples, see J. Hagan and A. Palloni, "Sociological Criminology and the Mythology of Hispanic Immigration and Crime," *Social Problems*, Vol. 46 (1999), pp. 617–632; L. J. Hickman and M. J. Suttorp, "Are Deportable Aliens a Unique Threat to Public Safety? Comparing the Recidivism of Deportable and Nondeportable Aliens," *Criminology and Public Policy*, Vol. 7 (2008), pp. 59–82; D. P. Mears, "The Immigration-Crime Nexus: Toward an Analytic Framework for Assessing and Guiding Theory, Research, and Policy," *Sociological Perspectives*, Vol. 44 (2001), pp. 1–19.

Glossary

Following are the text's key terms and their definitions. The number in parentheses at the end of each definition indicates which chapter the term is found in.

abandonment The desertion of a vulnerable elder by anyone who has assumed the responsibility for care or custody of that person.[1] (16)

absolute immunity The total immunity of a prosecutor from a suit. (8)

accusation rule The U.S. Supreme Court holding that the Sixth Amendment's guarantee of a right to a speedy trial attaches only *after* a person has been accused of a crime. (13)

Actual Innocence Awareness Database A computer-based resource maintained by the University of Texas at Austin's Tarlton Law Library that contains a wealth of information on the subject of wrongful convictions.[2] (15)

actus reus A term that literally means "the criminal act." The prosecutor has to show that an accused person (as a principal offender, an accessory to the crime, or an accomplice) committed a criminal act. (1)

***ad hoc* assigned counsel system** A method for appointing legal assistance in which the judge chooses a defense attorney on a case-by-case basis. (9)

***ad hoc* plea bargaining** A term coined by one legal scholar that refers to some strange concessions defendants agree to make as part of the prosecutor's decision to secure a guilty plea.[3] (12)

adjournment The continuance of a scheduled event. The verb "adjourn" means "to put off." (4)

adjudication "[T]he process by which a court arrives at a decision regarding a case."[4] (1)

adjudicatory hearing The fact-finding process by which the juvenile court determines whether there is sufficient evidence to sustain the allegations in a petition. (5)

Administrative Office of the U.S. Courts The federal agency that carries out the policies of the Judicial Conference and "provides a broad range of legislative, legal, financial, technology, management, administrative, and program support services to the federal courts."[5] (3)

administrative regulations Rules promulgated by government agencies that have been given their authority by the executive branch or legislative branch. (1)

adversarialism The element incorporated into the American judicial system by the founding fathers to promote argument, debate, and openness as a defense against oppressive government. (1)

adversarial justice system The functional construct of the American court system that features two competing sets of interests (the defendant's and the government's) working against each other in pursuit of the truth, from which stems the many protections our Constitution and laws afford people. (1)

affirmative defense A defense that goes *beyond* simply denying that a crime took place (e.g., alibi, duress, entrapment, or self-defense); also, an answer to a criminal charge in which a defendant takes the offense and responds to the allegations with his or her own assertions based on legal principles. Affirmative defenses must be raised and supported by the defendant independently of any claims made by the prosecutor. (13)

aggravating circumstances Factors that increase the seriousness or the outrageousness of a given crime (e.g., a homicide preceded by a period of prolonged torture). (14)

alibi A type of defense against a criminal charge wherein the defendant argues that he or she was somewhere else at the time of the crime, making it impossible for him or her to have committed it. (1)

Allen charge A set of instructions given to jurors after they become deadlocked that instructs them to reexamine their opinions in an effort to reach a verdict. (13)

allocution The defendant's explanation to the judge, usually in open court, of exactly what he or she did and why. An allocution is documented in court records and can be used against the defendant in related civil proceedings. (11)

alternative dispute resolution (ADR) "[A]ny means of settling disputes outside of the courtroom."[6] (16)

American Bar Association (ABA) A professional organization founded on August 12, 1878, whose mission today is "to be the national representative of the legal profession, serving the public and the profession by promoting justice, professional excellence and respect for the law."[7] (2)

American Judicature Society (AJS) A professional association for judges, lawyers, and concerned citizens that is involved in judicial ethics through efforts to promote the independence and integrity of the courts. (7)

amicus curiae A term that literally means "a friend of the court." It is a legal brief filed by a "person [or group] with strong interest in or views on the subject matter of an action,"[8] seeking to influence the court "ostensibly on behalf of a party but actually to suggest a rationale consistent with its own views."[9] (2)

anticipatory socialization The law school–based process of teaching an aspiring judge important analytic and communication skills and arming him or her with much of the information he or she will need in his or her future job.[10] (7)

Antiterrorism and Effective Death Penalty Act (AEDPA) The U.S. legislation that was passed in the wake of the bombings at the World Trade Center in 1993 and the Oklahoma City federal building in 1995 that sought to toughen federal antiterrorism capabilities. (14)

apology penalty A form of shaming penalty that requires offenders to express remorse, usually publicly, for committing a particular crime. (14)

appeal of right An appeal that is automatically granted to the defendant by law (i.e., one that *must* be heard by an appellate court); also called *direct appeal*. (14)

appellate jurisdiction "[T]he lawful authority of a court to review a decision made by a lower court; the lawful authority of a court to hear an appeal from a judgment of a lower court."[11] (2)

arbitration A simplified version of a trial without discovery and with modified rules of evidence. (16)

arbitrator A private, neutral person, typically trained in alternative dispute resolution, chosen to arbitrate a disagreement and empowered to impose a binding judgment or decision. (16)

arrest The taking of an adult or juvenile into physical custody by authority of law for the purpose of charging the person with a criminal offense or a delinquent act or status offense, terminating with the recording of a specific offense.[12] (11)

Article I tribunals Federal courts established by Article I of the U.S. Constitution that are not considered part of the federal judicial branch; also called *legislative courts*. (3)

Article III court A special category of federal courts established by Article III of the U.S. Constitution and considered part of the federal judicial branch. They include the U.S. Court of International Trade and the Foreign Intelligence Surveillance Court authorized by the Federal Intelligence Surveillance Act of 1978 (FISA). (3)

articles of impeachment The formal allegation of judicial misconduct, akin to an indictment in a criminal case. (7)

assigned counsel Lawyers appointed from a list of private bar members who accept cases on a judge-by-judge, court-by-court, or case-by-case basis.[13] (9)

assistant U.S. attorney One of more than 5,600 subordinate attorneys assigned throughout the various offices of the U.S. attorneys in the 94 federal judicial districts to perform the brunt of litigation work involving the federal government. (8)

attorney general The head of the U.S. Department of Justice and the chief law enforcement officer in the federal government; also, the chief law enforcement officer in each of the state- and territorial-level governments. (8)

authorized case One of three conditions that must be met to elevate a state matter to federal jurisdiction, mandating that the dispute in question must be one the court in which relief is sought is authorized to resolve. (2)

bail "To effect the release of an accused person from custody, in return for a promise that he or she will appear at a place and time specified and submit to the jurisdiction and judgment of the court, guaranteed by a pledge to pay to the court a specified sum of money or property if the person does not appear."[14] It is the money or property pledged to the court or actually deposited with the court to effect the release of a person from legal custody. (11)

bail bondsman A person, usually licensed, whose business it is to effect release on bail for people charged with offenses and held in custody by pledging to pay a sum of money if the defendants fail to appear in court as required. (11)

bench trial A trial in which the judge is both the trier of law *and* the trier of fact; also called *finder of law* or *finder of fact*. (13)

bifurcated trial A criminal trial in which issues relevant to the case (e.g., guilt and punishment, guilt and sanity) are tried separately. (14)

Bill of Rights The first ten amendments to the U.S. Constitution, placing important limitations on government authority with respect to the investigation of crime. (1)

***Blakely* bounce** The modest increase in the number of cases that required resentencing that arose from the U.S. Supreme Court's holding in *Blakely* v. *Washington* (2004)[15] that the right to a jury trial barred judges from increasing criminal sentences based on facts not decided by the jury or admitted by the defendant. (4)

blended sentence A form of offense-based sentencing that requires the juvenile to serve both a term of probation and time in an adult correctional facility.[16] (5)

Blockburger rule A complicated issue in double jeopardy jurisprudence concerning the definition of "same offense," resolved by the U.S. Supreme Court's development of a test that states, "Where the same act or transaction constitutes a violation of two distinct statutory provisions, the test to be applied to determine whether there are two offenses or only one is whether each requires proof of an additional fact which the other does not."[17] (11)

booking A law enforcement or correctional administrative process officially recording an entry into detention after arrest and identifying the person, the place, the time, the reason for the arrest, and the arresting authority. (11)

Capital Jury Project An ongoing research program in which in-depth post-trial interviews are conducted with members of capital juries. (13)

case-flow management "[T]he court supervision of the case progress of all cases filed in that court. It includes management of the time and events necessary to move a case from the point of initiation (filing, date of contest, or arrest) through disposition, regardless of the type of disposition."[18] (4)

Center for Court Innovation   "[A nongovernmental] nonprofit think tank that helps courts and criminal justice agencies aid victims, reduce crime and improve public trust in justice."[19] (2)

chain of custody   A documented record of custodial preservation of evidence in the original condition in which it was discovered during an investigation. (11)

challenge for cause   A prosecutor's or defense attorney's call for removal of a potential juror from service on a jury based on bias or a similar reason demonstrated by the potential juror. (13)

chancery courts   English courts created in the fifteenth century by the lord high chancellor to address cases that could not be decided in other common law courts[20]; also known as *equity courts*. (5)

change of venue   A motion to move a trial to another jurisdiction. (13)

charge bargaining   The prosecutor's ability to negotiate with the defendant in terms of the charges that could be filed. (12)

child savers   A group of reform-minded individuals in the United States that sought to improve the living conditions of poor urban children from about 1850 to 1890. (5)

circuit judicial council   A council established within each federal circuit that is charged, by law, with the task of making "all necessary and appropriate orders for the effective and expeditious administration of justice within its circuit."[21] (3)

circuit riding   The early practice of requiring two U.S. Supreme Court justices and one district judge to ride between each of the three districts established within the 13 judicial circuits to preside over trials. (3)

circumstantial evidence   "[E]vidence that *indirectly* proves a fact."[22] (13)

city attorney   The city-level official charged with providing legal services to other city-level agencies. (8)

civil forfeiture   A seizure, resulting from a civil court proceeding, of money, negotiable instruments, securities, property, or other things of value. (14)

Code of Conduct for Federal Public Defender Employees   A publication of the Administrative Office of the U.S. Courts. (9)

Code of Federal Regulations   The group of rules and regulations adopted by U.S. federal agencies and departments. (1)

Code of Hammurabi   The earliest-known example of a formal written legal code. (1)

collateral attack   An attempt to avoid or invalidate a judicial determination. *Habeas corpus*, a form of collateral attack, seeks to invalidate a criminal conviction by declaring one's confinement unconstitutional. (14)

Commission on Trial Court Performance Standards   A commission established by the National Center for State Courts in 1987 that was charged with developing performance standards that could be used by the state courts. (4)

common law   The law originating from usage and custom rather than from written statutes; also, a term that referred to the law "in common" throughout England following the Norman Conquest in medieval times. (1)

community court   A neighborhood-focused court that attempts to harness the power of the justice system to address local problems by using creative partnerships and problem solving, creating new relationships within the justice system and with outside stakeholders (e.g., residents, merchants, churches, and schools), and testing new and aggressive approaches to public safety rather than merely responding to crime after it has occurred.[23] (6)

community prosecution   An approach intended to improve cooperation and collaboration between prosecutors and individuals outside the criminal justice system (e.g., community members and business leaders). More formally, it is "an organizational response to the grassroots public safety demands of neighborhoods, as expressed in highly concrete terms by the people who live in them. They identify immediate, specific crime problems they want addressed and that the incident-based 911 system is ill suited to handle."[24] (8)

competency   A specific evidentiary requirement for witness testimony that requires witnesses to possess certain characteristics (e.g., be "of age") that render them legally qualified to testify. (13)

compulsory process   A defendant's constitutional entitlement to use subpoenas to obtain witnesses, documents, and other objects that are helpful to his or her defense. (10)

conciliation   An alternative dispute resolution process that seeks to reach agreement between parties to a dispute but differs from other techniques discussed in that the conciliator plays a relatively direct role in the actual resolution of a dispute and even advises the parties on certain solutions by making proposals for settlement.[25] (16)

concurrent jurisdiction   The legislative authority to try juvenile cases in either juvenile or adult court, with the prosecutor deciding where the case should be tried. (5)

concurrent sentence   One of two or more sentences imposed at the same time, after conviction for more than one offense, and served at the same time; also, a new sentence for a new conviction, imposed on a person already under sentence for a previous offense, and served at the same time as the previous sentence. (14)

concurring opinion   An opinion that supports the opinion but offers different reasoning. (3)

conditional guilty plea A negotiated arrangement whereby a defendant can sometimes preserve certain rights following a plea agreement. (12)

conferencing An extended conversation between the victim and the offender, usually with the assistance of a mediator or arbitrator, about the crime and its consequences. This approach differs from victim–offender mediation by inclusion of other parties, such as family members and community support groups. (16)

consecutive sentence One of two or more sentences imposed at the same time, after conviction for more than one offense, and served in sequence with the other sentence; also, a new sentence for a new conviction, imposed on a person already under sentence for a previous offense, and added to the previous sentence, thus increasing the maximum time the offender may be confined or under supervision. (14)

consent decree A judgment by consent of the parties to a lawsuit where the defendant agrees to stop the alleged improper or illegal activity. (3)

contract law The category of civil law that involves lawsuits to resolve unfilled legal obligations between parties. (1)

contract model A method of appointing counsel that uses non-salaried individual private attorneys, bar associations, law firms, consortiums or groups of attorneys, or nonprofit corporations that contract with a funding source to provide court-appointed representation in a jurisdiction, excluding public defender programs primarily funded by an awarded contract.[26] (9)

control conditions Probation or parole conditions that are intended to ensure adequate monitoring and supervision of a probationer or parolee. (14)

cooperative federalism A system of government wherein some of the lines between federal and state power are blurred. (1)

coordinated assigned counsel system A method for appointing legal assistance that relies on a coordinator who chooses the attorney. (9)

corpus delicti A term that literally means "the body of crime." While this could mean the literal body of a murdered individual, it more generally refers to the objective proof (i.e., the reality) of a crime. (1)

court "[A]n agency or unit of the judicial branch of government, authorized or established by statute or constitution, and consisting of one or more judicial officers, which has the authority to decide upon cases, controversies in law, and disputed matters of fact brought before it."[27] (1)

court-martial A criminal trial conducted by the military. (3)

court of appeal The colloquial name given to the U.S. Court of Appeals (formerly, the U.S. circuit court, renamed by the Judicial Code of 1948) within each respective federal circuit. (3)

courtroom work group The professional courtroom actors, including judges, prosecuting attorneys, defense attorneys, public defenders, and others who earn a living serving the court. (2)

Courts of Appeals Act of 1891 The federal law that created the 13 U.S. Circuit Courts of Appeals[28]; also called *Judiciary Act of 1891*[29] or *Evarts Act*. (3)

court-stripping "[T]he attempt to take jurisdiction away from courts to review matters"[30]; also called *jurisdiction stripping*.[31] (2)

court unification The simplification of state court structures to address such problems as overlapping jurisdiction and to achieve centralized control over state judiciaries. (4)

credibility A specific evidentiary requirement for witness testimony that is concerned with whether the witness's testimony should be believed. (13)

crime Any conduct in violation of the criminal laws of the federal government, a state, or a local jurisdiction for which there is no legally acceptable justification or excuse. (1)

criminal forfeiture A seizure, resulting from a criminal court proceeding, of money, negotiable instruments, securities, property, or other things of value that derived from or was used to facilitate a crime or criminal activity. (14)

cross-examination The questioning of a witness at trial by the opposing counsel. (10)

Customs Courts Act of 1980 The most significant federal legislation affecting international trade disputes. (3)

day fine A system for determining monetary fines that involves attaching a "unit value" to the seriousness of a given offense that is then multiplied by a fixed percentage of the offender's income. The result is a proportional fine that is not unnecessarily burdensome on an offender but is still sufficient to serve a punitive purpose. (14)

death-row volunteering A phenomenon involving a death-row inmate making a decision to stop appealing and let the sentence be carried out.[32] (9)

debasement penalty A form of shaming penalty that seeks to lower an offender's social status by requiring him or her to perform humiliating acts. (14)

declarant One who makes a statement or declaration. (10)

declaratory judgment A type of exception to the general rule that judges cannot initiate legal disputes or cases on their own. In the civil context, when one party is threatened with a lawsuit but the lawsuit is not yet filed, the party may ask the court to clarify its rights under some statute, will, or contract. A declaratory judgment is more preventive than reactive. A dispute usually occurs after some right has allegedly been violated, but a declaratory judgment is intended to be made before this occurs to ensure that one party does not violate the law or terms of a contract. (7)

defense attorney   "[T]he lawyer who advises, represents, and acts for the defendant (or, in post-conviction proceedings, the offender)."[33] (9)

deferred prosecution diversion   A delay in the actual in-court prosecution of an offender until the offender completes treatment or some other program. (8)

deferred sentencing   A twist on deferred prosecution that puts off sentencing instead of putting off charges. (8)

demonstrative evidence   Any evidence that seeks to demonstrate a certain point (e.g., drawings, diagrams, illustrations, and computer simulations) to help jurors understand how a crime was likely committed. (13)

deposition   The testimony of a witness given under oath and recorded for use in court at a later date. A problem with depositions is that they can be difficult to schedule at a time when all parties are readily available. (16)

determinate sentence   A model of criminal punishment in which an offender is given a fixed term of imprisonment that may be reduced by good time or gain time. Under the model, for example, all offenders convicted of the same degree of burglary would be sentenced to the same length of time behind bars. (14)

direct control   The ability of legislative bodies to directly control the courts through the power to create them, to set the rules they must follow, and to limit their jurisdiction.[34] (2)

direct evidence   "[E]vidence that proves a fact without the need for the juror to infer anything from it."[35] (13)

direct examination   The questioning of a witness by the attorney for the side (prosecution or defense) that originally scheduled that witness to testify. As a general rule, the questions on direct examination must be specific but not leading. (10)

discovery   The process whereby both parties to a case learn of the evidence that the opposition will present. (11)

discretionary appeal   An appeal that the appellate courts can decide—based on their own discretion—whether to grant a hearing. (14)

discretionary waiver   A type of juvenile waiver that "give[s] juvenile court judges discretion to waive jurisdiction in individual cases involving minors, so as to allow prosecution in adult criminal courts."[36] (5)

discrimination   The unfair treatment of a person or group because of prejudice about race, sex, age, sexual orientation, religion, or other distinguishing characteristics. (15)

disparity   "[A] difference [in how a person or group is treated] . . . that does not necessarily involve discrimination."[37] (15)

disposition plan   A document that includes recommendations concerning the juvenile's education, training, counseling, and support services needs. (5)

dissenting opinion   An opinion that disagrees with the main opinion. (3)

district attorney   The chief local (typically, county-level) prosecutor charged with bringing criminal cases to trial; also called *county attorney*, *state's attorney*, *prosecuting attorney*, *commonwealth attorney*, *county prosecutor*, *district attorney general*, *county and prosecuting attorney*, *solicitor*, or *circuit attorney*.[38] (8)

diversion   An informal or programmatic method of steering an offender out of the criminal justice system. (8)

diversity jurisdiction   One of three main types of federal court jurisdiction. This refers to the authority of federal courts to hear cases where the parties are from different states. (2)

domestic-violence court   A special state, county, or municipal court that focuses on tailoring interventions to meeting the needs of victims, closely monitoring the offender, and enlisting community participation.[39] (6)

double agent   An attorney who appears to work for one side but instead works for another; also, a defense attorney who looks out for his or her own interests more than the interests of the defendant. (9)

double jeopardy   The Fifth Amendment requirement that a person cannot be reprosecuted after acquittal, reprosecuted after conviction, or subjected to separate punishments for the same offense. (11)

drug court   A special state, county, or municipal court that offers first-time substance abuse offenders judicially mandated and court-supervised treatment alternatives to prison. (6)

Drug Treatment Alternative to Prison (DTAP) program   The Brooklyn, New York, deferred sentencing program.[40] (8)

dual court system   A judicial system comprising federal- and state-level judicial systems. (1)

dual federalism   A system of government wherein the only powers of the federal government are those explicitly listed, with the rest being left to the states. (1)

due process clause   The portion of the Fourteenth Amendment that has been used by the U.S. Supreme Court to make certain protections specified in the Bill of Rights applicable to the states. (1)

early neutral evaluation   The use of "a neutral or an impartial third party to provide an objective evaluation, sometimes in writing, of the strengths and weaknesses of a case. Under this method, the parties will usually make informal presentations to the neutral party to highlight their respective cases or positions."[41] It is also called *neutral evaluation*. (16)

elder abuse   "[A]ny knowing, intentional, or negligent act by a caregiver or any other person that causes harm or a serious risk of harm to a vulnerable adult."[42] (16)

electronic discovery "[A]ny process in which electronic data is sought, located, secured, and searched with the intent of using it as evidence in a civil or criminal legal case"[43]; also called *neutral evaluation*. (16)

electronic filing "[T]he process of transmitting documents and other court information to the court through an electronic medium, rather than on paper"[44]; also called *e-filing*. (16)

emotional abuse The infliction of mental pain, anguish, or distress on an elder person through verbal or nonverbal acts.[45] (16)

***en banc* proceeding** A term that literally means "in bench." This proceeding is typically called when there is a problem with conflicting decisions by different panels of appellate court judges and is attended by all of the judges within the circuit. (3)

error of justice A term coined by Forst to describe the many types of mistakes the criminal justice system can make. It is further described as "any departure from an optimal outcome of justice for a criminal case."[46] (15)

ethnicity "[D]ifferences between groups of people based on cultural customs, such as language, religion, foodways, family patterns, and other characteristics."[47] (15)

exclusionary rule The requirement that evidence obtained in violation of the Constitution during an illegal arrest, search, or other process cannot be used in a criminal trial. (11)

excuse defense A type of defense against a criminal charge in which the defendant claims that some personal condition or circumstance at the time of the act was such that he or she should not be held accountable under the criminal law. (1)

executive control A measure of control over the courts exercised through the executive's power to appoint judges to the bench and the daily presence of the prosecutors—each of whom is a member of the executive branch—who work in the courts. (2)

exoneration A subsequent declaration by the appropriate legal authority that a person who was wrongfully convicted of a crime is not guilty of having committed that crime.[48] (15)

exploitation The illegal taking, misuse, or concealment of funds, property, or assets of a vulnerable elder.[49] (16)

extended jurisdiction The legislative authority for juvenile court judges to commit a juvenile to a correctional facility beyond the age of 18.[50] (5)

family law The category of civil law that is concerned with matters of marriage, divorce, child custody, and children's rights. (1)

Federal Bail Reform Act The U.S. legislation that authorized judges to revoke pretrial release for firearm possession, failure to comply with curfew, or failure to comply with other conditions of release and that permitted detention for up to ten days of an individual who "may flee or pose a danger to any other person or the community."[51] (11)

Federal Intelligence Surveillance Act of 1978 (FISA) The U.S. legislation that spelled out procedures for conducting foreign intelligence surveillance. (3)

Federal Judicial Center The education and research agency for the federal courts.[52] (3)

Federal Judiciary Act of 1789 The federal law that established the organization of the federal courts, which emerged from the first meeting of the first Congress.[53] (3)

federal jurisdiction An exception to the general rule that federal courts have jurisdiction over federal matters and state courts have jurisdiction over state matters that gives the U.S. Supreme Court jurisdiction over certain cases arising from the states. (2)

federal question jurisdiction One of three main types of federal court jurisdiction that refers to the authority of federal courts to hear cases touching on the U.S. Constitution or other federal laws. (2)

felony A serious criminal offense generally punishable by more than one year of incarceration. (1)

felony case processor model A model of criminal prosecution that consists of the elements of mission, source of authority, demand, organization, tactics, environment, and outcomes. (8)

final judgment rule A general restriction that bars the filing of an appeal until after the court hands down its final judgment as to the defendant's guilt. (14)

fine The most common punishment used by the criminal justice system today.[54] Used primarily in cases involving minor offenses, fines involve the assessment of a monetary amount to be forfeited as a punishment for commission of an offense. (14)

fixed-fee contract A fee agreement for appointed legal defense fees whereby a law firm contracts to provide defense representation in a fixed number of cases for a fixed fee per case. (9)

fixed-price contract A fee agreement for appointed defense counsel fees whereby a law firm agrees to accept an unspecified number of cases for a single annual flat fee. (9)

forfeiture The authorized seizure of money, negotiable instruments, securities, property, or other things of value. (14)

freshman effects The phenomenon experienced by new U.S. Supreme Court justices wherein they are said to be overwhelmed—even bewildered—by the Court's caseload and their own responsibilities. The senior justice allegedly eases their opinion-writing burden, and the new justices are believed to avoid alignments with established voting blocs during their early years on the Court.[55] (7)

freshman socialization An informal phase of the socialization of a judge during which he or she learns and adjusts to his or her new role over the short term. (7)

fruit of the poisonous tree doctrine A legal principle that excludes from introduction at trial any evidence later developed as a result of an illegal search or seizure. (11)

gag order A judge's order to keep the media quiet concerning a particular matter. (13)

general court-martial A type of court-martial that is reserved for the most serious violations of the Uniform Code of Military Justice, including cases that may result in a penalty of death. (3)

geographical jurisdiction The organization of courts in distinct geographic regions. (2)

going rate An unwritten informal agreement between members of the courtroom work group (judge, defense attorney, and prosecutor) as to what the appropriate punishment should be for a particular type of case.[56] (14)

good-faith exception An exception to the exclusionary rule. Law enforcement officers who conduct a search or who seize evidence on the basis of good faith (i.e., when they believe they are operating according to the dictates of the law) and who later discover that a mistake was made (perhaps in the format of the application for a search warrant) may still provide evidence that can be used in court. (11)

graduated sanctions Sanctions imposed by the juvenile justice system such that first-time offenders who commit relatively minor offenses are treated leniently (with probation or some other form of community treatment). This system may also result in harsher sanctions for those who commit ensuing or repeat offenses or for offenders who commit severe offenses. (5)

grand jury "[A] body of persons who have been selected according to law and sworn to hear the evidence against accused persons and determine whether there is sufficient evidence to bring those persons to trial, to investigate criminal activity generally, and to investigate the conduct of public agencies and officials."[57] (11)

guided-discretion laws Laws enacted after *Furman* v. *Georgia* (1972) aimed at curbing the discretion of judges and jurors in death penalty cases to ensure fairness and evenhandedness in the process.[58] (15)

habeas corpus A term that literally means "you have the body." It is a form of collateral attack that allows someone to challenge the constitutionality of his or her confinement.[59] (14)

Harlem Parole Reentry Court A court that was developed as part of the U.S. Justice Department's Reentry Court Initiative to "test the feasibility and effectiveness of a collaborative, community-based approach to managing offender reentry, with the ultimate goal of reducing recidivism and prison return rates."[60] (6)

harm One of two restorative justice concepts (the other term being *repair*).[61] The term refers to material damage to property, lost wages, physical injury, emotional damage, damaged relationships, increased fear, and a reduced sense of community experienced by victims of a crime. It is also a characteristic that distinguishes damage to public places and community cohesiveness (public harm) from damage or injury shouldered by individual victims of crime (private harm). (16)

harmless error A mistake at the trial court level that has little practical consequences in terms of deciding whether the defendant is guilty or innocent. (14)

hearsay Anything that is not based on the personal knowledge of a witness. (10)

hearsay rule The long-standing practice that hearsay is inadmissible as testimonial evidence in a court of law. (10)

hierarchical jurisdiction The courts' distinct functions and responsibilities at different levels within a single (state or federal) judiciary. (2)

homeless court A special state, county, or municipal court whose purpose it is to resolve outstanding misdemeanor criminal warrants against homeless people so as to ease court case backlogs, reduce vagrancy, and meet a fundamental need of homeless people by eliminating obstacles to their reintegration into society that deter them from using social services and impede their access to employment. (6)

human trafficking A term used to refer to "sex trafficking in which a commercial sex act is induced by force, fraud, [or] coercion or in which the person induced to perform such act has not attained 18 years of age"[62]; also, the recruitment, harboring, transportation, provision, or obtaining of a person for labor or services through the use of force, fraud, or coercion for the purpose of subjection to involuntary servitude, peonage, debt bondage, or slavery.[63] (16)

hung jury A jury that is so irreconcilably divided in opinion after long deliberation that it is unable to reach any verdict. (13)

identity theft "[T]he unlawful use of another's personal identifying information."[64] (16)

impeachment "[A] written accusation by the House of Representatives of the United States to the Senate of the United States against the President, Vice President, or an officer of the United States, including federal judges."[65] (7)

impeachment exception An exception to the exclusionary rule that renders otherwise inadmissible evidence admissible if the prosecution seeks to use such evidence for the purpose of impeaching (i.e., attacking the credibility of) a witness. (11)

incorporation The legal doctrine based on the due process clause of the Fourteenth Amendment that makes various protections listed in the Bill of Rights, which is binding only on the federal government, binding on the states as well. (1)

independent source exception A limitation on the fruit of the poisonous tree doctrine that renders admissible any witness testimony that had been offered totally independent of an illegal search. (11)

indeterminate sentence A type of sentence imposed on a convicted criminal that is meant to encourage rehabilitation through the use of relatively unspecific punishments (e.g., a term of imprisonment of from one to ten years). (14)

indictment "[A] formal, written accusation submitted to the court by a grand jury, alleging that a specified person(s) has committed a specified offense(s), usually a felony"[66]; also called *true bill.* (11)

indirect control The ability of legislative bodies to indirectly control the courts through the power to confirm judicial appointees and to set the budget for the judiciary. (2)

inevitable-discovery exception A limitation on the fruit of the poisonous tree doctrine that renders admissible evidence that would be found regardless of unconstitutional police conduct. (11)

information The prosecutor's formal charging document and the alternative to a grand jury indictment that informs the defendant of what crime he or she is charged with. (11)

infraction An offense that is less serious than a misdemeanor, that usually consists of a violation of a state statute or local ordinance, and that is punishable by a fine or other penalty but not by incarceration.[67] (1)

initial appearance An appearance before a magistrate during which the legality of the defendant's arrest is initially assessed and the defendant is informed of the charges on which he or she is being held; also called *first appearance* or *presentment.* At this stage in the criminal justice process, bail may be set or pretrial release arranged. (11)

injunctive relief A court order directing one party in a civil suit to perform or refrain from performing certain acts. (1)

Innocence Network A series of organizations that provide free legal and investigation services to individuals seeking to prove their innocence and overturn wrongful convictions. (15)

Innocence Project An organization that, in collaboration with the Cardozo Law School in New York, seeks to exonerate wrongfully convicted persons through DNA testing.[69] (15)

inquisitorial system A judicial system that is the philosophical opposite of the adversarial system. (1)

intake The first step in decision making regarding a juvenile whose behavior or alleged behavior is in violation of the law or could otherwise cause a juvenile court to assume jurisdiction. (5)

interest group An organized private nongovernmental group whose mission is to influence political decisions and policy. (2)

interlocutory appeal An appeal filed prior to adjudication. (14)

intermediate appellate court "[A]n appellate court of which the primary function is to review the judgments of trial courts and the decisions of administrative agencies, and whose decisions are in turn usually reviewable by a higher appellate court in the same state" (e.g., the state supreme court).[70] (4)

intermediate sanctions Punitive measures (e.g., intensive supervision probation, shock probation, boot camps, electronic monitoring, and home confinement) that are tougher than probation but less harsh than a prison sentence. (14)

judicial activism The philosophy of using one's power as a judge to do more than interpret the Constitution or laws by avoiding precedent and handing down decisions with sweeping implications for the future. A judicially active judge favors "judge-made" law and looks more to the future than the past. (2)

Judicial Conduct and Disability Act of 1980 The U.S. legislation that permitted any person to file a written complaint alleging that a federal judge has engaged in "conduct prejudicial to the effective and expeditious administration of the business of the courts" or "is unable to discharge all duties of office by reason of mental or physical disability."[71] (7)

Judicial Conference of the United States The main policymaking body of the federal judiciary. It was formerly called the Conference of Senior Circuit Judges. (3)

Judicial Councils Reform and Judicial Conduct and Disability Act of 1980 The 1980 U.S. legislation that provided a mechanism for the federal judiciary to respond to allegations that a particular judge is unfit. (7)

judicial ethics "[T]he standards and norms that bear on judges and [that] cover such matters as how to maintain independence [and] impartiality and avoid impropriety."[72] (7)

judicial federalism A term used to refer to the sharing of judicial power between the 50 states and the federal government. (4)

judicial restraint The philosophy of limiting decisions to the facts of each case, deciding only the issue or issues that need to be resolved in a particular situation. (2)

jurisdiction The power of a court to resolve a dispute. (2)

jury consultant An individual who claims the ability to determine, based on various demographic and behavioral characteristics, how prospective jurors will decide. (13)

jury list The list of potential jury members; also called *jury pool* or *master jury wheel.* (13)

jury nullification The practice, exercised by some juries, of either ignoring or misapplying the law in a certain situation. (13)

jury panel The people selected from the jury list for service as members of a jury in a trial; also called *panel* or *venire*. (13)

jury vilification "The return of a jury verdict that reflects prejudiced or bigoted community standards and convicts when the evidence does not warrant a conviction."[73] (13)

justice of the peace (JOP) courts Low-level courts, found only in Arizona, Delaware, Louisiana, Montana, and Texas,[74] that have original jurisdiction over so-called Class C misdemeanors (e.g., various traffic violations, bail jumping, and bad check writing) and minor civil matters and that sometimes issue search and arrest warrants, perform wedding ceremonies, and even serve as coroners in the least populous counties. (4)

justification defense A type of defense against a criminal charge in which the defendant admits committing the act in question but claims that it was necessary in order to avoid some greater evil. (1)

juvenile A young person who has not yet attained the age at which he or she is treated as an adult for purposes of the law. More formally, a juvenile is "a person subject to juvenile court proceedings because a statutorily defined event or condition caused by or affecting that person was alleged to have occurred while his or her age was below the statutorily specified age limit of original jurisdiction of a juvenile court."[75] Under the federal Juvenile Delinquency Act, a juvenile is a person who has not yet turned 18 years of age.[76] Most states have followed the federal lead, but several states treat 16- and 17-year-olds as adults.[77] (5)

Juvenile Delinquency Prevention and Control Act (JDPCA) The U.S. federal legislation that encouraged states to develop community-level plans to prevent juvenile delinquency.[78] (5)

Juvenile Justice and Delinquency Prevention Act (JJDPA) The U.S. federal legislation that replaced the Juvenile Delinquency Prevention and Control Act of 1968, created several new entities, and enacted key reforms that affected juvenile justice in general and juvenile courts in particular.[79] (5)

juvenile waiver A juvenile judicial action that waives jurisdiction over a juvenile charged with committing a particularly harsh crime to adult court. (5)

law of succession The category of civil law that is concerned with how property is passed from one generation to the next. (1)

leading question A question "that suggests to the witness the answer that the examining party desires."[80] (13)

legislative exclusion A type of juvenile waiver whereby legislative action prohibits trying a juvenile as a juvenile for commission of a specific type of crime[81]; also called *statutory exclusion*. (5)

liberation hypothesis The tendency for jurors to fall back on their own gut instincts when presented with evidence that is vague.[82] The term derives from the phenomenon of jurors feeling "liberated" when the meaning or application of evidence is unclear. (13)

live testimony A defendant's constitutional entitlement to have witnesses physically appear in the courtroom to give their testimony. (10)

Magistrate Courts Low-level courts found only in Alaska, Georgia, Idaho, New Mexico, South Carolina, South Dakota, and West Virginia,[83] with responsibilities similar to those of justice of the peace courts. While magistrate judges also hold preliminary hearings in felony cases and issue warrants, there are no jury trials in magistrate courts. (4)

mandatory sentence A statutorily required penalty that must be set and carried out in all cases on conviction for a specified offense or series of offenses. (14)

mandatory waiver A type of juvenile waiver that requires a case to meet certain age, offense, or other criteria to be waived to adult court. A mandatory waiver differs from legislative exclusion because the case begins in a juvenile court (which is not the case with statutory exclusion). (5)

material evidence "[T]hat which is relevant and goes to substantial matters in dispute or has legitimate influence or bearing on the decision of the case."[84] (13)

mediation An alternative dispute resolution process that is less formal than arbitration. (16)

mediator A person (similar to an arbitrator) who is trained to help disputing parties come together and reach an agreement that is satisfactory to both. However, unlike an arbitrator, a mediator has no power to impose a decision on the parties. (16)

mens rea A term that literally means "a guilty mind." The prosecutor has to show that there was a degree of intent on the offender's part. (1)

mental health court A special state, county, or municipal court that is intended to bring together justice system and mental health agencies to provide services to mentally ill offenders. (6)

Midtown Community Court One of the earliest community courts (October 1993) whose purpose was to provide "accessible justice" for various quality-of-life crimes occurring in and around Times Square.[85] (6)

military tribunal A group authorized by an executive military order shortly after the September 11, 2001, terrorist attacks on the World Trade Center and the Pentagon to deal with alleged terrorists and individuals the government alleges could threaten national security. (3)

misdemeanor A less serious criminal offense generally punishable by less than one year of incarceration. (1)

Missouri Plan One of the more common merit-based selection systems for state judges, based on Missouri Bar Plan adopted in 1940, that combines appointment and election systems. (7)

mistrial A trial that has been terminated and declared invalid by the court because of some circumstance that created a substantial and uncorrectable prejudice to the conduct of a fair trial or that made it impossible to continue the trial in accordance with prescribed procedures. (13)

mitigating circumstances Factors that reduce the seriousness or outrageousness of a given crime (e.g., stealing to feed one's family). (14)

Model Code of Judicial Conduct A code of judicial conduct, adopted by the American Bar Association in 1972, that replaced the so-called Canon of Legal Ethics, which had been created some 50 years earlier. (7)

monetary damages A court-ordered payment of money by one party in a civil suit to the other party. (1)

municipal court A type of city-level court, found in most large cities, which typically has jurisdiction over misdemeanors. (4)

National Association of Criminal Defense Lawyers (NACDL) The leading professional organization for defense attorneys in the United States. (9)

National Center for State Courts A nongovernmental research, consulting, publishing, and educational service that seeks "to improve the administration of justice through leadership and service to state courts and courts around the world."[86] (2)

National Legal Aid and Defender Association (NLADA) A professional organization for defense attorneys in the United States that is roughly equivalent to the National Association of Criminal Defense Lawyers but that is focused mainly on defense attorneys who provide aid to indigent defendants. (9)

neglect The refusal or failure by those responsible to provide food, shelter, health care, or protection for a vulnerable elder.[87] (16)

net widening The expanding control that is exercised over the lives of more and more people who find themselves on the wrong side of the law, often seen as an unfortunate side effect of intermediate sanctions. (14)

neutral evaluation A method of alternative dispute resolution in which the parties make informal presentations to a neutral party who then examines the strengths and weaknesses of each side's case and informs the parties of them. (16)

New Jersey Plan The plan for a new national government drafted by opponents of Madison's Virginia Plan.[88] (3)

New York House of Refuge The first juvenile reformatory in America. (5)

no-drop prosecution The practice of not dropping charges against domestic-violence victims that emerged as a response to the high rate of dismissals in domestic-violence cases[89]; also called *evidence-based prosecution*. (8)

nolo contendere A plea to a criminal charge that means "I do not desire to contest the action." While it resembles a guilty plea, it is different in the sense that it may not be used against the defendant in any later civil litigation arising from the act that gave rise to the criminal charges. (11)

noncriminal proceeding rule A rule recognizing that there is no Sixth Amendment constitutional right to a jury in noncriminal proceedings, based on the amendment's wording, which states, "In all *criminal prosecutions*, the accused shall enjoy the right to a . . . trial, by an impartial jury" (emphasis added). (13)

norm of consensus A phrase used by political scientists to refer to unanimity in appellate court decisions that results from a concern for strengthening the authority of the court. (7)

occupational socialization An informal phase of the socialization of a judge during which he or she undergoes on-the-job training over the course of his or her career.[90] (7)

offense-based sentencing The practice of sentencing a juvenile based on the severity of his or her crime rather than following the traditional practice of sentencing the juvenile based on his or her need for treatment and rehabilitation. (5)

online deposition An alternative to the conventional process of deposing a witness in person that employs communications technology to depose the witness from a remote location. (16)

opening statement The initial statement of the prosecutor or the defense attorney, made in a court of law to a judge or jury, describing the facts that he or she intends to present during a trial to prove the case. (13)

opinion The court's decision in written form with supporting rationale, reference to appropriate precedent, and so on. (3)

original jurisdiction "[T]he lawful authority of a court to hear or act upon a case from its beginning and to pass judgment on the law and the facts."[91] (2)

Palm Sunday Compromise A significant piece of U.S. legislation that signaled not only legislative meddling in judicial affairs but also federal meddling in state affairs.[92] (4)

parens patriae A medieval doctrine that allowed the Crown to replace natural family relations whenever a child's welfare was at risk.[93] (5)

per curiam opinion An appellate opinion that is agreed to by judges and tends to be short. (3)

peremptory challenge The right to challenge a potential juror without disclosing the reason for the challenge. Prosecutors and defense attorneys routinely use peremptory challenges to eliminate from juries individuals who, although they express no obvious bias, are thought to be capable of swaying the jury in an undesirable direction. (13)

petition "[A] written request made to a court asking for the exercise of its judicial powers or asking for permission to perform some act where the authorization of a court is required."[94] (5)

physical abuse The infliction, or the threat to inflict, physical pain or injury on a vulnerable elder or the act of depriving him or her of a basic need.[95] (16)

plea bargaining "[T]he process whereby the accused and the prosecutor in a criminal case work out a mutually satisfactory disposition of the case subject to court approval. It usually involves the defendant's pleading guilty to a lesser offense or to only some of the counts of a multi-count indictment in return for a lighter sentence than the sentence possible for the graver charge."[96] (12)

poor law Several laws introduced by the English parliament throughout the 1500s (culminating in 1601)[97] that reflected an increasingly compassionate attitude toward the poor, as people came to realize that there were legitimate reasons why some people found themselves destitute (e.g., weak harvests); also called *Poor Law Act* or *Elizabethan Poor Laws*. (5)

postincarceration diversion A structured treatment or program typically reserved for chronic low-level offenders immediately following their release from incarceration that is aimed at getting these offenders to stop committing crimes.[98] (8)

precedent A legal principle that ensures that previous judicial decisions are authoritatively considered and incorporated into future cases. (1)

precharge diversion The diversion of an offender out of the criminal justice system before he or she is charged. (8)

preliminary hearing "[T]he proceeding before a judicial officer in which three matters must be decided: whether a crime was committed; whether the crime occurred within the territorial jurisdiction of the court; and whether there are reasonable grounds to believe that the defendant committed the crime."[99] (11)

preponderance of evidence The standard of proof in a civil trial. (13)

presumption A fact assumed to be true under the law. (1)

presumption of innocence The bedrock U.S. legal principle that assumes that every person charged with a crime is innocent until proven otherwise. (1)

presumptive waiver A type of juvenile waiver that involves statutory designation of a category of cases in which waiver to

criminal court is presumed to be appropriate but that may be rebutted by the defense.[100] (5)

preventive detention A statutory authorization to deny bail to dangerous persons charged with certain offenses for up to 60 days. (11)

probable cause A cause defined by the U.S. Supreme Court as more than bare suspicion. A probable cause exists when "the facts and circumstances within [the officers'] knowledge and of which they [have] reasonably trustworthy information [are] sufficient to warrant a prudent man in believing that the [suspect] had committed or was committing an offense."[101] To this the Court added, "The substance of all the definitions of probable cause is a reasonable ground for belief of guilt."[102] (11)

probation A sentence of imprisonment that is suspended; also, the conditional freedom granted by a judicial officer to a convicted offender as long as the person meets certain conditions of behavior. (14)

procedural due process The constitutional provision that is concerned with ensuring fairness.[103] (1)

progressive era A period in the evolution of the U.S. criminal justice system that occurred in the early twentieth century and was marked by reform efforts aimed at removing corruption and political favoritism from the criminal process. (8)

proof beyond a reasonable doubt The standard of proof in a criminal case. (13)

property law The category of civil law that is significantly concerned with the acceptable uses of property, such as those uses spelled out in zoning laws. (1)

prosecutor "[A]n attorney who is the elected or appointed chief of a prosecution agency, and whose official duty is to conduct criminal proceedings on behalf of the people against persons accused of committing criminal offenses, also called 'district attorney,' 'DA,' 'state's attorney,' 'county attorney,' and 'U.S. Attorney,' and any attorney deputized to assist the chief prosecutor."[104] (8)

prosecutorial discretion "[T]he decision of a prosecutor to submit a charging document to a court, or to seek a grand jury indictment, or to decline to prosecute."[105] (8)

pro se **defense** The act of representing oneself at trial. (10)

public client A client who receives a court-appointed attorney.[106] (9)

public defender The counsel appointed from a salaried staff of full- or part-time attorneys who renders criminal indigent defense services through either a public or a private nonprofit organization or as a direct government-paid employee.[107] (9)

public-exposure penalty A form of shaming penalty that seeks to make a criminal's conviction publicly visible so that the public can respond with disapproval, thereby heightening the offender's sense of shame. (14)

purged taint exception A limitation on the fruit of the poisonous tree doctrine that may permit, when sufficient time elapses between an initial unconstitutional search and later seizure of derivative evidence, the admissibility of such derivative evidence at trial. (11)

qualified immunity The immunity that attaches when a prosecutor acts as an administrator or investigator and makes reasonable mistakes. (8)

quorum The minimum number of judges required to decide a particular matter. (3)

race "[The] major biological divisions of mankind, [particularly those that are] distinguished by color of skin, color and texture of hair, bodily proportions, and other physical features."[108] (15)

real evidence "[A]ny tangible item that can be perceived with the five senses."[109] (13)

rebuttal witness A witness whose testimony is intended to attack the credibility of the previous witness. (13)

reform conditions Probation or parole conditions that are intended to facilitate a probationer's or parolee's rehabilitation. (14)

release on recognizance The unsecured pretrial release of an accused person with the assumption that he or she will show up for subsequently scheduled court hearings. (11)

repair One of two restorative justice concepts (the other term being *harm*).[110] The term refers to measures taken by an offender to repair damage incurred by his or her victim or the community during a crime so as to restore the victim or the community (as closely as possible) to a previctimization state. (16)

restorative justice A term that has been used interchangeably with related approaches such as community justice, peacemaking, relational justice, and therapeutic jurisprudence.[111] It is "a process whereby all the parties with a stake in a particular offence come together to resolve collectively how to deal with the aftermath of the offence and its implications for the future"[112]; it includes "every action that is primarily oriented toward doing justice by repairing the harm that has been caused by a crime."[113] (16)

retainer An amount paid by a criminal defendant to his or her defense attorney in order to engage the attorney's services; also called *retaining fee*. (9)

reverse waiver A legislative mandate that certain cases initiated in an adult court be sent to a juvenile court for an adjudicatory hearing.[114] (5)

Rule of 80 A retirement rule (established in 1984) that allows a federal judge to retire with full pay and benefits if the sum of his or her age and years of service on the bench equals 80, subject to certain restrictions. A sliding scale allows a judge to retire earlier for less pay.[115] (7)

rule of four The U.S. Supreme Court rule that requires the agreement of four justices to grant a writ of *certiorari*. (3)

Rules Enabling Act of 1934 The U.S. federal legislation that gave Congress the authority to set the rules of practice, procedure, and evidence in the federal courts.[116] (2)

scope of direct rule A rule that restricts the questions that may be asked on cross-examination to only those matters addressed on direct examination or to inquiries into the credibility of the witness. (10)

senatorial courtesy A tendency among U.S. presidents to defer to the judgment of senators and local party leaders regarding the qualifications of individuals for appointments to the lower courts. (7)

senior status A category of federal judgeship permitted by the U.S. Congress to federal judges who do not formally retire but who effectively give up their seats and work part-time, handling cases based on need. Senior status judges essentially volunteer their services and, together, handle about 15% of the federal courts' workload in a given year.[117] (7)

sentence bargaining A defendant agreement to plead guilty in exchange for a less serious sentence. (12)

sentencing circle A type of victim–offender interaction that moves beyond mediation and conferencing by involving the community in the decision[118]; also called *peacemaking circle*.[119] (16)

sentencing diversion The requirement that an offender participate in drug treatment, anger management, or some other program in lieu of going straight to jail or prison. (8)

sentencing guidelines Voluntary or involuntary (depending on state or federal law) sentencing policies that are used to determine appropriate sentences and that serve to reduce disparities between sentences by recommending a certain term of imprisonment for certain types of offenders. (14)

sexual abuse Any kind of nonconsensual sexual contact.[120] (16)

shaming A creative judicially imposed punishment that seeks to deter crime by imposing embarrassment or disgrace on an offender.[121] (14)

solicitor general The federal official charged with representing the government both in suits and appeals in the Supreme Court and in all lower federal trial and appellate courts in cases where the interests of the U.S. government are at stake. (8)

special court-martial A type of court-martial that is akin to civilian courts of general jurisdiction. This type of court is adversarial and tries more serious offenses than those tried by summary court-martial. (3)

specialized court   A type of nontraditional and experimental U.S. court that targets special problems (e.g., drug addiction, domestic violence, and child neglect) but shares a similar mission—to shift the focus from processing cases to achieving meaningful results for defendants by formulating creative, individually tailored sentences; also called *problem-solving courts*, *special jurisdiction courts*,[122] or *boutique courts*. (6)

special law   Any law of specific villages and localities that was in effect in medieval England and that was often enforced by canonical (i.e., religious) courts. (1)

specific question   A question that does not call for a narrative. (13)

standby counsel   An attorney who is "standing by" to assist an accused individual when necessary when the accused has elected to waive his or her right to counsel. (10)

stare decisis   A term that literally means "to stand by things decided." In the law, it is the formal practice of adhering to precedent. (1)

status offense   An act or conduct that is declared by statute to be an offense only if it is committed by or engaged in by a juvenile. (5)

strict liability   A standard of guilt that holds a party liable regardless of culpability.[123] (1)

subject matter jurisdiction   The type of case that individual courts can adjudicate. (2)

substantive due process   The constitutional provision that is concerned with protecting people's life, liberty, and property interests. (1)

summary court-martial   A type of court-martial that handles charges of minor misconduct. (3)

supplemental jurisdiction   One of three main types of federal court jurisdiction that refers to the right of some federal courts to hear a case for which they would not ordinarily have original jurisdiction[124]; also called *ancillary jurisdiction* or *pendent jurisdiction*. (2)

test case   A court case that is likely to test the legality or constitutionality of a particular tactic or statute. (2)

testimonial evidence   The information that someone supplies, usually referring to someone who is under oath and giving testimony in a trial. (13)

therapeutic jurisprudence   A core component of the specialized courts movement that "amounts to seeing law as a helping profession."[125] (6)

tort   A civil wrong recognized by law to be grounds for a lawsuit; also, conduct that leads to injuries not considered acceptable by societal standards. (1)

tort law   The category of civil law that involves lawsuits to resolve civil wrongs. (1)

trial *de novo*   A term that literally means "a new trial." The term is applied to cases that are retried on appeal as opposed to those that are simply reviewed on the record. (14)

trial jury   "[A] statutorily defined number of persons selected according to law and sworn to determine, in accordance with the law as instructed by the court, certain matters of fact based on evidence presented in a trial, and to render a verdict"[126]; also called *petit jury* (in contrast to a grand jury). (13)

trier of fact   The role of a juror (in a jury trial) or a judge (in a bench trial) that requires one or the other to listen to the facts presented by the prosecution and the defense and then render a decision based on which side made the more convincing case; also called *finder of fact*. (7)

trier of law   A description often applied to a judge that means he or she is generally tasked with resolving any legal matter that comes before the court; also called *finder of law*. (7)

true bill   The grand jury's endorsement that it found sufficient evidence to warrant a criminal charge. (11)

Twelve Tables   The first secular (i.e., not regarded as religious) written legal code, dating from 450 B.C.[127] (1)

Uniform Code of Military Justice   The military's criminal code, akin to state penal codes or the U.S. Code.[128] (3)

U.S. attorney   An attorney appointed by the president and serving under the direction of the U.S. attorney general to supervise the attorneys and staff of the U.S. Attorney's Office in each of the federal judicial districts. (8)

U.S. Court of Appeals for the Armed Forces   An Article I appellate court created by the U.S. Congress in 1950 to extend a measure of civilian authority into military law. (3)

U.S. Court of Appeals for Veterans Claims   An Article I court that reviews decisions from the Board of Veterans' Appeals, which itself makes decisions on appeals arising from decisions made by the secretary of veterans affairs. (3)

U.S. Court of Federal Claims   An Article I court that is authorized to issue decisions involving (1) claims for just compensation arising from government taking of private property (eminent domain), (2) refunds of federal taxes, (3) constitutional and statutory rights of military personnel and their dependents, (4) damages for breaches of contract with the U.S. government, (5) claims for back pay from dismissed civil servants, (6) claims involving patent and copyright infringement, and (7) certain claims involving the Indian tribes. It was formerly the U.S. Claims Court. (3)

U.S. Court of International Trade   An Article III court that is an outgrowth of the Customs Courts Act of 1980. The court's geographic jurisdiction extends throughout the United States, and it is also authorized to hear some cases in other nations. Its subject matter jurisdiction is rather limited; generally, it can decide any dispute arising out of laws pertaining to international trade. (3)

U.S. district court The federal trial court that is the "entry point" into the federal judicial system within each federal judicial district. (3)

U.S. Foreign Intelligence Surveillance Court An Article III court established by the Federal Intelligence Surveillance Act of 1978 that oversees requests for surveillance warrants against suspected foreign intelligence agents operating inside the United States; also called *FISA court*. (3)

U.S. magistrate judge A federal trial judge who is appointed to serve an eight-year term in a U.S. district court, who decides certain civil cases with the consent of the parties, and who assists in pretrial matters. (3)

U.S. Sentencing Commission A federal agency created in 1984 to deal with sentencing problems in the federal courts. The commission devised a "sentencing grid" used by federal judges to determine appropriate sentences. (14)

U.S. Supreme Court The final arbiter in the U.S. judicial system and the highest court in the United States; also called *the Court*. (3)

U.S. Tax Court An Article I court that specializes in settling disputes over federal income taxes. (3)

vanishing trial The phenomenon of a 15% decrease in criminal jury trials and a more than 30% decrease in civil jury trials[129] that occurred between 1976 and 2002.[130] (16)

vertical prosecution The practice of having the same prosecutor represent the state from the point that criminal charges are filed all the way through to sentencing.[131] (8)

vertical representation The appointment of a single attorney to represent the defendant from the case's inception until its end. (9)

victim impact statement The in-court use of victim- or survivor-supplied information by sentencing authorities seeking to make an informed sentencing decision. (14)

victim–offender mediation A version of the mediation approach to alternative dispute resolution that involves a meeting between victim and offender facilitated by a trained mediator. This approach differs from traditional mediation in that it carries underlying goals of restorative justice. (16)

Victims of Crime Act (1984) The federal legislation that spearheaded the establishment of victims' assistance programs nationally. (10)

Virginia Plan The plan for a new national government drafted by James Madison.[132] (3)

voir dire A term that literally means "to see what is said." It refers to the jury selection process whereby the prosecutor and the defense attorney question members of the jury panel in an effort to seat a jury that achieves the Sixth Amendment goal of impartiality. (13)

wedding cake model A model of differential treatment, first introduced by Lawrence Friedman and Robert Percival,[133] that uses an image of a layered cake to illustrate how the seriousness of an offense relates to the manner in which the case is processed by the criminal justice system. (15)

will A legal document wherein a person spells out the rights of others with regard to his or her property following his or her death. (1)

wired court A court that employs one or more technologies to improve its operations; also called *technology-enabled court*. (16)

writ of *certiorari* An order from a higher court that requires a lower court to send a case and a record of its proceedings to the higher court for review. (3)

NOTES

1. National Center for Elder Abuse, available at www.elderabusecenter.org/default.cfm?p=faqs.cfm (accessed August 8, 2009).
2. *Actual Innocence Awareness Database*, Jamail Center for Legal Research, available at http://web.austin.utexas.edu/law_library/innocence/index.cfm (accessed July 15, 2008).
3. J. A. Colquitt, "Ad Hoc Plea Bargaining," *Tulane Law Review*, Vol. 75 (2001), pp. 695–776.
4. U.S. Department of Justice, *Dictionary of Criminal Justice Data Terminology*, 2nd ed. (Washington, DC: U.S. Department of Justice, Bureau of Justice Statistics, 1981), p. 12. We use this dictionary throughout this book for definitions where appropriate.
5. L. R. Mecham, *Understanding the Federal Courts* (Washington, DC: Administrative Office of the U.S. Courts, Office of Judges Programs, 2003), p. 28.
6. Legal Information Institute, available at http://topics.law.cornell.edu/wex/ADR (accessed August 3, 2009).
7. American Bar Association, available at http://www.abanet.org/about/history.html (accessed September 22, 2009).
8. *Black's Law Dictionary*, 6th ed. (St. Paul, MN: West, 1990), p. 82.
9. Ibid.
10. M. J. Friedman, *Outline of the U.S. Legal System* (Washington, DC: U.S. State Department, 2004), available at http://usinfo.state.gov/products/pubs/legalotln/judges.htm (accessed September 22, 2009).
11. U.S. Department of Justice, *Dictionary of Criminal Justice Data Terminology*, p. 117.
12. Adapted from U.S. Department of Justice, *Dictionary of Criminal Justice Data Terminology*, p. 22.
13. C. J. DeFrances and M. F. X. Litras, *Indigent Defense Services in Large Counties, 1999* (Washington, DC: Bureau of Justice Statistics, 2000), p. 2.
14. U.S. Department of Justice, *Dictionary of Criminal Justice Data Terminology*, p. 28.

15. *Blakely v. Washington*, 542 U.S. 296 (2004).

16. P. W. Greenwood, "Juvenile Crime and Juvenile Justice," in J. Q. Wilson and J. Petersilia, eds., *Crime: Public Policies for Crime Control* (Oakland, CA: Institute for Contemporary Studies, 2002).

17. *Blockburger v. United States*, 284 U.S. 299 (1932), p. 304.

18. State Court Administrative Office, *Caseflow Management Guide* (Lansing, MI: State Court Administrative Office, n.d.), p. 1/1.

19. Center for Court Innovation, available at http://courtinnovation.org/index.cfm?fuseaction=page.viewPage&pageID=471 (accessed January 4, 2009).

20. J. Seymour, "*Parens Patriae* and Wardship Powers: Their Nature and Origins," *Oxford Journal of Legal Studies*, Vol. 14 (1994), pp. 159–188.

21. 28 U.S.C., Section 332 (d)(1).

22. J. L. Worrall and C. Hemmens, *Criminal Evidence: An Introduction* (Los Angeles: Roxbury, 2005), p. 71.

23. Center for Court Innovation, *Community Courts* (New York: Center for Court Innovation, 2008), available at www.communityjustice.org/index.cfm?fuseaction=page.viewPage&pageID=570&documentTopicID=17 (accessed July 7, 2009).

24. Barbara Boland, "What Is Community Prosecution?," *National Institute of Justice Journal* (August 1996), pp. 35–40.

25. Alessandra Sgubini, Mara Prieditis, and Andrea Marighetto, *Arbitration, Mediation and Conciliation: Differences and Similarities from an International and Italian Business Perspective*, available at www.mediate.com/articles/sgubiniA2.cfm (accessed August 8, 2008).

26. C. J. DeFrances and M. F. X. Litras, *Indigent Defense Services in Large Counties, 1999* (Washington, DC: Bureau of Justice Statistics, 2000), p. 2.

27. U.S. Department of Justice, *Dictionary of Criminal Justice Data Terminology*, p. 53.

28. R. Wheeler and C. Harrison, *Creating the Federal Judicial System*, 3rd ed. (Washington, DC: Federal Judicial Center, 2005).

29. 26 Stat. 826.

30. D. S. Dobkin, "Court Stripping and Limitations on Judicial Review of Immigration Cases," *Justice System Journal*, Vol. 28 (2007), pp. 104–108.

31. T. J. Weiman, "Jurisdiction Stripping, Constitutional Supremacy, and the Implications of *Ex Parte Young*," *University of Pennsylvania Law Review*, Vol. 153 (2005), pp. 1677–1708.

32. C. L. Harrington, "A Community Divided: Defense Attorneys and the Ethics of Death Row Volunteering," *Law and Social Inquiry*, Vol. 25 (2000), pp. 849–881.

33. U.S. Department of Justice, *Dictionary of Criminal Justice Data Terminology*, p. 27.

34. Mecham, *Understanding the Federal Courts*.

35. Worrall and Hemmens, *Criminal Evidence*, p. 71.

36. P. Griffin, P. Torbet, and L. Szymanski, *Trying Juveniles as Adults: An Analysis of State Transfer Provisions* (Washington, DC: U.S. Department of Justice, 1998), available at http://ojjdp.ncjrs.org/pubs/tryingjuvasadult/transfer.html (accessed February 28, 2009).

37. S. Walker, C. Spohn, and M. DeLone, *The Color of Justice: Race, Ethnicity, and Crime in America*, 4th ed. (Belmont, CA: Wadsworth, 2007), p. 18.

38. S. W. Perry, *Prosecutors in State Courts, 2005* (Washington, DC: U.S. Department of Justice, 2006), p. 11.

39. K. Little, "Specialized Courts and Domestic Violence," *Issues of Democracy: The Changing Face of U.S. Courts*, Vol. 8 (2003), pp. 26–31; J. Weber, "Domestic Violence Courts: Components and Considerations," *Journal of the Center for Families, Children, and the Courts*, Vol. 2 (2000), pp. 23–36.

40. We will discuss other treatment-oriented components elsewhere. Treatment is discussed here in the context of law enforcement only insofar as it heavily involves prosecutors.

41. Equal Employment Opportunity Commission, *Early Neutral Evaluation*, available at www.eeoc.gov/federal/adr/neutralevaluation.html (accessed August 8, 2009).

42. National Center for Elder Abuse, available at http://www.elderabusecenter.org/default.cfm?p=faqs.cfm (accessed August 8, 2008).

43. *Definitions*, SearchFinancialSecurity.com, available at http://searchfinancialsecurity.techtarget.com/sDefinition/0,sid185_gci1150017,00.html (accessed August 8, 2009).

44. J. E. McMillan, *A Guidebook for Electronic Court Filing* (Alexandria, VA: National Center for State Courts, 1999), p. 2.

45. National Center for Elder Abuse, available at www.elderabusecenter.org/default.cfm?p=faqs.cfm (accessed August 8, 2009).

46. B. Forst, *Errors of Justice* (New York: Cambridge University Press, 2004), pp. 3–4.

47. Walker et al., *The Color of Justice*, p. 10.

48. S. R. Gross, K. Jacoby, D. J. Matheson, N. Montgomery, and S. Patil, "Exonerations in the United States 1989 through 2003," *Journal of Criminal Law and Criminology*, Vol. 95 (2005), pp. 523–560.

49. National Center for Elder Abuse, available at www.elderabusecenter.org/default.cfm?p=faqs.cfm (accessed August 8, 2009).

50. P. W. Greenwood, "Juvenile Crime and Juvenile Justice," in Wilson and Petersilia, *Crime*, p. 86.

51. 18 U.S.C., Sections 3141–3150.

52. Federal Judicial Center home page, available at www.fjc.gov (accessed September 17, 2009).

53. 1 Stat. 73.

54. S. T. Hillsman, "Fines and Day Fines," in M. Tonry and N. Morris, eds., *Crime and Justice: A Review of Research*, Vol. 12 (Chicago: University of Chicago Press, 1990); S. T. Hillsman, J. L. Sichel, and B. Mahoney, *Fines and Sentencing: A Study of the Use of the Fine as a Criminal Sanction* (New York: Vera Institute of Justice, 1984); S. G. Casale and S. T. Hillsman, *The Enforcement of Fines as Criminal Sanctions: The English Experience and Its Relevance to American Practice* (New York: Vera Institute of Justice, 1986).

55. E. V. Heck and M. G. Hall, "Bloc Voting and the Freshman Justice Revisited," *Journal of Politics*, Vol. 43 (1981), pp. 852–860; A. P. Melone, "Revisiting the Freshman

Effect Hypothesis: The First Two Terms of Justice Anthony Kennedy," *Judicature*, Vol. 74 (1990), pp. 6–13.

56. S. Walker, *Sense and Nonsense about Crime and Drugs*, 5th ed. (Belmont, CA: Wadsworth, 2001).

57. U.S. Department of Justice, *Dictionary of Criminal Justice Data Terminology*, p. 99.

58. Walker et al., *The Color of Justice*, p. 293.

59. U.S. Constitution, Article I, Section 9, clause 2.

60. D. J. Farole, *The Harlem Parole Reentry Court Evaluation: Implementation and Preliminary Impacts* (New York: Center for Court Innovation, 2003).

61. The discussion in this paragraph borrows liberally from D. R. Karp, "Harm and Repair: Observing Restorative Justice in Vermont," *Justice Quarterly*, Vol. 18 (2001), pp. 727–757.

62. 22 U.S.C. Section 7102.

63. S. M. Strickland, "Beyond the Vanishing Trial: A Look at the Composition of State Court Dispositions," in T. Peters, N. Kauder, C. Campbell, and C. Flango, *Future Trends in State Courts, 2005* (Williamsburg, VA: National Center for State Courts, 2005), pp. 89–92.

64. J. Bellah, "Training: Identity Theft," *Law and Order*, Vol. 49 (2001), pp. 222–226.

65. *Black's Law Dictionary*, p. 753.

66. U.S. Department of Justice, *Dictionary of Criminal Justice Data Terminology*, p. 108.

67. Ibid.

68. Innocence Network home page, available at www.innocencenetwork.org (accessed July 15, 2009).

69. Ibid.

70. U.S. Department of Justice, *Dictionary of Criminal Justice Data Terminology*, p. 55.

71. American Judicature Society, *Federal Judicial Conduct* (Des Moines, IA: American Judicature Society, 2008), available at www.ajs.org/ethics/eth_fed-jud-conduct.asp (accessed August 28, 2009).

72. Legal Information Institute, *Judicial Ethics: An Overview*, available at http://topics.law.cornell.edu/wex/judicial_ethics (accessed April 21, 2009).

73. I. A. Horowitz, N. L. Kerr, and K. E. Niedermeier, "Jury Nullification: Legal and Psychological Perspectives," *Brooklyn Law Review*, Vol. 66 (2001), p. 1210.

74. D. B. Rottman and S. M. Strickland, *State Court Organization, 2004* (Arlington, VA: National Center for State Courts, 2006), pp. 16–20.

75. U.S. Department of Justice, *Dictionary of Criminal Justice Data Terminology*, p. 118.

76. 18 U.S.C., Section 5031.

77. For more details, see the "Shifting Conceptions of Age" section later in this chapter.

78. 42 U.S.C., Section 3801; for additional details, see G. Olson-Raymer, "The Role of the Federal Government in Juvenile Delinquency Prevention: Historical and Contemporary Perspectives," *Journal of Criminal Law and Criminology*, Vol. 74 (1983), pp. 578–600.

79. 42 U.S.C., Section 5601.

80. California Evidence Code, Section 764.

81. Griffin et al., *Trying Juveniles as Adults: An Analysis of State Transfer Provisions* (Washington, DC: U.S. Department of Justice, 1998). Available at http://ojjdp.ncjrs.org/pubs/tryingjuvasadult/transfer.html (accessed March 12, 2009).

82. H. Kalven and H. Zeisel, *The American Jury* (Chicago: University of Chicago Press, 1966).

83. Rottman and Strickland, *State Court Organization, 2004*, pp. 16–20.

84. Kalven and Zeisel, *The American Jury*, p. 407.

85. For additional information, see M. Sviridoff, *Dispensing Justice Locally: The Implementation and Effects of the Midtown Community Court* (New York: Center for Court Innovation, 1997).

86. National Center for State Courts, available at http://ncsconline.org/D_About/index.htm (accessed March 4, 2009).

87. National Center for Elder Abuse, available at www.elderabusecenter.org/default.cfm?p=faqs.cfm (accessed August 8, 2008).

88. M. Ferrand, ed., *The Records of the Federal Convention of 1787*, rev. ed., 4 vols. (New Haven, CT: Yale University Press, 1937).

89. J. R. C. Davis, B. E. Smith, and H. J. Davies, "Effects of No-Drop Prosecution of Domestic Violence upon Conviction Rates," *Justice Research and Policy*, Vol. 3 (2001), pp. 1–13.

90. Friedman, *Outline of the U.S. Legal System*.

91. U.S. Department of Justice, *Dictionary of Criminal Justice Data Terminology*, p. 117.

92. C. Babington and M. Allen, "Congress Passes Schiavo Measure," *Washington Post*, March 21, 2005, p. A1, available at www.washingtonpost.com/wp-dyn/articles/A51402-2005Mar20.html (accessed March 4, 2009).

93. D. Besharov, *Juvenile Justice Advocacy: Practice in a Unique Court* (New York: Practicing Law Institute, 1974); also see J. Albanese, *Dealing with Delinquency: The Future of Juvenile Justice* (Chicago: Nelson-Hall, 1993).

94. U.S. Department of Justice, *Dictionary of Criminal Justice Data Terminology*, p. 157.

95. National Center for Elder Abuse, available at www.elderabusecenter.org/default.cfm?p=faqs.cfm (accessed August 8, 2008).

96. *Black's Law Dictionary*, p. 1152.

97. For further details, see www.elizabethan-era.org.uk/the-poor-law.htm (accessed February 18, 2009).

98. See, e.g., S. Fairhead, *Persistent Petty Offenders* (London: HMSO, 1981).

99. U.S. Department of Justice, *Dictionary of Criminal Justice Data Terminology*, p. 161.

100. Griffin et al., *Trying Juveniles as Adults: An Analysis of State Transfer Provisions* (Washington, DC: U.S. Department of Justice, 1998). Available at http://ojjdp.ncjrs.org/pubs/tryingjuvasadult/transfer.html (accessed April 1, 2009).

101. *Beck v. Ohio*, 379 U.S. 89 (1964), p. 91.

102. *Brinegar v. United States*, 338 U.S. 160 (1949), p. 175.

103. *Geddes v. Northwest Missouri State College*, 49 F.3d 426 (8th Cir. 1995).

104. U.S. Department of Justice, *Dictionary of Criminal Justice Data Terminology*, p. 176.

105. Ibid., p. 177.

106. R. B. Flemming, "Client Games: Defense Attorney Perspectives on Their Relations with Criminal Clients," *Law and Social Inquiry*, Vol. 11 (1986), pp. 253–277.

107. DeFrances and Litras, *Indigent Defense Services in Large Counties, 1999*, p. 2.

108. Walker et al., *The Color of Justice*, p. 6.

109. Worrall and Hemmens, *Criminal Evidence*, p. 71.

110. The discussion in this paragraph borrows liberally from Karp, "Harm and Repair," pp. 727–757.

111. G. Bazemore and L. Walgrave, "Restorative Juvenile Justice: In Search of Fundamentals and an Outline for Systematic Reform," in G. Bazemore and L. Walgrave, eds., *Restorative Juvenile Justice* (Monsey, NY: Criminal Justice Press, 1999).

112. Tony Marshall, "Criminal Mediation in Great Britain 1980–1996," *European Journal on Criminal Policy and Research*, Vol. 4 (1996), p. 21.

113. Bazemore and Walgrave, *Restorative Juvenile Justice*, p. 48.

114. H. N. Snyder and M. Sickmund, *Juvenile Offenders and Victims: 2006 National Report* (Washington, DC: U.S. Department of Justice, Office of Justice Programs, Office of Juvenile Justice and Delinquency Prevention, 2006), p. 110.

115. Friedman, *Outline of the U.S. Legal System*.

116. 28 U.S.C., Sections 2071–2077.

117. Friedman, *Outline of the U.S. Legal System*.

118. The discussion in this paragraph borrows liberally from Karp, "Harm and Repair," pp. 727–757.

119. Ibid.

120. National Center for Elder Abuse, available at www .elderabusecenter.org/default.cfm?p=faqs.cfm (accessed August 8, 2008).

121. D. R. Karp, "The Judicial and Judicious Use of Shame Penalties," *Crime and Delinquency*, Vol. 44 (1998), pp. 277–294, 280–283.

122. J. Petrila, "An Introduction to Special Jurisdiction Courts," *International Journal of Law and Psychiatry*, Vol. 26 (2003), pp. 3–12.

123. Arguably the most famous case in this area was *Greenman v. Yuba Power Products*, 59 Cal. 2d 57 (1963).

124. For two leading cases, see *Owen Equipment and Erection Co. v. Kroger*, 437 U.S. 365 (1978) and *United Mine Workers of America v. Gibbs*, 383 U.S. 715 (1966).

125. D. P. Stolle, B. J. Winick, and D. B. Wexler, *Practicing Therapeutic Jurisprudence: Law as a Helping Profession* (Durham, NC: Carolina Academic Press, 2000).

126. U.S. Department of Justice, *Dictionary of Criminal Justice Data Terminology*, p. 208.

127. O. J. Thatcher, ed., *The Library of Original Sources, Vol. III: The Roman World* (Milwaukee, WI: University Research Extension Co., 1901), pp. 9–11.

128. 10 U.S.C., Sections 801–941.

129. See *Journal of Empirical Legal Studies*, Vol. 1, No. 3 (November 2004), for articles presented at the American Bar Association Section of Litigation's "Vanishing Trials" symposium.

130. S. M. Strickland, "Beyond the Vanishing Trial: A Look at the Composition of State Court Dispositions," in Peters et al., *Future Trends in State Courts, 2005*, pp. 89–92.

131. J. M. Dawson, S. K. Smith, and C. J. DeFrances, *Prosecutors in State Courts, 1992* (Washington, DC: National Institute of Justice, 1992).

132. Ferrand, *The Records of the Federal Convention of 1787*.

133. L. M. Friedman and R. V. Percival, *The Roots of Justice: Crime and Punishment in Alameda County, California, 1870–1910* (Chapel Hill: University of North Carolina Press, 1981).

Table of Cases

Name Index

A

Acker, J., 426
Acree, M., 366
Adams, Benjamin, 120, 121, 125
Adams, Charles Francis, 27
Adams, Guy, 120
Adams, John, 6, 54
Addams, Jane, 107
Adderly, Eleanor, 398
Adderly, Frank, 398
Administrative Office of the U.S. Courts, 37, 49, 77, 78, 102, 103, 168, 190, 241
Alanez, Tonya, 423
Albanese, J., 132
Albonetti, C., 222, 424, 425
Alexander, S., 160
Alexander, Travis, 22, 249
Alito, Samuel A., 170
Allen, Floyd, 379
Allen, M., 102, 103, 470
Allison, P., 222, 424
Alpert, G. P., 159, 423
Alpert, Geoffrey, 402
Alpert, L., 190
Alschuler, A. W., 332
American Bar Association, 32, 42–43, 49, 50, 190, 191, 202, 222, 223, 237, 238, 239, 242, 246, 321, 332, 365, 430, 443, 468
American Judicature Society, 190, 191, 470
Anderson, James M., 233
Anderson, S., 191
Anthony, Caylee, 349
Aquilino, W., 366
Arenella, P., 332
Arias, Jodi, 22, 249, 278
Arizona Commission on Judicial Conduct, 191
Ashenfelter, O., 192
Atkins, B. M., 190
Atlanta Long Term Care Ombudsman Program, 453
Atledge, P. C., 190
Auchter, Bernard, 395
Austin, A., 279

B

Baar, C., 49, 102
Babington, C., 102, 103, 470
Bailey, F. Lee, 401
Bailyn, B., 77
Baker, L., 77
Baker, N., 221
Baker, Tim, 120
Baldas, T., 279
Baldus, D. C., 412, 425, 426
Baldwin, A., 366
Balkin, S., 246
Balko, R., 426
Banks, D., 198, 215, 216, 223
Barnes, H. E., 395

Barrish, Cris, 433
Batemore, G., 452
Baum, L., 50, 191
Bazemore, G., 451, 471
Bearup, Patrick, 312
Beavers, S. L., 102
Beck, E., 452
Becker, R. T., 34, 49
Bedau, H. A., 426
Bedi, Petros, 210
Belenko, Steven, 143, 159
Belford, Christine, 433
Bellah, J., 451, 453, 470
Benesh, S. C., 50
Berk, R. A., 159
Berkson, L., 102
Berlow, A., 426
Berman, G., 159, 160, 161
Bernat, F., 279
Berzon, Alexandra, 49
Besharov, D., 132, 470
Bickle, G. S., 426
Bienen, L., 222, 424
Birckhead, Tamar R., 225
Black, D., 423
Blewett, Cornelius Demorris, 61
Blewitt, Jarreous Jamone, 61
Blomberg, T. G., 223
Bloomberg, Michael, 165
Blum, A., 366
Blumberg, Abraham, 235, 246, 247
Blumstein, A., 425
Boccaccini, M. T., 247
Bodenhamer, David J., 227, 246
Bogenshutz, J. David, 398
Boland, Barbara, 221, 222, 469
Boothroyd, R. A., 160
Borchard, E. M., 426
Bordt, R. L., 426
Bork, Robert, 34
Bos, C. D., 451
Bourge, Christian, 139
Bowers, B., 453
Bowers, W. J., 425
Boyce, Robert, 244, 245
Boyer, Jonathan, 353
Boylan, R. T., 223
Brace, Charles Loring, 107
Braithwaite, J., 452
Brandt, J., 453
Bratton, K. A., 191
Brennan, G., 27
Brennan, Michael, 152
Brennan, William, 171, 184, 378
Brennan, William J., 190, 192
Breyer, Stephen G., 169
Bridges, G. S., 424
Broder, J. M., 102
Brodsky, A., 279
Brodsky, S. L., 247
Broeder, D. W., 366
Bromage, C., 103

Bromet, E., 279
Brown, Linda, 40
Brown, Sherri, 270
Brownsberger, W. N., 161
Brundage, James A., 227, 246
Bruschi, C., 160
Buchanan, R., 366
Bull, James, 415
Bumiller, K., 425
Bureau of Justice Statistics, 93, 95, 229, 246, 250, 279, 409, 423, 424, 425, 426
Burek, M. W., 424
Burger, Warren, 65, 184
Burke, Kevin, 163
Burke, M. J., 222
Burke, Melissa Nann, 433
Burke, P., 424
Bursztajn, H., 279
Bush, George H. W., 37, 39, 166
Bush, George W., 43, 70, 99, 164
Bush, N., 366
Bynum, T. S., 307

C

Caldeira, G. A., 50, 192
Calhoy, D. R., 365
California Administrative Office of the Courts, 133, 160, 452
California Evidence Code, 365, 366, 470
California Penal Code, 395
Cameron, C. M., 50
Camp, C., 395
Camp, G., 395
Campbell, C., 103, 446, 451, 452, 453, 470
Campbell, Henry, 108
Canino, Robert, 270
Capital Jury Project, 365
Cappalli, Richard, 154
Carbon, S., 102
Carns, T. D., 332
Carrington, F., 279
Carson, E. Ann, 409
Carter, D., 423
Carter, Jimmy, 164
Carter, Terry, 313
Casady, Tom, 138
Casale, S. G., 395, 469
Casey, P., 103, 159, 160
Casey, T., 161
Casper, J. D., 236, 247
Castille, Ronald D., 182
Cauchon, D., 246
Cave, Jennifer, 349
Cave, Sharon, 349
Center for Court Innovation, 44, 49, 50, 144, 159, 160, 161, 469
Center for Legal and Court Technology, 431, 451
Center for Professional Responsibility, 239

Subject Index